Culinary Harmony

Favorite Recipes of the World's Finest Classical Musicians

Front cover photograph features the Emerson String Quartet

Culinary Harmony

Favorite Recipes of the World's Finest Classical Musicians

By David Rezits

Humorous Music/Food Illustrations by Lisa Scott
Food Drawings by Antoinette K. Lee
Text Editing by Gerald Deatsman
Cover Photo of Emerson Quartet by Wyatt Counts

"Culinary Harmony" cover layout designed in Bloomington, Indiana by:
Eric White and Rachel Whang, Daisybrain Media Center and Gallery;
Bruce and Diane David, The David Gallery

"Fish Soup" recipe reprinted with permission of Macmillan USA, a Simon & Schuster Macmillan Company, from TRATTORIA COOKING by Biba Caggiano. Copyright © 1992 by Biba Caggiano.

"Pate de Foie" recipe reprinted with permission of Simon & Schuster from THE JOY OF COOKING by Irma S. Rombauer and Marion Rombauer Becker. Copyright © 1931, 1936, 1941, 1942, 1943, 1946, 1951, 1952, 1953, 1962, 1963, 1964, 1975 by Bobbs-Merrill.

"Flan" recipe from PUERTO RICAN COOKERY by Carmen Aboy Valldejuli, © 1977, 1980, with permission of Pelican Publishing Company, Inc.

"Matthew Kenney's Summer Tomato with Grilled Jumbo Shrimp and Vidalia Onion" recipe reprinted by permission of Matthew Kenney of Matthew's Restaurant, 1030 3rd Ave., New York City.

"Indian Rice Salad" recipe reprinted with permission from author John Robbins, from MAY ALL BE FED: DIET FOR A NEW WORLD, © 1992.

"Paganini's Ravioli" recipe translation reprinted by permission of Judy Gardner, 1996.

"Ginger Sherry Crab Legs Andrea" recipe reprinted by permission of Andrea Gatov (former owner), Andrea's Old Town Café, Bandon, OR (1996).

"Lemon Custard Tart" recipe reprinted with permission of Alfred A. Knopf Inc. from NELA'S COOKBOOK by Nela Rubinstein. Copyright © 1983 by Nela Rubinstein.

Paragraph on Gioacchino Rossini from *The Pleasures of the Table* by George H. Ellwanger, M.A., Doubleday Page & Co., 1902.

*Every effort was made to receive copyright permission from the photographers listed in this book. In some cases, the photographers name and/or whereabouts was not known by either the artists' agency or the artist. In a few cases, neither the artist nor their agent was able to respond to my inquiries about their photographs.

ISBN: 0-9658851-0-0
Library of Congress Catalog Card Number: 97-91706

Copyright © 1997, David Rezits, Fort Wayne, Indiana
Copyright © 1997, Humorous Music/Food Illustrations, Lisa Scott, Indianapolis, Indiana

First printing: April, 1997
Second printing, revised: November, 1997

Culinary Harmony published by:
DIR Publishers
P.O. Box 11823
Fort Wayne, IN 46861-1823

This book is dedicated in loving memory of my dear friends Don Morrow, Maureen Snyder and Dzidra Ozoliņš, and wonderful cello teacher, Eva Janzer. Their compassion and kindness deeply touched all who knew them and whose joyful love for music and the arts was an inspiration to us all. To my loving grandparents, for their everlasting support of my music-making throughout life. And to the victims of AIDS, which has claimed the lives of so many of our brilliant gifted musicians and artists.

ACKNOWLEDGMENTS

I would like to thank the many people who made this book possible: Firstly, my dear friend Rosalyn Pollack Saz—for planting the seed that bloomed into this great endeavor. My parents Joseph and Roberta, for their support when I needed it the most. My dear friend Cindy Greider—for her encouragement and patience with me and my book during the past several years, and for her expert help with editing, ideas and cooking. Gifted pianist and editor of *Culinary Harmony,* Gerald Deatsman, for all the many devoted hours spent reading and editing this recipe book. Lisa Scott and her parents—for Lisa's incredible drawings that made this book come alive, and her mother Mary Bent's help with editing. The very gifted artist Antoinette Lee, for the many elegant food drawings. To my friends and colleagues of the Fort Wayne Philharmonic, for testing and tasting recipes in this book. To my devoted students' families, especially the Sarks, in Goshen, Indiana, for testing and tasting recipes. To Susi Sherman, for excellent culinary advice and help in testing recipes and Marialyn Bazile, for her many hours of expert recipe editing and cooking. And to Carol Anne McMillen (a master French cook) and her family, for testing and tasting many recipes—with the discriminating taste buds of her seven hungry boys.

To the generous and well-known cookbook authors Marcia Adams and Bernard Clayton, for their time and expert advice at the beginning stages of this book. Jewish artist Bruce David and his wife Diane, for their never-failing ideas and encouragement. Betsy Thal, for helping me through the many initial obstacles I experienced with my Compaq computer. Dessie Arnold and Rich Dunbar for expert help in formatting and editing. For writing the wonderful story and biography about Mr. Gingold, Lois Sabo Skelton.

I must especially thank all the management agencies for the many hours spent with my requests for photographs and biographies, as well as the many photographers who contributed photos to this book. In particular, Christian Steiner, whose contribution of over 25 photographs makes up the backbone of this book. And, of course, my deepest gratitude to all the wonderful musicians who contributed their recipes for this book.

Lastly, to all my friends and colleagues that have supported and encouraged me during the writing of this book. And, to God for giving me the patience to accomplish such an endeavor.

My thanks to the following individuals, managements and orchestras for their help in supplying photos, biographies and translations for this book.

AADVERT ASSOCIATES, INC: bio and photo of Nathaniel Rosen

ACADEMY OF SAINT MARTIN IN THE FIELDS: bio and photo of Neville Marriner

ALISON GLAISTER: bio and photo of Colin Davis

AMERICAN INTERNATIONAL ARTISTS MANAGEMENT: photo of Andrés Cárdenes

BALTIMORE SYMPHONY ORCHESTRA: bio and photo of David Zinman

BLOOMINGTON HERALD-TIMES: photo of Josef Gingold

BOOSEY & HAWKES: bio and photo of Ned Rorem

BOSTON SYMPHONY ORCHESTRA: bio and photo of John Williams

CAREY DOMB MANAGEMENT: bio and photo of Daniel Domb

CHARLES SENS (Library of Congress): photo of Niccolò Paganini

CHICAGO SYMPHONY ORCHESTRA: bio of Victor Aitay, bio and photo of Jay Friedman, photo of Alex Klein, bio of Donald Koss, photo of Donald Peck, photo of Charles Pikler, photo of Gene Pokorny

CINCINNATI SYMPHONY ORCHESTRA: bio and photo of Max Rudolf

CLARION/SEVEN MUSES: bio and photo of David Owen Norris

COLBERT ARTISTS MANAGEMENT: bio and photo of Phyllis Bryn-Julson

COLUMBIA ARTISTS MANAGEMENT: bio and photo of Manuel Barrueco, photo of Beaux Arts Trio, bio of Joyce Castle, bio and photo of Bella Davidovich, bio of Rudolf Firkušný, bio and photo of Adria Firestone, bio and photo of Hélène Grimaud, photo of Toby Hoffman, bio and photo of Jerry Hadley, bio and photo of Robert McDuffie, bio and photo of John O'Conor, bio and photo of Adrianne Pieczonka, bio and photo of Christopher Parkening, bio and photo of Florence Quivar, bio of Sharon Sweet, bio of Dawn Upshaw, bio and photo of Benita Valente, bio and photo of Frederica von Stade, bio and photo of Dan-Wen Wei, bio and photo of Lilya Zilberstein

CYNTHIA MEISTER/CHRISTINE BOURDELAIS (Office of Zubin Mehta): bio and photo of Zubin Mehta

DESSIE ARNOLD: writing bio of Jean Sibelius

DON MANILDI, (International Piano Archives at University of Maryland/College Park): photo of Rudolf Firkušný

DOROTHY RICHMOND: translation from Spanish of recipe from Rafael Frühbeck de Burgos

DEUTSCHE OPER BERLIN: bio and photo of Rafael Frühbeck de Burgos

E. SNAPP, INC. MANAGEMENT: bio of John Corigliano

EERO TARASTI (University of Helsinki): photo of Jean Sibelius

FOSTER CONCERT MANAGEMENT: bio and photo of Eugene Rousseau

FRITZ KRAMMER (office of José Carreras): bio and photo of José Carreras

GAMI SIMONDS MANAGEMENT: bio and photo of James Campbell

GERALD DEATSMAN: writing bios of Percy Grainger, Niccolò Paganini, and Gioachino Rossini

GURTMAN AND MURTHA ASSOCIATES: bio of Victor Borge, bio and photo of Robert Merrill

HARRISON PARROTT MANAGEMENT: bio and photo of Vladimir Ashkenazy, bio and photo of Steven Isserlis

HARLEQUIN AGENCY LIMITED: bio and photo of Bryn Terfel

HERBERT BARRETT MANAGEMENT INC: bio of Ida Kavafian, bio and photo of Jerome Lowenthal, bio and photo of Isabella Lippi, bio and photo of Susan Starr

HERBERT H. BRESLIN INC: bio and photo of Deborah Voigt

HOUSTON SYMPHONY ORCHESTRA: bio and photo of Christoph Eschenbach

ICM ARTISTS, LTD: bio and photo of Carter Brey, bio and photo of Pamela Frank, bio and photo of Janina Fialkowska, bio and photo of Grant Johannesen, bio and photo of Yolanda Kondonassis, bio and photo of Ruth Laredo, bio and photo of Anthony Newman, photo of Jon Kimura Parker, bio and photo of Roberta Peters, bio and photo of Peter Schickele, bio and photo of Ransom Wilson

INDIANA UNIVERSITY SCHOOL OF MUSIC PUBLICITY OFFICE: bio of Eva Czako Janzer

INDIANAPOLIS SYMPHONY ORCHESTRA: bio and photo of Raymond Leppard

INTERNATIONAL MANAGEMENT GROUP (IMG ARTISTS): bio and photo of Joshua Bell, bio and photo of John Horton Murray, bio and photo of John Nelson, bio and photo of Itzhak Perlman, bio and photo of William Shimell, bio and photo of Kurt Streit, photo of Dawn Upshaw

JANE DAVIS INC. MANAGEMENT: bio and photo of Bonita Boyd, bio and photo of Gary Karr

JANICE MAYER & ASSOCIATES: photo of Joyce Castle

JAY K. HOFFMAN & ASSOCIATES: bio and photo of Tzimon Barto, bio and photo of Sharon Isbin, bio and photo of Carol Wincenc

JIM COLIAS (office of Borge Productions, Inc.): photo of Victor Borge

JOAN JEANRENAUD: bio and photo of Kronos Quartet

JOANNE RILE ARTISTS MANAGEMENT, INC: bio and photo of Sergiu Schwartz

JUSTINE MACURDY: photo of John Macurdy

LOIS SABO SKELTON: story and bio of Josef Gingold

LOS ANGELES PHILHARMONIC: bio and photo of Jeffrey Reynolds

LUDWIG MUSIC PUBLISHING COMPANY: bio of Frederick Fennell

MARY JOHNSON: bio of Janos Starker

MASTER ARTISTS: bio of Italo Babini

M. L. FALCONE, PUBLIC RELATIONS: bio and photo of Eugenia Zukerman

MICHAL SCHMIDT ARTISTS INTERNATIONAL, INC: photo of Roberto Díaz

MIDORI AND FRIENDS (Rawn Harding): bio and photo of Midori

MILLER/CARTER ASSOCIATES: bio and photo of Barbara Nissman

PARSONS ARTIST MANAGEMENT: bio of Donald Peck

PASADENA SYMPHONY ORCHESTRA: bio and photo of Jorge Mester

PEER-SOUTHERN CONCERT MUSIC (Todd Vunderink): writing bio of David Diamond

PHILADELPHIA SYMPHONY ORCHESTRA: bio and photo of Wolfgang Sawallisch

ROBERT LESLIE: bio and photo of Salvatore Accardo

SAINT LOUIS SYMPHONY ORCHESTRA: bio and photo of Leonard Slatkin

SAN FRANCISCO SYMPHONY ORCHESTRA: bio and photo of Herbert Blomstedt, bio and photo of Raymond
        Kobler, bio and photo of Paul Renzi

SEATTLE SYMPHONY ORCHESTRA: bio and photo of Gerard Schwarz

SHEILA PORTER, PRESS AND PUBLIC RELATIONS: bio and photo of Robert Taub

SHAW CONCERTS, INC: bio and photo of Jessye Norman

SHELDON SOFFER MANAGEMENT INC: bio of Sidney Harth

SHIRLEY KIRSHBAUM & ASSOCIATES: bio and photo of John Browning, bio of Philip Setzer, bio and
        photo of Emerson Quartet (Cover Photo)

SHUMAN ASSOCIATES INC: bio and photo of Misha Dichter, bio and photo of John O'Conor

SUSANNE BAUMGARTNER AND VERA LAMPORT: bio and photo of Yehudi Menuhin

THEA DISPEKER, INC: bio of Jianyi Zhang

THEODORE PRESSER COMPANY: bio of George Rochberg

TRAWICK ARTISTS: bio of Dominic Cossa

URSULA KEMERY: translation from German of Wolfgang Sawallisch's recipe and bio of Rafael
        Frühbeck de Burgos

VIRGINIA SYMPHONY ORCHESTRA: photo of JoAnn Falletta

WESTMINSTER CHOIR COLLEGE: bio and photo of Joseph Flummerfelt

INTRODUCTION

CULINARY—relating to the kitchen or the art of cookery. HARMONY—a pleasing arrangement of notes or parts. That is what this book is about—a combination of food recipes in a very pleasing arrangement.

While I was working toward my music degree as an undergraduate at Indiana University back in the 1970's, I would have never dreamed that I would be writing a recipe book involving colleagues and teachers that I knew and so greatly admired. What remarkable lives these great musicians of today lead—their non-stop concert schedules—performing 100+ concerts a year—flying around the globe teaching countless numbers of students and learning voluminous pages of music. Do these artists have any time for activities besides performing and teaching? Well, yes! They have time to eat—and they thoroughly enjoy it!

This question was the impetus for writing this book. I began three years ago to contact the musicians appearing in *Culinary Harmony*. At first, I did not know who would be in this book or even if it would get off the ground. I needed to find out *which* artists were interested in sharing their culinary tastes (there is usually no mention of performers' eating habits written in symphony orchestra concert program biographies, or on record and CD jackets). I began by writing hundreds and hundreds of letters to famous classical musicians around the world. I sent faxes, made phone calls and personally contacted these musicians to see if they would contribute to my recipe book. Some of the musicians I contacted even made suggestions about others whom I might contact.

I did not ask for specific recipes in certain categories—only for the artists' *favorite* recipes; ones they enjoyed cooking or having prepared for them. Little by little, responses began to arrive and with a little prompting for a few (as in three or four letters to the same artist) this recipe book began to take shape. Aside from receiving recipes in the mail, I received phone calls and letters from all the over the globe apologizing for not responding sooner—"your letter was at the bottom of my 3-foot-high mail pile on my desk"...."I just returned from a twenty-three country/nine-month concert tour"—but usually the individual would eventually send back my recipe form. (I had several recipes that took two years to finally reach my mailbox). One musician from Germany sent back an envelope with the material I requested—well...almost—he thought *Culinary Harmony* was some sort of music theory book and sent his biography and photograph, but no recipe!

I have organized this book into chapters treating specific instrumentalists, conductors, composers and singers. This was the best way to organize the book because some of the musicians submitted more than one recipe, and it would have created an organizational problem if the chapters were listed by food categories. In addition to recipes, I asked the musicians for a biography and black and white photograph. I suggested an approximately one-page biography, but in a number of cases received quite a bit more or less (one biography was 38 pages long, one was 5 lines long). I decided that I would not drastically alter the biographies, unless overly long or short. I simply wanted to let the musician 'toot his or her horn' with the material presented. This resulted in different writing styles for the biographies, but which, I feel, would be of greater interest to the reader. Since many of the biographies were written by the musicians or their agents, they took the form usually seen in a symphony orchestra concert program. Some biographies included minute details concerning each performance given, while others gave a broad spectrum of generalized accomplishments during the artist's lifetime. It was also difficult to keep the biographies completely current, because the artists' lives can change drastically from week to week. With regard to their recipes, I suggested no particular number of recipes to contribute, only what they felt comfortable with. Again the range was wide—usually only one or two were sent, but from one musician I received forty recipes (unfortunately I could not print them all).

I have tremendously enjoyed testing these many recipes for the past several years. I have always had a passion for eating and cooking—and living and working on several continents has introduced me to a wide variety of cuisine. Being involved in the music profession makes it unavoidable not to eat foods from many different countries, especially since the musician population covers the planet. I was surprised that the array of recipes sent to me seemed to balance out just right in *Culinary Harmony.* I *would* make the observation that if there is one food that seemed to dominate the menu, it would be chicken. Musicians just love to eat chicken. (The dessert column tended to be popular as well!).

The artists' recipes in *Culinary Harmony* came from many sources. Some were 'passed down' family favorites, some were from favorite restaurants, many were the musician's own invention and some were from well-known recipe books. Some recipes were simple and quick; others took hours to prepare. A few cost a dollar or two for ingredients; others cost 30 to 40 dollars to prepare. I printed most of the recipes in this book as closely as possible to the way they were written out by the artist, but I occasionally needed to edit some recipes when a bit too much 'artistic freedom' was used.

One of my dreams with *Culinary Harmony* is to help support the music profession. As we approach the year 2000, with the difficult times the arts are experiencing, more and more types of fund-raising are needed. It is my hope that this recipe book will help contribute to this effort.

Enjoy the book and *Bon Appétit.*

David Rezits

With the great amount of correspondence I had during the writing of this book, I understandably received rejections from various artists who did not wish to be included. Even though some musicians did not wish to participate in my project, I still appreciated that they (or their agents) took time to respond to my requests. I found the reasons for declining to contribute to my recipe book to be quite sincere; and some were quite humorous. I thought I would share some of the responses that I received, without mentioning names.

Dear Mr. Rezits....I really feel I cannot help you with this as, over the years, I have contributed to about 20 recipe books with pretty much the same recipe!

(singer)

Dear David....Actually, had I been able in the course of my life to do more than boiling water for a kettle of tea or the odd hard-boiled egg, I would have definitely contacted you sooner; the creative in me would have wanted to 'share'...I don't seem to have developed a philosophical/therapeutic/cultural and/or enriching hobby such as cooking. I was spoiled all my life, everyone who loved me cooked (and well!) for me; I can attest some of them entered a mild state of TM while they chopped the parsley or diced their juliennes...

(pianist)

....The truth is that I am not only inactive in any way in the kitchen (my husband, thank God, does all the cooking), but am completely incompetent as well...

(singer)

Dear David....As far as your book about culinary harmony, I am afraid my wife and I will disappoint you. In fact we are very frugal, and no recipe is needed to cook some pasta, or a vegetable soup, or a couple of eggs....Believe it or not, we do not even have a book with recipes of any kind.

(violinist)

Unfortunately I cannot cook—although I enjoy fine food. My culinary skill is opening a can of soup. Sorry!

(pianist)

....I know nothing about food—nothing about cooking....Many of my colleagues will not let you down I trust....I once cooked dog food by mistake and ate it; so much for my taste buds.

(conductor)

....In all honesty, Ms._____has received so many requests that she is out of favorite recipes!!

(singer)

TABLE OF CONTENTS

BRASS

Photo: JIM CALDWELL

THOMAS BACON, HORN

Thomas Bacon's work in the United States, Europe, South America and Asia has placed him in the highest echelon of today's hornists. Born in Chicago, he began his musical studies on the piano at the age of five. At age nineteen, he had already performed with the Chicago Symphony, when he was invited to become principal horn of the Syracuse Symphony.

Then, in 1975, Lorin Maazel appointed him solo hornist of the Berlin Radio Symphony Orchestra. He lived in Berlin from 1975-1978 and performed with that city's leading musical organizations, including the Berlin Philharmonic, the Deutsche Oper Berlin, the Haydn Chamber Orchestra, and the Radio Free Berlin Big Band. Bacon was a frequent soloist on international tours with the Amati Ensemble and with the Berlin Radio Orchestra and made numerous recordings with the Radio Orchestra, including the virtuosic Horn Concertino by von Weber, and Dukas's "Villanelle."

In 1991, after serving for ten years as principal horn with the Houston Symphony Orchestra, Mr. Bacon was appointed to the faculty of Arizona State University, where he teaches horn and chamber music. With nearly one hundred performances annually, he continues concertizing in recital, chamber and orchestral engagements. Recent tours have taken him to Spain, Germany, Switzerland, Italy, Mexico, Canada and dozens of cities in the United States.

Mr. Bacon is also a founding member of Summit Brass, America's premier large brass ensemble. The group is comprised of principal players from major orchestras, including Chicago, New York, Los Angeles, San Francisco and St. Louis, as well as top soloists and recording artists from around the country. Summit Brass tours and records regularly, and hosts the annual Rafael Mendez Brass Institute in June. The institute draws students and professionals from around the world for two weeks of intensive coaching, performing, seminars and master classes.

A champion in the performance of contemporary music, Bacon has been involved in the premieres of hundreds of compositions and has inspired many composers to write new works for the horn. His recording *Dragons in the Sky* (Summit Records, 1992), includes several of the pieces that were composed for him. His most recent recording *Nighthawks,* with pianist Phillip Moll (Summit Records, 1994), features the complete horn and piano music of Alec Wilder.

Today, Mr. Bacon's presence is felt in every corner of the horn world through his many performances, publications and recordings. He is editor of *The Complete Hornist* for Southern Music Company, a series of music for horn solo and horn ensembles. He is widely sought after as a pedagogue and has given master classes and clinics on hundreds of university and college campuses around the world. Mr. Bacon has made over two dozen recordings on London, RCA, Telarc, Crystal, Centaur, Pro Arte, CBS, Gasparo, Vanguard, A&M, and Summit Records.

RED LIME CHICKEN FETTUCCINE
Serves 2 to 3

Mr. Bacon mentioned to the author that when he was principal horn of the Houston Symphony, he was the owner of the Munchies Café. The café was a chamber music nightclub and artists' hangout, which also served wonderful food. The following recipes were not on the café's menu, but nevertheless are favorites of Mr. Bacon.

2 tablespoons flour
2 skinless, boneless, chicken breast
   halves, cut into small cubes
⅓ cup fresh lime juice
1 tablespoon Cholula, (or other
   hot red sauce)
2 teaspoons honey

1 tablespoon chili powder
½ pound fettuccine or other pasta
2 or more tablespoons butter or oil
2 cloves garlic, crushed
1 medium-large tomato, chopped
1 medium red bell pepper, thinly sliced
Salt to taste

Mix flour with the chicken cubes. Mix together lime juice, red sauce, honey and chili powder. Prepare fettuccine or other pasta according to package directions. Melt butter or oil in large skillet over medium-high heat. Add garlic, cook briefly. Add sliced vegetables and sauté 3 to 4 minutes.

Push to one side of pan. Put chicken in skillet next to vegetables. Sauté and stir chicken until almost done. Stir vegetables and chicken together and reduce heat. Add lime juice mixture and stir until thickened. Remove from heat and salt to taste. Serve over cooked fettuccine, or other favorite pasta.

TUSCAN BEAN SOUP
Serves 8 to 10

1 pound ham and ham bones
1 pound dried marrow beans,
   or other plump white beans
2 to 3 tablespoons olive oil
2 cloves garlic, crushed
1 medium onion, finely chopped
1 carrot, finely chopped

1 celery rib, finely chopped
2 leeks, finely chopped
½ teaspoon dried rosemary, crushed
½ teaspoon fennel seed, crushed
½ teaspoon oregano, crushed
Salt and pepper to taste
Garlic croutons and Parmesan for garnish

Soak beans in water overnight. Drain the beans. Heat olive oil in large pot, cook vegetables and herbs over medium-low heat until they begin to brown. Add beans, ham and seasonings to the pot with vegetables. Cover with water and simmer gently until beans are very tender, about two hours, adding more water if needed.

Remove from heat and allow to cool enough to handle. Remove ham and bones from the pot and discard bones. Cut ham into very small pieces and set aside. Purée in blender about half of the beans and vegetables. Return purée to the pot. Return ham pieces to the pot and stir well. Season.

Photo: STEVEN A. EMERY

RONALD BARRON, TROMBONIST

Ronald Barron has been principal trombonist of the Boston Symphony Orchestra since 1975. He joined the orchestra in 1970, after being a member of the Montreal Symphony Orchestra, and also served as principal trombonist for the Boston Pops Orchestra for thirteen seasons. In 1974, he shared the highest prize awarded at the Munich International Competition for trombonists and appeared as soloist with the Bavarian Radio Orchestra. Mr. Barron has been soloist on many occasions with the Boston Pops, with regional New England orchestras, and has been a recitalist in the U.S., Europe, and Japan. In addition to numerous recordings with the Boston Symphony, and Boston Pops, he has recorded with the Canadian Brass, Empire Brass, and Summit Brass, and has three solo recordings: "Le Trombone Francais" and "Hindemith on Trombone" on the Boston Brass Series label, and "Cousins" on the Nonesuch label, with cornetist Gerard Schwarz.

Mr. Barron has been a faculty member for the International Trombone Workshop and the Keystone Brass Institute and teaches at Boston University and the Tanglewood Music Center.

SHASHLIK
(Barbecued Lamb)
Serves 8 to 10

Serve with red wine of some weight: Cotes du Rhone, Chateauneuf-du-Pape, Barbaresco, or Californian Petite Sirah or Zinfandel do well. Bordeaux or Californian Cabernet Sauvignon are fine, though slightly less well-matched to the flavor of the marinade.

Though good any time of year, summer evenings seem to match this wonderful outdoor style meal, served with cold salads of either pasta, potatoes, rice, or, of course fresh vegetables. --R.B.

1 **whole leg of lamb, 5 to 6 pounds, boned and flattened (ask your butcher to do this)**
2 **cups red wine**

½ **cup olive oil**
Garlic, at least one whole bulb, crushed
1 **teaspoon black pepper**
1 **tablespoon or more of oregano**

Combine red wine and oil (if you need more marinade, measure four parts wine to one part oil in whatever total volume you require to marinate the lamb). Use as much garlic in the marinade as possible, crushed, (at least one bulb), pepper, and a tablespoon or more of oregano.

Remove any outer membrane and marinate the lamb for some hours at room temperature, or overnight in the refrigerator. If you wish to cook the lamb on skewers, cut up into pieces or cubes *before* adding to marinade. It will make the cutting a little easier.

Grill lamb whole, or as small pieces or cubes, over a charcoal or wood fire, being careful not to overcook, medium-rare to medium is best for lamb (roughly 35 to 45 minutes).

The marinade can be used also on various vegetables cooked over the fire: eggplant, tomatoes, peppers, onions, mushrooms or any others usually associated with Mediterranean cuisine.

Rice pilaf makes a good starch with this meal.

Photo: ROSS PRESTIA

REBECCA BOWER, TROMBONIST

Rebecca Bower is currently co-principal trombone with the Pittsburgh Symphony Orchestra under the direction of Lorin Maazel. Ms. Bower is a founding board member of the International Women's Brass Conference and has been the editor of the IWBC newsletter since its inception in 1992. She is also currently on the faculty at Carnegie Mellon University.

Ms. Bower began her professional career at the age of 16, as trombonist with the San Jose Symphony. At the age of 17, she appeared as a soloist with the San Francisco Symphony as a result of winning first prize in their Young Musicians' Awards. Ms. Bower earned her B.M. from the California Institute of the Arts and her M.M. from the Yale School of Music. Before becoming a member of the Pittsburgh Symphony in 1989, Ms. Bower held the position of principal trombone with the Springfield Symphony in Massachusetts and the Rhode Island Philharmonic. She was also the trombone instructor at the University of Connecticut in Storrs, Hartt School of Music and Wesleyan University.

In September of 1993, Ms. Bower enjoyed the honor of appearing at The White House in Washington, D.C. as part of a 15-woman ensemble of brass and percussion players. The group performed the world premiere of the fanfare entitled *Celebration*, composed by Joan Tower and dedicated to Hillary Clinton. The occasion was the opening reception for the International Women's Forum Annual Conference. Ms. Bower was invited to participate as a result of her affiliation with The International Women's Brass Conference.

CINNAMON ROLLS
Makes 12 rolls

I love sweets, and breakfast is my favorite meal of the day, so I enjoy making this "Cinnamon Rolls" recipe quite often. --R.B.

Dough:
½ cup warm water
2 packages dry yeast
1 cup scalded milk
1 cup sugar
1 teaspoon salt
2 beaten eggs
4 cups sifted flour (more if needed)
1 tablespoon cinnamon
¼ cup butter or margarine, melted

Filling:
¼ cup melted butter
½ cup chopped walnuts or pecans
5 tablespoons chopped raisins
¾ cup brown sugar
½ tablespoon cinnamon

In a cup, add yeast to warm water. In a saucepan, scald milk (heat until almost boiling). Blend in sugar and salt until dissolved. Let stand until warm. Blend in yeast and eggs.

In a large bowl, combine yeast mixture with flour and cinnamon. Blend in butter. Knead dough on floured board for about 5 minutes (add more flour if necessary). Shape into ball, place in greased bowl and cover with towel or plastic wrap. (At this point, you can refrigerate dough overnight if you would like to prepare it the night before using). Let stand until its size has doubled, approximately 1 hour.

Knead again. Roll out into a ¼-inch thick rectangle (about 12 x 5-inches). Brush dough with melted butter, sprinkle with nuts, raisins, brown sugar, and an extra sprinkle of cinnamon, if you choose. Roll up lengthwise.

Cut into 1-inch slices and place each slice in a well-buttered muffin tin. Bake at 325 degrees for 20 minutes. Use toothpick to test center for doneness. Pick should come out clean. Do not overcook. Remove rolls from pan immediately and 'dig in'!

Photo: CHRISTOPHER MILLARD

BARBARA BUTLER AND CHARLES GEYER, TRUMPETERS

Barbara Butler and Charles Geyer have been performing as a double-trumpet duo since the mid 1970s, when they appeared as soloists under Leonard Slatkin with the Grant Park Symphony Orchestra in Chicago. At that time, they also began performing with a Chicago group called *Music of the Baroque*, an ensemble that is now syndicated and heard world-wide on broadcasts and recordings. Butler and Geyer solo with this ensemble every season in Baroque solos and duo-concerti by composers such as Bach, Vivaldi, Torelli, Pezel and Telemann.

Recently, the Butler-Geyer double-trumpet duo has appeared with the Des Moines Symphony, Grand Teton Music Festival, Rochester Philharmonic, Lincoln Symphony Orchestra and orchestras in New York, Michigan, Iowa and Montana.

Butler and Geyer are also involved in a recording project of music for two trumpets and organ and perform regularly in Boston, Chicago and New York with this group. Their first recording, music by Bach and Handel, has been released on the Gasparo label.

Both former full-time orchestral trumpet players, Butler and Geyer have devoted much of their successful careers to chamber music and solo performing. They are much in demand, touring and recording with the Eastman Brass, an all faculty brass quintet in residence at the prestigious Eastman School of Music in Rochester, New York. The Eastman Brass takes great pride in being the serious brass quintet, performing breathtaking transcriptions as well as recent commissions, such as the 1988 *The Three Wise Men* by Pulitzer Prize-winner John Harbison, recently featured on CBS TV with Charles Kuralt, narrator.

During the summer months, the Butler-Geyer duo performs with the Grand Teton Music Festival Orchestra, in Jackson Hole, Wyoming. Each summer they present a special event concert featuring a variety of trumpet spectaculars, always a sold-out event.

As professors of trumpet at the Eastman School of Music, Butler and Geyer have a great effect on the young trumpet players in America and abroad, giving master classes at various conservatories and universities when on tour, most recently in Italy, Spain, and Finland.

Though there is music available from the Baroque era for two trumpets (with organ and orchestral accompaniment), there is little from the 20th century. Butler and Geyer have begun commissioning music for this combination, such as the recent Suite for Two Trumpets and Orchestra by Jeff Beal, a trumpet soloist and film-writer from San Francisco, and the *Carmen Fantasia* for two trumpets and orchestra by Bizet, arranged by Donald Hunsberger.

Though Butler and Geyer began their careers separately and continue also to perform individually, they continue to draw attention from critics and audiences alike for their duo-performing style. When heard separately, each has a unique sound and style, but the years' experience of playing together has meshed their duo-style into a sound so alike that it has been noted that with eyes closed, the sound appears so continuous and flowing that you cannot tell them apart.

Butler and Geyer met in Chicago when Butler took over the principal trumpet position with the Grand Park Symphony Orchestra, when Geyer left it to expand his duties with the Chicago Symphony Orchestra at Ravinia. A year later, Butler left Chicago to be co-principal trumpet with the Vancouver Symphony Orchestra, returning in the summers to the Grant Park Symphony.

Two years later Geyer, who had been a member of the Chicago Symphony for 12 years, left Chicago to become principal trumpet with the Houston Symphony Orchestra. In 1980, both players resigned their orchestral posts to join the Eastman School of Music faculty in Rochester, New York.

They make their home on a farm in upstate New York, which they share with their young daughter, Jorie, and many dogs, cats and Arabian horses.

BABB'S COFFEE-BRANDY ICE CREAM

Eat only one large bowl per day, followed by 4 large garlic cloves to offset high cholesterol intake. --B.B. & C.G.

1 cup Kahlua
½ cup brandy
½ cup chocolate syrup
3 pints whipping cream

3 pints half-&-half
1 tablespoon vanilla
1 whole egg (optional)
Ice cream maker

Combine ingredients into chilled ice cream maker.

Photo: Courtesy of Chicago Symphony Orchestra

JAY FRIEDMAN, TROMBONIST/CONDUCTOR

Chicago native Jay Friedman attended Roosevelt University, where he majored in composition and studied conducting with Joseph Kreins. After two years in the Florida Symphony and four years with the Civic Orchestra of Chicago, he joined the Chicago Symphony Orchestra in 1962 and was appointed principal trombonist in 1964.

Mr. Friedman frequently has been a soloist with the Chicago Symphony, most recently in Ellen Zwilich's Trombone Concerto, which was commissioned for him by the Edward F. Schmidt Family. He is an exceptional arranger and his works are performed worldwide. He also is in demand as a conductor and as a teacher of orchestral style, and he has conducted orchestral seminars with such ensembles as the Danish Radio Orchestra, Stockholm Philharmonic, Gothenburg Symphony, Oslo Opera, and Helsingfors Symphony. His article on conducting was published in the September 1993 issue of *The Instrumentalist* magazine. In 1991, Jay founded the River Cities Philharmonic, a professional orchestra committed to the highest standards of music making.

A noted Sibelius interpreter, Mr. Friedman recently returned from Sweden, where he conducted Sibelius's First Symphony with the Universität von Gothenburg Symphony Orchestra and Mussorgsky's *Pictures at an Exhibition* with the world champion Gothenburg Brass Band. In 1994, he made his conducting debut with the Malmo Symphony.

JAY'S FORTISSIMO CHILI
Makes about 9 to 10 cups

This ain't no pussy-footin' up north "Stew." This is real Texas chili—just meat and spices, what the good Lord intended. The extras come right at serving time. It looks like some fantastic dessert. The paprika makes a mild chili and mild chili gives flavor, while hot chili gives heat. Do yourself a favor and buy some good quality pure chili powder. --J.F.

4 medium onions, finely chopped	Salt to taste
8 cloves garlic, finely chopped	1 chocolate bar
2 pounds ground beef	16 oz. can beans (your choice)
6 tablespoons chili powder	16 oz. can tomatoes (or fresh tomatoes)
6 tablespoons paprika (*secret ingredient*)	1 onion (for topping)
2 tablespoons cumin powder	Grated cheese
2 large cans of beer	Tabasco sauce

Take chopped onions and chopped cloves of garlic and sauté in some suet or vegetable oil until transparent. Add ground beef until it turns grey. Add the 6 tablespoons of chili powder, paprika and cumin powder.

Add 2 cans beer. Mixture should be watery (beery). Simmer uncovered as long as you can stand it (about 4 hours). Carefully add salt until chili flavor is at its best. Add more beer if necessary. Add a chocolate bar one hour before serving *(I don't know why)*.

Spoon chili into serving bowls one-half full. Put in a few cooked beans, some canned tomatoes, chopped raw onion and grated cheese on top; heat in the microwave or broiler until the cheese is melted all over the top. Pour on as much Tabasco sauce as you can stand and enjoy.

Photo: © GAIL NOGLE PHOTOGRAPHY

GREGORY HUSTIS, HORNIST

Gregory Hustis has been principal horn of the Dallas Symphony since 1976. A graduate of the Curtis Institute of Music, where he studied with Mason Jones, Mr. Hustis has performed as soloist with numerous orchestras, including the Utah Symphony, the Knoxville Symphony, the Dallas Chamber Orchestra, the Florida West Coast Symphony, the Latvian Chamber Orchestra, the Northwest Chamber Orchestra, and the Dallas Symphony.

As a clinician, chamber music player, and recitalist, he has been featured as a guest artist at many festivals, including the Sarasota Music Festival, Scotia Festival, Round Top, five International Horn Society Workshops, the Mainly Mozart Festival, the Santa Fe Chamber Music Festival, and the Lapplands Festspel in Sweden. He has

toured with the Summit Brass. In 1986, he performed with Lorin Maazel and the World Philharmonic Orchestra in Rio de Janeiro.

Besides the scores of orchestral recordings he has made as principal horn of the Dallas Symphony, Mr. Hustis can be heard as soloist on many recordings, including a compact disc for Crystal Records with the Dallas Chamber Orchestra and a recently released disc of Reinecke trios for clavier. Prior to joining the Dallas Symphony, he was principal horn of the Hamilton Philharmonic in Ontario, Canada. In addition to his varied performance schedule, Mr. Hustis teaches horn at Southern Methodist University and is a member of the Advisory Council of the International Horn Society.

COLD ORIENTAL NOODLES WITH PEANUT SAUCE

Serves 6

This recipe is great with beer!! --G.H.

FOR SAUCE:

6 large cloves garlic, minced

2 tablespoons fresh ginger root, peeled and finely chopped

1½ cups fresh cilantro, chopped (about 1 large bunch)

1 tablespoon peanut oil

1 tablespoon hot chili oil

½ cup smooth peanut butter (a natural brand is best)

½ cup regular (or low-salt) soy sauce

3 tablespoons rice vinegar, or more if needed

3 tablespoons sugar

FOR NOODLES:

1 **pound fine somen noodles***	6 **scallions, thin-sliced diagonally**
2 **tablespoons Oriental sesame oil**	1½ **pound package silken-firm**
½ **cup chopped fresh cilantro, plus**	**tofu, cut into ½-inch cubes**
sprigs for garnish	**Roasted peanuts, chopped**

To make sauce: add garlic with the ginger root and cilantro and mince in food processor. Add oils, peanut butter, soy sauce, vinegar and sugar, then blend together well. (If a thinner sauce is desired, stir in some hot water). The sauce will keep covered in the refrigerator for 3 to 4 weeks.

*To make noodles: In a pan of salted water, boil noodles for 3 minutes, or until tender, drain, and rinse in cold water until cooled. In a large bowl, toss the noodles well in oil, chopped cilantro, scallions and tofu. The noodles may be prepared a day in advance of making the recipe and kept covered and chilled. **Just before serving,** toss the noodles with the peanut sauce and coat them well and garnish them with the chopped peanuts and cilantro.

SHRIMP SALAD WITH BASIL AND LEMON

Serves 4

This dish leaves plenty of room for a big dessert.

1 **pound shrimp**	⅔ **cup olive oil, or to taste**
1 **cup peas, or more if desired**	2 **tablespoons fresh basil leaves**
1 **cup celery, sliced diagonally**	8 **small lettuce leaves**
2 **tablespoons grated lemon rind**	8 **lemon slices**
6 **tablespoons lemon juice**	8 **tomato slices**
Salt and white pepper to taste	

Cook, peel and clean shrimp, then chill. Boil some salted water in small saucepan and cook peas for 5 to 8 minutes, or until tender. Drain peas and refresh under cold water. Pat dry. Add peas to shrimp. Stir in celery and lemon rind. Blend lemon juice, pinch of salt, the oil and basil in blender until emulsified. Drizzle over the shrimp mixture and toss gently to coat. Add salt and pepper to taste. Divide the salad into four salad plates. Garnish with lettuce, lemon and tomato slices.

Photo: PIOTR GAJEWICZ

ANNE McANENEY, TRUMPETER, LONDON BRASS

London Brass grew out of the Philip Jones Brass Ensemble when Philip Jones retired from trumpet playing in 1986, 35 years after the formation of his first group.

The current members, which include: Mark Bennett-trumpet, John Barclay-trumpet, Andy Crowley-trumpet, Anne McAneney-trumpet, Richard Bissill-horn, Lindsay Shilling-trombone, David Purser-trombone, Richard Edwards-trombone, David Stewart-trombone, and Oren Marshall-tuba, lead busy individual careers as soloists, chamber, orchestral and jazz musicians. They devote a large part of each year to their work together, making regular tours to Europe, the Far East and the U.S.A., as well as giving concerts in London and around Great Britain, promoting their own educational events, as well as recording and broadcasting.

Highlights of recent seasons include a tour of British music conservatoires, celebrating their appointment as ensemble-in-residence at the Royal College of Music; a nation-wide tour for the Arts Council's contemporary music network; the release of a major recording of the works of Giovanni Gabrieli and other masters of renaissance Italy; a visit to the Far East, with concerts and master classes in Shanghai and Beijing; and the production of an hour-long documentary about the ensemble for TV and video.

The ensemble aims to stimulate interest in brass ensemble music through its policies of commissioning new music, giving encouragement and opportunities to young performers and composers, and, of course, by the excellence of its performance in the concert hall and on record.

LUNCHEON BRASS

*Like many international ensembles, **London Brass** spends more of its travel-time abroad than at home, and we are lucky enough to have a marvelous network of agencies around the world who organize tours for us. In January 1993, we had a particularly delectable trip to Italy, with eight concerts in ten days. The venues were close enough together that we were always able to leave our hotel comfortably after breakfast and arrive in the next town around midday, giving us ample time to find and enjoy a good restaurant before rehearsing for the evening's concert. We were joined on this occasion by the jazz trumpeter, **Guy Barker**, who was touring with us for the first time. Sitting down—slightly bemused—to his seventh successive (and excessive) midday meal, he said, "You've got the name of your ensemble wrong. You should call yourselves **Luncheon Brass**!"*

*The other side of the picture shows itself when one ends up short of time; this is a situation that will be horribly familiar, I'm sure, to many readers. Traveling recently in the Far East, we found ourselves in the unenticing position of having to undertake a one-night stand in Hong Kong—in more relaxed circumstances, a wonderful town to visit. Our inbound flight from Taipei was delayed by two hours; the coach driver got lost between the airport and the hotel, and we eventually arrived at the venue a scant hour before the concert was due to start, unfed, unwatered, and needing to rehearse. I asked the organizers—who were extremely sympathetic to our plight—whether they could arrange some food for us at the concert hall. Being aware of the local reputation as the gourmet center of the Far East, we requested that they bring us some **dim sum**-Chinese snacks. We went ahead with our rehearsal and came off-stage a little later to find ten chairs and a trestle-table set up for us, laden with Big Macs and cola. We left first thing the next morning for Beijing, and this remained our one "gourmet" experience of Hong Kong. Nonetheless, I think we can safely say that we had more three-course lunches than 'burger' suppers as we made our way around the world, so in the end, we still prefer to think of ourselves as **Luncheon Brass**.*

HARVEY G. PHILLIPS, TUBIST

Harvey G. Phillips, referred to by the press as "Paganini of the Tuba," "Mr. Tuba" "Tubameister," and "Iacocca of the Tuba," is described by Gunther Schuller as "...a legend among brass players and other instrumentalists...the major progenitor in his field...his efforts on behalf of other musicians never cease..." A world renowned artist, his performances include two dozen Carnegie Hall (NYC) recitals, the first solo tuba recital at the Library of Congress, over two hundred clinic/recitals at colleges and universities throughout the world, with international tours of Japan, Australia, Scandinavia and Europe.

Currently, Harvey Phillips is executive editor, *The Instrumentalist*; board chairman, Summit Brass and Rafael Mendez Brass Institute; consultant in the arts; founder/president, The Harvey Phillips Foundations, Inc. (OCTUBAFEST, TUBACHRISTMAS, TUBASANTAS, TUBAJAZZ, SUMMERTUBAFESTS), clinician, Warner Bros. Publications, Inc.

Formerly, Phillips was a freelance artist in New York City (radio/television, commercial recordings on every major USA label). Other positions have included: principal tubist with the Ringling Bros. and Barnum & Bailey Circus Band, Sauter Finegan Orchestra, New York City Ballet, New York City Opera, Band of America, Goldman Band, U.S. Army Field Band, Symphony of the Air, RCA Victor Orchestra, NBC Opera Orchestra, and the Festival Casals Orchestra. Phillips was a founding member (and tubist for 14 years) of The New York Brass Quintet; vice president for Financial Affairs,

The New England Conservatory of Music (1967-1971); co-founder/past, president, Tubists Universal Brotherhood Association (T.U.B.A.); chairman/host, First International Tuba-Euphonium Symposium (1973); chairman, First International Brass Symposium, Montreux, Switzerland (1974); influenced founding of the International Trumpet Guild (1975); chairman/director First International Brass Congress, Montreux, Switzerland (1976); co-chairman/host, Second International Brass Congress (1984); judge, First Solo Tuba Competition - Concours International d'Execution Musicale, Geneva, Switzerland (1991).

Harvey Phillips has received many honors which include: principal tuba, Circus Hall of Fame Band (selected by Merle Evans); Harvey Phillips Day & honorary doctor of music degree, New England Conservatory of Music (1971); Harvey Phillips Day - Bicentennial Celebration, Marionville, Missouri (1976); Kappa Kappa Psi Distinguished Service to Music Award (1978); Proclamation: Harvey Phillips Weekend, Office of the Governor, State of Missouri (1982); honorary doctor of humanities degree, University of Missouri (1987); "First" Mentor Award, Association of Concert Bands (1994); Sousa Foundation "Medal of the Order of Merit" (Sudler Award); elected to the Academy of Wind and Percussion Arts, National Band Association (1995).

Harvey Phillips currently resides in Bloomington, Indiana where he holds the title of distinguished professor of music emeritus at Indiana University.

TUBARANCH EGGNOG

TUBARANCH EGGNOG is the smoothest eggnog you will ever have. It brings out the best in friends and relatives. DO NOT GIVE TO STRANGERS; YOU MUST FIRST MAKE EVERYONE YOUR FRIEND—THEN SERVE GENEROUSLY! --H.P.

1 dozen eggs
1 cup sugar (to taste)
1 pinch salt
1 'fifth' Wild Turkey Bourbon
1 pint Meyer's Dark Jamaica Rum

3 pints heavy cream
1 pint milk
1 pint Remy Martin V.S.O.P. Cognac
Freshly ground nutmeg

Separate eggs, set whites aside. In a 2-gallon mixing bowl, beat egg yolks until frothy. Blend sugar and salt into the frothy yolks, stir until smooth.

Add Wild Turkey slowly and blend into yolks. Add Meyer's Dark Rum slowly and blend into yolks. Let mixture set for at least one hour (liquor will "cook" egg yolks.)

Very slowly add heavy cream and milk. Stir and blend well. Wait one-half hour.

Beat egg whites until stiff (peaked). Pour stiffly beaten egg whites onto top of mixture and dip through until well blended. *Patience will be rewarded!* Slowly add Remy Martin V.S.O.P. Stir until well blended.

Cover the bowl and set deep in clean snow to chill. When thoroughly chilled, serve with a dash of freshly ground nutmeg.

Share with family and friends, dip slowly. Enjoy!

Photo: Courtesy of Chicago Symphony Orchestra

GENE POKORNY, TUBIST

In September 1988, Sir Georg Solti appointed Gene Pokorny to succeed Arnold Jacobs in the coveted position of principal tuba of the Chicago Symphony Orchestra. One year later, Pokorny began playing with that ensemble full-time. He took a leave of absence in the 1992-93 season to play in the Los Angeles Philharmonic Orchestra as its principal tubist. In that year, he also participated in the film studios playing the scores for the movies, "Toys," "The Fugitive," "The Program," "Jurassic Park" and Tim Burton's *Nightmare Before Christmas.*

A proud native of southern California, he studied tuba with Jeffrey Reynolds, Larry Johansen, Tommy Johnson and Roger Bobo. After attending the University of Redlands and graduating from the University of Southern California, he played in the Israel Philharmonic, the Utah Symphony and the St. Louis Symphony. He is a founding member of Summit Brass, a large professional brass ensemble consisting of outstanding instrumentalists from all across America. He has played with the Colorado Music Festival in Boulder, Colorado and the Teton Music Festival in Jackson Hole, Wyoming.

Pokorny has given solo recitals across the country and is active in organizing activities for tubists. His performance of the Hindemith Sonata for bass tuba and piano (Summit); and his first solo recording, *Tuba Tracks* (Summit) released in 1992, have received rave reviews: "Gene Pokorny of the Chicago Symphony is absolutely flabbergasting," *Fanfare* magazine. "The results have to be heard to be believed" —*Salt Lake Tribune.* "Gene Pokorny, tuba, offers what may well be the most enthusi-

astic performance of the [Hindemith] Sonata for Tuba and Piano ever recorded." —*International Trombone Association Journal.* "Pokorny elevates solo tuba playing with these performances and displays some of the finest artistry ever recorded." —*The Instrumentalist* magazine. "Many players are intimidated by the work's stark structure, but Pokorny is one of that small number who realize it's okay to give this piece a personal interpretation, which he does to great effect." —*Stereophile* magazine. "The best part of this recording is the way Mr. Pokorny's personality is evident in every note he plays and every word in the program notes." —*T.U.B.A. Journal.*

Besides having written several articles for the *T.U.B.A. Journal,* Pokorny enjoys giving clinics and master classes to musicians who happen to be brass players. Recently, he wrote an exclusive chapter pertaining to orchestral auditions and auditioning in the *Tuba Source Book,* released in 1995. As a member of the William Herschel Society, he researched the music and life of that 18th century astronomer/musician from England and organized a concert honoring Herschel with the Chicago Symphony trombone section at the Adler Planetarium. He is also a member of the Union Pacific Historical Society and spends time railfanning (watching trains), cooking, studying astronomy, and being an avid enthusiast of not only "The Three Stooges" but also of his good friend David "Red" Lehr, the greatest Dixieland sousaphonist in the known universe.

He lives with his wife, Beth Lodal (a musician who happens to have a real job), in Oak Park, Illinois.

GUACAMOLE DIP

When I auditioned for the St. Louis Symphony in 1983, a portion of the application form asked for "Optional, additional information." This was requested after the usual "previous performance experience," "education," "formal teacher" questions.

*Since I figured most of the musical questions would be answered either in the application or by my audition on stage, I thought I would give them some **useful** information in the "Optional, additional information" category. I included this recipe. [I also got the job] --G.P.*

4 medium avocados	**3 to 4 green onions (scallions), diced**
Juice from 1 fresh lemon	**1 tomato, diced**
1½ teaspoons garlic powder	**¼ pound Monterey Jack cheese, grated**
¾ teaspoon salt	**¼ pound sharp Cheddar cheese, grated**
¼ teaspoon pepper	**Salsa (16 oz. jar)**
8 oz. sour cream	**Tortilla chips**

Mash the avocados and add lemon juice, garlic powder, salt and pepper to taste. Spread on bottom of a 2-quart (8 x 8 x 2-inch or similar-sized) serving dish (glass is visually attractive). Layer sour cream on top of avocado dip.

Layer onions on top of sour cream. Layer diced tomato on top of onions. Layer on cheeses and then salsa.

Serve with tortilla chips.

Photo: A. RENTMEESTER

JEFFREY REYNOLDS, TROMBONIST

Jeffrey Reynolds has been the bass trombonist with the Los Angeles Philharmonic since 1969. During these years, he has performed under Music Directors Zubin Mehta, Carlo Maria Giulini, André Previn and Esa-Pekka Salonen, and guest conductors including Vladimir Ashkenazy, Pierre Boulez, Erich Leinsdorf, Simon Rattle, Kurt Sanderling, Yuri Temirkanov and Franz Welser-Möst.

Reynolds grew up and was educated in the Los Angeles area, graduating from California State University at Long Beach in 1967. His orchestral experience includes the Young Musicians Foundation Debut Orchestra, the American Youth Symphony, the symphonies of Long Beach, Downey, Orange County, San Diego and St. Louis, and the San Francisco Ballet.

Jeffrey Reynolds has been a member of the California

Brass Quintet, the L.A. Brass society, the Los Angeles Brass, and the Hollywood Trombones, and has performed chamber music with students of the Los Angeles Philharmonic Institute and at the Ojai Festival. He has been heard on soundtracks for most of the major film studios, and has performed on recordings for labels such as Angel, CBS/Sony Classical, Crystal, Deutsche Grammophon, London, Philips, RCA Red Seal, Sheffield Lab, and Telarc.

Mr. Reynolds has long been a champion of the Moravian Trombone Choir, a church brass group of up to 100 players; he was its music director for 25 years. He teaches, composes, and arranges music for publication and is in demand as a clinician and soloist at brass festivals. His hobbies include model trains, mountain biking and four-wheel driving.

EL JEFE'S SALSA
Makes about 3½ cups

This salsa lasts several weeks under refrigeration. This recipe was developed over many years of "salsa testing" and refining! --J.R.

1 large onion, coarsely chopped (2 cups)	6 oz. can tomato paste
3 large cloves of garlic	2 oz. white wine vinegar
1 large green fresh Anaheim chili*	1 teaspoon ground cumin
3 small yellow fresh chilies*	2 tablespoons fresh oregano leaves
1 (or more) fresh jalapeño chili,*	1 teaspoon salt
½ cup fresh cilantro (coriander) leaves	1 teaspoon pepper
28 oz. can whole tomatoes, drained	Juice of 1 lime

Combine onion, garlic, and chilies in food processor. Process with metal blade until chopped medium-fine. Add cilantro leaves, tomatoes (save juice), tomato paste, vinegar, cumin, oregano, salt, pepper and lime juice. Blend again but do not over blend. It should be chunky. You may add juice from canned tomatoes to thin mixture, if too thick.

Refrigerate. Serve with tortilla chips.

*For milder salsa, remove seeds from chilies. If hotter salsa is desired, add more jalapeño and leave seeds in chilies.

Photo: HAROLD SINCLAIR

ROBERT ROUTCH, HORNIST

Robert Routch's diverse career includes performances in recital and chamber music, as soloist with orchestra, and as jazz improviser and composer. When he was seventeen, he performed the Strauss Horn Concerto No. 1 with the Philadelphia Orchestra; he has since appeared as soloist with numerous orchestras throughout the United States and Europe.

Now an artist of the Chamber Music Society of Lincoln Center, Mr. Routch began to perform with the society in 1973 and has recorded Poulenc's Elegy, Sextet, the Schubert Octet and the Mozart Horn Quintet with the society. He has also performed, recorded and toured with TASHI and has had a long association with Music From Marlboro and the Marlboro Music Festival. He has appeared as guest artist with such string quartets as the Tokyo, Emerson, Juilliard and Guarneri.

As a member of the Young Concert Artists roster, Mr. Routch gave recitals at the Metropolitan Museum and the 92nd Street "Y" in New York City, which included jazz improvisation. Mr. Routch is co-founder of Confluence, a jazz quartet, which has performed in Europe as well as the United States. He has collaborated with Ornette Coleman and is a member of Gerry Mulligan's "Rebirth of the Cool" jazz ensemble. His recordings appear on the RCA Red Seal, Columbia Masterworks, Polydar, Erato, Sunnyside, Musical Heritage, Arabesque, and Sony Classical labels.

"BERRIES" TUCKWELL

Select fresh seasonal berries—strawberries, raspberries, blueberries, blackberries and wild berries. Rinse, if necessary, and allow to air dry.

Drench with pear brandy, not pear liquor, as it is too sweet. Can be enjoyed solo, or nicely 'orchestrated' as an encore.

SALMON "ELLA"

Other than procuring only the finest, coolest, freshest salmon fillets, "sassy" ginger and a swingin', hot broiler, this recipe, in honor of Ms. Fitzgerald, must always be improvised as she would 'scat' chorus after chorus to Kern, Gershwin and Cole Porter—always honoring the beauty of the melody, while still adding a little something of herself. --R.R.

Photo: JOE HENSON

DOC SEVERINSEN, TRUMPETER

Doc Severinsen, best known to late night television audiences as the "Tonight Show's" flamboyant Grammy Award-winning music director, has established a multi-dimensional career beyond his late night repertoire, including symphonic, jazz and big band concert appearances, recordings, commercials and designing and manufacturing trumpets.

Though Severinsen's signature has been his superb trumpet playing, quick witted banter and original style of clothes on the "Tonight Show," he is one of today's preeminent instrumentalists. In a professional career that spans over 40 years, Severinsen has recorded over 30 albums, ranging in style from big band to jazz fusion to classical.

Severinsen's recent recordings have included the Grammy nominated, "Once More With Feeling" and "Merry Christmas from the Tonight Show Orchestra." Both recordings, from the Amherst label, were performed by Doc and the "Tonight Show" band and have received rave reviews. His last album, "Unforgettably Doc," on the Telarc label, highlights Severinsen's musical diversity with the trumpet to the backdrop of the Cincinnati Pops Orchestra.

Today, Doc continues to tour across the country performing concerts in an array of musical styles. He performs classical and pop music as a guest conductor/performer with symphony orchestras. In addition to guest stints, Doc is principal pops conductor of the Phoenix Symphony, the Buffalo Philharmonic, the Minnesota Orchestra and the Milwaukee Symphony. Severinsen also plays sizzling jazz with his jazz group, Facets, and big band tunes with the famous former "Tonight Show" Band, now known as Doc Severinsen and His Big Band.

Devoted to his instrument, Severinsen practices a minimum of two hours a day. He has been voted Top Brass Player more than ten times in *Playboy's* prestigious

annual music poll and received a Grammy Award in 1987 for Best Jazz Instrumental Performance-Big Band, for his world premiere digital recording on the Amherst label, "Doc Severinsen and the Tonight Show Band-Volume I" album. Other recordings on Amherst Label include "Facets," and "Merry Christmas from the Tonight Show Orchestra."

Severinsen's success dates back to his childhood hometown of Arlington, Oregon. Nicknamed "Little Doc" after his father, a dentist, Dr. Carl Severinsen, Little Doc had originally wanted to play the trombone, but senior Severinsen, a gifted amateur violinist, urged him to study violin. The younger Severinsen insisted on the trombone, but had to settle for the only horn available in their small community—a trumpet.

One week later with the help of his father and book of instructions, the seven-year-old was so good that he was invited to join the high school band. At the age of twelve, Little Doc won the Music Educator's National Contest and while still in high school, was hired to go on the road with the famous Ted Fio Rito Orchestra.

After completing his education and serving in the Army, Severinsen toured with Tommy Dorsey, Benny Goodman and Charlie Barnet bands. He finally settled down in New York as an NBC staff musician in 1949, joining the "Tonight Show" Orchestra in 1962, and becoming the music director in 1967. Somewhere along the line "Little" was lost, but "Doc" stayed and became known to late night audiences across America. Doc took his place in history in July of 1995, when he was honored with his own "star" on Hollywood's renown Walk of Fame.

In his non-musical moments, Doc enjoys horses, cooking (Italian is his specialty), collecting American art and keeping fit with daily runs and workouts—interests he shares with his wife, television producer/writer Emily Marshall.

DOC'S FAVORITE "FISH SOUP"

Serves 4 to 6

Doc's favorite recipe comes from the famous Italian cookbook "TRATTORIA COOKING" by Biba Caggiano. Make sure that all the fish in this recipe is fresh as possible. Doc added "optional" for the 6 oz. of squid. If you include the squid in the recipe, observe the cleaning instructions below from Ms. Caggiano's book.

¼ **cup olive oil, preferably extra virgin**
1 **small onion, finely minced**
3 **cloves garlic, finely minced**
2 **anchovy fillets, chopped**
½ **teaspoon dried red pepper flakes**
⅓ **cup red wine vinegar**
1 **cup dry white wine**
5 **cups canned imported Italian tomatoes**
 with their juice, put through a strainer
 or food mill to remove the seeds

Salt to taste
½ **pound each of the following fish fillets:**
 halibut, sea bass and swordfish steaks,
 all cut into 2-inch thick pieces
4 **oz. shrimp, peeled and veined**
4 **oz. sea scallops**
6 **oz. squid, cleaned* and cut**
 into 1-inch rings (optional)
2 **tablespoons chopped fresh parsley**
12 **small slices Italian bread,**
 toasted or grilled

Heat the oil in a large saucepan over medium heat. Add the onion and cook, stirring, until it begins to color, about 5 to 6 minutes. Add the garlic, anchovies, and red pepper and cook, stirring, about 1 minute.

Raise the heat to high and add the vinegar. When the vinegar is almost all reduced, less than 1 minute, add the wine. Cook and stir until it is reduced by half, 3 to 4 minutes. Add the tomatoes and season with salt. Bring to a boil, then lower the heat to medium-low and cook, uncovered, 5 to 6 minutes, stirring a few times.

Add the fish pieces and let simmer 2 to 3 minutes, then add shrimp and scallops and cook until the fish is cooked through, 2 to 3 minutes. Lastly, add squid and cook less than 1 minute. Stir in parsley, taste, adjust seasonings, and serve at once with slices of grilled bread or polenta.

*To clean the squid, hold it in one hand and gently pull away the tentacles. Cut the head off just below the eyes and discard it. Remove the little beak just inside the tentacles. Remove the squid bone from the body. (This is actually a piece of cartilage that resembles clear plastic). Clean the inside of the squid body under cold running water, pulling out any matter still inside. Wash and peel away the grayish skin from the body and tentacles and discard.

CELLO

Photo: HART HOLLMAN

ITALO BABINI, CELLIST

One of the nation's most outstanding artists and principal cellist of the Detroit Symphony Orchestra since 1960, Italo Babini occupies the Symphony's James C. Gordon Chair. A native of Brazil, he began his musical studies at the age of five with his father Tom Babini. As a youth, he gave many recitals throughout South America. In his late teens, Babini won a scholarship to study in Munich, which was renewed for three consecutive years. A later scholarship enabled him to study another year, this time at Yale. During that period, he was first cellist with the New Haven and Connecticut Symphony Orchestras and won the concerto competition at Tanglewood, appearing as soloist with the Berkshire Festival Orchestra. A scholarship to study with Pablo Casals took him to San Juan, Puerto Rico, where he appeared as soloist at the Casals Festival and in recitals with Jesus Maria Sanroma.

Babini has made several recordings and often appears as soloist with the Detroit Symphony Orchestra, in recital, and with chamber ensembles throughout the United States and Europe. He has collaborated with many famous conductors, including Antal Dorati, Paul Paray, Sixten Ehrling, Aldo Ceccato, Arthur Fiedler, Eleazar de Carvalho and Rafael Frühbeck de Burgos.

BABINI'S CAMARÃO

Serves 4 to 6

Everybody enthusiastically comments about this dish. The amount of spices used is relative to each person's taste. I use them in generous quantities. Shrimp is best served over plain rice. --I.B.

2 **pounds medium-sized fresh shrimp**
6 **cloves garlic, chopped**
3 **green onions, chopped**
1 **large green pepper, coarsely chopped**
3 **tablespoons virgin olive oil**
1 **teaspoon salt or to taste**

1 **teaspoon black pepper**
¼ **cup fresh cilantro, chopped**
2 **medium tomatoes, chopped**
3 **cups cold milk, plus a little extra to dissolve 1 tablespoon cornstarch**
½ **cup Heinz ketchup**

Cook shrimp in GENTLY boiling water (with shell) until nicely pink, but not overcooked (3 to 4 minutes). Drain shrimp, remove shell and clean, set aside. Combine garlic, onions, and green pepper and lightly sauté in olive oil for 8 to 10 minutes. Add salt, pepper, cilantro, and tomatoes, simmer an additional 5 minutes. In a 4-quart pot, combine milk, cornstarch, and ketchup with rest of ingredients; simmer on low heat, covered, for at least one-half hour.

Photo: JEFFREY ROTHSTEIN

CARTER BREY, CELLIST

From the time of his New York and Kennedy Center debuts in 1982, cellist Carter Brey has been regularly hailed by audiences and critics for his virtuosity, flawless technique and complete musicianship. As one of the outstanding instrumentalists of his generation—winner of such prestigious awards as the Gregor Piatigorsky Memorial Prize, an Avery Fisher Career grant, the Michaels Award of Young Concert Artists—he has been soloist with virtually all of America's major orchestras and has performed under the batons of such celebrated conductors as Claudio Abbado, Christian Badea, Semyon Bychkov, Sergiu Comissiona, Christoph von Dohnányi, Mstislav Rostropovich and Hugh Wolff. In 1996, Brey has added yet another road to his career by becoming the principal cellist of the New York Philharmonic Orchestra.

His career as an ensemble player is equally distinguished, marked by regular appearances with the Tokyo String Quartet, the Emerson Quartet and the Chamber Music Society of Lincoln Center, as well as at the Spoleto Festivals in the United States and Italy, the Santa Fe Chamber Music Festival and the La Jolla Chamber Music Festival, among many others.

During the 1993-94 season, Brey gave concerts with the Saint Louis Symphony, the Buffalo Philharmonic and the Indianapolis Symphony, among many other ensembles. He was also a featured soloist with the Dresden Philharmonic led by Philippe Entremont on that orchestra's United States tour, which included performances in more than 15 cities and an appearance at Carnegie Hall. He also joined pianist Christopher O'Riley, violinist Pamela Frank and violist Paul Neubauer in November of 1993 for a series of piano quartet concerts featuring the premiere of *Still Movement with Hymn* by Aaron Jay Kernis, a work commissioned for them by American Public Radio. In addition, he and Mr. O'Riley continued their highly successful collaboration with a series of duo recitals.

Brey's 1994-95 season was highlighted by performances with the National Symphony, the Colorado Symphony, the Milwaukee Symphony, the Saint Paul Chamber Orchestra, the Naples (Florida) Philharmonic, the New Jersey Symphony and the Sacramento Symphony. With Christopher O'Riley, he again gave a series of duo recitals, including appearances in Boston and St. Louis. He also participated in a program of music by Amy Beach at Alice Tully Hall, as part of a special Lincoln Center series of American music.

Carter Brey came to international prominence in 1981 when he took a prize in the first Rostropovich International Cello Competition. He attracted the attention of Rostropovich himself and their subsequent collaboration with the National Symphony Orchestra received enormous praise. His New York and Washington recital debuts followed in 1982 after his victory in the Young Concert Artists International Auditions.

Among other honors, this artist held the first Anne and George Popkin Cello Chair on the YCA roster. Brey was also the first musician to win the Performing Arts Prize of the Arts Council of America. In the fall of 1990, he was featured in a concert with cellist Yo-Yo Ma at Avery Fisher Hall which was broadcast nationwide on PBS's "Live From Lincoln Center."

Mr. Brey received his training at the Peabody Institute, where he studied with Laurence Lesser and Stephen Kates. Later study was with Aldo Parisot at Yale University, where he was a Wardwell Fellow and a Houpt Scholar. His violoncello is a rare J. B. Guadagnini made in Milan in 1754.

Carter Brey lives in New York City with his wife and their young daughter.

COFFEE PARADISE

*Living as I do with an Italian wife, I've learned to take seriously the Italians' half-jesting acronym for **caffè: amaro, caldo, forte, fresco, espresso** (bitter, hot, strong, fresh, fast). How sad to think that most Americans believe good coffee is that thin brown stuff setting for hours on the restaurant hotplate, or one of those silly, precious flavored "specialty" coffees that 'benighted yuppies' buy in droves.*

Here is how to achieve coffee paradise: start with fresh roasted whole beans from one of the better espresso roasters (I buy Lavazza or Illy here in New York). Measure out the beans, one palmful per person, into your burr grinder (the only kind capable of reducing the beans to the requisite even fineness), putting the rest into the freezer for storage. The resulting powder is gently tapped into a stainless steel filter cup and firmly twisted up into the maw of the espresso machine.

Once the steam pressure is such that it issues sibilantly from the escape valve, the handle is lifted momentarily, then brought down with great force to press the stream through the coffee, not so slowly as to extract bitter oils along with the flavor, not so quickly as to render the coffee too pallid. The espresso that flows smoothly into the cup should develop a crema, a top coating of light brown froth that enhances the look as well as the intense, brief savor of the coffee, gone from the cup in ten seconds but lingering in one's memory for the rest of the morning. --C.B.

DANIEL DOMB, CELLIST

Daniel Domb's outstanding achievements as soloist, teacher and principal cellist have earned him a place as Canada's preeminent cellist. Solo appearances have included the Chicago Symphony under Seiji Ozawa, the Boston Pops under Arthur Fiedler, the Toronto Symphony, the New York Philharmonic and the Cleveland Orchestra, as well as recitals in Carnegie Hall, Town Hall, Wigmore Hall, and the Concertgebouw.

Mr. Domb began his studies at the age of 11 with Paul Tortelier in Israel and Paris, and a few years later was chosen by Leonard Bernstein to appear with the New York Philharmonic. After studying with Leonard Rose at Juilliard, he earned a master of music degree at age 21 and became a professor at the Oberlin Conservatory that same year. After further studies with Gregor Piatigorsky,

Mr. Domb became acting principal cellist of the Cleveland Orchestra. A few years later, in 1974, he went to the Toronto Symphony as principal cellist. Since then, he has continued his solo career, performing with orchestras and in recitals, and has made dozens of solo appearances with the Toronto Symphony, both at home and on tour.

Daniel's most recent recording is the first Canadian release of the complete Bach Suites for solo cello (Mastersound). His previous releases include the successful *Meditations* (Pro-Arte), a collection of eighteen of his favourite melodies accompanied by harpist Judy Loman, also *Daniel Domb and Sheila Henig* (CBC), named "Best Broadcast of a Solo Artist" by the Canadian Music Council.

MEDITERRANEAN BARLEY
Serves 4

This earthy food cleanses your soul, and makes for a beautiful pure cello sound. Eat one portion, then play one Bach Suite. Eat two portions, and the Dvořák Concerto flows out of your fingers effortlessly. So, you live long, play beautifully, and enjoy great food. --D.D.

1½ cups *cooked* barley
1 medium onion, chopped (1 cup)
4 cloves garlic, chopped
½ cup broth or water
6 ripe plum tomatoes, diced, or a medium-
    sized can of diced tomatoes (14 oz.)
½ cup pine nuts, toasted

1 cup loosely packed chopped
    fresh basil
¼ cup loosely packed chopped
    fresh parsley
12 Greek black olives, pitted and torn
    into pieces

Once the barley is cooked, this recipe is fast and easy.

Cook onion and garlic in a large saucepan on stove (use a little oil if needed) until soft. Add water or broth and tomatoes, cook about 2 to 3 minutes. Add the pine nuts, basil, parsley, and olives; stir well and cook until heated through. Mix in barley and serve.

Photo: GARY BUEHLER

JUDITH GLYDE, CELLIST

Judith Glyde, cellist, studied with Bernard Greenhouse, formerly of the Beaux Arts Trio. A founding member of the Manhattan String Quartet in 1970, she left the quartet at the end of the 1991-92 season to be associate professor of cello and chamber music at the University of Colorado, Boulder.

Ms. Glyde has appeared throughout the United States, Europe, Canada, Mexico and South America, including three tours of the Soviet Union.

She has recorded for numerous companies, including a set of six E.S.SAY compact discs featuring the 15 string quartets of Dmitri Shostakovich. These recordings have received the highest praise, including *Time* magazine's "Best of 1991."

FETTUCCINE LIMON

Serves 5 to 6

This dish was prepared for me by my good friends, Jacqueline Flinker and Phil Hyde. The dish even surpassed the setting—a beautiful night high in the mountains outside of Boulder, Colorado. --J.G.

4 tablespoons butter
1 cup heavy cream
2 tablespoons freshly squeezed lemon juice
Grated peel from 3 small organic lemons
  (only colored part, not any of
   inner white layer)

1 pound fettuccine
Freshly ground pepper to taste
Salt to taste
½ cup freshly grated Parmesan, or to taste

Put butter and cream into a medium-large skillet, and turn on heat to medium-high. When cream begins to boil, reduce heat and add lemon juice and stir thoroughly. Add grated lemon peel. Stir until cream is reduced to **one-half** its original volume. Remove from heat.

After fettuccine is cooked, drain and return the pasta to pan, adding lemon sauce. Mix contents and reheat for 15 to 20 seconds. Add cheese after putting into serving bowl.

BERNARD GREENHOUSE, CELLIST

Bernard Greenhouse was born in New Jersey. He studied at Juilliard and made his New York recital debut at Town Hall to resounding critical acclaim. Mr. Greenhouse then went to Europe for an audition with Pablo Casals, which resulted in two years of study with the great Spanish master. Casals wrote, "Bernard Greenhouse is not only a remarkable cellist, but what I esteem more, a dignified artist."

Greenhouse was cellist with the famed Bach Aria Group, and, for thirty-two years, a founding member of the world acclaimed Beaux Arts Trio.

Mr. Greenhouse has won a reputation as one of the major interpreters on his instrument, making appearances in most of the major cities of Europe and America: in recital, with orchestras, and with chamber music ensembles; and recordings for CBS, RCA, Concert Hall, and the American Recording Society.

He has been a member of the faculties at the Manhattan School of Music and the State University of New York at Stony Brook, from which he received an honorary doctorate. He has recently retired emeritus from his position as WCSL professor at Rutgers University and from the New England Conservatory; Mr. Greenhouse now teaches master classes in the United States, Canada and Europe. His varied career has brought him recognition both as a soloist and as a chamber musician. He was recently awarded the National Service Award by Chamber Music America.

Mr. Greenhouse plays the famed "Paganini" Stradivarius cello, dated 1707.

BERNIE'S CHICKEN IN GIN
Serves 4 to 5

Having studied cello with Mr. Greenhouse for several years during the 1980's, the author can attest to the fine cooking abilities of Mr. Greenhouse. His wonderful cello parties at his home on Long Island were culinary delights. One can easily remember the taste of his lasagna, which was as rich and smooth as his beautiful cello tone. The "Chicken in Gin" recipe is just one of many creative dishes that Mr. Greenhouse invented.

**Parts from one small frying chicken, except
 back, or 2 medium-sized
 whole breast chicken fillets, cut up**
2 **tablespoons sesame oil**
3 **cloves garlic, pressed**
⅓ **cup gin**
¼ **cup soy sauce**

½ **cup or more chicken broth**
8 **oz. can water chestnut slices, drained**
4 **dried Chinese mushrooms (soak for
 20 minutes before cooking)**
8 **oz. can bamboo shoots, drained**
1½ **tablespoons cornstarch**
¼ **cup water**

Brown chicken parts in sesame oil, then add pressed garlic. Add gin and cover for 1 minute. Add soy sauce, chicken broth, water chestnuts, mushrooms and bamboo shoots. Cook about 30 minutes on medium-low heat, or until tender. Add additional chicken broth if needed. Near end of cooking time, mix cornstarch into ¼ cup cool water and add mixture to thicken sauce.

Serve on a bed of rice.

Photo: NATHANIEL LIEBERMAN

YEHUDA HANANI, CELLIST

Yehuda Hanani, artistic director of the "Close Encounters with Music" series, has distinguished himself throughout Europe, North and South America, the Orient, and his native Israel as soloist, chamber musician, master teacher and ambassador of the arts. An extraordinary recitalist, he is equally renowned for performances with orchestras such as the Chicago, Berlin Radio and BBC Welsh Symphonies, the Seoul, Israel, Belgrade and Buenos Aires Philharmonics, the St. Paul Chamber and Philadelphia Orchestras, I Solisti Veneti and the State Symphony of Mexico. His festival appearances have included Aspen, Chautauqua, Marlboro, the Robin Hood Dell and Festival Casals, as well as major international festivals.

He has collaborated in performance with preeminent fellow musicians, including Leon Fleisher, Andre Kostelanetz, Aaron Copland, Christoph Eschenbach, Sergiu Comissiona, and Itzhak Perlman, as well as members of the Cleveland, Colorado, Lark, Audubon, Muir, New World, and Vermeer Quartets, and the Cuarteto Latinamericano. His recording of the monumental Alkan Cello Sonata, the first ever, received a Grand Prix du Disque nomination. A Koch International CD of American works is the most recent addition to his discography. A recipient of three Rockefeller grants, he also received an American-Israel Cultural Foundation grant for studies at Juilliard and subsequently a scholarship for studies at Harvard.

Yehuda Hanani has had many contemporary composers write works specifically for him, most recently a cello concerto by Pulitzer Prize-winning composer Bernard Rands. Mr. Hanani is a professor of cello at the University of Cincinnati College-Conservatory, where he directs the annual international festival "Bach" Annalia.

BISCOTTI

Makes about 40, ½-inch slices

Mr. Hanani's recipe can also be called 'Italian nut' cookies. They are good at any time of the day. Variations with the ingredients can be made, such as using other varieties of dried fruits or nuts. The biscotti also freeze well.

2½ cups sifted unbleached flour
2 teaspoons baking powder
¼ cup butter (½ stick)
¾ cup sugar
4 eggs

1 tablepoon vanilla
2 tablespoons anise seeds
¼ cup slivered almonds
¾ cup dried cranberries

Preheat oven to 350 degrees. Mix sifted flour and baking powder. Set aside.

Beat butter and sugar until light. Add eggs one at a time, mixing well after each addition. Add flour mix, then vanilla, seeds, nuts, and fruit last.

Divide dough into two equal parts and place on greased and floured cookie sheet. Each loaf should be approximately 12 x 6 inches.

Bake 20 minutes or until golden brown. Remove from oven and slice on the diagonal into ½-inch pieces. Turn onto sides and place on cookie sheets. Bake about 15 more minutes or until biscotti are lightly toasted.

Remove and cool on racks.

Photo: ILAN BRUNNER

MICHAEL HARAN, CELLIST/CONDUCTOR

Michael Haran was born in 1944 in Jerusalem where he began his studies in cello, chamber music and conducting. His teachers have included Andre Navarra (cello), Joseph Calvet (chamber music) and Aldo Ceccato (conducting). Haran is a first prize laureate for both cello and chamber music from the Paris National Music Conservatory. He won top prizes in international cello competitions in Florence and Geneva, as well as the Antonio Janigro Award for best interpretation of Bach.

Michael Haran has been principal cellist of the Israel Philharmonic Orchestra (IPO) since 1976. As soloist, he has appeared with the IPO, the Pittsburgh Symphony, the Mexican National Symphony, the Academy of Santa Cecilia Orchestra, Milano R.A.I. Orchestra, the Suisse Romande Orchestra and the Bergen Philharmonic, among others. His solo appearances have been with distinguished conductors such as Leonard Bernstein, Paul Paray, Zubin Mehta, Christoph Eschenbach, Charles Dutoit, Rafael Frühbeck De Burgos, Mendi Rodan and James DePriest.

He has performed in chamber music concerts and recitals with Itzhak Perlman, Pinchas Zukerman, Sergiu Luca and Pnina Salzman, to name but a few. He has taught cello and chamber music at Temple University College of Music in Philadelphia, at the Rubin Academy of Music in Tel Aviv and has coached master classes in Israel, Norway, Brazil and North America.

Michael Haran has recorded a solo compact disc of Israeli music for cello in addition to various chamber music discs. He has directed his own chamber music series and marathons in Tel Aviv with the participation of Israel's foremost musicians. Haran is a frequent guest at chamber music festivals in Israel, Brazil and the U.S. In addition, he has presented various programs of different types of music, songs and jazz for Israeli radio.

Recently, Michael Haran embarked on a parallel career as a conductor. He has conducted and narrated a youth concert with the IPO; recorded Yan Freidlin's 2nd Symphony with the Jerusalem Symphony Orchestra; trained and conducted "M.A.T.A.N" (Israeli Young Artists) Strings and Symphony Orchestras; was soloist and conductor with the Kibbutz Chamber Orchestra, the Pro Arte Chamber Orchestra, and the Rishon Chamber Orchestra. He also conducted the Philocamera Ensemble (IPO players), which he founded in 1989.

Michael Haran has an extensive repertoire, ranging from Baroque to modern music.

MICHA'S SALAD
Serves 4 to 5

My favorite food is this salad that I make with a few variations. The dressing is usually made of pressed lemon and olive oil with some black pepper or Zatar. I prefer using Syrian olives when available. --M.H.

2 red tomatoes, (1½ pounds), cut up
   into medium-sized pieces
1 medium-sized head of green or red leaf
   lettuce, broken into small
   pieces by hand
¼ pound grated cheese, preferably Gruyère
   or a similar hard yellow cheese

15 pitted black or green olives,
   (beaten up and a little bitter)
1 just ripe avocado, sliced
   into pieces

Mix all ingredients gently together, add dressing to taste.

DRESSING

½ teaspoon black pepper or Zatar
¼ to ⅓ cup fresh lemon juice

½ cup olive oil
¼ teaspoon salt

Photo: CLIVE BARDA

STEVEN ISSERLIS, CELLIST

In 1993, Steven Isserlis was presented with the Royal Philharmonic Society's Instrumentalist of the Year Award for "performances with a quality of commitment that linger in the memory and for an unfailing gift for communicating the meaning of the music to the audience." Now, internationally recognized as one of the finest musicians of his generation, he has given audiences all over the world a new insight into the cello repertoire, from Baroque to contemporary.

In 1989, Isserlis gave the world premiere of John Tavener's *Protecting Veil* at the BBC Proms, followed by a recording, which reached number one on the classical charts and won the Gramophone Award for the best contemporary recording of 1992. The next year, he was presented with the Piatigorsky Artist Award and premiered *Protecting Veil* in the U.S. At the same time, he champions the nineteenth century cello repertoire, including lesser-known works by Glazunov, Rubinstein, Rachmaninov, Saint Saëns, Debussy and Liszt. Isserlis has enjoyed working with authentic instrument orchestras like the English Baroque Soloists and the London Classical Players on the concertos of Haydn and Schumann, as well as giving regular recitals with fortepiano player, Melvyn Tan, and harpsichordist, Maggie Cole.

He has given solo recitals in Amsterdam, London, Vancouver and San Francisco, and tours of Australia and Japan. His concerts in the 1993/94 season and beyond include performances in America with the Chicago Symphony, Los Angeles Philharmonic, St. Paul Chamber Orchestra, Philadelphia Orchestra, Cleveland Orchestra, St. Louis Symphony, New World Symphony, Atlanta Symphony, San Francisco Symphony, Orchestra of St. Luke, and the Houston Symphony.

In Europe, he is working, among others, with the Philharmonia and London Symphony, (BBC) Symphony, Czech Philharmonic, Belgian National Orchestra, Deutsche Kammerphilharmonie, Hessischer Rundfunk, Gulbenkian Orchestra, and the Finnish Radio Symphony Orchestra. Isserlis also plays regularly with the Australian Chamber Orchestra.

With an already full and varied solo career, Steven Isserlis enjoys both chamber music and teaching, performing extensively with Joshua Bell, Olli Mustonen and Tabea Zimmermann and giving master classes each year at Sandor Vegh's International Musicians' Seminar in Cornwall. An ardent champion of Robert Schumann, in 1989 Isserlis was the artistic director of the Schumann Festival at the Wigmore Hall, which opened with a special presentation of Schumann's life in words and music, devised by Isserlis and actor Gabriel Woolf. He also has been the subject of a number of television projects, including a 90 minute documentary by the Hessischer Rundfunk, Frankfurt, and was a featured soloist in the Channel Four series "Concerto!" with Michael Tilson Thomas and Dudley Moore—which was subsequently released as a CD and video and won a 1993 International Emmy Award.

In January 1994, Steven Isserlis signed an exclusive recording contract with BMG Classics, coinciding with the release of his CD single of Bloch's *From Jewish Life* and Tavener's *Eternal Memory*. Ongoing plans include recital albums with Pascal Devoyon, Melvyn Tan and Stephen Hough, and recordings of concertos by Barber, Saint Saëns, Schumann and Haydn.

Steven Isserlis plays a Guadagnini cello, ca. 1745.

STIR-FRY CHICKEN AND VEGETABLES
Serves 6

Pauline (my wife) prepares this for us when we can't think of anything else to eat and do not want anything fancy. It is always delicious! Even our 4-year-old son likes it—so it must be all right. --S.I.

2 whole chicken breast fillets, cut
    into 1-inch pieces
MARINADE SAUCE:
1 teaspoon chopped ginger
1 to 2 cloves crushed garlic
Juice of 1 lime or lemon
1½ tablespoons toasted sesame seed oil
3 tablespoons soy sauce

SELECTION OF VEGETABLES:
1 cup onions, sliced

1 cup mange tout, sugar peas
    or green beans
1 cup green/red/yellow pepper(s), sliced
1 cup carrots, sliced
1 cup mushrooms, sliced
½ teaspoon sugar
3 teaspoons cornstarch
2 teaspoons white wine vinegar
2 teaspoons soy sauce
2 tablespoons water

Marinate the chicken pieces in the *MARINADE SAUCE* for a minimum of one-half hour.

In a large frying pan, on medium-high heat, cook the vegetables in a little vegetable oil for approximately 3 to 4 minutes. Make a 'well' in the center of the vegetables and add chicken and marinade. Lower heat to medium and sauté until chicken pieces are almost cooked, then stir with vegetables until thoroughly cooked.

Mix the sugar and cornstarch into a thin paste with the white wine vinegar, soy sauce and water, and add to the chicken and vegetables, stirring until heated through.

Serve with rice or pasta.

EVA CZAKO JANZER, CELLIST

Eva Czako Janzer was born in India and studied cello at the Academy of Music in Budapest, Hungary, where she received a Diploma of Virtuosity. Twice winner of the Geneva Competition, Mrs. Janzer had a brilliant career as soloist and chamber musician. She played extensively together with her husband, the famed violist, Georges Janzer, whom she had met in Hungary and married shortly after World War II. She and her husband were members of such internationally famous chamber ensembles as the Grumiaux String Trio and the Vegh String Quartet.

Mrs. Janzer was equally well known as a distinguished teacher of cello. She taught at the University of Hanover before coming to the United States in 1972. She first came to Indiana University to teach for Janos Starker while he was on a sabbatical leave. Her husband Georges then joined the Indiana University School of Music faculty in 1972, to replace retired violist William Primrose. Eva became a full-time faculty member in her own right shortly afterward.

Eva Janzer was tremendously loved by all her colleagues

and students. In 1979, shortly after Eva Janzer's death, cellist Janos Starker, a lifelong friend and colleague, founded the Eva Janzer Memorial Center "to honor the memory of a great artist and much loved teacher." Each year the board of directors of the Eva Janzer Memorial Center selects a senior member of the international community of distinguished cellists to be honored for his or her contributions to cello playing and teaching. In addition, the center provides scholarships to assist young cello students during college.

The following quote from her late husband Georges best describes Eva Janzer:

"Eva was a great artist. She was very sensitive and had a wonderful feeling of style and phrasing....She was also a wonderful person. All her colleagues cherished her. I think Eva would say to these (Memorial Center cello) students 'you are gifted and talented enough to deserve this help, and I hope it helps you in your studies; because if you have financial problems, you cannot study with all your heart'..."

HUNGARIAN CHEESE SPREAD
(Körözött)
Makes 3½ cups

One recipe Mrs. Janzer prepared frequently was this cheese spread. Originally, a sheep-milk cheese was the basis of this recipe, but we changed it to cream cheese with a dollop of goat cheese added, feta or chevre. It can be spread on crusty bread or slices of green pepper. --Rae Starker

2 oz. goat cheese
18 oz. Philadelphia cream cheese
½ stick of unsalted butter, softened
1 tablespoon hot Hungarian paprika
½ teaspoon prepared Dijon mustard

½ teaspoon pounded caraway seeds
1 small onion, finely chopped
2 oz. can anchovies, minced,
    plus 1 tablespoon of the anchovy oil

Mix all of the above ingredients thoroughly and chill before serving.

Photo: CHRISTINE ALICINO

JOAN JEANRENAUD, CELLIST, KRONOS QUARTET

Joan Dutcher Jeanrenaud was born in Memphis, Tennessee in 1956. Her teachers have included Peter Spurbeck, Fritz Magg and Pierre Fournier. She completed her bachelor of music degree from Indiana University in 1977. One year later she was selected as the cellist of the Kronos Quartet.

Since its inception in 1973, the Kronos Quartet, which includes current members (from left to right): John Sherba-violin, David Harrington-violin, Joan Jeanrenaud-cello and Hank Dutt-viola, has emerged as a leading voice for new works. Combining a unique musical vision with a fearless dedication to experimentation, Kronos has assembled a body of work unparalleled in its range and scope of expression, and in the process, has captured the attention of audiences world-wide.

The quartet's extensive repertoire ranges from Webern, Shostakovich, Bartók and Ives to Astor Piazzolla, John Cage, Raymond Scott and Howlin' Wolf. In addition to working closely with modern masters such as Terry Riley, John Zorn and H.M. Gorecki, Kronos commissions new works from today's most innovative composers from around the world, extending its reach as far as Zimbabwe, Poland, Australia, Japan, Argentina and Azerbaijan. The quartet has worked with many composers, including Franghiz Ali-Zadeh, Foday Musa Suso, Scott Johnson, Sofia Gubaidulina, Steven Mackey, John Oswald, Steve Reich, Unsuk Chin, Gabriela Ortiz, Don Byron, Tan Dun, Peter Sculthorpe, Lois V. Vierk, Philip Glass and Dmitri Yanov-Yanovsky and Ben Johnston.

Kronos performs annually in many cities, including San Francisco, Los Angeles and New York, and tours extensively with more than 100 concerts each year in concert halls, clubs and at jazz festivals throughout the United States, Canada, Europe, Japan, Mexico, South America, New Zealand, Hong Kong and Australia. Recent tours have included appearances at the Concertgebouw in Amsterdam, Kennedy Center, Montreux Jazz Festival, Carnegie Hall, Sydney Opera House, Tanglewood, London's Royal Festival Hall, La Scala, Theatre de la Ville in Paris and Chicago's Orchestra Hall.

The quartet records exclusively for Nonesuch Records, and the catalogue includes *Howl, U.S.A. (1996), Released 1985-95 (1995), Kronos Quartet Performs Philip Glass (1995), Night Prayers* (1994), Bob Ostertag's *All The Rage* (1993), *At The Grave of Richard Wagner* (1993), Morton Feldman's Piano and String Quartet (1993), Henryk Mikolaj Gorecki's String Quartets No. 1 and 2 (1993), *Short Stories* (1993), *Pieces of Africa* (1992), Henryk Mikolaj Gorecki's *Already It Is Dusk* (1991), Astor Piazzolla's *Five Tango Sensations* (1991), Kevin Volan's *Hunting: Gathering* (1991), Witold Lutoslawski's String Quartet (1991), *Black Angels* (1990), which received a Grammy nomination for Best Chamber Music Performance, *Salome Dances for Peace* (1989), which received a Grammy nomination for Best Contemporary Composition, *Winter Was Hard* (1988), *White Man Sleeps* (1987), which received a Grammy nomination for Best Chamber Music Performance, and the *Kronos Quartet* (1986).

TONNO ALL' ALESSANDRO
(Pasta Sauce)
Serves 2

This recipe is from Alessandro Moruzzi, a native of Bologna now living with me in San Francisco. It is especially good late at night after a performance. --J.J.

5 or 6 oz. pasta, capellini suggested
6 oz. solid white tuna in water
   (dolphin-free)
2 tablespoons tomato paste
2 tablespoons virgin olive oil
A pinch of red pepper

2 dozen pitted black dried
   olives, chopped (if unavailable
   use pitted regular black olives)
Salt or soy sauce to taste
3 tablespoons milk or
   soy milk (optional)

Drain the tuna and put it in a pan with all the other ingredients except the pasta. Mix and cook over a medium flame for 4 to 5 minutes. If sauce is too dry, add a tablespoon or so of water to moisten. Set aside and boil pasta (capellini suggested). Combine pasta and sauce and then serve.

Photo: DON HUNSTEIN

NATHANIEL ROSEN, CELLIST

Nathaniel Rosen brings an awesome technical ability and no-nonsense musicianship to cello works. He is neither self-conscious nor posturing.

Rosen gained instant global recognition when, in 1978, he became the first American cellist ever to win the International Competition's Gold Medal. To this day, Rosen is the only American cellist to win this uniquely prestigious award. One year earlier, he had captured the attention of American musical circles by winning the Walter W. Naumburg Competition.

Rosen began studying the cello at the age of six. By age thirteen, his artistic gifts and unmistakable talent caught the attention of the legendary Gregor Piatigorsky, who became Rosen's teacher and mentor. At age twenty-two, Rosen became Piatigorsky's assistant, a post he retained until shortly before the master's death in 1976.

During his years with Piatigorsky, Rosen also enjoyed a close association with Jascha Heifetz and participated frequently as cellist in chamber ensembles under the great violinist's tutelage. At age seventeen, Rosen toured the Soviet Union as a finalist in the Third International Tchaikovsky Competition (1966). He was the youngest competitor among forty-two cellists and was one of only three Americans to win a prize. He returned to Russia twelve years later (1978) when he and Elmar Oliviera became the first American Gold Medal-winning instrumentalists since Van Cliburn.

He served as artistic director of the Interlochen Summer Chamber Music Festival in 1988-1989, is a founding member of the Sitka Summer Music Festival, was principal cellist of the Pittsburgh Symphony Orchestra for two years, and of the Los Angeles Chamber Orchestra

for eight years. Mr. Rosen has appeared as a guest on NBC-TV. He has performed as soloist on PBS with "Previn and the Pittsburgh" in Strauss's *Don Quixote*; in Mozart's G Minor Quartet with Isaac Stern, Pinchas Zukerman and André Previn; and with the Boston Pops and John Williams, playing Tchaikovsky's *Variations on a Rococo Theme*.

Audiences throughout North America, Central America, Europe and Asia have had the opportunity to enjoy Rosen's sensitive musicianship on recordings, in recital and as guest soloist with many of the world's greatest orchestras, including the New York, Los Angeles, and Czech Philharmonics; the Leipziger Gewandhaus, the Philadelphia, Minnesota and Dresdener Staats Orchestras; and the London, Pittsburgh, Seattle, Houston, Spokane, Columbus and Vancouver Symphonies.

Rosen is currently teaching at the Manhattan School of Music and holds the Chauncey Devereux Stillman Chair for distinguished visiting artist at Thomas More College, New Hampshire.

Some of his latest recordings: *Nathaniel Rosen in Concert*: Tchaikovsky, *Variations on a Rococo Theme, Pezzo Capriccioso,* and *Nocturne*; Shostakovich, Concerto No. 1 for violoncello and orchestra; *Rosen Plays Brahms*: Cello Sonatas in E Minor and F Major; Schumann: *Fantasy Pieces*; Mendelssohn: *Song Without Words,* Op. 109; Bach: Six Suites for violoncello; David Amram: Three Concertos, *Honor Song for Sitting Bull*; Sergey Taneyev: Piano Quintet, Op. 30 and String Quintet, op. 14.

Rosen plays a magnificent 1738 Montagnana cello, in both live performances and on recordings.

HUNK-O-MEAT
Serves 6

This is a comforting family meal on a cold night. We like it with horseradish on the side, and accompanied by parsley potatoes. --N.R.

All-purpose flour
4 pounds of chuck roast
2 tablespoons vegetable oil
2 tablespoons butter
1 bay leaf
2 teaspoons thyme
1 teaspoon pepper

2 beef bouillon cubes in 2 cups hot water
3 or 4 medium yellow onions, quartered
1 small bag of baby carrots (or 6 to 8
     carrots cut into 2-inch lengths)
3 ribs of celery, cut into 2-inch lengths
Red wine

Preheat oven to 350 degrees. Meanwhile, rub flour all over the roast and brown it in oil and butter, on medium-high heat, using a dutch oven or similar type pot. Do this step on top of the stove.

Add the bay leaf, thyme, pepper and bouillon broth, and bring to a boil. Cover and place pot in oven for 1½ hours.

Add onions, carrots, and celery and return to oven for 1 hour. In the last 15 minutes, add a generous dash of red wine. Remove from oven.

Transfer meat and vegetables to a platter. Skim drippings/cooking liquid and serve drippings as gravy.

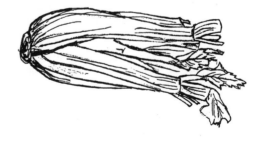

ELEONORE SCHOENFELD, CELLIST

Eleonore Schoenfeld earned her artist diploma at the famed Hochschule für Music in Berlin, Germany. An internationally renowned cellist, Eleonore Schoenfeld has concertized worldwide as soloist with leading philharmonic and radio orchestras, in recitals, and as a unique violin-cello duo with her sister, Alice Schoenfeld.

During forty-five European concert tours, she has made over 200 recordings of the solo and chamber music literature for the major radio stations in Europe. Among these recordings are works especially written for the Schoenfeld Duo and have been recorded by the BBC in London. In the United States, the duo has recorded for Everest and Orion Master Recordings.

Eleonore Schoenfeld is frequently guest artist at national and international festivals, including Schleswig-Holstein Music Festival in Germany; Centre d'Arts Orford in Canada; Bowdoin Summer Festival in the USA; Great Woods Festival Bonston in the USA; Music Academy of the West, Santa Barbara, CA and Morrowstone Festival in the USA. In 1980 and 1989, Eleonore Schoenfeld was artist-in-residence at the International Gregor Piatigorsky Seminar for Cellists, in Los Angeles, of which she also has been the director since 1979.

She has been much in demand to give master classes and seminars throughout the world. A renowned pedagogue, Eleonore Schoenfeld is professor of cello at the School of Music, University of Southern California, where she has been chairperson for eight years. She is also on the faculty of the R.D. Colburn School of Performing Arts in Los Angeles and the Arts Academy in Idyllwild, CA. In 1990, Professor Schoenfeld was the recipient of the prestigious Ramo Faculty Award as the

"Outstanding Teacher of the Year." In 1993, she received the Eva Janzer Memorial Award from the Indiana University School of Music.

Eleonore Schoenfeld continuously attracts talented students from all over the world; many of them became top prize winners in prestigious competitions: the Geneva Competition in Switzerland; the Schewenningen in Holland; the Casals Competition in Budapest, Hungary; the Tchaikovsky Competition, Moscow, USSR; Johannesburg in South Africa; Markneukirchen in Germany; the European Broadcasting Union in Germany; Concert Artist Guild, New York; Coleman Chamber Music Competition, Pasadena; and the Hammer-Rostropovich, University of Southern California in Los Angeles, CA. Her students perform repeatedly as soloists, among others, with the New York Philharmonic, Los Angeles Philharmonic, Los Angeles Chamber Orchestra, Georgian Chamber Orchestra, and the Bamberger Philharmonic under such eminent conductors as Zubin Mehta, Horst Stein, and Esa-Pekka Salonen. Her former students hold positions in American and European universities and are members of prestigious orchestras.

Eleonore Schoenfeld has frequently served as chairperson and American juror in national and international solo and chamber music competitions, such as ARD in Munich, Germany; First International Leonard Rose Cello Competition in Maryland; Piatigorsky, New York; International Chamber Music Competition in Caltanissetta, Italy; and the International Karl Klingler String Quartet Competition in Munich. In 1996, she was a juror in the First International Janigro Cello Competition in Yugoslavia, among others.

FORELLE BLAU
(Blue Trout)
Serves 4

I just love the way trout tastes. The "Blue Trout" recipe reflects a classic European way of preparing trout. One would typically find trout prepared in this manner in many of the finest restaurants in Germany. --E.S.

2 pounds fillet (any variety) of very fresh trout
1 cup vinegar
Saltwater

Slices of lemon (one lemon)
Tarragon, one pinch (eine Messerspitze)
Parsley (for garnish)

Touch only the fish with your wet hands.
Do not scale the fish, in order not to tear the very sensitive membrane, which would cause a change of color to blue.

Carefully clean the trout under running water and place it on a porcelain plate. Pour the vinegar over the trout. Then place trout in the boiling hot saltwater and let simmer 10 to 20 minutes, depending on the size of the fish. The fish should flake when done. Do NOT boil, do NOT cover.

Serve fish on a preheated platter; garnish with parsley and lemon slices.

This dish may be served with parsley, potato, herb butter or horseradish sauce.

Photo: SPECTRUM STUDIO

JANOS STARKER, CELLIST

The great virtuoso cellist and teacher Janos Starker is recognized throughout the world as one of the supreme musicians of the 20th century. Hallmarks of his performances and classes, given over the course of an extraordinary career spanning more than five decades, include peerless technical mastery, intensely expressive playing, and great communicative power. These qualities, combined with his rare musical intelligence, have made Starker the subject of hundreds of major news stories, magazine articles and television documentaries. His concerts have frequently been broadcast around the globe on radio and television.

Born in Budapest in 1924, Janos Starker came to the United States in 1948 where he subsequently held the principal cellist's chairs in three American orchestras, including the Chicago Symphony under Fritz Reiner. Starker resumed his international solo career in 1958. Since then, he has performed thousands of concerts with orchestras and in recitals throughout the world.

Starker has amassed a recording catalogue of more than 100 albums, containing over 165 works on various international labels. These recordings include a large portion of the standard repertoire for the cello, a number of lesser-known works and some of Starker's own transcriptions of works originally composed for other instruments. Several recordings also carry Mr. Starker's own jacket notes. Mr. Starker's recordings appear on the labels of, among others: Angel/EMI, BMG Classics/RCA Victor, CRI, Columbia, Decca/London, Delos, Denon, Deutsche Grammophon, Erato, JVC (Japan Victor), Laurel, Louisville First Editions, Musical Heritage Society, Pacific, Pantheon, Period, Philips/Mercury, Sefel, Star, Supraphon, Telefunken/Teldec, Trio and Virtuoso.

Since 1991, his releases on BMG's RCA Victor Red Seal label have included the first recording of the cello version of the Bartók Viola Concerto, plus the Dvořák Cello Concerto, both performed with the Saint Louis Symphony conducted by Leonard Slatkin, and Richard Strauss's *Don Quixote* with Slatkin and the Bavarian Radio Symphony. Recordings soon to be issued include the Elgar and Walton Cello Concertos with the Philharmonia of London and a new recording of the six unaccompanied Suites for cello by J.S. Bach. Starker's interpretations of sonatas for cello and piano of Brahms, Debussy, Martinu (nominated for a 1993 Grammy Award), Rachmaninoff, and Schumann's *Adagio and Allegro* and *Fantasy Pieces* have also been released by BMG on CD in performances with three virtuoso pianists: Rudolf Buchbinder, the late Rudolf Firkušný, and Shigeo Neriki. Other recent issues have come from Delos and CRI, as well as re-releases on CD of Starker's acclaimed recordings on labels including Mercury and EMI.

Mr. Starker has many awards to his name. In 1948, he received the Grand Prix du Disque, in 1972, the George Washington Award, in Washington D.C., and, during the late 1970's and 1980's, received the Herzl Award in Israel, the Ed Press Award, the Kodály Commemorative Medallion, the Arturo Toscanini Award, the Tracy Sonneborn Award and became a honorary citizen of Texas in 1986.

Janos Starker uses his 1705 Matteo Goffriller cello for most performances and all his recordings. Named "The Star," it has been the cellist's companion for more than a quarter of a century.

When not touring or recording, Janos Starker holds the title of distinguished professor at Indiana University in Bloomington, where his classes have attracted talented string players from around the world since 1958. His hobbies include swimming and writing.

CSOKOLÁDÉS MÁKTORTÁ

(Chocolate Poppy Seed Cake)

Serves 8 to 10

Mr. Starker has received many requests over the past decades for his favorite recipes. He invariably had to explain that he does not cook. While Mr. Starker says his very favorite recipe is Hungarian salami with hot banana peppers, here are some other special favorite recipes that come from the culinary hand of Janos Starker's wife, Rae Starker, described by Mr. Starker as "a legendary cook."

¼ cup butter	¼ pound melted semi-sweet chocolate
½ cup sugar	⅓ cup ground poppy seeds
6 egg yolks, beaten	6 stiffly beaten egg whites
½ cup bread crumbs	Jar of apricot jam for filling

Cream together butter and sugar. Add egg yolks, bread crumbs, semi-sweet chocolate and poppy seeds. Fold in the stiffly beaten egg whites. Pour batter into 2 buttered, floured 9-inch round pans, lined with wax-paper. Bake at 325 degrees for 20 to 30 minutes.

Layer apricot jam between cakes.

HUNGARIAN ICING

8 oz. semi-sweet chocolate	¾ cup water
¾ cup sugar	1 tablespoon sweet butter

For Hungarian icing, cook chocolate, sugar and water until a soft ball stage. As it cools, beat in the tablespoon of sweet butter.

RAE STARKER'S GLORIFIED PICKLES
Serves 8 to 10

1½ tablespoons gelatin (scant)
3 oz. dry white wine
1½ cans (14 oz.) artichoke hearts
9 large black pitted olives
9 medium-large sweet pickles
4 hard-boiled eggs

2 oz. black caviar (*I do prefer fine caviar, particularly in the decoration, however an inexpensive brand can be used in the mousse*)
½ cup mayonnaise

ICING:
½ cup mayonnaise
½ cup sour cream

Soak gelatin in wine. Finely chop artichokes, olives, pickles and eggs. Place in a bowl along with caviar and mayonnaise. Blend well. Add melted and slightly cooled gelatin mixture and blend. Pour into a well-oiled ring mold (5½ cup capacity). The mousse may remain in the refrigerator for a couple of days.

DECORATION:
Remove the mousse onto an attractive round platter. Ice with the mixture of one-half mayonnaise and one-half sour cream. Around the top of the mold place thin slices of hard-boiled egg whites. In the center of each egg white place a little caviar (about 1 or 2 oz. for the entire top).

Around the bottom of the mold place riced (pushed through a small sieve) hard-boiled egg yolks. In the open center, place watercress or the like. *I usually use a platter large enough to hold buttered and broiled cocktail rye and thin white crackers; the lemon slices separate rye from crackers.*

MOSAIC BREAD

1 long soft baguette
¼ pound piece of ham
¼ pound piece of salami
¼ pound piece of tongue (optional)
4 oz. of dill pickles

4 oz. of hard-boiled eggs
4 oz. piece of Swiss cheese
½ stick of soft butter
4 oz. of cream cheese

Scoop out centers of baguettes into short sections. Dice the following ingredients: ham, salami, tongue, pickles, eggs, and Swiss cheese. Mix all the ingredients together with butter and cream cheese and stuff the bread. Wrap in foil and chill. Cut into ¼-inch slices.

Photo: ROBERT F. GEORGE

DAVID WELLS, CELLIST

David Wells, cellist and master teacher, has been heard in major cities on both sides of the Atlantic in the great cello repertoire, spanning the Baroque to the modern, as a recitalist, soloist with orchestras and member of the Manhattan Trio, Columbia Concert Trio, Hartt String Quartet and Wells Duo. He studied with the noted pedagogue and colleague of Pablo Casals, Diran Alexanian, as well as with the celebrated soloist, Raya Garbousova. He is a winner of the America Artist Award, the Harold Bauer Award and other honors. Since making his debut in Chicago at the age of sixteen, he has concertized extensively throughout the world and is perhaps best known for his mastery of the Bach Suites for unaccompanied cello.

Mr. Wells is professor of cello at the Hartt School of the University of Hartford, where he served as co-chairman of the string department, and he is a faculty member at the New England Conservatory. He is a former faculty member of over thirty years tenure at the Manhattan School of Music, where he was head of the chamber music department for ten years. Mr. Wells has also taught at Princeton University as cellist-in-residence and at the Westminster Choir College, as well as at the University of Virginia at Richmond and the Music School of the 92nd Street Y in New York City.

Top honors taken by students of Mr. Wells: the Artists International, Coleman Chamber Music, Concert Artists Guild, MTNA, Naumberg Chamber Music, Vermont Symphony Orchestra/New England, Young Cellist, Young Concert Artists, Friday Morning Music Club and other important solo and chamber music competitions. His students have soloed with the Boston, Hartford, Hartt, Manhattan, New Orleans, Pittsburgh and Worcester Symphony Orchestras. Among his students are past and present members of the Boston, Chicago, Cleveland, Philadelphia and St. Louis Symphony Orchestras, as well as the New York Philharmonic and San Francisco Opera Orchestra.

As a member of the Manhattan Trio, Mr. Wells co-founded chamber music festivals at Hartwick College in Oneonta, New York and at New England College in Henniker, New Hampshire. He is also co-founder and co-leader of the Music Workshop at Cornwall Bridge, Connecticut, where personal issues and music are studied together.

In 1970, with his pianist wife, Janet Wells, he founded and still directs the Yellow Barn Music Festival in Putney, Vermont—a summer chamber music and soloist program dedicated to the presentation of emerging artists. Graduates hold posts as teachers, ensemble and orchestra players and have soloed with or are members of most of the major American orchestras. These students include first-place winners of the Artists International, Concert Artists Guild, Avery Fisher, Coleman, Dealy, MTNA, Naumberg, Performer of Connecticut Young Artists, Tchaikowsky and Young Concert Artists Competition.

David Wells has given master classes at the New England Conservatory, Longy School of Music and the Hartt Summer Youth Music Program. He also offers a week-long summer term mega-master class at the Hartt School of Music covering study techniques, interpretation development and stage fright, in depth, and solo and group playing.

He has recorded for CRI, Opus 1, Leonarda and Serenus. Mr. Wells is a member of ASTA, MTNA and VMTA.

FLUFFY SHORTCAKE DOUGH

Among my happiest memories from childhood are the dinners that were only strawberry shortcake. None of our friends or neighbors did it, but it was our favorite meal in springtime.

Here is a biscuit recipe we have enjoyed very much, with some thoughts about berries. It goes without saying that one should get the ripest berries possible. Cut off the tops and remove any rotten spots before rinsing the berries. We always put them in a bowl and crushed them with a potato masher. Sugar to taste and you end up with a wonderful strawberry sauce. The more 'modern' the berries are, the more sugar they seem to need! In the old days, strawberries were smaller and had more flavor. Nowadays they 'behave' more like celery and have less flavor, but you can enhance the flavor by adjusting the sugar. --D.W.

SIFT BEFORE MEASURING:
    2 cups cake flour or 1¾ cups all-purpose flour

RESIFT WITH:
    2½ teaspoons double-acting baking powder
    1 teaspoon salt
    1 tablespoon sugar

CUT IN WITH TWO KNIVES:
    ⅛ to ¼ cup butter

ADD:
    ¾ cup milk

Preheat oven at 450 degrees Stir lightly into flour mixture, using a fork. Turn dough onto a floured board and knead lightly for one-half minute. Pat to the thickness of 1 inch. Cut into typically-sized round segments. Bake on non-greased cookie sheet for 12-15 minutes at 450 degrees, until lightly brown.

COMPOSERS

Photo: JACK MITCHELL

JOHN CORIGLIANO, COMPOSER

Composer John Corigliano's first opera *The Ghosts of Versaille* was commissioned by the Metropolitan Opera in honor of its centenary and had its world premiere at the Metropolitan Opera on December 19, 1991. This opera received the International Classical Music Award for Composition of the Year in 1993.

Mr. Corigliano received the 1991 Grawemeyer Award for music composition for his Symphony No. 1, written as his response to the AIDS crisis. The symphony was commissioned by the Chicago Symphony Orchestra and Meet-the-Composer, Inc., and was the result of Corigliano's three-year term as the Chicago Symphony's first composer-in-residence. The work was recorded by Erato Records with Daniel Barenboim conducting the Chicago Symphony Orchestra, and received the 1991 Stereo Review Record of the Year Award and two 1992 Grammy Awards for Best Contemporary Classical Composition and Best Orchestral Performance. Among performances of the work during the 1991/1992 season were premieres with the San Francisco Symphony, the New York Philharmonic, and again with the Chicago Symphony in both Chicago and on tour in the United States and Europe.

Mr. Corigliano's other works include his Concerto for Clarinet and Orchestra, commissioned by the New York Philharmonic, which was premiered by that orchestra in 1977, with Leonard Bernstein conducting; his *Pied Piper Fantasy* for flute and orchestra, which had its premiere in 1982, was commissioned by James Galway and introduced by him with the Los Angeles Philharmonic; *Kaleidoscope* which was first heard at the 1961 Spoleto Festival; and Sonata for Violin and Piano, which won first prize at the 1964 Spoleto Chamber Music Competition. Corigliano's Concerto for Piano and Orchestra had its premiere at the opening concert of the 1968 Hemisfair and was played the following season by the Chicago Symphony Orchestra. The Chicago Symphony has also performed his Clarinet Concerto and

his *Tournaments Overture*. His Concerto for Oboe and Orchestra was given its premiere at Carnegie Hall in 1975. The following year, his hour-long *A Dylan Thomas Trilogy* for chorus, soloists and orchestra was given at the Washington Cathedral; and that same year his *Etude Fantasy* for piano was heard at the Kennedy Center.

In 1981, his *Promenade Overture*, commissioned by the Boston Symphony Orchestra in honor of its centennial celebration, had its first performance by the Boston Pops. The Miami Arts Festival commissioned *Summer Fanfare*, which was first performed by the Minnesota Orchestra conducted by Leonard Slatkin. In 1986, Mr. Slatkin conducted the New York Philharmonic in Corigliano's *Three Hallucinations*. His *Fantasia on an Ostinato* for solo piano was commissioned in 1985 by the Van Cliburn Foundation as a required competition piece for that year's concert, and in 1986 the work was expanded into an orchestral work, and performed by the New York Philharmonic conducted by Zubin Mehta. Mr. Corigliano has also written two film scores: for Ken Russell's *Altered States* (1981), for which he was nominated for an Academy Award; and Hugh Hudson's *Revolution* (1985), which earned him the Anthony Asquith Award for best score by the British Film Institute.

John Corigliano was born in Brooklyn, New York and studied with Otto Luening at Columbia University (where he received his bachelor of arts degree, cum laude, in 1959). Later studies were made with Victor Giannini at the Manhattan School of Music. Corigliano was recently elected to the Institute of Arts and Letters, is presently distinguished professor of music at Lehman College, City University of New York, and is on the composition faculty of the Juilliard School. His father, the late John Corigliano, Sr., was the concertmaster of the New York Philharmonic for twenty-three years.

JOHN'S RIGATONI WITH ANCHOVIES AND BEANS

Serves 3 to 4

2 tablespoons extra virgin olive oil
1 garlic clove, finely chopped
1 can (2 oz.) anchovies (flat)
1 can (19 oz.) cannelini beans (or if not
    available, use Great Northern beans)

8 to 10 oz. rigatoni
¼ teaspoon rosemary
½ teaspoon pepper
Grated Parmesan cheese

In a medium-sized skillet, on medium heat, brown chopped garlic in oil for about 5 minutes. Add one-half can anchovies and mix until dissolved in the oil. Then add beans, including the liquid in the can, and simmer for 10 minutes, until beans soften and mixture thickens.

Meanwhile, cook the pasta 'al dente'. Add rosemary and pepper to the sauce and remove pan from stove. Top with cheese and serve.

Photo: © JACK MITCHELL, 1988

DAVID DIAMOND, COMPOSER

"Composers, like pearls, are of three chief sorts, real, artificial and cultured. David Diamond is unquestionably of the first sort; his talent and sincerity have never been doubted by his hearers, by his critics, or by his composer colleagues."

Virgil Thomson, The *New York Herald Tribune*

The above quotation, following the 1941 premiere of David Diamond's Concerto for Small Orchestra, reflects the judgement of most critics of the day: that David Diamond would be, in Aaron Copland's words from 1936, "one to remember." Now in the 1990's, these statements from over 50 years ago still ring true. The *American Grove Dictionary* cites Diamond's "meticulous craftsmanship and his sensibility" as having "assured his position as a 20th century classicist."

David Diamond was born in 1915 in Rochester, New York. By the age of seven he was playing a violin borrowed from a family friend and writing original tunes in his own system of musical notation. In 1927, the Diamond family moved to Cleveland, Ohio, where David's talent came to the attention of an important figure in the musical world, André de Ribaupierre—a Swiss musician teaching in Cleveland—who arranged for him to receive his first formal training at the Cleveland Institute of Music, where he remained until 1929.

Diamond's works have been premiered by some of the great conductors and orchestras of the day: Dimitri Mitropoulos (Symphony No. 1, 1941, New York Philharmonic); Serge Koussevitzky (Symphony No. 2, Boston Symphony); Charles Munich (Symphony No. 3, 1950, Boston Symphony); Eugene Ormandy (Symphony No. 7, 1959, Philadelphia Orchestra); Leonard Bernstein (Symphony No. 8, 1961, Symphony No. 5, 1966, New York Philharmonic). Gerard Schwarz has begun a long-term revival of recording (Delos records) and performing

all of Diamond's some thirty orchestral works with the Seattle Symphony and the New York Chamber Symphony. In 1951, Diamond went to Europe as a Fulbright Professor. Peer-Southern Publishers signed him to an exclusive contract in 1952, which enabled him to remain in Europe, eventually settling in Florence, Italy. Except for brief visits to the United States, Diamond remained in Italy until 1965. When he returned to the United States, he was greeted by a series of country-wide concerts commemorating his fiftieth birthday.

In 1971, Diamond was given a National Opera Institute grant to write his opera *The Noblest Game*, an opera about the social intrigue in the Washington D.C. power set, taking place in the present. The New York City Opera gave the world premiere in the spring of 1995. Diamond's songs for voice and piano are among his finest achievements, sung by the likes of Jennie Tourel, Eileen Farrell, and Eleanor Steber. Hans Nathan has stated that "David Diamond has cultivated the art-song more consistently than any other American composer of his stature. Each of his songs is constructed with the same detailed care that is ordinarily given to an instrumental work."

In 1973, Diamond was appointed professor of composition at the Juilliard School, where, as of 1993, he remains a dedicated and much admired teacher of young composers. In 1986, Diamond received the William Schuman Lifetime Achievement Award. In 1991, he was awarded the Gold Medal of the American Academy of Arts and Letters and the Edward MacDowell Gold Medal for Lifetime Achievement.

Diamond's largest symphony to date, the Symphony No. 11, written from 1989-91, was one of the few major works commissioned by the New York Philharmonic in celebration of its 150th anniversary. David Diamond's creative energy continues unabated as he celebrates his 82nd birthday this year. He has been in the forefront of American composition for more than 50 years—a career perhaps unmatched in longevity of achievement by any other American composer.

DAVID DIAMOND'S SEAFOOD FUGUE
Serves 8 to 10

The fresher the fish the better. Do not overcook. If you prefer more firm fish bring oven cooking period up to 8 minutes. --D.D.

½ cup virgin thick olive oil
1 small Bermuda onion, thinly sliced
1 clove garlic, thinly sliced
1 small slice fresh ginger
1 small shallot, thinly sliced
1 jigger Old Grandad Bourbon (1½ oz.)
1 jigger lite soy sauce (1½ oz.)
1 jigger potato starch diluted
   in one cup warm water

2 cups chicken bouillon
1 pound sea scallops
6 large fresh shelled shrimp
2 fillets of cod (about 1 pound)
2 fillets of catfish (about ¾ pound)
2 fillets of whitefish (about 1 pound)
½ fresh lemon
6 fresh thin tomato slices
'Al dente' spinach noodles

In a large oven-proof frying pan or sauté skillet, pour in ½ cup of olive oil. Heat to moderate temperature. When bubbling, add sliced onion, garlic, ginger and shallot. When browned, raise heat slightly, add bourbon, soy sauce, potato starch and bouillon.

Bring to bubbling heat, stir, and reduce heat to low and let simmer for 3 minutes. Return heat to medium-high.

Immediately layer the fillets of fish crosswise and cover them with the shrimp and scallops. When bubbling, reduce heat to medium and let fish cook, covered, for 5 to 7 minutes.

Layer tomatoes on top and place pan, uncovered, in preheated oven at 325 degrees, for 6 to 8 minutes.

Squeeze lemon over everything. Serve with 'al dente' spinach noodles, buttered, but unsalted.

PERCY GRAINGER, COMPOSER/PIANIST

Grainger was born in Melbourne, Australia and eventually became a musical hero of that country. His first substantial studies were at the Hoch Conservatory in Frankfurt, Germany, from 1895-99. Subsequently, he enjoyed the advantage of a few lessons with the great Italian pianist, Ferruccio Busoni.

Early in his musical career, Grainger toured New Zealand, Australia and South Africa, winning great acclaim. He studied the Grieg Piano Concerto under the composer, but a planned performance with Grieg conducting was thwarted by Grieg's untimely death; Grainger remained strongly associated with this concerto throughout his lifetime. Grainger's New York pianistic debut was on February 11, 1915, which electrified the audience.

Grainger was a self-taught composer, learning from folk music, both Eastern and Western, and he built a large collection of recordings of ethnic music. He innovated what was termed 'free music', which adapted polyphonic technic to sliding intervals and non-metric rhythmic patterns. This became a powerful influence on several young composers during that period. During his eventful life, Grainger became an American citizen; his death in 1961 was in New York City.

ELLA'S MACARONI AND CHEESE

This is approximately how Ella, Percy's wife, prepared macaroni and cheese, although the quantities were always a handful here, a handful there, instead of by measuring cup. Percy Grainger called himself a meat-shunner. This recipe comes courtesy of Stewart Manville, archivist at the Percy Grainger Library in White Plains, New York.

Boil enough macaroni to fill your baking bowl or pan about halfway (without salt because the cheese will already have enough). Beat 2 or more eggs in enough skim milk just to come up to the surface level of the macaroni when it is poured on (the egg firms up the concoction so it won't sprawl when dished up).

Mix in some diced fresh tomato, if in season (having first peeled it, which is easy if it is first dunked in boiling water). As the final touch, cover the top with grated or sliced Cheddar and "don't be stingy, baby!"

Some Cheddar taste bitter when used in cooking and you have to experiment to find one that satisfies you. Bake plenty hot for about 25 minutes and then switch to the broil setting for an additional 10 to 15 minutes or so, to brown the cheese crust.

Photo: LOUIS OUZER

SYDNEY HODKINSON, COMPOSER

A native of Winnipeg, Manitoba, Sydney Hodkinson received his bachelor and master of music degrees from the Eastman School of Music where he studied composition with Louis Mennini and Bernard Rogers. He continued his studies in composition at the Princeton Seminars with Elliott Carter, Roger Sessions and Milton Babbitt. Hodkinson received his doctor of musical arts degree from the University of Michigan in 1968, studying with Leslie Bassett, Niccolo Castiglioni, Ross Lee Finney and George B. Wilson.

Dr. Hodkinson has taught at the University of Virginia, Ohio State University and the University of Michigan. Prior to his present appointment, Dr. Hodkinson served two years as artist-in-residence in Minneapolis under a grant from the Ford Foundation Contemporary Music Project. He joined the faculty of the Eastman School of Music in 1973, assuming direction of the Eastman Musica Nova, and, more recently, the Graduate Chamber Orchestra. During the academic years 1984-86, Hodkinson served as Meadows visiting professor of composition at Southern Methodist University. During the fall term of 1991, he was visiting professor of composition at the University of Western Ontario.

In addition to his activities as conductor, Mr. Hodkinson is one of the most prolific and widely performed contemporary composers. His most recent compositions include: String Quartet No. 2, commissioned by the Syracuse New Music Society and premiered by the Clinton Quartet; Symphony No. 7, for wind ensemble and piano, commissioned by a consortium of University Wind Ensembles, and premiered by Eastman Wind Ensemble, Donald Hunsberger, conducting; Symphony No. 6, for violin and orchestra; *Overture: A Little Travelin' Music,* commissioned for the Rochester Philharmonic Orchestra; the Clarinet Concerto, commissioned and premiered by Kenneth Grant; and an opera titled *Saint Carmen of the Main*, commissioned by Banff Centre for the Arts and premiered by Guelph Spring Festival. Three recently-released CDs include his *Expiration*, performed by the Dale Warland Singer, D. Warland, conductor; *Cortege: Dirge Canons* for solo cello, strings and percussion; and *Threnody*, for violin and orchestra—all performed by the University of Connecticut Symphony Orchestra with Mary Lou Rylands, cello, Theodore Arm, violinist, and Paul C. Phillips, conducting.

Awards include the Farnsley Prize of the Louisville Orchestra, Guggenheim Foundation, National Institute of Arts and Letters, Canada Council, The National Endowment for the Arts and the International Congress of Jeunesses Musicales Competition. Compositions by Dr. Hodkinson appear in the catalogs of American Composers Alliance, Associated Music publishers (G. Schirmer), Merion (Theo. Presser), Ludwig Music Pub. Co., Music for Percussion, Editions Jobert, Ricordi, Columbia University Music Press, Dorn Publications, and Transcontinental. Hodkinson is a member of BMI, a performing rights organization. Activities as composer/conductor are recorded on CRI, Grenadilla, Louisville, Advance, Nonesuch, Centaur, CBC, Novisse, Mark, Innova, and Pantheon labels.

"LIGHT MY FIRE" ORANGE ROUGHY

Serves 2 to 3

I came across this recipe back in the 1980's in a restaurant that no longer exists, named "Spice it up," in northeast Florida. It's hot!!! --S.H.

2 large orange roughy fillets
2 tablespoons olive oil
2 ribs celery, chopped
2 green onions, sliced
1 clove garlic, minced
1 large tomato, chopped
½ to ¾ cup (jarred) sliced
    jalapeños, drained

2 tablespoons fresh lime juice
1 leek, chopped (white part)
2 tablespoons fresh minced parsley
1 cup clam juice
2 tablespoons dry white wine
4 drops Tabasco sauce
¼ teaspoon basil

In large frying pan, over medium heat, add olive oil. Heat oil and add celery, onion, and garlic. Sauté until soft.

Add remaining ingredients (except fish) and bring to a boil. Reduce flame to low and simmer 15 minutes.

Add orange roughy and simmer on low heat for 20 minutes, or until cooked through and flaky. Gently remove fish to warmed dinner plates and 'nap' with sauce. Garnish with sprigs of parsley and lime wedges.

Photo: NANCY McINTOSH

JOEL HOFFMAN, COMPOSER

Joel Hoffman has emerged as one of the most significant American composers still producing musical works. His numerous awards include a major prize from the American Academy-Institute of Arts and Letters, two grants from the National Endowment for the Arts, three Ohio Arts Council Fellowships, the Bearns Prize of Columbia University, a BMI Award, fourteen ASCAP awards, three American Music Center grants, and two Juilliard composition prizes.

Currently, Mr. Hoffman is professor of composition at the University of Cincinnati's College-Conservatory of Music. During the 1993-94 season, he served as composer-in-residence with the National Chamber Orchestra of Washington, D.C. and in 1991-92, he held the position of new music advisor for the Buffalo Philharmonic. Mr. Hoffman has been a resident composer at the Rockefeller Foundation (Italy), the Camargo Foundation (France) and the Hindemith Foundation (Switzerland), as well as the MacDowell Colony and Yaddo (United States).

Hoffman is also an active concert pianist; he has appeared with the Chicago Symphony, the Belgian Radio and T.V. Orchestra, the Costa Rican Sinfónia Nacional and The Florida Orchestra. He has performed as recitalist and chamber musician on a number of university and festival series in the United States and throughout Europe. In April of 1994, he was soloist in his double concerto *Self-Portrait with Mozart* with the National Chamber Orchestra.

Mr. Hoffman's larger works have been performed by ensembles such as the Chicago Symphony Brass, the BBC Orchestra of Wales, the Cincinnati Symphony Orchestra, the Columbus Symphony, the National Repertory Orchestra, the Collegium Academicum of Geneva, Switzerland, the Cleveland Quartet and the Juilliard 20th Century Music Ensemble.

Hoffman's music has been performed frequently at summer music festivals such as Portogruaro (Italy), Chamber Music Northwest, the Seattle Chamber Music Festival, the Newport (R.I.) Festival, the Korsholm Festival in Finland and the Evian Festival in France. Several of Hoffman's works have been broadcast on the PBS, NPR, BBC and RAI networks. In February 1992, the Buffalo Philharmonic performed a commissioned work, *Music in Blue and Green.* Another recent work, *Cubist Blues*, was premiered by the Golub-Kaplan-Carr Trio. String Quartet No. 2, commissioned for the Shanghai Quartet, was premiered by that ensemble in January 1995. Hoffman's *ChiaSsO* was performed in April 1995 by the Cincinnati Symphony Orchestra. Other significant commissions have been awarded by the Berkshire Music Center at Tanglewood, the Fromm Foundation, the Hancock Chamber Players, the National Chamber Orchestra and the American Harp Society.

Currently, there are twelve works in print, from E.C. Schirmer in Boston (such as the Violin Concerto, Double Concerto and Chamber Symphony) and G. Schirmer in New York (*Music from Chartres*). Recordings include Duo for Viola and Piano on the CRI label and *Partenze* on the Koch International label.

Joel Hoffman was born in Vancouver, Canada in 1953. He received the B.M. degree (summa cum laude) from the University of Wales, Great Britain, as well as the M.M. and D.M.A. degrees in composition from the Juilliard School. His teachers include Easley Blackwood, Alun Hoddinott, Vincent Persichetti, Milton Babbitt and Elliott Carter.

Mr. Hoffman and his wife Dorotea have residences in both Cincinnati and Florence, Italy with their children Benjamin and Natania.

JOEL'S SEITAN SAN FREDIANO
Serves 5 to 6

Seitan is a wonderful meat substitute made from wheat. It can be made from scratch (recipes can be found in several macrobiotic and natural-foods cookbooks) or bought ready-made in sealed packages in most natural-food stores. Seitan is very flavorful and is an excellent source of protein. I enjoy eating vegetarian food; and this recipe I created is really a mixture of Jewish/Italian/vegetarian cooking. --J.H.

24 oz. of seitan (3, 8 oz. packages or home-cooked)	Cooking oil (canola or corn)
1 small can water chestnuts	1 tablespoon fresh garlic, minced
¾ to 1 cup white flour (enough to lightly coat the seitan)	2 medium shallots
	1 lemon (organic if possible), plus rind
	½ cup or more white wine
1 tablespoon each of fresh thyme and rosemary, minced	Tamari sauce
	½ cup fresh coriander, minced

Cut the seitan into thin pieces, not too large. Slice the water chestnuts into small pieces. Combine the flour, thyme and rosemary, and lightly dust the seitan pieces with this mixture.

Add enough oil to cover surface of heavy frying pan and set heat on medium-high. Sauté the garlic, shallots and minced rind of the lemon, adding a little of the wine. As soon as the shallots have begun to cook (2 to 3 minutes), add the seitan. Cook for 10 minutes, adding small amounts of tamari and wine from time to time to keep the seitan from drying. Add the water chestnuts, juice of the lemon, and cook for another minute.

Place everything in a large serving dish and evenly distribute the coriander on top.

Photo: CARL SCHURER, 1994

GEORGE ROCHBERG, COMPOSER

When George Rochberg was presented the Gold Medal of Achievement of the Brandeis University Creative Arts Award in 1985, the citation read in part: "We celebrate George Rochberg for his craft, poetry, and determination to melt the ice in contemporary music....Rochberg is a towering figure in American music. For over thirty years he had been a vibrant teacher and leading American composer—questioning, eloquent and deeply serious....His work reunites us with our musical heritage and provides a spiritual impetus to continue."

This recognition climaxed a long career during which Rochberg produced a large body of orchestral and chamber music, as well as works (including his opera *The Confidence Man*) which emerged first from his involvement with atonal and serial music during the late '40s, '50s, and early '60s, and then from a gradual reassessment of, and ultimately a turn to, tonal music in the middle-late '60s, '70s, and on into the '80s. It was this turn to a whole-hearted embrace of traditionally-oriented tonal possibilities which not only warmed up the musical climate for acceptance but also opened the way to greater freedom and latitude in the way composers could express themselves. Rochberg may have been speaking for others as well as himself when he declared serialism "finished, hollow, meaningless..."

The storm center of this change of 'hear and mind' came with the first performance and subsequent recording of his Third String Quartet—a work whose appeal, according to Donal Henahan of the *New York Times*, lay in its "unfailing formal rigor and old-fashioned musicality. Mr. Rochberg's quartet is—how did we use to put it?— beautiful."

Michael Walsh, then with the *San Francisco Examiner*, expressed the view that "Rochberg's Third Quartet may come to be seen as the work that defined the attitudes of a generation of composers....What is important about it was that it represented a way out of the maze. The defection of so prominent a serialist could not be ignored by all those young composers who were just developing their styles—composers who are now turning up on programs themselves."

Following the 1971 Third String Quartet, Rochberg produced new quartets, symphonies, and concertos which have added to his prominence in the concert hall. It is a body of work informed throughout by what Rochberg has called his "deep concern for the survival of music through a renewal of its humanly expressive qualities." International recognition has come to Rochberg through widespread performance of his works by leading orchestras, conductors and soloists. Many of his works have been recorded and his music has been the subject of discussion in journals and magazines in America and abroad, most recently in Australia and China.

Beginning with the first performances of his *Night Music* in 1953 by the New York Philharmonic with Dimitri Mitropoulos conducting, other works have subsequently achieved major attention, notably the Symphony No. 2 with George Szell and the Cleveland Orchestra (1959 and 1961); the Violin Concerto, which Isaac Stern performed in America, England and France during the middle '70s; the Oboe Concerto, commissioned for Joseph Robinson and performed by Zubin Mehta and the New York Philharmonic (1984); Symphony No. 5 premiered by Sir Georg Solti and the Chicago Symphony (1986); and Symphony No. 6, with Lorin Maazel conducting the first performances with the Pittsburgh Symphony (1987).

Born in Paterson, New Jersey, on July 5, 1918, Rochberg began his studies in composition at the Mannes School of Music. After serving as an infantry lieutenant in World War II, he resumed composition studies, this time at the Curtis Institute of Music. George Rochberg taught at the Curtis Institute from 1948 to 1954. In 1960, he joined the faculty of the University of Pennsylvania, serving as chairman of the Department of Music until 1968.

Rochberg retired from teaching in 1983 as Emeritus Annenberg Professor of the Humanities. He and his wife Gene make their home in Newtown, Square, Pennsylvania.

MAMA LUIGI'S MEAT LOAF FOR TWO
Serves 4 to 6

In the experience of my wife Gene and myself, according to our eating habits, this menu provides enough for a delicious dinner (add your own vegetables to taste) and leftovers for sandwiches the next day. --G.R.

1 **pound lean ground beef (or mixture of beef and veal; or beef, veal and pork)**
½ **cup old-fashioned Quaker oatmeal (or bread crumbs)**
½ **medium Vidalia onion, grated**

½ **cup Heinz salsa ketchup**
4 **slices of lean bacon**
6 **oz. can of V8 juice**
White wine (for additional sauce if desired)

Preheat oven to 375 degrees. Mix beef, oatmeal, onion and ketchup together. If too firm, loosen with a little white wine and/or salsa ketchup. Form loaf. Cover loaf with bacon strips. Place into shallow baking pan. Pour a can of V8 juice over loaf.

Bake uncovered at 375 degrees for about 50 to 60 minutes, until bubbly and brown. If more gravy is desired, add white wine.

Note ♪: Salt and pepper at your own discretion. We don't use any.

Photo: © JACK MITCHELL, 1992

NED ROREM, COMPOSER

Words and music are inextricably linked for Ned Rorem. *Time* magazine has called him "the world's best composer of art songs," yet his musical and literary ventures extend far beyond this specialized field. Rorem has composed three symphonies, four piano concertos and an array of other orchestral works, music for numerous combinations of chamber forces, six operas, choral works of every description, ballets and other music for the theater, and literally hundreds of songs and cycles. He is the author of thirteen books, including five volumes of diaries and collections of lectures and criticism.

Born in Richmond, Indiana on October 23, 1923, Rorem early moved to Chicago with his family; by the age of ten his piano teacher had introduced him to Debussy and Ravel, an experience which "changed my life forever," according to the composer. At seventeen, he entered the Music School of Northwestern University, two years later receiving a scholarship to the Curtis Institute in Philadelphia. Rorem studied composition under Bernard Wagenaar at Juilliard, taking his B.A. in 1946 and his M.A. degree (along with the $1,000 George Gershwin Memorial Prize in composition) in 1948. In New York he worked as Virgil Thomson's copyist in return for $20 a week and orchestration lessons. He studied on fellowship at the Berkshire Music Center in Tanglewood in the summers of 1946 and 1947; in 1948, his song *The Lordly Hudson* was voted the best published song of that year by the Music Library Association.

In 1949, Rorem moved to France and lived there until 1958. His years as a young composer among the leading figures of the artistic and social milieu of post-war Europe are absorbingly portrayed in *The Paris Diary of Ned Rorem* (Brazillier, 1966). He currently lives in New York City.

Ned Rorem has been the recipient of a Fulbright Fellowship (1951), a Guggenheim Fellowship (1957), and an award from the National Institute of Arts and Letters (1968). He received the ASCAP-Deems Taylor Award in 1971 for his book *Critical Affairs, A Composer's Journal*, in 1975 for *The Final Diary*, and in 1992 for an article on American opera in *Opera News*. Among his many commissions for new works are those from the Ford Foundation (for the String Symphony, 1985); the Chicago Symphony (for *Goodbye My Fancy*, 1990); and from Carnegie Hall (for *Spring Music*, 1991). Among the distinguished conductors who have performed his music are Bernstein, Mitropoulos, Reiner, Ormandy, Steinberg, Stokowski, and Mehta; his suite *Air Music* won the 1976 Pulitzer Prize in music. The Atlanta Symphony recording of the String Symphony, *Sunday Morning,* and *Eagles* received a Grammy Award for Outstanding Orchestral Recording in 1989.

Celebrations of the composer's 70th-birthday year began in February 1993 with the premiere of his Piano Concerto for Left Hand and Orchestra, which attracted international attention and critical plaudits; André Previn led soloist Gary Graffman and the Symphony Orchestra of the Curtis Institute of Music in performances at the Academy of Music in Philadelphia and Carnegie Hall in New York. In the months surrounding the birthday itself, all-Rorem concerts took place in New York, San Francisco, Philadelphia, Minneapolis, and Buffalo, along with major performances throughout the U.S., spanning the full range of his repertoire. In January 1994, Kurt Masur conducted English hornist Thomas Stacy and the New York Philharmonic in the first performances of Rorem's Concerto for English Horn and Orchestra, commissioned by the orchestra in honor of its 150th anniversary season. *Knowing When to Stop*, his newest book, was issued by Simon and Schuster in fall 1994; it is an autobiographical memoir of the composer's first 28 years.

Rorem has said: "My music is a diary no less compromising than my prose. A diary never less differs from a musical composition in that it depicts the moment, the writer's present mood which, were it inscribed an hour later, could emerge quite otherwise. I don't believe that composers notate their moods, they don't tell the music where to go—it leads them....Why do I write music? Because I want to hear it—it's (as) simple as that.

Others may have more *talent*, more sense of duty. But I compose just from necessity, and no one else is making what I need."

LIME BAVARIAN

Serves 4

*Now that I no longer smoke, or drink, make love, or use foul language, my sole reason for living, let alone for having a meal, is **DESSERT**. So here's one of my mother's recipes which dates back fifty years.* --N.R.

1 **package of lime JELL-O**
1 **cup hot water**
1 **cup freshly squeezed lime juice**

1 **pint of freshly whipped cream**
½ **pint lime yogurt**

Blend package of lime JELL-O with cup of hot water and cup of fresh lime juice. When ¾ hardened, add fresh whipped cream and lime yogurt. Refrigerate for 5 hours.

Serve with fresh raspberries, add whipped cream dollops and strawberry sauce (frozen strawberries mixed in a blender) presented in a silver bowl, and fudge squares. This recipe can be frozen in top of freezer and made into a sherbet.

Portrait by W. DRESER, Courtesy, Lilly Library, Indiana University

GIOACCHINO ROSSINI, COMPOSER

Rossini's early musical training was in harpsichord, singing and harmony. In 1807, he entered the Bologna Conservatory. Studies eventually were discontinued so he could devote his time to composing operas. His first grand success was in 1813, with the production of "Tancredi" in Venice. The year 1816 saw the "Barbiere di Siviglia" in Rome, which eventually proved to be his most widely known composition. In the opera, "Elisabetta," Rossini achieved a great innovation by dismissing 'secco recitative'.

From 1815-23, twenty operas were composed for the Neapolitan theaters.

Rossini married the celebrated soprano, Isabel Colbran. In 1822, Rossini was inspired by a meeting with Beethoven. Operatic sojourns were then made in England and France. Rossini wrote little music after the age of 37. A notable exception was his Stabat Mater; the first six parts were composed in 1832 and the remaining four parts appeared in 1841.

As described in the book, "The Pleasures of the Table," by George H. Ellwanger, Rossini, a contemporary and friend of Balzac and Dumas, was not alone a famous musician, but was also a distinguished 'fourchette' and cook of ability. One of his most celebrated compositions—that of a certain manner of preparing macaroni which is said to have vied in seductiveness with the sweetest strains of the "Barbiere di Siviglia"—is unfortunately lost to the world through a prejudice of Dumas.

One day the great romanticist, who never ate macaroni in any form, asked the noted composer for his recipe, being anxious to add it to his culinary repertoire. "Come and eat some with me tomorrow at dinner, and you shall have it," was the answer. But the host, perceiving that his guest would not touch a dish on which he had bestowed so much pains, refused to give him the formula, whereupon Dumas circulated the report that it was Rossini's cook, not Rossini himself, who was the master of the secret and forthwith presented at length a recipe given him by the famous Mme. Ristori as "the true, the only, the unique manner of preparing macaroni à la néapolitaine."

CONSOMMÉ ROSSINI

Many recipes have been named after Rossini. This particular dish, which uses goose livers, was one of his favorites. This recipe is recreated by concert pianist and master chef Alberto Portugheis.

9 oz. (250 g) *foie gras* (goose livers)
1 black truffle, finely chopped
30 small profiteroles, about
    1-inch (2-2½ cm) wide*
6 egg yolks

⅝ cup (150 ml) heavy cream
1½ quarts (1½ liters) chicken or beef
    *consommé**
2 tablespoons port (optional)
1 tablespoon flat parsley, finely chopped

Blend *foie gras* and truffle and with the help of a piping-bag (pastry bag), fill the profiteroles. Beat together egg yolks and cream.

Bring *consommé* to a boil, with port if being used. Add yolk/cream mixture, stirring continuously. Remove from heat source the moment it begins to thicken.

Pour *consommé* into individual soup plates or bowls, and garnish each with 5 profiteroles and sprinkle with parsley.

*See page 280 for profiteroles and *consommé* recipes.

Photo: © PETER SCHAAF

PETER SCHICKELE, COMPOSER/SATIRIST

Composer, musician, author, satirist—Peter Schickele is internationally recognized as one of the most versatile artists in the field of music. His works, now in excess of 100 for symphony orchestras, choral groups, chamber ensembles, voice, movies and television, have given him "a leading role in the ever-more-prominent school of American composers who unselfconsciously blend all levels of American music." (John Rockwell, *New York Times)*

In his well-known other role as perpetrator of the *oeuvre* of the now classic P.D.Q. Bach, Peter Schickele is acknowledged as one of the great satirists of the 20th century. In testimony, Vanguard has released 11 albums of the fabled genius's works; Random House has published eleven editions of *The Definitive Biography of P.D.Q. Bach* (which has also been translated into German); Theodore Presser has printed innumerable scores, and VideoArts International has produced a cassette of P.D.Q. Bach's only full-length opera "The Abduction of Figaro" which, late in the 1989 season, was given 28 successive sold-out performances in Stockholm, Sweden by the Dramatiske Ensemblen. That all adds up to "the greatest comedy-in-music act before the public today" (Robert Marsh, *Chicago Sun Times).* Although on an "indefinite sabbatical" from touring with the works of P.D.Q. Bach, he continues to present both old and new discoveries of his music at Carnegie Hall each December.

Peter Schickele created the musical score for the film version of Maurice Sendak's children's classic "Where the Wild Things Are," issued recently on videocassette along with Sendak classic "In the Night Kitchen" (Weston Woods), which Schickele narrates. He also has recorded for RCA Red Seal and CRI.

In 1993, Telarc released a recording of Prokofiev's *Sneaky Pete* (a.k.a. Peter) *and the Wolf* and *Carnival of the Animals* with newly written texts narrated by Peter Schickele, accompanied by the Atlanta Symphony Orchestra under Yoel Levi. Mr. Schickele gave the New York premiere of *Sneaky Pete and the Wolf* at Carnegie Hall as part of the Toyota Comedy Festival and has performed the Saint-Saëns work with several major American orchestras, including the New York Philharmonic at its gala New Year's Eve concert in 1991. He also continues to tour with a program of original songs, which he sings from the piano with the harmonizing assistance of David Düsing, and with a program entitled *The Condition of My Heart,* which combines Schickele's songs with the poetry of his wife, Susan Sindall.

Among his current projects is a weekly, syndicated radio program, "Schickele Mix," which has been heard nationwide over American Public Radio since January 1992 and which won ASCAP's prestigious Deems Taylor Award. During the 1994 to 1995 season, Schickele served as creative director and host for an innovative series of children's concerts with the American Symphony Orchestra.

Peter Schickele was born in Ames, Iowa, and brought up in Washington, D.C., and Fargo, North Dakota. He graduated from Swarthmore in 1957, having had the distinction of being the only music major (as he had been, earlier, the only bassoonist in Fargo). By that time, he had already composed and conducted four orchestral works, a great deal of chamber music and some songs. Schickele studied composition with Roy Harris and Darius Milhaud; at the Juilliard School of Music he studied with Vincent Persichetti and William Bergsma. Then, under a Ford Foundation grant, he composed music for high schools in Los Angeles before returning to Juilliard to teach in 1961. In 1965, he gave up teaching to become a freelance composer/performer which he has been ever since.

In the course of his career, Schickele has created music for four feature films, among them the prize-winning "Silent Running"; for countless documentaries; for television commercials; for several "Sesame Street" segments and for an underground movie that he has never seen. He has also created music and lyrics for "Oh, Calcutta," and has arranged for Buffy Sainte-Marie, Joan Baez and other folk singers.

Mr. Schickele and his wife, the poet Susan Sindall, reside both in New York City and at an upstate hideaway where he concentrates on composing. His son and daughter constitute two-thirds of an alternative rock band called Beekeeper that plays regularly in New York City.

GASTRONOMIC REMARKS FROM PETER SCHICKELE

The subject of food and drink has certainly been on the mind of Mr. Schickele for many years. There is evidence of this from Mr. Schickele's discovery and publication of various works of P.D.Q. Bach such as: *The Art of the Ground Round* (S. 1.19/lb.); *The Little Pickle Book* (S. 57); *The Stoned Guest, a half-act opera* (S. 86 proof); and the oratorio: *The Seasonings* (S. 1½ tsp.). Mr. Schickele has graciously shared some of his culinary insights with the author through their correspondence.

I like cooking. It's one of my favorite things to eat. I would much rather ingest someone's cooking, than say, the contents of his pencil sharpener.

My favorite kind of cooking? Heteroprepared.

I can't cook my way out of a paper bag. My idea of a recipe is the boiling instructions on the back of a package of frozen corn. I am, however, not typical in that respect; as you obviously know—many musicians are excellent cooks, and are as proud of their expertise as I am abashed by my lack of the same.

As my brother once said, "good food is better than bad food."

Thanks again for thinking of me, and here's to food and music.

Cheers,

Peter Schickele

University of Helsinki Department of Musicology

JEAN SIBELIUS, COMPOSER

Jean Sibelius was born in Tavastehus, Finland in 1865. In 1891, Sibelius returned to Finland after studying composition in Berlin and Vienna. He returned to find his country suffering under the oppression of Czar Nicholas II of Russia. Inspired by the national spirit of the Finnish people and their stance for truth and freedom in resisting the czar, Sibelius found his voice as a composer. In 1892 he wrote the symphonic poem *Kullervo* (based on an episode from the Finnish epic poem the *Kalevala*) in which he successfully expressed through music the feelings of the Finnish people. Sibelius married Aino Järnefelt in 1892. From 1892 until 1897 he played violin in a string quartet and taught music theory at both the Helsinki Conservatory and the orchestral school of the Philharmonic Society. In 1897 he became the first Finnish composer to be awarded an annual grant by the Finnish government which allowed him drop these other activities and to focus all of his energies on composing.

While remaining faithful to traditional approaches, Sibelius achieved originality through expressing both the spirit of Finland and his own deeply personal feelings gleaned through much introspection. He created music that expressed the essence of his country: its culture, geography, traditions, legends, its people and their love of freedom.

His last known work was completed in 1929, after which he withdrew from the world, internationally recognized as one of the most significant symphonists since Brahms, and regarded in his own country as a national hero and the voice of Finland.

Jean Sibelius died in Järvenpää, Finland in 1957. The house where he was born in Hämeenlinna as well as his former home (Ainola) in Järvenpää are now museums.

Major works of Sibelius include seven symphonies (written between 1899 and 1924), a violin concerto (1904), symphonic poems (*Kullervo, En Saga, Karelia, Four Legends* (including *The Swan of Tuonela*), *Pohjola's Daughter, Tapiola,* and *Finlandia*), *Valse Triste,* and *Voces Intimae* (*Intimate Voices*) for string quartet.

THE SIBELIUS SUPPER

Serves 2

Jean Sibelius liked a steak which calls for a contre-filet (bullock) of a young bull. To prepare the beef properly, the butcher must understand the European way of cutting and hanging the meat. In larger cities this may not be a problem, but it may be a problem in more remote areas. One can use beef tenderloin (filet mignon) as a substitute for this recipe, which is also quite common in many European countries. My great appreciation goes to Finnish natives Eva Haitto, for securing this recipe, and Telle Bayerle, for the above remarks and recipe editing.

In Finland, several years ago, advanced cooking students in a well-known cooking school prepared meals of the favorite dishes from the most important Finns in history. Each day a different menu was prepared for the dining-room customers. A "Sibelius Menu" was one of the featured items at the school.

1 **pound bullock of beef or**
   beef tenderloin (filet mignon)
1 **medium red onion, sliced**
3 **tablespoons salted butter**
Red wine

3 **medium red tomatoes**
Parsley for garnish
1 **tablespoon vegetable oil**
Salt and pepper
½ **pound brussels sprouts**

Sauté red onion slices in a small frying pan, using 1 tablespoon salted butter. When onions are soft, pour over some red wine. Keep warm.

Slice the filet. The slices should be rather thick and should be pounded a little. Heat a heavy skillet on medium-high flame, add vegetable oil and 2 tablespoons butter. When mixture turns light brown, add salt and black pepper and fry steaks until crusty and darkish outside, but still rather bloody inside, or at least pink, but never well-done. Set meat on a platter and spoon onions onto each steak.

Serve with steamed brussels sprouts, boiled potatoes and oven-baked tomatoes (top tomatoes with butter and salt, and bake for 35 minutes at 350 degrees). Garnish with parsley.

CONDUCTORS

Photo: DECCA/VIVIANNE PURDOM

VLADIMIR ASHKENAZY, CONDUCTOR/PIANIST

During the last thirty-five years, Vladimir Ashkenazy's richly active life has encompassed more than one career. In 1962, his already significant international reputation as a pianist was reconfirmed by winning the first prize in the Second Tchaikovsky Competition in Moscow. From then on, he has appeared each season in all of the great musical centers of the world.

During the last twenty years, Ashkenazy has also steadily increased his activities as a conductor; in 1987 he was appointed music director of London's Royal Philharmonic Orchestra. Since then, he has maintained an intensive schedule of engagements with the orchestra in London and abroad, and in future seasons he will continue to lead the Royal Philharmonic in its role as one of the most dynamic and innovative musical organizations in Europe.

Highlights of past performances with the Royal Philharmonic included two concerts in Moscow in November 1989, this being Mr. Ashkenazy's first return to the Soviet Union in twenty-six years. The concerts were recorded and broadcast and an international TV audience was able to share in the first performance by satellite link up. These concerts were followed by an equally successful tour of Japan. In September 1991, Mr. Ashkenazy and the orchestra completed the first tour of South America by a London orchestra in many years, performing to great acclaim in Mexico City, Buenos Aires, Rio de Janeiro, Brasilia and São Paulo. In January 1992, they made an acclaimed tour of all the EC capitals to mark the 1992 single European market. Beginning in 1995, Mr. Ashkenazy embarked on a global tour with the Royal Philharmonic to mark the orchestra's 50th anniversary. The tour has been chosen as a flagship project of the official 50th anniversary celebrations of the United Nations and will cover all five continents over a two-year period. Since September 1987, Ashkenazy has also been principal guest conductor of the Cleveland Orchestra, with whom he performs for several weeks each year, both in Cleveland and on tour in the United States.

In October 1989, Ashkenazy became chief conductor of the Radio Symphony Orchestra Berlin, now renamed the Deutsches Symphonie-Orchester Berlin, where his tenure currently extends to 1998. He has developed a particularly close association with this orchestra, giving many concerts and radio broadcasts in Berlin every season and touring extensively in Europe, Japan, and the U.S.A. Mr. Ashkenazy has also conducted the Berlin Philharmonic Orchestra in Berlin and Salzburg and is regularly invited as guest conductor by the Los Angeles Philharmonic, the Boston Symphony, and the San Francisco Symphony.

As a recording artist, Vladimir Ashkenazy's catalogue with Decca Records is enormous, covering almost all the major works for piano by Mozart, Beethoven, Chopin, Rachmaninov, Prokofiev, and Scriabin. As a conductor, his list of recordings is already substantial. Major projects already in progress include the Rachmaninov symphonies with the Royal Concertgebouw, Sibelius and Beethoven symphonies, Mozart piano concertos with the Philharmonia and Shostakovich symphonies with the Royal Philharmonic Orchestra. Ongoing plans include a major Stravinsky project with the DSO Berlin as well as Scriabin and Mahler cycles. With the Cleveland Orchestra, Ashkenazy has recorded the Brahms symphonies, as well as selected works by Prokofiev and Strauss. He is also active as a chamber musician, notably in partnership with Itzhak Perlman and Lynn Harrell, with whom he has performed and recorded many of the great works of the Classical and Romantic repertoire. Vladimir Ashkenazy lives with his family in Lucerne, Switzerland.

BEEF STROGANOFF
Serves 4

This dish can be served with rice, but we prefer puréed potatoes. Some people like mushrooms in the stroganoff, but that is not the original recipe. --V.A.

1½ pounds beef fillet or lean sirloin steak
1½ teaspoons salt, or to taste
1 to 2 teaspoons pepper
3 tablespoons butter
1 tablespoon flour

1 cup beef consommé
1 teaspoon hot prepared mustard
1 medium onion, sliced
3 tablespoons sour cream

Remove fat and gristle from meat, cut in narrow strips about 1½-inches long and ½-inch thick. Season with salt, pepper, and set aside for 2 hours at room temperature.

In medium saucepan melt half the butter and blend in the flour. Add consommé and boil up. Stir in mustard. Take pan off burner for the moment.

In a large pan, add remaining butter and brown the meat quickly with the onion until meat is cooked. Have sour cream at room temperature and add to the sauce, boil up again, then add meat to the sauce, after removing the onion. Cover the pan and keep hot for 20 minutes but make sure it does not boil or simmer. Heat up briskly just before serving.

Photo: TERRENCE McCARTHY

HERBERT BLOMSTEDT, CONDUCTOR

Since Herbert Blomstedt became music director of the San Francisco Symphony in September 1985, the partnership he and the orchestra have established has become recognized as one of America's most compelling artistic collaborations. This recognition has come in many forms, including acclaim on tour, a major recording contract with London Records, and coveted recording awards. Mr. Blomstedt relinquished his post as music director at the close of the 1994-95 season, after ten years with the orchestra, and assumed the post of conductor laureate.

Born in Springfield, Massachusetts in 1927, Herbert Blomstedt moved with his family to Sweden two years later. His mother, a pianist, gave him his first musical training. This led him to the Royal College of Music in Stockholm for studies in violin, piano, organ, theory, and conducting, and to the University of Uppsala for work in musicology. He continued conducting studies with the legendary Igor Markevitch, with Jean Morel at the Juilliard School, and with Leonard Bernstein at Tanglewood's Berkshire Music Center. Honors and accomplishments followed quickly: in 1953 the Koussevitzky Conducting Prize; in 1954, his conducting debut with the Stockholm Philharmonic and first appointment as a music director (with Sweden's Norrköping Symphony Orchestra); and in 1955, first prize at the Salzburg conducting competition. Mr. Blomstedt has held positions as music director of the Oslo Philharmonic, Danish Radio Symphony, and Swedish Radio Symphony. In 1975, the musicians of the Dresden Staatskapelle, the world's oldest orchestra, invited him to become their music director. In ten years at its helm, Blomstedt led the ensemble throughout Europe and in its first visits to the United States. He also dramatically extended the Staatskapelle's discography, with recordings that include the complete symphonies of Beethoven and Schubert and, in an ongoing series, orchestral music of Richard Strauss. He has led various orchestras in recordings of 150 orchestral works. His first set of the complete Nielsen symphonies, which he recorded with the Danish Radio Symphony in the early 1970's, played a key role in making that composer's music known in the United States.

Mr. Blomstedt is in constant demand as a guest conductor and has led many of the world's greatest orchestras, including the New York Philharmonic, the Berlin Philharmonic, the Royal Concertgebouw Orchestra of Amsterdam, Boston Symphony, Chicago Symphony, and the Philadelphia Orchestra. During the 1994-95 season, his conducting engagements included performances with the orchestras of Stuttgart, Stockholm, Hamburg, Leipzig, and Göteborg, also, major European tours with the San Francisco Symphony and the Bamberg Symphony. He has established an international reputation as a teacher of conducting and his many distinctions include membership in the Royal Musical Academy of Stockholm, of which Beethoven was a member. He is a Knight of the North Star, Stockholm, and a Knight of the Dannebrogen, Cöpenhagen. In 1989, Mr. Blomstedt received San Francisco's Cyril Magnin Award for Lifetime Achievement in the Arts, an award whose previous recipients include Isaac Stern and Leontyne Price. He was most recently a recipient of Columbia University's Ditson Award for outstanding service to American music (1992).

PORRIDGE

Serves 2 to 3

*For me, breakfast is the most important meal of the day. It usually starts with an apple and half a grapefruit, but the main course is always—***PORRIDGE.**

The ingredients can be varied ad infinitum, but my favorite is made of stone ground flour, or even better would be 'spelt', if you can find it. It keeps you in excellent shape the whole morning; it is cheap and it tastes wonderful. I never get tired of it—the flavor seems different every day. --H.B.

1 cup stone ground whole wheat flour or spelt flour	Pinch of salt
¼ cup unbleached white wheat flour	10 large dates, cut into small pieces
	3 tablespoons cut almonds

Fill a 3- or 4-quart sauce pan with a quart of water. Add a pinch of salt, and heat the water on medium-high.

When the water is boiling, turn down the heat to medium, add flour 'poco a poco' while stirring with a whisk. When porridge approaches the desired thickness (use less spelt flour for thinner porridge), add dates and 3 tablespoons of cut almonds. Let cook for about 10 minutes on very low heat, stirring occasionally.

Serve with low-fat milk or favorite juice.

Photo: © CLIVE BARDA, Performing Arts Library

COLIN DAVIS, CONDUCTOR

Sir Colin Davis is one of the most celebrated conductors in Europe today. In recent seasons, he performed and recorded with a number of different orchestras, including the Dresden Staatskapelle, and the London Symphony Orchestra. Sir Colin Davis became principal conductor of the London Symphony Orchestra in September 1995 having been principal guest conductor since 1975. He will become principal guest conductor of the New York Philharmonic in 1998.

In January 1996, Sir Colin Davis took part in a Bruckner/Mozart Festival with the London Symphony Orchestra and toured with them in the Canary Islands and Switzerland. He conducted Berlioz's *The Trojans* at La Scala, Milan in the spring and then returned to London for Mozart's *Die Entführung aus dem Serail* at the Royal Opera House, Covent Garden. In 1997, Sir Colin will take part in a Brahms Festival with the LSO and will be also working with the Dresden Staatskapelle, New York Philharmonic and Bavarian Radio Symphony Orchestra.

During the 1994-95 season, Sir Colin Davis appeared at the Proms with the Dresden Staatskapelle. In September 1994, he completed a tour with the Staatskapelle after concerts in Lucerne and Besancon and conducted the orchestra on a tour of Buenos Aires and São Paulo in the summer of 1995. In February 1995, Sir Colin led the London Symphony Orchestra through a 90th birthday celebration for Sir Michael Tippett, which featured the world premiere of his new work *The Rose Lake*.

Sir Colin Davis has recorded widely with Philips and BMG and has a continuing recording contract with them. This includes: *Fidelio* with the Bavarian Radio Symphony Orchestra and several live concerts from Munich, including Brahms's Violin Concerto with Kyoko Takezawa and Mahler's Eighth Symphony. A recording of the Sibelius Symphonies Nos. 1 and 4 with the London Symphony was released in 1996 as well the complete Schubert symphonies with the Dresden Staatskapelle. BMG released *Lohengrin* with the Bavarian Radio Symphony Orchestra, featuring vocalists Ben Heppner, Sergei Leiferkus, Bryn Terfel, Eva Marton and Sharon Sweet. Recently, Brahms's *German Requiem*, and the Beethoven *Missa Solemnis* and *Choral Fantasy* with Gerhard Oppitz have been released on video, CD and laser disc with the Bavarian Radio Symphony Orchestra. In the 1993/94 season, Sir Colin Davis completed recording the Beethoven symphonies on Philips Classics with the Dresden Staatskapelle.

Sir Colin Davis won the 1993 Evening Standard Award for outstanding artistic achievement in opera for the much acclaimed concert performances of Berlioz's *Trojans* with the London Symphony Orchestra and *Damnation of Faust* at the Royal Opera House. In the 1992/93 season, several international honours were bestowed on Sir Colin Davis for his services to music. He was awarded the Bayerischen Verdienstörden in Bavaria, the Freedom of the City of London and the Order of the Lion of Finland, Commander 1st Class. These awards are in addition to becoming Commander of the British Empire in 1965 and receiving a knighthood in 1980. He has also been honoured with the Commendatore of the Republic of Italy (1976); the French Legion d'Honneur (1982); the Commander's Cross of the Order of Merit of the Federal Republic of Germany (1987) and Commandeur dans l'Ordre des Arts et des Lettres of France (1990).

Sir Colin Davis is celebrated for his work in opera. For fifteen years until 1986 he was music director of the Royal Opera House, Covent Garden, following six years as music director of the Sadlers Wells Opera (now English National Opera). Former appointments with orchestras include principal conductor and music director of the Bavarian Radio Symphony Orchestra from 1984-1992.

Sir Colin was born in Weybridge, Surrey, in 1927.

FAST AND EASY SUPPER
For 4 to 6 people

STARTER AND MAIN DISH: DUCK WITH ALMONDS

Lettuce leaves—any variety washed and spun
Several rashers of smoked streaky bacon,
   fried until crispy, chopped

Chopped walnuts
Walnut oil or olive oil to taste
4 oz. Roquefort cheese, finely grated

Assemble lettuce, bacon and walnuts in a large salad bowl. Add the oil and toss. Serve on individual plates and garnish with grated Roquefort cheese.

1 pound lean duck meat (or if not available,
   fillet of pork, or chicken breast)
3 tablespoons of olive oil
2 cloves of garlic, crushed
2 slices of ginger root, shredded
4 spring onions (green onions)

4 oz. button mushrooms
4 oz. mange tout (snow peas)
2 tablespoons of sherry
2 to 3 tablespoons of soy sauce
2 teaspoons of cornstarch
Flaked almonds, toasted

Thinly slice the meat. In a bowl, add 1 tablespoon of olive oil with the garlic and ginger, mix well. Add the sliced duck into the bowl and marinate for 30 minutes. Meanwhile, slice onions and mushrooms.

In a deep frying pan, on medium-high flame, heat the remaining oil. Add the onions and the meat and cook for 3 minutes. (Cooking time may vary slightly depending on the choice of meat). Add the mushrooms and mange tout and cook for another 2 minutes. Add sherry and soy sauce, cook 1 to 2 additional minutes. Dissolve the cornstarch in a tablespoon of cold water and stir into the pan. Cook for 1 minute until thickened. Stir in the toasted almonds.

Serve with rice or potatoes.

DESSERT: SUMMER FRUIT

"The cleverest thing I ever did" said the White Knight to Alice "was inventing a new pudding during the meat course."

1 banana per person
2 oz. butter
3 to 5 oz. brown sugar

2 to 4 tablespoons lemon juice
3 tablespoons brandy (warm before
   lighting)

Slice the bananas in half, lengthwise, and fry for a few minutes in the butter. Sprinkle with brown sugar and lemon juice and cook for another 2 minutes. Pour brandy over them and serve, flaming!

Photo: © KLAUS WINKLER

RAFAEL FRÜHBECK DE BURGOS, CONDUCTOR

Rafael Frühbeck de Burgos, son of German parents, was born in the Spanish city of Burgos. He studied violin, piano, music theory and composition in Bilbao and Madrid. De Burgos studied to be a conductor in Munich, Germany, graduating summa cum laude and receiving the "Richard Strauss" Award. For four years, de Burgos was the music director of the Bilbao Symphony. From 1962-1978, he conducted the Spanish National Orchestra in Madrid. During that time, he also worked as general music director of the city of Düsseldorf, Germany (total of five years). Further along in his career, he took over leadership of the Montreal Symphony Orchestra and was principal guest conductor of the National Symphony Orchestra of Washington, as well as the Yomiuri Symphony Orchestra of Tokyo. As a guest conductor, he directed more than 100 international orchestras. These included the leading American and Canadian orchestras, the Berlin Philharmonic Orchestra, and the most important orchestras in Hamburg, Frankfurt, Cologne and Munich. He has been a guest conductor with all the London orchestras, as well as conducting in Italy, Switzerland, France, Sweden, Norway, Denmark and Finland. He is a guest conductor for the Israel Philharmonic Orchestra and the leading Japanese orchestras.

There are a large number of recordings of Rafael Frühbeck de Burgos available. Many of these recordings are regarded as milestones of interpretation: Mendelssohn's oratorios *Elias* and *Paulus,* Mozart's Requiem, Orff's *Carmina Burana.* The recording of Bizet's *Carmen* from the year 1970 with Grace Bumbry in the title role is still considered to be a definitive recording. In 1991, de Burgos became the chief conductor of the Vienna Symphony and in 1993 toured with the orchestra in Austria and Europe (Birmingham, Glasgow, London, Lucern, Toulouse, Seville, Valencia, Madrid, Lisbon, Maastricht, Nürnberg and Munich). That same year, he conducted the Israel Philharmonic Orchestra in Tel Aviv, Jerusalem and Haifa; the Göteborg Symfoniker in Göteborg and Stockholm; and the Wiener Symphoniker in Vienna.

At the beginning of the 1992-93 season, de Burgos was named general music director of the "Deutsche Oper" in Berlin. The first opera premiere was Verdi's *Don Carlos* in five acts. During that season, he directed a new study of Bizet's *Carmen,* as well as Wagner's *Meistersinger von Nürnberg*, and Verdi's *Ein Maskenball.* The 1994 season brought a new study of Verdi's *Otello.* More success was gained in Berlin with works by Richard Strauss (*Don Juan* and *Vier Letzte Lieder* with soprano Julia Varady), and Beethoven's Fifth Symphony. De Burgos has gained world-wide recognition for his conducting of works by Richard Strauss; he conducted the premiere of the opera *Ariadne auf Naxos* at the Zürich opera house, gaining music recognition. "His depth, character, and presence of details is of great value." In South America, the maestro gained praise for his interpretation of *Ein Heldenleben,* played with the Wiener Symphoniker. In Berlin, de Burgos directed the Radio Symphony Orchestra and has toured Japan with them.

The philosophy faculty of the University of Navarra in Pamplona, Spain bestowed an honorary doctoral degree on de Burgos in 1994.

PAELLA DE MARISCO
(Seafood Paella)
Serves 4 to 6

Maestro de Burgos's favorite recipe comes from one of his favorite restaurants: Rafa Restaurante-Marisqueria, in Madrid, Spain.

4 tablespoons olive oil	3¾ cups of very hot water
1 clove of garlic, minced	Salt and pepper to taste
1 red onion (about ¾ pound), chopped	1 pound of cleaned squid, coarsely chopped
1 large green pepper, coarsely chopped	½ pound fresh small clams
1 large red pepper, coarsely chopped	½ pound fresh giant prawns
2 cups of long-grain white rice	½ pound crayfish, precooked
Pinch of saffron and food coloring	

Finely mince the garlic and coarsely chop the onion and red and green peppers.

Add olive oil into a large, deep skillet (14-inch) with lid. Heat the oil on medium flame. Add the minced garlic, then the onion and peppers. Reduce heat and simmer for 12 minutes or until peppers are slightly soft.

Toss pan ingredients, then add the rice, a dash of saffron and yellow food coloring (enough to give the rice a pale yellow tone). Stir in hot water and distribute contents evenly. Salt and pepper moderately, or to taste. Cover pan and gently cook on medium-low heat for about 20 minutes.

Meanwhile, rinse and clean the clams. Remove the shell and veins from the prawns. When 20 minutes are completed, add both chopped squid and clams to pan, then prawns. Cook for 5 minutes, then add crayfish and heat 5 more minutes. Remove from stove, and let set for additional 10 minutes or longer to make rice fluffier. Serve hot.

Photo: SCOTT F. KOHN

CHRISTOPH ESCHENBACH, CONDUCTOR/PIANIST

Christoph Eschenbach became music director of the Houston Symphony on September 1, 1988. He follows a distinguished line of past music directors, including Leopold Stokowski, Sir John Barbirolli and André Previn. Christoph Eschenbach has regularly conducted the major orchestras of Europe and North America, including the Berlin Philharmonic, all the London orchestras, the Orchestre National de France, the Boston Symphony, the Cleveland Orchestra in Cleveland and on tour throughout the United States, the Chicago Symphony, the Philadelphia Orchestra, the National Symphony, the Pittsburgh Symphony, the San Francisco Symphony, and the Toronto and Montreal symphonies. He has also led the Vienna Symphony frequently in Vienna and on two tours in Japan, as well as one in the United States. In addition, he has conducted the Israel Philharmonic and all the German Radio orchestras.

In September 1994, Christoph Eschenbach was appointed music director of the Ravinia Festival, home of the Chicago Symphony Orchestra during its eight-week residency each summer. He follows James Levine, who held that post from 1971-1993. Maestro Eschenbach has also appeared at leading American summer festivals, such as Tanglewood, Blossom, Hollywood Bowl, and the Mostly Mozart festivals of both New York and Houston. He has appeared at many European summer festivals, including the Festival de Tours in France, the Schleswig-Holstein Festival with Sviatoslav Richter as soloist, and festival tours of Australia and Europe with the Australian Youth Orchestra.

In addition to conducting the Houston Symphony in Houston, Christoph Eschenbach regularly has led the orchestra on domestic and international tours. In 1992, he took his orchestra to Germany, Switzerland, and Austria, after a stop at New York's Avery Fisher Hall. In July 1991, they traveled to Japan for the Pacific Music Festival, where he and Michael Tilson Thomas are co-artistic directors, for six concerts in Sapporo, Chitose, Tokyo, and Osaka. He has led the orchestra on critically acclaimed tours of Florida (1989); the northeast United States, culminating with an appearance at Carnegie Hall (1990); Singapore, at the 1990 Singapore Festival of Arts, and the East Coast of the United States, including Florida, New York and Boston (1994).

In the summer of 1993, the Pacific Music Festival awarded him its Leonard Bernstein Award: an award presented during the festival to a musician who carries on the legacy of the late Leonard Bernstein, founder of the Pacific Music Festival.

Christoph Eschenbach had already earned a distinguished international reputation as a concert pianist before turning to conducting in 1972. Born in Breslau, Germany, he first studied piano with his mother. Subsequently, he continued his piano studies in Hamburg with Eliza Hansen and also studied conducting with Wilhelm Bruckner-Ruggeberg, both of whom he regards as the principal mentors of his artistic development.

Christoph Eschenbach's career has been highlighted by winning several major prizes, including the Steinway Young Pianist Competition at age eleven and the International Music Competition in Munich at age twenty-two. His career as a pianist was heightened by the award of first prize in the Clara Haskil Competition in Lucerne in 1965. After making his American debut in 1969 with the Cleveland Orchestra, conducted by George Szell, Eschenbach appeared as soloist with all the major orchestras throughout the world and was widely heard in recital.

With the Houston Symphony, Christoph Eschenbach currently records for both BMG's RCA Red Seal label and Koch International. He also recorded for Virgin Classics and Pickwick International. In 1990, the president of the Federal Republic of Germany, Richard von Weizsacker, awarded the Officer´s Cross of the Order of Merit to Christoph Eschenbach for his outstanding achievements as pianist and conductor; in 1993, he received the Commander`s Cross of the Order of Merit of the Federal Republic of Germany.

INDIVIDUAL ASPARAGUS SOUFFLÉS (OR MOUSSES)

*This recipe reflects Mr. Eschenbach´s love of asparagus in virtually any form, his preference for light, low-fat, yet intensely-flavored dishes, and, in its mousse variation, his fondness for warm salads and his dislike for anything more than a **hint** of vinegar. It is one of many asparagus concoctions I´ve made for him over the last eight years.*

These remarks and the eloquent recipe come from the kitchen of Elaine Cali, who is married to David Wax, executive director for the Houston Symphony.

2½ to 3 pounds asparagus
   (2 pounds trimmed)
1 cup water, reserved from cooking
   of the asparagus
1 tablespoon olive or almond oil
2 tablespoons flour
2 egg yolks (save whites)

Salt and pepper

FOR THE DISHES:
Butter or oil
Fine, dry bread crumbs or
   finely grated Parmigiano

1.   Preheat the oven to 400 degrees. Prepare 8 to 10 soufflé dishes or other molds of ½ to ¾ cup capacity by lightly wiping them with softened butter or oil and lining them with the crumbs or Parmigiano. Set the dishes on a cookie sheet or in a shallow pan, and set aside.

2.   Break off and discard the tough ends of the asparagus; wash the asparagus well and weigh it. You will need 2 pounds. Cut off and reserve the tips. Bring an oblong pan or deep skillet of water to a boil and lay in the asparagus stalks to cook until they are somewhat past crisp-tender, but not yet very limp. You may need to do this in two batches, in order for the asparagus to be completely immersed.

3.   When the asparagus is done, transfer it with tongs to another pan with ice water to stop the cooking and set the color. From the skillet, remove one cup of the cooking water, straining it through a very fine sieve or a paper coffee filter if it is at all gritty, and set aside.

4.   When the asparagus is cool, drain it and chop each stalk in halves or thirds. Transfer the pieces to a food processor and purée.

5.   Blanch the reserved asparagus tips in the cooking water for about 2 to 4 minutes, until just crisp-tender, and refresh in the ice water. Drain and reserve.

6.   In a saucepan, heat the oil, add flour, and stir or whisk for a few minutes, just long enough to remove any taste of raw flour. Do not let it brown. Add the reserved cup of cooking water and bring to a boil and cook, stirring or whisking for a few minutes. The mixture should be quite thick. Remove from heat and whisk in the egg yolks and salt and pepper to taste.

7.   Transfer the mixture to the processor and combine with the puréed asparagus until well-mixed. Transfer this to a large mixing bowl. Beat the egg whites until they are stiff. Stir about ⅓ of the beaten whites into the asparagus mixture to lighten it, then gently fold in the rest.

8.   Fill the soufflé dishes and set them on the middle shelf of the oven. Reduce heat to 375 degrees. After about 20 to 25 minutes, the soufflés will be well-risen and the tops lightly golden-brown. The dishes may be set on individual plates, garnished with the asparagus tips, and served immediately for a first course.

An additional way of handling the asparagus has the advantage of allowing ahead-of-time preparation and demanding no tricky scheduling: this results in mousses rather than soufflés.

1.   Continue baking the soufflés another 5 to 10 minutes. (Have them in a baking pan rather than on a cookie sheet for this method). During this time, they will sink. Remove them from the oven and set aside for up to several hours, or you may make them a day or two in advance and refrigerate them. Cover the pan with foil or wax-paper.

2.   Make a mixed green salad of arugula, watercress, endive, assorted lettuce, mizuna or dandelion greens, fresh tarragon and chives, etc. - sorrel is particulary nice with asparagus. When you are near serving time, dress it lightly with a vinaigrette of walnut oil and a splash of fruit vinegar, or of olive oil and lemon juice. Distribute among 8 to 10 salad plates, leaving a space in the middle of each.

3.   Preheat the oven to 350 to 400 degrees. Bring a kettle of water to boil. Pour it into the baking pan so that the water comes about halfway up the sides of the soufflé dishes. Bake, covered, for about 5 to 8 minutes or until the soufflés are heated through. They will have risen again just a bit. One at a time, remove them from the pan, run a thin knife around the edge, and release them onto the salad plates.

4.   If some soufflé is left in the dishes, remove it with a rubber scraper and pat it onto the tops. The surfaces do not have to be beautifully smooth, because you then cover the tops with the asparagus tips, lightly pressing them in. (Or, you could decorate the tops with parsley and spread them over the salad). Serve.

Photo: AARON RAPOPORT

JOANN FALLETTA, CONDUCTOR

"Widely recognized as one of the finest conductors of her generation" (*New York Times*) and called "one of the brightest stars of symphonic music in America," by the *Los Angeles Times*, JoAnn Falletta is remarkable not only for her musical awards and achievements but also for the breadth of both her experience and repertoire.

One of the most sought after and widely praised of American conductors, JoAnn Falletta is currently music director of the Virginia and Long Beach Symphony Orchestras, as well as the San Francisco-based Women's Philharmonic. At the same time, she also maintains an impressive schedule of guest conducting. In the United States, she has appeared on the podiums of the National Symphony Orchestra, the American Symphony, and the orchestras of Houston, Buffalo, Denver, Indianapolis, Honolulu, San Diego, Louisville, Phoenix, St. Paul, North Carolina, Sacramento, Florida, Rochester, Toledo, Tucson, Austin, Louisiana and Columbus. Foreign engagements include the Royal Philharmonic Orchestra of Belgium, the National Symphony Orchestra of Mexico, Edmonton Symphony Orchestra and the Central Philharmonic Orchestra of China, as well as orchestras in Italy, Austria, France and Denmark—often as the first woman to lead the orchestra in performance. Future seasons will see her returning to Europe, Asia and Canada for a heavy schedule of concerts with orchestras such as the Prague Symphony Orchestra, the Janáček Symphony and the Czech Philharmonic of Brno, the National Orchestras of Portugal and Taiwan, and for return engagements with the Philharmonic Orchestra of Bilbao in Spain and the historic Mannheim Orchestra—the favorite orchestra of Mozart.

Falletta is the winner of the most prestigious conducting prizes, including the Stokowski, Toscanini and Bruno Walter Awards. She has recorded with the London Symphony Orchestra, English Chamber Orchestra, the Women's Philharmonic, the Cabrillo Festival and the Virginia Symphony and she has been awarded the "Best Classical Recording" by the National Association of Independent Record Producers and given the "Most Creative Programming" award by *Classic CD* magazine. Falletta is the recipient of eight consecutive awards from ASCAP for creative programming, as well as the American Symphony Orchestra League's prized John S. Edwards Award for programming. Not only has Falletta an enormous repertoire (over 1,100 works performed in concert), but she also has been an indefatigable champion of new music. Sixty world premieres have been featured among the almost 300 works by American composers that she has performed.

Maestro Falletta has been music director of the Virginia Symphony since 1991. Her appointment in 1988 in Long Beach made her the first American woman ever appointed to the leadership of a regional orchestra. Under her leadership, the Long Beach Symphony achieved the remarkable accomplishment of selling out its entire 1989/90 season by subscription, a feat that has been regularly repeated. She is in her eighth season as music director of the Women's Philharmonic (specializing in works by women composers). Past positions include associate conductor of the Milwaukee Symphony, music director of the Queens (NY) Philharmonic, music director of the Denver Chamber Orchestra. Falletta has served as music advisor to the Nassau (NY) Symphony Orchestra and the Santa Cruz (CA) Symphony Orchestra. She received her doctorate in conducting from the Juilliard School in 1989 and was granted an honorary doctorate by Old Dominion University in 1994.

ZUCCOTTO ALLA FALLETTA
(A Traditional Italian Dessert)
Serves 6 to 8

The "Zuccotto alla Falletta" is an old family recipe that is a special favorite of mine. --J.F.

1 sponge cake
1 cup maraschino liqueur, crème de
     cocao, or brandy
3, 8 oz. cartons whipping cream
2 tablespoons sugar

½ teaspoon vanilla
4 oz. semi-sweet chocolate chips
4 oz. crushed black walnuts
1 tablespoon orange peel, finely chopped

Cut sponge cake into 1-inch thick slices and line a round casserole dish with the slices. The casserole dish should be wide enough to cover with a large plate. Dribble ¾ cup of the liqueur onto the cake slices, soaking them. Whip the cream until stiff, adding sugar and vanilla during mixing.

When the cream is stiff, fold in the chocolate chips, nuts and orange peel. Fill the cake-lined casserole dish with the whipped cream mixture. Top this mixture with more cake slices. Soak these slices with the remaining liqueur.

Put a plate on top of the casserole dish and invert. Freeze overnight. Allow one hour to thaw and remove from dish before serving.

Photo: INTERLOCHEN

FREDERICK FENNELL, CONDUCTOR

Frederick Fennell is one of the most famous wind ensemble conductors in the world. His numerous recordings, first with the Eastman Wind Ensemble (which he founded in 1952 and has over 30 record releases on the Mercury Living Presence label), and now with the Tokyo Kosei Wind Orchestra (with 25 record releases), are standards against which all other recordings are compared. However, Dr. Fennell is equally at home conducting opera and orchestra. Some of his conducting assignments in these fields are with the Cleveland Orchestra, the London Symphony, and the Denver, New Orleans, St. Louis, National, Buffalo, Houston, Calgary, Eastman, Hartford and San Diego Symphony Orchestras.

Dr. Fennell was an assistant to Serge Koussevitzky at Tanglewood, the assistant music director of the Minneapolis Symphony Orchestra (1962-64), a conducting fellow at the Mozarteum in Salzburg, Austria, and conductor-in-residence at the University of Miami. His opera conducting has included the Eastman Opera Theater and the Houston Light Opera Company. He has conducted the Boston "Pops" Orchestra, the Boston Esplanade and the Carnegie Hall "Pops" Concerts.

Dr. Fennel is editor of *Basic Band Repertory*, *The Instrumentalist* and *BDG*. He has edited many works for wind ensemble that are available through Ludwig Music Publishing Company as well as publications by Fox, Presser and Boosey & Hawkes. A book written about Dr. Fennell by Roger Rickson entitled "FFORTISSIMO" details 40 years of Dr. Fennell's exciting life.

During his most distinguished career, in addition to receiving almost every honor the world can bestow for conducting, he has earned the love and admiration of those who have been fortunate enough to play under his direction and who have come to know him through his appearances all over the world.

The Fennells make their home in Sarasota, Florida, while making frequent trips back to Cleveland to run their Music Publishing Company.

"WHAT'S IN THE FREEZER"?

For my favorite food and its preparation

1. Open the freezer door and select an appropriate item from previous shopping for the evening dinner.

2. Remove from the freezer; follow all instructions from the producer, especially those for piercing the outer plastic sheets with appropriate apertures in the desirable places.

3. Approach the microwave oven.

4. Place the evening's choice within, on micro-acceptable plates, if further garnish on heated plates is your preference.

5. Remove at the sound of the merry 'ting', adding items non-micro, top off with the beverage of choice, according to the foregoing.

Personally, I hate to boil water!

I find this recipe foolproof, inexpensive and frequently very enjoyable. --F.F.

Photo: DON HUNSTEIN

JOSEPH FLUMMERFELT, CONDUCTOR

For more than two decades, Joseph Flummerfelt's musical artistry has been acclaimed in many of the world's finest concert halls. Renowned as "an inspired and inspiring conductor," as well as a master teacher, his rich and varied career has included collaborations with such eminent conductors as Abbado, Bernstein, Boulez, Dohnányi, Giulini, Leinsdorf, Masur, Mehta, Muti, Ozawa, Penderecki, Shaw and Steinberg. His breathtaking artistry and endless passion for beauty have prompted critics and musicians alike to recognize him as "one of the world's greatest choral conductors."

A gifted orchestral conductor, Joseph Flummerfelt made his conducting debut with the New York Philharmonic in 1988 and he regularly guest conducts orchestras such as the Fort Worth Chamber Orchestra, the Spoleto Festival Orchestra, the Juilliard Symphony, the New Jersey Symphony Orchestra, the Westminster Festival Orchestra, the Orchestra of St. Luke's, and the San Antonio Symphony.

Maestro Flummerfelt is the director of choral activities for the Spoleto Festival U.S.A. in Charleston, South Carolina (since 1977), and for 22 years was the *Maestro del coro* for the *Festival dei Due Mondi* in Spoleto, Italy. He is the chorus master of the New York Philharmonic, the founder and conductor of The New York Choral Artists, and the music director of Singing City in Philadelphia. As the artistic director and principal conductor at Westminster Choir College of Rider University, Dr. Flummerfelt inspires countless young musicians to combine discipline and exemplary attention to detail with artistic spontaneity. One of the consistent results of his direction is a Westminster Choir that is critically acclaimed for its subtlety, robust rhythmic intensity and elegant balance.

Joseph Flummerfelt has made a number of recordings with the Westminster Choir including Gian Carlo Menotti's *Missa "O Pulchritudo," Christmas with the Westminster Choir, The Westminster Choir Sings Folk Songs, Favorite Hymns and Anthems,* and *O Magnum Mysterium.* Flummerfelt's choirs have been featured on over 30 major orchestral/choral recordings such as Haydn's *Lord Nelson Mass,* a Grammy Award-winning performance of Mahler's Symphony No. 3, Messiaen's *Le Transfiguration de Notre Seigneur Jesus Christ,* Puccini's *Tosca,* Verdi's *Nabucco,* and Beethoven's Symphony No. 9.

Mr. Flummerfelt's honors include *le Prix du President de la Republique of L'Academie du Disque Francais,* two Grammy nominations, the Mobil Pegasus Award for his "remarkable contribution to the Festival of Two Worlds," and inclusion in the International *Who's Who in Music* and in the seventh edition of Baker's *Biographical Dictionary of Musicians.* He has also received four honorary doctorates.

PÂTÉ DE FOIE DE VOLAILLE

Serves about 20, ½-inch slices

Mr. Flummerfelt's favorite recipe comes from the ever popular cookbook, "Joy of Cooking" by Irma S. Rombauer and Marion Rombauer Becker.

Divide **1½ pounds of chicken livers** into three parts. Blend one part (in blender) with **2 eggs**. Blend the second part briefly with ¼ **cup whipping cream**.

Blend the third part with:

3 tablespoons cognac	**2 tablespoons port wine**
4 slices chopped bacon	¼ **cup flour**
1 egg	

Mix these three blends together very lightly with:

1 teaspoon ginger	½ **teaspoon freshly ground black pepper**
2 teaspoons salt	**1 teaspoon allspice or nutmeg**
¼ **cup pistachio nuts or 1 to 2 minced truffles**	

Pour into a well-greased loaf pan and top with thin-sliced blanched salt pork. Cover tightly with heavy foil and place baking pan up to about half its depth in a larger pan of boiling water. Bake at 325 degrees about 1½ to 2 hours, or to an internal temperature of 180 degrees.

Serve cold, after removing some of the fat from the top surface if necessary. To store leftover pâté, be sure it is well covered with a layer of fat or clarified butter.

Photo: LORD SNOWDON

RAYMOND LEPPARD, CONDUCTOR

Guest conductor of many of the world's most famous orchestras, composer of film scores, Cambridge don, music scholar, conductor for more than 150 recordings, including a number of prize winners—this is Raymond Leppard, music director of the Indianapolis Symphony Orchestra since 1987.

Maestro Leppard has conducted most of the great symphony orchestras of the United States, including those in Boston, New York, Chicago, and Pittsburgh. He was principal guest conductor of the Saint Louis Symphony Orchestra and also principal conductor of the BBC Symphony. First identified with the English Chamber Orchestra, he also has conducted many of the renowned symphony orchestras of the Old World.

Leppard has had a long association with Glyndebourne, Covent Garden, and has conducted other opera companies in most European music centers as well as many American opera productions at such institutions as the Metropolitan Opera in New York, the New York City Opera, the San Francisco Opera and the Santa Fe opera.

Leppard and the Indianapolis Symphony Orchestra can be heard on a continuing series of compact disc recordings on the Koss Classics label. Prominent music critics have hailed Leppard's recordings with the orchestra as "elegant and warm," "a consistent pleasure," "exemplary" and "absolutely first-rate." Thus far, the orchestra has released recordings of music by Schubert, Elgar, Schumann, Vaughan-Williams, Tchaikovsky and Beethoven.

Maestro Leppard and the ISO have collaborated on a series of works broadcast on National Public Radio's "Performance Today" program. This was the first time that a major orchestra had been consistently featured on this nationally syndicated show.

Raymond Leppard was born in London and grew up in Bath. He was educated at Trinity College, Cambridge. Upon graduation, he returned to London and was subsequently appointed assistant conductor at Glyndebourne. In the late 1950's, about the time he became associated with the English Chamber Orchestra, Leppard accepted a post at Cambridge as university lecturer in music, beginning a distinguished joint career as academician and performer.

During that time, he was the first to bring operas of Monteverdi and Cavalli back to the professional stage, where they had not been seen in more than 300 years. In 1969, he delivered the Italian lecture to the British Academy. For his accomplishments in restoring early Italian music to the standard repertoire, Leppard was honored with the title of Commendatore by the Italian government.

Conductor of more than 150 recordings, Leppard has seen his albums win such international prizes as a Grammy, a Deutsche Schallplattenpreis, a Grand Prix Mondial du Disque, and an Edison Prize.

Films for which he has written scores include *Lord of the Flies, Laughter in the Dark,* and *Hotel New Hampshire.* He is the author of two books, *Authenticity in Music* and *Raymond Leppard on Music: An Anthology of Critical and Autobiographical Writings.*

Leppard has been honored with the title of Commander of the Order of the British Empire. He holds honorary doctorates from the University of Indianapolis and Purdue University.

GRAVAD LAX
Makes 2 large salmon fillets

Mr. Leppard greatly enjoys fresh salmon; smoked, grilled or as in this recipe, soused. This recipe reminds him of the happy times he spent in Sweden.

Center part of a whole fresh salmon
  cut into 2 equal-size fillets (about
  1½ pounds each) skin on and scaled
2 to 3 teaspoons whole white
  peppercorns, freshly ground

4 to 5 tablespoons of coarse salt
2 to 3 tablespoons of sugar
½ cup fresh dill or to taste
Mustard sauce*

Put the fillets together, skin side out, thick end to thin, after having rubbed in **half** of the peppercorn/salt/sugar mixture and some fresh dill. Put more dill on top of the joined fillets along with the other **half** of the mixture.

Place fillets into a heavy plastic bag and store in refrigerator under heavy pressure. Turn the bag at least every 12 hours during the sousing.

Thin fillets are ready in 24 to 36 hours, thick fillets in 48 to 56 hours. Pour off liquid, scrape off the spices and thinly slice.

*MUSTARD SAUCE

3 tablespoons dry mustard
1 tablespoon sugar
1 tablespoon white vinegar

1 tablespoon olive oil
3 tablespoons cut dill
Salt and pepper to taste

Mix well and spoon onto salmon fillets before serving.

NEVILLE MARRINER, CONDUCTOR/VIOLINIST

Sir Neville Marriner studied the violin at the Royal College of Music and then at the Paris Conservatoire. In 1949, he joined the Martin String Quartet and formed both the Jacobean Ensemble with Thurston Dart and the Virtuoso String Trio. He played with most of the London orchestras which gave him the experience of various legendary conductors—among them Toscanini, Furtwangler, Cantelli and Karajan.

While playing as concertmaster in the London Symphony Orchestra he founded the Academy of St. Martin in the Fields in 1959; from the concertmaster's seat as the director of this ensemble, he gravitated towards conducting. Pierre Monteux became his mentor and his first conducting appointment was Los Angeles Chamber Orchestra from 1969-1979. He then became music director of the Minnesota Orchestra until 1986, having already taken a similar post with the Radio Symphony Orchestra in Stuttgart.

Although the majority of his opera and symphonic performances and recordings are with the Academy of St. Martin in the Fields, one of the most comprehensively recorded chamber orchestras in the world, he works consistently with the major orchestras throughout the world.

Sir Neville Marriner has twice been honoured for his services to music. In 1979, he was made a Commander of the Order of the British Empire and received a knighthood in 1985.

The Academy of St. Martin in the Fields and Marriner have recently received the Queen's Award for Export Achievement in recognition of their considerable success in the field of international concert performance and recording.

The Academy of St. Martin in the Fields was founded in 1959 by Sir Neville Marriner and a group of London's leading orchestral players. Originally formed as a small conductorless string group, it spearheaded the 1950's Baroque revival.

The academy has a flourishing education programme and players take part in a wide range of educational projects with schools and community groups throughout the U.K. Projects are tailored to suit each group and provide people of all ages and abilities with the opportunity to work with many of the country's finest musicians.

The academy is constantly broadening its commitment to education work; future projects include residencies in Suffolk, Essex and Hertfordshire, where schemes will benefit youth orchestras, school groups, libraries, hospitals and community groups. Projects often encompass other art forms, such as art, dance, drama, creative writing, mime and puppet making. With Britain leading the way in music education projects, the academy is now involved in developing projects aboard.

With over 1000 releases to its credit, ranging from Baroque and Classical masterpieces to the major Romantic and 20th century works, the academy remains the most recorded chamber orchestra in the world.

This prestigious orchestra has won many coveted international awards—including eight Edisons, the Canadian Grand Prix and a multitude of gold discs—thirteen alone for the soundtrack of Milos Forman's film "Amadeus." In April 1993, the Academy of St. Martin in the Fields became the first orchestra to be honoured with the Queen's Award for Export Achievement.

SUMMER PUDDING
Serves 6

In this favorite recipe of Neville Marriner, the pudding can be made in a foil basin and then frozen after it has been pressed for 24 hours. To serve, stand at room temperature for about 6 hours and then turn out onto dish.

1½ pounds soft fruit:
   raspberries, blackberries,
   red currants, and loganberries
Roughly ½ loaf stale white bread
	6 to 8 oz. sugar
	½ cup of water
	Whipped cream for serving

Gently wash fruit and let dry. Have ready a basin or soufflé dish which holds about 1½ quarts. Cut bread lengthwise into thin slices, remove the crusts and completely line the basin with the slices.

On medium heat, in a medium-large saucepan or skillet, simmer the sugar and water until the sugar is dissolved. (The exact quantity of sugar will depend on what fruit you are using and its sweetness). Add fruit to uncovered pan and gently stew the fruit until soft (roughly 10 minutes). Stir occasionally. Test for sweetness and then pour the hot fruit into the prepared basin. Cover with a thin layer of bread, crust removed.

When cool, cover the container with a plate or flat saucer on top which exactly will fit the basin; place a weight on top of this so that the pressure will cause the juice to soak into the bread (but beware of overflow—it is a good idea to place the basin on a large plate for this reason). Refrigerate the pudding overnight.

To serve: turn onto a dish and serve with cream.

Photo: CHRISTIAN STEINER/SONY CLASSICAL

ZUBIN MEHTA, CONDUCTOR

Born in Bombay, India, Zubin Mehta grew up in a musical environment. His father, Mehli Mehta, currently music director of the American Youth Orchestra in Los Angeles, co-founded the Bombay Symphony. At the age of eighteen, Zubin abandoned his medical studies to pursue a career in music at the Academy of Music in Vienna. Seven years later, at the age of twenty-five, he conducted both the Vienna and Berlin Philharmonics, and, from 1961 to 1967, acted as music director of the Montreal Symphony. In 1962, the Los Angeles Philharmonic Orchestra appointed him its music director, a post he held until 1978, when he accepted the appointment of music director with the New York Philharmonic Orchestra.

In 1969, the Israel Philharmonic Orchestra appointed Mr. Mehta its music advisor, in 1977, its music director, and, in 1981, its music director for 'life'. Numerous concerts, recordings, and tours of all five continents have resulted in over 1500 concerts with the Israel Philharmonic. Since 1986, he has also acted as music advisor and chief conductor of the Maggio Musicale Fiorentino, the summer festival of Florence, Italy, where he recently completed a cycle of Mozart operas, produced and directed by Jonathan Miller.

During his thirteen-year tenure with the New York Philharmonic, Maestro Mehta conducted more than 1000 concerts and held the post longer than any other music director in the orchestra's modern history. He also conducted the philharmonic on a number of major tours. In June of 1988, he led a ten-day tour of the Soviet Union which culminated in a historic joint-concert with the State Symphony Orchestra of the Soviet Ministry of Culture in Moscow's Gorky Park. In May 1991, the Maestro concluded his tenure with three performances celebrating the 100th anniversary of Carnegie Hall, followed by a series of performances of Schoenberg's "Gurrelieder." In November 1992, he returned to conduct the New York Philharmonic in the world premier of Olivier Messiaen's last symphony "Eclairs sur l'Au Dela," and, in December joined in "A Philharmonic Celebration: 150th Anniversary Concert."

Mr. Mehta is continuing to accept guest conducting engagements with the world's major orchestras and opera companies, including the London, Vienna, and Berlin Philharmonics; the Royal Opera Covent Garden; and the Vienna Staatsoper. In fulfillment of his plan to conduct more opera, a collaborative achievement in Rome in 1990 produced the recorded performance of "Carreras, Domingo and Pavarotti in Concert"—a medley of show tunes and opera classics, including "Nessun dorma," "Tonight," and "O sole Mio." Mehta has conducted two productions of *Tosca*: the first—a live performance with Placido Domingo in early July 1992—viewed in forty-five countries, was performed at the exact locations and times of day specified by Puccini in his original score. Simultaneously, it was connected via television monitors and loudspeakers from a recording studio on the other side of Rome, the conductor leading the Rome Symphony Orchestra and Chorus of Italian Radio. A second production of *Tosca*, with Luciano Pavarotti, opened the Covent Garden season in London two months later. In the latter part of July 1992, Mr. Mehta joined the Israel Philharmonic Orchestra to produce a concert-version of *Aïda*.

Mr. Mehta realized a long-time ambition in November of 1994, when he brought the Israel Philharmonic Orchestra to his birthplace, India. By conducting in Bombay and New Delhi, he helped bridge a political gap that had prevented them from performing there for three decades. His affection for the orchestra so close to his heart, combined with the love of his motherland, made this tour one of the most memorable events of his life. In March of 1996, he completed a four-year commitment to perform Wagner's Ring Cycle with the Lyric Opera of Chicago. In 1998, Mr. Mehta will begin a five-year appointment as music director of the Bavarian State Opera in Munich.

The numerous honors that have been bestowed upon Zubin Mehta include the Nikisch Ring bequeathed to him by Dr. Karl Böhm, the Vienna Philharmonic Ring of Honor commemorating the twenty-fifth anniversary of his Vienna Philharmonic Orchestra conducting debut, and the Hans von Bulow Medal bestowed upon him by the Berlin Philharmonic Orchestra. The Maestro has been awarded a Padma Bhushan (Order of the Lotus) by the government of his native India, has received the Defender of Jerusalem Award, and is an honorary citizen of the City of Tel Aviv. In addition, he is the only non-Israeli ever to receive the Israel Prize.

NANCY MEHTA'S MOGLI CHICKEN
Serves 8 to 10

Included with this recipe was a cooking tip: "This dish is most successful if prepared while listening to music conducted by Maestro Mehta."

2 tablespoons warm milk
1¼ teaspoons ground cloves
1¼ teaspoons ground cardamom
¼ cup brown sugar, packed
¼ teaspoon or more of saffron
4 boneless, skinless, whole chicken breasts, slightly flattened (about 3 to 3¾ lbs.)
Seasoned flour
¼ cup butter
2 large onions, chopped

6 large cloves garlic, crushed
½ inch piece ginger root, ground
1¼ teaspoons ground cumin
1¼ teaspoons caraway seeds
1¼ teaspoons ground tumeric
1 green chile, split
1 teaspoon cayenne pepper
1 large tomato, chopped
1 hot cup water
1 cup sour cream

Place milk, cloves, cardamom, brown sugar and saffron into warming dish or pan and heat slowly until ingredients are dissolved. Keep warm. Dredge chicken breasts in seasoned flour.

Heat butter in heavy skillet over medium heat and brown chicken. Remove chicken, add onions, garlic, and ginger to skillet, sauté until onions are transparent. Add cumin powder, caraway seeds, turmeric, chile and cayenne to onion mixture. Cook over medium heat for 2 to 3 minutes, stirring until chile is brown, spices are mixed and seeds are fried lightly. Replace chicken breasts to the skillet, add tomato and cup of water, and simmer about 25 minutes, covered, until chicken is tender, stirring occasionally.

Move chicken breasts and sauce from skillet to baking dish. Pour warm milk solution and sour cream over chicken. Bake at 350 degrees for about 10 to 15 minutes, or until completely heated. *Enjoy*!

Photo: CHRISTIAN STEINER

JORGE MESTER, CONDUCTOR

Internationally renowned conductor Jorge Mester is in his second decade as music director of the Pasadena Symphony this season. He has served as music director of the Louisville Orchestra, the Kansas City Philharmonic and Festival Casals, and is conductor laureate of the Aspen Music Festival. A much sought after guest conductor in the United States and abroad, he has conducted such major ensembles as the Philadelphia Orchestra, the Boston, Pittsburgh, San Francisco, Detroit and Houston Symphonies, the Paris ORTF, Orchestre de la Suisse Romande and the Royal Philharmonic of London. He recently was chief conductor of the West Australia Symphony Orchestra in Perth and principal guest conductor of the Adelaide Symphony Orchestra.

Equally acclaimed as an opera conductor, Mester has made guest appearances at opera companies throughout the world, including New York City Opera, Philadelphia Opera, the Australian Opera in Sydney, and the Juilliard Opera Center. He has premiered many important American operatic works, and his critically hailed performance of Menotti's *The Medium* with the Washington Opera Society led Columbia Records to record the production.

During his 12-year tenure with the Louisville Orchestra, he completed 72 premiere recordings. He has recorded works for the CBS Masterworks, CRI, Desto, Seraphim, Vanguard and Varese Sarabande labels. Recent recordings with the West Australia Symphony are available in the U.S. on ABC Classics. His inaugural recording with the Pasadena Symphony is now available on the Newport Classic audiophile label and features Strauss's *Also Sprach Zarathustra* and Saint-Saëns's "Organ" Symphony.

Mentor over the years to an increasing number of young performers, Mester has introduced to the public many solo artists, including Nadja Salerno-Sonnenberg, Cho-Liang Lin, Midori and Robert McDuffie, and has assisted in the training of such gifted conductors as James Conlon, Dennis Russell Davies, JoAnn Falletta and John Nelson. A champion of contemporary composers, he served as artistic director of the National Orchestral Association's New Music Project, and received Columbia University's coveted Ditson Award for his "continuous and enthusiastic" showcasing of works by American composers.

Mester was born to Hungarian parents in 1935 in Mexico City. Encouraged by Gregor Piatigorsky and Leonard Bernstein, he enrolled at the Juilliard School to study conducting with Jean Morel. He joined the Juilliard faculty at age 22, and, in 1968, received the Naumburg Award in conducting. Most recently, he was awarded Mexico's prestigious Mozart Medal for his contributions to that country's cultural life.

Mester has been a frequent guest commentator and artist on National Public Radio and on programs for public television and Bravo, and is a frequent panelist on "First Hearing."

PASTA E CECI ALLA FREZZA-VARRATT

Serves 2 to 3

8 oz. package pasta corta (shells, etc.)
5 to 6 dried tomatoes, snipped,
   and softened in boiling water
2 tablespoons olive paste
1 tablespoon caper paste
   (or crushed capers)

1 anchovy, smashed (or a dash
   of anchovy paste
3 to 4 cloves garlic, crushed (more
   if small cloves)
15 oz. can of ceci (garbanzo beans)
Salt and Parmesan cheese (optional)

While the pasta is cooking, combine the drained tomatoes, olive paste, caper paste, anchovy and garlic in the serving bowl. Add enough of the pasta water to make this soupy (about 3 to 4 tablespoons). Blend well.

Heat the ceci, drain and coat with the sauce. Drain the pasta, add to the rest, mix well.

Coat lightly with olive oil and serve.

P.S. *Forgot the pepper flakes—you won't!!* --J.M.

Photo: CHRISTIAN STEINER

JOHN NELSON, CONDUCTOR

A popular guest conductor with the world's great orchestras, the American conductor John Nelson has recently led performances with the Chicago Symphony Orchestra, Boston Symphony Orchestra, Philadelphia Orchestra, Los Angeles Philharmonic, Dresden Staatskapelle, Florence Maggio Musicale, Orchestre de la Suisse Romande, and the Czech Philharmonic. His 1993-94 season has included debuts with the Orchestre de Paris, the New Japan Philharmonic, and the Chicago Lyric Opera; all three orchestras have invited him for return engagements.

As busy in the recording studio as he is on stage, John Nelson has made several recordings in the last few years which have earned him important international prizes and ecstatic critical praise. Among these are Berlioz's *Beatrice and Benedict* (Erato); which won the "Grand Diapaison d'Or de L'Annee;" Handel's *Semele* with Kathleen Battle (DG); which won a 1994 Grammy for Best Opera Recording; Gorecki's *Beatus Vir* (Decca); Bach arias with Kathleen Battle and Itzhak Perlman (EMI); an all Schoenfield album (Decca) and a Baroque album with Wynton Marsalis and Kathleen Battle (Sony Classical).

One of the world's leading Berlioz conductors, Mr. Nelson is currently completing a project to perform all of the composer's music. To date, he has conducted *Benvenuto Cellini,* and the Requiem, at the Berlioz Festival in Lyon, *Beatrice and Benedict, Romeo and Juliet*, and many of the symphonic works in Paris. His career was launched in 1972 with the first New York performances of *Les Troyens* at Carnegie Hall. Engagements immediately followed with the Metropolitan Opera and the Grand Theatre in Geneva in the same work. He recently conducted a new production of *Benvenuto Cellini* in Geneva. In addition to the orchestras mentioned above, Mr. Nelson's American engagements in the last several years have included the

Los Angeles Philharmonic, the Pittsburgh Symphony, the National Symphony, the San Francisco Symphony, the New World Symphony, the Mostly Mozart Festival Orchestra, and the orchestras of Houston, Dallas, Seattle, Atlanta, Buffalo, Detroit, Cincinnati, Baltimore, Denver and Rochester. His European engagements have been with the Royal Philharmonic, the Philharmonia, the Halle Orchestra, the Scottish National Orchestra, the Bavarian Radio Orchestra, the Berlin Radio Symphony, the Stockholm Philharmonic, the Oslo Philharmonic, the Helsinki Philharmonic, the Strasbourg Philharmonic, the French National Orchestra, Radio France's Orchestre Philharmonic, the Academia de Santa Cecilia in Rome, the Milan RAI and the orchestra of Venice's La Fenice.

Mr. Nelson was music director of the Opera Theatre of Saint Louis from 1977-87. For eleven years, he was music director of the Indianapolis Symphony Orchestra, during which time he elevated the orchestra to national prominence through tours, recordings and telecasts. He has also held the posts of music director of the Caramoor Festival (New York), principal conductor of the Orchestre National de Lyon in France, artistic advisor to the Louisville Orchestra and the Nashville Symphony, music director of the Pro Arte Chorale and the Greenwich Philharmonic and founder and director of the Aspen Choral Institute.

John Nelson also is committed to working with young musicians and conductors. He has conducted and given workshops at the Aspen Music Festival, Los Angeles Music Institute, Interlochen Academy, Tanglewood Institute at the Berkshire Music Center, and the New World Symphony, where he is the only guest conductor to have appeared every year since its inception in 1987. Mr. Nelson twice has been president of the jury at the Besancon International Competition for Conductors in France.

Born to American missionary parents in Costa Rica, John Nelson began piano studies at the age of six. He continued his training in the United States at Wheaton College, garnering awards in piano and composition, and at the Juilliard School, where he won the Irving Berlin Prize for conductors.

EVENING SALAD

The following recipe is just one simple sample of how we like to eat when 'on the road'. There are very definite tastes in John's palette, his favorite meal by far is pasta with pesto, the starter having been fresh mozzarella with the best ripe vine tomatoes. We locate the best pesto in any given city and when in Rome we often combine three different varieties for a unique taste.

A green salad with sautéed hot vegetables added at the last minute and then sprinkled with freshly grated Parmesan is the combination we most frequently find satisfying. The combination of hot and cold is wonderful, and the original (best) hot and cold salad that we have experienced is found in Lyon, France, SALADE LYONAISE...incredible. --Anita N.

2 heads Boston lettuce (washed and crisped)
Virgin olive oil
Grated fresh Parmesan cheese
Garlic cloves, sliced
4 to 6 fresh mushrooms, sliced

1 to 1½ cups cooked small brown lentils
    (leftovers!)
Fresh parsley
Tiny cherry tomatoes

Gently toss lettuce, coating it with olive oil. Follow with dusting of grated fresh Parmesan. **Set aside.**

Sauté several fresh garlic cloves (sliced) in hot oil with sliced mushrooms. Add lentils and heat through. Add fresh parsley leaves, torn, and pour this mixture over lettuce, adding additional Parmesan. Serve immediately. For color, add tomatoes.

Photo: Courtesy of Cincinnati Symphony Orchestra

MAX RUDOLF, CONDUCTOR

Max Rudolf was the music director of the Cincinnati Symphony Orchestra from 1958 to 1969. Maestro Rudolf had a deep and lasting influence on the musical life of Cincinnati and set a new standard or artistic achievement for the orchestra. His contributions to the Cincinnati Symphony Orchestra included initiation of the 8 O'Clock Pops Series in 1963, establishment of the Kinderkonzerts and in-school concerts for children, and numerous recordings with Decca Records. In 1966, he led the symphony in an historic ten-week world tour sponsored by the U.S. Department of State, the first such tour by an American symphony orchestra.

Maestro Rudolf commissioned several important compositions while music director in Cincinnati, fostering the careers of many young American composers. He also served as music director for the May Festival five times between 1963 and 1970.

Born in Frankfort-am Main, Maestro Rudolf's first American conducting post was with the Metropolitan Opera in 1945, where he remained as conductor and artistic administrator until he came to Cincinnati. Max Rudolf was appointed music director emeritus of the CSO in 1969 and more recently was named honorary music director for the Cincinnati Symphony Orchestra's Centennial season.

Maestro Rudolf passed away in 1995, at the age of 93. His warm personality had endeared him to the entire community and his extraordinary musicianship and commitment to his art left an indelible impression on the orchestra as well as the entire music world.

NUT ROLL
Serves 8 to 10

One evening when the Rudolf's were entertaining Pierre Monteux at dinner, Liese Rudolf proudly served this NUT ROLL as a climax to the meal. M. Monteaux noticed that his host took none, and inquired why. "Because I never eat desserts," replied Mr. Rudolf. M. Monteux appreciatively sampled his own serving. Then turning to Mrs. Rudolf he observed solemnly, "Madame, zees is raison for divorce."

4 eggs, yolks and whites separated
½ cup sugar
½ cup sifted flour
4 oz. ground walnuts
1 teaspoon vanilla
½ teaspoon salt

1 cup heavy cream, whipped

ICING:
2 teaspoons instant coffee
1 cup confectioner's sugar
2 tablespoons boiling water

Beat together egg yolks and ½ cup sugar. Work in flour. Fold in stiffly beaten egg whites, ground walnuts, vanilla and salt. Grease bottom of a 10½ x 15½-inch jelly-roll pan. Line with tin foil and grease foil. Pour mixture into pan and spread evenly. Bake at 375 degrees in oven for about 15 minutes.

Remove right away from pan and flip over onto a towel. Trim crusty edges. Let cool. Spread with whipped cream and roll up carefully.

Mix instant coffee in boiling water, add confectioner's sugar and stir until smooth. Spread immediately on top of roll. Keep roll in refrigerator until serving time.

MAX RUDOLF'S HAM CRESCENTS
Makes 16 crescents

1 cup boiled ham, chopped
1 cup sifted all-purpose flour
½ cup butter
¼ teaspoon salt

½ cup creamed cottage cheese
¼ to ½ cup grated cheese (your choice)
1 egg yolk, slightly beaten

Mix flour, butter (room temperature), salt and cottage cheese. Put dough into refrigerator for 1 hour. Spread dough on a floured board and cut into 3-inch squares. On each square, put 1 teaspoon of chopped ham and sprinkle with grated cheese, then fold square into a crescent.

Put crescents on a greased baking sheet and brush them with egg yolk. Bake at 375 degrees in oven for 15 to 20 minutes. To be served hot.

Photo: SABINE TOEPFFER

WOLFGANG SAWALLISCH, CONDUCTOR/PIANIST

Philadelphia Orchestra Music Director Wolfgang Sawallisch is considered one of the leading conductors of our time. "Sawallisch is unrivaled," wrote a critic of one of his recent recordings with the Philadelphia Orchestra, "in his ability to lend clarity to music and at the same time raise it to the most exalted heights." For more than twenty-one years, Sawallisch led the Bavarian State Opera in Munich as music director, serving during the last decade of his tenure also as general manager. The exemplary performances of great stage works under his directorship assured this institution its internationally acknowledged standard of excellence.

Born in Munich, Maestro Sawallisch graduated from the Munich Academy of Music. He began his conducting career in 1947 at the Opera Theater of Augsburg, where he served as vocal coach, chorus master, and conductor of ballet, opera, and concert music. From 1953, he held music directorships successively in Aachen, Wiesbaden, and Cologne. That year he also became the youngest conductor ever to lead the Berlin Philharmonic, an orchestra he is associated with to this day. From 1957 to 1962, he was on the podium at Bayreuth. For the decade beginning in 1960, he was music director of both the Hamburg Philharmonic and the Vienna Symphony; both orchestras have recognized his contribution by making him an honorary member and honorary conductor. He was artistic director of the Orchestre de la Suisse Romande in Geneva from 1973 to 1980. Having completed his tenure in Munich at the end of 1992, he became the sixth music director of the Philadelphia Orchestra in September 1993.

Many awards and honors testify to his artistic caliber and to the high esteem in which he is held throughout the world. Among them is the "Toscanini Gold Baton" Award which he received in recognition of his more than thirty-five year association with La Scala in Milan. He is the only "honorary conductor laureate" of the NHK Orchestra in Tokyo, where he has appeared as guest conductor every year since 1964; he is also "honorary conductor" of Santa Cecilia in Rome. A gifted pianist, Maestro Sawallisch is highly regarded as a chamber musician and as accompanist of many of the leading singers of our time. His recordings with orchestras and soloists, particularly recent releases made with the Philadelphia Orchestra, demonstrate—in the words of one critic—his "total command of every aspect of the score."

Frau Mechthild Sawallisch was born in Munich. She began a voice career at the age of eight, singing, speaking, making broadcasts for children and performing in children's operas. Frau Sawallisch studied at the Academy of Music in Munich. She became a well-known soprano on German radio until World War II, when most of the opera houses were destroyed, thus preventing her from furthering her career. She first met Maestro Sawallisch during this time and they married some years later, during 1952. She made the difficult choice at this time to leave her singing career and devote herself to raising a family and furthering her husbands conducting career.

The Sawallischs spend about four months of the year in Philadelphia. During the remainder of the year, they return to their country home in Grassau, Germany, to the company of many acres of forest and two large Bernese mountain dogs.

MEINE GEMUESESUPPE
(My Vegetable Soup)
Makes 4 quarts

If possible use fresh vegetables. I (Frau Sawallisch) like to use them from my own garden.

7 to 8 cups meat broth or stock
¼ cup olive oil
2 medium onions, finely chopped (3 cups)
2 medium-large carrots, sliced (1½ cups)
2 leeks, sliced into ½-inch rounds
1 medium celery rib, coarsely chopped
1 red bell pepper, chopped
1 green pepper, chopped

1 kohlrabi (tender leaves also), sliced
   (first remove outer layer if tough)
Salt and pepper to taste
1 cup green beans, sliced
1 cup cut broccoli florets
2 medium zucchini, sliced (3 cups)
1 to 2 skinned tomatoes, quartered
Parsley

Clean the vegetables and cut into suggested shapes and sizes. In a large pot, brown the onions in olive oil. Gradually add carrots, leeks, celery, red and green bell peppers and kohlrabi (except tender leaves) to cook with onions. Add 2 cups of the broth and spices to taste. Cover pot. Raise heat slightly and simmer for 5 minutes.

After 5 minutes, add beans, broccoli, zucchini, tomatoes, and remaining broth and cook very gently on low heat for 45 to 50 minutes, or until tender. When soup vegetables are still somewhat of a firm consistency, add kohlrabi leaves (chopped). Serve with plenty of chopped parsley.

APFELPFANNKUCHEN
(Apple Pancakes)

BATTER: (4 servings)
4 tablespoons flour
Pinch of salt

3 eggs
3 to 4 tablespoons milk

Roughly mix together flour, salt and eggs. Add milk, stir thoroughly. Let stand one-half hour.

PER PERSON: (one pancake)
½ apple, peeled

2 tablespoons butter
Sugar (regular and powdered)

Take one-half apple, already peeled, divide into quarters, then cut into 1/5-inch segments. Melt 2 tablespoons butter in a small frying pan (6-inch). When melted, cover bottom of pan with a single layer of apple slices and sprinkle with sugar, then cook. It is all right for sugar to caramelize. Pour batter over the above, just covering the apples. When underside is golden yellow, turn carefully. Let cook until golden. Turn out onto preheated plate. Sprinkle with powdered sugar and serve hot.

Photo: MARCO PROZZO

GERARD SCHWARZ, CONDUCTOR

The 1996-97 season marks Gerard Schwarz's fourteenth year with the Seattle Symphony and his twentieth season as music director of the New York Chamber Symphony. Maestro Schwarz was named 1994 "Conductor of the Year" by *Musical America International Directory of the Performing Arts*. His annual summer activities include Lincoln Center's Mostly Mozart Festival in New York City, where he has been music advisor and then director since 1982.

Gerard Schwarz began his conducting career in 1966 as music director for the Erick Hawkins Dance Company. In 1972, he was appointed music director of the Eliot Feld Dance Company. Four years later, he was named founding music director of the Waterloo Festival. His performances at that summer festival led to his appointment as music director of the New York Chamber Symphony when it was founded in 1977.

In 1978, Maestro Schwarz assumed the position of music director of the Los Angeles Chamber Orchestra. During his eight years there, he toured with the ensemble throughout the United States and at the Casals Festival and made numerous recordings. Maestro Schwarz established the Music Today contemporary music series in 1981 at Merkin Concert Hall in New York City and served as music director through the 1988-89 season.

In 1983, Maestro Schwarz came to the Seattle Symphony as music advisor. The following year, he was appointed principal conductor and since 1985 has held the post of music director. Over the past ten years, he has initiated several concert series, has led award-winning recordings and has introduced many new works to the Seattle Symphony's repertoire.

Highlights of his 1995-96 season with the Seattle Symphony included riveting performances of Mahler's Symphony No. 2, "Resurrection," Stravinsky's *Firebird Suite*, Bruckner's Symphony No. 4, Shostakovich's *The Execution of Stephan Razin* and Mozart's Piano Concerto

No. 24, K. 491. Continuing a strong tradition of championing the works of living composers, the subscription series included world premieres of works by Bright Sheng, William Kraft, Robert Starer and William Bolcom. Additionally, the symphony was awarded funding to mount a "New Seattle" series at the Intiman Theatre that included works by Deborah Drattell, Bernard Rands, Ernest Bloch and Ellen Taaffe Zwilich among others and featured the Seattle Symphony debut of flutist Jody Schwarz.

Maestro Schwarz's recordings for the Delos, Nonesuch, Angel and RCA labels constitutes an extensive discography. During his tenure, Schwarz and the Seattle Symphony have released over 60 compact discs. The 50th release on Delos label entitled "The Schumann Edition" is a four-disc package featuring the four complete symphonies of Robert Schumann. His first recording of music by Howard Hanson was a mainstay on the *Billboard* classical music best selling list for 41 weeks, including six weeks at number three. It was nominated for three Grammy Awards, including "Best Classical Album" of 1989, and earned a 1989 "Record of the Year" honor from *Stereo Review*. Since then, every Schwarz recording featuring Hanson's music has appeared on the *Billboard* best selling charts and has earned a Grammy nomination. In the past decade, Maestro Schwarz has received more than ten nominations for Grammy Awards. He has also received two Record of the Year Awards and a Mumms Ovation Award. Maestro Schwarz's recent recording, *Mount St. Helens Symphony,* by Alan Hovhaness, debuted on *Billboard's* chart at No. 17 and rose quickly to No. 5.

Gerard Schwarz's numerous television credits include several appearances on PBS' *Live from Lincoln Center* series with Mostly Mozart; a 1984 KCTS/9 (local PBS affiliate) broadcast of Mahler's Symphony No. 2; *Front Row Center,* KING-TV's (Seattle's NBC affiliate) award-winning 1985 broadcast featuring Copland's *Billy the Kid* suite; *A Grand Night,* PBS' March 1988 celebration of the performing arts, for which he served as music director; a KCTS/9 broadcast of the first Musically Speaking concert for the 1992-93 season; a nationally telecast performance in France with the Orchestre Philharmonique; and *A Romantic Evening,* a broadcast on KCTS/9 February 14, 1993, which received a Northwest Regional Emmy Award. Awards given to Gerard Schwarz and the Seattle Symphony during the 1995-96 season included a first place 1996 ASCAP (American Society of Composers, Authors and Publishers) Awards for Programming of Contemporary Music. Maestro Schwarz was honored by the Juilliard School with an honorary doctor of music degree during the conservatory's 91st commencement.

A graduate of the Juilliard School, Maestro Schwarz has received an honorary doctor of fine arts degree from Fairleigh Dickinson University and Seattle University, an honorary doctor of music degree from the University of Puget Sound and the 1989 Ditson Conductor's Award from Columbia University.

GERARD SCHWARZ'S FARMER'S SALAD

Serves 4

SUGGESTED MENU:

Farmer's Salad
Rye bread and butter—a hearty caraway rye
Beer—preferably a well-hopped micro-brew
(as opposed to well-malted)

1 large (must be sweet) cucumber, peeled
1 bunch scallions, both green and
   white segments
1 bunch radishes

Salt to taste
Tellicherry pepper*
1 pint sour cream (real)

Peel cucumber into 4-inch long strips and ½-inch chunks. Place in a large bowl. Cut scallions into 1-inch pieces, and radishes into not-too-thin round slices. Add to bowl.

The above can be assembled 1 to 2 hours ahead of the needed time. Cover and refrigerate. Add salt to taste and lots of tellicherry pepper. Add sour cream, stir and serve immediately.

*Found in markets offering food from India (if not available, use black or white pepper).

Photo: CHRISTIAN STEINER

LEONARD SLATKIN, CONDUCTOR

Throughout his career, Leonard Slatkin has been recognized internationally for his diverse abilities not only as a masterful interpreter of the standard repertory but also as a champion of new works. His imaginative, spirited programming is well-known, particularly with the Saint Louis Symphony Orchestra, which he has led to world prominence during his 16 seasons as music director.

At the close of the 1995-96 season of the Saint Louis Symphony, Leonard Slatkin became the new music director of the National Symphony Orchestra in Washington, D.C.

Mr. Slatkin began his appointment as music director of the Blossom Music Festival of the Cleveland Orchestra in the summer of 1992, a position he will hold through at least the 1996 festival. In November 1993, Maestro Slatkin made a triumphant three-week tour of Europe with the Saint Louis Symphony Orchestra. The *Frankfurter Allgemeine Zeitung* stated, "With total confidence, Leonard Slatkin imbues the orchestra with passion, he breathes with them and models sound with his hands, like a sculptor." Recent tours in this country have included stops in Chicago, Washington, D.C., Boston, San Francisco, Los Angeles and two concerts annually in Carnegie Hall.

Now an exclusive BMG/RCA recording artist, Mr. Slatkin has recently completed his first recording with the National Symphony Orchestra, a disc of music of John Corigliano, released last September. Mr. Slatkin's past recordings with the Saint Louis Symphony Orchestra have been nominated for 50 Grammy Awards over the last 16 years, winning three awards during this period. Additional honors received by Mr. Slatkin include ASCAP Awards in 1984, 1986 and 1990 for "adventuresome programming of contemporary music" with the Saint Louis Symphony Orchestra and

several honorary doctorates, including one from his alma mater, the Juilliard School. In 1993, he received the Laurel Leaf Award from the American Composers Alliance and was named an honorary member of the Royal Academy of Music.

In January 1989, Mr. Slatkin signed an exclusive, five-year recording contract with BMG Classics, which then included RCA Victor Red Seal, Eurodisc and Deutsche Harmonia Mundi. In 1992, the contract was extended, with the recordings to be completed by the 1995/96 season. The agreement, which was the most comprehensive and extensive in the classical recording industry today, called for a total of 40 discs—30 with the SLSO and 10 with orchestras in Europe.

Maestro Slatkin is in great demand worldwide as a guest conductor, with regular appearances over the last two decades with the New York Philharmonic, the Philadelphia Orchestra, the Chicago Symphony Orchestra, the Cleveland Orchestra, the Boston Symphony Orchestra, the Philharmonic (London), the Berlin Philharmonic, the Vienna Philharmonic, the Royal Concertgebouw Orchestra, the English Chamber Orchestra, the Orchestre de Paris and the Israel Philharmonic.

Equally acclaimed as an opera conductor, he has conducted the Metropolitan Opera, Vienna State Opera, Hamburg Opera, Stuttgart Opera, Lyric Opera of Chicago, and the Opera Theatre of Saint Louis.

Mr. Slatkin was born in Los Angeles, California. His parents, conductor-violinist Felix Slatkin and cellist Eleanor Aller, were founding members of the famed Hollywood String Quartet. After beginning his musical career on the piano, Mr. Slatkin first studied conducting with his father and continued with Walter Susskind at Aspen and Jean Morel at the Juilliard School.

CHINESE LETTUCE BURGERS
Serves 6

This recipe from Mr. Slatkin makes a tasty snack or a delicious lunch. For a variety of color and taste, try various kinds of lettuce, such as red leaf, green leaf or Boston. For salt-conscience eaters try using a low-sodium soy sauce. It contains half the salt but does not dramatically alter the taste.

1 **pound lean, finely ground pork**
3 **tablespoons soy sauce**
3 **tablespoons sugar**
3 **tablespoons water**
2 **teaspoons peanut oil**

**Small can (8 oz.) water chestnuts,
    drained and chopped**
Small can (8½ oz.) baby peas, drained
13 or 14 large romaine lettuce leaves

Mix pork in marinade of soy sauce, sugar and water. Let marinate for 1 hour.

In a frying pan, heat the oil for 30 seconds. Cook pork mixture on medium-high until done (about 15 minutes). Add peas and water chestnuts. Cook 2 additional minutes. Transfer to a warm baking dish.

Rinse, then chill lettuce in the freezer for 5 minutes. Remove and cut leaves in half. Spoon 2 tablespoons of the pork mixture into lettuce leaves and eat like a sandwich.

Photo: RON MAY

EDVARD TCHIVZHEL, CONDUCTOR

Edvard Tchivzhel (pronounced CHEEV-zhel) was born into a highly musical family in Leningrad in 1944. His father was a noted violinist and his mother was the organist for the Leningrad Kirov Theatre. His sister is a violinist for "Mussorgsky," the Leningrad State Theatre of Opera and Ballet.

Tchivzhel showed musical talent from an early age, graduating from the Leningrad Conservatoire in 1972 with the highest distinction in the areas of piano and conducting. He completed three more years of post-graduate study at the Leningrad Conservatoire's Higher Academy of Music in the prestigious conducting classes of Arvid Jansons. In 1971, while still a student, Tchivzhel scored a remarkable success by winning the Third Soviet Conductor's Competition in Moscow. From 1974 until 1977, Tchivzhel worked as assistant conductor to the legendary conductor Yevgeni Mravinsky with the Leningrad Philharmonic Orchestra. By the late 1970's, Tchivzhel appeared as permanent guest conductor with the Leningrad Philharmonic and conducted the Moscow Philharmonic, the Moscow Radio Symphony Orchestra, and Leningrad's Kirov Theatre of Opera and Ballet, as well as many other orchestras throughout the former U.S.S.R. In 1973, Tchivzhel became music director and principal conductor of the Karelian Symphony Orchestra of TV and Radio, a position he held until 1991. He had numerous performances in the Opera House of Leningrad (St. Petersburg) Conservatoire and appeared as a guest conductor at the Kirov Theatre of Opera and Ballet.

Since 1980, Tchivzhel's career has reached international status with appearances in England, Germany, Czechoslovakia, Poland, Romania and Scandinavia. In 1986, Tchivzhel became the principal conductor of the Umea Sinfonietta of Sweden, combining his work there with frequent appearances with the symphony orchestras of Helsinborg, Malmo and Norrkopping. In 1988, he made his operatic debut in Sweden with performances of Puccini's *Manon Lescaut* in Stockholm; Tchaikovsky's *Eugene Onegin*, and Kurt Weil's *Mahagony* in NorrLands Operan. Tchivzhel debuted with the Stockholm Philharmonic in 1989. That same year, he visited Australia for the first time to conduct the Australian Youth Orchestra on a tour through Sydney, Melbourne and Canberra.

As an associate conductor of the U.S.S.R. State Symphony Orchestra, Tchivzhel toured widely in Japan in 1990; in February of 1991, he achieved great success on a tour of the United States. Following this tour, Tchivzhel defected to the U.S. He has since performed as a guest conductor with various orchestras, including the Baltimore Symphony and the Atlantic Sinfonietta, a chamber orchestra based in New York, where he served as music director from 1992-94.

Tchivzhel continues to conduct regularly in Scandinavia, New Zealand and Australia. In February 1995, he made a successful debut with the Indianapolis Symphony and this past summer was invited to conduct two concerts at the prestigious Mozart Festival in Woodstock, Illinois.

Tchivzhel has compiled an extensive repertoire of both Classical and modern works and has made numerous recordings with the best orchestras of Moscow and St. Petersburg, several Swedish orchestras and American orchestras, including a recent CD with the Atlantic Sinfonietta and the Asheville Symphony.

Today, in addition to his main position as music director of the Fort Wayne Philharmonic, Tchivzhel is serving his third year as artistic advisor of the Auckland Philharmonia in New Zealand. Tchivzhel and his wife, Luba, a philharmonic violinist, have a 10-year-old son, Arvid.

EDVARD'S LEG OF LAMB
Serves 6 to 8

Edvard likes simple, fresh foods that are not spicy. Because of the lack of technology (in such areas as food packing or food preservatives) in Russia when we (Edvard and Luba) lived there, we always bought our meats, fish, and vegetables fresh from the 'farmers market'. We feel that the advancements in technology are perhaps not always for the better as we prefer to have fresh food. I also grew up by the sea, so fresh fish was part of my childhood, as it was always available.

Fresh (medium-small) leg of lamb (without preservatives or hormones, if possible)
1 to 1½ cups spring water

8 large grains black pepper (peppercorns)
2 to 2½ slices of lemon

Remove outer membrane from meat and cut leg of lamb into ¾-inch thick slices leaving most of the fat on meat. Start to brown meat in large dry frying pan, Teflon preferred, on medium-high heat. Keep turning lamb for about 5 to 6 minutes until it becomes golden and begins to emit a nice aroma.

Transfer lamb to a deeper, larger pan (with cover) and arrange meat slices side by side, or in layers if necessary. Pour in spring water; add lemon slices and grains of pepper around lamb. Cook on low heat (covered) for 1 to 1½ hours, or until tender.

Serve on top of green lettuce, cover with some diced onions that have been sautéed in butter. Also, complement lamb with cooked small red potatoes or mashed potatoes with a little sweet butter.

LUBA'S FAVORITE EGGPLANT
Serves 6

2 medium eggplants, very evenly shaped, firm, and fresh as possible
2 fresh green bell peppers
¾ cup or more sunflower oil

1 large, sour tasting red tomato
Salt and pepper to taste
Parsley for garnish

Cut each eggplant lengthwise into 3 or 4 segments, then cut crosswise into ⅓-inch thin chunks. Cut peppers into small pieces, but more rectangular than square.

Using a deep Teflon pan, put in sunflower oil and heat on medium to medium-high until oil is hot. Add eggplant and peppers to pan. Keep turning so they do not burn. Cook about 20 to 25 minutes without covering.

Meanwhile, remove skin and cut tomato up into very small pieces, retaining juice. When eggplant is cooked, add tomato, salt, pepper, and cook an additional 5 minutes. Cut up one-half bunch of parsley on clean plate, transfer contents to clean dish, garnish with parsley.

Photo: BACHRACH

JOHN WILLIAMS, CONDUCTOR/COMPOSER

In January 1980, John Williams was named nineteenth conductor of the Boston Pops Orchestra since its founding in 1885. He assumed the title of Boston Pops laureate conductor, following his retirement in December 1993, and currently holds the position of artist-in-residence at Tanglewood.

Mr. Williams was born in New York and moved to Los Angeles with his family in 1948. There he attended UCLA and studied composition privately with Mario Castenuovo-Tedesco. After service in the Air Force, Mr. Williams returned to New York to attend the Juilliard School, where he studied piano with Madame Rosina Lhevinne. While in New York, he also worked as a jazz pianist, both in clubs and on recordings. He then went back to Los Angeles, where he began his career in the film studios, working with such composers as Bernard Herrmann, Alfred Newman, and Franz Waxman. Williams went on to write music for many television programs in the 1960s, winning two Emmy Awards for his work.

John Williams has composed the music and served as music director for more than seventy-five films, including *Schindler's List, Jurassic Park, Home Alone, Far and Away, JFK, Hook, Home Alone 2, Presumed Innocent, Stanley and Iris, Always, Born on the Fourth of July, Indiana Jones and the Last Crusade, The Accidental Tourist, Empire of the Sun, The Witches of Eastwick, Indiana Jones and the Temple of Doom, Return of the Jedi, E.T. (the Extra-Terrestrial), Raiders of the Lost Ark, The Empire Strikes Back, Superman, Close Encounters of the Third Kind, Star Wars, Jaws,* and *Goodbye, Mr. Chips.* He has received thirty Academy Award nominations and has been awarded five Oscars and fifteen Grammies, as well as several gold and platinum records. In 1994, he was awarded an Oscar for Best Original Score for *Schindler's List.* Most recently, he was nomi-

nated for a Grammy for Best Instrumental Composition for a Motion Picture for *Schindler's List.* His most recent project has been scoring the remake of the film *Sabrina.*

In addition to his film music, Mr. Williams has written many concert pieces, including two symphonies, a flute concerto and a violin concerto, recorded by the London Symphony Orchestra, and a cello concerto written for Yo-Yo Ma and performed with the Boston Symphony Orchestra at the inaugural concert of Seiji Ozawa Hall at Tanglewood in 1994. A bassoon concerto, commissioned for New York Philharmonic Principal Bassoonist Judy LeClair, was premiered in April 1995, and the Cleveland Orchestra has commissioned a trumpet concerto for Principal Trumpeter Michael Sachs.

Many of Mr. Williams's film scores have been released as recordings; the soundtrack album to *Star Wars* has sold more than any non-pop album in recording history. Mr. Williams's highly acclaimed series of albums with the Boston Pops Orchestra began in 1990 on the Philips label, for which he recorded *Pops in Space, Pops on the March, Aisle Seat, Pops Out of This World, With a Song in My Heart* (a collaboration with soprano Jessye Norman), *America, The Dream Goes On* (a collection of favorite Americana), *Swing, Swing, Swing, Pops in Love, By Request...*(featuring music composed by John Williams), Holst's *The Planets, Salute to Hollywood,* and an all-Gershwin album entitled *Pops by George.* In 1990, John Williams and the Boston Pops started making recordings exclusively for the Sony Classical label. To date, these have included *Music of the Night* (an album of contemporary and classic show tunes), *I Love a Parade* (a collection of favorite marches), *The Spielberg/Williams Collaboration* (featuring John Williams's music for Steven Spielberg's films), *The Green Album* (which includes "This Land Is Your Land," "Simple Gifts," and "Theme for Earth Day"), a Christmas album entitled *Joy to the World,* an album of music by George Gershwin, Cole Porter, Richard Rodgers, and Jerome Kern entitled *Unforgettable,* a tribute to Frank Sinatra entitled *Night and Day,* an album featuring music by John Williams and Aaron Copland entitled *Music for Stage and Screen,* and most recently, *It Don't Mean a Thing If It Ain't Got That Swing,* with vocalist Nancy Wilson.

In addition to leading the Boston Symphony Orchestra at Tanglewood, Mr. Williams has appeared as guest conductor with a number of major orchestras, including the London Symphony, the Cleveland Orchestra, the Philadelphia Orchestra, the Chicago Symphony, the Pittsburgh Symphony, the Dallas Symphony, the San Francisco Symphony, and the Los Angeles Philharmonic, with which he has appeared many times at the Hollywood Bowl. Mr. Williams holds honorary degrees from Berklee College of Music in Boston, Boston College, Northeastern University, Oberlin College, Saint Anselm College, Tufts University, the University of South Carolina at Columbia, Boston University, the New England Conservatory of Music, and the University of Massachusetts at Boston.

WHOLE WHEAT PANCAKES

This serves the two of us with one left over. Use a non-stick griddle if possible. --J.W.

1 egg
1 cup non-fat plain yogurt
1 tablespoon butter
1 tablespoon maple syrup
1 teaspoon vanilla

1 cup whole wheat pastry flour
1 teaspoon baking powder
¾ teaspoon salt, or to taste
½ teaspoon baking soda
Nutmeg (optional)
Non-fat dry milk

Beat together egg, yogurt, butter, maple syrup and vanilla. Then add and whisk until blended, whole wheat flour, baking powder, salt, baking soda, and if desired, nutmeg. Add non-fat milk to achieve desired consistency.

Heat a non-stick griddle (or lightly oil a regular griddle) over medium heat. When hot enough to sizzle a drop of water, ladle batter onto griddle using about ½ cup batter per pancake. When pancake surface begins to bubble, flip and cook the other side until lightly brown.

Photo: TOM CUBBAGE

RANSOM WILSON, CONDUCTOR/FLUTIST

Long recognized as one of the world's leading instrumentalists, Ransom Wilson has in recent years become equally esteemed as an outstanding conductor of orchestral and operatic repertoire. He is music director and principal conductor of Solisti New York, a chamber orchestra he founded in 1981 with the aim of programming contemporary music alongside the classical repertoire. In addition to its annual concert series in New York City, Solisti tours the United States each season and is the resident orchestra each summer at the OK Mozart Festival in Bartlesville, Oklahoma, where Mr. Wilson serves as artistic director. He also served as music director of the Tuscaloosa Symphony from 1985 to 1992, a period that saw great artistic growth for that orchestra, and since 1991 has been the artistic director of the Mozart Festival at Sea on the M.S. Westerdam. More recently, Mr. Wilson was appointed music director of Opera/Omaha.

As guest conductor, he has appeared with the Saint Paul Chamber Orchestra, the Houston Symphony, the Denver Symphony, the San Francisco Chamber Symphony, the Budapest Strings, the Grand Rapids Symphony Orchestra, and the Berkeley Symphony; he has led a successful tour with James Galway and the Los Angeles Chamber Orchestra. Mr. Wilson has accompanied many internationally renowned artists from the podium, including Itzhak Perlman, Frederica von Stade, Nadja Salerno-Sonnenberg, Joshua Bell, Garrick Ohlsson and Jeffrey Kahane. An esteemed operatic conductor as well, Mr. Wilson has conducted new and highly acclaimed productions of Mozart's *Magic Flute* with the Tulsa and Omaha Operas and the American stage premiere of *Il Re Pastore*, also by Mozart, with the Glimmerglass Opera.

Ransom Wilson is the recipient of several prestigious honors. In 1988, The New York Times Foundation awarded him the first Alabama Prize, which is awarded to natives or residents of that state who have distinguished themselves in the performing or visual arts. The following year he received (with pianist Christopher O'Riley) a National Public Radio Award for best performance by a small ensemble on a national broadcast. More recently, he was honored last year by the Austrian government, which awarded him the prestigious Award of Merit in Gold, in recognition of his efforts on behalf of Mozart's music in America.

The artist's highly successful recording career, which has included two Grammy Award nominations, began in 1973 when he made a record with Mr. Rampal and I Solisti Veneti. More than 15 solo records have followed on the Angel/EMI, RCA, Orion and Musical Heritage Society labels. As conductor, he has made a best-selling recording of music by John Adams and Steve Reich with Solisti New York as well as a disc of Baroque music with the Los Angeles Chamber Orchestra.

A strong advocate of contemporary music, Mr. Wilson has commissioned new works by Steve Reich, Peter Schickele, Joseph Schwantner, John Harbison, George Tsontakis, Jean-Michel Damase, Jean Francaix and Carlos Surinach. A gifted arranger, he has transcribed much of the music for his Angel/EMI recordings and has conducted his own orchestrations of three of Ravel's *Five Greek Songs*, left unorchestrated by the composer, at Carnegie Hall with Frederica von Stade as soloist.

Educated at the North Carolina School of the Arts and at the Juilliard School, Ransom Wilson pursued postgraduate studies as an Atlantique Scholar in France with Jean-Pierre Rampal. He has studied conducting with Roger Neirenberg, James Dixon, Otto-Werner Mueller and received extensive coaching from the late Leonard Bernstein. He currently lives in rural Connecticut and is on the faculty of the Yale School of Music.

SZECHUAN COLLARD GREENS

Serves 4 to 6

I come from Alabama, where collard greens are eaten in great quantities. Collards are available almost everywhere these days, but remain surprisingly little-known. This recipe would probably be seen as a sacrilege by my ancestors (who would have boiled them to within an inch of their lives with a big ol'ham hock), but it is a delicious introduction to this versatile vegetable. --R.W.

2 tablespoons cooking oil (peanut, sunflower or canola)
3 to 4 scallions, minced
3 tablespoons unsalted peanuts (or pine nuts)
1 fresh hot pepper, minced (cayenne or jalapeño)
1 clove garlic, minced
1 bunch washed fresh collard greens, about 1½ pounds, coarsely chopped
    (sometimes just called "collards"). Include stems as well, but finely chop them.

COOKING SAUCE:
2 tablespoons Chinese dark soy*
1 clove garlic, minced
1 tablespoon dark sesame oil
1 tablespoon Chinese cooking wine *(I prefer using Japanese sake)*
2 tablespoons rice wine vinegar (or American white vinegar)
1 teaspoon Chinese red pepper paste (optional) - you could also substitute chili oil
1 teaspoon arrowroot powder or cornstarch (optional)

*Chinese dark soy is a commercial concoction containing molasses. (Japanese dark soy is not at all the same.) If you cannot find it, substitute 1 teaspoon molasses plus 1½ tablespoons soy sauce.

Prepare cooking sauce by combining all ingredients, then set aside. Heat oil in wok. Stir-fry scallions for 30 seconds, add peanuts, hot pepper, and continue to stir-fry for 1 minute, then add garlic. Add collard greens and stir-fry about 1½ to 2 minutes. Add cooking sauce, cook for 1 more minute, serve immediately.

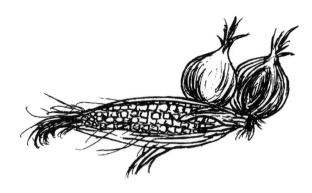

PASTA AL RACCOLTO
Serves 4

Corn as a food for humans is virtually unknown in Italy, but the insistence on the best and freshest ingredients is an integral part of Italian cuisine. I created this recipe, using ingredients fresh from my garden, and the proportion of tomatoes is purposefully low...the corn should dominate. This dish is paler, but still very good when made in the dead of winter with frozen corn (2 packages) and canned tomatoes (use only imported "San Marziano" type, and only one-half can, without the added juice or purée).

1　**large onion, chopped medium**
3　**tablespoons extra-virgin olive oil**
4　**ears fresh corn, kernels carefully cut off, preferably white or "butter and sugar"**
　　variety (roughly 2¾ to 3¼ cups)
2　**large cloves garlic, minced**
6　**sun-dried tomatoes (to soften, pour boiling water over them and let set 5 minutes,**
　　then drain)
3　**fresh ripe tomatoes, medium-sized, roughly chopped**
Fresh ground black pepper (*I like lots*)
Salt to taste (optional)
----
1 pound dry pasta (a substantial shape: fettuccine, tagliatelle or fusilli)

In a large deep frying pan, sauté onion in olive oil over medium heat for 2 minutes. Add corn and garlic, sauté, stirring frequently until the corn begins to look translucent. Add sun-dried tomatoes, sauté 1 minute. Add ripe tomatoes and fresh ground pepper, stir and reduce heat to low. Simmer 20 minutes. (If you are salting, add only at the very end, to prevent weeping of vegetables during cooking).

Meanwhile, bring a big pot of water with a dash of salt to boil and cook pasta. Drain and add directly to frying pan with sauce. Mix thoroughly, salt if desired, and serve immediately.

A LUXURIOUS VARIATION:
Substitute **butter** for **olive oil.** After adding ripe tomatoes, add 1 cup heavy cream, keep heat on medium for a few minutes until the cream has reduced slightly, then lower heat. White pepper works better in this version.

Photo: PETER HOWARD

DAVID ZINMAN, CONDUCTOR

David Zinman has emerged as one of the most admired conductors in America, both for his extraordinary success in building the artistic level and national reputation of the Baltimore Symphony Orchestra and for his highly praised guest performances with orchestras in Europe and North America. His stature was enhanced in 1990 by the winning of three Grammy Awards: for a Sony Classical disc of Barber and Britten Cello Concertos with the Baltimore Symphony and cellist Yo-Yo Ma; for a Nonesuch recording of 20th century vocal/orchestral music with soprano Dawn Upshaw and the Orchestra of St. Luke's; and for a Telarc "P.D.Q. Bach" disc (for which he used the pseudonym "Walter Bruno"). His recording of Henryk Gorecki's Symphony No. 3 with the London Sinfonietta continues to enjoy phenomenal success, having reached No. 1 on the classical music chart, No. 4 on the pop chart in England, and No. 5 in the U.S. This recording earned Mr. Zinman two Grammy nominations, as did the Baltimore Symphony's recent Argo/London recording of works by Samuel Barber.

Having entered its tenth year with the start of the 1994-95 season, Mr. Zinman's tenure at the Baltimore Symphony was renewed through the 1997-98 season. The symphony has been distinguished by David Zinman's programming of a remarkably broad repertoire, his strong commitment to the performance of contemporary American music, and his introduction of historically-informed performance practice for music of the 18th and early 19th centuries. He has brought new programming ideas to the orchestra's schedule including a summer music festival, the Discovery concerts devoted to contemporary music, Uncommon Concerts and Saturday-morning Casual Concerts, featuring informal commentary by the conductor and soloists.

Mr. Zinman has led the Baltimore Symphony on four highly successful tours, beginning in 1987 with a fourteen-city visit to Europe that included the first performances in eleven years by an American orchestra in the U.S.S.R.

An extensive David Zinman discography of more than 45 recordings holds, in addition to three Grammies, two Grand Prix du Disque awards and two Edison prizes. Under his direction, the Baltimore Symphony has expanded its recording activities and has already released 17 discs on the Telarc, Sony Classical, Argo/London and Nonesuch labels.

Since his American conducting debut with the Philadelphia Orchestra in 1967, David Zinman has pursued a busy guest-conducting career on the podiums of the world's leading orchestras and has served as music director of the Rochester Philharmonic, the Rotterdam Philharmonic, and the Netherlands Chamber Orchestra. He has performed with all the leading North American orchestras, including those of Philadelphia, Boston, Chicago, Cleveland, Minnesota, Montreal, New York, St. Louis, Los Angeles, Detroit, Pittsburgh, San Francisco, Toronto and the Saint Paul Chamber Orchestra. In addition, he has been a guest conductor at the Hollywood Bowl, Mostly Mozart, Ravinia, and Tanglewood Music Festivals and assumed the role of artistic director for the Minnesota Orchestra's Viennese Sommerfest, beginning with the 1994 season. He conducts the major European orchestras, including the Berlin Philharmonic, Royal Concertgebouw, Dresden Staatskapelle, London Symphony, Orchestre de la Suisse Romande, Royal Philharmonic and the Israel Philharmonic. Mr. Zinman has taken the post of music director at the start of the 1995-96 season of the Zürich Tonhalle Orchestra. This position will run concurrently with his leadership of the BSO.

Born in 1936, David Zinman graduated from Oberlin Conservatory and pursued advanced work in composition at the University of Minnesota, where he was recently granted an honorary doctorate of humane letters. His conducting studies at the Boston Symphony's Tanglewood Music Center brought him to the attention of the great Pierre Monteux, who guided his musical development and gave him his first important conducting opportunities with the London Symphony Orchestra and at the 1963 Holland Festival, where he was hailed by the critics as a major conducting discovery. Maestro Monteux said of his protégé: "I offer to the world my inheritance in the person of my beloved pupil David Zinman. In him the youth of an old maestro will live again."

AUSTRALIAN CHICKEN
Serves 12 to 14

This recipe comes from David's wife, Mary, who is Australian. She enjoyed preparing this favorite recipe during their courtship.

Meat from 2 cooked chickens
  (about 2, 3½ pound fryers)
3 tablespoons butter
2 sweet red bell peppers, chopped
2 green bell peppers, chopped
1 large onion (¾ pound), chopped
3 cups chopped mushrooms

Salt to taste
Freshly ground pepper to taste
3 tablespoons prepared mustard
3 tablespoons Worcestershire sauce
3 cups heavy cream
Paprika

In a large pot with cover, fill with 1 quart of lightly salted water and boil whole chickens for about an hour, or until tender. Remove meat and place chicken chunks in a greased 4-quart casserole dish.

Heat butter in a large skillet and sauté peppers, onion and mushrooms on medium-high flame, until tender. Add to chicken. Season with salt and pepper to taste.

Add mustard and Worcestershire sauce to cream and whip until cream is quite stiff. Spoon over vegetables, spreading gently with a knife. Sprinkle with paprika.

Bake uncovered at 350 degrees for 20 to 25 minutes, or until sauce is melted and top is slightly brown.

Serve with rice, salad and French bread.

DOUBLE BASS

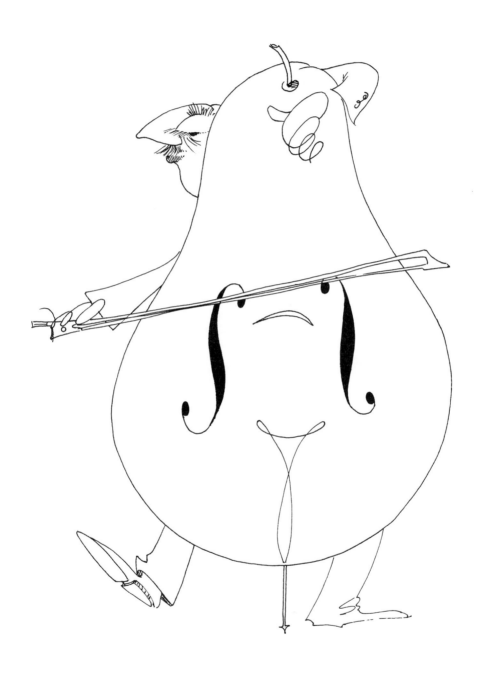

Photo: LISA SOUDERS

BARRY GREEN, DOUBLE BASSIST

Former principal bassist with the Cincinnati Symphony for 28 years, Barry Green has taught double bass at the University of Cincinnati from 1967 to 1992. Green was the first bassist to appear as soloist with the Cincinnati Symphony and has recorded several solo and chamber music albums for bass with this orchestra.

Green is founder and director of the International Summer Bass School (1977-81, 1989-90) and project director for the International Rabbath Institute held in Cincinnati in 1991, 1992 and 1995. For the past four years, Green has been studying with Francois Rabbath. Green presents a unique annual recital series called *The Big Green Machine* and in 1992 appeared as soloist with the Cincinnati Symphony in Jon Deak's *Jack and the Beanstalk Concerto*. Former director of International Society of Bassists, Green has written several books on bass pedagogy. He is also known to non-bassists as author of a series of educational publications on the mental aspects of learning and performing, called the *Inner Game of Music*. In the summer of 1995, Green moved to San Francisco to be the artistic director of a new Regional Art and Music Conservatory, as well as teach a beginning bass program for the San Francisco Youth Symphony.

MUSICIAN'S REFRIGERATOR/FREEZER PIZZA

Creativity is the key—your 'fridge' decides the ultimate recipe - always keep the crust frozen. You don't need salad with this! You will get full quickly—enjoy!! --B.G.

Begin with a **cheese pizza** (frozen). *I love Tony's four-cheese—each person should choose a kind that yields the preferred crust.* Scrape off the cheese and set the crust aside.

Empty your refrigerator of the following items: (substitutions are encouraged) To the top of the crust add extra salsa, or tomato sauce or hot sauce, then defrosted sausage links, ham, bacon, chicken, etc. and dice and spread to taste.

Add cut vegetables—celery, carrots, broccoli, onions (black or green), peppers (hot or bell), mushrooms or whatever else you have or like! Reapply frozen cheese that was scraped off and add additional Parmesan, mozzarella, and colby, cut or diced. If available, add blue cheese to taste.

On top of cheeses apply spices to taste: oregano, salad spices, basil, pepper, hot spicy peppers (red), veggie salt, etc. You may apply olive oil sparingly to top of pizza.

Bake until simmering. About 20 to 30 minutes at 425 degrees. Cheese should begin to brown and the crust should be crisp.

Photo: Courtesy of Chicago Symphony Orchestra

JOSEPH GUASTAFESTE, DOUBLE BASSIST

Joseph Guastafeste has been the principal string bass of the Chicago Symphony since the 1960-61 season, when he was appointed to that position by Fritz Reiner. Born in Brooklyn, New York, he began his musical education on violin and switched to the string bass on the persuasion of his older brother Eddie, who needed a bass player for his jazz band. Eddie arranged an audition with the beat bass teacher in New York City, Fred Zimmerman, of the Juilliard School and the New York Philharmonic. Joe was admitted to Juilliard on scholarship and secured his first orchestral position in the New Orleans Symphony at age 19. He moved on to the Dallas Symphony as principal bassist, under the direction of Walter Hendl and Paul Kletzki.

Mr. Guastafeste has performed in the Chautauqua Festival in New York state and the Casals Festival in Puerto Rico. He has also played chamber music with the Vermeer Quartet, New York Woodwind Quintet, Fine Arts Quartet, Emerson Quartet, and the Ravinia Institute Players.

Joe is currently a member of the Chicago Symphony Chamber Players and the Grammy Award-winning Chicago Pro Musica. He also performs with Music of the Baroque, conducted by Thomas Wikman. Students at Southern Methodist University and Northwestern University, as well as bassists who have attended his master classes, have benefited from his instruction. Proud of his rare instruments, Joe plays on a Dominico Buzon bass (circa 1749) for all orchestral work and owns a Gasparo Da Salo (1585), which he uses for Music of the Baroque, solo performances with the Chicago Symphony, and some chamber concerts.

Joe lives in Chicago with his wife, Yve Jorneaux, who is completing an MBA at the University of Chicago. While they enjoy biking and rock climbing together, Joe also pursues yoga as a way to keep in shape, mentally and physically. Joe's other creative outlets include cooking and painting.

Joe has two daughters: Camille, a first violinist with the Los Angeles Philharmonic Orchestra, and Manon, a jazz vocalist working with her husband Michael Spadaro in the Stu Hirsh Orchestra. Manon also teaches music and dramatics at the Bernard Zell Anshe Emet Day School in Chicago, while Camille is a visiting assistant professor of violin at U.C.L.A.

JOE GUASTAFESTE'S
SICILIAN MEAT BALLS
Serves 3 to 4

I prefer smaller sized meatballs (a little larger than golf balls), cooked medium-rare to medium in an uncovered pan. The meatballs can be eaten plain, after placing the cooked meatballs on paper towels to remove excess fat. The meatballs also can be placed in a favorite tomato sauce or even chopped into sauce to make a great meat sauce. They also make terrific Italian meatball sandwiches. --J.G.

1 pound ground chuck
   (for juicier meatballs) or 1 pound of
   (relatively fat-free) sirloin or filet
   mignon or round steak, ground
1 egg (use "Nest Eggs" from free range
   chickens) or 2 eggs if you prefer more
   compact meatballs
¾ cup of Italian-seasoned bread crumbs

½ cup grated Romano or
   Parmesan cheese
¼ cup fresh parsley, chopped
¼ to ½ cup pure water
2 or 3 cloves of garlic, minced and
   heated in 100% virgin olive oil
Oregano and basil to taste
Salt and pepper to taste

Put ingredients in a bowl, meat first, and mix well. Putting olive oil on your hands will make the mixing easier. Make meatballs of any desired size, again using olive oil on your hands. Cook in a frying pan in a thin layer of virgin olive oil, at medium heat, until 'darkish' brown on all sides. Serve with your favorite pasta.

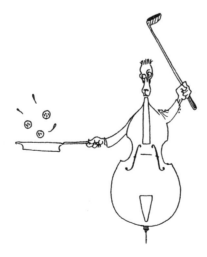

Photo: IRA NOZIK

GARY KARR, DOUBLE BASSIST

Gary Karr, acclaimed as "the world's leading solo bassist" (*Time* magazine), is in fact the first solo double bassist in history to make that pursuit a full time career. It is a career that adds new luster to his already lustrous 1611 Amati double bass, last owned by Serge Koussevitsky.

Karr, to expand the repertoire of works for the double bass with orchestra, commissions and premieres works from such American composers as John Downey, Robert Rodriguez, and Lalo Schifrin. These pieces help Karr to display the versatility of the instrument as no other artist has done before him.

Since his debut with Leonard Bernstein and the New York Philharmonic, Karr has performed with orchestras worldwide, including: the Chicago Symphony, the London Philharmonic, the Hong Kong Philharmonic, the McGill Chamber Orchestra (Montreal), the Simon Bolivar Orchestra (Caracas, Venezuela), the Jerusalem Symphony, the Olso Philharmonic, the Zürich Chamber Orchestra, and, on three tours there, each of the major orchestras of Australia.

On Italian cable TV, three Karr double bass recitals reached twenty million classical music lovers. Ten CDs of Gary Karr, made and released in Japan, are "top of the recording charts" favorites in the Far East. The BBC has featured two video films of Karr, one an illumination of his life and music ("*Amazing Bass*"), and one a children's series. On his third recording with the London Symphony Orchestra, Karr performed the John Downey Concerto. CBS *Sunday Morning* celebrated Gary Karr's career and the University of Wisconsin has released to the public a videotape demonstrating the double bassist's instructional approach ("*BASSically Karr*"), in addition to a special video concert for children ("*Karrtunes*").

Following thirty years of teaching at such schools as Juilliard, Yale, and the New England Conservatory, Karr is now retired to Canada to conduct a limited number of workshops around the world, including the continuation of his twenty-year stint at the Johannesen International School of the Arts in Victoria, British Columbia, where he now lives. Gary Karr's legendary influence on concepts of instrument design and of playing technique has raised the standards of performance of the double bass around the world.

The Karr Double Bass Foundation, Inc. was formed in 1983 to insure that its assemblage of fine instruments will be played by talented artists at no cost to them. Gary Karr's personal collection, including the 1611 Amati, will be in the foundation's legacy.

GARY'S GIFT HORSE CHICKEN

When ending a tour in Japan, I was given (graciously) five pounds of elegant pickled ginger, a bit of a gift horse redundancy in my occidental eyes. When home again and casting about for ways to use five pounds of pickled ginger, I devised a delicious "fusion cuisine" recipe—Gary's Gift Horse Chicken. --G.K.

Any number of chicken leg, thigh and split breast pieces, more or less uniform in size, skin left on. 1 tablespoon thin-sliced pickled ginger, drained slightly, for each piece of chicken. (SEE NOTE BELOW)

Preheat oven to 375 degrees. Wearing throwaway gloves, cram and distribute 1 tablespoon pickled ginger slices under the skin of each piece of chicken. Use no other seasoning. Spray shallow baking pan or dish with Pam. Place all chicken pieces in one layer, skin side up, in pan(s).

Spray Pam lightly over the top of the chicken pieces. Bake uncovered at 375 degrees for 35 to 45 minutes, or until chicken pieces are cooked—not dried out—and skin is browned.

Accompaniment:

Onions	**Snow peas**
Garlic slices	**Red bell pepper strips**
Broccoli florets	**Shiitake or other mushrooms**
Parsley	**Salt and pepper**
Thin carrot rounds	**Celery seed**

Stir-fry in olive oil 'enough' of the above ingredients, or 'ad lib' any vegetable inspirations of your own. Good color and texture are what you want. Toss with enough 'al dente' pasta and season with salt, pepper and celery seed to taste.

NOTE: Most Oriental grocers carry sliced pickled ginger in glass jars. Japanese brands are labeled "Sushi Yo Shoga." Brands from Thailand are labeled simply "Pickled Ginger Slices" or "Conserve Gingembre au Vinaigre." Color of the slices may vary from natural pale tan to slightly pink, but ingredients listed on every label will be "ginger, vinegar, sugar and salt," in no specific order. **If you can't find this product, you can make your own pickled ginger.**

PICKLED GINGER

3 pounds fresh ginger root	1 cup distilled white vinegar
2 quarts Oriental rice vinegar	3 cups sugar
1 cup cider vinegar	½ cup kosher salt

Peel the 3 pounds of fresh ginger root and slice thin across the grain (with a 1-mm slicer) in a Cuisinart, or on a mandoline or a Japanese Benriner, or, in a pinch, by hand. Cover slices with boiling water and let stand for 2 minutes. Drain. Place ginger in CLEAN glass or plastic container.

In a non-aluminum pot, combine rice vinegar, cider and distilled white vinegars with sugar and salt. Stir over moderate heat (or microwave) until sugar dissolves. Pour this hot mixture over ginger. Cool completely. Cover and refrigerate for at least 24 hours before using.

Photo: © PETER SCHAAF

JAMES VANDEMARK, DOUBLE BASSIST

One of the most brilliant virtuosi ever to perform on the double bass, James VanDemark began his musical studies at the age of 14 in his hometown of Owatonna, Minnesota. He made such rapid progress that just 18 months later he gave his solo debut with the Minnesota Orchestra. Subsequently, VanDemark has performed with the New York Philharmonic (Mehta), St. Paul Chamber Orchestra (Zukerman), Buffalo Philharmonic (Yoel Levi), Grant Park Symphony (James Paul), Rochester Philharmonic (Peter Bay), the San Antonio Symphony (Barrios), the Mostly Mozart Festival Orchestra (Rampal), the Chautauqua Festival Orchestra (Hugh Wolff), the Quebec Symphony, the National Symphony of Mexico, the Netherlands Radio Symphony, and in numerous other concerto appearances.

VanDemark's recitals with Andre Watts (including one on Lincoln Center's *Great Performers Series*), Samuel Sanders, Anthony Newman, Barry Snyder, and Robert Spillman have won him great acclaim. Chamber music collaborations with the Guarneri, Cleveland, Colorado, Muir, and Audubon Quartets, the Los Angeles Piano Quartet, members of the Tokyo Quartet, and pianists Gary Graffman, Alfred Brendel, Anton Nel, and Jeffrey Kahane highlight VanDemark's versatility. He is also a member of the Amadeus Ensemble of Toronto, one of Canada's most prestigious chamber music ensembles.

As a sought-after guest artist at summer festivals, VanDemark performs at the Mostly Mozart, Spoleto, Seattle, Round Top, Maverick, and Newport Festivals, also the Norfolk Chamber Music Festival and at London's South Bank Festival.

The recipient of numerous commissioned works, including those by three Pulitzer Prize-winners (Gian-Carlo Menotti, Joseph Schwantner, and Christopher Rouse), VanDemark received outstanding reviews for his world premiere performances of Jerod Sheffer Tate's *The Medicine Man and His Helper* (Ohio Chamber Orchestra), the Christopher Rouse Concerto (Buffalo Philharmonic), Sydney Hodkinson *Tango, Boogie, and Grand Tarantella* (Knoxville Symphony), and the Brian Fennelly *Lunar Halos* (Columbus Pro Musica Chamber Orchestra). His recent American premieres have included the Nino Rota *Divertimento Concertante* (Charlotte Symphony), and the Tubin Concerto (Queens Symphony).

An important direction in VanDemark's career has been his involvement with Native American performers in *Circle of Faith - the Words of Seattle*. VanDemark commissioned this unique collaborative work, and developed it in conjunction with respected Native artists and elders.

VanDemark has been professor of double bass at the Eastman School of Music since 1976, becoming, at age 23, the youngest person ever to hold such a position at a major music school.

As a recording artist, VanDemark can be heard on Philips, Telarc, Vox, and Pantheon. His second recording with the Cleveland Quartet (and John O'Conor) of the "Trout" Quintet was released recently on Telarc.

With other roles as artistic director of Music in Owatonna at the Gainey Center, a summer chamber music festival, director of Square Peg Productions, a film production company, and as a popular spokesman for the arts, VanDemark rounds out his career. In addition, he has been profiled in such diverse media as *Connoisseur* magazine, on the *MacNeil/Lehrer News Hour*, National Public Radio's *Morning Edition* and *All Things Considered*, and in the *Lakota Times*, the largest Native American newspaper in the United States.

CARROT YOGURT SOUP

Makes 7 cups

I found this recipe on a concert tour in Belgium; it has been a perennial favorite with guests at our home! Serve it hot or cold. --J.V.

A BLENDER IS NECESSARY
¼ cup butter or margarine
8 medium carrots, scraped and sliced
3 medium onions, chopped
4 cups chicken broth or stock (boiling)

1 cup plain yogurt
½ cup half-&-half
¼ cup chopped fresh chives or parsley
Salt and pepper (optional)

Melt butter or margarine in a large frying pan. Sauté carrots and onions until onions are tender. Add chicken broth to mixture, cover and simmer for 1 hour.

Purée carrots and onions with the liquid in a blender. Transfer the mixture to a 2-quart saucepan. Add yogurt and half-&-half, stirring until smooth. Keep on low heat until ready to serve, but do not boil. Sprinkle with chives or parsley. Add salt and pepper to taste if desired.

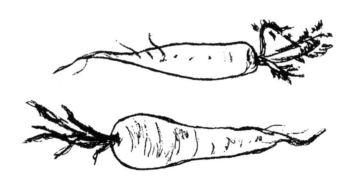

FLUTE

JULIUS BAKER, FLUTIST

Julius Baker was born in Cleveland, Ohio. After graduating from the Curtis Institute of Music in Philadelphia, he returned to Cleveland to play in the Cleveland Orchestra under Artur Rodzinski. Mr. Baker then went as solo flutist to the Pittsburgh Symphony under Fritz Reiner, leaving this orchestra to become solo flutist of the Columbia Broadcasting Symphony Orchestra in New York City. During this time, he joined the famed Bach Aria Group with which he was associated for eighteen years. When the CBS Orchestra was disbanded, Mr. Baker was appointed solo flutist for the Chicago Symphony Orchestra. Later he returned to New York to assume the solo flute position with the New York Philharmonic, where he remained until September 1983.

He now concentrates on solo performances and chamber music in addition to teaching. He is on the faculties of the Juilliard School, the Curtis Institute of Music—his alma mater—and Carnegie Mellon University.

During the summer of 1987, Mr. Baker was a member of the Yamaha International Soloists, a woodwind quintet whose members were invited by Yamaha to give concerts in the major cities of Japan in celebration of the 100th anniversary of the Yamaha Company. In 1988, he appeared in recital in Seoul, Korea and also spent two weeks teaching in Tokyo at Toho University. In October 1993, he performed in several Japanese cities as a guest of the Japan Flutists Association which is celebrating its 25th anniversary, giving master classes while there. Mr. Baker also gave master classes in both Spain and Italy, as well as in the United States, during the summer of 1993. April 1994 brought performances in Munich, Germany in celebration of the 200th anniversary of the birth of Theobald Böhm, the developer of the modern flute.

Mr. Baker has recorded for such labels as RCA Victor, Decca, Vanguard, Westminster and Vox Cum Laude. His latest CD was recently issued on the VAI label.

MUSHROOM SOUP
(French Country Style)
Serves 4

During the summer of 1994, the author had the pleasure of meeting, cooking for, and dining with Julius Baker, at a music festival in the state of Utah. One could not concentrate too much on eating a meal with Mr. Baker at the table since he would be reciting story after humorous story, not to mention his love of reading his self-created limericks. Mr. Baker's culinary tastes are as articulate as his musical tastes, as evidenced by this favorite recipe prepared by his wife, Ruth.

10 oz. package fresh mushrooms, sliced
1 small clove garlic, minced
2 or more tablespoons butter or olive oil
Dash of nutmeg
Salt and pepper to taste

2 slices firm bread
1 can condensed chicken broth
   or equivalent (21 oz.)
⅓ cup heavy or light cream
6 parsley sprigs, finely chopped

Sauté mushrooms and garlic in butter or olive oil for several minutes. Do not allow to brown. Add nutmeg, and salt and pepper.

Tear bread into small pieces and add to the chicken broth. Combine all ingredients, except cream and simmer for about 15 minutes.

Blend soup, a little at a time, in an electric blender. Pour back into saucepan and add heated cream. Serve garnished with additional chopped parsley.

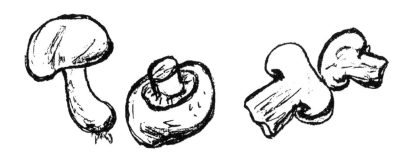

Photo: CHRISTIAN STEINER

JEANNE BAXTRESSER, FLUTIST

Jeanne Baxtresser, the brilliant principal flutist of the New York Philharmonic, enjoys a flourishing, multi-faceted career. As soloist and leading orchestral player, she has performed to critical acclaim in the music capitals of the world.

Miss Baxtresser made her professional debut with the Minnesota Orchestra at the age of fourteen. Following her graduation with honors from the Juilliard School, she was engaged as principal flutist of the Montreal Symphony, a position she later held with the Toronto Symphony. In 1984, at the invitation of the Music Director Zubin Mehta, she became the principal flutist of the New York Philharmonic, where she remains today.

A much sought-after soloist, Miss Baxtresser has performed at the Madeira Bach Festival, Mostly Mozart Festival, Spoleto and Aspen Music Festivals. She is a familiar figure on the "Live From Lincoln Center" broadcasts with the New York Philharmonic; last season marked her fourteenth appearance with the philharmonic as a soloist.

Among Miss Baxtresser's recordings are chamber music discs on the RCA and Philips labels. Her solo recordings include the Pro Arte release of Claude Bolling's Suite for Flute and Jazz Piano, *The Baroque Flute* and *The Magic Flute,* with conductor Andrew Davis.

In addition to presenting master classes all over the world, Miss Baxtresser is a faculty member of the Juilliard and Manhattan Schools. Her students occupy principal positions in orchestras in the United States, Canada, and Europe.

MARGY'S HOT CHICKEN SALAD
Serves 6 to 8

"Margy" is my mom and she is a wonderful pianist and dinner hostess. This is one of her many recipes that is 'easy and quick'. She can make a great meal for as many as twelve musicians with very little notice. --J.B.

4 cups cooked chicken breasts cut into large chunks (about 8 small breast halves)
4 cups celery, chopped into chunks, steamed until tender/crisp
2 cups grated Cheddar cheese

8 tablespoons minced onions or tops of green onion
1½ cups Hellman's mayonnaise
Potato chips, crushed

Mix together in bowl and sprinkle crushed potato chips on top. Cook in oven at 250 degrees for 10 to 15 minutes. Do not overcook, for celery will get mushy!

BONITA BOYD, FLUTIST

The combination of her sensitive musicianship and extraordinary technique makes Bonita Boyd one of today's most exciting flutists. The *New York Times* critic Donal Henahan wrote the following after her New York recital: "Bonita Boyd gave a flabbergasting account of her talents....Through it all, Miss Boyd's flute maintained its round, velvety sound at no expense to clarity of articulation....One could marvel, but still understand." Many other critics around the world have corroborated his opinion: *Los Angeles Times* critic Albert Goldberg wrote: "James Galway and Jean-Pierre Rampal are now joined in the forward ranks by a cheery young American girl name Bonita Boyd." *Frankfurter Allgemein* said: "...her Frankfurt debut in the Hindemith Hall of the Old Opera indeed confirmed that Bonita Boyd is a musician of great dimensions." The *Australian Advertiser* wrote: "Her technique and presence are those of an assured virtuoso and her command of the instrument's tonal possibilities, as with any major performer, had a very personal stamp."

Bonita Boyd's prodigious career has been studded with remarkable achievements. At age 21, her appointment with the Rochester Philharmonic made her the youngest first flutist with a major American orchestra. Her appointment at age 25 as flute professor for the Eastman School of Music made her the youngest professor at a major American conservatory. In addition, Ms. Boyd has performed widely-acclaimed recitals and concerts with orchestras throughout the United States, Europe, Latin America, Canada, Australia, Japan and Korea.

Bonita Boyd has premiered several works written for her as well as the recording premiere of these works: Samuel Adler's Flute Concerto, conducted by Sarah Caldwell and broadcast on National Public Television; Warren Benson's *Five Lyrics*, premiered with mezzo-soprano Jan DeGaetani in New York's Alice Tully Hall; and Miklos Rosza's Solo Flute Sonata, premiered in Los Angeles and recorded for Pantheon Records.

Ms. Boyd's recording of *Flute Music of Les Six* was awarded *Stereo Review* magazine's "Record of the Year" and was on *Hi-Fidelity* magazine's Critics Choice Column for three months. Her new recording of Samuel Adler's Flute Concerto and Solo Sonata was recently released on Vox CD.

MY MOM'S BRAN MUFFINS

Makes about 4½ dozen

Mix may be stored in refrigerator and baked fresh. These muffins are particularly moist and delicious. --B.B.

2 cups Kelloggs All-Bran	5 teaspoons baking soda
3 cups 100% Nabisco Bran	4 eggs
3 cups sugar	1 cup oil
5 cups flour	1 quart buttermilk
1 teaspoon salt	

Mix cereal, sugar, flour, salt, and baking soda in large bowl. Add eggs, oil, and buttermilk. Mix well. Pour into muffin tin, bake at 400 degrees for 20 minutes.

ERVIN MONROE, FLUTIST

1996 marks Ervin Monroe's twenty-eighth year as principal flutist of the Detroit Symphony Orchestra. Mr. Monroe has performed with the Mozarteum Orchestra (Salzburg, Austria), the Chamber Symphony of Philadelphia, the Royal Ballet, the Royal Danish Ballet, and the Bolshoi Ballet.

He has served as president of the National Flute Association and consulting editor for the *Flutist Quarterly*, that organization's official magazine. Ervin is the artistic consultant for Muramatsu Flutes U.S.A. He has numerous musical publications to his credit, including original compositions, and can be heard on solo and chamber music albums as well as orchestral recordings of the Detroit Symphony Orchestra. He has

also been featured in *The Instrumentalist* and *Flute Talk* magazines. Mr. Monroe has served as musical director and conductor of several Michigan orchestras and is an applied music studies teacher at the Oakland and Wayne State Universities. He has appeared as a soloist and clinician throughout North America and internationally and has served on the panel of judges for several world-wide music competitions. He has appeared in duo-concerts with such renown artists as Jean-Pierre Rampal.

In recent years, he has been a featured guest artist and given master classes at the Sewanee Music Festival in Tennessee, the Columbia Flute Society Flute Festival, the Fairbanks Fine Arts Festival, and the National Arts Camp in Interlochen, Michigan.

CHICKEN-RICE CASSEROLE
Serves 25 or more

I do a lot of entertaining here in Detroit, and this is my favorite recipe when hosting a large crowd. It's relatively easy to make and always turns out great. You can't miss on this one! --E.M.

8 whole (16 halves) chicken breast
5 cups white rice
10 cups chicken broth (best if
    used to cook rice)
5 ribs celery, sliced
4 large carrots, sliced
1 very large onion (a good 5-inch onion),
    cut in small pieces

4 to 5 tablespoons fresh parsley, chopped
2 cups slivered almonds
Salt and pepper to taste
5, 10½ oz. cans of cream-of-chicken soup
12 oz. can of condensed milk
¼-inch seasoned stuffing crumbs
3 to 4 sticks of butter, melted

Remove chicken skin and cook chicken in 2 to 3 quarts of water for about one hour. **SAVE THIS BROTH!** Debone chicken and tear into bite-size pieces.

Cook rice with chicken broth according to packaged rice instructions. If you do not have enough broth, add canned broth or water with bouillon.

In a covered 4-quart pot, partially cook celery, carrots, onion and parsley in 2 cups of water for 25 minutes, or until just tender, but still firm. Drain vegetables.

Mix these vegetables with the 2 cups of slivered almonds. **Do not skip this step!** Mix rice, chicken and vegetables in a very large pot or bowl, season with salt and pepper. Moisten all this with the cans of cream-of-chicken soup mixed with the can of milk. Press mixture into 2 or 3 large roasting pans. They heat faster with less content.

Sprinkle seasoned stuffing crumbs on top and drizzle generously with the sticks of melted butter. **The secret is in using the butter liberally!!** Heat until hot. Enjoy the party!

Photo: TERRY STEVENSON

MICHAEL PARLOFF, FLUTIST

Principal flutist of the Metropolitan Opera Orchestra since 1977, Michael Parloff is one of New York City's most versatile and sought-after musicians. As recitalist and concerto soloist, he appears regularly throughout the United States and Japan. In 1988, he was awarded the National Endowment for the Arts Solo Recitalist grant, which funded a major recital for flute with orchestral accompaniment at Lincoln Center's Alice Tully Hall.

Mr. Parloff is much in demand as a chamber musician, making frequent appearances with the Chamber Society of Lincoln Center, Music from Marlboro, and Bargemusic. He is the director of a series of New York City chamber concerts featuring James Levine and members of the Metropolitan Opera Orchestra.

Highly respected as a teacher, Mr. Parloff has been invited to present master classes at major conservatories and university music schools in the United States and abroad. He has been a member of the flute faculty at the Manhattan School of Music since 1985.

During the summers, Michael Parloff has been principal flutist, soloist, and faculty member at a variety of music festivals, including Marlboro, Waterloo, Grand Teton, Monadnock, Chautauqua, and Crested Butte.

Mr. Parloff has recorded extensively with the Metropolitan Opera for Deutsche Grammophon, Sony Classical, London, and Philips. He is a featured artist on baritone Thomas Hampson's popular album of Stephen Foster songs, *American Dreamer*, on Angel. His solo CD, *The Flute Album*, released in 1993 on E.S.SAY, surveys 200 years of classic repertoire for the instrument.

PICNIC PASTA

Serves 3 to 4

We have found this simple recipe to be consistently delicious, flexible, and appropriate for picnics, dinners, or after-concert parties. The amounts are easily extended for the occasion. --M.P.

1 box of bow tie pasta (8 oz.)
3 medium-sized fresh tomatoes
½ cup diced sun-dried tomatoes, soaked
    30 minutes in some olive oil
1 cup loosely packed fresh basil

1 teaspoon, finely minced fresh garlic
¼ cup olive oil
Salt and pepper to taste
OPTIONAL: steamed broccoli florets,
    diced cooked chicken or shrimp

Prepare and drain pasta. Remove and discard the inner seeds and pulp from the fresh tomatoes. Dice the remaining portion. Dice the sun-dried tomatoes. Chop the basil. Thoroughly mix the pasta and all the ingredients in a large bowl and salt and pepper to taste. Serve at room temperature.

Photo: Courtesy of Chicago Symphony Orchestra

DONALD PECK, FLUTIST

Recognized as one of the finest flutists in the world, Donald Peck is renowned for his performances, as principal flute, with the Chicago Symphony Orchestra in concert and on recordings. He is in great demand as guest artist with other orchestras and major music festivals. He has performed at the Casals Festival, Carmel Bach Festival, the Victoria International Festival in Canada, and at Festival Australia. He is a prominent figure in chamber ensembles, such as the Chicago Symphony Chamber Players and the Chicago Symphony Woodwind Quintet. As an acclaimed recitalist, he appears frequently in cultural centers throughout the United States and Europe.

Born in Seattle, Washington, Mr. Peck graduated from the Curtis Institute of Music. Before joining the Chicago Symphony at the invitation of Fritz Reiner, he played with the Washington National Symphony Orchestra and the Kansas City Philharmonic.

A faculty member of DePaul University, Mr. Peck travels to colleges throughout the United States, presenting master classes and flute clinics. Special summer master classes at DePaul University attract an international following of young professionals.

Mr. Peck was recently honored by Morton Gould, who wrote a concerto for flute and orchestra, expressly for Mr. Peck. Premiered in the spring of 1985 by Mr. Peck and the Chicago Symphony, the work and its performance met with critical acclaim. The *Chicago Tribune* wrote, "The hero of the evening clearly was Donald Peck....One could not imagine a finer, or more dedicated realization."

SHRIMP LINGUINE WITH GARLIC AND CUMIN
Serves 4 to 5

The best type of wine to serve with shrimp is probably a lighter red wine—maybe a Pinot Noir.
--D.P.

4 tablespoons virgin olive oil
½ pound mushrooms, sliced (fresh)
4 to 5 cloves garlic, chopped
1 pound medium-small shrimp, cooked, shell removed
¼ cup green onion, chopped
1 teaspoon grated lemon rind

½ teaspoon (or more to taste) cumin
1 cup sun-dried tomatoes*
Several sprinkles of ground or chopped red chili peppers (dried)
½ pound linguine
Parmesan or cheese Romano

On medium heat, sauté mushrooms and garlic in heated olive oil for 5 minutes. Add shrimp, chopped onions, lemon, cumin, tomatoes, and a few sprinkles of the ground or chopped red chili peppers, then salt to taste.

Cook the above for 5 or more minutes with a slightly lower heat. Stir occasionally. Moisten mixture with a little pasta water if too dry. Boil water for the pasta and cook until 'al dente'. Add linguine to sauce and toss. Add Romano or Parmesan cheese or sprinkle with some chopped stems from the green onions.

*You may wish to soften the tomatoes by pouring some boiling water over them, then letting them set for 5 minutes.

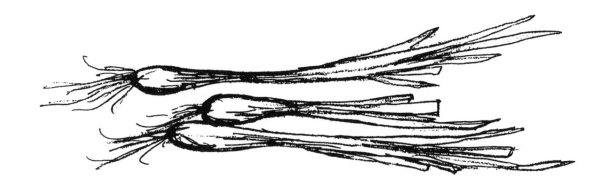

Photo: BOB ADLER

PAUL E. RENZI, FLUTIST

Paul Renzi was born in New York City and comes from a musical family. His father was principal oboist with Toscanini's NBC Symphony for many years, and his grandfather was organist of the Vatican for half a century. Carrying forward this extraordinary musical tradition, Renzi began studying piano at the age of eight and went on to study with John Wummer, principal flute of the New York Philharmonic. He attended the Juilliard School and Queens College in New York City.

At the age of eighteen, Mr. Renzi was chosen by Pierre Monteux for the position of principal flute with the San Francisco Symphony. He subsequently became principal flutist with the NBC Symphony under the direction of Arturo Toscanini and was with that organization and its successor, the Symphony of the Air, for nine years. He returned to his present position with the San Francisco Symphony in 1957.

Mr. Renzi has been on the musical faculties of Mills College, Stanford University, and San Francisco State University, where he is professor emeritus after teaching there for thirty-two years.

He can be heard on numerous Toscanini NBC Symphony recordings which are continually reissued by RCA Victor. Especially prominent are Renzi's solos in Gluck's *Orfeo*, the *William Tell Overture*, and Debussy's *Afternoon of a Fawn*. As a member of the NBC Symphony, he recorded the music for the TV series *Victory at Sea*, which is frequently shown on television.

Mr. Renzi has been a soloist for the past four consecutive seasons at the Monterey Mozart Festival. His arrangements of twelve arias from the Bach Cantatas for two flutes or two violins are published by CPP/Belwin, Inc.

The 1993-94 season marked the 50th year since Mr. Renzi began his career as principal flutist with the San Francisco Symphony. During that time, he has appeared as a soloist with the Symphony on more than fifty different occasions.

Mr. Renzi teaches privately and resides in San Francisco with his wife Roberta, who is a teacher at Notre Dame des Victoires. When not spending time with his six children and two grandchildren, he enjoys reading, playing and singing opera scores at the piano, walking, and throwing and batting a baseball (known as 'pepper practice' in his baseball circle) for exercise.

PASTA WITH VEGETABLES
(Pasta Primavera)
Serves 4

The below recipe should be treated as a musician playing a romantic piece of music; i.e. con rubato, a piacere, con slancio, etc. The amounts can be increased or decreased ad lib.; the ingredients can vary ad infinitum. --P.R.

3 tablespoons olive oil	2 cups yellow/red bell peppers, chopped
¼ cup chicken broth or water	1 medium-sized tomato, thinly sliced
4 cloves garlic, minced	1 cup any variety small squash, chopped
1 rib celery, minced	Salt and pepper to taste
1 small onion, chopped	½ cup white wine
1½ cups mushrooms, chopped	Favorite pasta (8 to 10 oz.)
1 cup broccoli tops, chopped	Parmesan or Romano cheese

Heat oil and chicken broth or water in a large skillet. Add garlic, celery and onion and simmer for about 5 minutes.

Then, add combination of the above vegetables, chopped. Salt and pepper to taste and add the white wine and cook on medium heat, uncovered, about 25 to 30 minutes, or until vegetables are tender.

Serve over your favorite pasta and sprinkle with cheese of choice. *BUON APPETITO!!*

Photo: CHRISTIAN STEINER

CAROL WINCENC, FLUTIST

The extraordinary range and breadth of Carol Wincenc's accomplishments worldwide attest to a fact well-known in music circles for many years: that she ranks as one of today's international stars of the flute.

A frequent guest of the major orchestras and festivals throughout the United States, Ms. Wincenc has appeared: with the St. Louis, Atlanta, Indianapolis, Houston and Seattle Symphonies; the Buffalo Philharmonic; the Los Angeles and Saint Paul Chamber Orchestras; and Mostly Mozart, Santa Fe, Spoleto, Caramoor and Marlboro Music Festivals. Equally in demand abroad, Ms. Wincenc has given acclaimed performances with the London Symphony, the English and Stuttgart Chamber Orchestras, and at the international music festivals in Aldeburgh, Budapest, Tivoli, Duisburg, Frankfurt and Montpellier.

Deeply committed to expanding the flute repertoire, Ms. Wincenc has commissioned concertos from Lukas Foss and Joan Tower (both of which she performed at Carnegie Hall), Pulitzer Prize-winner Christopher Rouse, Henryk Gorecki and Tobias Picker. During the 1994-1995 season, she gave the world premiere of Mr. Rouse's Flute Concerto with the Detroit Symphony and the U.S. premiere of the Gorecki work, Concerto-Cantata, with the Chicago Symphony. She also gave premieres of Concerto-Cantata in London, Amsterdam, Schleswig-Holstein, France and Poland, and will record it for Nonesuch. A composition by Tobias Picker, the Concerto for Flute and Voice, is being written for Ms. Wincenc and soprano Barbara Hendricks and will focus on the importance of saving the environment. Ms. Wincenc has also commissioned works from Peter Schickele, Paul Schoenfield and Roberto Sierra.

In great demand as a chamber musician, Ms. Wincenc has collaborated with the Guarneri, Emerson, Tokyo and Cleveland String Quartets, and has performed with such distinguished colleagues as Jessye Norman, Emanuel Ax, Yo-Yo Ma, Alexander Schneider and Elly Ameling. As

a result of her fascination with the flute and its family of instruments, Ms. Wincenc created and directed a series of International Flute Festivals at the Ordway theater in Saint Paul. The overwhelming success of these festivals, which featured such diverse artists as Jean-Pierre Rampal, Herbie Mann, American Indian flutist Carlos Nakai, and the Rumanian pan pipe virtuoso Syrinx, led to a sold-out U.S. tour which included performances at New York's 92nd Street Y, Stanford University, Dartmouth, UC Santa Barbara, and in San Francisco.

Equally active as a recording artist, Carol Wincenc can be heard on Nonesuch with pianist Samuel Sanders and composers/pianists David Del Tredici and Lucas Foss in music by American composers. Her first solo album for Musical Heritage Society, a collaboration with pianist Andras Schiff, was cited by Stereo Review as a "Recording of Special Merit" and was followed by albums in collaboration with guitarist Eliot Fisk and the Muir String Quartet in complete flute quartets of Mozart. In the fall of 1992, she recorded Paul Schoenfield's Klezmer Rondos, a concerto written especially for her, on the Decca label. Her most recent recordings include: Joan Tower's Flute Concerto with the Louisville Symphony Orchestra (d'Note); the Slovakian Children's Songs for flute and piano (London/Decca label), and a collection of 20th century chamber works by composers ranging from Samuel Barber to Heitor Villa-Lobos with tenor Douglas Webster and the Muir String Quartet (EcoClassics). In the spring of 1997, Telarc will issue Ms. Wincenc's recording of Christopher Rouse's Flute Concerto with the Houston Symphony conducted by Christoph Eschenbach.

Carol's husband, baritone Douglas Webster, was a winner of the Concert Artists Guild. He has appeared as the lead in "Les Misérables" on Broadway and can be seen currently performing in "Bravo Broadway." He also has appeared in a number of operatic roles, including Mozart's "Don Giovanni," and has been heard on a number of recordings, including Telarc Records's "Disney Spectacular," in which he created the voice of Prince Charming.

Carol Wincenc was first prize-winner of the Walter W. Naumburg Solo Flute Competition. She is presently professor of flute at the Juilliard School of Music in New York. She was vice-president of Chamber Music America and continues to be on the board of the organization.

Webster and Wincenc reside in New York City, with their young son, Nicola.

"A WHEATBERRYING A' BIT" SALAD

I'm very interested in 'whole' foods so this recipe fits that category! It even improves with age and is good several days later thus, I like to make large quantities for parties so I can enjoy the leftovers!!

The title came about as a result of a radio interview with New York host June LeBelle, where I was asked to bring in a favorite music composition and a recipe. The work I performed was Henry Cowell's "2 Bits for Flute and Piano." The movements are titled "A Blarneying a' Bit" and "A Tuneful Bit"—thus June called my dish "A Wheatberrying A' Bit" Salad.

This is a favorite of mine at our annual "WASSAIL"—a holiday party at Christmas time. It's easy to prepare in advance and can be served at room temperature. I more than double the recipe, like 5 times more, and intensify the flavors by adding more of everything, especially the orange zest and juice of the orange. --C.W.

4 cups water
2 cups wheat berries (the <u>whole</u> berry -
     these can be found at health
     food stores) hard or soft, winter
     or spring berries, (*I have
     experimented with both*)
1 generous cup of chopped pecans
1 generous cup of dried currants

4 tablespoons of freshly chopped
     Italian parsley
1 tablespoon best quality olive oil
Grated zest of 1 medium to
     large orange and most of
     the juice of that orange
Salt and pepper to taste

Rinse berries in cold water. Cook the berries in the 4 cups water until tender, but not overcooked—'al dente'. Use the same method as cooking any whole grain, e.g., brown rice.

Drain the cooked berries if necessary and put in large bowl and refrigerate overnight. The next day, add all remaining ingredients and toss. Serve at room temperature.

Photo: VIDAL

EUGENIA ZUKERMAN, FLUTIST

A flutist of international acclaim, Eugenia Zukerman has enthralled audiences for twenty-five years with her eloquent playing and graceful stage presence. An extraordinary musician, whose communicative gifts extend to other media, Eugenia Zukerman is in great demand worldwide for regular appearances with orchestras, in solo and duo recitals, and in chamber music ensembles. Ms. Zukerman is also a successful writer and television commentator.

As a soloist, she has appeared with the English Chamber Orchestra, Stuttgart Chamber Orchestra, Israel Chamber Orchestra, Royal Philharmonic, National Symphony, Denver Chamber Orchestra, Los Angeles Philharmonic, and the Minnesota Orchestra, to name a few, and she has toured Switzerland with the Slovakian Chamber Orchestra. Festival appearances have included the Aspen Music Festival, Mostly Mozart, OK Mozart International Festival, Ravinia, Tanglewood, Bravo Chamber Festival in Colorado, Edinburgh Festival, South Bank Festival in London, Spoleto Festival in Italy, Yehudi Menuhin's Gstaad Festival in Switzerland and the Schleswig-Holstein Festival in West Germany.

Highlights of Ms. Zukerman's past season include a series of chamber music concerts with Emanuel Ax, Yo-Yo Ma and others in New York, Boston, Washington D.C., Palm Beach and Stamford, Connecticut.

Following festival performances in August 1996 at Musiksommer Gstaad, OK Mozart and Angel Fire, highlights of Ms. Zukerman's 1996-97 season include six New York appearances: at Carnegie Hall with the New York Youth Symphony she premieres *Ophelia,* written for her by composer Teddy Shapiro; at Columbia University's Miller Theater she performs with harpist Yolanda Kondonassis and the Shanghai Quartet; with keyboardist Anthony Newman, she performs at Merkin Hall and in three concerts at the New York Public Library for the thirteenth season of their popular lecture/performance series.

Eugenia Zukerman has been the television commentator on the arts for CBS *Sunday Morning* since 1980, and has appeared on a variety of other television programs. As a writer, Ms. Zukerman has been published in a number of periodicals, including the *New York Times*, *Esquire* and *Vogue.* Her first novel, *Deceptive Cadence,* was published by Viking in 1981 and a second novel, *Taking the Heat*, was published by Simon & Schuster in March, 1991. Her first screenplay was purchased by 20th Century Fox, a second was commissioned by Universal Pictures and a third was sold to MGM.

As a recording artist, Eugenia Zukerman currently records for Delos and has recorded for CBS Masterworks, Pro Arte, Vox Cum Laude and Newport Classics. Recent releases include an all-Mozart CD recorded with Anthony Newman for Newport Classics and the Concerto for Flute by Jacques Ibert on a CD entitled "Vive Ibert." Her latest CD for the Deles label, *Incantation*, music for solo flute, was released in July 1996.

Born in Cambridge, Massachusetts, Ms. Zukerman began her flute training with Carl Bergner of the Hartford Symphony. She also studied with Albert Tipton at the Aspen Music Festival and continued studies under renowned flutist Julius Baker. Having entered Barnard College as an English major, Ms. Zukerman soon transferred to the Juilliard School. In 1971, she won the Young Concert Artists Award and made her formal New York debut to rave reviews.

SALADE DE TOOT
Serves hordes (makes about 4 quarts)

2¾ to 3 pounds boneless, skinless chicken breast cut into cubes, cooked and
    chilled (poach in 9 cups boiling water for 10 minutes, drain, then chill)

6 cups of cooked wild or brown long-grain rice, chilled (roughly 2½-3 cups dry)

2 medium-large red bell peppers, cut into small pieces
2 medium ribs of celery, chopped into small pieces
½ medium red onion, diced
½ cucumber, cut into small pieces
¼ cup green onion or scallion, chopped
1½ cups sliced mushrooms
½ cup chopped walnuts

Mix all together and add following dressing.

CURRY VINAIGRETTE DRESSING
(Ma Non Troppo)

1 cup olive oil
¼ cup blueberry vinegar
2 tablespoons Dijon mustard
Juice of ½ lemon (fresh)
2 cloves fresh garlic, crushed
1 teaspoon curry powder
¼ teaspoon each of pepper and salt

Chill first if using fresh ingredients and
* blend the following:*
¼ teaspoon dry basil, or fresh to taste
¼ teaspoon dry dill, or fresh to taste
¼ teaspoon dry parsley, or fresh to taste
Dollop of mayonnaise

Mix all ingredients in blender until smooth.

GUITAR

Photo: J. HENRY FAIR

MANUEL BARRUECO, GUITARIST

Guitarist Manuel Barrueco's astounding versatility extends from his quietly commanding performances of works ranging from the old Spanish masters, through Bach and Mozart, to his work with jazz greats Chick Corea and Keith Jarrett, and to his appearances on the Lexus television commercial. In addition, he continues his recitals and orchestral engagements each season in the major music centers on four continents. As a result, the demand for Manuel Barrueco has grown in exponential proportions worldwide. An exclusive recording artist for Angel/EMI, one of his latest recordings of Beatles arrangements with the London Symphony Orchestra was released in 1995. CBS *Sunday Morning* recently commented, "There are a huge number of terrific young players out there but it has been said that Manuel Barrueco is the reigning crown prince of the current dynasty and it's enormously exciting to hear his elegant, aristocratic, lyrical playing..."

Born in Santiago de Cuba in 1952, Manuel Barrueco began playing popular Latin-American music by ear at the age of eight. Encouraged to pursue more formal training, he attended the Esteban Salas Conservatory in Santiago, where at a young age he showed the facility to learn the most difficult repertoire. After Mr. Barrueco emigrated to the United States with his family in 1967, he studied with Juan Mercadal in Miami and Rey De La Torre in New York. At the Peabody Conservatory, he studied with Aaron Shearer and became the first guitarist ever to be awarded a full scholarship to Peabody.

In 1974 Manuel Barrueco also became the first guitarist ever to win the prestigious Concert Artists Guild Award, which resulted in his New York debut. He was soon performing extensively in both the United States and Europe.

Mr. Barrueco has since performed in all major North American cities, including Alice Tully Hall in New York City, The Kennedy Center in Washington D.C., the Ambassador Foundation in Los Angeles, and the Herbst Theater in San Francisco. He is heard regularly in recital in the music capitals of Europe, such as Vienna, Berlin, Munich, Hamburg, London, Rome, Milan, Paris, Madrid and Amsterdam. In the Far East, he has appeared in both Korea and Taiwan and made his sixth concert tour in Japan in 1993. He has also appeared at the summer festivals of Tanglewood, Mostly Mozart, Schleswig-Holstein, Ludwigsburg, Avignon and Echternach in Luxembourg.

Highlights of Mr. Barrueco's recent engagements included Staatsphilharmonie Rheinland-Pfalz in Salzburg, Austria, Budapest Symphony Orchestra in Vienna, Austria, Philharmonic Orchestra of Gran Carnaria in Spain, Orquestra de Camara de Bellas Artes in Mexico, Baltimore Symphony Orchestra in Maryland, Radio Symphony Orchestra Saarbrücken (giving the world premiere of *Images*, composed by Roberto Sierra), Russian State Symphony Orchestra and Moscow Virtuosi. Among the many recent recitals he has given are performances on tour in Japan and Korea, at Wigmore Hall in London, in Milan, Berlin, Vienna and Paris, and at the Metropolitan Museum of Art in New York City. Other recent engagements include a concert at the Great Performers Series at Lincoln Center in New York City, a recording with the London Philharmonic and a premiere of the Concerto for Violin, Guitar and Orchestra by Toru Takemitsu at the Schleswig-Holstein Festival in Germany with Frank Welser-Most conducting the Ensemble Actuell.

Mr. Barrueco's best-selling recordings have been critically acclaimed worldwide. In the spring of 1988, Angel/EMI released four solo albums: *Manuel Barrueco plays Mozart and Sor;* a recording with Latin-American composers Brouwer, Villa-Lobos and Orbon; *Manuel Barrueco plays Bach and De Visse;* and a recording of solo guitar music featuring *Suite Espanola* by Albeniz and the complete works for guitar by Turina. Other recordings include: an album of Mozart duets for flute and guitar with Ransom Wilson; a recording of music by

Johann Strauss II *On the Beautiful Blue Danube* with The King's Singers and Sabine Meyer; Annie Laurie, a recording of British Folk Songs with The King's Singers; and *Manuel Barrueco Plays Granados & Falla,* with singer Ann Monoyios. One of his latest releases contains the music of Paul Simon as well as Chick Corea and Keith Jarrett. Mr. Barrueco is on the faculty of the Peabody Conservatory of Music. He is the father of two young daughters, Anna and Emily.

ROPA VIEJA
(Old Clothes)
Serves 5 to 6

This traditional Cuban recipe from Mr. Barrueco is called 'old clothes' because the meat first is cooked, but when used again later, is torn up and shredded, like second-hand clothes.

2½ **pounds flank steak**
2 **bay leaves**
¼ **cup olive oil**
1 **large onion, cut in half, thinly sliced**
1 **large green bell pepper, cut into thin strips**

2 to 3 **cloves garlic, finely chopped**
28 **oz. can whole tomatoes, drained and chopped**
½ **cup sherry or white wine**
Salt and pepper

Cover the beef and one bay leaf with salted water and cook over low heat, covered, until meat is tender (about 1 to 1½ hours).

Remove the meat from the stock and let cool. Save the meat broth. Cut the meat into 2-inch chunks.

Meanwhile, cook the onion in the olive oil over medium heat, add bell pepper and garlic, cook until the onion is tender, but the pepper is still firm. Turn heat slightly lower, add tomatoes, sherry (white wine), and the remaining bay leaf and cook uncovered for about 15 minutes.

Take the cooled 2-inch chunks of meat, shred them with your fingers, season with salt and pepper, add to tomato mixture, cover and simmer over low heat for 30 to 40 minutes. Stir occasionally, add a little beef broth if mixture gets too dry. Remove bay leaves before serving. Serve with white rice.

Photo: STUART O'SHIELDS

SHARON ISBIN, GUITARIST

Acclaimed for her extraordinary lyricism, technique, and versatility, Sharon Isbin is considered one of the finest guitarists in the world. First prize winner of the Toronto Competition, the first guitarist ever to win the Munich Competition, and a winner of the Queen Sofia Competition in Madrid, Sharon Isbin has given sold-out performances as soloist for many prestigious concerts, including the Great Performers Series in New York's Avery Fisher Hall, the Great American Orchestra Series in Carnegie Hall, Boston's Celebrity Series in Symphony Hall, the Ambassador Auditorium Series in Pasadena, and the Mostly Mozart Festival at the Kennedy Center and Lincoln Center. She has served as artistic director and featured performer of Carnegie Hall's Guitarstream International Festival, the Ordway Music Theatre's Guitarfest in St. Paul, Minnesota, and the nationally acclaimed radio series *Guitarjam*. She was recently profiled on CBS television's *Sunday Morning* program.

Ms. Isbin's numerous recordings—from Baroque, Spanish/Latin, 20th century, cross-over, to jazz fusion—reflect her remarkable versatility. Her five recent recordings for EMI/Virgin Classics—*Nightshade Rounds,* Rodrigo *Concierto de Aranjuez* (Vivaldi and Rodrigo concerti), *Love Songs and Lullabies* (with soprano Benita Valente), J.S. Bach: Complete Lute Suites*, and *Road to the Sun/Latin Romances*—have received many awards, including "Critic's Choice Recording of the Year" in *Gramophone* and *CD Review*, and "Best Recording of the Month" in *Stereo Review*. Joaquin Rodrigo praised the recording of his concerti as "magnificent."

Sharon Isbin has been acclaimed for expanding the guitar repertoire with some of the finest new works of the century. She has commissioned and premiered more concerti than any other guitarist, and numerous solo and chamber works. Recent premieres include concerti written for her by John Corigliano, with the Saint Paul Chamber orchestra conducted by Hugh Wolff; Joseph Schwantner, with the Saint Louis Symphony conducted

by Leonard Slatkin; and Lukas Foss with the Orchestra of St. Luke's, conducted by the composer. Her EMI recording with the Saint Paul Chamber Orchestra of these works is the first-ever American guitar concerto recording. Among the many other composers who have written for her are Joan Tower, David Diamond, Ned Rorem, and Leo Brouwer. Upcoming premieres will include the Concerto for Violin, Guitar, and Orchestra by Aaron Kernis, with Nadja Salerno-Sonnenberg.

Ms. Isbin's festival appearances include the Aspen, Santa Fe, Vail, Grand Teton, Bermuda, Hong Kong, Montreux, Strasbourg, Paris, Athens, Cordoba (Spain), Amsterdam (Concertgebouw), Mexico City, Istanbul, Puerto Rico, Martinique, and Budapest international festivals.

In the United States, Ms. Isbin has appeared with many major orchestras, most recently including the Minnesota Orchestra, Indianapolis Symphony, Saint Louis Symphony, Houston Symphony, Milwaukee Symphony, St. Paul Chamber Orchestra, Utah Symphony, Rochester, Brooklyn and Buffalo Philharmonic Orchestras. She is a frequent guest on National Public Radio programs, including *St. Paul Sunday Morning*, and has often appeared on Garrison Keillor's *A Prairie Home Companion*.

As a chamber musician, Ms. Isbin has performed with Nadja Salerno-Sonnenberg, Nigel Kennedy, the Emerson and Cleveland String Quartets, Ransom Wilson, Gary Karr, Carol Wincenc, the Chamber Music Society of Lincoln Center, and the New York Philharmonic Chamber Series. She has made trio recordings with Larry Coryell and Laurindo Almeida, and duo recordings with Carlos Barbosa-Lima.

Sharon Isbin began her guitar studies in Italy, and later studied with Oscar Ghiglia. A former student of Rosalyn Tureck, Ms. Isbin collaborated with the noted keyboardist in preparing performance editions of the Bach Lute Suites for guitar, recognized as the first of their kind and published by G. Schirmer, Inc. She is the author of *The Acoustic Guitar Answer Book*, and is director of the Juilliard School Guitar Department (which she created in 1989) and the Aspen Music Festival Guitar Department.

SHARON'S MANGO BLUEBERRY PIE
Makes a 10-inch pie

This pie is luscious, juicy, and naturally sweet, even without adding any sugar. It is also probably low-fat. Once made, I could eat this pie for breakfast, lunch and dinner. --S.I.

PIE CRUST:

2½ cups whole wheat flour

¼ to ½ teaspoon salt or to taste

½ cup plus 2 tablespoons canola oil

3 to 4 tablespoons cold water

FILLING:

3 very sweet ripe mangoes (about 2 cups)

2 cups of blueberries

Cinnamon to taste

5 to 6 tablespoons fruit
    sugar (fructose) (optional)

Preheat oven to 425 degrees. Mix together the flour and salt with a fork. Stir in oil until coarse crumbs have formed. Gradually sprinkle in 3 or 4 tablespoons of cold water while mixing.

In empty 10-inch pie shell, evenly press down crumbs to make a pie mold. (You will have some crumbs left over to sprinkle on top of the pie before baking). Prick the bottom a few times with a fork, then bake crust at 425 degrees until slightly golden (about 10 minutes). Remove from oven.

Peel the mangoes and cut into 1-inch chunks. Sprinkle with a bit of cinnamon.

Wash the blueberries, then add to the mangoes in a bowl. Mix in optional fruit sugar. Sprinkle more cinnamon onto the baked bottom crust. Pour in the mango-blueberry mixture. Sprinkle lightly with additional sugar (if desired).

Cover pie top with remaining crumbs and bake 40 to 50 minutes at 425 degrees until golden. Serve warm or at room temperature.

Photo: TERRY DUGGAN

CHRISTOPHER PARKENING, GUITARIST

Christopher Parkening ranks as one of the world's preeminent virtuosos of the classical guitar. For more than two decades, his concerts and recordings have received the highest worldwide acclaim. The *Washington Post* has recognized "his stature as the leading guitar virtuoso of our day, combining profound musical insight with complete technical mastery of his instrument." His former teacher, the legendary Andres Segovia, proclaimed that "Christopher Parkening is a great artist—he is one of the most brilliant guitarists in the world."

Today Christopher Parkening is the recognized heir to the Segovia tradition. His rare combination of dramatic virtuosity and eloquent musicianship has captivated audiences from New York to Tokyo. He has played at the White House at the request of the President. In 1991 he performed in the 100th anniversary celebration season at Carnegie Hall. He has also performed twice on the televised Grammy Awards and with Placido Domingo on *Live from Lincoln Center.* Parkening has appeared on many nationally broadcast television programs, including *The Today Show, The Tonight Show, 20/20,* CBS *Sunday Morning,* and *The Good Morning America Show.* He has been voted "Best Classical Guitarist" in a nationwide readers' poll of *Guitar Player* magazine for many years.

Parkening has received two Grammy nominations in the category of Best Classical Recording for *Parkening and the Guitar* and *The Pleasures of Their Company*, a collaboration with soprano Kathleen Battle. Parkening's critically acclaimed *A Tribute to Segovia* was dedicated to the great Spanish guitarist and was recorded on one of the Maestro's own concert guitars. Other recent recording releases include a collaboration with Julie Andrews in *The Sounds of Christmas* with the London Symphony Orchestra on the Hallmark label, which sold over a million copies in its first year of release. In

January 1993, EMI released Parkening's first recording of the famous guitar concerto *Concierto de Aranjuez* by Joaquin Rodrigo, together with the *Fantasia para un gentilhombre.* The album also features the world premiere recording of William Walton's *Five Bagatelles* for guitar and orchestra. Maestro Rodrigo met with Mr. Parkening at London's famous Abbey Road Studios the week prior to the recording session. They discussed interpretation and refinements in the score to create as near definitive a performance as possible. Joaquin Rodrigo calls this recording "magnificent." He was also guest of honor at Parkening's performance with the Royal Philharmonic Orchestra at the Royal Festival Hall, a concert to celebrate the composer's 90th birthday.

Recently, in celebration of Parkening's 25 years with EMI, a collection of his most popular recordings, entitled *Christopher Parkening—The Great Recordings,* was released. One recent album, *Parkening plays Vivaldi,* includes favorite Vivaldi guitar concertos and features the world premiere of Peter Warlock's *Capriol* (suite for guitar and string orchestra) with the renowned soprano Kathleen Battle.

Parkening's commitment to the guitar extends beyond his demanding performance and recording schedule. Each summer, he teaches a master class at Montana State University in Bozeman, Montana (1994's class marked the 20th anniversary). He has also authored the Christopher Parkening *Guitar Method,* Volumes I & II. At the heart of his dedication to performance, recording, and teaching, is a deep commitment to his Christian faith.

Parkening has received commendations honoring his dedication and artistry: an honorary doctorate of music from Montana State University and the Outstanding Alumnus Award from the University of Southern California "in recognition of his outstanding international achievement and in tribute to his stature throughout the world as America's preeminent virtuoso of the classical guitar."

Christopher and his wife, Barbara, an avid equestrian, and their border collie "Miss T" reside in southern California. He is a "world class" fly-fishing and casting champion who has won the International Gold Cup Tarpon Tournament (the "Wimbledon" of fly-fishing) held in Islamorada, Florida.

JESSIE LEE MARSHALL'S BUTTERMILK COFFEE CAKE
Serves 10 to 12

Christopher's favorite, with many fond memories, is my mother's coffee cake, always known as "Grandmother's Coffee Cake." Mother began baking this simple cake in the 1930's. Her kitchen would smell of cinnamon and spices when the children and I came for a visit.

When Mom came to our house, in no time at all, my kitchen too would have the fragrance of those wonderful spices. (To this day, it is also my husband Duke's favorite cake.)

Chris and his sister, Terry, would look forward to warm coffee cake with butter in the morning or coffee cake with whipped cream and hot cocoa as dessert.

Today, Terry sees that Chris has "Grandmother's Coffee Cake" at Christmas and New Year's and always on his birthday, since I now live in Idaho and they both live in Los Angeles.

Good memories are such a blessing, and it always makes me smile inside to know that the children, who loved Mom dearly, still recall those lovely times of cake, cinnamon and spice.

--Betty Parkening

2 cups flour	1 egg
¾ teaspoon nutmeg	1 cup sugar
1 teaspoon cinnamon	¼ teaspoon salt
½ teaspoon baking soda	1 cup buttermilk
1½ teaspoons baking powder	Nuts (optional)
1 stick melted butter	

Preheat oven to 350 degrees. Sift flour, add spices, baking soda and baking powder, then sift again. Cream the butter, egg, sugar and salt together, then mix in buttermilk. Add sifted flour into buttermilk mixture, slowly, until it becomes a smooth batter. Place into 9 x 9-inch greased or non-stick pan. Cover with **TOPPING** (add nuts if desired) and bake at 350 degrees for about 45 minutes or until toothpick comes out clean. Let cool slightly and put on rack.

TOPPING:

½ cup brown sugar	Nuts (optional)
¾ teaspoon cinnamon	

Mix sugar and cinnamon together. Spread over batter before baking. Dot with butter and nuts.

HARP

Photo: TANIA MARA (N.Y.C.)

YOLANDA KONDONASSIS, HARPIST

Yolanda Kondonassis has become established as one of America's foremost solo harpists since her debut at the age of eighteen with the New York Philharmonic and Zubin Mehta. Praised by *American Record Guide* for her "rare combination of musicianship and virtuosity," she has appeared as a concerto soloist and recitalist in major cities throughout the United States, Europe, and the Far East. Her guest artist credits include concerto performances with the Cleveland Orchestra, the Detroit Symphony, the Houston Symphony, the North Carolina Symphony, and the New World Symphony. As a recording artist, Ms. Kondonassis has received the highest critical acclaim for her discs on the Telarc label, *Scintillation* and *A New Baroque*.

Ms. Kondonassis's long list of honors includes the distinction of being the first harpist ever to win first prize in prestigious competitions open to all instrumentalists, such as the Ima Hogg National Young Artists Competition and the Naftzger Competition. She has also garnered top prizes in other major competitions, including the Affiliate Artists National Auditions and the Maria Korchinska International Harp Competition in Great Britain. The recipient of two Solo Recitalist's grants from the National Endowment for the Arts, Ms. Kondonassis was the first harpist to receive the Darius Milhaud Prize and is actively involved in the commissioning and performance of contemporary music.

As a devoted chamber musician, Ms. Kondonassis has performed at the festivals of Marlboro, Spoleto, Tanglewood, and with members of the Vermeer, Guarneri, and Alban Berg String Quartets. She is co-founder and co-artistic director of the seventeen-member chamber music ensemble, *Myriad*, and also maintains a busy concert schedule as half of the Kondonassis/Zukerman Duo with flutist and CBS arts commentator, Eugenia Zukerman.

Yolanda Kondonassis was born in Norman, Oklahoma and began studying the harp at the age of nine. She attended Interlochen Arts Academy as a high school student and continued her studies at the Cleveland Institute of Music, where she received a bachelor and master degree in music performance as a student of Alice Chalifoux. Ms. Kondonassis is based in New York City.

POTATO-CRUSTED CHICKEN

Serves 4

Chicken and carbohydrates are a must for me before every performance; this is one of my favorite recipes that combines both and tastes wonderful! Since I rarely have time to get creative in the kitchen, "Potato-Crusted Chicken" is a specialty of one of my dearest friends and most-admired cooks, Jasmine Fiore. --Y.K.

2 whole chicken breasts, split, washed
    and patted dry
1 large Idaho potato, peeled and
    finely shredded (about 2 cups)
¼ cup finely diced onion

1 teaspoon olive oil
¼ cup chopped parsley
2 cloves garlic, peeled
¼ cup coarse grain white wine mustard
Cracked pepper to taste

Place potato shreds in a bowl and cover with cold water. Let stand 5 minutes, then drain and pat dry. Add diced onion, sprinkle with olive oil, and toss.

In a food processor or blender, place parsley and garlic and process until garlic is minced. Add mustard and blend 10 seconds. Evenly divide mustard mixture between the chicken breasts and spread to coat evenly. Spread potato shreds evenly over chicken breasts.

Place coated chicken breasts on broiler pan, fitted with a rack, and sprinkle with cracked pepper. Bake in preheated oven at 375 degrees for 30 minutes, or until chicken is cooked through. After chicken is cooked, turn on broiler for 3 to 5 minutes until potato crust is golden.

Photo: WARREN BOND

SUSANN McDONALD, HARPIST

Among those rare internationally celebrated artists who combine great depth of musical artistry with a rare ability to communicate with an audience, Susann McDonald must be counted in the top echelon. Possessing an enormous repertoire, her exciting recitals illustrate the incredible range of compositions which has been written for the harp over the centuries. Miss McDonald's fame is further enhanced by her numerous best-selling harp recordings.

A master teacher, she served as head of the harp department at the Juilliard School for ten years (1975-85) until she accepted the chairpersonship of the largest harp department in the world at Indiana University. She is one of two women presently at this famed School of Music to receive the rank of distinguished professor of music.

Miss McDonald's personal charm and enlightening commentaries about the harp and its intricacies result in musical delight for her audiences everywhere. She has toured coast to coast, captivating audiences in the United States, as well as performing and teaching master classes in South America, Europe, Japan, South Korea, Taiwan and China.

Her students hold important orchestral positions throughout the world, including the Philadelphia Orchestra, the New York Philharmonic, the Metropolitan Opera, the Berlin Philharmonic, the Orchestra Nationale de France, the Seattle Symphony, the Detroit Symphony, and numerous others. Many of her students are also major teachers and concert artists. Numerous well-known composers have written and dedicated new compositions for her and she has composed and published many volumes of harp music.

Susann McDonald has served as the artistic director of the World Harp Congress since its inception and is the founder and music director of the famed U.S.A. International Harp Competition. She is also honorary president of the Association Internationale des Harpistes in Paris.

Miss McDonald studied in Paris with Henriette Renie and Lily Laskine and was the first American harpist to receive the "premier prix" from the Paris Conservatory. She has a chalet near Villars, Switzerland, where she conducts annual summer harp master classes for students who come from throughout the world to study under her superb guidance. She also appears frequently on the *Joy of Music* television program and performs in duo-recitals with famed organist, Diane Bish.

KEY LIME PIE
Makes one 9-inch pie

I have a friend who brings me Key limes from Florida for this recipe, which is so easy to make and really delicious! If one wishes for a more tart taste, you can increase the amount of lime juice.
--S.M.

½ cup fresh Key lime juice
2 egg yolks
15 oz. can sweetened condensed milk

9-inch graham cracker pie crust
Whipping cream
Lime slices (for garnish)

Squeeze ½ cup fresh Key lime juice. Beat together 2 egg yolks and condensed milk with lime juice until mixture increases in volume and is frothy.

Pour into graham cracker crust and refrigerate or freeze. Top with whipping cream and garnish with small pieces of lime.

Photo: SUSAN WILSON

ANN HOBSON PILOT, HARPIST

Ann Hobson Pilot, principal harpist of the Boston Symphony Orchestra, began her musical education at the age of six with piano lessons from her mother, a former concert pianist and a teacher in the Philadelphia public schools. In her teens, Miss Hobson began studying the harp with Mary Ann Castaldo while attending the Philadelphia High School for Girls. She continued her training at the Philadelphia Musical Academy with Marilyn Costello.

In the summer of 1962, Ms. Hobson Pilot spent the first of many summers at the Salzedo Harp Colony in Camden, Maine, studying with Alice Chalifoux who was to become her major influence on the harp. Ms. Hobson later transferred to the Cleveland Institute of Music to continue her harp studies with Ms. Chalifoux and graduated in 1966 with a bachelor of music degree.

Ms. Hobson Pilot's first professional appointment came with the Pittsburgh Symphony in the 1965-1966 season when she was employed as substitute second harpist. In the fall of 1966, she became the principal harpist of the Washington National Symphony where she stayed until 1969, when she won the audition to join the Boston Symphony Orchestra. She was named principal harpist of the Boston Symphony Orchestra in 1980.

In addition to solo appearances with the Boston Symphony and the Boston Pops, she has been invited to appear as guest soloist with many American orchestras. In August of 1988, she performed the Mozart Flute and Harp Concerto with flutist James Galway and the Boston Symphony Orchestra for the "Tanglewood on Parade" concert. Ms. Pilot has participated in the Marlboro Music Festival, has performed with the Boston Symphony Chamber Players, is a member of the contemporary music ensemble "Collage," and is the founder of the New England Harp Trio.

Ms. Hobson Pilot is currently a member of the faculties of the New England Conservatory of Music and the Tanglewood Music Center. She delighted her Chinese hosts in 1979 by conducting master classes during the Boston Symphony Orchestra's historic tour of the People's Republic of China. She has also performed with the St. Trinity Orchestra of Port-Au-Prince, Haiti, as well as in Europe and Japan. Her numerous awards include presentations from the Pro Arts Society of Philadelphia in 1987 and the Boston Chapter of Girl Friends in 1988. Sigma Alpha Iota, an international music fraternity, presented Ann Hobson Pilot with its annual Distinguished Woman of the Year Award for 1991, and the Philadelphia College of Performing Arts School of Music (formerly called the Philadelphia Musical Academy) granted her the 1992 School of Music Alumni Achievement Award. In 1993 she was awarded the Distinguished Alumni Award from the Cleveland Institute of Music.

In addition to her many recordings with the Boston Symphony Orchestra and the Boston Pops, Ms. Hobson Pilot can be heard on many chamber music recordings: Debussy's Trio for Flute, Viola and Harp, released by Deutsche Grammophon; Thomas Oboe Lee's *The Mad Frog*, released by GunMar; and *Ennanga* for solo harp with accompaniment of piano and string quintet by William Grant Still on New World Records, are a few examples. She has recently released her first solo recording to critical acclaim on the Boston Records Classical label. She has also recorded the Norman Dello Joio Harp Concerto with the New Zealand Chamber Orchestra, James Sedares conducting, on KOCH International Classics.

Ms. Pilot is involved in community affairs in the Boston area. She and her husband, Prentice, have been instrumental in the formation of the Boston Music Education Collaborative, and she is directing a troubadour harp program at the Martin Luther King Middle School in Dorchester.

SAUTÉED VEAL SCALOPPINE WITH CREAM SAUCE

Serves 6

Ms. Pilot's recipe was inspired from her period of living in southern France.

8 veal scaloppine (1½ to 2 pounds) sliced
     ½-inch thick, against the grain, and
     pounded flat to ¼-inch thickness
Salt
Freshly ground black pepper
Flour
3 tablespoons butter

1 tablespoon vegetable oil
2 tablespoons finely chopped shallots
     or scallions
½ cup dry white wine
½ cup heavy cream
Several drops of lemon juice
Fresh parsley sprigs

Season the scaloppine with salt and a few grindings of pepper. Cover them with flour and then shake them vigorously to remove all but a light dusting. In a 10 to 12-inch enameled or stainless skillet, melt the butter with the oil over moderate heat. When the foam subsides, brown the scaloppine for 3 to 4 minutes on each side, or until they are a light golden color. Remove them from the pan and set aside. Pour off almost all the fat from the skillet, leaving just enough to make a thin film on the bottom.

Stir in the shallots and cook slowly for a moment. Pour in the wine and bring it to a boil over high heat, stirring and scraping in any browned bits that cling to the bottom or sides of the pan. Boil for 2 to 3 minutes until the wine has been reduced to about ¼ cup.

Reduce heat, stir in the cream and simmer, stirring constantly, for 3 to 5 minutes, or until the sauce thickens. Taste, then season with a few drops of lemon juice, salt and pepper.

Return the scaloppine to the skillet, baste with the sauce and cook just long enough to heat the scaloppine through.

Arrange the scaloppine, overlapping them slightly, down the center of a heated serving platter; pour the sauce over them, decorate with parsley, and serve at once.

HARPSICHORD

Photo: CHRISTIAN STEINER

ALBERT FULLER, HARPSICHORDIST

Since making his Carnegie Recital Hall debut in 1957, harpsichordist Albert Fuller has come to occupy a prominent position in American musical life, performing solo recitals and chamber concerts, conducting, and speaking throughout the United States and Europe. In addition to his reputation as improvisor of the *basso continuo,* he has made important contributions to the interpretation of solo harpsichord literature with his performances and recordings of Rameau, Scarlatti, Bach, Le Roux, and the Couperins.

Schooled initially at the Washington National Cathedral, and subsequently at the Georgetown, Johns Hopkins, and Yale Universities, he has served on the faculty of the Juilliard School since 1963, developing and sharing with students his philosophy that the understanding of music is sharpened and enriched by viewing it in historical, philosophical, and economic milieux.

In 1972, he founded the Aston Magna Festival that takes place each summer in Great Barrington, Massachusetts, where he served as artistic director and, until 1983, as president of the Aston Magna Foundation. Under his direction the annual concerts of the festival traversed the entire body of chamber and orchestral literature from Monteverdi to Beethoven, becoming the chief catalyst of the original-instruments movement in America. In 1978, Mr. Fuller expanded Aston Magna's vision with the institution of annual academies, designed as gathering places for the exchange of ideas among scholars, aestheticians, and humanists, as well as musicians, several generations of which have been influenced by his teaching and scholarship.

Mr. Fuller has conducted modern premiere productions of Rameau's *Les Indes Galantes* in Chicago, Rameau's *Dardanus*, and Handel's *Xerxes* (1984, in his new English translation) for the American Opera Center in New York, and, most recently, Bach's *St. John Passion* and Mass in B Minor, *Magnificats* by both J.S. and C.P.E. Bach, and Vivaldi, and Handel's *L'Allegro ed Il Penseroso* for the Connecticut Early Music Festival.

Fuller has been a member of the Visiting Committee to the Music Department of Harvard University (1977-83) and a member of the Yale University Council Committee on Music (1983-89). His present activities as president and artistic director of the Helicon Foundation aim to stimulate public interest in music and the other arts as the principal recorded sources of mankind's conscious awareness. Fuller is currently at work on a new musical CD-ROM concept.

GNOCCHI DI SEMOLINO ALLA ROMANA
(An Italian First Course)
Serves 6

I discovered this first dish, "Gnocchi di Semolino alla Romana," on my initial visit to Rome, and thereby found a glorified version of my first childhood cereal. Now I could drink a fine white wine, perhaps a Pino Grigio, with my Cream of Wheat as a first course, then go on to fine Roman entrées, etc. --A.F.

1 quart milk
Salt and pepper to taste
Pinch of nutmeg
1 cup *regular* Cream of Wheat, or,
    if possible, real Italian semolino

2 tablespoons butter
3 eggs, beaten
½ cup Parmesan cheese
Meat and tomato sauce (optional)

In 3 or 4-quart pan, bring milk to slow boil, season with salt, pepper and nutmeg. Gradually pour in Cream of Wheat or semolino. Stir constantly until thick and smooth. Remove from heat. Add 2 tablespoons butter and beaten eggs, a little at a time. Add Parmesan cheese. Mix well. Pour onto a buttered cookie sheet (at least 10 x 15-inch) and spread into a one-half-inch layer. Allow to cool for an hour.

Cut into rounds with a small glass or biscuit cutter. Overlap each piece in an attractive pattern in a buttered baking dish. Dot with plenty of butter and grated cheese.

Put dish into a hot oven and brown at 375-400 degrees. The rounds could be arranged in 2 layers, and/or spread with meat or tomato sauce, sprinkled with cheese and browned in oven.

CIVET DE MOUTON
(A French Main Course)
Serves 6

This second recipe, "Civet de Mouton," was a favorite of mine, discovered while living in Paris in the 50's. Although I had long liked to cook and often tried to make this dish, until Julia Child's "Mastering The Art of French Cooking" came out in 1961, I could not find the ultimate secret of it. That principal secret in Julia's recipe for me was, <u>drying the meat well before sautéing it, a few pieces at a time</u>, and then browning it further in the oven, as explained below. --A.F.

6 oz. bacon	1 tablespoon tomato paste
3 pounds well dried lamb (all one cut or a variety of cuts)	2 cloves garlic, mashed
1 large carrot, sliced	½ teaspoon thyme, dried
1 large onion, sliced	1 bay leaf, crushed
Salt and pepper to taste	2 dozen little white onions
2 tablespoons flour	1 pound fresh button mushrooms, cut into quarters
3 cups good red wine	
Beef broth (only enough to cover lamb)	

Preheat oven to 450 degrees. Cut bacon into slices the size of match sticks, simmer in water for 10 minutes, drain and dry. Sauté bacon in dutch oven 2 to 3 minutes until light brown, remove and set aside.

Cut lamb into 2-inch cubes and sauté in bacon fat, just a few at a time, until browned on all sides. When browned, set lamb cubes aside with bacon. In same fat, sauté carrot and onion until carrot is slightly tender. Set aside and pour out fat. Return lamb and bacon to casserole, toss with salt and pepper and sprinkle with flour. Place uncovered casserole in a preheated oven for 4 minutes, then remove. Toss meat and return to oven for 4 more minutes to brown flour to a light crust. Lower oven to 325 degrees.

Stir in 3 cups of wine and enough beef broth barely to cover lamb. Add tomato paste, garlic, thyme and bay leaf. Bring to simmer on stove, cover and place in oven, simmer slowly for 2 hours, until tender to the fork.

Meanwhile, braise white onions in brown stock, sauté in butter fresh mushrooms. Pour meat and sauce into a sieve set over a sauce pan. Wash out dutch oven, return lamb and bacon to it, with onions, carrots and mushrooms on top. Skim fat off sauce, it should coat a spoon lightly. If too thin, boil down rapidly. If too thick, add a little broth. Check for seasoning and pour sauce over meat and vegetables. Simmer covered for 2 to 3 minutes and serve with boiled potatoes, garnished with parsley.

Photo: KEN VEEDER

MALCOLM HAMILTON, HARPSICHORDIST

Malcolm Hamilton, critically acclaimed as a leading exponent of the harpsichord, has more than borne out the hopes and prophesies of his mentor and colleague, the renowned Alice Ehlers. Today his name falls easily within the elite of the 18th century instrument—Landowska, Ehlers, Kipnis, Kirkpatrick, and Puyana.

A native of Victoria, B.C., Dr. Hamilton earned his bachelor and master degrees in music at the University of Washington prior to moving to Los Angeles to study with Mme. Ehlers at the University of Southern California, where he completed his doctorate in music, founded the USC Baroque Society, and today is on the faculty as professor of harpsichord and piano.

He has appeared throughout North America with major orchestras under such distinguished conductors as Sir John Barbirolli, Sir Neville Marriner, Gerard Schwarz, and Gerard Samuel.

His recordings include the complete Well-Tempered Clavier of Bach on the Everest label, the complete Brandenburg Concertos on Angel, performances of Handel and Scarlatti on Delos, and concertos by C.P.E. Bach on Nonesuch.

His recitals are numerous and include appearances on such prestigious concert series as Ambassador Auditorium in Pasadena, the Carmel Bach Festival, and the Cabrillo Festival.

Dr. Hamilton, in his New York debut, prompted the *New York Times* critic to exclaim "...one of the best recitals this listener has ever heard."

MOUSSE OF RHUBARB

If you would like to serve a sauce with this, cook enough rhubarb to make an extra cup of the purée (about another half pound). Mix 1 cup of the purée and a little of the juice. Put through a sieve or whirl in a blender or food processor. Pour around the mousse. --M.H.

1¼ pounds rhubarb	**1 envelope plain gelatin**
1 cup sugar	**2 cups sweetened whipped cream**
Several tablespoons water	

Cut rhubarb into 1-inch lengths. Put into a saucepan with the sugar and water. Bring to a boil. Lower heat, cover pan and simmer until tender (20 to 25 minutes). Remove from heat and take out enough of the rhubarb to make one-half cup. Reserve. Drain the remaining rhubarb and purée it in a food processor.

Dissolve gelatin in ¼ cup boiling water and add to the 2 cups of purée. Cool slightly. Fold in the cut rhubarb and the whipped cream. Put it into a mold and chill thoroughly. Remove mold to serve and decorate top with pieces of rhubarb or strawberry.

ESCALOPES DE VOLAILLE A LA NORMANDE
(Chicken Breasts with Apples, Cream, and Calvados)
Serves 6

3 whole chicken breasts, split, skinned and boned	½ cup butter or margarine
½ cup all-purpose flour	½ cup Calvados or apple brandy
1½ teaspoons salt	1 cup heavy cream
¼ teaspoon pepper	1 can (20 oz.) pie-sliced apples, drained

Flatten chicken breasts between sheets of waxed paper to about ¼ inch thickness. Dredge in a mixture of flour, salt and pepper, shake off excess. Chill. Reserve 2 tablespoons flour. In large skillet, heat butter until sizzling and sauté the chicken cutlets, 3 at a time, 2 to 3 minutes per side, or until tender. Drain on paper towels and keep warm.

Stir reserved flour into pan drippings and add Calvados. Stir the pan to scrape away all brown particles, then blend in heavy cream and apples. Season generously with additional salt and pepper to taste.

Stir gently over low heat until sauce thickens. **Do not boil!** Pour sauce over chicken and serve with baby carrots and brandied applesauce. Garnish with watercress.

Photo: DRUCE REILEY

EIJI HASHIMOTO, HARPSICHORDIST

Born in Tokyo, Eiji Hashimoto graduated from the Tokyo University of Fine Arts and Music (B.Mus. in organ), the University of Chicago (M.A. in composition and musicology), and Yale University School of Music (M.M. in harpsichord). After a year of teaching at Toho Gakuen School of Music in Tokyo, he received a grant for musicological research in Paris in 1967; his ensuing U.S. tour resulted in an invitation in 1968 to join the faculty of the University of Cincinnati, College-Conservatory of Music, where he is now professor of harpsichord and harpsichordist-in-residence.

His concert activities have taken him to most major cities across the U.S.A. and produced over fifty international tours to Australia and the countries of Austria, Belgium, Brazil, Canada, Chile, England, Finland, France, Germany, Holland, Hong Kong, Iran, Italy, Japan, Luxembourg, Mexico, New Zealand, the Philippines, Spain, Switzerland, and Venezuela. He has received various prizes and awards, including the Prize of Excellence (Japanese Ministry of Cultural Affairs, 1978 and 1981); the Rieveschl Award for Excellence in Scholarly and Creative Works (University of Cincinnati, 1984); the Ohio Arts Council Solo Artist grant (Ohio Arts Council, 1987-present); and the Arts Midwest Performing Arts Touring Program (1990-present).

Hashimoto's recordings include a dozen solo LP or CD albums from the Musical Heritage Society, Fontec, Camerata Tokyo, and Klavier Records. He has published editions of eighteenth century keyboard works from Zen On, G. Schirmer, Heugel, and Oxford University Press.

He is director of the Ensemble for Eighteenth Century Music, a chamber orchestra at the University of Cincinnati's College-Conservatory of Music, and is actively involved in conducting various other chamber orchestras.

EIJI HASHIMOTO'S GOMOKU MESHI (FIVE-COLOR RICE)

Serves 4
Preparation time 2 hours

RICE:

2½ cups short-grain rice
   (Japanese rice is best)
2½ cups water

Several sheets of *nori*,
   (toasted seaweed) for topping
Dash of salt

Rinse rice in bowl until water becomes clear. Pour into a strainer and allow to stand for about 10 minutes until all excess water has drained. Put rice into a rice cooker (or a 2-quart pan with a tightly

fitting lid). Add 2½ cups of cold water with a dash of salt and cover. If using a rice cooker, turn on and cook until it shuts itself off. If using a regular pan, bring to a boil over high heat, then reduce heat and simmer with lid on until all of the water is absorbed. Do not stir as it is cooking. Be careful not to burn on the bottom, but rice should not be mushy. Once rice is cooked, allow to stand <u>covered</u> in the pan until you are ready to mix in the other ingredients.

GINGER:

"Knuckle" of fresh ginger root	**Dash of salt**
Rice vinegar (osu)	**Dash of sugar**

Wash and peel ginger. Slice lengthwise very thinly. Stack the slices and slice lengthwise again to make thin slivers. Place in a small bowl and pour over it just enough rice vinegar to cover. Add just a sprinkle each of salt and sugar. (Some rice vinegar already has salt and sugar added. If you are using this kind, you do not need to add more). Set aside and allow to marinate until serving time.

CARROT MIXTURE:

3 shiitake (Japanese mushrooms), fresh or dried	**4 medium-sized button mushrooms**
2 medium-sized carrots	**2 teaspoons sugar**
2 squares of *age* (pronounced "ah-gay"), which is fried tofu	**¾ cup water**
	¼ cup soy sauce (Japanese)
	½ cup *sake* (Japanese rice wine)

If using dried shiitake, cover with boiling water and allow to soak for about 10 minutes.

Wash and peel 2 carrots. Cut each into three pieces, then thinly slice each third lengthwise, and, like the ginger, cut each slice lengthwise again to make slivers about the size of wooden match sticks. Place in a 2-quart sauce pan. Thinly slice 2 squares of *age* to make strips a little longer than the carrot slivers and add these to the carrots. Squeeze water out of the shiitake (or simply wash shiitake, if using fresh ones). Reserve soaking water. Cut off tough stems and discard. Slice shiitake thinly and add to carrot mixture. Wash and thinly slice the 4 button mushrooms and add to carrots. Add the 2 teaspoons sugar, the shiitake soaking water plus enough additional water to make ¾ cup, Japanese soy sauce and *sake*. Cover and bring to a boil, then reduce heat and simmer for 15 to 20 minutes, or until carrots are tender but still slightly crunchy. (Water can be added during cooking if liquid evaporates too quickly). When done, pour into a bowl and set aside to cool. (Do not drain off liquid).

GREEN BEANS:

6 to 8 fresh green beans
Dash of salt

Wash green beans and slice diagonally very thinly to make 1-inch slivers. (One-half package of French style frozen green beans may be used instead, but fresh ones are better). Place in a small pan and cover with water. Bring to a boil and cook until just tender, but still crisp. If you cook them too long, they will lose their bright green color. At the very end of the cooking time, add a dash of salt. Remove from heat, drain and pour into a bowl to cool.

EGG:

2 eggs
1 teaspoon *sake*
2 teaspoons sugar and dash of salt
½ teaspoon soy sauce

Crack eggs into a small bowl. Add 2 teaspoons of sugar, a dash of salt, 1 teaspoon *sake,* and ½ teaspoon soy sauce and beat well. Pour a very small amount of oil into a 10-inch skillet (preferably with a non-stick coating). Heat over a low flame for about 1 minute, but do not let the pan get so hot that the egg mixture will scorch when it is poured in. (It should cover the bottom of the skillet, like a very thin pancake). Allow egg to 'set', but be careful not to let it turn brown on the bottom. If the top does not seem to be setting quickly enough, you can gently cut slits into the egg with a spatula and tip the pan slightly to allow the uncooked egg from the top to run into the slits. When the egg is set (it can still be slightly soft on top), cut it in half and very carefully turn each half so that the top cooks. When it is solid (but not browned), remove from pan and allow to cool on a plate. When cool, divide each half again. Stack and slice very thinly to make narrow strips. Set aside.

In a measuring cup or small bowl, combine ⅓ cup of rice vinegar, a sprinkle of salt and ½ teaspoon of sugar. (Again, if you are using seasoned vinegar, you will not need to add salt and sugar). While the rice is still fairly hot, transfer it into a large serving bowl (a wide, fairly shallow bowl works best). With a wooden spoon or shamoji (Japanese rice spoon), cut into the rice a number of times to separate the grains. Gradually pour the seasoned vinegar over the rice and mix it in by scooping rice from the sides of the bowl to the center and then cutting into the center with the shamoji. Rotate the bowl slightly and repeat. Be careful not to mash the rice. The idea is to toss it lightly so that the vinegar is distributed throughout. As you are mixing in the vinegar, fan the rice with a Japanese fan, or a magazine will work. *It helps to have another person do the fanning!* This makes the vinegar evaporate from the hot rice, leaving the flavor but keeping it from becoming mushy.

After the vinegar is mixed in, drain the liquid from the carrot mixture and set aside. Put the **carrot mixture** and **green beans** on top of the rice. In the same way that you mixed in the vinegar, gently cut in the vegetables until they are well distributed throughout the rice. Distribute the **slivered egg** over the top of the rice, but do not stir in. Just before serving, cut a sheet of the toasted seaweed (*nori*) into thin slivers and sprinkle them over the top of the rice. **Serve the ginger** as a condiment to be put on the rice. (It is quite spicy, so just a few of the slivers are enough to add a nice flavor).

Photo: TANIA MARA (N.Y.C.)

ANTHONY NEWMAN, HARPSICHORDIST/ORGANIST

For thirty years, the multifaceted Anthony Newman has been in the public eye as one of the country's leading organ virtuosos and as a prodigiously active harpsichordist, fortepianist, organist, conductor, composer, writer and recording artist. His more than 100 releases on such labels as CBS Masterworks/Sony Classical, Newport Classic Recordings, Moss Music Group, Musical Heritage Society and Connoisseur cover a full range of styles from the 17th century to the 20th century. Many of his recordings have been singled out for excellence, and his 1989 fortepiano performance of Beethoven's Third Concerto was chosen by *Stereo Review* as "Record of the Year."

In 1992, to mark the 25th anniversary of Mr. Newman's first public appearance, Newport Classics released five CDs covering the full range of his artistry: an album of popular Bach organ works; the complete Mozart sonatas for fortepiano and flute with Eugenia Zukerman; favorite hymns with trumpet descants; a recording of Newman conducting his own orchestral works; and the eight Suites for harpsichord by Handel. Recordings of the Brandenburg Concertos, with his period instrument Brandenburg Collegium, and of Bach's organ "Clavierubung III," are among his upcoming releases on that label. A frequent collaborator with many notable artists, Mr. Newman has also recorded recently for both Sony Classical and Deutsche Grammophon with Kathleen Battle, Itzhak Perlman and Wynton Marsalis.

In past years, his orchestral engagements included appearances as conductor and soloist with the Saint Paul Chamber Orchestra, the Calgary Philharmonic, the Colorado Symphony and the Rishon Symphony in Israel. During the summer of 1993, Mr. Newman performed on the new Fisk organ at the Meyerson Center with the Dallas Symphony, gave a recital on the Ahrend organ at the Oregon Bach Festival, and performed and taught in Poland and Eastern Europe.

Mr. Newman's duo recitals with flutist Eugenia Zukerman are heard from Washington to Los Angeles and are now in their thirteenth season at the New York Public Library. His performances with soprano Julianne Baird and the Brandenberg Collegium have been enthusiastically received in cities across the country, and his solo appearances as an organist and harpsichordist in New York, Atlanta, Chicago, Louisville, San Francisco, Mexico City, Paris, Prague and Vienna have confirmed his reputation as one of the keyboard masters of his generation.

In previous seasons, Anthony Newman has been a guest with many major orchestras and has appeared on national television in the "Gala of Stars" special. He has conducted the Los Angeles Chamber, Mostly Mozart Festival, and Scottish Chamber Orchestras. A frequent guest with the Chamber Music Society of Lincoln Center, he was a consultant in the selection of an organ for Alice Tully Hall and was invited to perform on the instrument for Miss Tully's 90th birthday celebration.

Born in Boston, Mr. Newman studied in Paris with Alfred Cortot, Nadia Boulanger and the famed organist Pierre Cochereau. He received a Diplome Superieur from the Ecole Normale de Musique with a special commendation from Cortot. In the U.S., Newman trained with pianist Edith Oppens, composers Leon Kirchner and Luciano Berio, and served as choral assistant to New York Pro Musica Director, Noah Greenberg. Mr. Newman's own teaching career has included positions at several distinguished institutions, and he currently heads the graduate music program at the State University of New York at Purchase.

CABBAGE SOUP

Makes 9 to 10 cups

1 medium green cabbage, cored and chopped
1¾ cups yellow onions, chopped
¼ stick unsalted butter
1 teaspoon rosemary
1 teaspoon dried thyme

5 cups fresh chicken broth
Salt and pepper to taste
¼ teaspoon cayenne pepper, or to taste
Chopped almonds for topping
Roquefort cheese for topping

In a large pot, sauté onions in butter until translucent. Add remaining ingredients through chicken broth.

Bring to a boil and simmer until cabbage is soft (about 30 minutes). Remove one-half of the ingredients with a slotted spoon and process in a blender until smooth. Return blended ingredients to pot. Mix well and season with salt, pepper and cayenne pepper.

Reheat and top with Roquefort cheese and almonds.

OBOE, BASSOON, CLARINET & SAXOPHONE

Photo: TIM LEYES

JAMES CAMPBELL, CLARINETIST

James Campbell is one of the few classical clarinetists today enjoying an international solo career. His concerts have taken him to the major concert halls of North and South America, East and West Europe, Japan, Asia and Australia.

He has performed as soloist with over 50 orchestras, including the London Symphony Orchestra, the Philharmonia of London, the London Philharmonic, the Toronto Symphony, the National Radio-Television Orchestra of Spain, the Belgrade Symphony, the Vancouver Symphony and the National Arts Centre Orchestra Ottawa, to name but a few. In 1989, he was named Canada's "Artist of the Year" and also received the Roy Thomson Hall Award. In the same year, his album "Stolen Gems" won a Juno Award, Canada's citation for outstanding recordings.

James Campbell has collaborated with many of the world's greatest musicians, including five television programs with the late Glenn Gould, performances with Elly Ameling, Janos Starker and Aaron Copland, as well as with the Amadeus, Guarneri, Fine Arts, Allegri, Colorado, Manhattan and Orford String Quartets. His CD/discography contains over 25 albums and includes the Weber Clarinet Concerto with the London Symphony Orchestra, Debussy's *Premiere Rhapsodie* with the Philharmonia of London, and the Mozart and Copland Concertos with the National Arts Centre Orchestra. His recording of the quintets of Mozart and Weber with the Orford Quartet and his CDs with the Borodin Trio have won much international critical acclaim.

James Campbell is the artistic director of the annual Canadian summer music festival "The Festival of the Sound" in Parry Sound, Ontario. He has taken the festival to England on three separate occasions, with concerts at the Wigmor Hall and St. John's Smith Square in London and the Pump Room in Bath. Under the directorship of James Campbell, the festival has been the subject of documentary programs on BBC Television, CBC Television and TV Ontario. His collaboration with jazz pianist Gene DiNovi has become very popular and a CD - "After Hours" - has just been released.

Campbell is one of the clarinetists featured in the book by British author and clarinet authority, Pamela Weston, entitled *Clarinet Virtuosi of Today*.

Highlights of recent seasons include chamber and solo tours of Britain, a recording with the London Symphony Orchestra, a tour of Australia and concerts and festivals coast to coast in Canada and the United States. During the past season, in addition to concerts in Europe and North America, James Campbell was in Japan for concerto performances. He is also recording a set of CDs for Cala Records of London, encompassing the complete repertoire of French chamber music for winds, and producing another CD for Marquis Records, of the Brahms sonatas with pianist Leonard Hokanson. James Campbell is professor of music at the Indiana University School of Music in Bloomington, Indiana.

WHOLE WHEAT BREAD

Makes 3 loaves

This recipe is my mother's, Margorie Campbell. The bread is so delicious my wife now cooks 3 loaves each week. --J.C.

1 egg, beaten
2 teaspoons salt
¼ cup oil

¼ cup honey
3½ cups white flour
4½ cups whole wheat flour

YEAST MIXTURE:
½ cup very warm water
½ teaspoon sugar

2 packages dry yeast (not instant)

Add 2½ cups **hot** water to egg, salt, oil and honey. Mix well. Add white flour and beat out lumps. Add **yeast mixture**, stir until mixed. Add whole wheat flour, knead for 5 minutes.

Cover bowl with damp cloth. Allow to rise in warm place for about 20 minutes.

When doubled in size and spongy to touch, turn onto floured surface, beat down and knead into shape. Put into greased pans. Let rise 20 plus minutes.

Bake at 350 to 375 degrees for 35 minutes, or until bread sounds hollow when tapped on bottom.

Some tips about cooking: save water used when boiling potatoes for use in bread. Use high-gluten white flour if possible. Substitute ½ cup fresh wheat germ for ½ cup whole wheat flour.

Photo: JOYCE WILSON

ELI EBAN, CLARINETIST

Eli Eban began his professional career as principal clarinetist of the Israel Radio Symphony under Lukas Foss. He subsequently joined the Israel Philharmonic Orchestra, where he played thirteen seasons under Mehta, Bernstein, Barenboim, Solti, Dohnányi, Masur, Tennstedt, Levine, and other internationally renowned conductors.

Mr. Eban's numerous concerto appearances with the Israel Philharmonic include the world premiere of Lalo Shifrin's Capriccio for Clarinet and Orchestra, dedicated to the State of Israel, with the composer conducting. He has also appeared as soloist with the Camerata Academica Orchestra of the Salzburg Mozarteum and the Concerto Soloists of Philadelphia.

In 1984, Eban performed the Mozart Clarinet Concerto with the City of London Sinfonia at Royal Festival Hall and has since returned to London as soloist with the English Chamber Orchestra. He also has been a participant in the IMS concert series directed by Sandor Vegh, drawing critical acclaim from the London Guardian for his "high-powered, electrifying performance." His subsequent CD recordings for Meridian records, London, were cited by the 1988 Penguin Guide as being "full of life and highly sensitive."

Mr. Eban has toured extensively as a chamber musician, performing in Israel, Europe, Singapore, Japan, Australia, Canada, and the United States. He has been guest artist with the Alexander, Audubon, Tel Aviv and Ying String Quartets, and a participant of the Marlboro, Carmel Bach, Chautauqua, Windsor (England) and Prague Music Festivals. Mr. Eban is currently a member of "Myriad," a chamber ensemble formed by members of the Cleveland Orchestra.

A graduate of the Curtis Institute of Music, Eli Eban served as visiting professor of clarinet at the Eastman School of Music and is currently on the faculty of the Indiana University School of Music. During 1994-95 he appeared as soloist at the Salzburg Mozarteum and performed and taught in Prague and Budapest at the invitation of the European Mozart Foundation.

BAKED GARLIC AND ONION CREAM SOUP

Serves 6 to 8

I consider this to be a very healthy recipe, particularly with all the garlic. It comes from my native country Israel. --E.E.

6 large onions, cut into ½-inch slices
2 heads of garlic, cloves separated and peeled
5 cups chicken stock (or canned broth)
1½ teaspoons dried thyme leaves
1 teaspoon coarse black pepper

1 teaspoon coarse (kosher) salt
4 tablespoons unsalted butter
2 cups heavy cream
2 tablespoons chopped parsley
Parsley for garnish

Preheat oven to 350 degrees. Place onion and garlic in shallow roasting pan, add 3 cups of chicken stock. Sprinkle with the thyme, pepper and coarse salt. Dot with butter. Cover pan with aluminum foil, bake for 90 minutes. Stir once or twice while baking.

Remove pan from oven, purée onions and garlic with the liquid in several batches, in blender or food processor until smooth. With the blender motor on, add remaining 2 cups of stock and the cream. Pour soup into large saucepan, adjust seasonings to taste and slowly heat through without allowing to boil. Sprinkle with parsley and serve.

Photo: JULIUS & LILI HAHN

SIDNEY FORREST, CLARINETIST

Sidney Forrest is a respected internationally-known clarinetist and educator. His educational background includes study at the Juilliard School as well as degrees awarded from the University of Miami, Florida, and Columbia University. He was professor at Peabody Conservatory of Music, John Hopkins University in Baltimore from 1946 to 1985, achieving the rank of professor of emeritus in 1985. Mr. Forrest was director of Placement and Counseling at Peabody from 1969 to 1985. He was clarinet soloist with the U.S. Marine Band and Symphony Orchestra of Washington from 1941 to 1945. From 1946-50, Forrest was principal clarinetist of the National Symphony. Since 1954, he has been adjunct professor on the faculty of Catholic University, Rome School of Music. He has been on faculty at the Interlochen Arts Camp, Interlochen, Michigan since 1959 as well as American University since 1961. He has taught at the Levine School of Music, Washington since 1980. He was adjudicator of the National Fulbright Commission from 1980 to 1984 and for the Quebec Canadian National Conservatoire from 1969-84.

Sidney Forrest has edited and arranged many clarinet solos. He has given major recitals at Carnegie Recital Hall, Brooklyn Music, National Art Gallery, Phillips Collection, Library of Congress, among others.

Sidney Forrest is married to Faith Levine and they have one daughter, Paula Forrest Helmuth, a gifted pianist and teacher. Mr. Forrest's avocations include photography, gardening, stamp collecting, and travel.

BREAST OF CHICKEN _CLARIBELLA_

Serves 10 or 12

Deelicious! Deelightful and very popular with our guests, friends and others. This is my favorite dish. --S.F.

5 or 6 skinless and boneless whole chicken
   breasts, cut into halves or quarters
1 head garlic, peeled and puréed
⅛ cup dried oregano
Coarse salt and fresh ground pepper
   to taste
½ cup lemon juice
½ cup olive oil

1¼ cups pitted prunes
¾ cup large Spanish green olives
½ cup capers
6 bay leaves
1 cup brown sugar
1 cup white wine
¼ cup finely chopped cilantro or parsley

In a bowl, marinate chicken and all ingredients except sugar, wine and cilantro. Cover and refrigerate overnight.

Preheat oven to 350 degrees. Arrange chicken, prunes, olives in a single layer in a large shallow baking pan and spread marinade over top. Sprinkle chicken parts with brown sugar and pour white wine around chicken breast pieces.

Bake at 350 degrees for 50 to 60 minutes, basting frequently with pan juices. Arrange attractively on platter in rows: chicken, olives, prunes.

Sprinkle with chopped cilantro or parsley. May be served hot or at room temperature.

Photo: GAIL NOGLE

STEPHEN GIRKO, CLARINETIST

Stephen Girko has been the principal clarinetist with the Dallas Symphony Orchestra since 1975. He made his solo debut with this orchestra, playing the Copland Clarinet Concerto with the composer conducting. Before joining the Dallas Symphony, Mr. Girko served as associate principal clarinetist with the Houston Symphony and as principal clarinetist with the Oklahoma City Symphony. While fulfilling his military obligation as a member of the United States Military Academy Band at West Point, N.Y., he served as principal clarinetist with both the Albany Symphony and the Hudson Valley Philharmonic.

Mr. Girko frequently appears in solo recitals as well as solo appearances with orchestras. He is on the faculty of Southern Methodist University and has given master classes throughout the country.

Aside from his musical activities, Mr. Girko is considered by many to be an accomplished cook and cooking instructor, specializing in classic Italian and French cuisine. He has a number of recipes published in cookbooks and gourmet magazines and has taught cooking classes at gourmet stores in the Dallas area. Mr. Girko has recently started a catering company called EAT MY PIZZA!, whereby "Symphony Steve" (his Nome de la cucina) prepares in advance all the makings of his New York inspired pizza, plus a gourmet salad. He then transports all the ingredients in his customized Citroen 2CV to the homes of his customers and assembles and bakes the pizzas on the premises. If his clients should desire some added entertainment, Steve will provide the guests with a formal recital (a tuned grand piano is mandatory) or play unaccompanied 'strolling' music.

MUSSELS MARINIÈRE

Serves 4

*The author had a difficult time deciding which recipes to include from Mr. Girko. While quite content to receive one or two recipes from most artists, I was pleasantly surprised to have received from Mr. Girko, **forty** delicious recipes from which to choose. The following recipes are only the tip of the iceberg of Mr. Girko's culinary creations.*

3 quarts cleaned mussels
¼ cup minced onions
3 cloves minced garlic
¼ teaspoon thyme

Salt and pepper to taste
1⅓ cups white wine
1 stick butter
2 tablespoons minced parsley

In a heavy pot, sauté onions, garlic and spices, covered, until slightly translucent. Add mussels, wine and parsley, cover and steam for approximately 6 minutes or until mussels open. Apportion mussels among 4 individual bowls and cover. Strain poaching liquid (liquor) into another pot, heat and reduce contents, then remove. Swirl in butter, 1 tablespoon at a time. Pour over mussels and garnish with parsley.

LA MOUCLADE
(Creamed Mussels)
Serves 4

Use recipe **MUSSELS MARINIÉRE**	2 egg yolks
¼ cup minced shallots	⅓ cup cream
3 tablespoons butter	6 tablespoons garlic butter
2 tablespoons flour	Lemon juice to taste
¼ teaspoon crushed saffron	

Keep mussels covered in a large bowl. **Do not reduce liquid or yet add parsley**, but strain the liquid. In a skillet, sauté shallots in butter until soft and slightly brown. Add flour and stir roux over moderate heat for about 2 minutes. Add mussel liquor and saffron and simmer for 5 minutes. In a bowl, mix yolks and cream. Mix into liquor and simmer (do not boil). Remove from heat, swirl in garlic butter, mix in lemon juice and pour over mussels. Sprinkle with parsley.

BOURBON CHOCOLATE PECAN PIE

½ cup chopped pecans	¼ cup melted butter
7 teaspoons bourbon	¼ teaspoon salt
3 eggs, beaten but not frothy	1 teaspoon vanilla
1 cup sugar	½ cup semi-sweet morsels*
¾ cup light corn syrup	10-inch unbaked pie shell

Macerate nuts in liquor for several hours. Combine eggs, sugar, corn syrup, butter, salt and vanilla. Mix well and stir in pecan mix and chocolate chips.

*You may melt chocolate with butter and stir in remaining ingredients (the resulting texture of the pie will be different). Pour mix into pie shell and bake at 375 degrees for about 1½ hours, or until set.

BAKED SEAFOOD AU GRATIN

Serves 4

2 cups sliced leeks
4 cloves garlic, minced
3 potatoes, quartered and sliced
¼ cup olive oil
¼ cup chopped olives
½ cup dry white wine
¼ cup minced parsley

Salt and pepper to taste
1½ pounds scrod fillet pieces
½ pound shelled shrimp
½ pound scallops
½ cup fresh bread crumbs
½ cup grated Gruyère cheese
2 tablespoons melted butter

Cook leeks, garlic and potatoes in olive oil until potatoes are tender. Stir in olives, wine, parsley, and salt and pepper to taste. Transfer to a baking dish large enough to hold fish in one layer. Fill with fish and then top fish with remaining seafood. Mix crumbs and cheese together, sprinkle over seafood and drizzle with butter. Bake gratin at 350 degrees until fish flakes and top is golden, about 30 minutes.

BRUSSELS SPROUTS/BEER
AND CHEESE SOUP

Serves 4

½ pound brussels sprouts,
   cooked and halved
6 slices bacon, cooked and
   broken (save bacon fat)
1 red pepper, diced
1 onion, diced
3 cloves garlic, minced

2¾ tablespoons flour
1 teaspoon dry mustard
12 oz. beer
1½ cups chicken stock
7 oz. shredded Cheddar cheese
Salt and pepper to taste

In reserved bacon fat, sauté pepper, onion, and garlic until soft. Add flour and mustard; cook until roux begins to brown. Add beer and stock and simmer for 5 minutes, stirring occasionally. Remove from heat, add cheese in small batches, stirring after each addition. Stir in brussels sprouts, season with salt and pepper and serve.

Photo: PATTY HEIMERL

ALAN GOODMAN, BASSOONIST

Alan Goodman began playing the bassoon at age 13. He studied with several renowned bassoonists in his native New York state, later receiving scholarships to study respectively at the Music Academy of the West in Santa Barbara, California and the Aspen Music Festival in Colorado, at ages 15 and 16. Mr. Goodman received a bachelor of music degree from New York State University at Potsdam and a master of music degree from the University of Wisconsin in Milwaukee. He served three years in the U.S. Army. Mr. Goodman played three years as principal bassoonist of the Milwaukee Symphony and one year as associate principal of the Pittsburgh Symphony, before being appointed co-principal bassoonist of the Los Angeles Philharmonic in the fall of 1970. He has been featured as soloist on several occasions with the Los Angeles Philharmonic.

Alan Goodman has four grown children. He enjoys jogging with his wife, Betty, is an avid fisherman; and enjoys reading, gardening and camping.

QUICK AND EASY STEAMED VEGETABLES

Serves 6

I always try to have a vegetable garden, which gives me both fresh vegetables and an excuse to go out and dig holes in the ground. In order to use these fresh vegetables, I enjoy preparing the following dish. --A.G.

3 cups white rice or about
  ½ cup per person
A variety of fresh vegetables,
  chopped or sliced

Different types of cheeses of your choice,
  sliced or grated

Prepare white rice for number of guests. Lightly steam assortment of fresh vegetables until they are slightly softened, usually no longer than 3 to 4 minutes. Place the steamed vegetables over a bed of rice on each dinner plate and place your favorite cheese on top of the vegetables. Place contents into hot oven or microwave until cheese is melted. Serve.

Photo: NORMAN BILISKO

ALEX KLEIN, OBOIST

Alex Klein was chosen in 1995 to become the new principal oboist of the Chicago Symphony Orchestra. Known for his innate musicality and complete mastery of oboe technique, Alex Klein boasts a repertoire which encompasses virtually every major concerto and recital work for oboe.

While residing on the West Coast, Mr. Klein performed Vivaldi's Concerto in C Major with the Northwest Chamber Orchestra in Seattle in March of 1995. In the last several years, he has won first prize in four international music competitions, including the International Competition for Musical Performers in Geneva, where he was the first oboist to be so honored in 29 years. He has appeared in recital on the Dame Myra Hess Memorial Concert Series, in both Chicago and Los Angeles, and at Weill Recital Hall in New York, as well as in Aspen, Boston and Cleveland. Featured as guest soloist for the 100th anniversary of the modern oboe at Carnegie Hall, Mr. Klein has also performed as soloist with the Philadelphia Orchestra, the Orchestre de la Suisse Romande, and the Winston-Salem Symphony Orchestra in the closing concert of the International Double Reed Society Convention. In addition, Alex Klein is a founding member of the Chamber Music

Society of Seattle and maintains a dynamic career as a soloist, recitalist, chamber musician and teacher. In addition to his recent appointment to the Chicago Symphony, Mr. Klein is currently on the music faculty at the School of Music at Northwestern University, in Evanston, Illinois.

Alex Klein began his musical education in his native Brazil when he was nine years old, as a student of Walter Bianchi. He made his solo debut at the age of ten. Awarded a scholarship by the Brazilian Government, he was a student of James Caldwell at Oberlin Conservatory of Music. In addition, he has studied at the Curtis Institute of Music and the São Paulo State University. The recipient of the first "Artistry in Oboe Performance Award" and the "Louis Sudler Prize in the Arts" at Oberlin, Mr. Klein also has won first prize in more than a dozen competitions. In Brazil, he has been honored as "Best Interpreter of Brazilian Music," and, in the Czech Republic, as "Best Interpreter of Czech Music."

Alex Klein's spouse, Marlise Klein, is a professional violist. She is an active musician; performing in orchestras, chamber groups and music festivals around the country. Marlise is also a native of Brazil.

TORTA DE BOLACHAS "MARIA"

This recipe has been traveling from generation to generation in my family. My mother Ruth Klein passed it on to me. "Maria" cookies are very popular in Brazil and throughout Latin America. They are made out of starch and are not too sweet, allowing us to mix it with plenty of chocolate for the perfect taste. --A.K.

4, 6 oz. packages of Maria cookies*

CREAM:
3 cups milk
2½ tablespoons cornstarch
4 tablespoons Nestlé Quick

TOPPING:
14 oz. can condensed milk
2 tablespoons margarine or butter
4 tablespoons Nestlé Quick

Note: You need a 9-inch springform pan

You will be able to find "Maria" cookies at imported food stores or at South American Food Stores.

To prepare **CREAM,** heat milk, Nestlé Quick and cornstarch (dissolve in 3 tablespoons of milk) in pan on medium heat. Bring to a boil, always stirring vigorously until cream is smooth and shiny, then set it aside.

You will now need the 9-inch springform pan. Fill a small bowl with some more milk. Dip each cookie in milk briefly, about 3 seconds at the most, to moisten them. Spread one layer of Maria cookies evenly on the bottom of the springform pan. You may want to break some cookies and use smaller pieces of them to fill in the larger holes between them. Cover cookies with a thin layer of cream. (Not too much and not too little). As a rule, make sure the layer of cream is flat and smooth, but also make sure that the outline of the cookies is still visible. That will tell you that you are using the right amount of cream.

Repeat this process, alternating layers of cookies and cream until either the cookies reach the top of the pan or you run out of cookies or the cream. The last layer should be of cookies. Put aside for the moment.

To prepare **TOPPING**, mix all the topping ingredients in a non-stick pan. Set on medium heat and stir gently and regularly with a wooden spoon. It takes expertise to find the right time to stop doing this. As you start stirring, you will notice that the consistency is very 'liquid' and easy to stir. At this point, while stirring, you should not be able to see the bottom of the pan. As the topping heats up you will notice the changing consistency. As you bring to a boil, you will notice that the topping comes off the pan easily, or that the pan is visible after the spoon touches the bottom. This means it is done. To be sure, take a teaspoon of the topping and drop into a small bowl with cold water. If it is firm and not runny, it is ready.

Pour the topping over the pie and sprinkle it with granulated chocolate. The pie is ready. *We generally lose our patience and eat at this point, but for better taste, you may want to place the pie in the refrigerator overnight.* That will allow the cream to soak more into the cookies and the topping to harden a little. Remove the sides of the pan and place pie in a serving dish.

Photo: BACHRACH

JUDITH LeCLAIR, BASSOONIST

Principal Bassoonist Judith LeClair has made more than thirty-five solo appearances with the New York Philharmonic, since joining the orchestra in 1981 at the age of twenty-three.

Ms. LeClair made her professional debut with the Philadelphia Orchestra at age fifteen, playing the Mozart *Sinfonia Concertante* with colleagues from the Settlement Music School in Philadelphia where she studied with Shirley Curtiss. A graduate of the Eastman School of Music, Ms. LeClair studied there with K. David Van Hoesen. Before joining the New York Philharmonic, she was principal bassoonist of the San Diego Symphony and San Diego Opera Orchestra.

Active as a recitalist and chamber music player, she has performed with such artists as Andre Watts and the Guarneri Quartet on the Great Performers series at Lincoln Center and has given solo recitals at the Eastman School, Oberlin College, Michigan State and Ohio University.

In April 1995, Ms. LeClair premiered the *The Five Sacred Trees* for bassoon and orchestra, a concerto written for her by John Williams, which was commissioned by the New York Philharmonic as part of its 150th anniversary celebration. She has since performed the work with the San Francisco Symphony and the Royal Academy Orchestra in London and has recorded it for Sony Classical with the London Symphony Orchestra, all with Mr. Williams conducting. The recording was chosen for an Editor's Choice review for *Gramophone* magazine in July, 1997. Ms. LeClair also has a solo recording, released in June, 1997, with CALA records.

Ms. LeClair is on the faculty of the Juilliard School and has given master classes throughout the country. She lives in New Jersey with her husband, pianist Jonathan Feldman.

QUICK-SET SALMON MOUSSE WITH CUCUMBER-YOGURT SAUCE

Makes about 3 cups

Serve with crackers and slices of cucumber. Dot a teaspoon of sauce on each cracker....The sauce is optional—I usually don't make it. The mousse is great on its own. --J.L.

14½ oz. can pink or red salmon
2 tablespoons white wine or rice
    wine vinegar
1 envelope unflavored gelatin
1 medium onion, quartered
½ cup low-fat mayonnaise

8 oz. container plain yogurt
¼ to ½ cup fresh dill, or 1 tablespoon
    dried
½ teaspoon salt or to taste
¼ teaspoon cayenne pepper

Combine juice from salmon and vinegar (should equal about ¼ cup). Stir in gelatin and heat in microwave or on top of stove until gelatin is dissolved. Keep warm enough so it does not solidify.

In the container of the food processor or blender, finely chop the onion. Add salmon, mayonnaise, yogurt, dill, salt and pepper; purée until smooth. Add gelatin mixture and blend once again.

Pour into fish mold (or any shallow dish) and refrigerate overnight or for several hours (or freeze one-half hour).

YOGURT SAUCE

½ pint yogurt
½ teaspoon salt

½ pint sour cream (low-fat)
½ finely chopped cucumber, seeded

Mix all ingredients together with a fork; chill and pour on salmon before serving.

RICHARD LESSER, CLARINETIST

Richard Lesser began his early music studies in 1944 in Los Angeles with Kalman Bloch and Mitchell Lurie. He graduated from the Curtis Institute of Music in Philadelphia in 1959, where he studied with Anthony Gigliotti.

Between the years of 1957 to 1964, Lesser participated in four summers of chamber music concerts and recordings at the famed Marlboro Festival in Vermont.

He recorded works of Stravinsky and Schoenberg with Stravinsky and Craft in Los Angeles between the years of 1961 to 1966. Lesser was engaged by Zubin Mehta to join the Israel Philharmonic in 1966 and appointed to principal clarinetist in 1968.

He has worked under such conductors as Mehta, Barbirolli, Steinberg, Kletzki, Paray, Kertesz, Leinsdorf, Giulini, Dorati, Ormandy, Munch, Bernstein, Maazel, Solti, Dohnányi, Barenboim, Levine, Abbado, Tennstedt, Dutoit and Masur.

Lesser has taught in the United States, Australia, Germany and Israel, and, in the summers of 1992 to 1993, in the Far East as clarinet coach with the Asian Youth Orchestra. He is the appointed woodwind coach of the Israel Philharmonic Youth Orchestra and has been chairman of the Clarinet Department at the University of Tel Aviv in Israel since 1968.

SINI'YE

Serves 8

This is our (my wife Yael and myself) own version of a traditional Arab dish. Tahini is a basic ingredient in Arab-Israeli cuisine. It can be used as a dip for pita bread or topping for falafel, or for any green salad. --R.L.

TAHINI SAUCE:

1 cup sesame seed paste (tahini is found in health food stores). Mix paste well before using
1 cup yogurt
1 cup water
Juice of ½ lemon

½ teaspoon garlic powder/salt or to taste
½ cup chopped parsley (parsley should have an aroma, such as Italian or uncurled type)
½ teaspoon salt or to taste
1 tablespoon olive oil

☞

Mix sesame paste, yogurt and water together—a Tupperware shaker is a good device for this. Next, add this to mixture of lemon, garlic powder or garlic salt, and parsley. Salt to taste. Finish by adding olive oil.

MEAT MIXTURE:

2 pounds lean ground beef
   (or half turkey, optional)
1 tablespoon mustard
1 tablespoon olive oil
6 cardamom pods peeled and black
   seeds crushed

Black pepper to taste
½ teaspoon sweet paprika
½ teaspoon cumin
2 tablespoons bread crumbs
Fried nuts for topping (optional)

Work spices and bread crumbs well into the meat. Arrange meat in flat baking dish (Pyrex or clay), do not press down or flatten.

Pour tahini mixture to cover all meat. Bake for one-half hour in preheated oven at medium-high heat (375 to 425 degrees). Sprinkle with fried nuts and serve immediately.

Photo: TOM RITTER

DAVID McGILL, BASSOONIST

David McGill, the newly appointed principal bassoonist of the Chicago Symphony Orchestra, was born in Tulsa, Oklahoma in 1963. Prior to beginning his tenure in Chicago, he was principal bassoonist of the Cleveland Orchestra (1988-97) and Toronto Symphony (1985-88). In 1980, at the age of 17, he won the principal bassoon position in his hometown orchestra, the Tulsa Philharmonic, remaining for one season before starting his studies with Sol Schoenbach at the Curtis Institute of Music in Philadelphia.

While a student at Curtis, Mr. McGill's woodwind instructors were John de Lancie and John Minsker; they were former principal oboist and English hornist of the Philadelphia Orchestra respectively. In 1983, McGill won first prize in the International Double Reed Society's "Fernand Gillet Competition."

Upon graduation from Curtis in 1985, David McGill was hired by Andrew Davis as principal bassoonist of the Toronto Symphony. In 1988, he accepted the principal bassoon position in the Cleveland Orchestra under the direction of Christoph von Dohnányi, remaining in that position until his appointment as principal bassoonist of the Chicago Symphony by music director Daniel Barenboim, effective the fall of 1997. In 1993 David McGill recorded Mozart's Bassoon Concerto for London/Decca with Christoph von Dohnányi and the Cleveland Orchestra; in 1994, he played the world premier performance of a work written for him, the Concerto for Bassoon and Chamber Orchestra by Oskar Morawetz. He has appeared as a soloist with the Cleveland Orchestra under the direction of both Dohnányi and Leonard Slatkin, and with the Toronto Symphony, the Oklahoma Symphony, the Tulsa Philharmonic, Orchestra London, Symphony New Brunswick, the Colorado Philharmonic and the student orchestras of the Curtis and Cleveland Institutes of Music.

David McGill was selected by Sir Georg Solti to participate and teach in the "Solti Orchestral Project" (an orchestra made up of students and principal players from major American orchestras) held for a 2-week period at Carnegie Hall in June, 1994. He was again selected by Maestro Solti to play principal bassoon in a hand-picked international orchestra, the "World Orchestra for Peace," put together to perform in Geneva in celebration of the 50th anniversary of the United Nations in July, 1995. Both of these unique orchestral gatherings were recorded by London/Decca. Also in 1995, a CD of orchestral excerpts for bassoon with spoken commentary by Mr. McGill was released to critical acclaim by Summit records.

Mr. McGill played in the American premier performance of Jean Francaix's *Trio for Oboe, Bassoon and Piano* at the 1996 convention of the International Double Reed Society. The same year, he participated in the world premier recording of the work.

David McGill has taught master classes in Canada, Finland, Hungary and throughout the United States. He has participated in summer music festivals in Aspen, Colorado (1982), the Colorado Philharmonic (principal bassoon, 1983, 1984), Tanglewood (1985) and Marlboro (1988).

David McGill credits the great operatic soprano, Maria Callas, as being the most inspiring influence in his musical life. He is also a great admirer of the historic recordings of violinist Fritz Kreisler and conductor Leopold Stokowski.

For future video release, McGill is documenting the reminiscences of the remaining students and colleagues of Marcel Tabuteau (1887-1966), the legendary principal oboist of the Philadelphia Orchestra and profoundly influential teacher of musical phrasing. David McGill is also writing a book on musical thought in performance.

INDIAN RICE SALAD

**Makes 2 main-course servings or
4 side-dish servings**

*I am a vegan. I abstain from all food products of animal origin for ethical, environmental and, being diabetic, especially for **health** reasons. This dish is one of my favorite recipes which I have unearthed in the four years I have eaten this way. It is also one of the tastiest dishes I have ever eaten. To anyone who is curious about this way of eating, I recommend reading "Diet for a New America" by John Robbins. This book has changed my life and the lives of my closest friends and relatives. I have never enjoyed food so much in my life. --D.M.*

The "Indian Rice" recipe from David McGill comes from another wonderful book by John Robbins; "May All Be Fed."

¼ cup canola or safflower oil

2 teaspoons yellow mustard seeds

2 teaspoons cumin seeds

2 garlic cloves, minced

1 teaspoon finely grated fresh ginger root

1 teaspoon turmeric

⅛ teaspoon cayenne pepper

2½ cups water

1 bay leaf

1 cinnamon stick

1 cup long-grain brown rice

½ cup raisins

3 tablespoons rice vinegar

2 tablespoons dark Oriental sesame oil

2 tablespoons tamari

1 medium carrot, finely chopped

4 green onions, with tops, thinly sliced

1 pound fresh peas, shelled, or

    1 cup (thawed) frozen peas

In medium saucepan, heat 1 tablespoon of the oil over medium heat. Add the mustard seeds, cumin seeds, garlic, ginger, turmeric and cayenne pepper and cook, stirring until the mustard seeds begin to pop, after about 30 seconds.

Add the water, bay leaf and cinnamon, cover, and bring to a boil. Add the rice, cover, reduce heat to low, and simmer until the water is absorbed, 30 to 40 minutes. Remove the rice from the heat and let stand, covered, for 10 minutes.

Put the rice into a medium bowl and remove the bay leaf and cinnamon stick. Stir in the raisins.

In a small bowl whisk the rice vinegar, the remaining 3 tablespoons of canola oil, the sesame oil and tamari until combined. Pour over the rice. Add the carrot, green onions and peas and stir well. Refrigerate until well chilled. Serve chilled.

FRANK MORELLI, BASSOONIST

After being introduced to the bassoon through the public school music programs in his hometown of Massapequa, New York, Frank Morelli studied with Stephan Maxym at the Manhattan and Juilliard Schools of Music. He holds the distinction of being the first bassoonist to be awarded a doctorate by the Juilliard School.

Since his Carnegie Hall concerto debut in 1973, Frank Morelli has been heard around the world as a soloist and with chamber and orchestral ensembles. One of the most active bassoonists recording today, he has over one hundred recordings for major record labels to his credit and can be heard on a number of television soundtracks, commercials and film scores. Morelli's performances and recording of the Mozart Bassoon Concerto with the Orpheus Chamber Orchestra on the Deutsche Grammophon record label met with international critical acclaim and his recording of Mozart's *Sinfonia Concertante* for winds and orchestra with Orpheus for Nonesuch Records was named "Recording of Special Merit" by *Stereo Review* magazine. The Orpheus CD of Copland's *Appalachian Spring*, which featured Frank Morelli, was a 1990 Grammy nominee for best classical recording.

Much sought after as a chamber musician, Frank Morelli has appeared with the Chamber Music Society of Lincoln Center on numerous occasions since his first appearance with them in 1978 at the Mostly Mozart Festival in New York. He has performed at the 92nd Street YMCA with violinist Jaime Laredo and at the Metropolitan Museum of Art with flutist Paula Robison. He also appeared on many occasions with oboist Heinz Holliger, as well as at the Spoleto, Newport, Caramoor, Grand Canyon, Grand Teton, Norfolk and Bridgehampton Music Festivals. He is a member of the North Country Chamber Players, Festival Chamber Music Society and the New York Wind Soloists.

Chosen to succeed his teacher, Stephen Maxym, Mr. Morelli serves on the faculties of the Juilliard School as well as the Yale and Manhattan Schools of Music. He participates often as a coach at the National Orchestral Institute and served as a judge at the Gillet International Competition in Frankfurt, Germany. Frank Morelli is the editor of the new *Orchestral Works of Igor Stravinsky for Bassoon,* published by Boosey & Hawkes. He is principal bassoonist of the New York City Opera Orchestra, Orpheus, Brooklyn Philharmonic and the American Composers Orchestra. Frank lives in Closter, New Jersey with his wife Bethany and son Anthony.

DORIS HORTON'S READY-TO-USE ROLLED OATS MIX FOR PANCAKES AND WAFFLES
Makes about 11 cups

I have these two recipes to offer, one from my mother and one from my mother-in-law! The oats mix is great for home use as well as on camping trips. Also, it makes a great gift when put into a handsome container and accompanied by a copy of the recipe and a bottle of maple syrup. --F.M.

4 cups flour	1 tablespoon salt
1½ cups dry milk	1½ cups shortening
¼ cup baking powder	4 cups quick oats

In a large mixing bowl, combine flour, dry milk, baking powder and salt. Cut in shortening and mix well by hand or machine until thoroughly blended. Mix in quick oats.

Store in an air tight container (such as gallon-size mayonnaise jar). The dry mixture does not need to be refrigerated unless it is being kept for months.

TO MAKE PANCAKES:
Combine 1½ cups mix, 1 cup water and 1 egg. Add nuts or fruit as desired. Let stand for 2 minutes. Cook on hot skillet. Thin the batter with a little water if necessary. Makes 9 medium pancakes.

TO MAKE WAFFLES:
Follow above directions, but add ½ teaspoon oil to mixture so that waffles will not stick.

MAMMA MORELLI'S FAMOUS ROASTED PEPPERS

Mamma suggests that you need to prepare this dish a few days ahead before eating!

8 thick-skinned, red bell peppers
Dried oregano
Salt and pepper

3 cloves of garlic
¼ cup olive oil
Brown paper grocery bag

Place whole red bell peppers on a cookie sheet and roast under the broiler, turning occasionally until skin is blistered, but not burned. Remove from broiler and place immediately in paper bag for one-half hour. As you remove peppers from bag, pull out stems, attempting to remove as many seeds as possible in the process. Peel off skin (which should just about fall off) and place in a bowl or container in which they will be stored. Tear into slices of approximately ¾ inch; at the same time, remove any seeds that may remain.

Sprinkle lightly with oregano, and salt and pepper to taste. Add sliced raw garlic and store in an air-tight container in the refrigerator for 2 to 5 days.

To serve, remove from refrigerator and allow to warm to room temperature. (You can remove garlic if you wish). Add olive oil and stir gently. Serve at room temperature in a bowl beside slices of Italian bread and a plate of anchovies (if you wish) as part of the antipasto or with the meal.

Photo of Charles Neidich © PETER SCHAAF

CHARLES NEIDICH AND AYAKO OSHIMA, CLARINETISTS

Charles Neidich has been mesmerizing audiences and critics alike since his unheralded, spectacular New York recital debut in 1974. A native New Yorker, he studied music with both parents—piano with his mother and clarinet with his father. As a child, his musical idols were not clarinetists, but violinists and pianists, such as Heifetz, Kreisler, and Schnabel. Eventually the clarinet won out and Neidich continued his studies with the famed pedagogue Leon Russianoff. Although quite active in music at an early age, he decided against attending a music conservatory but continued private lessons with Mr. Russianoff until graduating from Yale in 1974, with a major in anthropology. In 1975, Neidich became the first American to receive a Fulbright grant for study in the former Soviet Union. He studied with Boris Dikov for three years at the Moscow State Conservatory.

A winner of several top European prizes, including the 1982 Munich International Competition, Charles Neidich won the Walter W. Naumburg competition in 1985, the first major clarinet competition in the United States. Since then, he has performed with major orchestras throughout Europe, the United States, and the Far East, such as the American Symphony, Indianapolis Symphony, Berlin Radio Orchestra, Hong Kong Philharmonic, and National Symphony of the Republic of China. Recent highlights include performances with the Juilliard Quartet at the Library of Congress and with the American Quartet at Wigmore Hall in London.

An artist of highly acclaimed virtuosity and musicianship, Mr. Neidich performs a repertoire of well over 200 works, including pieces commissioned or inspired by him, as well as his own transcriptions of vocal and instrumental showpieces. He has given premieres of many of the leading composers of the twentieth century, including Ralph Shapey, Elliot Carter,

Edison Denisov, Joan Tower, and Meyer Kupferman. He has also become increasingly interested in performance on original instruments and currently devotes a significant portion of his concert activity to this fascinating field.

Mr. Neidich also maintains a busy teaching schedule and is on the artist faculties of the Juilliard School, the Manhattan School, S.U.N.Y. at Stony Brook and S.U.N.Y. at Purchase. He is a member of the Orpheus Chamber Orchestra and the New York Woodwind Quintet. His recent recordings include: the Mozart Clarinet Concerto, the Weber concerti and the Rossini *Introduction, Theme and Variations*, with the Orpheus Chamber Orchestra on Deutsche Grammophon; the Mozart and Weber quintets with the Mendelssohn String Quartet on Music Masters; Robert Schumann's violin sonatas (in his own transcription) with pianist Leonard Hokanson on Sony Classical, and on period instruments for the series Sony Vivarte; Mozart's quintet, quartet, and trio, with the quartet L'Archi Budelli and Robert Levin; with the wind ensemble Mozzafiato, period arrangements of Mozart's *Marriage of Figaro,* Rossini's *Barber of Seville*, and Beethoven *Wind Music*. Soon to be released are the Brahms Clarinet Quintet with the Juilliard String Quartet; on period instruments will be Weber, Reicha and Hummel quintets and quartets with L'Archi Budelli.

Ayako Oshima graduated from the Toho School of Music in 1983 as a student of Koichi Hamanaka and Kazuko Ninomia. In 1985, she came to the United States as a special student of Charles Neidich at the Eastman School of Music. She is the winner of numerous international competitions, including the 55th Japan Music Competition in Tokyo, 1986, the Winds and Percussion Competition in Japan, and third prize at the 17th International Jeunesses Musicales Competition in Belgrade, 1987. At that competition, she also received the "Golden Harp" Award given to the favorite of the audience and critics.

One of the most popular clarinet soloists in Japan, Ms. Oshima performs on a regular basis both in recital and in concerto appearances with orchestra. Highlights have included performances in Osaka, Nagoya, Kobe, at the Casals Hall and Bunka Kaikan in Tokyo, and with the Hiroshima and Osaka Symphonies. She was a featured artist at the 1990 International Clarinet Festival in Quebec and has participated in tours with the Orpheus Chamber Orchestra. She is also a founding member of the award winning ensemble, L'Art Respirant, the leading contemporary ensemble in Japan.

Since 1989, Ayako Oshima has recorded for Toshiba EMI. With L'Art Respirant, she has recorded for Victor Japan. In addition, she has made several recordings on original instruments for Sony Classical as a member of the ensemble, Mozzafiato.

Since her marriage to clarinetist Charles Neidich in 1989, Ayako Oshima makes her home in New York City while continuing a very active performing career in the Far East. In addition to her performing career, she maintains a high profile as a teacher and is on the faculties of the Juilliard School of Music, Queens College, and the State University of New York at Purchase. With her husband, she has written a book on the basics of clarinet technique for the publisher, Toa Ongaku, Inc.

YOSE-NABE
(Seafood Hot Pot)

This is a typical Japanese and Chinese winter dish. Really a whole meal in one pot. It is generally cooked at the table like fondue and is very democratic. You can use basically any ingredients which look (and taste) good to you, and you can cook them in any order you like. Your guests can eat either everything or whatever parts appeal to them. **For this recipe you need either a portable butane gas stove or electric hot pot.** --A.O.

1 **bunch watercress, cleaned, but not chopped**
1 **bunch scallions, cleaned and cut into 4-inch segments**
1 **small head Chinese cabbage, and/or head of green cabbage, cut into large pieces**
1 **package firm tofu (or if bought loose, 3 pieces), cut into small size cubes**
8 to 10 **shiitake mushrooms (if dry, soak in water at least 30 minutes and save the water in which they are soaked)**
These are the basic vegetables. You can add any green vegetables you like.

FISH: red snapper, monkfish, cod, salmon, shrimp (preferably with shells and heads intact), scallops, clams etc...*Basically you can use any seafood you like.*

Arrange the vegetables on one or two large plates and the seafood on one or two other large plates. Put aside.

FOR THE SOUP OR BOILING WATER: PACKAGE OF KOMBU (Japanese dried kelp)

JAPANESE SAUCE:

¾ cup lemon and/or lime juice squeezed from fresh fruit (or for the most authentic Japanese taste, yuzu, a Japanese lime)
½ cup soy sauce
¼ cup finely chopped scallions
½ teaspoon hot cayenne pepper or shichimi powder (Japanese seven-pepper and spice mixture)

Mix everything together in one bowl and put aside.

Fill a large pot, preferably a ceramic hot pot (in Japanese, donabe) approximately ⅔ full of water. If you have the water from the shiitake mushrooms, add now. Add kombu (Japanese dried kelp), heat until boiling, then place on the portable stove in the middle of your table and keep boiling the water. Place the vegetables and seafood plates on the table and put some sauce in a small bowl for each person. Then, when everyone is seated, put a portion of whatever needs to cook the longest into the pot gradually adding more ingredients. When cooked, place the vegetables and seafood in each person's bowl. When you have finished everything in the hot pot, simply start over, putting in more ingredients.

Leave a little watercress and scallion for the end. The soup is quite delicious, and you can add cooked Japanese or Chinese noodles. Boil one minute or less with the watercress and scallions and serve.

For a Chinese style hot pot, add any of the following ingredients which you like to the basic Japanese sauce:

Ground fresh ginger	**Chinese hot sauce**
Ground fresh garlic	**Chinese XO sauce (made from dried**
Sesame oil	**scallops, shrimp, garlic and**
Roasted sesame seeds	**red pepper)**

Also, if you can get to a Chinese market, it is very nice to include with the basic vegetables Chinese greens, such as snow pea leaves, Chinese flowered scallions, bok choy, Chinese broccoli and so on.

Photo: SPECTRUM STUDIO

EUGENE ROUSSEAU, SAXOPHONIST

Eugene Rousseau has performed across North America and on five continents since his Carnegie Hall debut and has distinguished himself as one of the world's great saxophonists and teachers. His artistry has inspired many "firsts," including numerous world premieres of works written for him. He performed the first classical saxophone recitals in Paris, Berlin, London, Vienna, and Amsterdam. An active recording artist, Rousseau's discography includes the first album of a saxophone recital on compact disc (Delos), as well as albums on the Coronet, Crystal, Golden Crest, Liscio, and McGill labels. He has appeared as soloist with the Minnesota Orchestra under Leonard Slatkin, the Pan-American Festival Orchestra under Lukas Foss, the Indianapolis Symphony under Raymond Leppard and Phillipe Entremont, the BBC Orchestra in London, the Kansai Philharmonic (Japan), the Janáček Philharmonic, the Prague Symphony, the Austrian Radio Orchestra, and the Bavarian Radio Orchestra, and has presented recitals and master classes in major cities throughout the world.

Rousseau holds the rank of distinguished professor of music at Indiana University and teaches a yearly master course at the Mozarteum in Salzburg. He has been a guest professor at Arizona State University, the Hochschule für Musik in Vienna, and the Prague Conservatory, where in a 1993 ceremony he was awarded the title of "Honorary Professor of Music."

ER'S PANCAKES

Makes 12 medium-small pancakes

With my difficult schedule, I need to have a substantial breakfast. This recipe takes care of that and offers a nice variety in the diet. It is something I do not eat every day, but will have it perhaps once or twice a week, while on other days I enjoy eggs or even some form of pasta for breakfast. --E.R.

1 egg
1 cup buttermilk
1 cup flour

4 tablespoons wheat germ
4 tablespoons wheat bran (or oat bran)
¾ teaspoon baking soda

Using a large mixing bowl, beat egg and buttermilk. Sift flour into liquid while stirring. Add wheat germ and bran, then add baking soda. Stir well. Preheat large iron skillet, brushed with light cooking oil. Fry pancakes until golden brown, using a large spatula to turn them. (If cakes are too thick or dry, add a dash of buttermilk. If they are not stiff enough in pan, stir in more flour).

Photo: CHRIS LEE

SHERRY SYLAR, OBOIST

Associate Principal Oboist Sherry Sylar joined the New York Philharmonic in 1984, after having performed with the Louisville Orchestra and having taught at the University of Evansville in Indiana. A native of Chattanooga, Tennessee, she earned her bachelor of music degree at Indiana University and her master of music degree from Northwestern University. In addition to her philharmonic concerts, Ms. Sylar performs chamber music and solo concerts regularly. During the 1989 Christmas season, she took part in the "Berlin Celebration Concerts," held in East and West Berlin to hail the dismantling of the Berlin Wall. One of eight philharmonic musicians chosen to represent the United States, she performed with an international orchestra led by Leonard Bernstein. Most recently, Ms. Sylar was a featured soloist with Kurt Masur and the New York Philharmonic in Bach's Second Brandenburg Concerto.

Among her outside interests are cats, garage sales, oil painting, and working on her new country home.

SIZZLING ICE CREAM

I have used this recipe on many occasions, and it is always successful. Cooking is my passion, though there's not much time in this profession for at-home entertaining. When I get a chance, I like to spend most of my preparation time on entrees and least time on dessert. --S.S.

1 **pint vanilla ice cream or frozen yogurt**
½ **stick butter (light butter will also work)**
1 **cup unsweetened coconut**

½ **cup crème de cacao, triple sec,**
   amaretto or any sweet dessert liqueur
   of your choice

Melt butter in skillet, stir coconut into melted butter and sauté until it begins to brown (careful, it burns easily). Have bowls ready with scoops of ice cream served in each.

Immediately pour hot browned coconut mixture over ice cream followed quickly by crème de cacao or other dessert liqueur.

*It will **sizzle** and delight your guests!*

Photo: BOB O'LARY

WILLIAM WINSTEAD, BASSOONIST/COMPOSER

William Winstead is principal bassoonist of the Cincinnati Symphony Orchestra and professor of bassoon at the Cincinnati College-Conservatory of Music. A native of western Kentucky, Winstead began his musical training as a pianist and composer before studying the wind instruments. He attended the Curtis Institute of Music in Philadelphia where he received a degree in bassoon later studying composition in New York City and at West Virginia University.

For seven years a participant at the Marlboro Music Festival, Winstead served as principal bassoonist under Pablo Casals, toured the United States and Canada representing the Marlboro Festival and released numerous chamber music and orchestral recordings. He has performed at other summer festivals including Spoleto, Italy's Festival of Two Worlds and the Sarasota Music Festival. As bassoon soloist, he has appeared with orchestras, including the Pittsburgh Symphony, and has held one-year residencies as principal bassoonist of the Lake George Opera Company, the Goldovsky Opera Festival and the Fort Wayne (Indiana) Philharmonic.

Winstead has been a featured recitalist both here and in Europe at several recent conferences of the International Double Reed Society—the world's principal organization of student, amateur and professional oboists and bassoonists; in 1987, Winstead was re-elected president of IDRS for a second term. He has also frequently served as a member of the National Endowment of the Arts (NEA) Music Advisory Panel for Solo Recitalists Grants. Winstead previously taught on the faculties of West Virginia University, Indiana-Purdue University, Florida State University, and Oberlin Conservatory of Music.

As a composer, Winstead has enjoyed premieres of major works by the Philadelphia Orchestra and the Pittsburgh Symphony. In 1976, he received an NEA grant for a bicentennial work for narrator and orchestra. His Concerto for Bassoon was an award winner in the Eastman Prize Competition. In addition, Winstead has collaborated with Sol Schoenbach in publishing three volumes of solo bassoon music, and has been the recipient of numerous commissions and awards.

REAL AMERICAN SWISS STEAK

Serves 8 to 10

In the last several decades, we have had an enormous variety of foods in our diet; in part, from the availability of many different ethnic foods. In addition, we are very conscience of healthy eating habits, such as reducing fats, lowering salt and sugar intake, etc. We do not seem to cook the American food of 50 years ago any more. Recipes like "Real American Swiss Steak" were the norm back then, but not so today. Once in a while I like to eat something from that past time period—food that is "home cooking." --W.W.

3½ pound round steak,
    (¾ to 1-inch thick)
2 to 3 cups all-purpose flour
Salt and pepper
¼ cup vegetable oil
1 cup green pepper, chopped

1 cup onions, chopped
1 cup carrots, chopped
1 cup celery, chopped
8 oz. can tomato sauce
14 oz. can beef broth

Trim fat from meat; cut into serving pieces. Season flour with salt and pepper. Pound as much seasoned flour into both sides of the steak pieces as they will hold (use edge of saucer or mallet). Heat ¼ cup oil in electric skillet or large regular skillet; brown meat on both sides, adding more oil if necessary. Remove meat to drain.

Arrange meat in one layer in baking/serving dish. Cover with chopped vegetables. Season to taste before adding tomato sauce and heated beef broth.

Cover and bake 2 hours or more at 300 degrees. After 1½ hours, check for liquid and tenderness, adding water if needed. To serve, scoop meat portions out carefully (covered with vegetable layer).

Wonderful with real mashed potatoes, baked potatoes, or noodles.

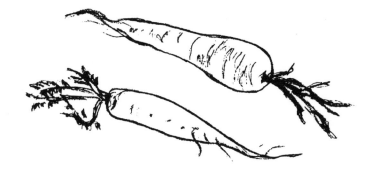

Photo: DAVID WEISS

MICHELE ZUKOVSKY, CLARINETIST

Soloist, chamber musician, and principal clarinetist of one of the world's major orchestras, Michele Zukovsky has garnered praise for her extraordinary talents in each capacity.

As soloist with numerous orchestras, Ms. Zukovsky has given the premiere performances of a number of important compositions, including the Berio transcription for clarinet and orchestra of the Brahms F Minor Sonata and the John Williams Clarinet Concerto, which was written for her. The Williams Concerto was performed at Tanglewood with the composer conducting the Boston Pops, in July of 1991.

Festival appearances have included Marlboro, Casals, Sitka, Chestnut Hills, Spoleto, Schlewig-Holstein in Germany, Korsholm in Finland, Lochinhaus in Austria, the Mostly Mozart Festival in New York and the Kapalua Music Festival of Maui, Hawaii. New York City appearances have included James Levine's Ravinia Concerts at Alice Tully Hall, the 92nd Street Y with Jamie Laredo, and the Lincoln Center Chamber Players.

Ms. Zukovsky's recent diverse activities include a recital for I Pomeriggi Musicall di Milano in Italy, chamber music performances in Japan, teaching at the Banff Centre of Fine Arts in Canada and a chamber music tour of Australia in January of 1991 with Pinchas Zukerman.

Ms. Zukovsky joined the Los Angeles Philharmonic Orchestra at the age of eighteen while still a student at the University of Southern California, having studied with her father, Kalman Bloch, who was principal clarinetist of the same orchestra for many years. She has recorded for Decca/London, Nonesuch, and Avant Records.

Frequently noted for the beautiful tone of her playing, Michele Zukovsky is unique in the United States for her mastery of the German System Wurlitzer instruments, and she has given master classes throughout the world.

GINGER SHERRY CRAB LEGS ANDREA

Serves 6

It's quick and it's a hit! For dessert, stew plums in a 200 degree oven for 3 to 4 hours. Put vanilla ice cream on top. This recipe comes from a favorite restaurant, Andrea's Old Town Café, in Bandon, Oregon. --M.Z.

4-inch length of ginger root, peeled and finely chopped (totaling about ⅓ cup chopped ginger)

1½ cups cream sherry

1½ cups salted butter (3 sticks) *(I like to use less)*

6 large cloves garlic, finely chopped

1½ pounds picked Dungeness crabmeat (from upper portion of legs) or 1½ pounds of sea scallops or shrimp

1½ cups light cream or half-&-half

Parsley and paprika as garnish

1 pound linguini

Marinate ginger in cream sherry at least 2 hours. Melt butter in large frying pan over medium heat. Sauté garlic, but do not brown. Add crabmeat or scallops or shrimp and sauté for 1 minute, turning lightly so meat does not break up. Add sherry and ginger and bring to a boil for 1 minute. Remove seafood and set aside.

Add cream to frying pan contents and bring to a hard boil, stirring frequently, until reduced to a rich, creamy sauce. Return seafood to sauce to reheat.

Serve, garnished with chopped parsley and paprika. Serve over linguini.

ORGAN

Photo: PIZZAZ

DIANE BISH, ORGANIST

Concert and recording artist, composer, conductor and international television artist, Diane Bish has displayed her dazzling virtuosity and unique showmanship around the world. Her performances have been hailed by critics internationally as "stunning, virtuosic, fiery and astonishing." Through numerous recordings, concerts and weekly television appearances, Diane Bish is the most visible organist in the world today.

In 1989, Diane Bish received the prestigious National Citation given by The National Federation of Music Clubs of America. "The highest honor for distinguished service to the musical, artistic and cultural life of the nation." Other past recipients of this prestigious award are Van Cliburn, Leonard Bernstein, Eugene Ormandy, Irving Berlin, Fred Waring and Robert Shaw.

On her own international television series, *The Joy of Music*, Diane Bish has brought together for the first time on a television platform the great music of the organ with world renowned solo artists, ensembles and orchestras. Combining exhilarating performances with entertaining, informative and inspirational narrative, the series appeals to people of all ages, musician or non-musician.

Diane Bish has produced, hosted and performed over 300 *Joy of Music* programs from famous churches, cathedrals, palaces, museums and monasteries of the United States, Israel and Europe. Over 100 million people worldwide are capable of seeing *The Joy of Music* on a weekly basis. The program is featured on six national cable networks, various independent and PBS stations, Armed Forces Network worldwide, Canada's Vision Network and various foreign countries.

Ms. Bish is also seen weekly on the international broadcasts of the Coral Ridge Presbyterian Church, Fort Lauderdale, where as senior organist, she directed the design and plays the majestic 117 rank Ruffatti organ. She is also featured weekly on the "Gloria" program hosted by Art Linkletter.

Diane Bish has made over 30 recordings on many of the great organs of the world, including St. Bavo Cathedral, Haarlem, Holland, and Freiburg Cathedral, Germany, where she was the first American woman to record. Recordings include music for: organ and orchestra; brass and organ; cello and organ; great organ masterpieces and original works and hymn arrangements.

The sparkling creativity and artistry of Diane Bish is equally evident in her composing as well as performing. Four major works include: *Festival Te Deum* for organ and orchestra; *Passion Symphony* for organ and narrator; *Symphony of Psalms* for organ, choir, orchestra and soloist and *Morning Has Broken* for organ, choir, orchestra and narrator. She is noted for her brilliant works for organ with seven books and numerous solo pieces. She is also the author of *Church Music Explosion* inspiring excellence in church music.

Diane Bish began her early study with Dorothy Addy in Wichita, Kansas. As a student of the famous Mildred Andrews, Diane Bish, while still in her teens, was the winner of national competitions in both organ and composition and recipient of Fulbright and French government grants in Amsterdam and Paris with Nadia Boulanger, Gustav Leonhardt and Marie Clarie Alain.

CHICKEN DIANE
Serves 4

This is a very quick and easy recipe. Whenever I have last minute guests, this recipe leaves the impression that I have been cooking for hours. It goes well with baked potatoes and green vegetables. --D.B.

6 medium chicken breasts or thighs,
   cut up into small pieces
2 tablespoons butter and oil
Garlic, fresh or powdered

Salt to taste
Pepper, freshly ground
4 bananas, cut in half and sliced
   in the middle

Debone chicken and cut into small pieces. Season chicken with salt, pepper, and garlic.

Preheat skillet with 2 tablespoons butter and oil, add chicken and brown quickly. Turn burner down to medium-low heat and cook for about 20 minutes. Return to high heat and add bananas. Fry one-half minute per side or until brown. Remove from heat and serve.

Photo: LOUIS OUZER

DAVID CRAIGHEAD, ORGANIST

David Craighead was born in Strasburg, Pennsylvania. His father was a Presbyterian minister and he received his first music lessons from his mother, who was an organist. At the age of eighteen, he became a pupil of Alexander McCurdy at the Curtis Institute of Music in Philadelphia, where he received the bachelor of music degree in 1946.

Mr. Craighead has maintained a balanced career as both a performer and teacher. Many of his students now hold positions in colleges and churches across the country. He has played recitals in seven national conventions of the American Guild of Organists and at the International Congresses held in London, Philadelphia and Cambridge, England. Recognized as one of America's great organ artists, David Craighead was voted the 1983 International Performer of the Year by the New York City Chapter of the American Guild of Organists.

In June, 1968, Mr. Craighead received an honorary doctor of music degree from Lebanon Valley College, Annville, Pennsylvania, and in 1975 was awarded the first such honorary degree from the Eastman School. His most recent award is that of honorary fellowship in the Royal College of Organists, London, England.

Recordings include a 1968 Artisan long-playing disc of compositions of Franck, Mendelssohn and Messiaen. He has subsequently made two recordings for the Crystal Record Company. The first includes works of Samuel Adler, Paul Cooper and Lou Harrison. The second consists of *The King of Instruments* by William Albright and the Sonata for Organ by Vincent Persichetti. Mr. Craighead also made two recordings for Gothic, one of late 19th century American composers and the other of Albright's Organbook I and Organbook II. His most recent recording, for Delos, is of the Second Sonata by Max Reger and Louis Vierne's Symphony No. 6.

David Craighead is married to Marian Reiff Craighead, who collaborates with him in duo organ recitals. They have two children and two grandchildren.

BEEF FROM THE NORTH OF SPAIN

Serves 8 to 10

This "Beef from the North of Spain" recipe was given to us by Ruth Mader, the wife of Clarence Mader, with whom I studied organ. He was one of this country's leading organ teachers. We remained friends of theirs until their deaths in 1971. --D.C.

¼ pound margarine
1 medium-sized onion, sliced
4 pounds round steak or good stewing beef
1 pint Burgundy wine

Medium-sized jar (8 oz.) stuffed olives
1 can (13 oz.) sliced mushrooms
4 oz. jar pimentos
Rice

Melt margarine and fry onion in it. Cut meat into bite-size pieces. Brown it with the onions. Add Burgundy wine. Cover and cook slowly for 4 hours. Uncover and add drained olives, mushrooms and pimentos. Raise heat slightly and simmer another 20 minutes, uncovered. Serve over rice (a rice pilaf recipe is recommended).

BAKED LASAGNA

Serves 8 to 10

1½ pounds ground beef
1 large onion, sliced
2 cloves garlic, crushed
1½ packages spaghetti sauce mix
1 teaspoon Accent
1 teaspoon oregano
½ teaspoon salt
¼ teaspoon pepper
28 oz. can peeled tomatoes, drained
15 oz. can tomato sauce

4 oz. can mushrooms, drained
1½ pounds large curd cottage cheese,
   cream-style
2 beaten eggs
½ teaspoon seasoned salt
½ pound lasagna noodles,
   cooked and drained
12 oz. mozzarella cheese
½ to 1 cup grated Parmesan cheese

In a large skillet, sauté onion and garlic in a little corn oil for several minutes, then add meat and brown. Drain fat. Sprinkle with spaghetti sauce mix, Accent, oregano and seasonings. Add tomatoes, tomato sauce and mushrooms.

Cook over low heat **at least** 30 minutes, stirring occasionally. Longer cooking improves flavor. In a separate bowl, combine cottage cheese, eggs and seasoned salt. In greased 13 x 9 x 2-inch pan, alternate layers of half of each: noodles, mozzarella cheese, cottage cheese mixture and meat sauce. Repeat layers, ending with the sauce.

Bake at 350 degrees for 30 minutes. Sprinkle with Parmesan cheese. Bake for an additional 15 minutes. Let stand 10 to 15 minutes before cutting. (Can be prepared well ahead of time and reheated).

Photo: HERBERT ASCHERMAN

LARRY SMITH, ORGANIST

Larry Smith is a member of the organ faculty at Indiana University, Bloomington, Indiana. He is a concert organist of national reputation, having performed solo recitals for three consecutive national conventions of the American Guild of Organists, in 1982, 1984 and 1986. He also served as one of the judges for the National Organ Playing Competition held during the national AGO convention in Houston in 1988.

Dr. Smith began his musical studies at Guttenberg, Iowa with John G. Lammers. He was graduated in 1965 from Drake University, Des Moines, Iowa where he studied with Russell Saunders. He continued formal education degrees at Syracuse University as a student of the late Arthur Poister and was graduated from the Eastman School of Music with a doctor of musical arts degree. His work at Eastman was with David Craighead; he also earned that school's prized Performer's Certificate in Organ.

Before his appointment to Indiana University in 1981, Dr. Smith served on the faculties of Kent State University, Kent, Ohio and Converse College, Spartanburg, South Carolina. Prior to his work in academia, he was full-time director of music at the First United Methodist Church in Des Moines, IA. He was appointed chairman of the Organ Department at Indiana University, a position he held until the fall of 1992. Dr. Smith's recording of *Troisieme Symphonie*, Opus 28 by Louis Vierne is available on VQR Digital records. His most recent CD is *The Martin Ott Organ at St. Brigid's Church, San Diego*, and includes works by Bruhns, Buxtehude, Handel, Bach, Schumann and Heiller.

Larry Smith is married to Caroline Bradley Smith, an adjunct member of the voice faculty of DePauw University. They have a young daughter, Johna.

CORNSTARCH PUDDING

This is one of the recipes (my mother) used as I grew up. She wanted me to think of her when I would prepare this recipe. It makes a nice dessert for 3 people. --L.S.

2 cups milk
¼ teaspoon salt
½ teaspoon sugar

2 heaping tablespoons cornstarch
1 egg

Heat milk, salt and sugar in double boiler until large bubbles form and it is near boiling. Blend cornstarch with a little cold milk. Break 1 egg into the mixture and blend well with egg beater. Add to hot milk, stirring constantly until thickened. Serve with strawberries or raspberries.

JOHN WEAVER, ORGANIST

John Weaver has been director of music at Madison Avenue Presbyterian Church since 1970, head of the Organ Department at the Curtis Institute of Music in Philadelphia since 1972 and chair of the Organ Department at the Juilliard School since 1987.

Weaver's early training was at the Peabody Conservatory which awarded him its 1989 Distinguished Alumni Award. He is a graduate of the Curtis Institute and Union Theological Seminary's School of Sacred Music. He has been on the faculties of the Westminster Choir College, Union Seminary and the Manhattan School of Music. For eleven years he was at Holy Trinity Lutheran Church in Manhattan where he founded that church's Bach Vespers.

He often appears in recitals with his wife, Marianne, a flutist.

John Weaver has been an active concert artist since coming under management in 1960, playing throughout North America and western Europe. He has played at numerous regional and national conventions of the American Guild of Organists and at the 1987 International Congress of Organists in Cambridge, England. His numerous published compositions are performed worldwide.

His other interests include railroad trains (both model and prototype) and hiking mountain trails.

CARROT PUDDING

Serves 8 to 10

This is my grandmother Weaver's recipe which has been passed down through several generations. The fact that it takes a very long time to prepare makes it all the more desirable from the consumer's standpoint—just like a fine musical performance! Part of the pleasure of this delicacy is in savoring the aroma of the kitchen while the pudding is steaming on a cold winter's day. --J.W.

1 cup flour	½ cup butter (one stick)
¼ teaspoon ground cloves	1 cup sugar
½ teaspoon nutmeg	1 cup grated raw carrots
½ teaspoon cinnamon	½ cup raisins
1 cup grated white potatoes	½ cup currants
1 teaspoon baking soda	Hard sauce*

In a medium-sized bowl, sift together flour, cloves, nutmeg and cinnamon. In separate bowl, stir soda into grated potatoes.

In separate bowl, cream together butter and sugar. Mix in with the flour and spices; grated potatoes, creamed butter and sugar, then finally carrots, raisins and currants. Grease a 9 x 9-inch or similar-sized baking dish or cake pan. Put in mixture and cover tightly. Bake with moist heat for 3 hours in oven set at 225 degrees, by placing in pan or Pyrex dish surrounded by an inch or so of boiling water.   .

*Good served with hard sauce. Mix together: **2 tablespoons butter, 1 tablespoon of milk, 1 teaspoon of vanilla** and **1 cup powdered sugar**. Chill in refrigerator until firm.

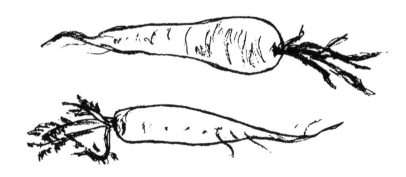

PERCUSSION

Photo: JEAN BRUBAKER

MICHAEL BOOKSPAN, PERCUSSIONIST

Principal percussionist and associate timpanist of the Philadelphia Orchestra, Mr. Bookspan is a graduate of the Juilliard School, where he studied with Morris Goldenberg, Saul Goodman and Fred Albright. Prior to coming to Philadelphia in 1953, Mr. Bookspan played with the Little Orchestra Society of New York, the New York City Ballet and the Goldman Band. He has participated in the Marlboro, Casals, Aspen and Grand Teton Music Festivals. He commissioned and premiered Robert Suderburg's Concerto for Solo Percussionist and Orchestra with the Philadelphia Orchestra in 1979, repeating it in 1993. Mr. Bookspan joined the Curtis Institute of Music faculty in 1980.

BOOKSPAN CAESAR SALAD

Serves 6 to 8

These recipes are 'passed down' family favorites of Michael and his wife Shirley.

2 cloves garlic, minced	Worcestershire sauce
6 tablespoons olive oil	3 tablespoons wine vinegar
2 heads romaine lettuce	1 egg
½ teaspoon salt	½ lemon
¼ teaspoon dry mustard	1 cup garlic croutons
Black pepper, freshly ground	3 tablespoons Parmesan cheese, and/
6 anchovy fillets	or grated Romano cheese

Mix garlic with olive oil and set aside. Break up romaine lettuce and spin dry in salad dryer. Remove and place in large salad bowl. Combine salt, dry mustard, black pepper, mashed anchovy fillets, a few shakes of Worcestershire sauce, and wine vinegar. Stir into oil mixture.

Slowly simmer egg in shell for 1½ minutes, gently beat and stir into oil mixture. Drizzle over romaine lettuce, tossing quickly. Add garlic croutons and Parmesan cheese. Toss and serve immediately.

SALAD NIÇOISE

Serves 8

3 cups potatoes, cooked and sliced
¼ cup dry white wine
3 cups French-cut green beans,
   cooked 'al dente'
1 cup French dressing
1 head Boston lettuce

2, 6 oz. cans tuna in oil
2, 2 oz. cans anchovy fillets
3 eggs, hard-boiled, quartered
½ cup black olives, pitted
1 tablespoon parsley, chopped
1 tablespoon chives, chopped

Marinate warm potatoes in wine for at least 1 hour. Place beans in glass bowl and pour ⅓ cup French dressing over them. Marinate 1 hour or more. Carefully remove large outer leaves of lettuce until you have 5 lettuce cups. Drain tuna and break into bite-size pieces. Drain and separate anchovy fillets.

On a platter, arrange a mound of potatoes in center. Encircle with lettuce. In lettuce cups, arrange alternately: green beans, tuna, eggs, olives, and anchovy fillets. Sprinkle with parsley and chives. Serve with a cruet of the remaining French dressing.

STRAWBERRY SOUP

Serves 6

2 cups fresh strawberries, rinsed
½ cup sugar
½ cup sour cream

2 cups water
½ cup red wine

Place strawberries in blender and process to a pulp. Add: sugar to taste, sour cream, water and wine. Chill for several hours.

Photo: ERIC ARBITER

BRIAN DEL SIGNORE, PERCUSSIONIST

Brian Del Signore was born in Pittsburgh, PA and studied with the percussionists of the Pittsburgh Symphony and Philadelphia Orchestra. Brian has performed in numerous orchestras along the way, including the two fine orchestras of his teachers. He also was a finalist in percussion auditions of the Chicago Symphony and the New York Philharmonic before accepting his present position as principal percussionist with the Houston Symphony, commencing duties on New Year's Eve of 1987 (December 31, 1986).

Brian Del Signore's Houston Symphony duties include performance on all percussion instruments. (That means if he doesn't know how to play it already, he'd better learn...QUICK!) During his tenure to date, Houston Symphony has toured both Europe and Japan twice. He has also toured Japan with the Houston Symphony Players, a chamber group made up of principal players from the orchestra and it's music director Christoph Eschenbach.

Brian also teaches graduate students majoring in percussion performance at the University of Houston. He produces and performs music for children, with and without orchestral accompaniment. Children know him as "Brianboy." Along with his wife Leah, he has two children, Damian and Jacquelyn.

LEAH'S FRESH VEGETABLE AND CHEESE ENCHILADAS
Serves 3 to 4

This is my wife Leah's recipe....Living in Houston, which has a large Hispanic population, has enabled us to enjoy many excellent Mexican restaurants. One very important secret of these chefs, so close to the border, is <u>fresh</u> ingredients. Fresh cilantro (a Mexican parsley) is always available for green salads and for cooking. --B.D.S.

15 oz. can tomato sauce
1½ teaspoons chili powder
1 teaspoon paprika
Dash of comino (cumin)
⅓ pound grated Cheddar cheese
⅓ pound grated Monterrey Jack cheese
1 medium-large onion, chopped

2 ribs celery, chopped
½ green bell pepper, chopped
½ jalapeño pepper, chopped (optional)
6 to 8 corn tortillas (small size, 6-inch)
¼ to ½ cup cilantro, chopped

Combine tomato sauce, chili powder, paprika and comino in a skillet and bring to a simmer. Combine all cheese, onion, celery, bell pepper, and jalapeño pepper in a bowl.

Grease a 2 to 3-quart baking dish. Dip corn tortilla into sauce to warm. Fill with 2 to 3 tablespoons of cheese mixture and roll up. Place seam-side down in baking dish. (Be sure to reserve some cheese mixture for the top). Cover with the remaining sauce and reserved cheese mixture.

Cover with foil during first half of baking time. Bake at 350 degrees for at least 20 minutes, or until heated through. Top with cilantro before serving.

Serve with Spanish rice, beans and green salad; use ranch dressing.

GEORGE GABER, PERCUSSIONIST

George Gaber holds the title of distinguished professor of music emeritus from Indiana University. Mr. Gaber joined the faculty of the Indiana University School of Music in 1960.

Mr. Gaber was born and educated in New York City. He attended Cooper Union and the Juilliard and Manhattan Schools of Music and studied privately with teachers from the major orchestras in New York City. He received an honorary degree from Escuela Mocidade of São Paulo, Brazil. Mr. Gaber has performed with many symphony, opera and ballet orchestras, as well as jazz and Latin groups, modern dance ensembles and the major networks. These include the Ballet Russe Orchestra, Pittsburgh, NBC, Israel, Los Angeles, ABC and CBS Symphony Orchestras. Among the conductors and composers with whom he has worked are Paul Hindemith, Aaron Copland, Fritz Reiner, Leopold Stokowski, Gian Carlo Menotti, Stan Kenton, Duke Ellington, Walter Susskind, Zubin Mehta, and Igor Stravinsky. In the course of his network activities, Mr. Gaber performed on the Bell Telephone, Firestone, U.S. Steel, Omnibus, Alcoa and Sid Caesar shows.

His experience with the jazz-Afro-Latin recording and film fields includes associations with many outstanding band leaders. Mr. Gaber has composed music for the CBS series "Look Up and Live," for the African play "Song of a Goat" by John Pepper Clark, and for the American theater production of "Phaedra." Other works include etudes and ensemble pieces for percussion.

George Gaber is widely known as a pedagogue, having played and taught at the Aspen, Colorado, and Banff, Canada, Summer Festivals. He has been invited to lecture, teach, and perform in a number of foreign countries, including Japan, Australia, Israel, Mexico, Canada, Brazil, China, Haiti, and Chile. He has also served as advisor for UNESCO, the United National Educational, Scientific and Cultural Organization. George and his wife Esther live in Bloomington, Indiana.

DANISH APPLE CRISP
Serves 8

This is a great recipe for unexpected company, as one usually has the ingredients in the closet. It is quick and easy, and very tasty. It was given to me (Esther Gaber) by my friend Leah Grodner, (now deceased) after her year in Denmark.

1 large tart apple, peeled, cut into bits (1 cup)	¾ cup sugar
1 teaspoon baking powder	½ cup walnuts, chopped
⅛ teaspoon salt	1 egg, slightly beaten
	½ cup flour

Blend all ingredients together. Pour into 8-inch pie pan. Bake for 25 minutes at 400 degrees. Top should be nicely browned.

Serve in wedges. Top with whipped cream, ice cream or frozen yogurt.

Photo: © STUART-RODGERS-Photography

DONALD KOSS, TIMPANIST

Donald Koss is presently the principal timpanist of the Chicago Symphony Orchestra. He is a graduate of Northwestern University, where he received a degree in mathematics. He played with the Fifth Army Band for three years, before returning to Northwestern for graduate work in mathematics. Koss performed with the Evanston Symphony under Sidney Harth and Frank Miller, the North Side Symphony of Chicago under Milton Preves, the Civic Orchestra of Chicago under John Weicher and the Grant Park Symphony, before joining the Chicago Symphony in 1963 as principal timpanist. In addition to his duties with the Chicago Symphony, Mr. Koss is in demand for timpani and percussion coachings in the various orchestras around Chicago. He also has served as a consultant for the Ludwig Drum Company and as advisor for the Zildjian Cymbal Company.

Mr. Koss has performed chamber works featuring percussion and timpani at the Ravinia Festival, including Bartók's Sonata for Two Pianos and Percussion and Stravinsky's *L'histoire du Soldat* and *Les noces*. The Stravinsky pieces were recorded by the Ravinia Chamber Players with Mr. Koss as solo percussionist. In addition, he has performed and recorded with Chicago Pro Musica, including Walton's *Façade*, *L'histoire du Soldat* and Lovondi's *The Nightingale*. In 1985, the *Façade* and *L'histoire du Soldat* won a Grammy Award as Best New Classical Artist for Mr. Koss and the other members of the Chicago Pro Musica. During past seasons, he has appeared as soloist on the Chicago Symphony subscription concerts in Bartók's Concerto for Two Pianos and Percussion and Poulenc's Concerto for Organ, Strings, and Timpani. On the orchestra's trip to Japan, he performed as solo percussionist with the Chicago Pro Musica.

Donald met his wife Mary when she was the timpanist of the Civic Orchestra; she was instrumental in getting him to join the Civic, inviting him to play timpani while she served as percussionist. Mary continues to perform as a professional percussionist.

FRENCH DRESSING

Makes about 2 cups

This recipe, our current favorite salad dressing, was given to us by the charming ladies of the Co-op Acadean Restaurant in Cheticamp, Nova Scotia. --D.K.

1 can tomato soup (10 oz.)	½ teaspoon pepper
⅓ cup salad oil	1 teaspoon paprika
⅓ cup vinegar	1 tablespoon Worcestershire sauce
⅓ cup sugar	1 teaspoon mustard
1 teaspoon salt	1 medium onion

Mix all ingredients well in blender.

Photo: BEN SPIEGEL

STANLEY S. LEONARD, TIMPANIST

Stanley Leonard was the principal timpanist of the Pittsburgh Symphony Orchestra from 1956 to 1994. His performances received acclaim from colleagues, conductors, and critics. The *Pittsburgh Press* called him "a jewel of the orchestra," the *Christian Science Monitor*, "the finest timpanist in the country." André Previn stated that Stanley Leonard "is not only a virtuoso, but a consummate musician." Perhaps one of the most impressive critiques of his artistry is quoted from the late William Steinberg; "Stanley Leonard is not just a timpanist, he is the embodiment of tympanum playing."

Mr. Leonard appeared as soloist with the Pittsburgh Symphony in the world premieres of Raymond Premru's Celebrations for Solo Timpani and Orchestra (1984), and Byron McCulloh's Symphony Concertante for Timpanist and Orchestra (1973). He performed the American premieres of Andrzej Panufnik's Concertino for Timpani, Percussion, and Strings (1981), and Werner Thaerichen's Concerto for Timpani and Orchestra (1964). Mr. Leonard was soloist in Darius Milhaud's Concerto for Percussion and Small Orchestra (1958). He has made many recordings with the orchestra for Capitol, Command, Columbia, Phillips, Angel, and Sony records.

Mr. Leonard's musical goals include an interest in presenting the timpani as a 'solo' instrument. He and his wife Margaret have sponsored commissions for new works for solo timpani and orchestra through the Eastman-Leonard invitational commission at the Eastman School of Music of the University of Rochester. They also have assisted Duquesne University in commissioning a new solo work for timpani and wind symphony in which Mr. Leonard appeared as soloist.

Mr. Leonard was senior lecturer in percussion at Carnegie Mellon University for twenty years. Since 1989, he has been adjunct professor of percussion at Duquesne University. His teaching has included presenting percussion clinics and master classes at colleges and universities throughout the United States. His former students are members of major symphony orchestras, and educators in universities and public schools nationwide. His musical compositions for solo timpani, percussion, percussion ensemble, and handbells are published in the United States and England and performed throughout the world. Leonard is a published author of the widely respected method book *Pedal Technique for the Timpani*. He is *Percussion Review* editor for Ludwig Music Publishing Company.

Stanley Leonard was born in Philadelphia, Pennsylvania, and grew up in Independence, Missouri. He studied at Northwestern University and is a graduate of the Eastman School of Music. His first performance as an orchestral timpanist was with the Independence Little Symphony in November 1945. His wife of 42 years, Margaret, is a guidance counselor in the Chartiers Valley School District; a son, Mark, is paintings conservator of the John Paul Getty Museum in Los Angeles. Steven is a computer programmer in Birmingham, Alabama.

Mr. Leonard's favorite avocation is fishing, especially for trout.

STUFFED TROUT

Serves 3 to 4

This recipe reflects Mr. Leonard's taste in food and his love of the outdoors. He prefers to eat fresh fish, especially when he has made the 'catch'.

14 to 16-inch freshly caught trout or
    2, 9 to 10-inch freshly caught trout
½ teaspoon olive oil
2 tablespoons softened butter
¼ cup white wine (Chardonnay)
2 tablespoons fresh lemon juice
4 cloves garlic, crushed

1 teaspoon ground dill weed
¼ teaspoon salt
¼ teaspoon pepper
1 cup fresh, sliced mushrooms
½ cup chopped onions
¼ cup fresh, chopped parsley
3 lemon slices
Paprika to garnish

Clean trout, remove head. Cover bottom and sides of a **Swedish baking dish*** or heavy baking dish with **aluminum foil**. Brush the aluminum foil with olive oil. Place cleaned and beheaded trout in the dish.

Butter the inside and outside of the trout; do not worry if the butter is not completely smooth over the surface of the fish. Wet the inside and outside of the trout with white wine and fresh lemon juice. Brush the crushed garlic on all inside and outside surfaces of the trout. Sprinkle all surfaces with dill weed, salt and pepper.

Place mushrooms, chopped onion and parsley inside the fish. Place any remaining onions or mushrooms around the outside of the fish. Arrange lemon slices on the top of the fish, sprinkle with parsley and paprika.

Cover the dish with a second piece of aluminum foil, and seal the edges. Place dish in a preheated oven at 325 degrees. After 20 minutes, check for doneness. When the fish is done, remove foil and place fish on a serving plate and lightly cover with the remaining liquid. Serve immediately.

* A Swedish baking dish is a cast iron dish with a porcelain finish.

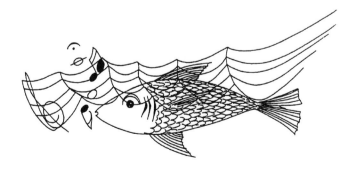

Photo: LEO KNIGHT

ROBERT PANGBORN, PERCUSSIONIST

Born in Painesville, Ohio, Robert Pangborn, principal percussionist and assistant principal timpanist of the Detroit Symphony Orchestra, began studying piano at age seven and percussion at nine. His early training was with William Hruby at the Hruby Conservatory of Music in Cleveland. He later studied with Cloyd Duff at the Cleveland Institute of Music, Roman Sculz at the Berkshire Music Festival, William Street at the Eastman School of Music, and Morris Goldenberg at Juilliard. His military service was spent as a percussionist with the United States Military Academy Band at West Point.

Before joining the Detroit Symphony Orchestra in 1964, Pangborn held the positions of principal timpanist with the Indianapolis Symphony, mallet percussionist with the Cleveland Orchestra, and timpanist/percussionist with the Metropolitan Opera Orchestra in New York City.

An accomplished soloist, Mr. Pangborn performed the American premiere of the Rolf Lieberman Concerto for Bass Drum and Orchestra with the Cleveland Orchestra, George Szell conducting. Donald Erb's Concerto for Solo Percussionist and Orchestra, which bears a dedication to Robert Pangborn, was given its world premiere by Mr. Pangborn with the Detroit Symphony Orchestra under the baton of Sixten Ehrling. He has also performed *The Worried Drummer*, a humoresque for solo percussionist, at numerous children's concerts. In addition to his duties with the orchestra, Mr. Pangborn has organized and directed several chamber percussion groups in Cleveland and Detroit, including the Detroit Percussion Trio, 4 for Percussion, and Mostly Mallets.

Mr. Pangborn serves on the Board of Trustees of Detroit Symphony Orchestra Hall and the Metropolitan Detroit Friends of Interlochen. He also is a member of the International Percussive Arts Society. He and his wife, Brenda, own an international marketing company and enjoy working with HO trains and miniature doll houses.

VEGETARIAN CHILE

Serves 12 to 14

15 oz. can tomato purée
6 oz. can tomato paste
2, 28 oz. cans crushed tomatoes
1 cup tomato juice
1 can fine beer
3 to 4 large cloves garlic
¼ cup chile powder, or to taste
1 bay leaf
1 teaspoon each; oregano, basil and pepper
2 teaspoons salt (to taste)
1½ cups carrots, thinly sliced
2 cups chopped onions
2 teaspoons cumin
⅛ teaspoon cayenne pepper

1 cup chopped green pepper
1 cup sliced celery
½ head broccoli, cut in small florets
1 zucchini, cut in small pieces
3, 31 oz. cans Brooks spicy chili beans
OPTIONAL:
Sliced mushrooms, shredded cabbage, peas
   or green beans
GARNISHES:
Tortilla chips, chopped tomato,
   chopped onion, sour cream,
   shredded Cheddar cheese

Combine the tomato purée, paste, crushed tomatoes, tomato juice, beer, garlic, chili powder, bay leaf, oregano, basil, salt and pepper, and simmer for 30 minutes. Add carrots and onions and simmer for 15 minutes.

Stir in the cumin, cayenne and remaining vegetables, except the beans, and simmer at least 10 minutes. Drain, add the chili beans and heat through.

PIANO

Photo: Courtesy of Jay K. Hoffman & Associates

TZIMON BARTO, PIANIST

Since his appearances as pianist at the Vienna Musikverein and the Salzburg Festival at the invitation of Herbert von Karajan and his U.S. debut with the Boston Symphony Orchestra under the direction of Christoph Eschenbach, Tzimon Barto has repeatedly brought dynamic and highly acclaimed performances to audiences worldwide.

Among the leading orchestras with which he has performed are the National Symphony Orchestra, the NHK Symphony Orchestra, the Berlin Philharmonic, the Czech Philharmonic, and the Orchestre National de France. He has had five standing-ovation successes with the Philadelphia Orchestra and triumphs with the Milwaukee and Indianapolis Symphonies, as well as appearances with the National Symphony under the direction of Zdenek Macal, and the San Jose Symphony. His recital schedule included performances in Houston, Munich, Istanbul, and Berlin. Additional highlights from previous seasons include his New York debut as soloist with the Houston Symphony at Lincoln Center and an acclaimed recital at the Salzburg Festival.

Tzimon Barto's 1995-96 concert season include a performance of Grieg's celebrated Piano Concerto with the Philadelphia Orchestra and a performance of Tchaikovsky's monumental Piano Concerto No. 1 with the Chicago Symphony; both under the direction of Christoph Eschenbach. In February, Barto was the featured soloist in a six-city U.S. tour by the Atlanta Symphony Orchestra conducted by Yoel Levi. In April, Barto and Eschenbach joined forces again on two pianos for a ten recital tour of Germany and Austria which included appearances in Dresden, Stuttgart, Berlin, Munich and Vienna. They also presented their unusual recital program, which traces impressionism from Schumann to Messiaen, at the Ravinia Festival on August 12.

Highlights of Tzimon Barto's 1994-95 concert season include concerto appearances with the symphony orchestras of San Francisco, Milwaukee, Houston, San Antonio, San Jose, Phoenix and Anchorage. In October, Barto toured South America with the Bamburg Symphony conducted by Christoph Eschenbach and in January 1995, he toured Germany with London's Philharmonia Orchestra. Barto made a second German tour in March with the Rundfunksinfonieorchester Frankfurt.

An exclusive EMI recording artist, Mr. Barto has recorded Ravel's G Major Concerto, Prokofiev's Third Concerto, Gershwin's *Rhapsody in Blue*, Rachmaninoff's Third and Bartók's Second Concerto, Liszt's Second Concerto and a collection of his solo music, Schumann's *Kreisleriana* and Symphonic Etudes, Chopin's Preludes and First Concerto, Saint-Saëns's *Carnival of the Animals*, and de Falla's *Nights in the Gardens of Spain*. His latest CD, *Popular Encores,* features music by J.S. Bach, Debussy, Janáček, Gershwin, Scott Joplin, Felix and Fanny Mendelssohn, and others.

Despite his active performing and recording career on the piano, Tzimon Barto is also an accomplished conductor and a composer of a variety of music ranging from operas, to a 27 minute piece for chamber orchestra based on the story of creation. Possessing an insatiable appetite for knowledge, he is fluent in seven languages and is currently studying the biblical Hebrew in order to read the Bible in its original language.

GERMAN SWEET CHOCOLATE CAKE
Makes a 9-inch, three layer round cake

Tzimon chose this wonderful recipe because he grew up with this cake—his mother's specialty.

1 package (4 ounces) Baker's
   German sweet chocolate
½ cup water
2 cups flour
1 teaspoon baking soda
¼ teaspoon salt

1 cup (2 sticks) margarine or butter
2 cups sugar
4 eggs (yolks and whites separated)
1 teaspoon vanilla
1 cup buttermilk
4 egg whites

Heat oven to 350 degrees, line bottoms of 3 (9-inch) round cake pans with wax-paper. Heat chocolate and water in heavy 1-quart saucepan on very low heat, stirring constantly until chocolate is melted and mixture is smooth. Remove from heat. Mix flour with baking soda and salt, then set aside. Beat margarine and sugar in large bowl with electric mixer set on medium speed, until light and fluffy. Add egg yolks, one at a time, beating well after each addition. Stir in chocolate mixture and vanilla. Add flour mixture alternately with buttermilk, beating after each addition until smooth.

Beat egg whites in another large bowl with electric mixer set on high speed until stiff peaks form. Gently stir into batter. Pour into prepared pans. Bake 30 minutes or until cake springs back when lightly touched in center. Immediately run spatula between cake and sides of pans. Cool 15 minutes, remove from pans. Remove wax-paper. Cool completely on wire racks.

COCONUT-PECAN FILLING AND FROSTING

1 can (12 oz.) evaporated milk
1½ cups sugar
¾ cup (1½ sticks) margarine or butter
   or 50/50 mixture

4 egg yolks, slightly beaten
1½ teaspoons vanilla
1 package (7 oz.) Baker's angel
   flake coconut
1½ cups chopped pecans

Mix milk, sugar, margarine/butter, egg yolks and vanilla in large saucepan, cook and stir on medium heat about 12 minutes or until thickened and golden brown. Remove from heat. Stir in coconut and pecans. Beat until cool and of spreading consistency. (Makes about 4½ cups).

Photo: JORGE BOLET

RALPH BERKOWITZ, PIANIST

Ralph Berkowitz was born in New York City in 1910. He was graduated from the Curtis Institute of Music in 1935, and was on the staff until 1940. He joined the legendary cellist Gregor Piatigorsky in 1940 for thirty years of association, making innumerable tours all over the world and many recordings for RCA Victor and Columbia Records. Mr. Berkowitz became executive assistant to Serge Koussevitzky in 1946 and was later chosen for the position of dean of the Boston Symphony Orchestra's Tanglewood Music Center, a post he held until 1965.

He performed extensively from 1930 to 1970 with a wide variety of artists, including Felix Salmond, Janos Starker, Raya Garbousova, Jan Peerce, Josef Gingold, Leonid Kogan, Joseph Silverstein, Phyllis Curtin, Zara Nelsova and Eudice Shapiro. Ralph Berkowitz has transcriptions and arrangements published by G. Schirmer, Elkan-Vogel Associated and Galaxy in U.S.A.; in Europe, Universal Editions, Austria; Durand et Cie, France; and B. Schott Söhne, Germany. His articles have been published by Penguin Books (London), *Etude* magazine and the *Juilliard Review*.

Mr. Berkowitz has lectured at Columbia University, the University of Southern California, Albright Museum, Buffalo, Franklin Institute, Philadelphia, and Tanglewood. He appeared in the June Music Festival, in Albuquerque, New Mexico for twenty-six years (1946-1972), appearing 250 times in 123 works.

Mr. Berkowitz was manager of the Albuquerque (now New Mexico) Symphony Orchestra from 1958 to 1969. His other interests include an avid love and talent for painting, as seen from his several art exhibitions in the Berkshire Museum in Philadelphia, and the Jonson Gallery in Pittsfield, Massachusetts.

Martin Bookspan, radio and TV commentator, said in a letter to Mr. Berkowitz for his 80th birthday celebration:

"Ralph Berkowitz is a man of impeccable manners and taste, awesome erudition, unflappable temperament, and a pixieish sense of humor that combine to make him a true Superman of our time. Long may he enrich the lives of all who know and love him."

BROILED SWORDFISH
(Turkish Style)
Serves 2 to 3

I love food very much, and enjoy dishes that are healthy and beneficial, especially for musicians.
--R.B.

1 pound swordfish steaks (1-inch thick)	**6 bay leaves**
½ tablespoon paprika	**3 medium tomatoes**

8 tablespoons lemon juice

4 tablespoons olive oil

Salt and pepper to taste

2 green peppers

2 medium onions

Skin fish, cut into 1-inch cubes and place in bowl. Mix paprika, lemon juice, oil, salt, pepper and bay leaves and marinate fish with this mixture in refrigerator for three hours.

Cut tomatoes, peppers and onions into chunks. When ready to cook, place fish, tomatoes, peppers and onions in broiler pan, cover with marinade and place three inches below broiler in preheated oven. Broil about 5 minutes, turn, broil several more minutes so both sides of fish and vegetables are cooked through. Serve with lemon sauce.

LEMON SAUCE (beat well)

¼ cup olive oil

5 tablespoons lemon juice

½ cup chopped fresh parsley

Salt and pepper to taste

STUFFED RED PEPPERS

Serves 4

1 pound lean ground beef

1 large onion, chopped

¼ cup uncooked instant rice

1 small tomato, chopped

1½ tablespoons dried dill

1½ tablespoons dried parsley

Salt and pepper to taste

Worcestershire sauce to taste

6 tablespoons ketchup

Large dash of margarine

4 large red bell peppers

1½ cups beef bouillon

On medium heat, lightly brown the beef and onion. Boil rice according to package directions in separate pan with chopped tomato. Place meat, onion, rice, tomato, dill, parsley, salt and pepper, Worcestershire sauce, ketchup and margarine in bowl and knead well.

Wash and slice tops off peppers, but save to use as covers. Using a sharp knife, carefully cut and remove ribs and seeds from inside of peppers. Fill peppers with mixture and replace tops. Place in deep saucepan with lid. Add beef bouillon, cover, and cook over medium heat until peppers are tender, about 45 to 60 minutes. Serve with yogurt sauce.

YOGURT SAUCE

½ pint plain yogurt

½ teaspoon salt

1 clove garlic, crushed

Photo: MARTIN REICHENTHAL

VICTOR BORGE, PIANIST/HUMORIST

Victor Borge's unique combination as musician and humorist has made him a legend in his own time. Affectionately known as "The Great Dane," Mr. Borge is an ambassador of goodwill for both his native Denmark and his adopted America. In fact, he was awarded the Medal of Honor by the Statue of Liberty Centennial Committee at a gala ceremony on Ellis Island. He has been knighted by the Scandinavian countries of Denmark, Iceland, Norway, and Sweden, as well as Finland, and he was honored by both the U.S. Congress and the United Nations.

Each season, Maestro Borge performs with and leads a number of the world's foremost orchestras, including at times the New York Philharmonic, Cleveland, Philadelphia, London Philharmonic, the Royal Danish, and others. Some orchestras have actually had their seasons rescued by the inclusion of a Victor Borge appearance in their programs or by special benefit performances.

Borge has written two books with Robert Sherman—*My Favorite Intermissions* and *My Favorite Comedies in Music*. He made his operatic acting "debut" by performing as both Prince Orlovsky and the jailer Frosch in Sarah Caldwell's Boston Opera Company production of *Die Fledermaus* with Beverly Sills. He has conducted five S.R.O. performances of Mozart's *The Magic Flute* for the Cleveland Opera—Borge has also presented his own concert adaptation of Bizet's *Carmen*, which he narrated and conducted to critical accaim.

His numerous television appearances include several recent events on PBS. One is with the Chicago Symphony Orchestra hosted by Itzhak Perlman, featuring Borge as the special guest star performing his famous "Borgeism" on Mozart and a duet with Perlman. The "On Stage at Wolf Trap" series presented "Victor Borge: A Birthday Celebration," which is now available on home video. Also running on PBS is the Tanglewood special "Bernstein" which features Borge in

a hilarious duet with the Boston Symphony Orchestra. "Victor Borge: Then & Now," a new program taped in Detroit in April 1992, was featured as the PBS fundraiser special for the summer and fall of 1992. It combines new, live concert footage and early television and movie clips from Borge's fifty years in the entertainment industry. This new program is also now available on home video. "Victor Borge Tells Hans Christian Andersen Stories" is a new project and was created especially for the children's home video market. It was released in November of 1992 and is available in both a 110-minute version and a 55-minute version.

Born in Copenhagen to a musical family, Borge's mother introduced him to the piano when he was three years old. He was hailed as a prodigy and given a scholarship to the Copenhagen Music Conservatory. While still in his teens, he was awarded scholarships to study with Frederic Lamond and Egon Petri in Berlin and Vienna. Yet Borge's incredible sense of humor, combined with his musical ability, established him already in his early twenties as one of the leading film and stage personalities in Scandinavia. Humorist Borge was noted for his biting satire; when the Nazis invaded his homeland, his barbs about Hitler earned him position Number 1 on the Nazi blacklist. From Finland, he escaped on the S.S. American Legion, the last American passenger ship to leave northern Europe before the war.

In the fifty-one years he has lived in the United States, Victor Borge has performed on radio, in films, on television, on Broadway (where, with rave reviews, he made theatrical history with his *Comedy in Music,* which, according to *The Guinness Book of Records,* holds the record for the longest running one-man show, 849 performances), presented in huge sports arenas, in opera houses, and at the White House.

Borge has established scholarships at universities and colleges; with the eminent New York lawyer Richard Netter, he created in 1963 the Thanks to Scandinavia scholarship fund in gratitude for the heroic deeds of the Scandinavians, who, while risking their own lives, saved the lives of thousands of the persecuted and doomed during the Holocaust. The multimillion dollar fund has already brought more than a thousand students and scientists to America from the Scandinavia countries for studies and research. In memory of his parents (Borge's father was an honored member of the Royal Danish Philharmonic Orchestra), he has established a special music scholarship; one of the highest study grants in his native country, it is awarded each summer at a gala ceremony in the Concert Hall of the famous Tivoli Gardens. He has given innumerable benefits to help worthy causes.

Mr. Borge spends his treasured free time with his wife, Sanna, their five children and nine grandchildren. An expert skipper, Borge says, "with me the three B's are Bach, Beethoven and Boats." Deeply devoted to his native country, he is no less grateful for being a citizen in the one he adopted. "The smile," he says, "is the shortest distance between people."

VICTOR'S ROCK CORNISH HENS

Serves 3

3 Rock Cornish hens
Salt and pepper
½ stick of butter
¾ cup water
3 teaspoons flour

¼ cup light cream
Tasteless sauce coloring (a browning
    agent such as Kitchen Bouquet)
½ teaspoon sugar

Rub insides of pullets with salt and pepper. Sear hens in butter in a large (5-quart or greater) dutch oven until golden brown, about 10 to 12 minutes. *("If a clock is not available, play the 'Minute Waltz' 10 to 12 times").*

Add ¾ cup water and let hens simmer, with pot covered, on stove top, until tender (approximately 35 minutes). Just before the birds are finished, in a small cup, dissolve 1 tablespoon of cool water and 3 teaspoons flour. Remove birds, stir in like crazy the drippings paste made with water and flour. Stir in cream, salt to taste, sauce coloring and sugar. Pour sauce over pullets and serve.

Photo: CHRISTIAN STEINER

JOHN BROWNING, PIANIST

In the tradition of the great romantic pianists, John Browning is renowned for his exceptional interpretive skills, brilliant technique and deep commitment to musicianship. Mr. Browning has made more than twenty European concert tours and has performed repeatedly with such orchestras as the Concertgebouw of Amsterdam, London Philharmonic, London Symphony, and the Scottish National Symphony. He has toured the Soviet Union on four occasions and has concertized in Japan, South America and Africa. In this country, Mr. Browning appears regularly with the Boston Symphony, Chicago Symphony, Cleveland Orchestra, Philadelphia Orchestra, New York Philharmonic, St. Louis Symphony, Pittsburgh Symphony, and the Los Angeles Philharmonic, to name only a few.

In 1962, John Browning was soloist at the inaugural celebration at New York's Lincoln Center in the world premiere performance of Samuel Barber's Pulitzer Prize-winning Piano Concerto, which had been written especially for Mr. Browning. He recorded it with the Cleveland Orchestra in 1964, George Szell conducting. A new recording of the Barber Piano Concerto was released in 1991 by BMG Classics with Mr. Browning and the St. Louis Symphony, Leonard Slatkin conducting. This earned John Browning his first Grammy Award for Best Instrumental Soloist with Orchestra; the recording also received a Grammy nomination for Best Classical Album. In 1992, Mr. Browning began recording for Music Masters; a disc of the complete Barber solo piano repertoire was released in

September 1993 which earned him a second Grammy award for Best Classical Instrumental Soloist Without Orchestra. He has recently recorded two Mozart concerti with the Orchestra of St. Luke's, under Julius Rudel, and an all-Scarlatti recording was released last year. Browning's latest recording of the complete Barber songs, with baritone Thomas Hampson and soprano Cheryl Studer, was released to great acclaim on the Deutsche Grammophon label.

Current listings in the John Browning discography also include three CDs on the Delos label: one devoted to music of Mussorgsky, one to Liszt, and one to Rachmaninoff. Other recordings appear on the CBS Masterworks, RCA, Capitol and Phoenix labels.

John Browning celebrated his 60th birthday with a three-concert series at Lincoln Center in New York: his first performance with Leonard Slatkin and the Juilliard Orchestra, the second in recital, and the third with Thomas Hampson and the Ridge Ensemble. Each concert included a world premiere (by Richard Cumming and Benjamin Martin respectively) and at least one work by composer Samuel Barber, with whom Mr. Browning has been closely identified over the years. The recital program included the first New York performance in 50 years of the Barber Interlude I, and the final concert included the premiere performance of three of the composer's unpublished songs. During the 1996-97 season, Browning will continue to appear in recital and in concert with major orchestras across the United States and Europe.

SWEET POTATO RUM CASSEROLE
Serves 6

It's great!! --J.B.

4 cups boiled sweet potatoes
   (about 3 pounds)
4 tablespoons butter
4 tablespoons cream

¼ teaspoon nutmeg
¼ cup rum
4 tablespoons dark brown sugar
Salt and pepper to taste

Boil potatoes in a 4-quart pot, slightly covered, until tender, for about 25 to 30 minutes. Peel off skins and mash up potatoes in a bowl.

Measure out 4 cups of sweet potatoes into a mixing bowl. Beat in butter and cream, then nutmeg, rum and brown sugar. Season with salt and pepper.

Pour into 2-quart casserole dish and sprinkle with melted butter. Bake at 400 degrees, uncovered, until lightly browned.

Photo: CHRISTIAN STEINER

BELLA DAVIDOVICH, PIANIST

Before emigrating to this country, Bella Davidovich was one of the Soviet Union's preeminent artists, as well as one of the few women to be admitted to the inner circle of Russian cultural life. Since coming to the United States more than a decade ago, Mme. Davidovich has established herself as one of her adopted country's premiere keyboard artists, as well as one of few women to achieve such international prominence. Her October 1979 American debut at Carnegie Hall before a standing-room-only crowd heralded a new chapter in a career of major importance.

Throughout her extraordinary career, Mme. Davidovich has performed with the world's leading conductors, including Rudolf Barshai, Semyon Bychkov, Sergiu Comissiona, James Conlon, Andrew Davis, Lukas Foss, Christoph von Dohnányi, Charles Dutoit, Christoph Eschenbach, Mariss Jansons, Neeme Järvi, Kiril Kondrashin, Raymond Leppard, Neville Marriner, Kurt Masur, Riccardo Muti, Eugene Ormandy, David Oistrakh, Mstislav Rostropovich, Kurt Sanderling, Maxim Shostakovich, Gerard Schwarz, Leonard Slatkin, Yevgeny Svetlanov, Yuri Temirkanov, Klaus Tennstedt, Michael Tilson Thomas, Edo de Waart, and David Zinman, among many others.

Each year Bella Davidovich continues to affirm the high esteem of the thousands who have become her followers during her career in the West. The East, however, has also reclaimed her in the spirit of "perestroika;" in December, 1988 she became the first Soviet emigre musician to receive an official invitation from Goskoncert to perform in her native country. Mme. Davidovich played concertos, a recital and chamber music with the Borodin String Quartet to sold-out halls filled with her fans of many years, as well as with the new generation hearing her live for the first time. Her triumphant first visit to Poland in thirteen years took place in the spring of 1988. The Polish musical and cultural community celebrated her return jubilantly: the concerts were broadcast on national radio live and

televised by several European countries; they were followed by an immediate reinvitation for February of 1989.

Mme. Davidovich's recent engagements include performances with the Pittsburgh Symphony, the Seattle Symphony, the Puerto Rico Symphony and the New York Chamber Symphony at the Tisch Center of the 92nd Street Y. She toured throughout Austria and Switzerland with Walter Weller and Leopold Hager conducting; to Copenhagen with Otto Kamu, performing the Chopin Second Piano Concerto; to the Edinburgh Festival and Glasgow; to Saint Petersburg to perform the Schumann Piano Concerto with the St. Petersburg Philharmonic under Mariss Jansons; to Hague to perform Beethoven's First Piano Concerto with Yevgeny Svetlanov; and to Germany to perform the Saint-Saëns Second Piano Concerto with the Hessische Rundfunk under Paavo Berglund. After the close of the season she served as judge at the Queen Elizabeth and Clara Haskil Competitions.

Born into a family of musicians—her mother and sister were accompanists and her grandfather was concertmaster at the local opera house—in Baku, Russia, Bella Davidovich displayed rich musical talent by the age of three and began formal training at the age of six. Davidovich was 18 when she entered the Moscow Conservatory where she studied with Konstantin Igumnov and Jacob Flier. In 1949, she won first prize in the Chopin Competition in Warsaw, earning her the title "Deserving Artist of the Soviet Union."

During her remarkable career in Russia, Mme. Davidovich appeared with every major Russian conductor and performed as soloist with the Leningrad Philharmonic for 29 consecutive seasons.

She was a member of the faculty of the famed Moscow Conservatory for sixteen years. Mme. Davidovich came to the West in October of 1978 and became an American citizen in the fall of 1984. She is a member of the faculty of the Juilliard School. Mme. Davidovich can be heard on the Philips, Orfeo, Novalis and Delos Records labels.

HAMENTASCHEN
Makes 40 hamentaschen

This favorite pastry recipe comes from Bella Davidovich's sister, who enjoys baking it for Bella. If you are unable to find lekvar in the store, just buy regular plump pitted prunes and run them through a food processor, using the chopping blade, until pulpy.

DOUGH:
¾ cup oil
1½ cups sugar
4 eggs
2 teaspoons vanilla extract
3 teaspoons baking powder
½ teaspoon salt
5½ cups flour

FILLING: (mix together the following)
1 pound lekvar (prune filling)
4 tablespoons honey
½ pound chopped walnuts
1 tablespoon lemon juice

In a large bowl combine oil and sugar, mix well. Add eggs one at a time, beating until mixture is light and fluffy. Stir in vanilla extract. Sift dry ingredients and add gradually. Knead until smooth enough to be rolled out on floured board. Roll to ¼-inch thickness.

Cut into circles with 3-inch cutter. Place full teaspoon of filling in center of each circle. Pinch bottom right side and top right side of circle of dough together, bring open left edge into middle and seal all edges. You should have raised triangles, shaped like a slightly flattened 3-sided pyramid. A little filling should be exposed in middle.

Bake on greased cookie sheet at 350 degrees for 20 minutes until lightly brown.

Photo: J. HENRY FAIR

MISHA DICHTER, PIANIST

Now in the fourth decade of a highly distinguished international career, Misha Dichter has established himself as one of the foremost musicians of our time. Renowned for his powerful musical vision and his keyboard mastery in the grand virtuoso tradition, Mr. Dichter's performances of music, ranging from Mozart through Schoenberg, have made him a favorite of audiences around the world. He appears annually in recital, orchestral and chamber music concerts in the major music capitals.

Mr. Dichter has entered into a multi-record agreement with MusicMasters Classics, which in March 1994 released his first solo recording for that label, an all-Brahms disc that includes the *Variations and Fugue on a Theme of Handel*, waltzes and fantasias. Among Mr. Dichter's acclaimed recordings for Philips and RCA Records is the complete cycle of Liszt's Hungarian Rhapsodies, the two Brahms Piano Concertos with Kurt Masur and the Leipzig Gewandhaus Orchestra, the Lizst Concerto with André Previn and the Pittsburgh Symphony, as well as music of Beethoven, Brahms, Chopin, Gershwin, Mussorgsky, Schumann, Stravinsky and Tchaikovsky.

Mr. Dichter is an active chamber musician and has collaborated with most of the world's leading string quartets. In addition, he regularly performs with his wife, pianist Cipa Dichter, in duo-recital and with leading orchestras in the United States and Europe. Mr. Dichter has given master classes at music festivals, conservatories and universities, including Juilliard, Curtis, Aspen, Ravinia, Harvard and the Amsterdam Conservatory.

Following performances this past summer with the Chicago Symphony, Baltimore Symphony, and Minnesota Orchestra, Misha Dichter's 1996-97 schedule includes appearances with the St. Louis and National Symphony Orchestras, as well as both solo and duo recitals.

Mr. Dichter's recent concert schedule included 25 recitals across the United States, as well as orchestral performances at Carnegie Hall in New York, the Kennedy Center in Washington, D.C. and Symphony Hall in Boston, and appearances with the Chicago, Atlanta, Utah and Oregon Symphonies. He also made a European concert tour in the spring of 1995 that included an orchestral performance in Paris.

Misha Dichter's 1994 summer engagements included his 26th consecutive season at the Ravinia Festival, where he performed the Grieg Piano Concerto with the Chicago Symphony; a cycle of Beethoven piano concerti with the Atlanta Symphony; performances of the Brahms D Minor Concerto on tour in Brazil; and a chamber music program at the Caramoor Festival. Mr. Dichter also marked his 21st summer at the Aspen Music Festival, where he gave chamber music performances, played a duo-recital with Cipa Dichter, and performed Stravinsky's Concerto for Piano and Winds, a work he also played at the Eastern Music Festival in North Carolina.

Among the highlights of Misha Dichter's performances during the 1993-94 season were a recital at the Academy of Music in Philadelphia and a performance with Wolfgang Sawallisch and the Philadelphia Orchestra, a Carnegie Hall concert, and a recital in Paris. Mr. Dichter also returned to Russia, the scene of his 1966 Tchaikovsky Competition victory, after an absence of 20 years, to perform with the St. Petersburg Philharmonic Orchestra (formerly the Leningrad Philharmonic) led by Mariss Jansons. In addition, he joined his wife, Cipa, in duo-recitals throughout the United States.

Misha Dichter was born in Shanghai in 1945, his Polish parents having fled Europe at the outbreak of World War II. He moved with his family to Los Angeles at the age of two and took his first piano lessons four years later. Mr. Dichter's principal teachers were Aube Tzerko, a pupil of Artur Schnabel, and at the Juilliard School, Rosina Lhevinne. His stunning triumph at the 1966 Tchaikovsky Competition in Moscow launched his international career.

An accomplished writer, Mr. Dichter has contributed many articles to leading publications such as the *New York Times*. He has been seen frequently on national television and was the subject of an hour-long television documentary that was broadcast in Europe. An avid tennis player and jogger, Mr. Dichter is also a talented sketch artist. His drawings, which have served as a sort of visual diary, have been exhibited in New York art galleries.

MISHA'S 24 HOUR OMELET
Serves 12

1 loaf of long day-old French bread, broken into small pieces
6 tablespoons unsalted butter, melted
¾ pound Swiss cheese, shredded
½ pound Monterey jack, shredded
9 thin slices of Genoa salami, chopped, (or 4 oz. smoked salmon)
16 eggs

3½ cups milk
½ cup white wine
4 scallions, minced
1 tablespoon German mustard
¼ tablespoon ground pepper
½ tablespoon cayenne pepper
1½ cups sour cream
⅔ to 1 cup grated Parmesan cheese

Butter or grease two shallow 3-quart (13 x 9 x 2-inch) baking dishes. Spread bread over the bottom of the 2 pans and drizzle with butter. Divide evenly and sprinkle cheeses and meat. Beat together eggs, milk, wine, scallions, mustard and peppers. Pour evenly into pans over cheese. Cover with foil. Refrigerate overnight. Remove from refrigerator 30 minutes before baking.

Preheat oven to 325 degrees. Cover and bake one hour. Uncover and spread with sour cream and sprinkle with Parmesan. Bake again until brown, about 10 to 13 minutes.

Photo: CHRISTIAN STEINER

JANINA FIALKOWSKA, PIANIST

Hailed as one of the leading pianists of her generation, Janina Fialkowska has been recognized for her exceptional artistry with enthusiastic accolades worldwide. Celebrated for her interpretations of the Classical and Romantic repertoire, she is particularly distinguished as one of the great interpreters of the piano works of Chopin and Liszt.

Past engagements have included a major North American tour in February 1993 with the Cracow Philharmonic Orchestra under Gilbert Levine that took her to Boston, Philadelphia, Detroit, Toronto, the Kennedy Center in Washington, D.C., and Avery Fisher Hall in New York. She also appeared in 1993 with the Royal Philharmonic Orchestra, both in London and on tour in England, and with the BBC Symphony Orchestra of London.

In previous seasons, the artist has appeared with the Chicago Symphony, the Cleveland Orchestra, the Detroit Symphony, the Los Angeles Philharmonic, the Minnesota Orchestra, the National Symphony, the Philadelphia Orchestra, the Pittsburgh Symphony and the Seattle Symphony, among others, as well as with all of the principal Canadian orchestras. She has won special recognition for a series of important premieres, most notably the world premiere performances of a newly discovered Liszt Piano Concerto, Op. Posth., with the Chicago Symphony in May 1990. She has also given the world premiere of the Piano Concerto by Libby Larsen with the Minnesota Orchestra (October 1991) and the North American premiere of the Piano Concerto by Sir Andrzej Panufnik with the Colorado Symphony (February 1992).

In touring Europe each year, Miss Fialkowska has appeared as guest artist with such prestigious orchestras

as the Royal Concertgebouw Orchestra of Amsterdam, the Bonn Philharmonic, the Halle Orchestra, the London Philharmonic, London's Philharmonia Orchestra, the Royal Philharmonic, the Scottish National Orchestra, the Warsaw Philharmonic and the French and Belgium National Radio Orchestras. She has also played with the Israel Philharmonic and the Hong Kong Philharmonic.

Janina Fialkowska has recently founded "Piano Six," a group of internationally renowned Canadian pianists who are committed to a ten-year program that will bring important recitals to specific areas, at an affordable price, and in locations throughout Canada where classical music performances are a rarity.

Born to a Canadian mother and a Polish father in Montreal, Janina Fialkowska started to study the piano with her mother at the age of five. Eventually she entered the Ecole de Musique Vincent d'Indy, studying under the tutelage of Yvonne Hubert. The University of Montreal awarded her both bachelor and master of music degrees by the time she was 17. The next year, 1969, her career was greatly advanced by two events: winning the first prize in the Radio Canada National Talent Festival and traveling to Paris to study with Yvonne Lefebure. One year later, she entered the Juilliard School of Music in New York, where she studied with Sascha Gorodnitzki, later becoming his assistant for five years. In 1974, she took top prize at the First International Arthur Rubinstein Master Piano Competition in Israel.

In 1992, the CBC produced a sixty-minute television documentary, "The World of Janina Fialkowska," that aired to great acclaim throughout Canada. This program was awarded a Special Jury Prize at the 1992 San Francisco International Film Festival.

LEMON CUSTARD TART

Serves 6 to 8

This recipe comes from Mrs. Arthur Rubinstein's cookbook. Long before writing the book she used to make me this tart when I was a guest in their house in Paris or in Marbella, Spain. She knew it was my favorite! --J.F.

10-inch tart shell (see below)	**3 eggs**
3 to 4 lemons	**1 cup (200 grams) sugar**
3 tablespoons unsalted butter, softened	**1 cup (¼ liter) heavy cream**
⅓ cup (¾ deciliter) bread crumbs	

TART SHELL:

1 stick (115 grams) unsalted butter	**1 cup (140 grams) flour**
at room temperature	**plus 3 tablespoons**
3 tablespoons sugar	**½ teaspoon salt**
2 egg yolks	

To make tart shell, cream together softened butter and sugar. Mix in egg yolks. Slowly add flour and salt, mixing well. Gather dough into a ball and place in an ungreased tart mold. Use the heels of your hands to press and mold the dough into the pan. If you are using a slip-bottom tart mold (one in which the side will be removed) be sure to keep the sides approximately ⅜-inch thick so it will hold its shape. When the dough is in place, "dimple" the bottom by quickly jabbing it all over with your fingertips. Mix together 1 lightly beaten egg with 1 tablespoon water and lightly brush over the dough. Place the tart shell in a preheated oven 400°F (205°C) and bake for about 8 minutes or until very pale gold.

Grate the lemons carefully, using the 'fine' side of your grater and applying very little pressure to be sure of avoiding the bitter white pith. You should have 3 to 4 tablespoons. Squeeze the lemons to make ¾ cup (1¾ deciliters) juice.

Preheat oven to 350°F (180°C). Pour the lemon juice, grated zest, butter, bread crumbs, eggs, sugar and cream into blender, and running it just long enough to mix contents thoroughly.

Pour the custard into the half-baked tart shell, not quite filling it since the lemon custard expands during baking. Bake it for 20 to 30 minutes. It is done when the filling has risen somewhat, all over. It will be uniformly set and golden brown. Let the tart cool for 10 minutes before you serve it.

Photo: INTERNATIONAL PIANO ARCHIVES

RUDOLF FIRKUŠNÝ, PIANIST

Acclaimed as one of the premier keyboard artists of our time, Rudolf Firkušný came from a richly varied background of Czech and Central European musical traditions, including studies with Leos Janáček and Artur Schnabel. Hailed for his masterful performances of the Classical, Romantic, and early 20th century repertoires, he is also considered the world's foremost exponent of Czech music and has championed the works of Smetana, Dvořák, Janáček, and Martinu throughout his distinguished career.

Mr. Firkušný has recorded a richly varied repertoire for several major labels and earned three consecutive Grammy nominations—in 1991, 1992 and 1993—for his RCA Victor Red Seal recordings. These include solo works by Janáček, his teacher and mentor; music of Martinu, his close friend and colleague; and a disc of Dvořák piano quintets with the Ridge Quartet. His 1992 RCA disc of his "signature piece," the Dvořák Piano Concerto, paired with two chamber concertos by Janáček, was named "Best of the Month" by *Stereo Review.*

Mr. Firkušný was an active performer on the international scene. Mr. Firkušný performed regularly on five continents in recital and as soloist with virtually every major orchestra and many of the legendary conductors of this century, among them Otto Klemperer, Serge Koussevitzky, Fritz Reiner, George Szell, Leopold Stokowski and Bruno Walter. He had also collaborated in chamber music performances with such distinguished artists as Gregor Piatigorsky, William Primrose, Lynn Harrell and the Juilliard Quartet.

Mr. Firkušný began his 1993-94 season in Europe, where he performed with the Gurzenich Orchestra of Cologne, giving recitals in Toulouse, France, and in Brussels at the Flanders Festival, then returned to the Czech Republic for an all-Janáček recital in the composer's home city of Brno. He also toured major German cities with the German Chamber Philharmonic. In Prague, in

December, 1994, Mr. Firkušný performed chamber music with Itzhak Perlman and Yo-Yo Ma at a Dvořák Gala Concert marking the 100th anniversary of the premiere of the *New World Symphony.* A Peter Gelb production for CAMI Video, the program was televised in Europe, aired over PBS in North America and released as a home video by SONY. Additional European engagements included recitals in London and Paris and a return to the Prague Spring Festival.

Mr. Firkušný had entered a period of renewed recording activity in the past several years. His RCA Victor Red Seal recording of Czech songs by Dvořák, Martinu and Janáček with soprano Gabriela Benackova was released in September 1993. He recently recorded the Martinu Piano Concertos Nos. 2, 3 and 4 with Libor Pesek and the Czech Philharmonic in Prague; it was Mr. Firkušný who gave the world premieres of all three concertos, two of which are dedicated to him. He has recorded Janáček's *Diary of One Who Disappeared* and a Dvořák piano quartet (with the Ridge Ensemble) for BMG/RCA Victor, as well as late Schubert sonatas for MusicMasters.

In May 1990, Mr. Firkušný returned to perform in Czechoslovakia for the first time in forty-four years, ending his self-imposed exile and acknowledging the triumph of democracy. He continued to make frequent trips to his native country to perform, record and receive numerous honors. In 1991, Mr. Firkušný was awarded the highest civilian honor bestowed by the Czech Government, the Order of T.G. Masaryk, First Class, which was named for the country's first President, who sponsored Mr. Firkušný's initial trips abroad in the 1930s.

One of the most important figures in American musical life, Rudolf Firkušný made his home in New York City. His untimely death in 1994 was a tremendous loss to the music world.

ANNA'S VITELLO TONNATO

Serves 6 to 7

This recipe comes from my friend Anna Malamood. Her "Vitello Tonnato" is my favorite dish. It goes very well with a cold rice salad. --R.F.

2½ pounds veal
½ cup olive oil (Berio if possible)
1 cup white wine
2 cups water
Small tube of anchovy paste
1 onion, quartered
1 carrot, sliced

1 or 2 celery ribs, sliced
Juice of 1 lemon
Mayonnaise (*use a good ready made*)
Small can tuna fish (6½ oz.), drained
2 anchovies
Capers for garnish
Sliced pickles and lemons for garnish

Put veal into a heavy enamel or earthenware dutch oven-type pot. Mix olive oil, white wine, water, several tablespoons of anchovy paste, onion, carrot, celery and lemon juice. Pour over veal, cover pot and simmer for about an hour or until cooked.

Remove veal from liquid, place on rack, put liquid through strainer, place in smaller pan or dish and add veal. Let cool completely, remove veal and place once again on rack.

Put pan with liquid over flame and let contents thicken slightly, then cool.

In blender, add tuna fish to about ½ cup mayonnaise, or more to taste and add some of the sauce from veal; it must not be too dense, it must flow, then add 2 anchovies. Blend well. Slice veal and place on platter. Cover with the tuna sauce, decorate with capers and sliced pickles, put capers on top and sliced pickles around platter with some lemon slices.

Photo: STEPHEN DEUTCH

JEROLD FREDERIC, PIANIST

Jerold Frederic has played over 3,500 recitals in the United States, Mexico and Canada, plus three far reaching tours of western Europe. As a soloist, he has performed with the Cleveland, Chicago, Minneapolis, Houston, Portland, Denver and Los Angeles Symphony Orchestras.

Mr. Frederic received a master of arts degree from Chicago Musical College and a doctoral degree from Boston University.

Mr. Frederic established an early record of concert activity when he played 257 engagements in his first

three seasons. Mr. Alexander W. Greiner, artistic director for Steinway and Sons, said, "Frederic's rise and extensive concertizing throughout the United States, accomplished as it was without preliminary debut in New York or Europe, presents an achievement without precedent in the history of the field." Jerold Frederic is a Steinway Artist.

Jerold Frederic is professor of music at College of Mount Scholastica in Duluth, Minnesota; director of the Milwaukee School of Music, Milwaukee, Wisconsin; and artist-in-residence, Ohio State University, Columbus, Ohio.

FRUIT STUFFED CORNISH HENS WITH CUMBERLAND SAUCE

Serves 8

I hope that others will enjoy this menu as much as we have. --J.F.

8 Cornish hens
Lawry's garlic salt (to taste)
½ cup sesame seed oil
3 teaspoons of soy sauce
2 sticks of sweet butter
1 cup yellow onion, peeled, and diced
2 tart apples, peeled, cored and diced

1 cup golden raisins
1 cup walnuts, finely chopped
1 chicken flavored bouillon cube
   dissolved in one-half cup hot water
½ cup sherry or vermouth
16 oz. package of Pepperidge Farm
   herb stuffing

Rinse hens well under cold running water and pat dry. Sprinkle garlic salt inside and outside. Rub with sesame seed oil and sprinkle soy sauce inside and outside. Set hens aside.

Melt butter in large skillet, then add diced onions, apples, golden raisins, walnuts and bouillon cube dissolved in one-half cup boiling water. Sauté for approximately 15 minutes, add sherry or vermouth. Add 6 cups Pepperidge Farm dry stuffing and 1¾ to 2 cups boiling water to pan. Stir until moist and water is absorbed. Add additional water if necessary.

Preheat oven to 350 degrees. Prepare hens with stuffing and arrange them in shallow pan (if large enough). Otherwise, use 2 baking pans. Set in middle of oven and bake for one-half hour, covered, then uncovered for 1 hour or until golden brown and done.

CUMBERLAND SAUCE

10 oz. jar of currant jelly
¾ cup of orange juice
½ cup of sherry
1 teaspoon of dry mustard

½ teaspoon ginger, finely chopped
¼ teaspoon garlic salt
½ tablespoon of shredded lemon peel
  or lemon zest

Add all ingredients and bring to boil while stirring. Reduce heat and simmer for 20 minutes, then cool for 10 minutes. Arrange birds on serving platter and pour sauce over hens. Garnish with parsley and green grapes.

Photo: CHRISTIAN STEINER

GARY GRAFFMAN, PIANIST

Hailed by *Newsweek* as "one of the great living pianists," Gary Graffman has been one of the most popular and peripatetic performers on the international concert circuit for over three decades: witness summer 1988 when Mr. Graffman performed at the Hollywood Bowl and at Philadelphia's Mann Music Center before return engagements with both the Cleveland and Philadelphia Orchestras in the fall of that year.

Ever since his debut at the age of 18, with Eugene Ormandy and the Philadelphia Orchestra, he has circled the globe almost nonstop, playing the most demanding works in the piano literature. His recordings of concertos by Tchaikovsky, Rachmaninoff, Prokofiev, Brahms, Chopin and Beethoven with the orchestras of New York, Philadelphia, Cleveland, Chicago and Boston have been acclaimed as definitive, and his album of Gershwin's *Rhapsody in Blue* with Zubin Mehta and the New York Philharmonic became one of the best-selling disks ever made by that venerable orchestra.

In 1979, however, Graffman's performing career was interrupted by an ailment affecting the fourth and fifth fingers of his right hand. Considering the grueling tasks these fingers had been conquering for so many years, any problems that might have developed along the way would not seem surprising. Nevertheless, a frustratingly protracted search for informed medical help was necessary before the cause of Graffman's affliction—emphasizing once again the relationship between performing artist and performing athlete—was finally related to a sprained knuckle received some fifteen years earlier when the pianist was dealing with a balky instrument.

During the slow and often agonizing process of rehabilitating his right hand, Gary Graffman has been far from idle. He has returned to the concert stage to play the few, but brilliant, piano concertos written for left hand alone (most of them commissioned early in the century by Paul Wittgenstein, who lost his right arm in World War I). In addition to the famous Ravel Piano Concerto, these include major works by Prokofiev, Britten, and, in September 1985, the North American premiere, with Zubin Mehta and the New York Philharmonic, of the coruscatingly virtuosic Piano Concerto by Erich Wolfgang Korngold, written in 1924.

Graffman's enforced semi-retirement from the keyboard has provided him with remarkable opportunities to expand his horizons, literally as well as figuratively. In June, 1986, after six years as a faculty member (after ten earlier years as a student), Gary Graffman was appointed to the post of director of Philadelphia's esteemed Curtis Institute of Music, following such illustrious predecessors as Josef Hofmann, Efrem Zimbalist and Rudolf Serkin. Extra-musically, he continues his lifelong study of Oriental art, adding to his collection of ancient Chinese ceramics and paintings and traveling to exotic destinations for archeological rather than pianistic pursuits.

Gary Graffman is also a popular writer, whose articles on non-musical subjects have appeared in such diverse publications as *Connoisseur* and *The Village Voice*. He is also the author of a highly praised book of memoirs, *I Really Should be Practicing*, published by Doubleday in 1981 and issued in paperback by Avon in 1982. It has become a classic, earning for its author the same kind of critical praise that he has received as a pianist.

Gary Graffman was born in New York of Russian parents and first climbed to the piano bench at the age of three. His violinist father had given him a small fiddle, but the instrument proved too cumbersome for the toddler and piano lessons were substituted with the idea that Gary would eventually return to the violin. However, the youngster's affinity for the piano soon became evident, and at age seventeen he won a scholarship to the Curtis Institute of Music for study with the renowned Isabelle Vengerova. After graduation from Curtis, Graffman studied intensively for several years with Vladimir

Horowitz, and, in the summers, at the Marlboro Music Festival with Rudolf Serkin. In 1949, Graffman won the prestigious Leventritt Award and made his debut with the leading American orchestras.

NAOMI'S NALISTNIKI
(Meat-filled Crêpes with Mushroom Sauce)
Serves 8 to 10

The preparation of this dish can be stopped before baking. Just put the baking dish in the refrigerator until time to bake. This makes it a good party dish—all you have to do before serving is put the pan into the oven. --Naomi G.

FILLING:
3 pounds beef
Salt and pepper (to taste)
Butter
2 onions, finely chopped
Substantial amount of fresh dill, chopped
1 pound of fresh button mushrooms (for
      mushroom sauce below), finely chopped
Parsley, chopped (for mushroom sauce)
2 cups meat stock (for mushroom sauce)

CRÊPES:
1 cup flour
3 tablespoons sugar
Pinch of salt
3 eggs, beaten
1½ cups milk
Vegetable oil

Simmer beef in stock seasoned with salt and pepper for 2 to 3 hours, or until very tender. Reserve stock. Cool beef and put through meat grinder. Sauté in butter 2 onions, until golden, and add to meat. Season to taste with salt and pepper and goodly amount of chopped fresh dill. Mix well and add a little of the meat stock, so that it is not dry. The consistency should be like cottage cheese.

Mix together flour, sugar and pinch of salt, and add to this eggs and milk. Mix until smooth and let stand for 2 or 3 hours. Using a cast-iron skillet 6 to 7 inches in diameter (*I use 2, which cuts the cooking time in half*), heat a tablespoon of vegetable oil until bubbling. Then pour in 1 tablespoon of the batter, rotating the pan quickly until batter covers the bottom of pan thinly as possible. Cook for about a minute and then flip over and do the same on other side. Set completed crêpes aside.

Next, put about 1 tablespoon of the meat filling into the center of each crêpe, fold crêpe like a little envelope. Arrange the crêpes in a buttered baking dish and dot the top of each with butter. Bake in a 350 degree oven for about 20 minutes, or until tops of crêpes are crisp. **Serve with mushroom sauce (see next paragraph).**

Sauté mushrooms in 1 stick of melted butter. When mushrooms have shrunk and released their liquid, remove from pan. Either remove water or add butter to pan to equal approximately 2 tablespoons. Add 2 tablespoons flour to pan and cook, stirring, until flour looses its raw smell. Slowly add 2 cups meat stock, stirring continuously, and cook until sauce thickens. Return mushrooms to pan. Add chopped dill and parsley, season to taste.

Photo: J. HENRY FAIR

HÉLÈNE GRIMAUD, PIANIST

Hélène Grimaud first came to international attention in 1986 with her debut recording of the Rachmaninoff Second Piano Sonata for Denon; she was fifteen years old. She has since been applauded by audiences and critics throughout the world for her ravishing command and passionate enthusiasm at the keyboard.

Miss Grimaud has performed recitals in the major cities of Japan, Europe and North America and has appeared with all of the orchestras of France, as well as many of Europe's leading orchestras, including, but not limited to: the London Symphony Orchestra, Munich Philharmonic, Berlin Staatskapelle, Bamberg Symphony, Zürich Tonhalle Orchester, Lausanne Chamber Orchestra, Oslo Philharmonic, St. Petersburg Philharmonic, Leipziger Gewandhaus, Frankfurt Radio Orchestra and Gothenburg Symphony. In North America, Miss Grimaud has appeared as soloist with the symphony orchestras of Los Angeles, San Francisco, Atlanta, Baltimore, Buffalo, Toledo, Vancouver and Montreal and has collaborated on both continents with such distinguished conductors as Daniel Barenboim, Herbert Blomstedt, Kurt Masur, Myung-Whun Chung, Jesus Lopez-Cobos, Neeme Järvi, Charles Dutoit, Andrew Davis, David Zinman, Michel Plasson, Yuri Temirkanov, Wolfgang Sawallisch, Marek Janowski and Lawrence Foster.

Highlights of Miss Grimaud's 1994-95 season included performances in Paris and a tour of Germany with the Orchestre de Paris, as well as a recital at New York City's 92nd Street Y. During the 1996 season Miss Grimaud made her debut with the Berlin Philharmonic. Among her numerous concert appearances during the 1993-94 season, Miss Grimaud performed with the Bayerische Rundfunk Orchester under the direction of Kurt Sanderling. She also made her debut with the Mostly Mozart Festival, appearing at New York's Lincoln Center with Gerard Schwarz, conducting, as well as touring with the Mostly Mozart Orchestra to Japan.

Miss Grimaud's United States recital debut in March, 1990 at Washington, D.C.'s Kennedy Center and her New York recital debut the following year were met with critical acclaim. She made her United States orchestral debut in summer, 1990 with the Cleveland Orchestra.

Hélène Grimaud first appeared with Gidon Kremer at the violinist's Lockenhaus Festival in Austria in 1988 and has returned since then to collaborate with Mr. Kremer, pianist Martha Argerich, violist Gerard Causse and the Hagen Quartet.

Miss Grimaud's discography for Denon Records includes Brahms's Third Sonata and Piano Pieces, Op. 118, as well as works by Chopin, Liszt, Schumann and Brahms. She recently recorded Rachmaninoff's Second Concerto with Jesus Lopez-Cobos and the Royal Philharmonic Orchestra. Her debut Rachmaninoff disc won the Grand Prix de L'Academie du Disque. In October, 1995, Denon released her recording of the Schumann Piano Concerto and Strauss Burleske with the Berlin Radio Orchestra, conducted by David Zinman.

Hélène Grimaud was born in 1969 in Aix-en-Provence, France. She attended the Conservatoire National Superieur de Musique in Paris, graduating with top honors. She is grateful for the artistic guidance she has received from Jacques Rouvier, Leon Fleisher and Daniel Barenboim.

PASTA A LA PIEMONTAISE
(From a Region of Northern Italy)
Serves 4

The below recipes are inspired by my mother's wonderful gift of cooking. To this day, still the best cook I have ever met. --H.G.

4 oz. unsalted butter
8 oz. 'crème fraiche'*
3 to 4 oz. grated fresh Parmesan cheese
Salt to taste

Nutmeg
1 tablespoon flour
Ham, cut into small cubes (optional)
14 oz. of egg and spinach pasta

Put butter, crème, Parmesan, a little salt, a little nutmeg, flour and optional ham into a pan. Let it warm up on low heat while stirring. Do not boil. Cook pasta and drain. Mix with sauce.

*If 'crème fraiche' is unavailable, substitute 8 oz. of sour cream instead.

PASTA SAUCE NAPOLITANA
Serves 2 to 3

⅓ cup olive oil (cold pressed)
1 medium onion, finely chopped
1 or 2 cloves garlic, crushed
1 tablespoon flour
1¼ cups water
¾ pound fresh tomatoes, quartered

¼ teaspoon thyme
¼ teaspoon laurel
1 clove
Salt to taste
Choice of Italian seasonings
8 oz. pasta of choice

Heat olive oil in medium-large skillet, add onion, and cook on medium heat for one minute or so, then stir in crushed garlic and the flour. Let the onion become 'blond' in the pan (about 5 to 6 minutes), then add 1¼ cups water.

Add the tomatoes, thyme, laurel and clove. Feel free to add any of your favorite Italian spices (oregano, basil...). Let it cook for 30 minutes, uncovered, on low heat. Stir occasionally.

CAROLA GRINDEA, PIANIST

Carola Grindea studied piano at the Bucharest Music Academy, then came to London where she was privileged to meet Myra Hess who arranged for her to study with Tobias Matthay, with whom she worked for over two years. After her Wigmore Hall debut in a programme of French music, she was launched on her career, giving many recitals and playing in chamber music ensembles in the UK and in other European countries. Grindea was broadcast on the BBC and other radio stations during her travels and appeared on many television stations. She joined the staff of Guildhall School of Music and Drama, London, in 1969 and succeeded in combining her career as performer with that of teacher.

Ms. Grindea became greatly involved in music education and published several methods on piano teaching: *The First Ten Lessons* (Oxford Univ. Press); *We Make Our Own Music* (Kahn & Averill; Pro-Am Music Resources, N.Y.—Also on video); and *The Adult Beginner* (K.K. Tapes).

She became engaged in research in a new area of exploration—problems caused by excessive tension in performance—and, with a group of scientists (doctors, psychiatrists, psychologists) and performing artists (musicians, actors, dancers), she founded, in 1981, the International Society for the Study of Tension in Performance (ISSTIP). Her studies in this field have appeared in the book *Tensions in the Performance of Music*—a Symposium, with foreword by Yehudi Menuhin and contributions by outstanding musicians.

For her pioneering work, she was awarded the Fellowship of the Guildhall School of Music by the Lord Mayor of London at a ceremony at Mansion House.

Ms. Grindea founded EPTA—European Piano Teachers Association—in 1978, which has grown into a most prestigious organization, with 34 national associations in Europe, and associate members throughout the world. Affiliations also were established with Piano Teachers Associations in the U.S.A., Japan, Canada, Hong Kong, Australia, and New Zealand. In 1980, she founded *Piano Journal*—the only magazine of this kind in Europe—which she edits.

In 1990, Grindea retired from Guildhall School and set up the first "Performing Arts Clinic" in the UK at the London College of Music, where she also teaches several piano students. With a team of medical specialists, psychologists and other therapists, she has helped over 500 musicians with their physical or psychological problems.

Ms. Grindea gives consultation lessons on both sides of the Atlantic and lectures and broadcasts often on "How to Cope with Physical and Psychological Problems in Performance." She conducts master classes in music faculties and conservatoires.

Carola has translated and edited the book *Dinu Lipatti* by Dragos Tanasescu and Grigore Bargauanu, now available in paperback (Kahn & Averill; Pro-Am Music Resources N.Y.)

CHEESE PLACHINTA (Pie)
(A Simplified Romanian Recipe)
Makes 16 pastries

Alternatively, one can use other cheeses like Gruyère, Ementhal, etc., combined with feta or curd cheese. If in a hurry, just slice the cheese with a Swedish slicer, into thick slices, placed along the middle of the pastry. It tastes very good even without egg....Proceed with folding the pastry and bake. --C.G.

2 packages (17 oz. each) frozen Pepperidge Farm puff pastry sheets
⅔ pound Cheddar cheese, grated
⅓ pound feta cheese, crumbled with a fork
1 large whole egg
½ to 1 tablespoon fresh chopped dill
Salt to taste

⅛ teaspoon pepper
Pinch of paprika
Pinch of cayenne pepper
Flour to spread on board
2 dessert spoons of milk (optional)
Sour cream or yogurt to taste

Defrost the 4 pastry sheets according to package directions. Mix together the cheeses with the egg, dill, salt, pepper, paprika and cayenne pepper. Cut each rolled up pastry sheet into 4 equal pieces. Gently unroll each piece into oblong shape on floured surface.

Place a heaping tablespoon of the cheese mixture in the center of each piece of pastry. First fold one side of the pastry over the mixture and then the other side. Pinch the open edges together. Repeat process with the rest of the pastry and mixture.

Place the 16 pastries on a non-stick baking tray(s), with the seams facing down. If desirable, brush pastry with milk to cause extra glow. Place the tray in a preheated oven at medium heat (350 degrees) for about 20 minutes, until the pastry is golden.

Serve hot with 1 or 2 teaspoons of sour cream or natural yogurt.

Photo: CHRISTIAN STEINER

LEONARD HOKANSON, PIANIST

Leonard Hokanson, internationally recognized as a recitalist, soloist with orchestra and chamber music player, is a welcome guest in the world's major music capitals. Winner of the Steinway Prize of Boston and prize winner at the International Piano Competition "Ferruccio Busoni," he has performed at such festivals as Aldeburgh, Berlin, Frankfurt, Lucerne, Prague, Salzburg, Schlewswig-Holstein and Vienna.

Among the orchestras with which he has appeared are the Bavarian Radio Symphony Orchestra, the Berlin Philharmonic, the Halle Orchestra, the Philadelphia Orchestra, the Rotterdam Philharmonic and the Vienna Symphony. He is a founding member of the Odeon Trio and has been guest artist with such ensembles as the Vermeer Quartet, the Fine Arts Quartet, the Ensemble Villa Musica, and the Wind Soloists of the Berlin Philharmonic.

Mr. Hokanson appears regularly in joint recital with the clarinetist, James Campbell and the hornist, Hermann Baumann, and collaborates for the song cycles of Schubert and Schumann with the German baritone, Hermann Prey. One of the last pupils of Artur Schnabel, Hokanson also studied with Karl-Ulrich Schnabel, Claude Frank and Julian DeGray. A native of Maine, Mr. Hokanson has concertized extensively in North and South America, Europe, and Southeast Asia.

Leonard Hokanson is professor of piano at the prestigious Indiana University School of Music in Bloomington, Indiana, a rank he previously held for ten years at the Hochschule für Musik in Frankfurt, Germany. He is often invited to give master classes for solo piano, chamber music, or for works of Schubert with piano (solo, chamber music, Lied).

His many recordings are on labels such as Bayer, Denon, Deutsche Grammophon, EMI, Naxos, Northeastern, Philips, RCA, and Sony.

OLD FASHIONED AMERICAN CHEESE CAKE

Serves 6 to 8

These favorite recipes of Mr. Hokanson are old established recipes that his wife Rona has enjoyed making for many years.

32 graham cracker squares
¼ pound butter
12 oz. cream cheese
¾ cup sugar
2 eggs, separated
2 teaspoons vanilla

Topping:
1 pint sour cream
2 tablespoons sugar
1 teaspoon vanilla

Crush graham crackers. Mix melted butter and graham cracker crumbs. Line bottom and up the sides of a 9-inch spring form pan with ¾ of mixture and bake 3 minutes at 350 degrees.

Mix cream cheese and ¾ cup sugar. Add beaten egg yolks and 2 teaspoons vanilla. Fold in stiffly beaten egg whites. Pour into crust and sprinkle the rest of the graham cracker crumbs on top. Bake for 25 minutes at 350 degrees. Remove and cool for 30 minutes.

For topping, mix sour cream, sugar and vanilla. Pour on top of cake and bake for 5 minutes at 350 degrees. Let cool and refrigerate.

PECAN BALLS

Makes approximately 30

¼ pound butter
2 tablespoons sugar
1 teaspoon vanilla

4 oz. ground pecans
1 cup flour

Blend the butter and sugar. Add vanilla, pecans and flour. Roll into balls and bake on a greased cookie sheet approximately 20 minutes at 350 degrees. Sprinkle on confectioners sugar while still hot and again when cool.

Photo: MEG OTTO

GRANT JOHANNESEN, PIANIST

Grant Johannesen is one of this country's most important and distinguished artists. Harold Schonberg of the *New York Times* wrote "One is apt to forget how strong a technician Mr. Johannesen is because he so seldom engages in sheer display. He remains one of the finest American pianists and is a superior musician. Few pianists give so satisfactory a recital."

In a career that spans fifty years, Grant Johannesen has secured for himself international status of the highest order. Continual engagements with the great American orchestras, together with annual appearances with distinguished European symphonic organizations, and on the national and international recital circuit, have elicited the highest critical praise. In addition, Mr. Johannesen was chosen to be the only soloist on two international tours with the New York Philharmonic and the Cleveland Orchestra; this included a tour of the Soviet Union. These and many other tours abroad have prompted the United States government to comment repeatedly on the artist's superior abilities as a "cultural ambassador" of the United States.

Known for his expansive and diverse repertoire, Mr. Johannesen has played with most of the important conductors of our time, a list that includes Solti, Maazel, Leinsdorf, Tennstedt, Ozawa, Boulez, Sawallisch, and Abravanel. He made his New York orchestral debut under the baton of George Szell with the New York Philharmonic, a collaboration which marked the beginning of a long and distinguished affiliation.

The catalog of Grant Johannesen's recordings (for HMV, Vox, Pantheon and Golden Crest) reveals the wide range of his musicianship. He has recorded works by Bach, Mozart, Beethoven, Schubert, Chopin and Schumann and displayed a special affinity for the French repertoire—he was the first artist to record the complete piano works of Gabriel Faure—and is a staunch champion of the works of American composers as well.

A recipient of many honorary doctoral degrees, Mr. Johannesen has served as a panelist with the National Endowment for the Arts in Washington, D.C. and has judged many international piano competitions. In addition to a consistently active performing career, he served from 1977 until 1985 as president of the Cleveland Institute of Music. Mr. Johannesen was made a Chevalier des Arts et Lettres by the French Government for his substantial contribution in the area of the performance and extensive recording of French music.

A native of Salt Lake City, Mr. Johannesen and the Utah Symphony recently performed the world premiere of *Pentameron*—a piano concerto he commissioned from composer Crawford Gates in honor of the 100th anniversary of the statehood of Utah. In February 1995, Mr. Johannesen celebrated the 50th anniversary of his debut recital with a concert in Carnegie Hall.

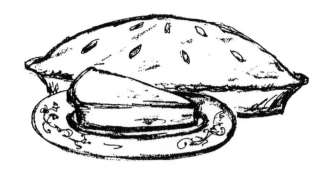

PIEPLANT
(Rhubard Cream Pie)
Makes one, 10-inch pie

The old word for rhubarb was "Pieplant" in my family's vocabulary. This recipe dates from an 1850 church cookbook. --G.J.

3 cups rhubarb	**CUSTARD:**
¼ teaspoon salt	1 cup white syrup
2 tablespoons flour	4 tablespoons sugar
1 cup sugar	1 cup sweet cream
2 eggs, beaten	3 eggs
10-inch double-crust pie shell	1½ tablespoons cornstarch
1 tablespoon butter	

Cut rhubarb into ½-inch lengths. Add salt and flour to sugar, then add the 3 cups of rhubarb and beat in the 2 eggs. Mix and turn into the unbaked pie shell. Dot with butter.

Mix custard ingredients and cook in a sauce pan on low heat until thickened. Pour into pie shell over rhubarb. Cover with a top crust, glaze it lightly with a combination of sugar and milk and bake in a hot 450 degree oven for 15 minutes. Reduce the heat to moderate, about 325 degrees and bake for 25 to 40 minutes, or until the rhubarb is tender and the crust is brown.

Photo: TRIX ROSEN

GILBERT KALISH, PIANIST

Gilbert Kalish has drawn international acclaim for his presentation of piano literature spanning the 18th century to the present. An eloquent spokesman for the music of his countrymen, Mr. Kalish's concert appearances throughout Europe, Asia, Australia and the United States have been influential in presenting the emerging American tradition. As soloist, chamber player, teacher, and perhaps most importantly, dedicated proponent of 20th century music, Kalish's performances and recordings have exerted considerable influence on the younger generation of musicians.

Born in New York in 1935, Gilbert Kalish graduated from Columbia University and pursued piano studies with Leonard Shure, Isabella Vengerova, and Julius Hereford. His most active collaborations have been as a member of the *Contemporary Chamber Ensemble*, in duo with cellist Joel Krosnick, in duo with violinist Paul Zukofsky, and as the life-long duo partner of the late mezzo-soprano, Jan DeGaetani. For many years, Mr. Kalish also has been the pianist of the Boston Symphony Chamber Players. His impressive discography of some eighty recordings documents all of these associations, as well as his solo performances. Notable discs include his five volume traversal of Haydn sonatas (Nonesuch), his Ives Concord Sonata (Nonesuch), and his many award-winning recordings with Jan DeGaetani (Nonesuch, Arabesque, Bridge).

Mr. Kalish's close association with the Boston Symphony Orchestra includes his position as chairman of the faculty as well as director of chamber music activities at Tanglewood. He has appeared as soloist with the Boston Symphony Orchestra in concerti by Berio, Carter, Bach and Mozart. He is professor of piano at the State University of New York at Stony Brook, where he also heads the performance faculty.

PASTA SAUCE

Other vegetables can be added near the end, such as zucchini and chopped parsley for flavor and color. The onions become totally sweet after slow cooking, as the recipe indicates. --G.K.

3 large onions, sliced thinly (about 6 cups)
¼ cup olive oil

¼ cup dry vermouth or dry white wine

Slow-cook the onions in olive oil on very low heat in a covered pan until entire lump is caramelized (this can take as long as 1 to 2 hours, or even longer). Stir occasionally. Close to the end, add dry vermouth or dry wine, raise flame and cook until the liquid has evaporated, while stirring continuously. Add to pasta of your choice. **Makes about 1¼ cups of sauce.**

Photo: © PETER SCHAAF

RUTH LAREDO, PIANIST

Hailed as "America's first lady of the piano" (*N.Y. Daily News*), Ruth Laredo has a distinguished worldwide reputation as a leading soloist, recitalist and recording artist. While she is particularly renowned for her pioneering recordings of the complete solo piano music of Rachmaninoff and the complete piano sonatas of Scriabin, her broad repertoire ranges from Beethoven to Barber.

She has appeared at Carnegie Hall, Alice Tully Hall, the Kennedy Center, the Metropolitan Museum of Art, the Library of Congress and the White House, and with such prestigious orchestras as the New York Philharmonic, the Philadelphia Orchestra, the Cleveland Orchestra, the Boston Symphony and the St. Louis Symphony. She has also performed with the Detroit Symphony, the National Symphony, the American Composers Orchestra, the American Symphony and the principal orchestras of Baltimore, Indianapolis, Houston and Buffalo. Additionally, she has played with the leading chamber orchestras, including the St. Paul Chamber Orchestra, the Orchestra of St. Luke's and the Orpheus Chamber Orchestra.

Noted for her strong commitment to chamber music, Miss Laredo frequently collaborates with the Tokyo String Quartet and was a founding member of the Music from Marlboro concerts. Each season she also devotes part of her schedule to performances with flutist Paula Robison. In March 1992, Ms. Laredo served as artistic director of a thirteen-hour Robert Schumann marathon at Symphony Space in New York City.

Her recent tour of Russia and the Ukraine, highlighted by recitals in Moscow, St. Petersburg and Odessa, formed part of an extensive television profile on CBS "Sunday Morning," with Charles Kuralt.

A three-time Grammy Award nominee, Ruth Laredo has been widely lauded for her numerous recording projects. She was the first pianist to record Rachmaninoff's complete solo works, a five-year undertaking for CBS Masterworks which produced seven discs and earned her a "Best Keyboard Artist" award from *Record World*. The final album in this series won her a Grammy nomination and was chosen "Best of the Month" by *Stereo Review*. Her Scriabin recordings—the first in North America of the complete sonatas—have garnered equal praise, being named "Best of the Month" by *Stereo Review* and one of "The Year's Best Recordings" by the *Saturday Review* (Sonatas Nos. 5, 7 & 9 and Etudes, Op. 42). Her recording of the music of Samuel Barber on Nonesuch earned her another Grammy nomination.

In great demand as an eloquent and authoritative commentator on the arts and piano literature, Ms. Laredo is a regular columnist for *Keyboard Classics* magazine, a frequent "guest critic" on WQXR's long-running "First Hearing" program and a special arts correspondent for National Public Radio's "Morning Edition." Additionally, she was commissioned by the international publishing firm of C. F. Peters to edit a new Rachmaninoff Urtext edition. A volume containing the Prelude, Op. 3, No. 2 and the ten preludes, Op. 23, inaugurated the series. The second volume, containing the complete preludes, Op. 32, has just been issued. Also published recently is "Ruth Laredo's Become a Musician Book," a guide for aspiring young artists drawn from Ms. Laredo's own experiences.

As the preeminent woman pianist in the United States, Ruth Laredo is a role model for women in the arts. A champion of women composers, she has performed and recorded works by Clara Schumann, Cecile Chaminade and Lili Boulanger, alongside music of their more celebrated male contemporaries. Nominated for "Woman of the Year" by *Ladies Home Journal*, she was also a guest speaker at the Second Annual Harvard/Radcliffe Women's Leadership Conference in September 1989 at the John F. Kennedy School of Government.

Born in Detroit and now residing in New York City, Ruth Laredo has been playing the piano since early childhood. She studied under Rudolf Serkin at the Curtis Institute and made her New York Philharmonic debut in 1974 under Pierre Boulez. Her New York orchestral debut took place at Carnegie Hall under Leopold Stokowski; in 1984 she was selected as the special guest soloist at the gala Carnegie Hall American Symphony Orchestra concert, marking the centennial of Stokowski's birth. She also has the honor of being one of only five pianists chosen by Carnegie Hall to perform in a concert as part of its 90th anniversary celebration.

RUTH LAREDO'S EASY QUICHE LORRAINE

Serves 6 (with meal)

This recipe was made in the days when we hadn't heard about cholesterol. Nevertheless, it's delicious and foolproof. I suppose you can substitute light cream cheese, light butter or Land O'Lakes spread instead of butter, egg beaters instead of eggs, and half-&-half instead of cream, or even whole milk. --R.L.

CRUST:
3 oz. cream cheese
1 cup flour
¼ pound butter
You will need an empty 8-inch pie tin

Mix together. Form into ball. Chill in refrigerator for about an hour. Roll out and place in 8-inch pie tin. Bake at 450 degrees for 10 minutes (or until slightly brown)

FILLING:
1 pint light cream
½ cup grated Cheddar cheese
2 eggs, beaten
½ pound fried bacon, crumbled
Salt and pepper to taste

Scald cream in a sauce pan, *do not burn or boil it,* cook slowly on low heat but stop just before boiling (when bubbles form around edge). Add grated cheese, eggs and bacon, then salt and pepper to taste. Pour into baked pie shell.

Bake for 30 to 45 minutes at 325 degrees (until quiche is set). Serve as hot hors d'oeuvres or with meal.

Photo: CHRISTIAN STEINER

JEROME LOWENTHAL, PIANIST

Jerome Lowenthal has distinguished himself as an artist of rare musical vision and integrity. His wide-ranging presence in a career spanning more than three decades has made him one of the important figures on the international music scene today. Critics have described him as "An extraordinary technician and a superb stylist, [who] plays with the sort of authority that seems instinctive" (*New Yorker*), or simply as "A pianist in the grand manner" (*New York Times*).

Mr. Lowenthal has recently recorded four pieces by Liszt for piano and orchestra with Sergiu Comissiona and the Vancouver Symphony Orchestra for the Music and Arts label. He will also record solo works by great composers who played the Steinway piano. For this recording he will play the music of Rachmaninov, Rubinstein, Paderewski, and Godowsky on ten different Steinway pianos that date from 1857 to the present. He previously recorded on two compact discs the complete works of Tchaikovsky for piano and orchestra with the London Symphony Orchestra and Sergiu Comissiona. He has performed these and other works recently with the New York Philharmonic, the Philadelphia Orchestra, the Pittsburgh Symphony, the San Francisco Symphony, the Radio Television Orchestra of Madrid, Orchestre de la Suisse Romande, and at the Catalonian Festival of Perelada. Mr. Lowenthal's 1993-94 season took him to Vancouver, Los Angeles, Amsterdam, Copenhagen and New York. In January 1991, Mr. Lowenthal performed as soloist in the New York premiere of Liszt's newly discovered Third Piano Concerto, with Zubin Mehta and the New York Philharmonic.

Born in Philadelphia, Jerome Lowenthal made his debut at the age of 13 with the Philadelphia Orchestra. He studied with three now-legendary figures: William Kapell; Edward Steuermann at the Juilliard School; and Alfred Cortot at the Ecole Normale de Musique, which Lowenthal attended on a Fulbright grant. His studies in Paris culminated in a premiere license de concert, a recording contract with Pathe Marconi, and performances

with the Orchestre de la Societe des Concerts du Conservatoire. While in Europe, Mr. Lowenthal won prizes in the international competitions of Brussels, Bolzano and Darmstadt. Moving then to Jerusalem, he became concert-lecturer at the Jerusalem Academy and an annual performer with the Israel Philharmonic. In 1961, Mr. Lowenthal returned to the United States, performing the Bartók Concerto No. 2 under the direction of Josef Krips with the New York Philharmonic, the Philadelphia Orchestra and the San Francisco Symphony.

Since then, Jerome Lowenthal has appeared with virtually every major orchestra in the United States, including the Chicago Symphony, Boston Symphony, Philadelphia Orchestra, New York Philharmonic, Los Angeles Philharmonic, National Symphony, Baltimore Symphony, Cleveland Orchestra, St. Louis Symphony and the Minnesota Orchestra. He has performed with some of the most distinguished conductors of our time, including Barenboim, Bernstein, Comissiona, Dorati, Giulini, Mehta, Monteux, Ormandy, Ozawa, Steinberg, Stokowski and Tennstedt.

Mr. Lowenthal's voluminous repertoire includes 59 performed concerti. He plays works by many living composers, three of whom—George Rochberg, Jay Reise and Ned Rorem—have composed works expressly for him. He has given all-Rochberg recitals and presented the world premiere of Rorem's Piano Concerto in Six Movements with the Pittsburgh Symphony, later recording it with the Louisville Orchestra.

Chamber music, too, is an important part of Jerome Lowenthal's musical life. He has played duo recitals with cellist Nathaniel Rosen and violinist Itzhak Perlman, as well as two-piano programs with his late wife, the Israeli pianist, Ronit Amir. Mr. Lowenthal is a regular participant in the festivals of Sitka, Alaska, the Reizend Muziekgezelschap in Holland, Chamber Music of Los Angeles, and the Music Academy of the West in Santa

Barbara. He and his family spend their summers in Santa Barbara and otherwise live in Manhattan where Mr.

Lowenthal is on the faculty of the Juilliard School.

LEORA'S FRUIT CAKE

*This cake has been prepared for me by my daughter Leora, and eaten by me, as well as by my other daughter Carmel. For maximum pleasure, it should be consumed, **NEITHER BEFORE** nor **AFTER**, but **INSTEAD OF** giving a concert. --J.L.*

2½ cups dried currants
3¾ cups seedless raisins
1 cup sliced citron
½ cup glacé lemon peel
1½ cups dried figs, chopped
1 cup dried pears, chopped
1½ cups blanched whole almonds,
   toasted and sliced
1 cup dried dates, chopped and pitted
1 cup glacé whole cherries, sliced
½ cup glacé pineapple wedges, chopped

½ cup glacé orange peel
5 cups dark Jamaican rum
1 cup butter
2 cups dark brown sugar, firmly packed
½ teaspoon *each* of cinnamon,
   allspice and nutmeg
5 eggs
2 cups all-purpose flour, sifted
2 teaspoons baking powder
½ teaspoon salt

Soak fruit and almonds in 3 cups of rum. Stir well and *soak for one week*.

Soften butter in a large mixing bowl and gradually mix in sugar and spices, then beat in 2 eggs. Sift flour, baking powder and salt. Add 1 cup to butter-sugar mixture and beat in remaining eggs. Stir in the soaked fruit, undrained, and add the remaining flour. Mix well.

Line greased pans (either two, 9-inch by 3-inch bread pans or three, 7-inch tube pans) with brown or waxed paper. Grease paper lightly and divide butter equally between pans. Place shallow pan of hot water beneath cake pans in oven to prevent cake from drying. Bake cake in preheated oven at 275 degrees until toothpick or cake-tester inserted in center comes out clean (about 2½ hours).

Cool in pans 1 hour. Remove to a wire-cooling rack. Remove paper and let set until cold. Wrap in aluminum foil and store in tightly-closed tin box. Moisten occasionally with remaining rum. *Age at least 1 month* before serving.

Photo: © ANGELA LLOYD-JAMES B.A.

JEREMY MENUHIN, PIANIST

Jeremy Menuhin made his New York recital debut as winner of the Young Concert Artist's Piano Competition in 1984 and soon afterwards gave the first of a number of concerts with the Berlin Philharmonic. He has regularly given recitals in the Kennedy Center in Washington, the Berlin Philharmonie, the Amsterdam Concertbouw and the Salle Pleyel.

Jeremy Menuhin's wide musical education has included composition with Nadia Boulanger in Paris, piano studies with Mindru Katz in Israel and conducting with Hans Swarowsky in Vienna. He has played with many of Europe's leading orchestras, notably the Royal Philharmonic, the Orchestre Nationale, the Israel Philharmonic, the Czech Philharmonic, the English Chamber Orchestra, the Prague Chamber Orchestra, the Zürich Chamber Orchestra and the Salzburg Mozarteum, under such conductors as Rudolf Barshai, Sergiu Comissiona, Eliahu Inbal and Evgeny Tchakarov.

In 1994, Jeremy performed the Bartók Third Piano Concerto with the Halle and Zürich Tonhalle Orchestras and Beethoven's Fifth Piano Concerto with the Sinfonia Varsovia; from these concerts a recording was released later that year. He has toured with Philharmonia Hungarica in the Czech Republic and Poland, playing Mozart's Piano Concerto, K. 488 with the English String Orchestra and Beethoven's Piano Concerto "Emperor" with the Orchestra of St. John's Smith Square. He also gave a series of recitals in Germany and Poland.

Chamber music represents an important part of Jeremy Menuhin's career and he regularly performs with many leading instrumentalists and singers. This past season, he appeared at festivals in Bath, Leicester, St. Nazaire, Bad Harzburg, St. Yrieux and Gstaad amongst others.

A varied discography includes works by Schubert, Mozart, Debussy, Beethoven and Bartók, the last of which consisted of the two Sonatas for Violin and Piano recorded with his father, Yehudi Menuhin, which received the Grand Prix du Disque. In 1993, his recording of the Dvořák Piano Quintet with the Chilingirian Quartet was released by Chandos. Last year an additional disc of works by Schubert was released by Dinemec UK.

SALADE TIEDE AUX FOIES DE VOLAILLE

Serves 4

This recipe requires one-half hour to prepare and is an hor d'oeuvre. --J.M.

Olive oil

6 shallots, finely chopped

6 oz. streaky bacon

1 pound chicken livers

1 wineglass Madeira

2 tablespoons mild balsamic vinegar

Sea salt

Freshly ground pepper

Small cup high quality olive oil (for dressing)

½ a radicchio lettuce, leaves torn
   into 3 or 4 pieces

12 oz. young spinach leaves

Stew finely chopped shallots in a small amount of olive oil until soft without burning and remove. Fry bacon until crisp without burning and discard fat.

In another very hot frying pan, fry the cleaned chicken livers in 1½ tablespoons hot olive oil until browned on both sides. Finish cooking the livers by simmering them briefly in the Madeira. They must remain pink inside.

Make a simple dressing from the vinegar, seasonings and olive oil. Add the radicchio leaves and spinach. Then add the rest of the ingredients and mix.

Photo: © ARCHIE KENT

PHILLIP MOLL, PIANIST

As a partner and accompanist for such celebrated artists as Kyung Wha Chung, James Galway, Anne-Sophie Mutter, Jessye Norman, Margaret Price, Thomas Bacon, and Kyoko Takezawa, Phillip Moll has performed in many of the world's most important concert halls. He has also won critical praise as a soloist.

Born in Chicago in 1943, Mr. Moll received his first instruction in piano and violin from his father, a violinist in the Chicago Symphony Orchestra. He was awarded a bachelor of arts degree in English literature from Harvard University in 1966 but continued his study of music throughout his university years. Among his teachers were Alexander Tchereprin, Claude Frank and Leonard Shure. At the University of Texas, where he earned his master of music degree, Mr. Moll became a teaching assistant in the opera workshop. He subsequently spent one year in Munich on a grant from the German Academic Exchange Service.

Mr. Moll records and performs frequently as ensemble pianist and harpsichordist with the Berlin Philharmonic Orchestra and also plays in a trio and chamber group with members of the orchestra. As soloist, he has performed with the Berlin Philharmonic, the Philharmonic Chamber Music Collegium of Berlin, the English Chamber Orchestra, the Orchestra of St. John's Smith Square and with major Australian orchestras.

Moll has recorded for BMG, Capriccio, Decca, Denon, Deutsche Grammophon, EMI, Koch International, Philips, Schwann, Summit, Tacet and Teldec.

FRESH GRAPEFRUIT JUICE WITH MINT

This is a joyously refreshing hot-weather drink, which I first bought from a street-vendor in Aix-en-Provence. Squeeze juicy grapefruits into the jar of your blender. Add mint leaves and some ice, along with a little sugar if necessary. Blend until slushy. --P.M.

TAGLIATELLE WITH WHITE TRUFFLES AND BUTTER

Fresh (not dried) pasta should be used. Fresh pasta cooks very quickly. The drained noodles are seasoned only with butter and salt: no pepper or cheese. After they are dished up, the raw truffle is shaved into razor-thin slices over each person's portion. If you get a good truffle, this dish can send those partaking of it into paroxysms of ecstasy. White truffles grow in northwestern Italy and can be found in gourmet stores.

Photo: J. HENRY FAIR

BARBARA NISSMAN, PIANIST

"Barbara Nissman is one of the last pianists in the grand Romantic tradition of Liszt, Rachmaninoff, and Rubinstein." So wrote a leading New York critic on the occasion of a recent performance of the Tchaikovsky Piano Concerto No. 2.

Ms. Nissman's international career was launched in 1971 with a highly acclaimed European tour, personally sponsored by Eugene Ormandy, who had previously engaged her as soloist with the Philadelphia Orchestra. In Europe, Ms. Nissman has appeared as soloist with such major orchestras as the London Philharmonic, the Royal Philharmonic, the BBC Symphony, the Rotterdam Philharmonic and the Munich Philharmonic, among others. In the United States, she has appeared with the New York Philharmonic, the Pittsburgh Symphony, the St. Louis Symphony, the Philadelphia Orchestra, the Chicago Symphony and the Cleveland Orchestra. She has worked with some of the world's major conductors such as Eugene Ormandy, Riccardo Muti and Leonard Slatkin.

In 1989, Ms. Nissman made history by becoming the first pianist ever to perform the complete piano sonatas of Sergei Prokofiev in a series of three recitals, both in New York and London. In the wake of these historic performances, the complete sonatas and other major solo piano works of Prokofiev were released in a three-volume recording by Newport Classic and were chosen by the BMG Compact Disc Club as their featured selection. Ms. Nissman's set represents the first such set of Prokofiev ever made on compact disc.

A noted Prokofiev scholar and authority in her own right, Ms. Nissman was invited by the former Soviet Union to travel to Moscow and collaborate with leading Soviet

musicians on a detailed study of the Prokofiev manuscripts housed in the Central State Archives. In commemoration of the composer's 100th birthday, she performed the complete cycle of his piano sonatas throughout Europe and the U.S. during the 1991-92 season.

Ms. Nissman has long been associated with the music of Alberto Ginastera. In 1976, she was invited by the composer to play his Piano Concerto No. 1 with l'Orchestre de la Suisse Romande in celebration of his sixtieth birthday. Ms. Nissman's recording of Ginastera's complete solo and chamber works for the piano, including the Sonata No. 3 written expressly for her, is available as a 2-CD recording on the Newport Classic label. Both *Gramophone* magazine and the *American Record Guide* chose the Ginastera recording as one of the best in 1989.

Ms. Nissman's recording of Liszt's piano music, including the Sonata in B Minor, six Paganini etudes, and the *Rhapsodie Espagnole,* was recently released on the Newport Classic label. Her recording of the complete Chopin nocturnes was released in the fall of 1994. In addition to performing and recording, she has contributed numerous articles to music publications and is currently completing a book on Béla Bartók and recording his complete piano music. Barbara Nissman, along with Leonard Slatkin, was one of the participants at the Kennedy Center 25th Anniversary Gala Concert which was broadcast on PBS television.

Born in Philadelphia, Ms. Nissman received her doctoral degree from the University of Michigan. She now resides in the mountains of eastern West Virginia.

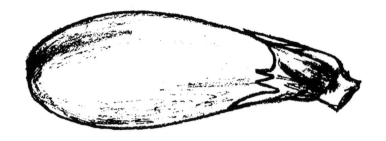

BARBARA'S GREEK CHICKEN
Serves 4

This is a wonderful dinner party recipe and you can make it before the guests arrive. It tastes better if made the day before and then reheated. I always make more so I'll have leftovers—it really is good, and easy to make! --B.N.

2 whole breast chicken fillets (about 1¼ lb.)	3 cloves fresh garlic, chopped
Salt and black pepper	1 tablespoon dried oregano, or to taste
1 medium-sized eggplant	28 oz. can Italian tomatoes
Flour	Red pepper bits, to taste
Olive oil	Feta cheese
1 medium-sized onion, sliced	Rice of choice

Salt and pepper the chicken and put to one side. Cut the eggplant lengthwise into 4 slices (approximately ¾-inch thick), salt and pepper and cover lightly with flour. Brown eggplant in olive oil and place in bottom of a 2-quart casserole dish.

Brown chicken breasts in olive oil and place on top of eggplant. Sauté onion and garlic until onions are transparent. Add oregano, tomatoes (drain a little of the juice from the can before adding), and red pepper bits. Pour over the chicken, then top with broken bits of feta cheese.

Bake in preheated oven at 425 degrees for about 20 to 25 minutes, or until tender.

Serve over rice.

Photo: HANYA CHLALA

DAVID OWEN NORRIS, PIANIST

David Owen Norris is one of Britain's most enterprising pianists whose career has embraced broadcasting, teaching and artistic directorships in addition to his work as a performer.

He was the first recipient, in 1991, of the Irving S. Gilmore Award, accorded him after a long search among many of the world's finest pianists. The award, from an American foundation based in Kalamazoo, has taken him to concert halls and universities all over the United States and has led to debut recitals in New York and Washington D.C. as well as concerto performances with the Chicago Symphony Orchestra.

Norris has appeared with orchestras in France, Switzerland and Germany and has performed with both the BBC Scottish and BBC Symphony Orchestras at the Proms. He has also given over two hundred piano broadcasts as a soloist and accompanist.

Norris has presented many programmes for BBC Radio, including *The Works* and *In Tune* for Radio 3, and has made appearances on BBC television programmes, including *Jim'll Fix It* and *Cardiff Singer of the World*.

Norris is chairman of the faculty of the Steans Institute at the Ravinia Festival in Chicago. He was artistic director of the 1995 Cardiff Festival.

Born in 1953 in Northampton, David Owen Norris attended the Royal Academy of Music before entering Keble College, Oxford, as an organ scholar. There he won a First Class Honours in music and received a Halstead Leaving Scholarship in composition. He is a Fellow of the Royal Academy of Music, and of the Royal College of Organists. In 1993, he became the Gresham Professor of Music in the City of London. He has delivered a series of lectures on his philosophy of music during the past three academic years.

MARMALADE AND CORIANDER CHICKEN
Serves 4

It saves a lot of washing up if you place the chicken on aluminum foil, inside a metal pan with sides, before cooking. This is because once the sauce cooks and then cools, it becomes like toffee and is almost impossible to remove from the tin. This recipe is very quick and easy, but is sufficiently unusual to impress your guests.

SERVING TIP: Do not reveal the ingredients to your guests until after the meal!! --D.O.N.

2 whole (4 breast halves), boneless, skinned, breast of chicken (about 2 pounds)
4 cloves of garlic, crushed
Ground black pepper

2 tablespoons ground coriander
12 oz. jar of thin-shred orange marmalade
Fresh coriander to garnish

Wash the chicken and lightly score with a sharp knife. Rub one of the crushed garlic cloves onto the chicken pieces and sprinkle with ground black pepper.

Mix the ground coriander into the marmalade until you have a thick paste, add 2 or 3 cloves of the crushed garlic to the paste and mix well. Spread the paste generously onto the chicken pieces and place in a 2½ to 3-quart baking tin or Pyrex dish.

Preheat oven and bake at 350 degrees, covered, for 40 minutes, or until tender. Remove from tin and serve, pouring spare marmalade and coriander juices left in the tin onto chicken pieces.

If one wishes to thicken the sauce, add one tablespoon of cornstarch with one tablespoon of cool water and mix until starch is dissolved. Add to remaining pan juices and simmer on stove top until thickened.

This recipe is ideal with baked potato and green salad.

Photo: © LAURA LYNN MINER

JOHN O'CONOR, PIANIST

Irish pianist John O'Conor has been acclaimed for his eloquent phrasing, impeccable technique and mastery of keyboard color, particularly in the Classical and early Romantic repertoires. He first gained widespread attention in the United States in 1986 with the initial release in his complete cycle of Beethoven sonatas on the Telarc label. The complete nine-volume recording was released as a boxed set in October 1994, and *CD Review* called Mr. O'Conor's playing "piano recording of the highest caliber and Beethoven playing at its best. This Beethoven series should become the complete set of choice for the next decade." In addition to his recorded Beethoven cycle, Mr. O'Conor has performed complete, chronological sonata cycles in New York and Boston.

Mr. O'Conor is currently recording Mozart piano concertos with Sir Charles Mackerras and the Scottish Chamber Orchestra, the latest of which is the fourth volume featuring Concertos No. 20 in D Minor, K. 466, and No. 22 in E-flat Major, K. 482. In addition, he has recorded Schubert's A Major Piano Sonata, Op. Posth., D. 959 and *Moments Musicaux*, as well as Schubert's "Trout" Quintet with members of the Cleveland Quartet.

In addition to the Beethoven and Mozart cycles, Mr. O'Conor is recording all the major piano works of Irish composer John Field. Telarc released his recording of the Field concertos in the spring of 1994. In 1993, his disc of four sonatas was released, and in 1990, his disc of fifteen Field nocturnes was featured on the *Billboard* classical charts for several weeks. Other recordings by Mr. O'Conor on the Telarc label include: *Autumn songs;* a volume of short piano pieces by Bach, Chopin, Lizst, Mozart, Mendelssohn, Grieg, Schumann, Rachmaninoff, Debussy and Gershwin, which was released in August 1995 as a companion volume to his earlier "Piano Classics."

Mr. O'Conor performs extensively in Europe, having appeared with orchestras including the Royal Philharmonic, the Vienna Symphony, the Czech Philharmonic, l'Orchestre National de France and the Stuttgart Chamber Orchestra. In addition, he has made several tours of North America, including appearances with the Cleveland Orchestra, the National Symphony and the orchestras of Montreal, Detroit and Dallas. In Japan, Mr. O'Conor has performed both in recital and in concert with the NHK Symphony, and has toured the countries of the former Soviet Union twice.

Highlights of Mr. O'Conor's 1993-94 season include recitals in Washington, D.C., at the Kennedy Center, and in Chicago, Seattle and Atlanta, as well as a series of recitals and orchestral appearances in Hawaii. In Europe, he has performed in Great Britain, Germany, Poland and Czechoslovakia. Last season, Mr. O'Conor's engagements included recital and orchestral performances across the United States. He returned to Central America and toured major cities in New Zealand with the New Zealand Symphony Orchestra.

Mr. O'Conor's early studies began with J.J. O'Reilly at the College of Music in Dublin. He was subsequently awarded an Austrian government scholarship that enabled him to study in Vienna with the respected pianist and instructor, Dieter Weber and with noted Beethoven interpreter, Wilhelm Kempff. In 1973, Mr. O'Conor was unanimously awarded first prize in the International Beethoven Competition in Vienna, an achievement followed by another prestigious award that year—first prize at the Bösendorfer Piano Competition.

Mr. O'Conor is actively involved in improving educational and performing opportunities for young musicians in his native Ireland. He also has been instrumental in the establishment of the GPA Dublin International Piano Competition. John O'Conor lives in Dublin, Ireland with his wife and two sons.

SAUCE POSITANO
(For Pasta)
Makes about 2½ cups

I enjoyed this recipe while studying Beethoven with Wilhelm Kempff at his summer home in Positano, Italy. Whenever I eat the sauce, I am right back in that beautiful spot. --J.O.

2 pounds tomatoes
2 oz. butter
¼ teaspoon dried oregano
½ teaspoon dried thyme

1 tablespoon fresh basil
Salt and freshly ground black pepper
Garlic—*as many cloves as you dare*, but
    at least 4 or 5, very finely chopped

Peel and remove seeds from the tomatoes. Melt butter on medium heat and very gently cook the garlic which has been very finely chopped. After about 5 minutes, add the tomatoes, herbs and seasonings and cook gently for 10 to 15 minutes.

Serve with freshly cooked spaghetti.

Photo: JACK MITCHELL

JON KIMURA PARKER, PIANIST

Since winning Great Britain's Leeds International Piano Competition in 1984, Jon Kimura Parker has become one of the most sought-after artists in his native Canada, as well as throughout Europe, the United States and the Far East. Whether performing as recitalist, soloist with orchestra or chamber musician, he has won unanimous praise for his brilliant technique, exquisite tone and thoughtful musicality.

Mr. Parker's career has already encompassed performances with many of the world's leading conductors and orchestras, among them André Previn and the Los Angeles Philharmonic, Leonard Slatkin and the San Francisco Symphony, Mstislav Rostropovich and the National Symphony, and Günther Herbig and RSO Berlin. His recital and chamber music appearances have taken him to such festivals as Aldeburgh, Ravinia and Tivoli.

The recipient of many international awards, Parker has been honored repeatedly in his native Canada, where in 1985 the Canadian Music Council named him "Performer of the Year." In 1991, he was invited by Prime Minister Brian Mulroney to give a televised solo recital to open officially the new Canadian Embassy in Tokyo.

A well-known personality in Canada, Mr. Parker has hosted radio and television programs for the CBC. An enthusiastic advocate of new music, he has commissioned several works for piano by Canadian composers and has written a major recital work himself.

Born in Vancouver, Jon Kimura Parker appeared with the Vancouver Youth Orchestra at the age of five. He began his training with his uncle, Edward Parker, and also studied with Robin Wood at the Victoria Conservatory of Music and with Marek Jablonski at the Banff School of the Arts. After four years of advanced study with Lee Kum-Sung at the Vancouver Academy of Music and at the University of British Columbia, Mr. Parker was admitted to the Juilliard School on full scholarship as a student of the renowned piano pedagogue, Adele Marcus.

TERIYAKI SHISH KEBABS

I learned this recipe from cellist Bruce Uchimura while a student at Juilliard. It is perfect for parties since all the work is done the day before; when people get hungry, you need only to throw them (the 'babs') under the broiler for a few minutes. If you use wooden skewers, they are also convenient to eat with while standing. This is a flexible recipe which can be tailored to those who don't eat red meat (total vegetarians, etc.). I prepared these for my colleagues at the Seattle Chamber Music Festival one summer and received the ultimate compliment from cellist and gourmand Gary Hoffman, who pronounced the recipe "as good or better than the standard of New York's best restaurants." I also once prepared this recipe for my piano class at the Banff School of Fine Arts; I found every ingredient at the grocery store except the sesame oil, which is crucial to the texture and flavor of the marinade. At the last minute, I hit on the idea of going into the kitchen of the one Chinese restaurant in town, and the chef gladly sold me 1 tablespoon for $1.00! --J.K.P.

MARINADE:

2 to 3 cups soy sauce
½ cup water
Several cloves garlic, chopped
1½-inch ginger root (skinned and chopped)

2 to 3 oz. sherry
¾ cup sugar
1 tablespoon sesame oil
Several stocks scallions (chopped)

SHISH KEBABS:

2½ pounds London broil
3½ pounds chicken breast (boneless)
2 Spanish onions
3 green bell peppers

3 red bell peppers
1 pound mushrooms
Whatever else you might like to include

UNUSUAL EQUIPMENT:

Dozens of skewers
Large bowl

Flat trays deep enough to marinate
   the skewers

All preparations should be done the day before serving. Prepare the marinade in a large bowl. Feel free to adjust all quantities of ingredients to taste. (You may wish to use low-sodium soy, honey instead of sugar, etc.). You must stir very well to dissolve the sugar, etc. Let stand.

Chop all other ingredients into 1½ inch cubes, and place on skewers, alternating beef or chicken with the various vegetables. Definitely make a few veg-only 'babs' as well.

Place the skewers in flat pans, pour the marinade over them, cover with plastic wrap, and place in fridge. The marinade will probably only soak the 'babs' halfway, so after one-half day rotate all the skewers. *To cook* the 'babs', simply place under the broiler, rotate after 4 to 5 minutes, cook to your doneness preference and remove. Best accompanied by rice and over a lettuce garnish.

Photo: ROSANGELA MASSA

ALBERTO PORTUGHEIS, PIANIST

The distinguished pianist Alberto Portugheis was born in La Plata, Argentina, to parents of Russian and Rumanian descent. He studied in Buenos Aires, Geneva—here also the violin and conducting—and London.

After winning first prize at the Geneva Concours de Virtuosité, Portugheis embarked upon an international career, visiting over 40 countries. He performed in recitals, chamber music concerts and as soloist with many major orchestras, including the Royal Philharmonic, London Symphony, London Mozart Players, Philharmonia, English Chamber, Lausanne Chamber, Paris and Israel Sinfoniettas, Suisse Romande, Sinfónica Nacional of Argentina and Filharmónica de Buenos Aires. He has frequently broadcast on radio and television and has given regular master classes. As a conductor, Portugheis has appeared, among others, with the London Mozart Players and Philharmonia Orchestras.

Alberto Portugheis has a particularly wide repertoire, with music ranging from Baroque—including his own transcriptions—to Contemporary. Many works have been specially written for him. His acclaimed recordings include the four Chopin Ballades, Alfred Nieman's Second Sonata, the complete piano music and chamber music with piano of Ginastera, the Khachaturian Piano Concerto, with the London Symphony Orchestra, also solo piano works by the same composer, the Cello and Piano Sonatas of Rachmaninov and Shostakovich, and a CD dedicated entirely to the piano music of Rossini.

Like Gioacchino Rossini, the creator not only of the opera, *The Barber of Seville,* but also of Cannelloni and Tournedos Rossini, Alberto has always shared the same two passions: Music and Food.

He has an interest in the culinary and gastronomic traditions of the whole world and a special love of British cookery, which he feels has been wrongly neglected and discredited. In 1988, he devoted himself to the creation of an original British menu, for the *Manor at the Gate* restaurant, in Queensgate SW7, based on researched recipes from various centuries. In 1992, Alberto presented the British Food Festival in Buenos Aires. At his restaurant, *Rhapsody,* Alberto has held four food festivals: Welsh, Swedish, Sicilian and Argentine.

Alberto is also a food-writer and broadcaster, contributing regularly to the *Cronica Latina* newspaper, the *I.S.M. Journal* and various other publications, and has appeared regularly on *the Pete Murray Show* on London Talkback Radio, as well as on BBC Radio 3.

PASTEL DE CHOCLO CON GALLINA
(Bolivian Chicken and Sweet-corn Pie)

Depending on the rest of the menu, this recipe will serve from 6 to 8 people. If ripe, flavorsome tomatoes are not available, use tinned instead. If you prefer, use lard instead of butter. You will need at least a 10-inch (25 cm) pie dish [more than 1-inch thick (3 cm)] for this recipe. --A.P.

1 chicken or broiler, 3½ pounds (1½ kg)
Chicken stock for boiling chicken
4 tablespoons olive or vegetable oil
1 large onion, chopped
10 oz. (300 g) fresh tomatoes, peeled
   and chopped
2 oz. (50 g) seedless raisins, soaked in
   water for 15 minutes and strained
2 oz. (50 g) green stoned
   olives, coarsely chopped

6 eggs (3 hard-boiled and chopped)
Pinch of ground cinnamon
Salt to taste
Black pepper to taste
4 oz. (120 g) butter
1½ pounds (750 g) packaged corn
   kernels, cooked and reduced to a
   purée in food processor
1 dessertspoon sugar
Mild paprika

Cook the chicken or broiler in stock until tender, about 50 to 60 minutes. (Cut into pieces first, it cooks faster, particularly the broiler). Leave chicken to cool, then strain, skin, bone, and cut in small pieces (you will need about 2½ cups, lightly packed). Reserve stock for other use.

In large skillet, heat the oil and cook the onion until soft. Add tomatoes and cook for an additional 5 to 6 minutes. Add chicken, raisins, olives, hard-boiled eggs, and cinnamon to pan. Season with salt and pepper. Remove and place this mixture in greased (or non-stick) pie dish.

In a saucepan, melt the butter, add the sweet-corn purée, sugar, salt and pepper. Cook, stirring all the time, until quite thick. Remove from the heat and add the remaining raw eggs, lightly beaten.

Pour the sweet-corn topping over all the chicken filling, sprinkle with paprika and bake in a moderately hot oven at 350 degrees (180° C) for 1 hour or until the topping sets and becomes a little brown.

OCOPA AREQUIPEÑA
(Peruvian Potatoes with Walnut and Cheese Sauce)
Serves 4

This dish makes a wonderful, succulent vegetarian main course; but it can also make a perfect first course, using (if you stick to the measurements above) half a potato per person. You could also use 8 small to medium potatoes. If the sauce is too thick, you can thin it down with milk, oil, or a bit of both.

4 large potatoes, boiled, peeled and
   halved lengthwise
4 dry chillies, seeded
6 tablespoons (100 ml) peanut oil
1 medium onion, sliced
2 cloves garlic, finely chopped
4 oz. (120 g) walnuts
4 oz. (120 g) crumbly cheese (Lancashire,
   Caerphilly, Cheshire, etc.)

1¼ cups (300 ml) milk
Salt to taste
Pepper to taste
Lettuce leaves
4 hard-boiled eggs, halved lengthwise
8 black olives
1 red pepper, cooked and
   cut in strips (fresh or tinned)

Prepare potatoes as directed above. Soak chillies in hot water for 30 minutes and drain. Fry onion in the oil until slightly colored; add garlic and fry for an additional 20 seconds. Add chillies, walnuts and crumbled cheese. Remove from flame and blend the ingredients in a mixer or food processor.

Put back in frying pan or saucepan, adding milk, salt and pepper, cooking while stirring until you reach the consistency of a thick white sauce.

To serve, first arrange a bed of lettuce and place hot potatoes on top (cut side down). Mask the potatoes with the sauce and decorate with the eggs (cut side up), the olives and strips of pepper.

CONSOMMÉ
Makes about 2 quarts liquid

Alberto's "Consommé" and "Profiteroles" recipes will come in handy with several other dishes featured in this recipe book including: "Beef Stroganoff" from Vladimir Ashkenazy and Consommé "Rossini."

4 quarts (4 liters) water
4½ pounds (2 kg) beef (skin and bones)*
1 onion, peeled and halved
1 whole leek, cut into 1-inch (3 cm) pieces
1 celery rib, cut into ½-inch (2 cm) pieces
1 carrot, cut into ½-inch (2 cm) pieces
1 small bunch of parsley

1 small bunch tarragon
2 tablespoons (50 g) tomato purée
½ cup dry white wine
20 black peppercorns
3 egg whites (optional)
Salt to taste

Bring pot of water to a boil, with beef inside pot. Do not cover. Boil for 20 minutes, skimming as necessary. Add vegetables, herbs, tomato and peppercorns. Cook gently with pot slightly covered for 3 hours, or until liquid has reduced by half. Add wine and cook for an additional 40 minutes. Season with salt.

Strain—Remove all impurities in the classical way, with egg whites or strain through a double muslin (cloth strainer made of coarse cotton).

*NOTE: The beef can be replaced by a large 'boiling fowl'.

PROFITEROLES

3 oz. (80 g) butter
1 cup plus 1 tablespoon (250 ml) water
Pinch of salt

1 cup (125 g) all-purpose flour
4 medium eggs

Put butter, water and salt in a saucepan and bring to a boil. At this point, remove from heat, add flour and mix well. Return saucepan to low heat and stir uninterrupted (to help dry out dough) with wooden spoon until the contents resemble a ball and the mixture does not stick to the bottom and sides of the pan. Let cool down a bit (5 minutes or so), then add eggs, one by one, mixing well.

Measure out little mounds of dough with a teaspoon or pastry bag on a greased baking tin, and place in a preheated *hot* oven at 450 degrees (230° C) for about 8 to 10 minutes, or until profiteroles have risen, are firm to the touch, and have a golden color.

Photo: VICTORIA PRESTON

ROBERT PRESTON, PIANIST

Robert Preston enjoyed an extensive career as a concert pianist during the years 1960 to 1985. A graduate of Juilliard, he performed in every major city of the United States and throughout Europe as recitalist and soloist with major symphony orchestras. He was the Gold Medal-winner of the International Busoni Competition, recorded the Kabalevsky and Rubinstein Piano Concerti and Bach-Busoni transcriptions, and gave dozens of chamber music concerts with many renowned instrumentalists. As a serious avocational photographer, Preston eventually came into personal contact with Ansel Adams, whose influence and encouragement caused him to change his career. Mr. Preston now works as a full-time photographer in Stamford, Connecticut. Some of his many portraits of musicians appear elsewhere in this book.

SPICED SHRIMP

Serves 4

One of Mr. Preston's hobbies is cooking and entertaining. He has perfected many tasty recipes which he has served on various occasions to distinguished colleagues and friends.

1   **pound fresh shrimp shelled and veins removed (or about 40 shrimp)**
1   **teaspoon of sesame oil (for use at very end of recipe)**

MARINADE:

1   **egg, slightly beaten**
2   **tablespoons flour**
1   **tablespoon cornstarch**

¼   **teaspoon baking soda**
1   **teaspoon soy sauce**
1   **teaspoon dry sherry wine**

SEASONINGS: (Prepare in advance on a separate plate)

2 scallions cut crosswise in small bits	1 teaspoon minced fresh ginger
2 teaspoons minced garlic	1 dried red chile pepper torn into small pieces

SAUCE: (Mix together in advance in a small bowl)

3 tablespoons tomato ketchup	2 teaspoons dry sherry wine
1 tablespoon water	4 teaspoons soy sauce
1 teaspoon white cider vinegar	2 tablespoons sugar

Mix the shrimp with the marinade and refrigerate for 2 hours before use.

Heat a wok over medium heat until hot. Add 4 tablespoons vegetable oil. Add the shrimp and stir-fry briskly until they turn whitish-pink. Remove with a slotted spoon and place in a bowl.

Add 2 more tablespoons of oil to the wok. Heat, then slightly brown the seasonings. Stir in the sauce ingredients and continue to cook and stir until contents begin to bubble. Return the shrimp to the wok. Stir-fry for several more seconds. Swirl in a teaspoon of sesame oil. Serve immediately over rice.

PORK TENDERLOIN ROAST

Serves 4

The simple secret to this recipe's success is to marinate the pork overnight in the refrigerator, then take it out the following afternoon to gain room temperature prior to the evening meal. --R.P.

2 pork tenderloins (1 pound or slightly more)

Marinade:	1 minced scallion
¼ cup safflower oil	½ teaspoon minced garlic
3 tablespoons soy sauce	½ teaspoon minced fresh ginger
½ teaspoon sesame oil	3 tablespoons honey

The night before, place the tenderloins in a baking dish just large enough to accommodate them, so the marinade rises about halfway up the sides. The next morning, pierce the meat with a fork and turn it several times throughout the day.

Place baking dish containing the meat and marinade into a preheated oven at 350 degrees. Bake for 20 to 30 minutes, until cooked and tender. Transfer pork onto a cutting board, cover immediately with foil and let stand for 5 minutes before carving crosswise into half-inch thick medallions. Spoon a little of the remaining marinade onto the top of each serving.

This entree goes well with almost any type of vegetable dish, as well as all kinds of potato and rice recipes.

CHICKEN WITH TARRAGON SAUCE

(a la Preston)

Serves 4

1¼ pounds of chicken breast tenderloins cut into bite-sized cubes

¼ cup sherry wine (for marinade)

4 tablespoons or more of olive oil

½ package mushrooms (approximately 6 oz.), thinly sliced

1 medium onion, thinly sliced (when in season Vidalia is best)

½ small red bell pepper, sliced into julienne strips

½ small yellow bell pepper sliced into julienne strips

1 scallion chopped crosswise into pea-sized bits (leave uncooked)

2 cups canned chicken broth

⅓ cup Marsala cooking wine

1 generous tablespoon cornstarch mixed with a little cold water to dissolve it

1 tablespoon butter

½ cup flour for dredging—have ready on flat plate

1 generous tablespoon dried tarragon crushed between the fingers

Marinate the chicken pieces in sherry wine *overnight* in the refrigerator. Remove from fridge the next day to gain room temperature.

In a 10-inch skillet, with a cover available, heat a generous tablespoon of olive oil in the skillet. Sauté the mushrooms over medium heat, until lightly golden. Transfer to a bowl.

Add another tablespoon of olive oil to the skillet. Add the sliced onions and the bell peppers. Stir briefly until all ingredients are well coated. Reduce heat to very low and cook covered, stirring occasionally, until onions and peppers are soft and sweet (about 20-25 minutes). (During this waiting period, in a suitable container, blend together the broth, Marsala wine, and stir in the dissolved cornstarch). When the onions and peppers are finished, transfer them to the same bowl as the mushrooms and put the uncooked scallions on top of these ingredients.

Having all the remaining ingredients prepared as above, put about 2 tablespoons olive oil in the skillet as well as 1 tablespoon butter. While it is heating, drain the sherry wine from the chicken pieces and dredge the chicken in the flour. Turn the heat to medium-high and brown the chicken on all sides, turning constantly.

As soon as the chicken is browned and sizzling, give the broth a good stir to remix the cornstarch. Pour the broth onto the chicken. Immediately add the bowl of onions, scallions, peppers and mushrooms. Add the dried tarragon. Add salt and pepper to taste and stir everything well. Reduce heat to low and cook covered at least 30 minutes. (But it can stay an hour with no harm done while you tend to your other items, i.e. rice or potatoes, vegetables, even your guests!)

Photo: ROBERT M. TALBOT

JOSEPH REZITS, PIANIST

Joseph Rezits, professor emeritus of music at the Indiana University School of Music, received his primary training with Isabelle Vengerova at the Curtis Institute of Music. He also studied with Rudolph Ganz, Percy Grainger, Howard Wells, Florence Frantz and Dorothy Taubman. He studied chamber music with Gregor Piatigorsky, William Kroll, Samuel Mayes, William Primrose and others. At the age of 23, he made his North American debut with Eugene Ormandy and the Philadelphia Orchestra as winner of the Philadelphia Orchestra Youth Auditions. On this occasion, Max de Schauensee of the Philadelphia Bulletin wrote:

"Mr. Rezits is a pianist of the highest promise; he is an instinctive artist. One is constantly conscious of the technical prowess of today's crop of young pianists, but few of them have the grace and the natural poetic quality that Mr. Rezits displayed in his playing. Soft passages carried perfectly, and the tone was warm and musical. Light quick scales and embellishments were accomplished with the brio of the real artist. Mr. Rezits also exhibited massive power when this quality was demanded, though the Saint Saëns Concerto is a delightfully lyric composition, on the whole."

Subsequently, Dr. Rezits entered a highly successful solo career and ultimately specialized primarily in duo and chamber music repertoire. In addition, he became internationally known as a clinician and lecturer. In these multiple capacities, he has appeared in virtually every one of the United States and in Canada, as well as in Europe, South America, Asia and Australia.

Dr. Rezits has also achieved special prominence as an author. In 1974, *The Pianist's Resource Guide* (written in collaboration with Gerald Deatsman) was published by Neil A. Kjos and elicited enthusiastic reviews such as "the arrival of this giant work is like the arrival of television in the world of radio communications....Any 'review' of its 993 pages of facts and information must proceed first from a feeling of awe that it's 'all there', like the Himalayas, and then, to the mundane business of taking one step after another in the direction of a climb." [Robert Dumm, *Piano Quarterly*]. Several more books followed. In the recent past, his latest book, *Beloved Tyranna: the Legend and Legacy of Isabelle Vengerova,* paid tribute to his former teacher at the Curtis Institute. A review by Angela Brownridge for the *European Piano Teachers Association Piano Journal* stated "This book, which was in preparation for over forty years, is as intensive a study as one could hope for....However hard a time 'Madame' may have given him during lessons, I am sure that she will be smiling down at him from heaven, and should be grateful to him for the production of such a comprehensive document which leaves no stone unturned....This book is a must for pianists and teachers alike."

Rezits has recorded for the Audiophile, Festival, Avant-Garde and Coronet labels, and has contributed to ten major periodicals on three continents.

Dr. Rezits resides in Bloomington, Indiana with his wife Roberta. His various hobbies include photography, traveling and collecting recordings and films of legendary musicians of the past.

SWEET AND SOUR CHICKEN
Serves 4

This wonderful recipe comes from Eugene and Lucy Gee, who live in Albany, New York, and who are the parents of one of my former piano students, Larry Gee. This recipe was one of the main dishes at a dinner that they prepared for my son and me while we were on a concert tour on the East Coast in the early 1980's. It was one of the finest meals that I have ever eaten. --J.R.

BATTER:

½ cup flour
¼ cup cornstarch
1 teaspoon baking powder
1 tablespoon beaten egg

½ cup *minus* 1 tablespoon water
1 teaspoon oil
½ teaspoon salt

Mix above ingredients and set aside.

CHICKEN:

1 pound fresh chicken meat cut up into 1-inch pieces. *Dip into batter and deep-fry in oil until lightly browned and cooked through (about 7-8 minutes).*

SAUCE:

½ cup sugar
¼ cup vinegar
½ teaspoon soy sauce
¼ teaspoon bead molasses
1 can (8 oz.) pineapple chunks, undrained

¼ cup coarsely chopped sweet pickle
1 small green pepper cut into small pieces
1 tablespoon cornstarch dissolved in
    1 tablespoon cool water
1 small tomato cut into wedges

In a small sauce pan, mix the sugar, vinegar, soy sauce and bead molasses and simmer a few minutes to allow sugar to dissolve. Add pineapple, sweet pickle and pepper. When mixture comes to a boil again, add the cornstarch dissolved in the water. Mix in the tomato wedges and simmer until mixture thickens and vegetables become tender. Pour the sauce over the deep-fried chicken. Serve with rice.

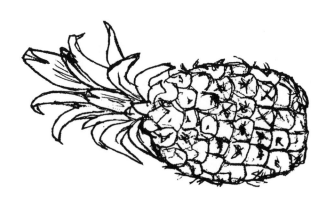

BRUCE AND DIANE'S
CREAM CHEESE EGGS
Serves 3 to 4

This recipe is really a favorite of my son, David. While I enjoy eggs very much (during my youth I would eat sometimes 2 or 3 a day) these days I tend to go with egg substitutes such as egg beaters, or eating just the egg whites which have no cholesterol. Bruce David is a well-known Jewish artist living in Bloomington, Indiana, and both he and his wife Diane are good friends of the family. They are primarily vegetarians, and this dish is one of their most tasty.

5 eggs, beaten
4 oz. cream cheese (we use ⅓
　　less-fat type)
4 tablespoons milk

1 tablespoon mayonnaise (we use
　　low-fat)
1½ teaspoons parsley flakes
⅛ teaspoon thyme
Salt and pepper to taste

Beat eggs in medium bowl. Add to eggs, pea-sized chunks of cream cheese, then milk. Add mayonnaise and beat mixture until mayonnaise is broken up into very small parts. Add spices and mix well.

Cook in well greased frying pan, COVERED, over very low heat. *Do not stir.* Cook approximately 15 minutes (watch closely toward end of time). Eggs are done when top of the mixture looks dry and puffs up. Garnish with fresh parsley.

MY SON'S MIDDLE EASTERN HUMMUS

Makes 2½ cups

I learned to make hummus during my tenure of two years as the principal cellist of the Haifa Symphony Orchestra, in northern Israel. I was taught by a close friend, Nina Benzoor, who is an Israeli. She lived in Iraq originally, but emigrated from Iraq during turbulent times there many years ago.

The true secret of this recipe is in the saving of the water after the chick-peas have been cooked. This flavored liquid gives an extra special taste to the hummus. One can experiment with different amounts of ingredients: more garlic, extra cumin, etc....No ingredient quantity is set in stone.

YOU WILL NEED A MEDIUM OR LARGE CAPACITY FOOD PROCESSOR

8 oz. (½ package) dried chick-peas (garbanzo beans)

1 to 2 large cloves fresh garlic

⅛ cup coarsely chopped fresh parsley

2 to 3 heaping tablespoons tahini (crushed sesame seed oil)

Juice from ½ medium lemon

1 to 1½ tablespoons olive oil

2 or more teaspoons ground cumin

¼ teaspoon salt or to taste

¼ teaspoon black pepper or to taste

In spring or distilled water, soak chick-peas overnight, using a 2 to 3-quart bowl. The water level should be several inches above beans to allow beans to swell.

Drain chick-peas. In 2-quart sauce pan, add swelled chick-peas and new water to pan, covering peas by about 1 inch. Add 1 teaspoon salt to water, cover pan, and simmer peas on low heat for 2 hours, or until tender. Add additional water if level goes below the beans.

Drain chick-peas, but **SAVE** the water. Let peas cool slightly. In food processor, finely chop garlic and parsley. Add 2¼ cups cooked chick-peas and rest of ingredients; process until mixture is creamy in texture. (You will need to add some reserved bean water, a little at a time, to attain this consistency, roughly 8 to 12 tablespoons). The hummus should be thickened slightly, yet creamy and not runny. Salt and pepper to taste. (I like less salt than most people, so take the suggested amount 'with a grain of salt'.

Serve in an attractive bowl with additional chopped parsley, a layer of olive oil around outer edge of the hummus and any extra chick-peas dotting the top of the hummus. Delicious with pita bread and/or fresh vegetables and crackers.

Photo: MICHAEL SANDOR

GYORGY SANDOR, PIANIST

Acknowledged today as one of the world's leading masters of great virtuoso playing, Gyorgy Sandor's career has spanned six continents through five decades, bringing the celebrated Hungarian-born pianist the highest critical acclaim both in the concert field and as a recording artist.

After his Carnegie Hall debut in 1939, Sandor's concert tours featured him throughout the U.S.A., Europe, Latin America, Canada, Australia, New Zealand, the Far East, India, the Middle East and South Africa. His concert tour in the U.S.A. in 1990 included Chicago (world premiere of Bartók's recently found piano version of his Concerto for Orchestra), San Francisco, Miami, Boston, Washington, D.C. and New York City (Carnegie Hall, East Coast premiere of the piano version of the Bartók Concerto for Orchestra).

Of the numerous world premieres presented by Sandor, including works by Barber, Bernstein, Lukas Foss, Fuleihan and Jacques de Menasce, the most significant ones are some major works by Bartók. First, the *Dance Suite*, adapted for piano and revised by Bartók for its world premiere by Sandor at Carnegie Hall in January 1945. The composer was present at the performance, shortly before his untimely death. Sandor also presented the world premiere of the Third Piano Concerto in January 1946, with the Philadelphia Orchestra, Eugene Ormandy conducting. In 1975, he presented his piano version of Bartók's Sonata for Solo Violin as well as that of the *Intermezzo Interrotto* from the Bartók Concerto for Orchestra, both heard for the first time in this version.

Sandor was a Grand Prix du Disque winner for his recording of the entire piano output of Bartók, in 1965.

He also recorded all the piano works by Prokofiev and Kodály, as well as a wide selection of works by Bach, Beethoven, Chopin, Schumann, Brahms, Liszt, de Falla, Debussy; concertos with the New York Philharmonic Orchestra (Rachmaninoff's Second), the Philadelphia Orchestra (Chopin's First, Bartók's Third), the Vienna Symphony (Bartók concertos), the Luxemburg Radio Orchestra (de Falla's *Nights in the Gardens of Spain*) etc. Recently (1990), Sandor re-recorded the three Bartók piano concertos with the Hungarian State Orchestra and Adam Fischer in Budapest, released by SONY/Classical on CD. CBS/SONY also released his new recording of the piano version of Bartók's Concerto for Orchestra and the piano versions of the *Dance Suite* and the *Petite Suite* (from the 44 violin duos) on compact disc.

At the Liszt Academy in Budapest, Gyorgy Sandor graduated in piano under Bartók; in composition under Kodály. It was during his four years of study with Bartók that he prepared the first two piano concertos under the composer's guidance. After Bartók's passing away in 1945, Sandor was given the manuscript of the Third Piano Concerto, by Tibor Serly, who completed the orchestration of the last 17 measures, for presentation of the concerto's premiere in January 1946.

Sandor is the author of the book *On Piano Playing* published by Schirmer Books, in which his ideas on technique and interpretation ("motions and emotions") give a comprehensive guide to achieve accomplished piano playing, without allowing undue force and stress to the muscular system, as well as expressiveness without distortions.

THESE ARE A FEW OF MY FAVORITE DRINKS

One of my favorite appetizers is actually a drink: orange juice, with quite a few carrots blended into it, and with crushed ice. You may try to mix it with your favorite alcoholic drink.

Another preferred drink is coffee (warmed or iced), also put in the blender for a few seconds, milk or cream added to it. Very much like a cappuccino, but it is ready much quicker.

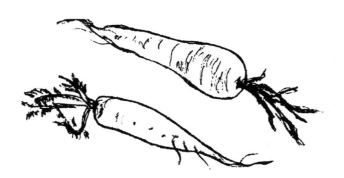

Photo: SPECTRUM STUDIO

GYORGY SEBOK, PIANIST

Gyorgy Sebok, born in Szeged, Hungary, has distinguished himself as an international figure in the musical world. His appearances with orchestra and his solo performances have taken him to three continents. He began his musical studies at the age of five and gave his first solo piano recital at age eleven. When Sebok was 14, he appeared as soloist with orchestra in Beethoven's First Piano Concerto under the direction of Ferenc Fricsay. Two years later, he entered the Liszt Academy in Budapest where he was active as pianist, accompanist and coach, also studying composition with Kodály and chamber music with Leo Weiner. He remained at the Liszt Academy until 1943, when the war reached Hungarian territory. For the next ten years, he toured eastern and central Europe and the Soviet Union, giving his first important performance in 1946, in Bucharest under Enesco. During this time, Sebok was chosen as soloist at the first Bartók Memorial Concert (Budapest, 1950), won the coveted International Prize in Berlin and received the Liszt Prize from Hungary. In 1949, he was appointed professor of piano at the Béla Bartók Conservatory in Budapest. In 1957, Paris served as his home base while his concert tours extended to cover the entire globe. He has appeared as soloist with major orchestras in Paris, Tokyo, Strasbourg, Geneva, Luxembourg, Lisbon, Athens, Moscow, Kiev, Lausanne, Algiers, Prague, Monte Carlo, Bucharest and Edmonton, as well as Chicago and Rochester and many other cities in the United States.

Mr. Sebok's first recording for Erato Records in 1957 received the Grand Prix du Disque in Paris. He has made solo, concerto and chamber music recordings on Erato, Mercury, Hispavox, Fonoring, Philips, Musical Heritage, Nippon-Columbia, Nippon-Westminster and other labels. He now has some 40 long-play recordings to his credit, representing every era of piano literature, encompassing solo, concerto and chamber music, the latter medium with his colleague and long time friend, the distinguished

cellist Janos Starker, and also with Arthur Grumiaux.

For the past 30 years, Mr. Sebok has been a distinguished professor of music at Indiana University in the United States. He is guest professor at the Hochschule der Künste in Berlin, the Toho School of Music in Tokyo, and the School of the Arts in Banff, Canada. He also is founder and director of Ernen Musikdorf and the Festival der Zukunft in Ernen, Switzerland, where he was presented with "Honorary Citizenship," only the third such citizenship to be given in 800 years. He gives annual master classes in Barcelona, Amsterdam and at Linfield College in Oregon. He has been a jury member of several major competitions and many of his former students have become renowned soloists and successful teachers in important positions around the world.

Janos Starker writes about Sebok's teachings as follows:

"Hundreds of young musicians pursue useful, contributive lives due to Sebok's giving them the tools to be real pianists and true musicians. Hundreds are forever indebted to him, having been exposed to his universal views, knowledge and wisdom embracing the arts and sciences in order to enhance musical understanding. Counting those in Germany, Canada, Japan, Finland, France, Holland, Spain, Hungary and all over the United States, the number grows to the thousands. His crowning feat of putting the little village of Ernen on the musical map as a haven and joy for musicians and music lovers from far away, wrote him into history."

Gyorgy Sebok is listed in "Who's Who in America," "Who's Who in Music," "Who's Who in the Midwest," the "Register of Prominent Americans" and the Riemann Music Lexicon. Mr. Sebok was awarded the Cross of Merit from the Hungarian government in 1993.

SAJTOS POGÁCSA
(Small Round Cheese Pastry)
Makes about 80, 1-inch pastries

We enjoy making this Hungarian pastry—particularly for our friends. They always comment about how much they enjoy this recipe. Sajtos Pogácsa is especially nice during the holidays. --G.S.

1¾ cups all-purpose white flour	½ teaspoon salt
3 sticks butter, softened (unsalted)*	½ teaspoon baking soda
4 oz. grated Parmesan cheese	3 egg yolks
4 oz. grated Swiss cheese	1½ oz. tube of anchovy paste

Mix flour, 2 sticks of butter, both cheeses, salt, baking soda, and egg yolks in Cuisinart food processor until well mixed. Refrigerate for 1 hour.

Roll out onto floured pastry board. (If dough is too sticky, add flour as necessary to aid in rolling process). Roll to ¼-inch thickness. Use a 1-inch diameter cookie cutter and cut into rounds. Put onto baking sheet(s), allowing at least ¼ inch between each pastry, and glaze the top surface of half the rounds lightly with an egg yolk and water mixture. Bake all slowly at 325 degrees for about 20 to 25 minutes or until color is tan and pastry is slightly crisp.

Let cool at room temperature. Mix 1 stick of unsalted butter with a ¼ tube of anchovy paste, take a knife and spread anchovy butter on the bottom of each glazed pastry. Adhere the bottom of each glazed pastry to the bottom of an unglazed pastry, making a secure fit. Serve at room temperature.

*Author's note: Do not substitute margarine for the butter because the taste will become somewhat bitter.

Photo: ROBERT PRESTON

KAREN SHAW, PIANIST

Wherever she appears, Karen Shaw receives a sensational response for the authority and compelling emotional power of her performances. In a series of appearances at Carnegie Hall, this dynamic soloist was repeatedly recognized as a "persuasive interpreter of Romantic music," possessing a virtuosity "as dazzling as accurate, and a sensitivity tenderly poetic" (the *New York Times*).

American-born, Ms. Shaw inherits the background of a musical family. Karen Shaw first appeared in New York as winner of the Concert Artist Guild Award, her debut recital prompting unusual critical acclaim from Donald Henahan of the *New York Times*. Since then, the artist has distinguished herself in performances across the U.S., Europe, Canada, Mexico and East Asia as recitalist and soloist with orchestra. As a result of her successful series of recitals at Carnegie Hall, Shaw embarked on her recording of Rachmaninoff's complete etudes.

A dedicated teacher, Ms. Shaw has produced many prize-winning students and enjoys presenting lectures, master classes and workshops throughout the country. She is also director of the Silvermine Young Artists Series in Connecticut.

Ms. Shaw has been professor of piano at the Indiana University School of Music since 1968. Ms. Shaw dedicates herself to her dual careers as a teacher and performer, while her prize-winning pupils continue to grow in number.

Ms. Shaw makes her home in Bloomington, Indiana.

BAKED STUFFED FILLET OF SOLE

Serves 4

This recipe is easy, delicious and low in fat and cholesterol. --K.S.

4 medium-sized sole fillets
1 cup Pepperidge Farm herb stuffing
1 beef bouillon cube dissolved in
   1 cup hot water
½ cup chopped celery
½ cup chopped onions

½ cup chopped parsley
Garlic powder to taste
Salt and pepper to taste
Parmesan cheese (optional)
Fresh lemon juice
Paprika

Prepare stuffing as package directs, using beef bouillon for moistening (butter is optional). Sauté celery and onion in a little butter or oil until softened, then add to stuffing along with chopped parsley, garlic powder, salt and pepper to taste, and optional Parmesan cheese. Mix together.

Lightly grease medium-sized Pyrex or baking dish and cover with foil. Lay each fillet flat in dish and spoon stuffing onto the middle. Fold ends over and secure with a toothpick. Squeeze a bit of lemon juice over the fillets and sprinkle with paprika.

Bake for 25 minutes in preheated oven at 350 degrees or until fish becomes flaky.

ZADEL SKOLOVSKY, PIANIST

Zadel Skolovsky, internationally renowned pianist, began his career as a child prodigy, appearing in recital at age eleven as both pianist and violinist in his home city of Los Angeles. That same year, he won a scholarship at the Curtis Institute of Music in Philadelphia in both piano and violin, studying piano with Isabella Vengerova and later also studying conducting with Fritz Reiner. He graduated from the Curtis Institute with a diploma in both piano and conducting and subsequently continued studying conducting with Pierre Monteux.

Skolovsky was the youngest and favorite student of the great pianist, composer, and pedagogue, Leopold Godowsky. He was taken in by Godowsky like an adopted son and was Godowsky's last student during the five remaining years of his life.

Skolovsky made his debut in New York at Town Hall as winner of the much-coveted Naumburg Award, also winning awards from the National Federation of Music Clubs, the National Music League, and the Robin Hood Dell Young American Artist Award.

His dramatic orchestral debut was as soloist with the New York Philharmonic at Carnegie Hall as a last minute replacement for ailing pianist Josef Hofmann. So successful was his debut, he appeared as soloist with the New York Philharmonic for three successive years and with virtually every great orchestra of the world, including the Philadelphia, Boston, Chicago, San Francisco, Toronto, the London Philharmonia, Royal Philharmonic, BBC Symphony, the French National Orchestra, Lamoureux, and the Israel Philharmonic (replacing pianist Rudolf Serkin in 12 subscription concerts) under such noted conductors as Pierre Monteux, Charles Munch, Leonard Bernstein, Lorin Maazel, Erich Leinsdorf, Jan Kubelik, and Paul Kletzki.

Skolovsky also appeared in Mexico and South America and in the most prestigious recital series in the musical capitals of the world, which included Allied Arts Piano Series in Chicago, Aaron Richmond Celebrity Series in Boston, and the Eaton Series in Toronto.

He introduced the first performance at the New York Philharmonic concerts of Prokofiev's Second Piano Concerto, under Munch, being the first pianist to perform this work in the United States since Prokofiev himself played it with the Boston Symphony seventeen years previously.

Skolovsky gave the world premiere of Darius Milhaud's Fourth Piano Concerto (dedicated to Skolovsky) with the Boston Symphony under Munch. After the performance, Charles Munch wired Darius Milhaud and spoke of this "pianiste extraordinaire." When Milhaud heard Skolovsky's Columbia recording of his *Saudades do Brazil*, he wrote the pianist saying, "The record is just perfection."

Considered one of the greatest living interpreters of Gershwin's music, to quote Ira Gershwin: "Zadel Skolovsky is a pianist without a peer." Philips Records in Holland signed Skolovsky to a contract, his first record to be an all Gershwin album of the Concerto in F and *Rhapsody in Blue*, with Skolovsky both playing and conducting the Lamoureux Orchestra in Paris.

Skolovsky started teaching early in his youth and his first student was the daughter of Mischa Schneider, cellist of the Budapest Quartet. Soon afterward, the pianist Vladimir Horowitz asked Skolovsky to teach his young daughter Sonia, making it clear that the lessons were to take place at the home of her grandfather, Arturo Toscanini.

Mr. Skolovsky retired in 1987 as professor of music at the Indiana University School of Music. He continues to concertize and give master classes throughout the world. He now makes his home in New York City.

TURKEY/CHICKEN/VEAL LOAF
Serves 4 to 6

My favorite kosher recipe comes from Chavi Miller, owner of Michdan Inc., Glatt Kosher Meat and Deli, in Manhattan. --Z.S.

1 tablespoon margarine	½ cup flour (mix with 1 cup broth)
1½ tablespoons grated onion	½ cup finely chopped celery
2 cups cooked diced turkey, chicken or veal	¾ teaspoon chile powder
½ teaspoon salt	¾ cup gravy
1 cup bread crumbs	Chopped olives, parsley or chives
1 cup chicken or turkey broth	

Preheat oven to 350 degrees. Add margarine to a pan and cook and stir onions for one minute. Briefly add to pan 2 cups of turkey, chicken or veal and mix with onions. Remove from heat.

In a separate bowl, add contents of pan and mix in salt, bread crumbs, flour, celery and chile powder.

Place ingredients in a well-greased medium loaf pan, set loaf pan in tray of hot water, and cook loaf in oven at 350 degrees for 45 minutes.

Serve with gravy, chopped olives, and plenty of chopped parsley or chives.

Photo: CHRISTIAN STEINER

SUSAN STARR, PIANIST

Susan Starr, called by the *New York Times* "a star of the first magnitude," is one of America's most celebrated pianists. Since her triumph in Moscow's Tchaikovsky Competition, she has played to standing ovations in recital and with the world's most distinguished orchestras and conductors.

Miss Starr made her concert debut with the Philadelphia Orchestra at age six and has since performed with the orchestra on more than 50 occasions. She has also appeared with such orchestras as the New York Philharmonic, Chicago Symphony, Minnesota Orchestra, Baltimore Symphony, Atlanta Symphony, National Symphony, and the American Symphony, as well as the symphonies of Dallas, Denver, Indianapolis and New Orleans. Among the eminent conductors who have chosen her as soloist are Eugene Ormandy, Robert Shaw, Maxim Shostakovich, Leopold Stokowsky, Sergiu Comissiona, Leonard Slatkin, Aldo Ceccato, Raphael Frühbeck de Burgos, and Sir Neville Marriner.

Audiences throughout the world have been enthralled by Susan Starr's artistry, and her active international career has taken her on three tours of the Soviet Union, ten tours of the Far East and more than a dozen trips to South America, as well as tours throughout England, Belgium, Germany, Sweden, Greece and Italy. Miss Starr's many festival appearances include Ravinia, Ambler, Robin Hood Dell, Saratoga, Chautauqua and the Ann Arbor May Festival.

A native of Philadelphia, Susan Starr began her studies with Eleanor Sokoloff. She later entered the Curtis Institute of Music, where she studied with Rudolf Serkin until her graduation in 1961. Miss Starr has been artistic chairperson of the piano faculty at the Philadelphia Colleges of the Arts and is a visiting professor at the University of Michigan in Ann Arbor. She has recently been chosen to be on the piano faculty at Florida International University in Miami.

Susan Starr is well-known for her recordings for RCA and Orion Master. She has received tremendous acclaim for her two most recent recordings, an album featuring the Schumann G Minor Sonata and the Fantasiestücke, and a Ravel/Griffes recital, both on the Orion label.

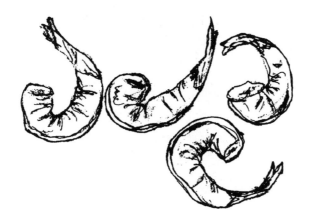

"SHRIMP BOSTON SYMPHONY"

Serves 4

This recipe was given to me by a member of the Boston Symphony when I played with them for the first time many years ago. It was handed around from one musician to the other within the orchestra, which is why I gave it the name "Shrimp Boston Symphony." It is ideal for people who don't want to spend a lot of time in the kitchen. --S.S.

3 cloves of garlic, minced or pressed
1 stick butter (less may be used)
1 jar Progresso roasted red peppers,
    sliced in strips, or 1 small red pepper

1 pound of fresh or frozen shrimp
½ cup white wine
¼ cup lemon juice
Salt and pepper to taste

Sauté garlic in butter until soft. Add red peppers and cook until also soft (if using jarred peppers, no added time is needed).

If using frozen shrimp, cook 1 minute in boiling water before adding to sauté pan. Add shrimp and sauté for 2 minutes. Add remaining ingredients and cook 1 or 2 minutes longer.

Serve over rice or linguine.

Photo: RITA NANNINI

ROBERT TAUB, PIANIST

Robert Taub, an internationally acclaimed leader in the new generation of virtuoso pianists, made his debut on the Great Performers Series at Lincoln Center in February 1994. Since his first recital at Lincoln Center's Alice Tully Hall in 1981, he has performed throughout the United States, Europe, the Far East and Latin America; he is the winner of some of the most coveted international prizes, including the 1981 Peabody-Mason Award of Boston.

In recent seasons, Taub has performed with the San Francisco Symphony (concertos of Bach and Stravinsky), Philadelphia Orchestra (Persichetti Concerto), Los Angeles Philharmonic (Powell Concerto), Montreal Symphony (Bartók Concerto No. 3), BBC Philharmonic (Prokofiev Concerto No. 3), Bonn Philharmonic (Mozart Concerto K. 503), Orchestra of St. Luke's (Beethoven Concerto No. 4), and Hong Kong Philharmonic (Brahms Concerto No. 1).

His New York recital of October 1992 was the only recital highlighted by the *New York Times* in its year-end review "Year in the Arts." In addition, he has performed solo recitals in Boston, San Francisco, Los Angeles, Seattle, London, Amsterdam, Berlin, Hong Kong, and Manila.

During recent summers, he has participated in major festivals: the Saratoga Festival where he collaborated with Charles Dutoit, the Lichfield Festival in England with Sir Edward Downes, San Francisco's Midsummer Mozart Festival, the Geneva International Summer Festival, and others.

Robert Taub's repertoire embraces music from the Baroque era to the present day, and he has been chosen by contemporary American composers to recreate their music. In January 1990, with the Los Angeles Philharmonic he gave the world premiere of Mel Powell's Two Piano Concerto, which won the 1990 Pulitzer Prize and has since been released on the

Harmonia Mundi label; two months earlier, in London's Queen Elizabeth Hall, Taub had given the world premiere of "Emblems," a major solo work composed for and dedicated to him by Milton Babbitt; further performances followed in New York, Seattle, San Francisco, and Berlin. Between the two premieres he played the Persichetti Piano Concerto with the Philadelphia Orchestra and Charles Dutoit, a performance which has been released on the New World label.

Mr. Taub gave the premiere of Preludes, Interludes, and Postlude, the fourth work Milton Babbitt composed for him, in Seattle in March 1992; the Boston premiere followed three weeks later; in October he gave the New York premiere. In January 1994, Mr. Taub made the first recording of Roger Sessions' Piano Concerto (1956), with Paul Dunkel and the New Orchestra of Westchester, for New World Records. He has recorded the sonatas of Scriabin for Harmonia Mundi; in February 1994, the cycle was reissued as a 2-CD set. Other recordings on this label, of Beethoven, Schumann, Liszt, and Babbitt, have been selected as "critic's favorites" by *Newsweek,* the *New York Times,* the *Washington Post, Gramophone, Ovation,* and *Fanfare.* Mr. Taub won *Opus* magazine's 1986 "Record of the Year" award in the solo piano category for his recording of Babbitt's music.

Mr. Taub is a Phi Beta Kappa graduate of Princeton, where he was a University Scholar. As a Danforth Fellow, he was awarded his doctoral degree from the Juilliard School, where he received the highest award in piano. His principal teacher was Jacob Lateiner.

Mr. Taub has just been appointed artist-in-residence at the Institute for Advanced Study in Princeton—a singular honor, since he is the first musician to be acknowledged in this way during the institute's sixty-year history. The prestigious appointment will involve Mr. Taub in performing the complete cycle of Beethoven sonatas in nine concerts over the next three years in the institute's newly opened Wolfensohn Auditorium. From 1990 to 1992, Mr. Taub served as Blodgett Artist-in-Residence at Harvard University, an appointment that entailed a week of performances and master classes four times during each academic year. Last season, he led the chamber music program at Princeton University.

BOB'S FAMOUS GRILLED CHICKEN

*This recipe works best if the grill is truly hot before placing the chicken upon it. Variations include using hickory wood/charcoal combination for the fire; **fresh** basil works best; a little more soy can be added to suit one's palette. --R.T.*

Quartered chicken (about 3½ pounds)

CHICKEN MARINADE:

¼ cup soy sauce	½ teaspoon sweet basil
¼ cup extra-virgin olive oil	Dash of Hungarian paprika
¼ cup red wine vinegar	Dash of black pepper
1 teaspoon oregano	Juice of ½ lemon

Pour marinade over chicken pieces in glass bowl. Cover and refrigerate for 10 to 12 hours, turning occasionally.

Arrange coals around perimeter of grill, with drip pan in center.

Place marinated chicken pieces on hot grill, directly above coals. After cooking for 5 minutes per side, rearrange chicken pieces to center of grill, over drip pan. Turn pieces as needed and baste with marinade while cooking (approximately 45 to 50 minutes).

Photo: © PETER SCHAAF

IRMA VALLECILLO, PIANIST

Irma Vallecillo is that rare pianist who puts a prodigious solo technique and remarkable musical gifts at the service of chamber music. "She plays with beautiful sound, directness and warmth of impulse, and absolute instrumental competence" (Dyer, *Boston Globe* 1991). Her repertoire is extensive and spans every style from Baroque to contemporary. She has premiered more than thirty works and actively enjoys finding out-of-the-way works from every period. Ms. Vallecillo, a student of Adele Marcus, Angelica von Sauer and Joanna Graudan, attended the Juilliard School.

In recent years, Ms. Vallecillo has appeared in concert with some of the most distinguished artists of this century, as well as participating in numerous chamber music festivals. She has been heard across the United States, Europe and Japan at such halls and festivals as Carnegie Hall, Avery Fisher Hall, Kennedy Center, Ravinia Festival, Hollywood Bowl, Casals Festival, Pacific Music Festival, Lincoln Center Chamber Society, Chamber Music Northwest, Schleswig-Holstein Festival, and the Aspen Music Festival. She appeared on the television special "Leonard Bernstein's 75th," as well as in the 17th Annual Gala from Wolftrap National Park.

Ms. Vallecillo has recorded extensively on the BMG, Moss Music, Albany Records, Delos, Louisville Orchestra, Desmar, Orion, Laurel, and Avanti labels. Currently, she is chairperson of the Accompanying Departments at the Hartt School and the New England Conservatory, as well as director of Chamber Music and Piano at the Pacific Music Festival in Sapporo, Japan.

EVAPORATED MILK CUSTARD
(Flán de Leche Evaporada)
Serves 8

This is a Puerto Rican version of "flan" from a cookbook by Carmen Valldejuli. --I.V.

2¼ cups of sugar (1 cup to caramelize)

5 eggs

1 teaspoon vanilla extract

13 oz. can of evaporated milk, undiluted

Preheat oven to 350 degrees. Caramelize 1 cup of sugar in an 8 x 3-inch round aluminum pan (without tube) by melting sugar, slowly, until a light gold color. (Be careful not to burn the sugar). Remove from heat and tilt the pan to allow the caramelized sugar to cover the bottom and sides evenly. Set on wire rack.

In a saucepan, break eggs, without beating, just enough to mix egg yolks and whites. Add to the unbeaten eggs the 1¼ cups sugar, vanilla and evaporated milk, and mix well. Strain the mixture.

Pour into the caramelized aluminum pan. Set the pan in a large shallow baking pan containing about 1 inch of hot water and bake at 350 degrees, uncovered, for about 1 hour until set and golden.

Remove pan from the oven and let set at room temperature for 45 minutes to an hour, then invert onto a serving plate. Or if the flan is to be eaten at a later time, allow to cool, cover, and set in refrigerator. Invert onto platter when ready to serve.

Irma's Note ♪ When serving right away, if the flan is too hot it will break apart. If it's too cold the caramel will harden and the flan won't release from the pan.

Photo: BURAY PHOTOS, Budapest

BÁLINT VÁZSONYI, PIANIST

Bálint Vázsonyi possesses the unique ability to recreate music, as if the composer were speaking directly to the audience. His scope is not limited to any particular style. He made his piano debut in Budapest (at age 12) with the Bach´s F Minor Piano Concerto, in London´s Royal Festival Hall with the "Emperor" and at Carnegie Hall with Chopin´s Piano Concerto No. 1. This unique ability proved particularly significant when Mr. Vázsonyi made performance history in playing chronological cycles of the 32 Beethoven piano sonatas in a series of appearances in New York, Boston and London.

Having left Hungary in 1956, Bálint Vázsonyi completed his studies with Dohnányi in Florida. Being the last pupil of the *master* of all Hungarian musicians, Vázsonyi became the last link in a tradition which stretches back to Liszt himself.

He maintains a repertoire of some 40 concertos and has been soloist with many great orchestras: the London Symphony orchestra, the New Philharmonia, the Vienna Symphony, the Suisse Romande—to mention but a few. He also appeared frequently in the prestigious South Bank Series in recitals. His numerous radio and television engagements included NBC and BBC telecasts. Vázsonyi´s first recording offer came from Vox (a set of Liszt Rhapsodies, hailed by *High Fidelity* as the best performances available), followed by mostly large-scale masterpieces of the 19th century on Pye Virtuoso, DGG, Genesis and Desmar. Over the past three decades, his tours took him most frequently to the countries of Europe, North and Central America and Africa. Bálint and his wife Barbara now reside in Washington, D.C.

BARBARA'S SALMON MOUSSE

This recipe always seems to work and looks and tastes wonderful. Bálint enjoys this recipe for its flavor and consistency. One can make a lovely presentation of this dish. Use a fish mold rather than a plain mold, use an olive for an eye. Decorate around fish with nice green alfalfa. Lay strips of dill weed for a pattern on the fish and lightly dust with paprika. Your guests will enjoy just looking at the salmon mousse! --Barbara V.

1 pound red salmon, cooked in any
   fashion, but poached is best,
   (canned is ok also)
1 can Campbell's beef consommé
1 packet Knox unflavored gelatine
1 small onion, finely chopped

8 oz. mayonnaise
Juice of 2½ lemons
1 tablespoon vinegar
1 teaspoon soy sauce
1 teaspoon Worcestershire sauce
A few drops Tabasco sauce

Heat one-half can consommé and dissolve gelatine in it. Put all ingredients into blender plus remaining half of consommé. After blending, test for additional amounts of above flavoring. Oil the mold, turn whole mixture into it, then refrigerate. Will be ready to release from mold in approximately 2 hours.

Photo: TOM NAKIELSKI

RALPH VOTAPEK, PIANIST

Ralph Votapek is one competition winner (Gold Medal, First Van Cliburn International Piano Competition, 1962) who has emerged a winner in the more competitive field of professional concertizing. Critics and audiences alike extol his artistic maturity, technical brilliance, and the charm of his relaxed platform manner. He performs in repeat engagements throughout the length and breadth of the Americas. Reviews from Canada to Argentina remark on his ever-consistent artistic growth since his prize-winning days, when he also captured the prestigious Naumburg Award in 1959 and gave his New York debut in Town Hall.

At this juncture in his career, Ralph Votapek's appearances with the major orchestras of the United States alone number in the hundreds, including many performances with the Chicago Symphony and the Boston Pops. With the latter orchestra, he performed on the last recording conducted by Arthur Fiedler (a Gershwin album). His biennial tours of Latin America are sold out events. In Buenos Aires, Votapek plays repeated engagements on each tour, always performing a different repertoire. In the summer of 1994, he made his 16th tour of South America. U.S. audiences frequently hear him on the PBS-TV and National Public Radio Network.

Mr. Votapek has performed throughout the European Continent, including appearances with the London Philharmonia, the National Orchestra of Spain, the Orchestra of Monte Carlo, in Lisbon, and in Germany. At the invitation of the former Soviet Government, he performed throughout the U.S.S.R. in recital and as a soloist with orchestras in St. Petersburg and other major Soviet cities. Audiences in the Soviet Union were tremendously responsive, and his concerts were sellouts.

Born in Milwaukee, Mr. Votapek began his musical studies at the age of nine at the Wisconsin Conservatory of Music. Later, he studied four years at Northwestern University, a year at the Manhattan School of Music, and another year at the Juilliard School. His principal teachers were Rosina Lhevinne and Robert Goldsand. He presently serves as artist-in-residence at Michigan State University in East Lansing.

In recent seasons Ralph Votapek has had numerous appearances in recital on the Chicago Symphony's Allied Arts Piano Series at Orchestra Hall, the Van Cliburn Series in Ft. Worth, the Pabst Theatre Recital Series in Milwaukee, and at Alice Tully Hall at Lincoln Center. His performance at the Lincoln Center Out of Doors Series drew the largest crowd in its history. During the summer of 1992, he was soloist with the World Youth Symphony at Interlochen and in the summer of 1993 made his first Asian appearance in recital in South Korea. In 1995, he performed with orchestra and in recital in Taiwan.

In 1989 and in 1993, Mr. Votapek served on the jury of the eighth and ninth Van Cliburn Competitions; during the summer of 1990, he was one of two American judges at the Tchaikovsky International Piano Competition in Moscow. He has been a guest on chamber concerts of the Juilliard, Fine Arts, New World, and Chester String Quartets. He also makes frequent two piano appearances with his wife, Albertine. He has recorded for RCA Victor and London, and has CDs on the Music and Arts and Pickwick labels.

ARGENTINE EMPANADAS

Serves enough for an orchestra

Though each province of Argentina has its own style of recipes for making empanadas, this is a standard one that you might find in Buenos Aires. Empanadas go well with any dry or semi-dry red wine. --R.V.

Note: This recipe makes 12 cups of filling, and if one chooses to use up all the filling (only 1 teaspoon of filling per empanada is necessary), it will require many packages of Pillsbury Crescent Rolls (see Empanada Pastry below). However, the filling freezes well. It can be kept for months in the freezer if the olives are omitted.

EMPANADA FILLING:

3 pounds of ground beef
4 to 5 cloves garlic
4 medium onions, chopped
¾ large green pepper
2 cups raisins, chopped
2 teaspoons chili powder

1½ teaspoons cumin
6 drops Tabasco sauce
2 tablespoons flour
1 tablespoon sugar
2 tablespoons capers
3 tablespoons tomato paste
1 to 2 cups green olives, sliced

In a very large skillet brown the meat. Add garlic, onions and green pepper; cook uncovered over medium to medium-low heat until onions are clear and green pepper is just tender. (About 20 to 30 minutes). Add remaining ingredients except olives. Cook together until blended. (Add 1 tablespoon water if mixture seems very dry). Add olives at end, but do not cook.

EMPANADA PASTRY:
Use prepared **PILLSBURY CRESCENT ROLLS** for pastry. Each package comes with 8 crescent rolls (*I like to cut each roll in half to make appetizer-size empanadas*). Unroll the refrigerated pastry. Separate on the perforated lines.

Press each section out on a cutting board in order to make them a little larger. Place at least 1 teaspoonful of filling on each pastry section, wet edges, shape into a crescent and press together.

Bake at 400 degrees until pastry is lightly browned—about 10 minutes. May be baked a day ahead and rewarmed at 325 degrees for 5 minutes.

Photo: STEVEN ANDERSON

DAN-WEN WEI, PIANIST

Dan-Wen Wei, a native of the People's Republic of China, began his piano studies at age four and gave his first public concert at age nine. At the age of twelve, he was one of only fourteen pianists among 17,000 applicants accepted for admission to the prestigious Central Conservatory in Beijing. At the age of seventeen, Wei was asked by the government of China to perform for Margaret Thatcher on her first visit to Beijing. After graduation, he was sent as cultural ambassador from China to play concerts in Moscow, Odessa, Prague, Sophia, and Lisbon, among other cities throughout eastern Europe.

In 1986, Mr. Wei began his studies at the Juilliard School under Martin Canin. During his years at the Juilliard School, Mr. Wei was twice-named the winner of the Gina Bachauer Prize as well as winner of the Juilliard Concerto Competition. Dan-Wen Wei graduated in 1991 with both bachelor and master degrees and received the Helen Fay Award for outstanding achievement and character. In 1991, Mr. Wei was chosen by Maestro Zubin Mehta to perform the Piano Concerto in D Major by Mozart with the New York

Philharmonic at the opening concert of the Mozart Bicentennial in Avery Fisher Hall at Lincoln Center. His performance was broadcast internationally as part of the Live from Lincoln Center series.

This past season saw Mr. Wei in performance with the Minnesota Orchestra as well as a return engagement in recital as part of Lincoln Center's Mostly Mozart Festival. In the 1994-95 season, Mr. Wei performed on the Portland State University Piano Series in recital, as well as an extensive solo recital tour. Mr. Wei also performed with the Seattle Symphony Orchestra.

Dan-Wen Wei has been awarded prizes at numerous piano competitions, including the Montreal International Piano Competition, the Robert Casadesus International Competition, and the Marguerite Long International Piano Competition. As a result of these competitions, Mr. Wei has performed as soloist with the Montreal Symphony Orchestra, Orchestre Philharmonique de Radio France, the National Broadcasting Orchestra of China, the Canton Symphony and the Juilliard Symphony.

SHRIMP AND BEAN CURD
(Shanghai Style)
Serves 4

This dish has a variety of colors, and it is very light yet tasty, and delicious with sesame oil.
--D.W.

1 pound medium-sized fresh shrimp
½ pound tofu (sliced into
   1-inch cubes)

GROUP A:
1 tablespoon cooking wine
1 teaspoon salt
½ teaspoon white pepper
1 egg white
¾ tablespoon cornstarch

GROUP B:
1½ tablespoons peanut oil
1 teaspoon ground ginger
1 tablespoon scallions, cut very thin,
   almost like ground pieces

GROUP C:
1 tablespoon green peas
½ teaspoon soy sauce
1 tablespoon cornstarch mixed
   with 3 tablespoons cool water
Sesame oil
Rice (optional)

Clean shrimp and peel off shrimp shell. Dry the shrimp with a kitchen cloth or paper towel. Use a clean bowl and mix together GROUP A ingredients, then add shrimp and coat well, store them in the refrigerator for about one-half hour.

Slice tofu into small pieces (about 1-inch squares).

In cool wok, first add 1½ tablespoons of peanut oil, heat up wok and add rest of GROUP B. Stir-fry for ½ minute.

Put marinated shrimp into wok and stir well until the shrimp turn slightly pink (about 1 minute or so, depending on the temperature, the higher the faster). Put sliced tofu in quickly, cook about 1½ minutes. From GROUP C add green peas and ½ teaspoon soy sauce, cook about another ½ minute, then add cornstarch mixed with water and cook an additional minute, or until thickened.

Turn off heat and add 1 teaspoon sesame oil. If you like, you can add some chopped parsley or green onion. Serve with rice or alone.

Photo: ANNETTE LEDERER

LILYA ZILBERSTEIN, PIANIST

Born in Moscow in 1965, Lilya Zilberstein started playing piano at age five. In 1971, she went on to study at the Gnessin Music School in Moscow with Ada Traub and graduated from there with a gold medal in 1983. She continued her studies with Alexander Satz at the Gnessin Pedagogical Institute, where she took her final examination in 1988. Lilya is a winner of the Russian Republican Competition and the All Union Competition and her international success came in 1987 when she won first prize at the Feruccio Busoni International Piano Competition.

In May, 1988, Ms. Zilberstein took her first tour of the West, with performances in Italy, the United States, Germany, Austria and France. The 1991 season featured Lilya's debuts in Amsterdam's Concertgebouw and in Berlin, where she performed Rachmaninov's Piano Concerto No. 3 with the Berlin Philharmonic Orchestra under the direction of Claudio Abbado. In the summer of 1992, she made her debut at the Ravinia Festival with James Levine and the Chicago Symphony Orchestra, playing Prokofiev's Piano Concerto No. 3. Other recent performances have brought Ms. Zilberstein to the music centers of Germany, Italy, France and Japan.

In the fall of 1993, Lilya toured Germany as soloist with the Moscow Philharmonic Orchestra. That same season also featured her debuts in London with the London Symphony, in Brussels, where she performed with the National Orchestra, as well as in recital, and in Copenhagen with the National Radio Symphony.

An exclusive Deutsche Grammophon artist since 1988, Lilya Zilberstein has recorded solo works by Rachmaninov, Shostakovich, Brahms, Liszt, Schubert, Mussorgsky, Taneyev and Medtner as well as the Grieg Piano Concerto with Neeme Järvi and the Göteborg Symphony. Her performance of Rachmaninov's Second Piano Concerto with Claudio Abbado and the Berlin Philharmonic Orchestra in 1991 was recorded live by Deutsche Grammophon; it was coupled with Rachmaninov's Piano Concerto No. 3 and released in 1994.

STRUDEL
Serves 6 to 8

I received these recipes from my Russian grandmother, Tatjana Schwarzstein. --L.Z.

1 cup sour cream
8 oz. margarine or butter (or half and half)
2 cups flour
Sugar

1 cup plum jam
1 cup raisins
1 cup walnuts, crushed

Mix sour cream, margarine and/or butter (melted) and flour. Work into a ball. Put into refrigerator, covered, for 2 to 3 hours.

Remove dough and separate into four equal pieces. Roll out each piece of dough onto a floured board. Dough should not be too thick or thin and somewhat oblong shaped.

Sprinkle some sugar over each rolled out piece of dough and spread about ¼ of each ingredient, beginning with the jam, then raisins, then walnuts. Wrap up dough. Make several little holes in dough for pie pieces. Sprinkle again with sugar and place in oven on a 11 x 14-inch greased or non-stick cookie sheet for 35 to 40 minutes at 350 degrees. When done, cut into pieces.

GRANDMOTHER'S RUSSIAN SALAD
Serves 4

2 to 3 medium-sized onions
4 hard-boiled eggs, sliced
4 apples, sliced

Mayonnaise
½ cup Edam cheese, grated

Boil whole onions, with skin, in water for 20 minutes. Gently add eggs to same water and cook until hard-boiled (about 12 minutes). Remove eggs and put into some cold water until ready to use. Remove onions and peel off skins. Let cool. Separately slice apples, eggs, and onions. Layer, on an attractive plate, first the onions, then apples, then eggs. Add a light coating of mayonnaise over salad and sprinkle cheese over mayonnaise.

SINGERS

Photo: CHRISTIAN STEINER

MICHAEL BALLAM, TENOR

"Tenor Michael Ballam performed with an abundance of intensity, intelligence and musicality as well as a personable stage manner and a strong ability to communicate," proclaimed the *Los Angeles Times* about his recital at the music center.

Intelligence and musicality are adjectives that well describe this young tenor, who, at the age of 24, was the youngest recipient of the degree of doctor of music with distinction in the history of the prestigious Indiana University School of Music. His voice has been described as "splendid" by the *Washington Post*, "commanding" by the *Chicago Tribune*, and "superb" by the *Philadelphia Inquirer*, in an amazing repertoire that includes over 60 major roles.

An insatiable musician, he is an extraordinary pianist and accomplished oboist.

Today, Mr. Ballam has already participated in three operatic world premieres, including Krysztof Penderecki's *Paradise Lost* at the Lyric Opera of Chicago. In 1979, Mr. Ballam debuted with the San Francisco Opera in *Elektra,* having become somewhat of a Strauss specialist with that renowned company, sharing the stage with Monserrat Caballe, Kiri Te Kanawa, and Birgit Nilsson, also appearing in the international telecast of *Samson and Delilah* with Shirley Verrett.

He has appeared regularly with the Chicago Lyric, San Francisco Opera, Pennsylvania Opera Theater, Kentucky Opera, Philadelphia Opera, Washington Opera, Dallas Opera, and with the Santa Fe, San Diego, and St. Louis Operas, also the Michigan Opera Theater and the Mississippi Opera. He has gained great distinction for singing major roles in Busoni's *Doktor Faust,* Haydn's *Il Mondo della Luna* (sung at the Kennedy Center's Haydn Festival), Cavalli's *L'Ormindo* (title role), Barber's *Vanessa*, Offenbach's *La Belle Helene* and David Amram's *Twelfth Night*. In the more standard repertoire he also has garnered much praise for his work in *Madama Butterfly, La Bohème, Faust, Tales of Hoffmann, Gianni Schicchi, Un Ballo in Maschera, Rigoletto, La Traviata, Pelléas et Melisande, and Die Fledermaus.*

As a recitalist, Michael Ballam has performed with astounding critical success in the most important concert halls in the country, including the Kennedy Center (Washington D.C.), Orchestra Hall (Chicago), Jordan Hall (Boston), Jones Hall (Houston), and Music Center (Los Angeles). He has also given recitals throughout Europe, Asia and the Soviet Union, and gave command performances at the Vatican and the White House. With a wide orchestral repertoire ranging from the Verdi Requiem to Haydn's *Creation*, he has drawn considerable attention, appearing with such orchestras as the Houston Symphony, Utah Symphony, Dallas Symphony and the Minnesota Orchestra.

PEGGY'S ITALIAN SPAGHETTI

Serves 4 to 6

It is true that I was attracted to opera because of Mr. Puccini, Bellini, and Rossini, but I think it was the other "ini" boys that attracted me as well...linguini, tortellini, and the like. Here is my favorite pasta sauce, which was given to me by a lifetime friend, Peggy Carey...we know it as Peggy's Spaghetti. --M.B.

1½ pounds hamburger	28 oz. can whole tomatoes, drained
1 large green pepper, sliced	14 oz. can mushrooms, drained
2 medium onions, sliced	Long spaghetti (1 pound)
Salt and pepper	Grated cheese of choice

Slice green pepper and onion across (to form rings). In large skillet, sauté onion and pepper in Crisco until just starting to brown. Combine with hamburger that is broken into pieces, and brown. Add salt and pepper, cook until almost done.

Mash tomatoes through fingers and add to above mixture. Cover and cook slowly for 2 hours.

Add mushrooms to sauce. Cook spaghetti in plenty of water (salted). Do not break up. Heat plates; add spaghetti on plates in neat arrangement. Cover with grated cheese.

One can add seasonal steamed vegetables such as carrots or peas to sauce.

Photo: MARY NOBLE OURS

PHYLLIS BRYN-JULSON, SOPRANO

Known for her lustrous voice and her pitch-perfect three-octave range, Phyllis Bryn-Julson commands a remarkable amount of vocal literature that spans many centuries.

Highlights of recent seasons include the world premiere of *A Winter's Tale* at Rutgers University, followed by a Lincoln Center performance of the work with the Chamber Music Society of Lincoln Center. Miss Bryn-Julson also sang this composition in Baltimore, Los Angeles and at the Santa Fe Chamber Music Festival. She also premiered a work by Margaret Meachem with the Atlantic Sinfonietta in New York's Merkin Hall. She has appeared frequently with symphony orchestras throughout North America including the Boston and Chicago Symphony Orchestras, the Cleveland, Philadelphia and Minnesota Orchestras, the Toronto, Atlanta and Dallas Symphonies and the New York and Los Angeles Philharmonics. With the latter, she most recently returned for concerts with Pierre Boulez, with whom she frequently collaborates.

Phyllis Bryn-Julson has appeared extensively in Europe where she sang Bernstein's Symphony No. 3 *(Kaddish)* at the Flanders Festival, Kurtag's *Kafka Fragments* in Badenweiler and at the Warsaw Autumn Festival and appeared with the Lausanne Chamber Orchestra in Lausanne and Geneva, Jesus Lopez-Cobos conducting. With the Ensemble Inter-Contemporain, she has traveled to Canada, Barcelona, Madrid, the Soviet Union and the Salzburg Festival, among other cities. Miss Bryn-Julson has also appeared with the Berlin Philharmonic, conducted by Claudio Abbado; sung a concert of Gershwin, Porter, Glen Miller and Copland songs with the London Sinfonia and Richard Hickox; appeared at the Festival de Musique Sacree de Fribourg with the Arditti String Quartet; portrayed Vitellia in a concert version of Mozart's *La Clemenza di Tito* in Baden-Baden, Freiburg and Frankfurt; participated in performances of Mahler Symphony No. 2 in Antwerp and was the soloist in Schoenberg's *Pierrot Lunaire* in Vienna. She has

appeared in cities such as London, Paris, Stockholm, Amsterdam, Copenhagen, Stuttgart, Hamburg, Berlin and at La Scala in a variety of repertoire.

A member of the Peabody Conservatory faculty, Phyllis Bryn-Julson appeared as soloist with the Peabody Symphony in Moscow in February 1988. During the orchestra's brief one-week residency, she became the first American ever to give a master class at the Moscow Conservatory of Music.

Born in North Dakota of Norwegian parents, Phyllis Bryn-Julson began her musical life as a pianist. It was not until she was called upon to sight-read a difficult contemporary score for Gunther Schuller that her extraordinary voice was discovered, then nurtured, at Tanglewood and at Syracuse University.

Miss Bryn-Julson made her opera debut in the 1976 world premiere of Roger Session's *Montezuma* with the Boston Opera Company and in 1983 made her Covent Garden debut in Stravinsky's *Le Rossignol*. Later, at Covent Garden, she performed in both *Le Rossignol* and Ravel's *L'enfant et les sortileges*. In concert she has sung the role of Vitellia in *La Clemenza di Tito* with the Baden-Baden Radio Orchestra and was one of the divas in the *Impresario* at the Mostly Mozart Festival in New York.

Her lengthy list of recordings, many of them award-winning, includes works on CBS Masterworks, CRI, Decca, Edici, London, Louisville, New World, Nonsuch, Odyssey, Orion, RCA and Deutsche Grammophon. Miss Bryn-Julson and Pierre Boulez have recorded his compositions *Le Visage Nuptial* and *Le Soleil des Eaux*, Elliott Carter's *A Mirror on Which to Dwell* and *Le Rossignol,* all on the Erato label. She has recorded Britten's *Our Hunting Fathers* with the English Chamber Orchestra for Collins Records and Schoenberg's *Cabaret Songs* with pianist Ursula Oppens for the Music and Arts Label. Additional recordings include

Beethoven's *Missa Solemnis* with Michael Gielen; "Stravinsky Chamber Music" with Pierre Boulez; Griffes's *Poems of Fiona MacLeod* with the Boston Symphony, Seiji Ozawa conducting; and most recently, *Ewartung* with Simon Rattle and the City of Birmingham Symphony for EMI Classics, and a disc of Miss Bryn-Julson singing solo works by Schuller, Dallapiccola, Carter, and Messiaen, Mark Markham, piano, from Music and Arts.

NORWEGIAN PINWHEEL
Serves 8

Ms. Bryn-Julson suggests using this recipe as a delicious hor d'oeuvre. It is a colorful recipe to make during the holiday season.

15-inch cooked pizza crust, cooled
1 pound cream cheese, softened
1½ cups chopped green bell peppers
1 cup chopped yellow bell peppers
6 large hard-boiled eggs, yolks and whites chopped separately

1 cup chopped red bell peppers
1 cup chopped black olives
2 cups flaked cooked salmon, or chopped lox

Spread pizza crust with cream cheese. Starting at the outside, place alternate circles of green and yellow peppers, egg whites, red peppers, black olives, egg yolks, and salmon on the crust. Use whatever order looks most attractive in color. Keep chilled until ready to serve. Cut into wedges.

An alternative method for another hor d'oeuvre is to mix 1 cup mayonnaise and 1 cup Parmesan cheese, add seasoning of choice, spread on pizza crust and bake until just melted and slightly bubbly (about 10 minutes at 350 degrees). Serve with vegetables and chips.

Photo: © SONY CLASSICAL

JOSÉ CARRERAS, TENOR

Very few singers can have made their debuts in an international house at the age of eleven, as was the case with José Carreras. This was no small undertaking, moreover, for he sang the role of El Trujitnan, the boy narrator in de Falla's Master Peter's Puppet Show, whose music is so difficult that it is more frequently entrusted to a high mezzo. José Carreras made this important first appearance at the Liceo in his native Barcelona with José Iturbi conducting. "It was an exciting experience," he recalls. Uniquely, perhaps, Carreras made his adult debut in the same opera house at the age of twenty-two, by which time he was a highly promising tenor.

The music student, who at his parent's wish had also read chemistry for a few semesters, won the International Verdi Singing Competition in Parma, important test for opera debutantes. Among the audience for the final competition concert was the world famous tenor Giuseppe di Stefano, who prophesied a glittering career for the young Catalan. After the competition, Carreras sang his first Rodolfo (La Bohéme) in Parma and received rapturous ovations from the demanding Teatro Regio audience. In 1971 he was invited to London to make his international debut in a concert performance of Donizetti´s *Maria Stuarda* at Festival Hall. Later, Mr. Carreras took part in the British premiére of *Caterina Cornaro,* when on only two days notice he stepped into what was for him a new role in this difficult lesser-known role.

Debuts in important roles and cities followed. In 1972, he sang his first Pinkerton in Puccini's *Madame Butterfly* in the United States, with the New York City Opera, and in 1974, he celebrated deserved triumphs in no less than three opera houses - at London's Royal Opera House with Alfredo *(La Traviata),* at Vienna's State Opera House with The Duke in Verdi's *Rigoletto* and then at the Metropolitan Opera House in New York with Cavaradossi in *Tosca*. San Francisco, Philadelphia, Chicago and Houston are just a few of the many cities where Mr. Carreras performed in operatic repertoire as well as in recitals and concerts.

Maestro von Karajan engaged José Carreras in 1976 for his Easter Festival singing the tenor part in Verdi's Requiem and their artistic and personal relationship lasted over 12 seasons, resulting in performances and recordings with the Maestro in Salzburg, Vienna, Lucerne and Berlin. The José Carreras discography includes recordings of over 60 complete operas, including *Un Ballo in Maschera, Trovatore, Aïda, Turandot, Don Carlos, La Bohème, Lucia di Lammermoor, Andrea Chenier, Werther, Carmen, Tosca,* as well Rossini's difficult and virtuosic *Otello* and Nemorino in Donizetti's *L'Elisir d´ Amore.*

During his career, Carreras has made a number of excursions into 'light' repertoire, not just popular Spanish and Italian songs, but Lloyd Webber, West Side Story and South Pacific as well. Then, of course, there was The Three Tenors concert in Rome before the World Cup Final in 1990, an event which was seen by one billion people on television. From World Cup 1994 in Los Angeles, The Three Tenors - Encore! concert has attracted record television audiences around the world.

Mr. Carreras' position as musical director of the opening and closing ceremonies at the spectacular 1992 Olympics kept him busy in his hometown of Barcelona. Also in the same year, José Carreras made his stage debut in the part of Loris in Giordano's opera *Fedora*, which he performed again in May 1993 with the Teatro alla Scala, and will sing at a later date in London and Vienna. In January 1993, he made his acclaimed stage debut in Verdi's *Stiffelio* at the Royal Opera House in London. This triumphal performance, heard for the first time ever in this version, won the 1992/93 Sir Laurence Olivier Award. This production with Mr. Carreras was repeated in Milan (1995) and in Vienna.

Among the many international awards and recognitions which have been bestowed upon José Carreras are:

Doctor Honoris Cause for the Medical Faculty of the University of Barcelona; Honorary Member of the Royal Academy of Music in London; Lifetime Honorary Member and "Kammersänger" of the Vienna State Opera House; Grande Ufficiale della Republica Italiana; Gold Medal of the Generalitat of Catalunya; Spain's Medalla de Oro de las Bellas Artes; Commandeur de l'Ordre des Arts et des Lettres de la République Francaise; Grand Prix du Disque from the Academy of Paris and winner of 1991 Grammy Award. Mr. Carreras

portrayed in the motion picture "Romanza Final" the life of the tenor Julian Gayarre. His video portrait "A Life Story" won the International Emmy Award.

In 1988, The José Carreras International Leukemia Foundation was established in Barcelona, with the collaboration of a highly qualified world-wide team which included Professor E.D. Thomas, the winner of the 1990 Nobel Prize for Medicine. José Carreras is a popular and effectual president of his own foundation.

CALDERETE DE CORDERO
(Lamb Stew)
Serves 3 to 4

Mr. Carreras's "Calderete de Cordero" recipe originates from Jerez, Spain, and is made with lamb less than a year old.

2 **pounds lean, boneless lamb**	1 **tablespoon flour**
½ **cup wine vinegar (for marinade)**	8 **oz. cup boiling water**
4 **tablespoons extra virgin olive oil**	4 **peppercorns**
4 **cloves garlic**	1 **tablespoon finely chopped mint**
2 **large sliced onions**	**Salt and pepper to taste**

Cut up lamb into 1½-inch stew-size pieces; allow to marinate for one hour in equal parts water and wine vinegar. Drain and wash in clean running water and dry thoroughly.

Heat oil in a large saucepan, brown cloves of garlic, then remove and save. Add meat to oil and brown carefully, then add sliced onions together with the flour. Sauté onions several minutes while stirring in flour. When flour is dissolved, add boiling water to contents of pan, cover, and simmer over low heat for about 1½ to 2 hours.

Meanwhile, pound the fried garlic into a mortar with the peppercorns, mint and a little salt. Stir 2 tablespoons of the broth from the meat into the mortar. When the meat is cooked and tender, remove it from pan and keep warm. Add the garlic mixture to the pan and cook sauce on medium heat, until reduced and thickened. Pour over the meat and serve.

Photo: SADGE LEBLANG, METROPOLITAN OPERA

WALTER CASSEL, BARITONE

Baritone, Walter Cassel, is considered one of the great singing actors of this century. His "fine dark baritone, commanding figure, and polished style of characterization," as the *San Francisco Chronicle* put it, won him an international reputation as an artists of unique versatility and accomplishments.

He has been in demand for every dimension of the standard European repertoire. Mr. Cassel scored with the New York City Opera in modern works, such as the American operas "The Ballad of Baby Doe," and "The Devil and Daniel Webster" both by Douglas Moore, and in "The Taming of the Shrew" by Vittorio Giannini, receiving unanimous critical acclaim from the New York Press.

Mr. Cassel's former Wagnerian roles at the Metropolitan Opera were especially cited by the critics. The multi-faceted aspects of his artistry were noted by the *Saturday Review* after his first of many Kurvenals in *Tristan und Isolde* performances at the Metropolitan Opera. "A singer who can follow his Scarpia with a German role on this level is clearly one to be cultivated." Cassel continued to add to his repertoire with Jochanaan in *Salome*, Telramund in *Lohengrin*, Wolfram in *Tannhäuser*, and the Dutchman in *The Flying Dutchman* until the *New York Tribune* extolled, "Walter Cassel would get an accolade from Wagner himself."

As a guest artist from the Metropolitan, Walter Cassel made his European debut during the 1964 summer festival in Zürich in one of his most famous roles, Jochanaan in *Salome,* in the company of other notable American artists, including Felicia Weathers and Glade Peterson. That was to be the beginning of ten years of alternating periods of performances at the Metropolitan Opera and throughout the United States. He sang also in many opera houses abroad, including the Deutsche Oper am Rhein in Düsseldorf, the Vienna Staatsoper, the Lyceo in Barcelona, the Massimo in Palermo, culminating in a joyous hit revival of *The Great Waltz* in the old Drury Lane Theatre in London, England in which he starred as the elder Johann Strauss. The show ran for 21 months in that wonderful old theatre and was considered the greatest hit since *My Fair Lady*.

Musicals and operettas have been a part of his musical career since the beginning of it, having starred in most of the important summer theatres in the United States. In one of these engagements, he played opposite the beautiful blonde soprano Gail Manners, and they fell deeply in love and later married. They have appeared together since then so frequently that in some quarters they were considered the Lunt and Fontaine of the musical theatre.

The amazing vocal stamina with which his American training has endowed him was dramatically demonstrated at the Metropolitan, when Mr. Cassel set a new record at the house by singing *three* of the taxing roles in the baritone repertoire, Scarpia in *La Tosca*, Kurvenal in *Tristan und Isolde*, and Jochanaan in *Salome,* in the space of 24 hours.

It was during rehearsals for his first *Gianni Schicci* in Seattle, Washington, that Dean Charles Webb phoned him about sharing some of his time and talents with the School of Music at Indiana University. Webb stressed the fact that today's young singers need to learn from the experience and skills of the performing artist. Cassel then added a new dimension to his career, that of professor of voice at the top rated and renowned School of Music. Walter Cassel finds life more fulfilling than ever, as a teacher of the great promising voices in America, while he still is active as a performer throughout the world.

CHICKEN SANS SOUCI

Serves 4 to 5

This recipe was brought to us by our son Dietrick. He received it from his wife Shelly who had attended chef school and found it to be an outstanding recipe.

We find that as time passes our culinary tastes get simpler. This recipe is very much a favorite of Walter and myself. --Gail C.

3 **pounds chicken parts**	1 **can condensed chicken consommé**
3 **tablespoons oil**	1 **pound button mushrooms, quartered**
3 **tablespoons butter**	2 **tablespoons dried onion flakes**
3 **tablespoons flour**	3 **tablespoons dried parsley flakes**
½ **cup dry white wine**	**Salt and pepper to taste**

Heat oil and butter, add chicken and brown. Place chicken into casserole dish. On low heat, using same skillet, add flour, stirring until smooth. Add consommé and wine, simmering until smooth. Add mushrooms, onion and parsley, simmer several minutes. Pour over chicken and bake uncovered in oven for 1¼ to 1½ hours at 375 degrees or until chicken is tender.

Photo: CAROL CASTEL

NICO CASTEL, TENOR

Nico Castel was born in Lisbon, Portugal, to a set of multi-lingual parents who inculcated in him from the cradle, a love of languages. He grew up with Portuguese and Spanish and spoke German with his nanny. Later in his childhood he lived in Venezuela, where he attended a French school, adding French, Italian and English to his language collection. At age 16, he traveled to New York to pursue his career as a singer. In 1958, he won the "Joy in Singing" Award of a New York Town Hall debut recital, and his career was launched. Castel soon made his debut with the Santa Fe Opera and since then his services have been in demand by many opera companies, including the New York City Opera and the Metropolitan.

Mr. Castel is a true polyglot, a man of vast culture, a multi-talented artist and scholar, who in addition to having carved himself a career as one of the world's pre-eminent character operatic tenors, with over 200 roles in his repertoire, has also developed a parallel career as a vocal coach and teacher of multi-lingual lyric diction. His 25 years at the Metropolitan Opera Company include 14 years as staff diction coach. He is on the faculties of the Juilliard School of Music, Mannes College of Music, and Manhattan School of Music in New York, as well as the Israel Institute of Vocal Arts in Tel Aviv, the AIMS program in Graz, Austria and the Aspen Festival. Mr. Castel is a visiting professor at universities and conservatories throughout the United States, Canada and South America, including the Eastman School of Music, the University of Maryland at College Park, Baylor University, University of Texas at Austin, Indiana University at Bloomington, and many more. He is adjunct professor at Boston University and the New England Conservatory of Music in Boston. For two years he has been invited to coach the singers of the Finnish National Opera in Helsinki, as well as the singers associated with the Palacio de Bellas Artes in Mexico City.

Mr. Castel's lifetime of knowledge and experience in the fields of language and vocal music have finally come together in a Spanish vocal music book for singers and coaches; *A Singers' Manual of Spanish Lyric Diction*. It is lovingly researched and written especially for singers wishing to perform the Spanish and Hispanic repertoire. Published by Excalibur Press, this book is currently available.

Mr. Castel is also now in the process of completing translations and phonetic (I.P.A) transcriptions of all the known operas for Leyerle Publications. His first volume of the complete Puccini libretti is already published. After the Puccini, Mr. Castel will translate all 28 Verdi operas, all of Mozart's operas and later a Verismo set, a Bel-Canto set, a French set, the Handel operas, and finally, German opera and the Wagner music dramas.

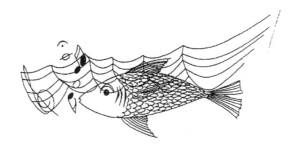

BACALHAU À GOMES-DE-SÀ
Serves 8

Garnish with wedges of hard-boiled eggs, black olives and parsley sprigs. Serve with a crusty white bread, a good Portuguese "Vinho Verde" or Spanish Rioja. Quantities can be varied for the number of persons served. It does not alter the flavor of the dish. --N.C.

2 **pounds salted, boneless cod** *(bacalhau can be found in Latin bodegas or special fish markets)*
4 **pounds red or russet potatoes**
4 **large red or yellow onions (about 3 pounds), thinly sliced**

½ to ¾ **cup olive oil**
Black pepper
4 **hard-boiled eggs, for garnish**
Black olives, for garnish
Parsley, for garnish

Soak codfish in cold water for 24 hours, changing the water at least twice. Cover fish with water and boil until it starts to flake. Drain water and set aside.

Wash and then boil potatoes with skins on for about 30 minutes, or until tender. When done, test with a knife to see if it goes through a potato smoothly. When cooled, peel off skin and cut into approximately ½-inch slices.

Meanwhile, add a little corn oil to large frying pan and cook onions on medium heat for about 25 minutes, until golden brown.

In 4-quart casserole dish, start layering ingredients. First, lightly coat the bottom of casserole with some olive oil and then cover with a layer of potato slices. Coat with a little more olive oil. Then layer one-half of the codfish pieces over it and then a layer of fried onions. Add a little more oil and some pepper. Repeat process until the casserole is full and all the components are used. You should have 2 complete layers, ending with the onions. Make sure you have added enough oil every time you build a layer.

The dish then can be set aside until company comes. When needed, bake the casserole in a 350 degree oven for 30 minutes, covered, then 10 minutes, uncovered. Garnish with eggs, olives and parsley.

Photo: CAROL ROSEGG

JOYCE CASTLE, MEZZO-SOPRANO

A gifted mezzo-soprano, also praised for her inspired acting abilities and excellent musicianship, Joyce Castle is aptly described as a "mezzo of a thousand faces" in the *Opera Monthly* cover story on this versatile artist.

Since her Metropolitan Opera debut in 1985, Miss Castle has performed in Met productions that range from Strauss operetta to Wagner's Ring Cycle, and include *Die Fledermaus, Eugene Onegin, Il Tabarro, Gianni Schicchi, Andrea Chenier, Boris Godounov, Falstaff, Faust, Der Rosenkavalier, Götterdämmerung and Die Walküre.* Frequently heard on Saturday afternoon Texaco broadcasts, Miss Castle also appeared in the Metropolitan Opera's nationally televised performances of *The Ring*, conducted by James Levine. Joyce Castle returned to the Metropolitan Opera during the 1993-1994 season for its production of *Rusalka*.

After centering her career in Europe for six years, in 1983 Joyce Castle was recruited by Beverly Sills and Hal Prince to return to the United States for principal roles at the New York City Opera and for the role of Mrs. Lovett in Mr. Prince's production of Stephen Sondheim's *Sweeney Todd,* slated for the Houston Grand Opera. In addition to her critically acclaimed performances of Mrs. Lovett in *Sweeney Todd,* with both the New York City Opera and the Houston Grand Opera, Miss Castle has enjoyed tremendous success at the New York City Opera as Augusta Tabor in *The Ballad of Baby Doe,* Madame d'Urfe in the heralded New York premiere of Dominick Argento's *Casanova,* and the Old Lady in *Candide.* Joyce Castle has also appeared with the City Opera as Baba the Turk in *The Rake's Progress,* Fata Morgana in *The Love for Three Oranges,* Meg in *Brigadoon,* Emma Jones in *Street Scene,* and Katisha in *The Mikado.* Ms. Castle's association with the New York City Opera continues this season with the world premiere of Hugo Weisgall's *Esther* in which she will perform the role of Zeresh.

North American opera engagements include her Canadian debut at the Manitoba Opera with her first performances of Herodias in *Salome,* followed by her Calgary Opera debut in the same role in performances conducted by Mario Bernardi. In the United States, Ms. Castle has appeared at the Washington Opera as Madam de la Haltiere in *Cendrillon,* as the Marquise in *The Daughter of the Regiment,* and as Herodias in the acclaimed Peter Hall production of *Salome.* Frequently engaged by the Seattle Opera, Joyce Castle sang her first performances of Mother Marie in *Les Dialogues des Carmélites* with this company and returned for heralded performances of Augusta Tabor in *The Ballad of Baby Doe.* She returns to Seattle this season as Mrs. Grose in *The Turn of the Screw.* Miss Castle has also appeared with the opera companies of San Francisco, Houston, Dallas, Long Beach (CA), Cleveland, Arkansas, Anchorage, Alaska and Philadelphia.

Miss Castle has been privileged to participate in the first performances of several operatic works during her career. These performances include the first opera house performances *Sweeney Todd* mentioned previously, the New York premieres of *Casanova* by Argento, *Die Soldaten* by Zimmermann at the New York City Opera, and the American premieres of *A Night at the Chinese Opera* by Weir. She sang in *The Black Mask* by Penderecki, and *The King Goes Forth to France* by Sallinen at the Santa Fe Opera, and sang the world premiere of *Where's Dick* at the Houston Grand Opera (directed by Richard Forman). She was also fortunate to give her first performances of Begbick in *Mahagonny* at the Kennedy Center under the direction of Ian Strasfogel, with Lotte Lenya as artistic consultant. In concert, the artist sang the world premiere of Leonard Bernstein's *Arias and Barcarolles,* with Maestro Bernstein and Michael Tilson Thomas at the keyboard, and made her New York Philharmonic debut performing the challenging *Aventures et Nouvelles Aventures* by G. Ligeti in the first performances of this work at Lincoln Center. She was also pleased to have the opportunity to perform Lili Boulanger's *Faust et Helene,* accompanied by the composer's sister Nadia Boulanger.

Miss Castle may be heard on the Grammy Award-winning New World Records recording of *Candide* as the Old Lady, the Book-of-the-Month recording of Sondheim (singing "Send in the Clowns" and *Sweeney Todd* selections), the recently released Koch recording of *The Music of Stefan Wolpe*, and the Albany Records album of *The Vocal Music of Joseph Fennimore*.

Joyce Castle holds a B.F.A. degree from the University of Kansas (major in voice theater) and a masters degree in voice and music literature from the Eastman School of Music.

This Kansas native currently resides in New York.

PEGGY'S POULET A L'AIL
Serves 6

I was born in Texas, raised in Kansas, and lived 8 years in France—thus these recipes. --J.C.

1 medium-sized chicken, whole
3 heads (bulbs) of garlic, whole, not peeled
3 tablespoons Pastis (French alcoholic
    beverage flavored with anise)

Thyme
1 bay leaf
Salt and pepper

Brown the chicken in butter and oil. Put into a heavy casserole with **3 heads** (not 3 cloves) of garlic, unseparated. Sprinkle over with spices. Pour 3 tablespoons Pastis over the contents. Cover and cook at 350 degrees for one hour. *(Don't Peek)!*

MOTHER'S OKRA CREOLE
Serves 4

4 or 5 slices bacon
1 small onion, sliced or diced
12 small whole okra (about 1¼ cups, cut)
Salt and pepper to taste

¼ teaspoon oregano
1 to 3 teaspoons sugar to taste
4 fresh medium tomatoes, thinly sliced

Fry slices of bacon until brown. Remove bacon to a clean plate and tear into small pieces when cool (**do not** lay bacon on paper towel to soak up grease).

Pour off almost all the grease from pan and fry the small onion until clear.

In the meantime, cut off stem ends of the okra and slice the okra into ½-inch thick rounds. Add cooked bacon and okra to pan and season with salt, pepper, oregano and sugar. Lay tomatoes on top.

Simmer, covered for 45 minutes, then uncovered for 15 minutes. **Do not stir.**

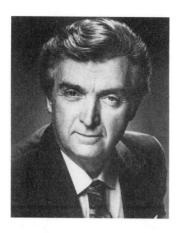

DOMINIC COSSA, BARITONE

Dominic Cossa, "who possesses one of the most beautiful baritone voices you are likely to come across anywhere," in the words of the *New Yorker*, is well known to American opera audiences. Since making his debut at New York City Opera, Mr. Cossa has sung in more than 20 new productions for the company. The wide variety of his roles there includes Figaro in *Il Barbiere di Siviglia*, Dr. Falke in *Di Fledermaus*, Dr. Engel in *The Student Prince*, Fritz in *Die Tote Stadt*, Germont in *La Traviata*, and Zurga in *Les Pêcheurs de perles*. In 1970, he made his debut at the Metropolitan Opera and at San Francisco Opera and has subsequently sung a variety of roles with the Met, including Figaro, Valentin in *Faust*, Yeletzky in *Pique Dame*, Marcello in *La Bohème*, Lescaut in *Manon Lescaut*, Albert in *Werther*, and Mercutio in *Roméo et Juliette*.

When Dominic Cossa performed his show-stopping Figaro in the Miami Opera production of *Il Barbiere di Siviglia*, he was widely praised for his vocal and dramatic expertise. Enthusiastic reviews follow him everywhere, and his mastery of style, from Brahms to Broadway, receives constant acclaim. Although Mr. Cossa is known primarily for his work in this country, he has appeared at London's Albert Hall, with the Opéra du Rhin in Strasbourg, as Falke in *Die Fledermaus* in Catania, Italy, and in frequent engagements at the major opera centers of North and South America. He made his European debut at Milan's Teatro Nuovo.

In addition to performing a repertoire of more than 50 operatic roles, Dominic Cossa is frequently invited to appear in recital and concert venues, and has sung with the New York Philharmonic, the Chicago Symphony, the Boston Symphony, the National Symphony, and the Israel Philharmonic. He has worked with many eminent conductors including Seiji Ozawa, Georg Solti, and Leonard Bernstein. He has toured East Asia extensively with concerts in Beijing, Shanghai, Hong Kong, Seoul, Taiwan and Singapore.

Mr. Cossa was featured as soloist on Broadway with Martha Graham in the world premiere of *Heloise and Abelard* and can be heard on numerous recording labels singing opposite some of the greatest names in opera, including Beverly Sills in *Giulio Cesare* on RCA, Joan Sutherland in *Les Huguenots* on London, and Luciano Pavarotti in *L'elisir d'amore* on London. He has also recorded *When Lilacs last in the Dooryard Bloom'd* with the Boston Symphony for New World Records, and the original recording of *Mass,* conducted by Leonard Bernstein. He was chosen by Gian Carlo Menotti to appear in two of his premieres, *The Hero* in which he sang the title role, and *Tamu Tamu* in Spoleto, Italy.

Born in Jessup, Pennsylvania, to Italian parents, Dominic Cossa was surrounded by music from early childhood, and soon developed a special love for great Italian operas. As much as he loved music, however, he had no intention of making a career of it, choosing instead to pursue a degree in psychology. He received both his B.S. and his Ph.D. degrees from the University of Scranton and his M.A. from the University of Detroit. On the advice of a friend, Cossa courageously entered the Metropolitan Opera regional auditions and received one of the top awards, plus much encouragement. Three years later, he auditioned for New York City Opera and was immediately offered a contract. He has been listed in 'Who's Who' for many years and was recently included in the International *Who's Who in Music*.

Mr. Cossa is a professor of music at the University of Maryland and resides there with his wife Jan. His hobbies include gardening, wine-making and cooking.

SAUSAGE AND BEAN CASSEROLE
Serves 8

If the sausage is well-drained, this is a fairly low-fat meal. The ¼ cup olive oil can be cut down to a couple tablespoons or less for very restricted diets. In any event the beans make a perfect accompaniment to the sausage. Buon Appetito! --D.C.

1 pound dried Navy beans	1 tablespoon minced parsley
2 pounds Italian sausage	¼ teaspoon oregano
1 large onion, chopped	1 bay leaf
2 cloves garlic, chopped	½ teaspoon rosemary
1 green bell pepper, chopped	¼ cup olive oil
8 oz. can tomato sauce	Salt and pepper to taste

Soak beans overnight. Drain, cover with water and simmer 1 hour, or until tender. Drain but save liquid. Slice sausage into bite-size pieces and bake (uncovered) in oven at 350 degrees for 45 minutes. Drain grease.

Cook chopped onion, garlic and green pepper in olive oil very slowly until they *melt,* stirring frequently. Add tomato sauce and herbs. Let simmer for 10 minutes.

*(Use a large dutch oven). Add the beans and sausage to the tomato sauce mixture and add the bean liquid as needed. Cook uncovered on stove top over low heat for 1 hour. Salt and pepper to taste. Best when reheated.

*Author's note: if a dutch oven-type pot is not available, an alternative way to cook the casserole could be to bake at 325-350 degrees in a covered 4-quart casserole dish for about an hour.

Photo: ANNE KIRCHBACH

COSTANZA CUCCARO, SOPRANO

Soprano Costanza Cuccaro has won high acclaim for her performances in many of the world's opera houses and concert halls. A native of Ohio and a graduate of the University of Iowa, she was one of the youngest contestants ever to win first place in the Metropolitan Opera National Auditions

After study in Rome as a Fulbright scholar, Cuccaro sang at the Zürich Opera and later became the leading lyric-coloratura at the Deutsche Oper Berlin. She has made frequent guest appearances in the opera houses of Munich, Hamburg, Vienna, Boston, Toronto, Montreal and Buenos Aires in a repertoire including *Lucia di Lammermoor, Rigoletto, The Rake's Progress* and *The Magic Flute*. Her Metropolitan Opera debut was as Rosina in *The Barber of Seville*. Ms. Cuccaro has appeared with the orchestras of Chicago, Cleveland, Detroit, Paris and Tel Aviv and has been heralded for her interpretations of the music of J. S. Bach in such cities as Moscow, Prague, Leipzig, Cleveland, Buenos Aires and Rio de Janeiro. Her recording and video credits include numerous oratorios and Bach cantatas as well as seven operas. Television appearances include *The Tonight Show* with Johnny Carson and *The Today Show.*

Costanza Cuccaro performed at the International Congress of Voice Teachers in Philadelphia in July of 1991 and at the National Convention of NATS held in Boston in July of 1992. Miss Cuccaro is the 1993 recipient of the Maxine Christopher Schutz Distinguished Teaching Award from Missouri University. In July 1994, Costanza Cuccaro presented the opening recital for Richard Miller's Institute of Vocal Performance Pedagogy at Oberlin. Cuccaro's students include numerous district and regional NATS and Metropolitan Opera Contest winners.

Costanza Cuccaro is the wife of Edwin Penhorwood, composer and pianist, who accompanies her in recital. She was artist-in-residence and professor of voice at Missouri University from 1987 to 1993 and is now professor of voice at Indiana University.

APPLE CRANBERRY RAISIN PIE
Serves 8 to 10

I found that this recipe was a wonderful alternative to a regular apple pie recipe. It is delicious, particularly over the holiday season. Its origins are from the 18th century. --C.C.

½ cup sugar	2 large tart apples, peeled and cut
¼ teaspoon salt	into small pieces (about 3 cups)
2 tablespoons flour	1 medium lemon
½ cup golden raisins	2 tablespoons butter
1 cup cranberries	Ready-made unbaked pie crust (9-inch)*

Mix sugar, salt and flour together, then toss with fruit. Add zest of lemon. Fill up the pie crust with apples, cranberries and raisins until about even with rim of crust, with the middle of the pie higher than the edges. Dot with butter. Preheat oven and bake at 425 degrees for about 45 minutes. Juices should be bubbling nicely when done.

*Use foil around edge of crust.

Photo: J. HENRY FAIR

ADRIA FIRESTONE, MEZZO-SOPRANO

Adria Firestone's artistry combines a voice of unusual color and exceptional timbre with the performance mastery of an accomplished actor and dancer. She has appeared on stage and in concert in a variety of dramatic roles, encompassing the repertoire of opera, musical theater, operetta and contemporary works.

Miss Firestone is especially acclaimed for her portrayal of Bizet's legendary *Carmen*. She has played the gypsy more than eighty times with companies throughout the world, including: Houston Grand Opera, San Diego Opera, Miami Opera, Auckland Opera, New York City Opera's National Company and the Singapore National Opera, to name only a few.

Miss Firestone returned to the Houston Grand Opera during the 1988-89 season to sing Julie in *Show Boat*, followed by performances of the production in Egypt celebrating the opening of the new Cairo Opera house.

An accomplished recitalist as well, Miss Firestone has traveled throughout the Far East with the Ambassadors of Opera, singing in such countries as Hong Kong, Singapore, Malaysia, Indonesia, Sri Lanka, the Philippines and Korea. During the 1990-91 season, Miss Firestone returned to Manila and Singapore for concerts and traveled through the Middle East, singing in such cities as Cairo, Abu Dhabi and Bahrain, as well as for our Desert Storm troops in the Persian Gulf.

In addition to recital appearances, the 1993-94 season included appearances for Opera Omaha's Toulouse-Lautrec Concerts (Scenes from *Perichole* and *Mon Coeur* from *Samson et Dalila*), Julie in *Showboat* for the Gold Coast Opera and her return to the Greater Miami Opera for their awaited *Fiesta Espanola*, in which she sang both Candelas in *El Amor Brujo* and Abuela in *La Vida Breve*. In the summer of 1994, Miss Firestone was heard as *Abuela*—this time in concert performances under the baton of Maestro Mata at the Grant Park Festival in Chicago.

Other engagements included Amneris in *Aïda* for the Utah Opera, *Carmen* for the Sacramento Opera (with her dear colleague Rico Serbo in the role of Don José), Beethoven's 9th Symphony for Las Cruces, and her debut in the role of Santuzza in *Cavalleria Rusticana* with the Kentucky Opera. In addition, she made her Australian debut in an extensive number of *Carmen* performances at the Lyric Opera of Queensland. In 1996-97, she will return to the San Diego Opera to repeat her portrayal of *Carmen* (with Ricky Leech and Maestro Bonynge) and to sing the role of Donna Francisca in the world premiere of Myron Fink's *Il Conquistador* with Jerry Hadley.

The compact disc recording of contemporary composer John Cage, featuring Miss Firestone in *5 Songs for Contralto* and *Experiences*, was released on the Wergo Label.

Born in California and educated in Florida, Miss Firestone is of Spanish-Italian heritage. She studied with Sara Sforni-Corti at the Giuseppe Verdi Conservatory in Milan and with Edward Zambara, Beverly Johnson, and presently Mary Henderson Buckley in New York. She was regional finalist in the San Francisco Opera Auditions and first prize winner in the Palm Beach Opera Scholarship contest, where as a company member she made her debut as Siebel in *Faust* and performed such diverse roles as *Cenerentola, Ulrica* and *Lola*. She was also the recipient of first prize in the Center for Contemporary Opera's International Voice Competition and was a finalist in opera and musical comedy in the 1985 National Institute for Musical Theater Competition.

Miss Firestone presently makes her home in New Jersey.

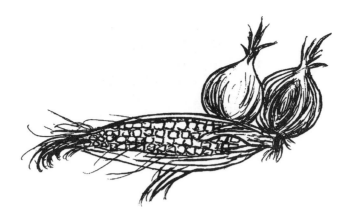

CHICKEN PICCATA

Serves 6 to 8

Because I have a wheat allergy, I am always looking for wheatless dishes that still have crispness and flavor. This one is yummy. If you can't find corn flour, you can grind cornmeal in your food processor with the metal blade until very fine. You may of course substitute regular flour. --A.F.

3 whole chicken breasts, skinned,
   boned and halved (about 2½ pounds)
½ cup corn flour (can be found as harina
   de maiz by Goya foods) or cornmeal
1½ teaspoons salt
¼ teaspoon freshly ground pepper
1 teaspoon paprika
Seasoned salt to taste
¼ teaspoon red pepper

½ cup butter
2 tablespoons virgin olive oil
4 to 6 tablespoons dry Madiera or
   vermouth or water
4 to 5 tablespoons fresh lemon juice
1 lemon thinly sliced
4 tablespoons capers
¼ cup minced fresh parsley

Flatten chicken breasts between 2 sheets of wax-paper until ¼-inch thick. Combine corn flour or cornmeal, salt, pepper, paprika, seasoned salt, and red pepper in a bag. Wet chicken in additional lemon juice and add to bag. Coat well. Shake off excess.

Heat butter and oil in large skillet until bubbling. Sauté chicken breasts a few at a time, 2 to 3 minutes on each side. Do not overcook. Drain and keep warm. Drain off all but 3 tablespoons of butter and oil, stir Madeira, vermouth or water into drippings, scraping bottom of skillet to remove any particles. Add lemon juice and heat briefly. Return chicken to skillet. Add lemon slices and heat until mixture thickens. Add capers and sprinkle with minced parsley.

Serve with a crisp green salad, buttered steamed carrots and a cold bottle of Italian or French dry white wine. Voilá, a beautiful, flavorful dinner.

HERTA GLAZ, MEZZO-SOPRANO

Herta Glaz made her debut at the age of nineteen in Breslau (then Germany) as Erda in Wagner's *Das Rheingold.* After two years and some 300 performances in opera and light opera roles, Ms. Glaz returned to Vienna, Austria, her hometown. Subsequently, she sang many recitals including contemporary works by Berg, Schoenberg, Bartók and Krenek. With Krenek at the piano, she introduced several of his compositions. For the next few years, she performed with Krenek in several European cities. Ms. Glaz performed Schoenberg's "Lied der Waldraube" from Gurrelieder with the Vienna Philharmonic Orchestra under the baton of Otto Klemperer. This resulted in an invitation from Mr. Klemperer to make her United States concert debut in Mahler's *Das Lied von der Erde* and Bach's *St. John's Passion* with the Los Angeles Philharmonic. Ms. Glaz toured the United States as leading mezzo-soprano of the Salzburg International Opera under management of Sol Hurok.

Hitler's army moved into Austria on the last day of the company's performance in New York City. Ms. Glaz remained in this country, immigrated legally and became an American citizen in 1943. Her American opera career began with the Chicago Opera in 1938 as Brangäne in *Tristan und Isolde* and as Fricka in *Die Walküre* opposite Kirsten Flagstad and Lauritz Melchior. In the same year,

she joined the San Francisco Opera. During the following years, Ms. Glaz continued with recital and orchestral engagements throughout the United States and Canada. On Christmas day in 1942, Ms. Glaz made her Metropolitan Opera debut singing Amneris in *Aïda.* Several years later she made a concert tour in Australia, New Zealand and the Hawaiian Islands.

Ms. Glaz has recorded with Victor, MGM, and Columbia records. In 1955, Ms. Glaz married Professor Frederick Redlich, then chairman of the department of psychiatry at Yale University in New Haven. A year later she retired from the Metropolitan Opera and dedicated herself to teaching. She joined the voice faculty at the Manhattan School of Music where she remained until 1977. She is presently adjunct professor on the voice faculty at the University of Southern California. Miss Glaz received an honorary degree of fine arts from the University of New Haven. Several of her students are now members of the Metropolitian Opera and European opera houses. Ms. Glaz first performed in Aspen in 1949 and continued to teach and perform at the Aspen Music Festival and School until 1954. She returned to join the Aspen voice faculty in 1987 and now returns each year. Herta Glaz and her husband received the Cross of Honor for the Arts and Science from their native Austria.

SEAFOOD À L'OPERA

Serves 4

This dish is always a success!! --H.G.

30 medium-sized fresh shrimp
      (about 1½ lb.) or 2 cans of crab meat
1½ tablespoons onion, chopped
3 tablespoons butter
3 tablespoons flour
1¼ cups liquid (from cooked shrimp)
¼ cup milk

1½ tablespoons curry powder
1 teaspoon paprika
1 egg, slightly beaten
⅔ cup cream
3 tablespoons sherry
Salt to taste

Drop shrimp with shell on into 4 cups of gently boiling water, cook for 3 to 4 minutes, or until tender. Drain, save liquid (if crab meat is used, save some of can liquid). Peel and clean the shrimp.

In medium-large skillet, brown onions lightly in butter, dissolve flour with 1¼ cups liquid from shrimp and add to pan. Pour in milk. Slowly cook ingredients until smooth, add curry powder and paprika.

Before serving, add slightly beaten egg, cream and sherry. Stir sauce and bring to a slow boil. Add shrimp or crab meat and salt. Mix and heat slowly. Do not boil.

Serve over boiled rice.

JERRY HADLEY, TENOR

Jerry Hadley has been called "the great tenor hope of the post-Pavarotti generation" and remains one of the most sought-after singers of our time. He has received international acclaim for his interpretations of the great Mozart tenor roles and those of the French Romantic and Bel Canto eras, as well as for his frequent ventures into Broadway musical theater, operetta, and American popular song.

American born and trained, and of Italian and English ancestry, Mr. Hadley exhibits the warm, vibrant sound and easy-going good looks that have made him a 'natural' as a romantic leading tenor.

A stalwart of the New York City Opera in his formative years, Jerry Hadley's burgeoning international career was launched with his debut at the Vienna State Opera in 1982, as Nemorino in *L'elisir D'amore*. Debuts in the great opera houses of the world followed quickly, and he is now a regular visitor to the Metropolitan Opera, the Royal Opera at Covent Garden, the Hamburg State Opera, Deutsche Oper Berlin, the Lyric Opera of Chicago, the San Francisco Opera, the Glyndebourne Festival, the Festival d'Aix-en-Provence, and the Salzburg Festival, to name but a few. 1995 saw his debuts at Teatro alla Scala in Milan in Berlioz's *Damnation de Faust*, opposite Jose van Dam and Frederica von Stade, under Seiji Ozawa; and at the Lyon Opera in Stravinsky's *The Rake's Progress*.

Neither is he a stranger to the concert stage, appearing regularly with the great orchestras of the world, under the batons of such luminaries as Seiji Ozawa, Wolfgang Sawallisch, Kurt Masur, Claudio Abbado, Charles Dutoit, Robert Shaw, André Previn, Sir Georg Solti, Sir Colin Davis, Sir Charles Mackerras and Sir Neville Marriner. He was particularly close to the late Leonard Bernstein, with whom he collaborated often in the last decade of the composer/conductor's life.

Hadley is an accomplished recitalist, appearing throughout North America and Europe, both as a soloist (with pianist Cheryll Drake Hadley) and in frequent collaboration with baritone Thomas Hampson.

Television and radio audiences have regularly thrilled to his appearances on such programs as *Live from Lincoln Center; Great Performances; An Evening at Pops;* and Garrison Keillor's *American Radio Theater.*

Mr. Hadley is a prolific recording artist, with dozens of titles to his credit. He is a two-time Grammy-winner and frequent nominee. His classical credits include *La Bohème* (DGG) with Leonard Bernstein; *Anna Bolena* (Decca), opposite Joan Sutherland and Richard Bonynge; *Il Re Pastore* (Philips); *Così fan Tutte* (Telarc); *Hadley and Hampson, Operatic Duets* (Teldec), a collaboration with his friend and colleague, baritone Thomas Hampson; *Il Barbiere de Siviglia* (EMI), again opposite Thomas Hampson; Britten's *Nocturne, Les Illuminations, Serenade for Tenor, Horn and Strings* (Nimbus); Verdi's *Requiem* (Telarc), for which he won a Grammy; Mozart's *Requiem* (Telarc and DGG); Schubert's *Mass in E-flat* (DGG); and Beethoven's *9th Symphony* (Pro Arte). Upcoming are Stravinsky's *The Rake's Progress* and Massanet's *Werther* for Erato; Mozart's *Don Giovanni* for Telarc; Lehar's *Land of Smiles, Giuditta, Czarevich and Paganini,* in English, for Sony; and Mendelssohn's *Elijah,* with Thomas Hampson, under the baton of Robert Shaw, for Telarc.

Regarded as the undisputed "king of crossover," Mr. Hadley was selected by Leonard Bernstein to record the title role in *Candide,* for which he won his second Grammy, and by ex-Beatle Paul McCartney to create the leading role in *Liverpool Oratorio.* His impressive list of credits also includes the landmark recording of *Showboat* (EMI); *Kismet* (Sony); *My Fair Lady* (Decca); and Weill's *Street Scene* (Decca).

For BMG Classics/RCA Victor and Red Seal, with whom he records extensively in a wide range of repertoire, Mr.

Hadley has released the following: *Golden Days,* a collection of Romberg, Herbert and Friml, whose title song boasts a duet with the great Mario Lanza; *Standing Room Only,* a collection of Broadway favorites; *In The Real World,* an elegy of popular and jazz standards; *The Men In My Life,* where he, Thomas Hampson, Samuel Ramey and Spiro Malas join Marilyn Horne in a potpourri of popular favorites; as well as guest appearances on the all-star *Sondheim: A Celebration,* the Richard Tucker Foundation's *A Celebration of American Music;* the latest Canadian Brass Christmas album; and *Symphonic Rolling Stones.* Future releases on the label include *The Art of Bel Canto* with Richard Bonynge and the English Chamber Orchestra; two discs of arias from Viennese operettas, again with Bonynge, and the Bayerische Rundfunk Orchestra; *Italian Sonnets* for voice and piano; *Arias from American Opera*; and a complete *West Side Story*, opposite Dawn Upshaw.

SESAME COOKIES

Makes 35 cookies

This delicious cookie recipe from Jerry Hadley requires tahini, which is a creamy paste produced from crushed sesame seeds. The author would recommend using one of the Middle Eastern brands of tahini, such as Ziyad brand, which comes from Lebanon. It is important that the tahini is stirred before using, because the oil, as in some brands of natural peanut butter, rises to the top of the jar.

¼ **cup peanut butter**
¼ **cup crushed sesame seed oil (tahini)**
   (found at most health-food stores)
½ **cup butter (1 stick) softened**
½ **cup granulated white sugar**
½ **cup brown sugar, patted firmly**

½ **teaspoon vanilla**
1 **large egg**
1½ **cups flour**
1 **teaspoon baking powder**
½ **teaspoon salt**

Blend together peanut butter, sesame tahini and butter. Slowly work in the brown and white sugars. Add the vanilla and the large egg, mix well together.

Sift together all the dry ingredients. Add to batter, mixing thoroughly. Form the dough into small balls and place 2 inches apart on a greased baking sheet. Press the tops of each cookie with the fork tines to make a checkerboard pattern. Do not press the cookies too flat.

Preheat oven to 350 degrees. Bake 12 to 14 minutes. Remove to cooling rack.

Photo: BORIS

JANICE HARSANYI, SOPRANO

Janice Harsanyi is a professor of voice at Florida State University. She was formerly on the faculty at North Carolina School of the Arts and head of the voice department at Westminster Choir College. Some of her former students are now singing at the Metropolitan, New York City, Chicago Lyric, San Francisco and Houston Opera Houses. She has performed in 45 of the 50 states and six European countries and has appeared with many of the leading American orchestras, including 40 performances with the Philadelphia Orchestra under Eugene Ormandy. Other conductors with whom she has sung include Robert Shaw, Leopold Stokowski and Sir John Barbirolli. She has also introduced music by more than 50 living American composers, including Roger Sessions, Milton Babbitt, Robert Ward and John Harbison. She has appeared in the Alaska, Saratoga Springs, and Meadowbrook Festivals, as well as many Bach festivals, including the Bethlehem Festival in Pennsylvania. Mrs. Harsanyi has performed lecture recitals and conducted master classes at universities and colleges throughout the United States, including New England Conservatory, University of Michigan and Oberlin. She is listed in the International *Who's Who in Music* and the *New Grove Dictionary of American Music*.

APPLE RAISIN SOUR CREAM PIE
Serves 8 to 10

This is a recipe which I concocted and which my guests have enjoyed on many occasions. MacIntosh apples are my favorite. You can make this pie the night before; it keeps well when refrigerated. --J.H.

1½ cups graham cracker crumbs
6 tablespoons butter (melted)
3 eggs, beaten
¾ cup sugar
¾ cup sour cream

1½ cups apples, peeled, cored
    and cut into small pieces
3 oz. raisins
¾ teaspoon almond flavoring

Place graham cracker crumbs and melted butter into a 9-inch pie plate. Press crumbs on the bottom and sides of the pan, then set aside. In a mixing bowl, add beaten eggs, sugar and sour cream. Mix well. Add the apples, raisins and almond flavoring. Pour into pie pan.

Bake in a preheated oven at 325 degrees for approximately 1 hour or until the mixture is firm. **Do not overbake!** Ovens vary, so check after 50 minutes. Cool to room temperature, then refrigerate for a minimum of 1½ hours.

Evelyn Lear and Thomas Stewart

EVELYN LEAR, SOPRANO

Consider the legacy that Miss Lear carries forward: forty operatic roles sung in most of the major opera houses in the U.S. and throughout the world, including the Metropolitan Opera (where her debut in 1967 was in the role of Lavinia in the world premiere of Marvin David Levy's *Mourning Becomes Electra*), Lyric Opera of Chicago, The Royal Opera at Covent Garden, Teatro alla Scala Milan, The Paris Opera, the Vienna State Opera, the Teatro Colon in Buenos Aires, and in Germany at the famed houses in Berlin, Hamburg and Munich. Her concert appearances have been legion; she has performed with every major symphony orchestra and conductor (including Karl Böhm, Claudio Abbado, James Levine, Sir Colin Davis, James Conlon, Seiji Ozawa, Zubin Mehta, Michael Tilson Thomas and Edo de Waart), and at a multitude of important festivals both here and abroad.

Miss Lear's association with the Metropolitan Opera endured for fourteen seasons; she performed twelve roles in ten works and was heard in ninety-one performances. Among important roles she sang at the Met were Tosca, Donna Elvira, Alice Ford, Marie in *Wozzeck*, the Composer in *Ariadne auf Naxos*, the Countess in *Le Nozze di Figaro,* and the Marschallin in *Der Rosenkavalier*.

Miss Lear has been the recipient of numerous awards for her artistry, including being named "Kammersängerin" by the Senate of Berlin and winning the Max Reinhardt Award in Salzburg.

Her extensive discography of complete operas, operatic excerpts, and Lieder has been honored with several Grammy awards. A critic writes of her latest release, *A Celebration of Twentieth Century Song*, "The revelation here is Evelyn Lear, she sings with passion... the opening vocalise is simply ravishing, the recording is remarkable....I hope there are more where that came from."

In addition to her well-known complete opera recordings of *Der Rosenkavalier, Lulu, Wozzeck, The Magic Flute, Boris Godunov* and *Le Nozze di Figaro*, there are four new CDs available now on the Video Arts International label: *Evelyn Lear and Thomas Stewart Sing Wagner & Strauss* (VAIA 1011); *Evelyn Lear, A Celebration of Twentieth-Century Song* (VAIA 1049); *Evelyn Lear, Songs My Mother Taught Me* (VAIA 1057); and *Des Knaben Wunderhorn* (VAIA 1061). A fifth, *Salzburg Lieder Recital, Richard Strauss* will be released shortly.

From stage to master classroom to pen, Miss Lear's latest turn as writer is a logical extension of her success as a teacher. The result to date are three pedagogical books, published by G. Schirmer and distributed by Hal Leonard Publishing. Written in collaboration with her husband Thomas Stewart, *Romantic Duets* includes extensive interpretive comments and study translations, as well as six sample programs intended as a guideline for both singers and coaches. The book features twelve duets that run the gamut from Schubert and Brahms to Saint Saëns and Stephen Foster.

Selections from Der Rosenkavalier lives up to its name with interpretive insights, photographs, and a new translation of the plot from this beloved opera. Miss Lear's rare versatility has allowed her the unique distinction of having performed all three principal roles in more performances of *Der Rosenkavalier* than any other artist.

A comprehensive two-volume set, *Lyric Soprano Arias,* presents twenty of the most popular soprano arias, encompassing the span of centuries from the Baroque era to the present. Slated for this year is a new publication on Strauss Lieder with an accompanying CD of master classes, which was recorded last fall at the Houston Grand Opera when Miss Lear worked with artists in that company's studio program. Published along with the text will be song accompaniments for additional personal intensive study, as well as insights into the art of the Lied. In addition to Miss Lear's writing and her master class work, she is still very much a performer as narrator/actor of works for orchestra or chamber groups. In 1995, Miss Lear made a guest appearances as the "Baroness" at the Kennedy Center in Washington Opera's production of Samuel Barber's *Vanessa*.

Miss Lear is one of the most highly sought-after teachers, with a resumé that speaks for itself: Juilliard, Peabody, Santa Fe, London, Houston, Chicago, New England Conservatory, Amsterdam, San Francisco and Miami. Her classes have covered a wide geographical area, throughout the United States, Canada and abroad.

CHICKEN DIVAN

Serves 4

To be eaten while listening to Mozart's Jupiter Symphony. --E.L.

4 medium chicken breast halves (par-boiled)	1½ cups grated Parmesan cheese
2 cups of fresh broccoli	½ cup bread crumbs
11 oz. can creamed chicken soup	½ cup melted margarine
1 tablespoon lemon juice	

Par-boil chicken in pot of boiling water for about 20 minutes. In greased 2-quart casserole dish, place in layers: broccoli, par-boiled chicken, soup, lemon juice, cheese, bread crumbs and margarine.

Bake uncovered at 350 degrees for 35 minutes until it is brown. Serve with noodles of choice.

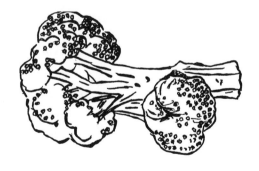

Photo: LOUIS MÉLANÇON, METROPOLITAN OPERA

JOHN MACURDY, BASS

Internationally acclaimed bass John Macurdy is considered one of the finest artists on the opera and concert stage. Since his debut at the Met in 1962, Macurdy has performed over forty different roles with this company, including most major bass parts: Gurnemanz, Pogner, *Trovatore*/Ferrando, Friar Laurent, and the Inquisitor. He knows 60 roles and has 15 to 20 so well prepared he can do them on short notice. More than once he rushed in to save a performance; when he replaced an ailing colleague as Mephistopheles in Gounod's *Faust*, the *New York Times* wrote, "On a few hours' notice, Mr. Macurdy not only saved the day but also stole the show. His characterization had shape, dimension and style. He moved on stage with complete confidence and generated a refreshing touch of humor in his mock-wooing of Marthe." He has participated in five opening nights and in over a dozen new Met productions including Samuel Barber's *Anthony and Cleopatra,* performed for the inaugural of the new house at Lincoln Center; Chagall's *Magic Flute,* the Karajan *Ring, Les Troyens, Lohengrin* and the Schneider-Siemsen/Otto Schenck *Tannhäuser,* and *The Tales of Hoffmann,* among others.

Since his operatic debut, which took place in New Orleans, singing the Old Hebrew in *Samson et Dalila,* he has performed with most major companies in the U.S., making debuts in 1958 in Santa Fe (Colline); in 1959 in Houston (Comte des Grieux), Baltimore (Sparafucile), and the New York City Opera; 1962 in San Francisco (Trulove); 1975 in Miami (Sparafucile); 1977 in Tulsa (Ramphis); and 1980 in Washington, D.C. (Marke). In 1960, he sang the Commendatore with Leontyne Price and Cesare Siepi in *Don Giovanni,* which was the first color telecast of an opera, produced by NBC Studios and shown throughout the United States.

Mr. Macurdy has also performed with festivals at Ravinia, Tanglewood, the Hollywood Bowl, Central City, Newport, Grant Park, and at Temple University in Ambler, Pennsylvania.

As popular in the concert hall as in the opera house, Macurdy has sung with many of the major orchestras of the world, among them the Chicago, Boston, Detroit, Montreal and San Francisco Symphonies, the New York (Beethoven Ninth), and Los Angeles (Verdi Requiem) Philharmonic Orchestras; with the Orchestre de Paris, he sang in the Mahler Eighth Symphony under the baton of Sir Georg Solti. He is also heard in the Beethoven Ninth Symphony on Columbia Records with Eugene Ormandy conducting the Philadelphia Orchestra.

His European debut took place in France in 1965, singing Prince Gremin in *Eugene Onegin* with the Marseille Opera, and Banquo in *Macbeth* with the Nice Opera. In 1974, he returned to Europe to sing Sarastro for the Scottish Opera, followed in rapid succession by debuts in Geneva: Narbal/*Les Troyens*; La Scala in Milano and Strasbourg: Inquisitor/*Don Carlos*; Paris Opera: Arkel/Pelleas and Melisande; and, Commendatore/Don Giovanni; Lisbon: Heinrich/*Lohengrin,* and Madrid: Hunding/*Die Walküre.*

At the Salzburg Festivals of 1977 and 1978, Mr. Macurdy sang the Commendatore in the new production of *Don Giovanni* with Karl Böhm. This highly successful production was later recorded by Deutsche Grammophon and has received unanimous critical acclaim. He repeated the role in the motion picture "Don Giovanni," directed by Joseph Losey and recorded by CBS under the baton of Maestro Maazel.

Other noted conductors he has performed with include Richard Bonynge, Claudio Abbado, Riccardo Chailly, Sixten Ehrling, Berislav Klobucar, Rafael Kubelik, Erich Leinsdorf, Charles Munch, Gustav Kuhn, James Levine, Zubin Mehta, Seiji Ozawa, Giuseppe Patane, Leopold Stokowski, Mstislav Rostropovich, John Pritchard, Julius Rudel and Robert Shaw.

In 1985, Mr. Macurdy performed Sarastro in *Die Zauberflöte,* Christoph von Dohnányi leading the

Cleveland Orchestra in the first staged production of an opera at the Blossom Festival. Also in 1985, he was named to the Academy of Vocal Arts Hall of Fame and received the AVA's Medal for Great American Singers.

The career of John Macurdy, a native of Detroit, is the story of a steady rise to success. It all began with the song "O Tannenbaum," which he learned from his Prussian grandfather. From boy soprano to alto, Macurdy's voice descended to the bass register at age 12, and he sang throughout his youth for the sheer enjoyment of music. An engineering student at Wayne State University, he served four years in the Air Force, after which he began attending the Opera Workshops of Boris Goldovsky. Soon he was performing with the Experimental Opera Theater in New Orleans and the Santa Fe Opera, where he sang in the world premiere of Carlysle Floyd's *Wuthering Heights*. Macurdy subsequently moved to New York but now resides in Connecticut, where he enjoys adding to his antique clock collection, a fine wine cellar, and looking after his garden.

ORANGE SAUCE FOR SPONGE CAKE

I have no clue as to the origin of this "Orange Sauce" recipe, but it has been in my family for over one hundred years. I have never seen, in the many cookbooks that I own, one equal to it.

The sauce is improved if you whip the custard before you add the whipped cream. I also like to add touches of both lemon and orange rind, which is for taste and not mere ornamentation. This "Orange Sauce" is for either angel food or sponge cake. --J.M.

½ cup sugar
1 tablespoon lemon juice
Juice of 1 orange

4 egg yolks
Pinch of salt
1 cup cream (whipping cream)

Mix and whip sugar, lemon juice, orange juice, egg yolks and salt. Cook in a double boiler until thick. Cool and add cup of cream (stiffly whipped).

ROBERT MERRILL, BARITONE

Acclaimed by critics as "one of the great natural baritones of the century," Robert Merrill has truly become a legend in his own time. From the grand stages of the world's great opera houses, to Broadway, records and television, he has set a standard for musical excellence.

His 1991 "I LOVE AMERICA" concert with the United States Air Force band and the Singing Sergeants performed at Constitution Hall in Washington, D.C. received rave notices throughout the country when it aired over PBS stations. It set a record for biggest money maker during pledge week for PBS-WLIW/21 in the New York area. Other recent television appearances include a celebration of the 20th anniversary of the Boston Pops, under the direction of John Williams, and as special guest star on the "Victor Borge at 80" salute, both of which are currently airing on PBS nationwide. He performed on and hosted a PBS special from Carnegie Hall in tribute to his colleague, the late Richard Tucker. He is a favorite of Johnny Carson and appears on many variety specials.

One of the few performers who has been able to balance both opera and popular music styles with phenomenal success, Merrill opened the new Rainbow and Stars Room in New York City's Rockefeller Center with a standing-room-only one week engagement. The critics raved. Bob Harrington wrote in the *New York Post* that "Robert Merrill's voice—a rich, mellifluous baritone—remains one of the wonders of the Western world," while *Variety* reported that "Merrill's baritone still booms. It has vibrancy and is adaptable to music far removed from the Met. He designed a program to catch the middle brow as well as the high brow and made it a night to remember."

The Brooklyn-born baritone, who has received every accolade that critics can bestow, has been honored throughout the United States as one of this country's greatest artists. He has performed many times for visiting heads of state at the invitations of every President from Truman to Ronald Reagan. In October 1993, President Clinton honored him by bestowing the National Medal of the Arts on the baritone and hosting a State Dinner at the White House in honor of the recipients. Merrill is also the recipient of the Handel Medallion, New York's highest cultural award, as well as an honorary doctorate of music degree from Gustavus Adolphus College in St. Peter, Minnesota. Also, he holds a place of honor in Philadelphia's Academy of Vocal Arts Hall of Fame for Great American Opera Singers. The Metropolitan Opera honored him with the hanging of his portrait in the Hall of Fame, recognizing his record setting 787 performances with the company.

Mr. Merrill made his Metropolitan Opera debut as the elder Germont in Verdi's *La Traviata*; he was the youngest artist to sing this role at the Met. Shortly thereafter, he was heard by Toscanini, who was so impressed that he invited Merrill to sing Germont in his historical *Traviata* broadcast with the NBC Symphony. Merrill became a favorite of Toscanini, and when the conductor was 87 and preparing for his final opera broadcast, *Un Ballo in Maschera*, he asked Merrill to sing the role of Renato. Throughout his career, Merrill has performed as soloist with every major orchestra in the United States and most of the world's great conductors, among them Arturo Toscanini, Leonard Bernstein, Herbert von Karajan, Fritz Reiner, Erich Leinsdorf, Sir Georg Solti, Leopold Stokowski, George Szell, Eugene Ormandy, Zubin Mehta and William Steinberg. His annual coast-to-coast recital tours in recent seasons have included performances at Wolf Trap, the Hollywood Bowl and Philadelphia's Mann Music Center, as well as participation in a tribute to the late tenor Jussi Björling in Stockholm, Sweden. In addition to opera, Merrill has recorded music of the Broadway stage, including *Porgy and Bess, Show Boat, Carousel* and *Fiddler on the Roof.* He has performed popular music in Las Vegas and Atlantic City with Joan Rivers, Don Rickles, and Alan King, and with Frank Sinatra in numerous charity and television appearances.

Robert Merrill's autobiography (written in collaboration with Sanford Dody and published by Macmillan) was an immediate bestseller, and he has subsequently completed two additional books: *Between Acts* (published by McGraw-Hill), and *Divas* (published by Simon and Schuster). Merrill's enthusiasm for baseball is legendary and, but for a God-given voice, he undoubtedly would have pursued a baseball career; in fact, he once pitched for a semi-pro team to help pay for singing lessons. His recent recording of *God Bless America* is regularly played at home games of the New York Yankees, and it has become a tradition of Merrill to sing the national anthem live at Yankee opening games. 1994 marked the 25th year he had done so.

Mr. Merrill is married to the former Marion Machno, a concert pianist and Juilliard graduate, who frequently plays for him when he appears in recital. They have two children, David and Lizanne, who appeared with Merrill on television when he was named National "Father of the Year" in 1983. Both children are married and the Merrill family has expanded with the addition of three grandchildren.

QUICK HOME-MADE BORSCHT
Serves 6

This is a favorite summertime refresher that both my mother, mother-in-law, and now my wife Marion makes that seems to hit the spot on a hot day after a game of golf. --R.M.

1 **can (16 oz.) whole beets, chilled**
1 **can cold water**
1 **pint (16 oz.) sour cream**

¼ **cup fresh lemon juice or to taste**
Salt to taste
2 **tablespoons fresh dill, chopped**

Remove beets from can and grate. Reserve juice. Put sour cream into a bowl and gradually add beet juice and water. Add grated beets, lemon juice, salt and dill and mix to blend. Adjust seasonings between lemon juice and salt. Should have a tart taste. **Serve chilled.**

For variation:
For lower-fat diets, use a low-fat sour cream or sour cream substitute.

If you are really in a hurry, all of the above can be done in a blender rather than grating the beets. A small cold, boiled and peeled potato can be added to each serving if desired.

Photo: THOMAS O'KRIEGSMANN

JOHN HORTON MURRAY, TENOR

A graduate of the Curtis Institute of Music in Philadelphia, John Horton Murray joined the Metropolitan Opera Young Artists Development Program at the beginning of the 1990-91 season. Mr. Murray grew up in West Berlin, where his father, William, is a Kammersänger with the Deutsche Oper Berlin.

In the summer of 1996 tenor John Horton Murray's engagements include the title role in Mozart's *La Clemenza di Tito* with Opera Theatre of Saint Louis followed by the young servant in *Elektra* at the Salzburg Music Festival with Lorin Maazel conducting and Florestan in *Fidelio* with Opera Northern Ireland. While touring Italy this summer he attended a performance of *Carmen* at Verona's 18,000-seat arena and when the residing tenor at the arena fell ill, Mr. Murray finished the performance by singing Act IV—making headlines across Italy and notice in the international press. Upcoming engagements in his 1996-97 season include a return to the Metropolitan Opera to cover both Plácido Domingo as Don José in *Carmen* and the role of the Prince in *Rusalka*; he will also appear as Narraboth in *Salome* with the Houston Grand Opera and Rodolfo in *La Bohème* with the Austin Lyric Opera.

In the 1995-96 season Mr. Murray stepped in to sing two performances of the role of Walther at the Metropolitan Opera in their production of *Die Meistersinger von Nürnberg* conducted by James Levine; later that season at the Met he appeared in their production of *Salome*. In past seasons John Horton Murray appeared at the Metropolitan Opera in a variety of roles, including Nathanael and Spalanzani in *Les Contes D'Hoffman*, Normanno in *Lucia Di Lammermoor*, 1st Armored Man in *Die Zauberflöte*, Froh in *Das Rheingold* and Moser in *Die Meistersinger*. In the summer of 1993, he sang Janáček's *Glagolitic Mass* with the Royal Philharmonic Orchestra and Libor Pesek at Royal Festival Hall in

London; Stravinsky's *Les Noces* with the San Francisco Symphony and Michael Tilson-Thomas; and Beethoven's Ninth Symphony with the Atlanta Symphony Orchestra and Yoel Levi. In the 1993-94 season, he appeared as Don José in *Carmen* at the New York City Opera, Nando in D'Albert's *Tiefland* with the Washington Opera, and a return to the Metropolitan Opera in their productions of *Les Troyens, Lucia Di Lammermoor* and *Aïda*.

In the 1991-92 season, John Horton Murray appeared in over sixty performances at the Metropolitan Opera in roles which included Heinrich in *Tannhäuser* and Gran Sacerdote in *Idomeneo*, and he sang in the ensemble and covered the role of Bégearss in the world premiere of John Corigliano's *The Ghosts of Versailles,* conducted by James Levine. His concert engagements that season included his first appearance with the Atlanta Symphony Orchestra and Yoel Levi (also as soloist in Beethoven's Ninth Symphony). In the summer of 1992, he appeared in the role of David in *Die Meistersinger* and as soloist in Haydn's *Creation* at the Spoleto Festival in Italy.

Mr. Murray has been heard on the radio in thirteen nationally broadcast Lyric Opera of Chicago performances. He has also appeared as a featured soloist on a national PBS broadcast of J. S. Bach's *Magnificat*. He gave hundreds of performances as the Italian tenor, Ubaldo Piangi, in the Broadway production of Andrew Lloyd Webber's *The Phantom of the Opera*.

Mr. Murray appeared at Alice Tully Hall as a winner in the Musician's Emergency Fund tribute to Leonard Bernstein. His other opera awards include two National Institute of Music Theater prizes: the 1988 George London Award and a three-year Sullivan grant. He was a national finalist in the 1989 Metropolitan National Council Auditions.

MARSHMALLOW PAVLOVA SLICE
Serves 10

I discovered this wonderful dessert while singing in New Zealand. It's a favorite there. I prefer it without kiwi fruit. --J.H.M.

4 egg whites
1 cup sugar
½ teaspoon vanilla
1 teaspoon white vinegar
2, 10 oz. containers thickened cream
2 bananas

2 tablespoons lemon juice
1 small container strawberries
2 kiwi fruit (optional)
1 passion fruit (optional)
2 tablespoons strawberry jam

Beat egg whites until soft peaks form, gradually add sugar, beating well after each addition until all sugar is dissolved. Add vanilla and vinegar, beat an additional 1 minute. Spread meringue into greased, greased-paper lined 7 x 11-inch tin pan that has been dusted lightly with cornstarch. Bring paper over sides of tin so it is easy to remove slice when cooked. Bake in slow oven for 45 minutes or until meringue is crisp and has a hard shell.

Lift out carefully onto wire rack to cool. (You will notice the top of the pavlova has fallen slightly, giving room for the topping). Trim edges with sharp knife. Beat one carton of cream until soft peaks form, spread cream over top of meringue. Peel bananas and cut into diagonal slices, put into the lemon juice to keep their color. Remove stems from strawberries, cut in half. Peel kiwi fruit, cut into slices. Remove pulp from passion fruit.

Heat strawberry jam in small saucepan, push through sieve to remove seeds, brush jam over strawberry halves to give a glaze. Arrange banana slices, strawberries and kiwi fruit decoratively on top of pavlova, spoon passion fruit pulp over bananas. Whip remaining cream, pipe decoratively around edge of pavlova.

Photo: CHRISTIAN STEINER

JESSYE NORMAN, SOPRANO

"Art on nature's scale, at once grand and intimate," is how one reviewer aptly described the vocal phenomenon that is Jessye Norman. Whether portraying operatic heroines, interpreting Lieder, or appearing with the world's premier orchestras and conductors, her exquisite artistry invariably enthralls capacity audiences across the globe.

Born in Augusta, Georgia, Miss Norman's teachers have included Carolyn Grant at Howard University in Washington, D.C., Alice Duschak at Baltimore's Peabody Conservatory, and Pierre Bernac and Elizabeth Mannion at the University of Michigan. She began her professional life as a member of the Deutsche Oper Berlin, making her first appearance on the operatic stage in 1969, as Elisabeth in *Tannhäuser*.

Jessye Norman has sung a widely varied operatic repertoire at La Scala, Milan; the Teatro Comunale, Florence; the Royal Opera House, Covent Garden; the Stuttgart Opera, Vienna and Hamburg State Operas, Opera Company of Philadelphia, and the Aix-en-Provence Festival. Her Metropolitan Opera debut, in Berlioz's *Les Troyens* (in which she sang both Dido and Cassandra), opened the Met's 100th anniversary season in 1983. At the Met, her roles have included Jocasta in Stravinsky's *Oedipus Rex*, the title role in Strauss's *Ariadne auf Naxos*, Madame Lidoine in Poulenc's *Dialogues of the Carmelites*, Kundry in *Parsifal* and Elisabeth in Wagner's *Tannhäuser*. During 1988-89, she made company history appearing in the company's first presentation of a one-character opera, Schoenberg's *Erwartung*, a *Live from the Met* telecast that also featured her as Judith in Bartók's *Bluebeard's Castle*.

In addition to her *Live from the Met* and *Live from Lincoln Center* appearances, Miss Norman is known to television audiences worldwide for her two Christmas specials: *Jessye Norman at Notre Dame* (telecast in Christmas 1992) and *Christmastide* (a Thames Television and PBS joint production telecast in 1987), and for the film, *Jessye Norman Sings Carmen,* a documentary chronicling her recording of the Bizet opera, released in 1990. In 1993, P.B.S. telecast the Saito Kinen Festival's electrifying production of *Oedipus Rex,* conducted by Seiji Ozawa and featuring Miss Norman as Jocasta. Millions worldwide saw her sing the *Marseillaise* at the spectacular Bastille Day festivities, celebrating the 200th anniversary of the French Revolution in July 1989.

Miss Norman has been presented many prestigious awards and distinctions, including honorary doctorates from Howard University, the University of Michigan, the Boston Conservatory, the University of the South, Sewanee; Brandeis University, Harvard University, Cambridge University, the American University of Paris, the Juilliard School, Yale University, Western New England College, Kenyon College, Paine College (Augusta, Georgia), the New School for Social Research (New York City), LaSalle University (Quebec), Amherst College, Spelman College, Dartmouth College, and the University of Edinburgh. She was also a recipient of the 1990 Albert Einstein College of Medicine Annual Achievement Award. In 1984, the French Government invested Miss Norman with the title "*Commandeur de l'Ordre des Arts et des Lettres.*" Also in 1984, the National Museum of Natural History in Paris honored her by naming an orchid for her. She is an Honorary Fellow of Pierson College, Yale University, and Jesus and Newnham Colleges, Cambridge University. Miss Norman is a member of the Board of Trustees at Paine College in her hometown of Augusta, Georgia. In October 1989, she was awarded the *Legion d'Honneur* by French President Mitterand, and in June 1990 she was named Honorary Ambassador to the United Nations by U.N. Secretary Xavier Perez de Cuellar. Most recently, Ms. Norman was winner of an "Ace" Award from the National Academy of Cable Programming for *Jessye Norman at Notre Dame*, and the Grand Prix at Japan's Symphony Hall 1992 International Music Awards.

One of the most distinguished and prolific recording

artists of our day, Jessye Norman's recordings have won numerous awards, including the Paris *Grand Prix National du Disque* for albums of Lieder by Wagner, Schumann, Mahler and Schubert. She has also received the prestigious Gramophone Award in London for her outstanding interpretation of Strauss's *Four Last Songs*, the Edison Prize in Amsterdam, and recording prizes in Belgium, Spain and Germany. In the United States, Miss Norman's Grammy Award-winning recordings include *Songs of Maurice Ravel*, Wagner's *Lohengrin* and *Die Walküre*, and Beethoven's Ninth Symphony. Her long-standing association with Philips Classics continues with the release of *Brava, Jessye!*, a new compilation disc of some of the singer's most ravishing performances recorded for Philips over the past two decades. Other recent issues include *Cavalleria Rusticana* (Santuzza), *Fidelio* (Leonore), a Salzburg Recital with James Levine, *Amazing Grace, Lucky to Be Me* (her second anthology of popular songs) and *Jessye Norman at Notre Dame*. She has also recorded for Angel, EMI, CBS Masterworks, Decca, DG and Erato.

JESSYE NORMAN'S QUICK DESSERT CAKE

This cake makes a fine accompaniment for fresh fruit salad or ice cream. --J.N.

1¾ cups self-rising flour
3 teaspoons baking powder
¾ teaspoon salt
3 eggs, well beaten
6 oz. unsalted butter, softened
¾ cup brown sugar, packed

¼ cup chopped almonds
¼ cup raisins
1½ teaspoons lemon essence
2 oz. Grand Marnier
2 to 3 oz. milk

Mix all ingredients together (except milk) for 4 minutes in electric mixer, at medium speed. Then add milk to make a sufficiently moist cake mixture (about 2 to 3 oz.). Set aside for ten minutes.

Butter and flour a metal baking tin large enough to contain the whole mixture (9 x 9-inch cake pan). Mix again for 2 to 3 minutes at high speed. Bake in preheated oven at 350 degrees for 40 to 45 minutes.

ROBERTA PETERS, SOPRANO

A singer of incandescent vocal radiance, Roberta Peters illuminates the opera and concert stages as one of America's favorite artists of this century. Her beautiful voice, great showmanship and winning charm have continued to captivate a worldwide public since her sensational debut at the Metropolitan Opera, when, as a completely unknown and unheralded New Yorker, she made a surprise debut as Zerlina in Mozart's *Don Giovanni*. She immediately became one of the Metropolitan's most-prized sopranos, noted especially for her coloratura roles. Miss Peters was honored in 1985, in a special ceremony on the occasion of her 35th anniversary with the Metropolitan Opera.

Roberta Peters has maintained a tremendous schedule of concerts, recitals and personal appearances throughout her career, singing an average of forty engagements each season. She has performed with the world's major orchestras, on its major recital stages, and at such celebrated summer festivals as the Salzburg Festival, Ravinia, the Hollywood Bowl and Robin Hood Dell. She has made her mark on national television with her unprecedented sixty-five appearances on the "Ed Sullivan Show" and her equally unprecedented twenty-five performances on "The Voice of Firestone."

Roberta Peters was born in New York City, where as a young girl she exhibited an amazing natural voice which attracted the attention of the famed tenor Jan Peerce. Upon his recommendation, she began voice lessons at the age of 13, deciding to make singing her career. Her parents, despite moderate means, arranged for extensive private tutoring, including language, piano, drama and ballet.

After six years of intensive study, Ms. Peters was auditioned at her teacher's studio by the late impresario Sol Hurok, who was so impressed with her talent that he immediately signed her despite her youth and complete lack of professional experience. He subsequently arranged an audition with Rudolf Bing, then the general manager of the Metropolitan Opera, who was equally impressed with the young singer and immediately invited various conductors to hear her. Shortly thereafter, the 19-year-old was offered a contract to make her debut as the Queen of the Night in Mozart's *The Magic Flute*. Fate decreed otherwise, and before her scheduled debut, Miss Peters replaced an indisposed colleague as Zerlina in *Don Giovanni*, on six hours notice. Since then, she has achieved the longest tenure of any soprano in the history of the Metropolitan Opera, including fifty-seven Saturday afternoon Texaco broadcasts as well as in the telecast Centennial Gala of the company.

Miss Peters' recital and concert appearances have taken her throughout the world. Her repertoire is extensively varied, ranging from the Baroque masterworks of Bach and Handel, through Mozart and German romantic Lieder, to the *Four Last Songs* of Richard Strauss. Her recitals include not only Lieder, but also French art songs, Italian *arie antiche*, Spanish and English songs, as well as American folk songs. She has had works dedicated to her by such leading contemporary composers as Aram Khatchaturian, Paul Creston and Roy Harris; in 1973 at Carnegie Hall, she premiered Darius Milhaud's *Ani M'amim*, set to words by Elie Weisel.

Roberta Peters was first invited to appear at the White House by President John F. Kennedy, and she has appeared to sing for every President at the Executive Mansion since then, the most recent being at a state dinner hosted by President Bush for the King of Morocco in 1992. She became the first American-born artist to receive the coveted Bolshoi Medal. In 1979, she traveled to the People's Republic of China for recitals and master classes. She has often appeared in Israel, performing in a benefit concert for the Roberta Peters Scholarship Fund of Hebrew University of Tel Aviv and for soldiers in the Six-Day War, when she and her colleague, the late Richard Tucker, were caught in Israel during that conflict.

Roberta Peters has also devoted herself to social causes, such as the National Cystic Fibrosis Foundation, for which she served as national chairperson for a number of years, to Israel Bonds, and most recently to appearances and concerts benefiting AIDS research. She has taken an active part in efforts by Congress to aid in government funding for the arts, and she serves on the Boards of the Metropolitan Opera Guild and the Carnegie Hall Corporation. In 1991, she was appointed by President Bush to the National Council on the Arts, a post to which she has been confirmed by the Senate for a term through 1996.

Roberta Peters greatly enjoys tennis, playing in charity tournaments and on her own court in Scarsdale, New York. In private life, she is Mrs. Bertram Fields, the wife of a prominent real estate investor, and the mother of two sons, Paul and Bruce.

TOFFEE COOKIES - ROBERTA

Makes about 40 cookies

1 **cup of butter at room temperature**
1 **cup of brown sugar**
1 **egg yolk**

1 **cup flour**
6 **Hershey Bars (six to box)**
⅔ **cup chopped pecans**

Cream together butter, sugar and egg yolk, add flour and stir until mixed. Spread in a 10 x 15-inch jelly roll pan which has been lined with greased foil. Bake 20 minutes in a 350 degree oven or until brown. Immediately top with candy bars.

When melted, spread bars with a spatula. Top with pecans and cut on diagonal into diamond shapes.

Photo: ELIANE ZILKHA

ADRIANNE PIECZONKA, SOPRANO

Canadian-born lyric soprano, Adrianne Pieczonka, has firmly established herself as one of the foremost young talents on the European scene. As a recipient of a Canada Council Award in 1988, she studied in England under Vera Rosza. She went on to win the first prize in both the 's-Hertogenbosch (Netherlands) and Pleine-sur-Mer (France) international vocal competitions in that same year.

In 1989, Adrianne Pieczonka became a member of the Vienna Volksoper and in 1990 won great critical acclaim for her portrayal of Tatyana in Harry Kupfer's production of Tchaikovsky's *Eugene Onegin*, conducted by Donald Runnicles. In 1991, she became a solo artist at the Vienna Staatsoper where she performed as the Countess in *Le Nozze di Figaro*, as Donna Elvira in *Don Giovanni*, as Micäela in *Carmen*, and as Freia in *Das Rheingold*. She has most recently sung the role of the Countess in *Le Nozze di Figaro* under the baton of Maestro Muti in Vienna and Maestro Harnoncourt in Zürich.

Ms. Pieczonka appears frequently as a guest artist in many of Europe's leading houses, such as Barcelona, Dresden, Amsterdam and Stuttgart. In 1992, she created the role of Freida in Aribert Reiman's world premiere of *Das Schloss* (based on the Kafka novel) at the Deutsche Oper Berlin, and she also portrayed Tatyana at the Semperoper of Dresden, a role she most recently performed under James Conlon in a new production by Willy Decker at the Cologne Opera House. Miss Pieczonka recently made a brilliant debut in the part of

Mimi in *La Bohème* in Stuttgart and repeated the role in Toronto in the fall of 1994. She will perform in Amsterdam as Rosalinde in *Die Fledermaus*. She will also portray the Tochter in Hindemith's *Cardillac*; Marenka in *The Bartered Bride*; Eva in *Die Meistersinger;* and Antonia in *Tales of Hoffman* in her next season in Vienna. During the 1995-96 season, she made her Glyndebourne debut as Donna Elvira in *Don Giovanni* and will return in the title role of Strauss's *Arabella*.

As a concert artist, she took part in the opening concert of the Edinburgh International Festival, performing Mozart's Mass in C Minor, conducted by Sir Yehudi Menuhin, a concert she repeated in the Swiss town of Gstaad. Adrianne has appeared with orchestras in Amsterdam, Vienna, Paris and Toronto. She has most recently performed Strauss's *Four Last Songs* at the Palais des Beaux-Arts in Brussels with David Shallon and the Belgian National Orchestra and made her debut at the London Proms, singing Beethoven's *Ah, pefido* with Sir Neville Marriner and the Academy of St. Martin in the Fields at Royal Albert Hall. As a recitalist, Ms. Pieczonka has performed in the United Kingdom, Switzerland, France, Brazil and throughout the United States and Canada. She made her Vienna recital debut in 1992 with Charles Spencer.

Adrianne Pieczonka can be heard as the First Lady on Sir Georg Solti's most recent recording of Mozart's *Die Zauberflöte.*

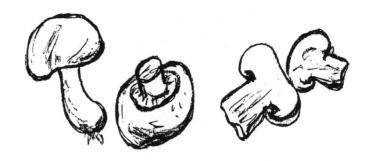

PENNE ALL 'ARRABBIATA
(Angry Penne!)
Serves 8

As a singer, I particularly like to eat pasta a few hours before my performance. It's the best energy food and tastes great. --A.P.

1 pound (or slightly more) penne (1½-inch long, pencil-thick noodles)

5 oz. lean unsmoked bacon, diced

2 to 3 tablespoons olive oil

10 oz. fresh button mushrooms, finely sliced

2 cloves garlic, crushed

1 fresh or dried chili pepper (HOT!), finely chopped

18 oz. fresh or canned tomatoes, skinned and chopped

6 to 7 fresh basil leaves

Salt and pepper to taste

3 to 4 oz. butter

4 oz. Parmesan cheese, grated

Sauté the diced bacon in olive oil until golden. Lift out and keep warm. Cook mushrooms in the same heated oil for a few minutes, then remove and keep warm. Discard excess liquid (from cooking mushrooms) from pan and add an additional teaspoon of olive oil. Sauté garlic and chili, let them color slightly. Add tomatoes and torn basil leaves. Season with salt and pepper, let simmer, uncovered, for 20 to 30 minutes.

Taste and adjust seasonings.

Have a large pan of boiling salted water for the pasta. When the sauce is ready, cook the pasta 'al dente' (not too long). Drain, place in a warmed pasta bowl, add the sauce, bacon, mushrooms, and the butter in flakes. Toss, top with grated cheese.

Photo: CHRISTIAN STEINER

FLORENCE QUIVAR, MEZZO-SOPRANO

Renowned for her vibrantly rich mezzo-soprano voice, Florence Quivar is considered one of America's most distinguished artists. A singer of international stature and a woman of striking physical beauty, she is a regular guest of the world's leading opera companies, orchestras, and music festivals.

A perennial favorite of New York audiences, Miss Quivar has enjoyed many seasons at the Metropolitan Opera. In the past, she has portrayed Mother Marie in Poulenc's *Dialogues des Carmélites*, Jocasta in *Oedipus Rex*, Isabella in *L'Italiana in Algeri*, Fidès in *Le Prophète*, Frederica in *Luisa Miller*, La Zia Principessa in *Suor Angelica* and Serena in the company's first production of *Porgy and Bess*. Miss Quivar has appeared in a telecast performance of *Un Ballo in Maschera*. With the Met, she traveled to Seville, Spain for more performances of this same opera. Florence Quivar appeared with the Metropolitan Opera in the 1994/95 Gala Opening in the role of Frugola in *Il Tabarro*, a spectacular event that was televised nationally on PBS.

Miss Quivar has collaborated with most of the leading conductors of our time. She has performed with Leonard Bernstein, Herbert von Karajan, Pierre Boulez, James Conlon, Erich Leinsdorf, James Levine, Zubin Mehta, Helmut Rilling, David Zinman, Giuseppe Sinopoli, Lorin Maazel, Carlo Maria Giulini, Christoph Eschenbach, Zubin Mehta, Seiji Ozawa, Colin Davis, Riccardo Muti, James Conlon, Robert Shaw, Sir David Wilcox, André Previn, Simon Rattle, Bernard Haitink, John Nelson, Christoph von Dohnányi, and Rafael Frübeck de Burgos.

Miss Quivar has appeared with the Chicago Symphony, Houston Symphony, Berlin Philharmonic, London Philharmonic, New York Philharmonic, Detroit Symphony, Cincinnati Symphony Orchestra, Philadelphia Orchestra, Cleveland Orchestra, National Symphony in Washington, Buffalo Symphony, Baltimore Symphony, Montreal Symphony, L'Orchestre de Paris, L'Orchestre Nationale de Radio, Metropolitan Opera Orchestra, San Francisco Symphony, Nouvel Orchestre Philharmonique, City of Birmingham Symphony Orchestra, National Academy Santa Cecilia in Rome, BBC Symphony Orchestra, Czech Philharmonic, Los Angeles Philharmonic, Boston Symphony Orchestra, Philadelphia Orchestra, Stuttgart Bach Academie, Israel Philharmonic, the Rundfunk-Sinfonie-Orchester of Cologne, Symphonieorchester des Bayerischen Rundfunks and Flanders Philharmonic.

She has toured the festivals of Caracas, Salzburg, Lucerne, London, Frankfurt, Bonn, Edinburgh, and Florence with Zubin Mehta and the Israel Philharmonic. She has also appeared at Lincoln Center's Mostly Mozart Festival, Cincinnati May Festival, Japan's Saito Kinen Festival, San Sebastian/Santander Festival, Florence's Maggio Musicale, Ravinia Festival, Lille Festival, Helsinki Festival and BBC Promenade Concerts, and Tanglewood, among others.

Miss Quivar presents an impressive discography including a solo album of spirituals, *Ride on King Jesus* (Angel/EMI); *Luisa Miller* (Sony) and *Oedipus Rex* (Deutsche Grammophon), conducted by James Levine; two recordings of the Verdi Requiem with Carlo Maria Giulini (Deutsche Grammophon) and Sir Colin Davis (BMG); Rossini's *Stabat Mater* with Thomas Schippers (Vox); a highly-acclaimed recording of *Porgy and Bess* with Lorin Maazel (London); two recordings of Mahler's Eighth Symphony, one with Seiji Ozawa (Philips), and one with Lorin Maazel (Sony); Mahler's Third Symphony with Mehta (Sony); Mahler's *Gurrelieder* with Mehta (Sony); Virgil Thomson's *Four Saints in Three Acts* (Nonesuch); Handel's *Messiah* with Andrew

Davis (Angel/EMI); and Manuel de Falla's *Three-Cornered Hat* with Jesus Lopez-Cobos (Telarc). She has recorded a Ravinia Festival performance of Mendelssohn's *A Midsummer Night's Dream* with James Levine (Deutsche Grammophon), Verdi's *Un Ballo in Maschera* with von Karajan (Deutsche Grammophon), Szymanowski's *Stabat Mater* with Simon Rattle (Angel/EMI), Berlioz's *Roméo et Juliet* with Charles Dutoit (Erato), Mahler's Second Symphony with Mehta (Teldec), and Mendelssohn's *Elijah* with Robert Shaw (Telarc).

A native of Philadelphia, Florence Quivar is a graduate of the Philadelphia Academy of Music and a former member of the Juilliard Opera Theatre. She is a winner of the National Opera Institute Award, the Baltimore Lyric Opera Competition, and the Marian Anderson Vocal Competition.

MATTHEW KENNEY'S SUMMER TOMATO RISOTTO WITH GRILLED JUMBO SHRIMP AND VIDALIA ONION

Serves 4

This delicious and favorite recipe of Ms. Quivar comes from Matthew's Restaurant in New York City.

8 jumbo shrimp
2 tablespoons olive oil
1 teaspoon balsamic vinegar
Pinch of crushed red pepper
1 Vidalia onion, sliced and grilled
1 pound of tomatoes
6 tablespoons unsalted butter
2 shallots, minced

1½ cups Arborio rice
1 cup dry white wine
1½ quarts tomato broth
⅓ cup julienne strips of basil
   plus 4 sprigs for garnish
1 cup grated Parmesan-Reggiano
   cheese
Salt and pepper to taste

Peel and clean shrimp. Rinse and marinate in the oil, vinegar and red pepper. Grill for about 3 minutes on each side. Grill onion until just brown. Slice tomatoes into quarters and set aside.

Over medium heat, melt 3 tablespoons butter in 6-quart pot. Add shallots and cook until translucent. Add rice. Cook for 3 minutes, stirring often. Add wine. Cook until liquid is nearly evaporated. Add tomato broth, 1 cup at a time. Simmer, stirring constantly. When rice is slightly firm, but cooked through, add tomatoes, onion, remaining butter, Parmesan, herbs and salt and pepper. Serve topped with grilled shrimp and garnished with basil sprigs.

WILLIAM SHIMELL, BARITONE

William Shimell is one of Britain's most accomplished operatic baritones. Since beginning his career in the United Kingdom, Shimell has earned himself an international reputation in the world's leading opera houses.

As Count Almaviva in *Le Nozze di Figaro*, Shimell has appeared at La Scala, Milan under Riccardo Muti, at the Vienna Staatsoper and the Paris Bastille, in Geneva, Zürich, Munich, Chicago and Glyndebourne. He has sung Guglielmo in *Così fan Tutte* at Covent Garden, in Geneva, Zürich, Tokyo, and on tour with La Scala, at the Bolshoi in Moscow.

He is becoming increasingly well known for his interpretations of *Don Giovanni*, which he first sang in Britain for Welsh National Opera and ENO, and he has since sung at opera houses throughout the world,

including Amsterdam and Zürich (with Nikolaus Harnoncourt), Frankfurt, Madrid, Hong Kong, Santiago, Lyon and the Aix Festival. His recording of the role for EMI with Riccardo Muti was released in 1992.

William Shimell's reputation has been further enhanced by his performances of Marcello in *La Bohème* at Covent Garden, the Vienna Staatsoper and San Francisco, of Nick Shadow in *The Rake's Progress* in San Francisco, and Dourlinski in Cherubini's *Lodoiska at La Scala*, recorded live for Sony. He is greatly in demand on the concert platform and has recorded Bach's B Minor Mass with Solti and Stravinsky's *Pulcinella* with Riccardo Chailly.

In the near future, Mr. Shimell will sing *Don Giovanni* in Munich and Berlin, and *Le Nozze di Figaro* in Paris and Vienna.

BREAD PUDDING

Makes 20 or more servings

This recipe for BREAD PUDDING was handed down to my mother and has been a family favorite for many generations. I would not recommend that these recipes be served on the same evening, as they are rather rich! --W.S.

2 pounds bread crumbs (any kind)
1 pint milk
½ cup soft brown sugar
1½ cups mixed dried fruit, diced or cubed

8 oz. margarine (2 sticks)
2 tablespoons light molasses
1 tablespoon orange marmalade
2 large beaten eggs

½ cup orange peel, grated (about 2 oranges)
¼ cup all-purpose flour sifted with
   3 teaspoons allspice

2 tablespoons Demerara sugar mixed
   with 1 teaspoon ground cinnamon

Soak the bread crumbs in the milk overnight. Put the mixture into a very large bowl, breaking any lumps, mix in the sugar, dried fruit, peel, flour and allspice, keeping back the Demerara sugar. Add the margarine, molasses, marmalade and eggs and mix well. Grease a large tin (a meat tin 11 x 13-inches and about 3 inches deep is ideal). Transfer the mixture into it, pressing it down and flattening the top.

Preheat oven and bake the pudding for about one-half hour, at medium heat (gas 4, 350 degrees). Take out of the oven and sprinkle Demerara sugar/cinnamon mixture, then put back in the oven for about another 20 minutes. Serve hot or cold, cut into slices.

LIVER PÂTÉ

Serves 6

1 pound pig's liver
½ pound belly of pork
1 teaspoon anchovy essence
1 level teaspoon salt
Freshly milled pepper
1 clove garlic, crushed

½ pint milk
½ onion
Bay leaf
1 oz. butter
1 oz. flour
2 eggs

Trim the liver and remove rind from the pork. Pass both meats through a mincer twice and add anchovy essence. Add salt, pepper and crushed garlic.

Infuse the milk with the onion and bay leaf. Melt butter in a pan and add flour to make roux. Stir in strained milk and bring to a boil to thicken. Season to taste. Pour white sauce into minced ingredients and add beaten eggs and blend well. Put mixture into 2-pint pâté dish and stand in a bain marie in the oven at about 325 degrees for 1½ to 2 hours. Pâté is cooked when center begins to firm and no pink juices flow when center is pressed. Place a weight on the pâté to compress it and cover the container. When pâté is cool, pour melted butter over the top to seal the contents.

Photo: ED MOSS

CAROL SMITH, MEZZO-SOPRANO

Carol Smith's career was launched at the age of eighteen, when she won the Chicago Tribune Music Festival Contest. This was followed by a series of oratorio and orchestral engagements with most of the major symphony orchestras, including the New York Philharmonic, the Boston Symphony, and the Chicago Symphony. The operatic field opened with appearances with the New York City Opera and the Chicago Lyric Opera. A member of the highly respected Bach Aria Group, Miss Smith toured both America and Europe; in 1964, she was engaged for three years by the La Scala Opera in Milan. Miss Smith moved her residence to Europe, where she sang at Vienna, Berlin, Hamburg, Munich, Marseille, Monte-Carlo and Zürich Opera Houses.

She has sung with many major opera companies including: Salzburg Festival and Vienna Staatsoper in Austria; Aix-en-Provence Fest in Marseille, France; Athens Festival in Greece; Berlin Deutsche Oper, Düsseldorf, Frankfurt, Hamburg, Karlsruhe, Kiel, Munich Staatsoper, Stuttgart, Wiesbaden in Germany; Milan La Scala, Naples San Carlo in Italy; Monte Carlo; Basel, Geneva and Zürich in Switzerland; as well as Chicago, Cincinnati, Miami, New York City Opera, and Washington, D.C. in the U.S.A.

Roles with these companies include: *Carmen* (Bizet); Kontchakovna in *Prince Igor* (Borodin); Neris in *Medea* (Cherubini); Geneviève in *Pelléas et Melisande* (Debussy); Sara in *Roberto Devereux* (Donizetti); Pantasilea in *Bomarzo* (Ginastera); Lucretia in *Beatrix Cenci*; Santuzza in *Cavalleria Rusticana* (Mascagni); Charlotte in *Werther* (Massenet); Ottavia in *Incoronazione di Poppea* (Monteverdi); Guilietta in *Contes d'Hoffmann* (Offenbach); La Cieca in *Gioconda* (Ponchielli); Frugola in *Tabarro* (Puccini); Zita in *Gianni Schicchi*; Pythia in *Melusine* (Reimann); *Panthesilea* (Schoeck); Comtesse in *Pique Dame* (Tchaikovsky); Maddalena in *Rigoletto* (Verdi); Ulrica in *Ballo in Maschera*; Azucena in *Trovatore*; Eboli in *Don Carlos*; Amneris in *Aïda*; Emilia in *Otello*; Quickly in *Falstaff*; Brangäne in *Tristan und Isolde* (Wagner); Ortrud in *Lohengrin*; and Mary in *Holländer*.

Miss Smith performed the world premiere of the role of Lucretia in Ginastera's *Beatrice Cenci* in Washington, D.C. in 1971. She has recorded for BASF, Harmonia Mundi and has been filmed for the video *Penthesilea* by Schoeck. Several past recordings of Miss Smith's have been recently been reissued on CD, including Beethoven's *Missa Solemnis* with Leonard Bernstein conducting and Mascagni's *Cavalleria Rusticana*, singing opposite to Milanov and Björling, with Renato Cellini directing.

In 1944, Miss Smith received the *Chicago Tribune* Best Singer Award and in 1967 she received the Woman of the Year Award (Vera Dougan, NFWC).

Miss Smith has been teaching voice at the Indiana University School of Music in Bloomington, Indiana since 1984.

FIVE-CHEESE SAUCE FOR PASTA
Serves 8

I invented this recipe while living in Zürich because my husband is Italian. The grana and parmesan-reggiano cheese may be hard to find, but should be available at Italian food shops. --C.S.

Place in a double boiler the following ingredients:

11 oz. can cream of chicken soup
1 cup grated parmesan-reggiano cheese
8 oz. package Philadelphia cream cheese
2 cloves garlic, finely minced
Milk (use to attain desired consistency)

½-inch wedge Gorgonzola cheese, crumbled
½ cup grana cheese, grated
1 cup sharp Cheddar, crumbled

Melt over boiling water, stirring often, adding milk just enough to make it pour. Pour over hot pasta. Enjoy!!

SWEDISH "BEAR" CAKE
Serves 8 to 10

This recipe was given to me by my Swedish landlady Mrs. Holmer, while I was singing in New York City. She used to listen to me sing from outside my front door, but would never come inside. She said she liked to hear my singing better from outside the door.

2 eggs
1½ cups sugar
1½ cups flour
2 teaspoons baking powder
1 teaspoon cardamom powder

2 teaspoons cinnamon
¼ pound butter *minus*
      1 tablespoon
¾ cup milk

Beat eggs and sugar. Mix dry ingredients and add to sugar and egg mixture. Beat in cooled, melted butter and milk. Pour into greased 9-inch floured square pan and bake at 325 degrees for 45 minutes. Good just plain or with ice cream.

Photo: CHRISTIAN STEINER

THOMAS STEWART, BARITONE

Thomas Stewart is unique in the world of opera. He is one of the few American singers to perform leading roles in the major opera houses of both the United States and Europe, in the German, Italian and French repertoire.

Thomas Stewart was the recipient of the 1985 San Francisco Opera Medal for 25 years of distinguished performance with that company. Recently, he sang Wotan in their cycle of Wagner's *Der Ring dies Nibelungen* and King Lear in Jean Pierre Ponnelle's production of Reimans's opera *Lear*. His recent performances in *Die Meistersinger* and *The Magic Flute* with the Lyric Opera of Chicago marked a triumphant return to this company, which presented his professional debut in 1954 (also the company's inaugural season) in Giannini's *Taming of the Shrew* and opposite Maria Callas in *Lucia de Lammermoor*. At the Metropolitan Opera, his repertoire included Wagner's Sachs, Wotan, the Wanderer, Wolfram, Holländer, Amfortas, Kurvenal and Gunther. In the Italian and French repertoire he was represented by Golaud in *Pelléas et Melisande* and the Four Villains in *Tales of Hoffman*, Escamillo in *Carmen,* Amonasro in *Aïda* and Ford in *Falstaff* (Met debut, 1966). Mozart's Count and Giovanni, Strauss's Orestes

and Jokanaan and Britten's Balstrode, were also starring roles in the new productions at the Metropolitan.

After a Fulbright Scholarship, he and his wife Evelyn Lear were engaged by the Deutsche Oper Berlin in 1958. Mr. Stewart soon became world-renowned for his repertoire of Wagnerian roles, including thirteen years at the Bayreuth Festival and as the first American baritone to sing all four leading roles in the Ring Cycle of Wagner at the festival. In addition, Thomas Stewart has sung *Der Ring der Nibelungen* with the Vienna, Berlin, Buenos Aires, Hamburg, Paris, San Francisco and Metropolitan Operas and at the Salzburg Festival with Karajan. He has sung with many other eminent conductors, including Kempe, Knappertsbusch, Solti, Davis, Mehta, Ozawa, Leinsdorf, Pretre, Maazel, Levine and Böhm.

Thomas Stewart has recorded many of his operatic roles, including the Bayreuth Festival's *Parsifal, Die Walküre, Siegfried* and *Götterdämmerung* with von Karajan; *Lohengrin* with Kubelik and *Der Fliegende Holländer* with Böhm. Other recordings include *Nabucco, Les Contes d'Hoffmann* and *Tiefland.*

PORK AND VEGGIES OVER RICE

Serves 4

This dish is easy, but it fools your guests into thinking you worked very hard. --T.S.

4 boneless pork chops (not too thick)
Salt and pepper
2 tablespoons margarine
2 cups sliced fresh mushrooms
¼ teaspoon crushed rosemary

10 oz. can cream of mushroom soup
4 to 6 tablespoons water
½ pound fresh green beans,
     sliced into 1-inch pieces.

Season pork chops with salt and pepper. In a medium-large frying pan on medium-high heat, brown pork chops in 1 tablespoon of margarine. Remove pork from pan and set aside.

Add an additional tablespoon of margarine to the remaining pan juices, reduce heat to medium and cook mushrooms for about 4 minutes, or until tender. Add rosemary and stir well. Add soup, 4 to 6 tablespoons of water and the freshly cut beans. Heat until mixture starts to boil. Put in pork chops, surrounding all sides with liquid, cover pan, and cook for about 15 minutes, until beans are soft and pork is cooked and tender.

Serve with rice of choice. *Enjoy*!

Photo: MARTY SOHL

KURT STREIT, TENOR

American tenor Kurt Streit began studies and professional singing in his home state of New Mexico. He moved to Hamburg, Germany in 1987 for a four-year contract with the Hamburg State Opera, where he sang the repertoire of Mozart and Donizetti. During his tenure in Hamburg, he made his debut on many of the European and American stages, including the Royal Opera at Covent Garden, Vienna State Opera, Munich, San Francisco, and Rome, as well as at the festivals of Glyndebourne, Aix-en-Provence, Schwetzingen and Salzburg.

He has appeared in concert with the London and St. Petersburg Symphony Orchestra, Orchestre National de France, BBC Orchestra, National Orchestra of Spain, London Philharmonic, Concentus Musicus in Vienna, Orchestre de Paris and the Academy of St. Martin in the Fields. Since leaving Hamburg, he has expanded his repertoire at the Liceu in Barcelona, La Fenice in Venice, Chicago, San Francisco and Geneva, singing Britten, Berlioz, Rossini and Strauss, while continuing to sing Mozart at the Metropolitan Opera, Los Angeles Opera and La Scala in Milan.

Streit's recordings include *Die Entführung aus dem Serail*, Bruno Weil conducting (Sony); *Così fan Tutte*, Daniel Barenboim conducting (Erato); *Die Zauberflöte,* Arnold Ostman conducting (L'Oiseau-Lyre); a collection of Brahms quartets for EMI; and Gilbert & Sullivan's *The Yeoman of the Guard;* with Sir Neville Marriner conducting (Philips).

SWEET POTATO BOURBON PECAN PIE
Makes a 9-inch deep-dish pie

My sister Cheryl and I acquired this recipe over Thanksgiving. She wanted to prepare the recipe one way and I another. This is the resolution of that dispute. --K.S.

2 medium-sized sweet potatoes (2 cups)
1 teaspoon nutmeg
⅓ cup sugar, packed
⅓ cup brown sugar
5 oz. can of evaporated milk
2 eggs
1 teaspoon lemon juice
Dash of salt
Dash of cinnamon

⅓ cup bourbon
9-inch unbaked deep-dish pie shell

TOPPING:
2 tablespoons butter
1 cup whole pecans
⅓ cup brown sugar, packed
¼ cup bourbon
Dash of cinnamon

Boil potatoes with skin on until tender, about 20 to 25 minutes. Peel and mash well. Measure out 2 cups of potatoes and add with rest of ingredients. Stir until smooth. Pour into the unbaked pie shell and set aside.

Preheat oven to 450 degrees. For topping, melt over medium heat 2 tablespoons of butter in a small metal skillet, add pecans and stir until they are roasted (don't burn them). Add brown sugar and stir until melted. Add bourbon and (here's the fun part!) FLAMBÉ! When the fire goes out (*and you still have a kitchen*) spread pecans evenly over the top of the pie. Bake at 450 degrees for 15 minutes then at 325 degrees for 30 minutes, or until done. (Knife inserted should come out clean).

SHARON SWEET, SOPRANO

Soprano Sharon Sweet is internationally recognized as one of the most important artists of our day and has been heard at leading opera houses, including the Vienna State Opera, Paris Opera, Metropolitan Opera, Chicago Lyric Opera, San Francisco Opera, Hamburg State Opera, Bavarian State Opera, Theatre Royal de la Monnaie, Cologne Opera and at the Salzburg Festival and the Arena di Verona. Sweet has won acclaim as a Verdi soprano of the very first rank for her portrayals of roles, including the title role in *Aïda,* Leonore in *Il Trovatore,* Desdemona in *Otello* and Amelia in *Un Ballo in Maschera.* Her Elisabeth in Wagner's *Tannhäuser* has received high praise in Vienna, Berlin and Cologne and at the Metropolitan Opera. Sharon Sweet has also established herself as a soloist in the orchestral repertoire and has collaborated in that capacity with such conductors as Carlo Maria Giulini, Claudio Abbado, Sir Colin Davis, Lorin Maazel, Helmut Rilling, Sir Georg Solti, Zubin Mehta, Giuseppe Sinopoli, Marek Janowski, Kurt Masur and Rafael Frübeck de Burgos.

Sharon Sweet has had a special collaboration with conductor Carlo Maria Giulini, with whom she has performed several concerts of Verdi's Requiem and with whom she also recorded the work for DGG. She has sung Schoenberg's *Gurrelieder* in Munich under Zubin Mehta, appearing there also in Mahler's Symphony No. 8 under Lorin Maazel, followed by a recording of the work for Sony Classical. She opened the 1992 Wiener Festwochen in the *Gurrelieder* under Claudio Abbado and also gave highly successful Liederabends in both Vienna and Paris. Sweet has been a frequent guest to London since her debut in 1990, singing the *Four Last Songs* of Strauss under Rafael Frübeck de Burgos with the LSO. Also in London, she has often been heard in Verdi's Requiem under the conductors Giulini, Sir Colin Davis, Frübeck de Burgos, and others. Sweet made her New York Philharmonic debut in May of 1993, as Agathe in *Der Freischütz,* under Sir Colin Davis.

Sharon Sweet's growing discography also includes two

complete operatic recordings: Donna Anna in Mozart's *Don Giovanni* under Sir Neville Marriner for Philips and Alice Ford in Verdi's *Falstaff* under Sir Colin Davis for BMG. She also can be heard in Schmidt's *Psalm 47* under Janowski on Erato; in Schumann's *Das Paradies und die Peri* and Mahler's Symphony No. 8 under Maazel for Sony; as well as in Strauss's *Four Last Songs* under de Burgos on Collins Classics. Future recording projects include complete recordings of *Lohengrin* and *Der Freischütz* for BMG. Other works in her orchestral repertoire include Wagner's *Wesendonk Lieder*, the Liebestod from *Tristan und Isolde*, Rossini's *Stabat Mater*, Beethoven's Symphony No. 9 and Dvořák's *Stabat Mater,* which introduced her to the Salzburg Festival.

Sharon Sweet made her North American stage debut in the autumn of 1989, when she appeared as Aïda for the San Francisco Opera. She performed at the Metropolitan Opera in the spring of 1990 as Leonora in *Il Trovatore,* returning in following seasons as Elisabeth in *Tannhäuser* and as Amelia in *Ballo.* Sweet made her first stage appearances in Italy appearing at the Arena di Verona in *Aïda* and in concerts of the Verdi Requiem opposite Luciano Pavarotti, conducted by Lorin Maazel.

In the 1995/96 season, Sharon Sweet sang Leonora in a new production of *La Forza del Destino* at the Metropolitan Opera, conducted by James Levine and directed by Gian Carlo del Monaco. She also appeared at the Met as Amelia in *Ballo* and as Donna Anna in *Don Giovanni.* She made her debut as Aïda at the Teatro Colon in Buenos Aires and also returned to the Vienna State Opera as Elisabeth in *Tannhäuser.* The artist also appeared as Norma in *Bilbao* and at the Hamburg State Opera as Leonora in *Il Trovatore.* Sharon Sweet made her Chicago Symphony debut in May of 1996 in Mahler's Symphony No. 8 under Christoph Eschenbach.

Plans for the 1996/97 season include productions of *Turandot* at the Maggio Musicale Fiorentino under Zubin

Mehta and at the Royal Opera House, Covent Garden under Daniele Gatti. Sweet will also return to the Metropolitan Opera as Aïda. She will appear as soloist with the Israel Philharmonic Orchestra under Zubin Mehta and with the Cincinnati Symphony Orchestra under Jesus Lopez-Cobos. The artist will make her Bastille Opera debut in fall of 1997 in a new production of *Turandot*.

Born in New York State, Sharon Sweet attended the Curtis Institute of Music in Philadelphia and completed her vocal studies in New York with renowned vocal instructor, Mme. Marenka Gurewich.

CHICKEN PINWHEELS
Serves 6

This recipe came to me from Aunt Wilma of Greenville, South Carolina. My husband changed the biscuit recipe (for the better). Our three children love this dinner a great deal. We hope you do!
--S.S.

3 to 4 pound whole chicken
SAUCE:
5 tablespoons margarine
1 medium onion, chopped
6 to 7 tablespoons flour
6 cups skimmed milk
½ teaspoon salt or to taste
¼ teaspoon pepper or to taste
2 cups carrots, frozen or fresh (be sure they are diced small if fresh)
1 cup peas, frozen

BISCUITS (Pinwheels):
2 cups flour
2 teaspoons baking powder
½ teaspoon baking soda
⅛ teaspoon salt
¼ cup shortening
¾ cup buttermilk
1½ cups shredded Cheddar cheese

Boil whole chicken in covered pot for at least 40 to 50 minutes. (The meat when cooked should easily come off the bones). Cool and remove bones. (If desired, return bones to stock and cook for 6 to 8 hours. This makes great stock for soup). Cut chicken into bite-size pieces and set aside.

For Sauce: Melt margarine over medium heat and add onion. Sauté until clear and soft. Take off heat and stir in 6 to 7 tablespoons flour. Put back on heat, add milk gradually, stirring continuously until it thickens and starts to boil. Season with salt and pepper. Add peas and carrots. Mix chicken into sauce and pour into a large, shallow casserole dish about 9 x 13 x 2-inches.

For Biscuits: In a large mixing bowl, mix together 2 cups flour, baking powder, baking soda and salt. Cut ¼ cup shortening into dry ingredients until it starts to form pea-shaped balls. Add buttermilk and stir 10 to 12 strokes with spatula.

Onto a floured surface, turn out batter and roll out to a long, thin shape with rolling pin. About 18 inches long and 6 to 8 inches wide. Cover top with 1½ cups of shredded Cheddar cheese and curl up like a jelly roll. Separate into ¾-inch slices. Place on top of sauce in casserole dish. Bake at 400 to 425 degrees in oven for 20 minutes or until biscuits are golden brown. Serve with fresh tossed salad and a large glass of iced tea.

MICHAEL SYLVESTER, TENOR

Michael Sylvester has won international acclaim as one of the most important Spinto tenors of our day, in important debuts at theaters including the Metropolitan Opera, La Scala, Milan, Teatro La Fenice in Venice, the Grand Theatre de Geneve, the Paris Opera, San Francisco Opera, Hamburg State Opera, Vienna State Opera, Royal Opera at Covent Garden, Deutsche Oper Berlin, Frankfurt Opera, Oper der Stadt Bonn, Staatstheater Stuttgart and the Canadian Opera Company.

In the 1996/97 season Sylvester will appear in the title role of *Don Carlos* in Chicago and in *Aïda* at the Metropolitan Opera. He will add the role of the Kaiser in Strauss's *Die Frau Ohne Schatten* to his repertoire in performances with the Geneva Opera and with the Flemish Opera. Sylvester will also appear at the Hamburg State Opera in *Tosca* under Byschkov and at the Berlin State Opera in *Aïda* under Mehta.

Michael Sylvester made his Metropolitan Opera debut in the spring of 1991 in Verdi's *Luisa Miller,* under James Levine. He returned to the Metropolitan in the 1991/92 season in the title role of *Don Carlos* and in the 1992/93 season for *Madama Butterfly.* Sylvester made his debut at the Teatro La Fenice in Venice in December of 1991. The artist sang at the Royal Opera, Covent Garden in London as Samson in Saint-Saëns *Samson et Dalila* in 1991 and returned as Gabriele Adorno in a new production of *Simon Boccanegra,* conducted by Sir Georg Solti. He appeared for the first time at the Grand Theatre de Geneve in June of 1992 as Foresto in *Attila* and then appeared with the Seattle Opera in *Aïda.* Other recent engagements have included a new production of *Aïda* at the Hamburg State Opera and his Houston Opera debut in the same work.

Michael Sylvester made his actual European debut in May of 1987 in Stuttgart as Pinkerton in *Madama Butterfly,* where he has also been heard as Radames in a new production of *Aïda,* Cavaradossi in *Tosca* and as Florestan in Beethoven's *Fidelio.* Sylvester debuted at the Paris Opera in the autumn of 1987 as Pollione in the new production of Bellini's *Norma,* and his subsequent significant debuts followed in quick succession: he bowed in Bonn in 1989 in a new production of *Butterfly,* at the Hamburg State Opera in June of 1989 as Rodolfo in *La Bohème* and in Toronto in *Tosca.* Sylvester appeared for the first time at the Frankfurt Opera as Bacchus in a new production of Strauss's *Ariadne auf Naxos,* in the autumn of 1989. He then debuted at La Scala, Milan as Pinkerton in *Butterfly* under veteran Maestro Gianandrea Gavazzeni in the spring of 1990. He had appeared previously with the forces of La Scala under Riccardo Muti, in concerts of Verdi's *Requiem* in the Soviet Union. Sylvesterdebuted at the Deutsche Oper Berlin as Radames and then appeared at the 1990 Bregenz Festival in the new production of Catalani's *La Wally.*

Michael Sylvester was born in Noblesville, Indiana and holds degrees from Westminster Choir College and Indiana University, where he studied with famed Wagnerian soprano Margaret Harshaw. He began his career in the United States where he first appeared with companies such as the New York City Opera, San Diego Opera, and the Cincinnati Opera. Sylvester also has appeared in concert, in works including Beethoven's *Leonore*, the Symphony No. 9 and Mahler's Symphony No. 8. He has recorded the last mentioned for Telarc under Robert Shaw and has also recorded the title role in *Don Carlos,* under James Levine, for Sony Classics.

WEIHNACHTS MATSCH
(Christmas Mud)
Serves 4 to 6

A friend in Germany gave me this recipe. I do not know its origins, although with curry, bananas and pork, it does not sound especially German—perhaps it is Middle Eastern. It is not to everyone's liking, but I think it is delicious! --M.S.

1 to 1½ pounds pork fillet (tenderloin)
Salt and pepper to taste
3 bananas
1 pint heavy cream
4 tablespoons tomato paste

6 tablespoons ketchup
3 to 4 teaspoons curry powder
¼ pound Gouda cheese, grated or
   thinly sliced

Cut the pork fillet into 1-inch thick slices. Season with salt and pepper, then brown on both sides in a frying pan. Put them into the bottom of an oven-safe casserole dish (2 to 2½-quart capacity). Cut the bananas vertically, down the center, into 2 pieces each. Lay them on top of the meat.

Mix together the cream, tomato paste, ketchup and curry, then salt and pepper to taste. It should be spicy. Pour this mixture over the pork and bananas. Top with the cheese.

Bake at 425 degrees, uncovered, for 20 to 25 minutes. Serve over rice.

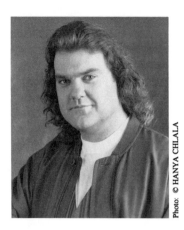

Photo: © HANYA CHLALA

BRYN TERFEL, BASS-BARITONE

Bryn Terfel, a native of North Wales, Britain, is now one of the most highly sought after bass-baritones. He studied at the Guildhall School of Music and Drama with Arthur Reckless and later with his current teacher, Rudolf Piernay. While at college, he was awarded the 1989 Gold Medal Award and won the 1988 Kathleen Ferrier Memorial Scholarship.

In 1989, Bryn represented Wales in the Cardiff Singer of the World Competition, winning the Lieder Prize. In 1992, he became the first recipient of an award conferred by members of the music section of the British Critics Circle, as the person whom the members considered to have made the most outstanding contribution to musical life in Great Britain. In the same year, he was voted Young Singer of the Year in the *Gramophone* Magazine Awards. In 1993, Bryn was voted Newcomer of the Year in the inaugural International Classical Music Awards, held at the Birmingham Symphony Hall.

He has performed Figaro in *Le Nozze di Figaro* at most of the major opera houses, including Hamburg, Vienna (conducted by Muti), Santa Fe, Welsh National Opera, English National Opera, Chatelet, Lisbon and the Royal Opera House, Covent Garden. He also performed the role in his debut with the Metropolitan Opera, New York in the autumn in 1994. Bryn's recording of the role for Archiv, conducted by John Eliot Gardiner, was released in 1994.

In 1992, Bryn made his debuts at the Royal Opera House, Covent Garden, singing Masetto in *Don Giovanni,* and at the Salzburg Festival, singing Jochanaan in *Salome* and Geisterbote in *Die Frau Ohne Schatten.* He made his debut in 1993 at the Lyric Opera, Chicago, singing Donner in *Das Rheingold* and returned to sing Lindorf, Coppelius, Dapertutto and Dr. Miracle in *Les Contes D'Hoffmann.* In 1994, Bryn made his debut in the role of Leporello in the Salzburg Festival. In 1996, he performed the role of Nick Shadow for the Welsh National Opera and Sharpless in Japan. Future opera

engagements include his debuts in La Scala and San Francisco as Figaro, Sydney Opera House as Falstaff with the Australian Opera, Ferrara Festival as Leporello, at the Bastille, Paris in the title role in Don Giovanni and for the Netherlands Opera, Amsterdam as Scarpia. Other future engagements include Wolfram and Papageno at the Metropolitan Opera, and Wozzeck in the Salzburg Festival.

On the concert platform, Terfel has sung Mahler's Eighth Symphony with James Levine at the Ravinia Festival and Brahms's Requiem with Claudio Abbado at the Salzburg Easter Festival. In 1994, he gave recitals in New York, Florence, Berlin and at the Wigmore Hall, London, and was the soloist in the BBC Last Night of the Proms at the Royal Albert Hall, London, a video and CD recording of which has been released on the Teldec label. Terfel also performed Mahler's *Kindertotenlieder* with Giuseppi Sinopoli at La Scala, to which he returned this year to give a recital. Last year, he was a soloist in the Berlin Philharmonic Orchestra's New Year's Eve Gala Concert (of which both CD and video recordings have been released).

Operatic recordings include Jochanaan in *Salome,* conducted by Giuseppe Sinopoli, Stravinsky's *Oedipus Rex* and Britten's *Gloriana.*

Concert recordings include: Beethoven's *Choral Symphony,* and Elgar's *Starlight Express,* with Sir Charles Mackerras; Handel's *Messiah* and Delius's *Sea Drift* with Richard Hickox; Mahler's 8th Symphony; Schumann's *Faust Szenen,* with Claudio Abbado; and Brahms's *Ein Deutsche Requiem,* with Sir Colin Davis, for BMG Classics. Solo recordings include Schubert's *Schwanengesang* with Malcolm Martineau for Sain, *Kindertotenlieder* with Giuseppe Sinopoli, and a recording of Schubert Lieder entitled *An die Musik,* with Malcolm Martineau.

His latest recording of songs by Rodgers and

Hammerstein, *"Something Wonderful"* was released by Deutsche Grammophon in September. Future plans with Deutsche Grammophon include a solo operatic album with James Levine.

LEEK AND POTATO SOUP

Serves 6 to 8

Just the meal to serve on St. David's Day with garlic bread! It is easy to remember and to cook. --B.T.

2 large leeks (white part with 2"of green)	2 oz. margarine or butter
1 large onion	Season with salt and pepper to taste
4 medium-sized potatoes	Milk or cream

Dice all vegetables. Melt margarine or butter over medium-heat in medium-sized pot. Add vegetables and sauté for about 5 minutes. Add water to cover and bring to a boil. Simmer until tender and of desired consistency (about 15 to 20 minutes). Remember to stir occasionally, avoiding any sticking on saucepan! Just before serving, add the milk to color, or use cream on special occasions.

Photo: CHRISTOPH KLAUKE

DAWN UPSHAW, SOPRANO

Soprano Dawn Upshaw's unusual career can be traced back to the year of 1984, when, already a winner of the Young Concert Artists International Auditions, she was invited by James Levine to join the studio of the Metropolitan Opera. From these dual vantages grew a career measured equally between operatic stages and concert halls. This versatility, combined with diverse musical tastes, a silvery lyric soprano voice, and a natural, ineffable charm, has enabled Dawn Upshaw to capture the respect and affection of an extraordinarily broad segment of music lovers throughout the world. As a two-time Grammy Award-winning recording artist, her work has been documented by over two dozen albums.

Within a few seasons of her debut at the Met, Miss Upshaw was engaged there and elsewhere for many leading roles in her repertoire, including Pamina in *Die Zauberflöte,* Zerlina in *Don Giovanni,* both Susanna and Cherubino in *Le Nozze di Figaro,* Ilia in *Idomeneo,* Sophie in *Werther* and both Constance and Blanche in *Dialogues des Carmélites.* Pamina was her debut role in Amsterdam, Hamburg and Vienna, while for Glyndebourne she sang Hero in *Béatrice et Bénédict.* At Aix-en-Provence, she appeared as Despina in *Così fan Tutte,* and, more recently, as Anne Trulove in *The Rake's Progress.* Her debut at the Salzburg Festival in 1986 was as Barbarina in a new *Figaro,* conducted by Levine and directed by the late Jean-Pierre Ponnelle, and she quickly graduated to Susanna in another new Salzburg *Figaro,* conducted by Sir Bernard Haitink. In the summer of 1992, she had one of Salzburg's greatest successes as the Angel in a triumphant Peter Sellars production of Messiaen's *St. Francois d'Assisi.* The production also appeared in Paris at the Bastille.

On the concert platform, she has been engaged by many of the world's leading conductors—among them Ashkenazy, Andrew Davis, de Waart, Dohnányi, Gardiner, Harnoncourt, Marriner, Mehta, Norrington, Ozawa, Nagano, Salonen, Sawallisch and Sinopoli: she has appeared with many of the world's finest orchestras, including the Berlin Philharmonic, the Boston Symphony, the Chicago Symphony, the Cleveland Orchestra, the Los Angeles Philharmonic, the New York Philharmonic, the Philadelphia Orchestra, the Rotterdam Philharmonic, and the Concentus Musicus. Her repertoire ranges from the sacred works of Bach and Handel to the music of contemporary composers, such as Jacob Druckman and John Harbison. Ms. Upshaw frequently performs contemporary music in concerts and on recordings with a variety of colleagues, including the Kronos Quartet and the Arditti Quartet, and she has appeared in New York and on tour with the Chamber Music Society of Lincoln Center.

From the moment of her first recital at Alice Tully Hall in 1986—a result of winning the 1985 Naumburg Competition—Dawn Upshaw was recognized as a recitalist of limitless potential. In her programming as well as her presentation can be found the imagination and integrity that are the hallmarks of her success. She has appeared at London's Wigmore Hall, the Vienna Konzerthaus, the Edinburgh Festival, and literally dozens of North American venues. Her recital partners have included such diverse pianists as Malcolm Bilson, Margo Garret and Gilbert Kalish. James Levine, with whom she has given several programs in New York and elsewhere. Baritone Olaf Baer, and pianist Richard Goode, with whom she has toured throughout North America and recorded a program of songs with texts by Goethe for Elektra/Nonesuch Records, have become prized collaborators.

Dawn Upshaw's first solo album for Nonesuch won the 1989 Grammy Award for Best Classical Vocal Album. This recording, which contains Barber's *Knoxville: Summer of 1915,* as well as music by Harbison, Menotti and Stravinsky, was on the *Billboard* top 10 list for nearly half a year. Her second solo recording for Nonesuch, *The Girl with Orange Lips,* which features chamber music by Delage, de Falla, Earl Kim, Ravel, and Stravinsky, won a second Grammy Award, in 1991. In

August 1994, Nonesuch released Miss Upshaw's album *I Wish It So*, a musical theater collection of Weill, Blitzstein, Bernstein and Sondheim, as a further testimony to Miss Upshaw's artistic diversity and interest in her country's musical culture.

Dawn Upshaw has also recorded leading roles in numerous operas, among them Susanna in *Le Nozze di Figaro* under James Levine for Deutsche Grammophon; Pamina in *Die Zauberflöte* under Roger Norrington for EMI; both Delia in *Lucio Silla* and Serpetta in *La finta giardiniera,* under Nikolaus Harnoncourt for Teldec; and Nina in Massenet's *Cherubin*, with Frederica von Stade, for BMG. With David Zinman and the London Sinfonietta, she has recorded Henryk Gorecki's Third Symphony, which has sold over half a million copies worldwide and which has appeared frequently on both popular and classical best-seller lists. She recorded on a Sony Classical release of Claude Debussy's *La Damoiselle elue,* with the Los Angeles Philharmonic Orchestra led by Esa-Pekka Salonen; and Gustav Mahler's Symphony No. 4, with the Cleveland Orchestra led by Christoph Dohnányi, on London Records.

"ANN'S DIP"

My friend and college roommate used to make this recipe, which is why I call it "Ann's Dip." I enjoy it quite often for it is so easy to make. It makes enough to serve 5 to 6 people. --D.U.

1 cup mayonnaise (*in these more health conscience days I substitute ½ cup, or more, non-fat yogurt for ½ cup mayo*)
1 cup Parmesan cheese

8 oz. marinated artichoke hearts, drained and finely chopped
Salt and black pepper to taste

Mix all ingredients together and bake at 350 degrees in a small casserole dish for 30 minutes, or until browned. Serve with crackers or cut vegetables.

Photo: ROBERT LEWIS

BENITA VALENTE, SOPRANO

The distinguished American soprano Benita Valente is one of this era's most cherished musical artists. An internationally celebrated interpreter of Lieder, chamber music, and oratorio, she is equally acclaimed for her performances on the operatic stage. Her keen musicianship encompasses an astounding array of styles, from the Baroque of Bach and Handel to the varied idioms of today's leading composers.

The California-born soprano has held the spotlight since she won the Metropolitan Opera National Council Auditions. As a participant in the prestigious Marlboro Festival, her performances and recordings with the legendary pianist Rudolf Serkin won great renown. Other major instrumental collaborators have included the Guarnari and Juilliard String Quartets, cellist Yo-Yo Ma, clarinetist Richard Stoltzman, and pianists Emmanuel Ax, Leon Fleisher, David Golub, Richard Goode, Lee Luvisi, Cynthia Raim and Peter Serkin.

Benita Valente has been sought as an orchestral soloist by nearly every great conductor of the last two decades, including Claudio Abbado, Daniel Barenboim, Mario Bernardi, Leonard Bernstein, Sergiu Comissiona, James Conlon, Edo de Waart, Christoph Eschenbach, Nikolaus Harnoncourt, Rafael Kubelik, Erich Leinsdorf, Raymond Leppard, James Levine, Kurt Masur, Nicholas McGegan, Riccardo Muti, Seiji Ozawa, Julius Rudel, Robert Shaw and Klaus Tennstedt. With these conductors, she has appeared with the great symphonies of the United States, Canada and Europe, including orchestras such as the Philadelphia Orchestra, the New York Philharmonic, the Chicago Symphony Orchestra, the Boston Symphony Orchestra, the Cleveland Orchestra, the Los Angeles Philharmonic, the Montreal Symphony, the Toronto Symphony, the Munich Philharmonic, the Orchestre de Paris, the London Symphony, the Rotterdam Philharmonic, the Concertgebouw Orchestra, and others.

The operatic stage has figured prominently in Benita Valente's career. A long association with the Metropolitan Opera began with her debut in 1973 as Pamina in *Die Zauberflöte*. Other roles included Gilda in *Rigoletto*, Nanetta in *Falstaff*, Susanna in *Le Nozze di Figaro*, Ilia in *Idomeneo*, and Almirena in *Rinaldo*. Other notable operatic engagements include Ginevra in a Santa Fe production of *Ariodante*, opposite Tatiana Troyanos; Euridice in a Santa Fe production of *Orfeo*, opposite Marilyn Horne; the Countess in *Le Nozze di Figaro* in the Jean-Pierre Ponnelle production, conducted by Daniel Barenboim, for the Washington Opera; Dalilah in Handel's *Samson* for the Teatro Comunale in Florence; Almirena in *Rinaldo* in a Pier Luigi Pizzi production in Parma and other Italian theaters; and concert performances of *Pelléas et Melisande* with the Philadelphia Orchestra. In recent seasons, Miss Valente has been acclaimed for her performances as the Countess in *Le Nozze di Figaro* at the Metropolitan Opera, at the Teatro Colon in Buenos Aires and at Opera Pacific in California. She returned to the Santa Fe Opera in summer 1995 as the Countess.

Benita Valente was the guest soloist for the inaugural concert of Lincoln Center's Mostly Mozart Festival, and she has returned to that established series nearly every season since. She also has appeared often at the Tanglewood and Ravinia Festivals, the Cincinnati May Festival, the Mann Music Center, the Grant Park Festival, and, in Europe, at the Vienna, Edinburgh, and Lyon Festivals.

Benita Valente is particularly beloved by connoisseurs of song literature. She has maintained an active solo recital schedule every season, with frequent appearances with the country's leading recital presenters.

Her recorded repertoire includes six highly regarded Lieder albums, three with pianist Cynthia Raim, for Pantheon (Wolf, Strauss, Handel, Mozart, and Schubert Lieder), Gerhard songs with Tan Crone for Etcetera; Schubert and Schumann Lieder with Lee Luvisi for Eurodisc/BMG; and Mozart, Wolf, Schubert and Brahms

Lieder with Richard Goode for Telefunken. Two solo albums, one with Mozart and Handel works and the other featuring the Spanish and French repertoire, are also available on Pantheon. Symphonic works include the Beethoven Symphony No. 9 with Robert Shaw and the Atlanta Symphony (Pro Arte); Mahler's Symphony No. 2 "Resurrection" with Gilbert Kaplan and the London Symphony Orchestra (MCA Classics); and the Liszt *Christus* with James Conlon and the Rotterdam Philharmonic (Erato). A record of her acclaimed collaboration with mezzo-soprano Tatiana Troyanos is available on the Music Masters disc Handel and Mozart arias and duets, which was conducted by Julius Rudel. Miss Valente received a Grammy nomination for her Sony Classical recording of Haydn's *Seven Last Words of Christ* and a Grammy Award for her Columbia recording of Schoenberg's Quartet No. 2, both performed with the Juilliard String Quartet.

BENITA VALENTE'S CRANBERRY RELISH

Serve over whatever you like—sweet potatoes, for example—or eat as is. --B.V.

2, 12 oz. bags of whole fresh cranberries
16 oz. package of frozen strawberries
16 oz. package of frozen blueberries

½ cup date sugar
Small container (6 oz.) apple
juice concentrate

Cook cranberries in juice concentrate until they start to pop. Add frozen fruit and date sugar. If you prefer, add a few slices of lemon. Cook about 10 minutes, then leave on stove, covered, until the relish reaches room temperature.

Photo: CHRISTIAN STEINER

DEBORAH VOIGT, SOPRANO

Deborah Voigt is a soprano poised at the brink of great international stardom. The elegance of her performances, the stunning power of her genuine Straussian voice and the impressive range of her repertoire, encompassing Verdi as well as Wagner, have won her a rare distinction among critics and audiences around the world. Often compared to the renowned soprano Eileen Farrell, Miss Voigt has in just a few years established herself as one of the world's most sought-after dramatic sopranos, inspiring John Rockwell of the *New York Times* to call her "the most important singer to come along in years."

Ms. Voigt's 1996-97 season began with performances and a live recording for Teldec of a great Strauss role—the Kaiserin in Richard Strauss's *Die Frau ohne Schatten* with Maestro Giuseppe Sinopoli at the Dresden Semperoper. She will also perform and record for EMI Zemlinsky's *Eine florentinishe Tragödie* with Maestro James Conlon and the Gürzenich Orchestra. American forthcoming engagements for the soprano include Mahler's *Das klagende Lied* with the American Symphony Orchestra at Avery Fisher Hall. In the spring of 1997, Ms. Voigt reprises the role of Amelia in *Un Ballo in Maschera* with Maestro Levine, Luciano Pavarotti and Juan Pons, followed by performances of Sieglinde in her first full *Ring des Nibelungen* at the Metropolitan Opera.

Ms. Voigt's 1995-96 season began with a much-anticipated recording of one of her signature roles—Chrysothemis in Strauss's *Elektra* under the baton of Maestro Sinopoli for Deutsche Grammophon. In January and February of 1995, Ms. Voigt sang Verdi's *Lady Macbeth* at the Teatro Comunale in Bologna, Italy. In March, she returned to the United States for performances of Honegger's *Jeanne d'Arc au bûcher* with Maestro Charles Dutoit, first with the Philadelphia Orchestra, in both Philadelphia and Carnegie Hall, then with the Pittsburgh and Montreal Symphonies. In April, however, came the highlight of

the season: Ms. Voigt's long-awaited debut with the Royal Opera, Covent Garden, as Amelia in *Un Ballo in Maschera,* opposite legendary tenor Luciano Pavarotti.

The 1994-95 season saw performances on four continents, including her long-awaited debut at the Royal Opera, Covent Garden as Amelia in *Un Ballo in Maschera* with Luciano Pavarotti, and her spectacular South American debut at the Teatro Cólon in Buenos Aires as Chrysothemis in *Elektra* with Hildegard Behrens and Leonie Rysanek.

Highlights of the 1993-94 season included her debut with the Berlin Philharmonic, conducted by James Levine, in Zemlinsky's *Lyrische Symphonie,* performances of the Verdi Requiem—in Washington with the National Symphony under Maestro Mstislav Rostropovich and with Maestro Edo de Waart and the Minnesota Orchestra—and her debut with the Philadelphia Orchestra in a series of highly acclaimed Wagner concerts, under the baton of Maestro Wolfgang Sawallisch in Philadelphia and Carnegie Hall.

Among her past recording achievements is her first interpretation of the great French heroine—Cassandre. In October 1993, she performed live and recorded the role for Decca London in a rare, uncut production of Berlioz's epic *Les Troyens,* with Maestro Charles Dutoit conducting the Orchestre Symphonique de Montreal.

Miss Voigt's 1992-93 season included a triumphant televised appearance in the Richard Tucker Gala, a concert honoring her as the winner of the 1992 Tucker Award for vocal excellence. Other celebrated engagements in 1992-93 included a title role performances with the Metropolitan Opera production of *Ariadne auf Naxos.* In addition, Ms. Voigt had her debut in May at La Scala as Reiza (Rezia—in German) in Weber's *Oberon* under the baton of Maestro James Conlon. Miss Voigt made her Metropolitan Opera House debut to great acclaim in October of 1991, as Amelia in

Verdi's *Un Ballo in Maschera.*

A native of Illinois, Deborah Voigt has attracted world-wide attention by winning many of opera's most prestigious awards, including the first prize in Italy's Verdi Competition and the Gold Medal in Moscow's Tchaikovsky Competition. Ms. Voigt's interest outside the world of opera include her devotion to bringing the beauty of music to children, which she pursues through master classes and other programs coordinated by <u>Young Audiences</u>. The soprano's new Internet Website can be visited at: **http://www.artsinfo.com/deborah_voigt.**

HUMMINGBIRD CAKE
Makes a 10 x 12-inch two-layer cake

Ms. Voigt received this rich delicious recipe from a long time friend of the family. She simply describes this cake as being "really yummy!"

CAKE MIXTURE:
3 cups plain flour
2 cups sugar
1 teaspoon salt
1 teaspoon baking soda
1 teaspoon ground cinnamon
3 eggs, beaten
1½ cups oil
1½ teaspoons vanilla extract
8 oz. can crushed pineapple (with juice)
2 cups chopped bananas (the riper the better)

CREAM CHEESE ICING:
2 sticks butter*
8 oz. package cream cheese
1 teaspoon vanilla
16 oz. powdered sugar
A little milk, if necessary
Some pieces of mango (optional)
  *Some people prefer to use more cream cheese and less butter, for a 'cheesier taste'.

Combine dry ingredients in a mixing bowl and add eggs and oil, stirring well until dry ingredients are moistened. Do not beat. Stir in vanilla, crushed pineapple and bananas.

Spoon the batter into two, 10 x 12-inch square cake pans that are well greased and floured. Bake at 350 degrees for 25 to 35 minutes or until lightly brown on top. Test with a toothpick in the center to check if it comes out clean. Remove from oven and let cool for 10 minutes before placing on cooling racks.

To make icing, process the butter, cream cheese and vanilla together. (Let butter and cream cheese soften first.) Add powdered sugar and process again. If too stiff, add a little milk. Use a little icing and pieces of mango for the center layer. Cover the cake with rest of icing.

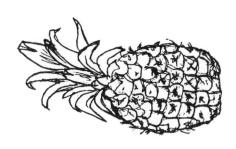

Photo: MARCIA LIEBERMAN

FREDERICA VON STADE, MEZZO-SOPRANO

As she enters the third decade of an extraordinary career, Frederica von Stade continues to reign as one of the music world's most beloved figures. With seemingly effortless versatility, she traverses an ever-broadening spectrum of musical styles and dramatic characterizations. A noted bel canto specialist, she excels as the heroines of Rossini's *La cenerentola* and *Il Barbiere di Siviglia* and of Bellini's *La sonnambula*. She is an unmatched stylist in the French repertoire, a delectable Mignon or Perchole, and, in one critic's words, "the Melisande of one's dreams." Her elegant figure and keen imagination have made her the world's favorite interpreter of the great 'trouser' roles, from Strauss's Octavian and Composer to Mozart's Idamante and—magically, indelibly—Cherubino.

Her career began at the top, when she received a contract from Sir Rudolf Bing during the Metropolitan Opera Auditions. Since her debut at the Met in 1970, she has sung nearly all of her great roles with that company, as well as with the Lyric Opera of Chicago, the San Francisco Opera, and many other leading American theaters. Her career in Europe has been no less spectacular, with new productions mounted for her regularly at La Scala and the Paris Opera, both productions visited the United States during our bicentennial. Frederica von Stade was the only American to appear as a guest not just with one company but with both—as Cenerentola with La Scala and Cherubino with the Paris Opera.

She is invited regularly by the world's top conductors—among them Claudio Abbado, James Levine, Riccardo Muti, and Seiji Ozawa—to appear with the world's top orchestras: the Boston Symphony, the Chicago Symphony, the Philadelphia Orchestra, the London Symphony, the orchestra of La Scala, and many others.

Ms. von Stade has made over three dozen recordings on major labels, including Sony, CBS Masterworks, London/Decca, Deutsche Grammophon, Telarc, Philips, EMI/Angel, Erato and BMG Classics, which include complete operas, aria albums, symphonic works, solo recital programs, and popular crossover albums. Her recordings have garnered five Grammy nominations, two Grand Prix du Disc Awards, the Deutsche Schallplattenpreis, Italy's Premio della Critica Discografica, and "Best of the Year" citations by *Stereo Review*, *Opera News*, and other journals. Recently, she enjoyed the distinction of holding simultaneously the first and second places on the national sales charts, for Angel/EMI's *Showboat* and Telarc's *The Sound of Music*.

She also appears regularly on television, with "Live from the Met" performances of Cherubino, Hansel, and Idamente, as well as a Unitel film of the classic Jean-Pierre Ponnelle production of *La cenerentola*. She created the role of Tina in the world premiere production of Domenick Argento's *The Aspern Papers* (a work written for her) which was broadcast from the Dallas Opera on PBS. A holiday special, "Christmas with Flicka," was shot on location in Salzburg and appeared on PBS. In the spring of 1990, Ms. von Stade was the focal point of another PBS special, "Flicka and Friends," in which she was joined by bass Samuel Ramey and tenor Jerry Hadley for an evening of operatic and musical theater selections. In December 1991, she appeared with Kathleen Battle and Wynton Marsalis in a "Carnegie Hall Christmas Concert," which was conducted by André Previn and broadcast internationally on television; audio and home video recordings were issued by Sony Classics. She was the guest soloist for the Berlin Philharmonic's 1992 New Year's Eve gala, conducted by Claudio Abbado, which was also telecast worldwide and recorded in audio and video formats by Sony.

Frederica von Stade is the holder of honorary doctorates from Yale University, Boston University, the Georgetown University School of Medicine, and her alma mater, the Mannes School of Music. In 1983, she was honored with an award given at the White House by former president Ronald Reagan in recognition of her significant contribution to the arts.

QUICK AND EASY SALAD DRESSING
Makes ⅔ cup

⅓ cup of the best olive oil available
2 tablespoons cider vinegar
Crushed juice of 1 lemon
Salt to taste
⅛ teaspoon pepper
3 large fresh basil leaves

⅛ teaspoon dried dill weed
2 teaspoons regular or low-salt soy sauce
2 cloves garlic
⅛ teaspoon thyme
5 very small fresh mint leaves

Mix above ingredients together in small food processor. Toss with salad just before serving.

Author's Suggested Salad
Serves 8

1 medium head red-leaf lettuce, torn
2 green onions, about ½ cup, chopped
1 medium red bell pepper, chopped
2 medium carrots, thinly sliced
1 small bunch arugula,
    about ½ cup, torn
1½ cups red cabbage, shredded

2 medium fresh red tomatoes,
    sliced in wedges
½ cup fresh parsley, chopped
1½ cups sliced fresh button mushrooms
1 medium cucumber, peeled and sliced
4 large romaine lettuce leaves, torn

Photo: © PETER SCHAAF

ROBERT WHITE, TENOR

Tenor Robert White was born into a New York family that enjoys a strong tradition of song. He studied at the Juilliard School, earning a master degree in voice. European studies included work with Nadia Boulanger at Fountainebleau.

Versatility has been the tenor's trademark throughout his career. Just after college, he toured Europe and America as soloist with Noah Greenberg's New York Pro Musica, while also performing premieres of 20th century works by Menotti, Schuller, Babbitt, Corigliano and Hindemith (under this latter composer's direction).

His wide ranging interest in musical styles continues today. In this past season alone, Mr. White sang two New York premieres of modern works; he appeared with the Juilliard Quartet and pianist Samuel Sanders at Lincoln Center in a chamber-music setting of Gabriel Faure's cycle *La Bonne Chanson*; and he performed in a staged performance of William Boyce's 18th century opera *The Chaplet* at Caramoor.

In the 1980's, Mr. White attracted a large concert-following in the UK and Ireland through his frequent appearances on BBC television and radio. In fact, following a month-long musical tour with flutist James Galway, Mr. White was given the opportunity, rare for an American artist, to host his own BBC radio series—with orchestra—in repertoire ranging from Mozart to Dvořák and Kern to Berlin. In New York, his sold out, three-

concert tribute to the art of the legendary John McCormack received unanimous critical acclaim.

Mr. White has participated in major festivals, including New York's Mostly Mozart, and those at Edinburgh, Spoleto, Prague, Hong Kong and Aspen. He has sung with such orchestras as the New York Philharmonic, the National Symphony Orchestra, the Houston, Baltimore and Dallas Symphonies, and the Monte Carlo Philharmonic. His work in opera ranges from Baroque pieces to Mozart's *Don Giovanni*, Smetana's *The Two Widows*, Bizet's *Carmen*, Moussorgsky's *Boris Godunov*, and modern operas such as Hindemith's *The Long Christmas Dinner*, and Menotti's *Labyrinth*.

Today, Robert White is one of America's most recorded tenors. His albums of Schubert Lieder and Handel arias for the Virgin Classics label have received outstanding reviews in the *New York Times*, *Gramophone* and *Fanfare* magazines, and in many other publications in the U.S. and Europe. He has recorded a dozen solo albums for RCA and EMI-Angel. Mr. White's next release will be an album of Edwardian songs performed with pianist Stephen Hough on the Hyperion label. Robert White has sung for five U.S. Presidents, Britain's Queen Mother and Prince Charles, and Pope John Paul II.

Robert White is a member of the voice faculty of the Juilliard School of Music.

PASTA PORTOBEL-CANTO OR "ZITI AL TENORE"

Serves 3 to 4

This is my favorite meal before a concert (a few good <u>hours</u> before, to be sure!). I learned it when I was a student in Rome back in the 60's, and I have never tired of it. It is quick and easy to prepare, is filling and luscious in taste and texture, and does not cost "il patrimonio" to pay for it! It's the fresh sage that gives this dish its special perfume and flavor. --R.W.

8 to 10 oz. ziti or rigatoni
3 tablespoons extra virgin olive oil
2 large fresh Portobelo (or porcini)
    mushrooms—caps whole (6 oz.),
    or 6 oz. fresh button mushrooms
2 cloves garlic, crushed or thinly sliced
1 spray of fresh sage leaves, chopped
    leaving a few leaves whole (about 1½ oz.)
1 medium onion, thinly sliced

1 teaspoon flour
Fresh chopped parsley, plus a few
    sprigs for garnish
1 teaspoon butter or
    margarine (optional)
Parmesan cheese, freshly grated
Salt or (salt substitute) to taste
Pepper to taste

Cook pasta 'al dente' (approximately 12 minutes) in lightly salted water. Drain and reserve 1 or 2 cups pasta water.

While pasta cooks, remove and slice caps from mushrooms and chop the stems. Sauté garlic, sage and onion in olive oil over medium-high heat for 4 to 5 minutes, or until golden brown. Reduce heat slightly, add mushrooms to pan and cook 10 minutes, turning occasionally. Mushrooms should be nicely browned. Mix flour with ½ cup reserved pasta water. Add to mushrooms and cook an additional 4 or 5 minutes.

Toss pasta with mushroom sauce, parsley and butter, adding reserved water as necessary for moistening. Sprinkle with Parmesan and serve.

Photo: SHERI JACOBS, Indiana Daily Student

CAMILLA WILLIAMS, SOPRANO

Since her spectacular debut with the New York City Center Opera in the title role of "Mme. Butterfly," Camilla Williams' glorious voice and consummate artistry have won for her an enviable reputation of truly international dimensions.

A native of Danville, Virginia, Ms. Williams is an honor graduate of Virginia State College, where she prepared for a teaching career. After a year, the petite and charming soprano began the study of serious music in Philadelphia under the guidance of Mme. Marion Szekely-Freschl, who remains her vocal mentor to this day. Only six months had passed under Madame Freschl's tutelage when Camilla Williams emerged winner of the coveted Marian Anderson Scholarship Award, and subsequently, the Philadelphia Orchestra Youth Auditions. These two signal honors had launched the lovely young soprano on what was to be a career of substance and enormous fulfillment.

In addition to having the distinction of being the first major artist to tour Alaska before it gained statehood, Ms. Williams has sung in every state in the Union, with the exception of Mississippi and Hawaii. She later toured South America.

Having established herself as an artist of the first magnitude in both the Americas and Canada, Camilla Williams embarked on her first tour of Europe, where she was an instant success in England, Germany, Holland, Switzerland, Austria and Italy. She has, subsequently, made no less than 12 tours in Europe in six years, a feat many a veteran artist could envy.

Her debut with the Vienna State Opera, as with the New York City Center Opera, was in the role of "Butterfly," causing the musically discriminating *Arbeiter Zeitung* critic to exclaim: "Camilla Williams is a sensation!" *Bilt Telegraff* wrote: "So moving is the intensity of this singer that it is unique." On the occasion of her first all-German recital in that legendary musical city, *Osterreischer Neue Tageszeitung* declared her "A magnificent artist!" At this point, the announcement of an appearance by the diminutive soprano from Virginia spelled box-office magic throughout Europe.

At the invitation of the State Department, Camilla Williams made an unprecedented tour of fourteen northern and central African countries—performing in new cities and capitals where a first class musical attraction had never before appeared—defending America in hostile areas and winning countless new friends for the land she loves so dearly. So enormous was her success on that continent that she was again invited to tour Ireland and all the real "danger spots" of Southeast Asia (Vietnam, Korea, Laos, Formosa [Taiwan]), the Far East, Australia and New Zealand. Her initial visit to Israel was so warmly received that she was reengaged for a second tour of that new nation.

Now a full-fledged celebrity, Ms. Williams began to receive many honors, including those from her alma mater, New York University, and the New York Newspaper Guild's "Page One Award," to name a few. The latter was bestowed upon her for "bringing democracy to opera" in that she was the first Afro-American woman to sing grand opera with a professional American company, thereby "opening the door" for her now distinguished colleagues, Mattiwilda Dobbs, Leontyne Price, and, ironically enough, her early benefactress, Marian Anderson! The story of Camilla Williams is truly a success in the true American tradition.

Ms. Williams has now devoted much of her life to teaching and currently holds the title of professor of voice at the prestigious School of Music at Indiana University. She resides in Bloomington, Indiana.

STUFFED GREEN PEPPERS

Serves 6

This recipe was often made by my mother. When she used to make it for me in her later years, it would be reminiscent of my childhood. While I use potatoes in this recipe now, she would use corn instead. --C.W.

6 fresh medium-sized firm
   green bell peppers
6 medium potatoes, (about 2 pounds)
   mashed, with cream and butter

6 heaping tablespoons of grated sharp
   Cheddar cheese
Salt and pepper to taste

Wash peppers thoroughly and remove stems and white segments from inside. Drop whole peppers into boiling water until soft but still firm (5 to 6 minutes).

Prepare the fresh mashed potatoes by mashing or whipping potatoes with 3 tablespoons butter and ¼ cup cream. Salt and pepper to taste. Stuff peppers with hot mashed potatoes, mounding up about ½ inch above the opening. Top the potatoes with 1 heaping tablespoon of grated sharp Cheddar cheese.

Bake in 350 degree oven until cheese melts.

Photo: METROPOLITAN OPERA

VIRGINIA ZEANI, SOPRANO

"She sings like Melba and acts like Bernhardt." A rare combination, indeed, but this critic's comment capsulizes perfectly the unique artistry of soprano Virginia Zeani. In a career that spans some thirty years and more than sixty-five extremely diverse roles, Zeani has established herself as one of the last and greatest exponents of the true Bel Canto art of singing.

Virginia Zeani was born in Bucharest, Romania and began her vocal studies at the age of 13 with Lucia Anghel. She continued with famous Russian soprano Lydia Lipkovskaya, who had been a noted colleague of Enrico Caruso and Fedor Chaliapin. At age 19, Ms. Zeani traveled to Italy and there finished her formal studies with Aureliano Pertile, the internationally acclaimed tenor and personal favorite of Arturo Toscanini. The vocal technique and music education Virginia Zeani learned from her maestri has enabled her to maintain a standard of excellence throughout her career. The soundness of her vocal approach, in particular, has allowed her to explore almost every type of soprano role.

Zeani made her stage debut at the age of twenty in Bologna, Italy. The role was Violetta Valery in Verdi's *La Traviata* and the combination of voice, dramatic commitment and rare physical beauty made the debut a tremendous success. This performance was the first of Zeani's long association with this role, which she has performed all across the world in every major opera house, including the Metropolitan Opera, the Bolshoi of Moscow and Covent Garden in London.

After her debut, Zeani added many other roles to her repertoire, including Mimi in *La Bohème*, Marguerite in *Faust* and the title role in Massenet's *Manon* which she sang with Beniamino Gigli, then in the last years of his career. Her performances in *Lucia de Lammermoor*, *L'Elisir d'Amore*, *Don Pasquale*, *Il Barbiere di Siviglia*, *La sonnambula* and *I Puritani* were hailed throughout Europe. She has sung a tremendous variety of roles in

Rome, from Bellini's *I Puritani* through Verdi's *Aïda*. Two especially important productions were mounted for her there—Verdi's *Alzira* and Rossini's *Otello*. Both works had not been performed in the 20th century until these revivals. Zeani's Desdemona was one of the greatest triumphs of her career, one which she repeated when the Rome Opera appeared in Berlin and at the Metropolitan Opera House in New York in 1968.

In 1956, Virginia Zeani was invited to make her debut at La Scala in a new production of Handel's *Guilio Cesare*. Opposite her Cleopatra was the Cesare of Nicola Rossi-Lemeni, the Cornelia of Giulietta Simionato and the Sesto of Franco Corelli. The following spring, she performed Blanche De La Force in the world premiere of Poulenc's *Dialogues des Carmélites* at La Scala. Zeani was personally chosen for this exacting role by the composer, Francis Poulenc, with whom she had a long musical relationship. In recent years, Poulenc's monodrama *La Voix Humaine* has become one of the staples of her schedule. Zeani sang many other roles at La Scala, including *Madama Butterfly* and a famous production of *Les Contes D'Hoffman* in which she performed all four female protagonists opposite the four villains of famous basso, Nicola Rossi-Lemeni. She also performed *Manon*, *Thais*, *Werther* and other French works.

Maturity and the excellence of her vocal technique allowed Virginia Zeani gradually to broaden the scope of her repertoire to encompass many more roles of a heavier texture. As she recalls in an interview in 1978, "Looking back, I believe it was right to begin as a coloratura and at 30 to begin singing as a lyric soprano, and then at age 40 to undertake the dramatic repertoire. This is the right development for a singer trained by the Italian singing school."

Virginia Zeani has recorded albums for London and Phillips, and complete versions of *La Traviata* and *Tosca* for Electrecord. Many of her exciting live performances including *Dialogues Des Carmélites, Otello, and Tosca.* *Fedora* and *Mefistofele* have been captured on the Legendary Recordings label.

At present, Zeani resides in Bloomington, Indiana where she teaches a select group of gifted students at Indiana University and holds the title of distinguished professor of voice.

STUFFED CABBAGE LEAVES
Serves 6

This recipe is for diet lovers—very low in calories—and very tasteful. --V.Z.

1 medium cabbage, about 3 pounds	1 pound of lean ground beef or chuck
1 tablespoon vinegar	Salt and pepper
1 bouillon cube	½ cup parsley
1 medium-large onion, chopped	4 cups of V8 juice
½ cup white rice	½ cup small peanuts

Core cabbage and drop into a large pot of boiling water for 10 minutes with some salt and vinegar. (Add enough water to cover about ¾ the cabbage). Remove as many outer leaves as possible, then add rest of cabbage again to boiling water briefly and remove more leaves. You will need around 14 leaves. Divide the leaves and let cool.

Dissolve bouillon cube in 1 cup hot water and keep water hot. In a medium pan, sauté the onion and rice in a small amount of oil until they become colorful, about 3 minutes. Add bouillon water to pan and cook rice until it is half-cooked. Put the pans contents over the meat, salt and pepper to taste and add parsley. With this mixture, stuff the cabbage leaves into the form of a sausage.

Place in a 4-quart casserole dish; cover all with 2½ cups V8 juice, cover dish with lid or tin foil and cook in the oven at 325 degrees for 1½ hours. Remove cover and add more V8 juice, cooking dish for an additional one-half hour at 375 degrees.

Serve hot, with sour cream on the side.

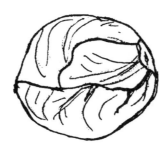

Photo: © CAROL PRATT, 1994

JIANYI ZHANG, TENOR

Jianyi Zhang has been acclaimed in Europe and the United States for the beauty and expressiveness of his singing. Engagements in his 1995-96 season have included a return to the Stuttgart Opera to sing Macduff in *Macbeth*, the role of Riccardo in Verdi's *Oberto* at the Opéra de Nice, the Duke in *Rigoletto* with Florentine Opera, and Rodolfo in *La Bohème* at the Utah Opera. In the summer of 1996, following further performances of *Macbeth* in Stuttgart, he performed the Verdi Requiem in Nice, the title role in "Faust Medley" at Canada's Lanaudière Festival (including excerpts from the Boito, Berlioz and Gounod versions of the Faust story) and concert performances of Alfredo in *La Traviata* with the Kansas City Symphony.

He began his 1994-95 season singing Rodolfo in *La Bohème* at Stuttgart Opera and returned there for performances as Macduff in *Macbeth*. Other engagements include Alfredo in *La Traviata* for Hamburgische Staatsoper, *Faust* for Washington Opera, Cavaradossi in *Tosca* for Tampere Opera in Finland, and the Verdi Requiem for the Atlanta Symphony.

During the 1993-94 season, he was chosen by Maestro Rostropovich to sing in his farewell concert with the National Symphony as the tenor soloist in the Verdi Requiem. Other appearances include the title role in *Faust* at the Bastille in Paris, and the same role for the Michigan Opera Theatre and the Greater Miami Opera, Rodolfo for Sherbrooke Symphony, San Antonio Symphony, and the Minnesota Orchestra, Don José in *Carmen* for the Springfield Symphony, and Lisboa 94 (Lisbon), Beethoven's Symphony No. 9 for the Jacksonville Symphony, an Evening of Arias for the Ft. Wayne Philharmonic, an Opera Evening for the Napa Valley Symphony, and Pinkerton in *Madama Butterfly* for Art and Music in the Philippines.

In the 1992-93 season, the tenor was acclaimed in Bizet's

The Pearl Fishers at the Washington Opera, Don José in *Carmen* for the Bastille in Paris, Donizetti's *L'Elisir d'Amore* with the Connecticut Opera, *La Bohème* at Opera Pacific and the Michigan Opera Theatre, and *La Traviata* in Stockton. He sang Verdi's Requiem with the Vancouver Symphony, the RTVE of Madrid, the Festival Solfeges de Deauville in Paris, and with the Helsinki Symphony in Finland.

Mr. Zhang's extensive operatic repertoire includes many principal tenor roles which he has sung with such venues as Opera de Lyon, Opera de Nice, Opera Comique de Paris, the Chatelet Music Theatre of Paris, Palais de Paris Bercy, Teatro Communale di Firenze, Choregies d'Orange Festival, New York City Opera, Opera Dayton, Sacramento Opera, Summer Opera Theater of Washington, Aspen Music Festival, Il Piccolo Teatro, and the Minnesota Orchestra.

Mr. Zhang's orchestral appearances in recent years have included the London Philharmonic, the Radio Symphony Orchestra of Berlin, Vancouver Symphony Orchestra, Helsinki Philharmonic, Radio France, KRO-Amsterdam, RTVE-Madrid, the Puerto Rico Symphony Orchestra, Pittsburgh Symphony, Colorado Symphony and Tucson Symphony Orchestra, in major works of the orchestral repertoire. Also a recitalist, Mr. Zhang made his Carnegie Hall debut in 1986 and was heard recently in a concert in Denver, Colorado.

Mr. Zhang was trained at the Shanghai Conservatory and the American Opera Center of the Juilliard School. In 1984, Mr. Zhang won the first prize in the Third Belvedere International Opera Competition in Vienna. In 1988, he received the "Grand Award" in the Luciano Pavarotti International Vocal Competition in Philadelphia. He is a Sullivan Award winner, as well as a recipient of the Sullivan Foundation grant and the Cravath Memorial Award.

"GLASSY" SHRIMP
(Chinese Cuisine)
Serves 2

⅔ pound prawns or jumbo shrimp
2 teaspoons baking soda
1 cup water
1 teaspoon shredded ginger root
2 tablespoons green onion, shredded
1 tablespoon shredded hot red pepper

SAUCE:
¾ teaspoon salt
¼ teaspoon sugar
3 tablespoons water
1 teaspoon cornstarch

Remove shells and veins from prawns and remove all pink outer skin, rinse and drain. Soak prawns in 1 cup water with baking soda for 2 hours. Remove and rinse well to rid prawns of any baking soda. Cover prawns with fresh water and let soak for 1 hour, then drain.

Boil 5 cups of water and cook prawns for 1½ minutes, remove and drain.

Place ginger root, green onions and hot red pepper on serving plate.

Heat **SAUCE** in a pan (no oil) and bring to a boil. Add prawns; and when mixture has thickened, pour onto serving plate. Toss lightly and serve.

VIOLA

Photo: JOE MYERS

ALAN DE VERITCH, VIOLIST

Alan de Veritch is one of the most respected violists in the world today. Currently serving as professor of music at Indiana University, he has performed in almost every major concert hall in the United States and Europe and appeared as soloist with such orchestras as the Los Angeles Philharmonic, National Symphony Orchestra and the Philadelphia Orchestra.

A student of and teaching assistant to William Primrose, Alan's career has also included almost ten years as principal violist of the Los Angeles Philharmonic, guest principal violist of the New York Philharmonic and membership in An die Musik, the Aldanya String Quartet and the White House String Quartet. Additionally, he has performed on literally hundreds of motion picture soundtracks and recorded for almost every major record label.

In high demand as a teacher, coach and lecturer, Alan de Veritch's previous faculty positions have included: California Institute of the Arts, California State University, Idyllwild School of Music and the Arts, R.D. Colburn School of Performing Arts and the University of Southern California, where he developed the orchestral repertoire/audition preparation program for strings.

His students hold many of today's most prestigious viola positions and include such names as Paul Neubauer, James Dunham, and Nokathula Ngwenyama, the rising new star of the viola.

The recipient of numerous awards and commendations from local, state and federal government, Alan de Veritch served from 1990-1994 as the national president of the American Viola Society and has recently established the de Veritch Institute of Viola Studies, a school designed to set the standard for excellence in consistent viola training at all levels and be national in scope.

In June 1995, Alan was the co-host of the International Viola Congress XXIII, held on the campus of Indiana University in Bloomington, Indiana. At that time he was presented the coveted America Viola Society Award for "Outstanding Achievement" - Personal Contributions to the Legacy of the Viola."

Simultaneously, Alan has spent the past few years rapidly building a reputation as a highly respected orchestral conductor. In March 1996, he was officially appointed to the conducting staff at the Indiana University School of Music.

CHICKEN PICCADILLY

Serves 4 to 6

This is an old modified English recipe. By eliminating the step of straining out liquid from cream corn, the recipe becomes an excellent stew! A good option. --A.D.

**2 skinless boneless whole chicken
    breasts (about 1½ pounds)**
2 small bananas

3, 15 oz. cans cream-style corn
¼ to ⅓ cup sliced almonds
¾ cup Baileys Irish Cream liqueur

Divide whole breasts into halves. Marinate chicken breasts in ¼ cup of Baileys Irish Cream at least 4 hours prior to cooking. Turn chicken over several times and puncture lightly with fork to assure saturation. After straining out all liquid, empty corn into baking dish, approximately 8 x 12-inches.

Add ¼ cup of Baileys to corn. Mix well and spread corn evenly, covering bottom of baking dish. Let stand.

Put whole chicken breast, including any excess marinade, into stove top skillet. Turning regularly, cook until both sides are nicely browned. (As a great alternative, barbecue the chicken on an outdoor grill). Cut browned chicken breasts into bite-sized chunks and mix with additional ¼ cup of Baileys.

Slice bananas and add along with chicken to corn mixture. Mix contents of baking dish well and spread evenly. Sprinkle sliced almonds over top. Place baking dish in preheated oven and bake at 350 degrees for 30 to 35 minutes, uncovered. Chicken should be tender. Serve hot.

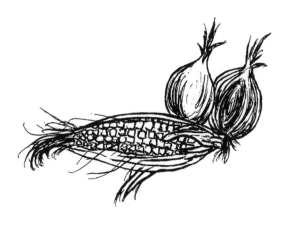

CHERRY TRIFLE
Serves 8

This is super! Works best if chilled overnight.

2 cups vanilla cream custard, divided*

2 dozen ladyfingers or layer of sponge
    or pound cake cut into
    fingers, divided

1 cup cherry jam, divided

Rind of 1 lemon, grated and divided

½ cup sherry, divided

3 tablespoons brandy, divided

1 quart fresh cherries or
    1 can (1 pound, 5 oz.) of
    cherry pie filling, divided

1 dozen macaroons, crushed and divided

1 cup whipping cream

Maraschino cherries

Prepare the custard sauce. Coat one-half of the ladyfingers with ½ cup of cherry jam and place in the bottom of a crystal bowl 8-inches in diameter and 3½-inches deep, and sprinkle with one-half of the lemon rind.

Sprinkle with ¼ cup sherry and half of the brandy. Cover with a layer of half cherries or pie filling and half macaroons. Allow to stand an hour or so.

Pour half of the custard sauce over the top, repeat the layers of ladyfingers, cherry jam, lemon rind, sherry, brandy, cherries and the remaining macaroons. Repeat the custard layer. Chill.

Just before serving, top with whipped cream and maraschino cherries.

*VANILLA CREAM CUSTARD

5 egg yolks

½ cup sugar

2 tablespoons cornstarch

2 cups milk

1 teaspoon vanilla

Combine beaten egg yolks with sugar and mix well. In a saucepan, dissolve the cornstarch in ½ cup milk. Add the rest of the milk and the vanilla and bring to a boil, stirring continously. Pour gradually into the egg mixture and blend well. Return to the heat and boil, stirring constantly for 2 minutes. Cool in the refrigerator until required.

Photo: CHRISTIAN STEINER

ROBERTO DÍAZ, VIOLIST

Rapidly becoming one of the most sought-after violists, Roberto Díaz enjoys a successful career in solo, chamber music, teaching, and orchestral performance. He has been the recipient of numerous awards and prize winner in several competitions, including the Naumburg, Munich and Washington International Competitions.

Mr. Díaz was principal violist of the National Symphony Orchestra in Washington, D.C. He was selected recently by the Philadelphia Orchestra to be their new principal violist.

Mr. Díaz has performed in the United States, Europe, and Central and South America in recital and as a soloist with such orchestras as the Bayerischer Rundfund (Germany), the National Symphony, the Boston Pops, and the Savannah Symphony, to name a few. Recital engagements have taken him to Boston, Los Angeles, Washington, D.C., Chicago, Baltimore, Atlanta, and Moscow, where he was reengaged immediately to perform in the city's Great Hall. He has also toured extensively in his native Chile as soloist and recitalist.

As a chamber musician, Mr. Díaz has collaborated with many of today's leading artists such as Isaac Stern, Yo-Yo Ma, Emanuel Ax, Yefim Bronfman, and Samuel Sanders at festivals, including Mostly Mozart, Tanglewood, El Paso, Newport, Cape and Islands, and Marlboro. As a member of the Díaz Trio, along with violinist David Kim and cellist Andres Díaz, he has performed throughout the United States, Mexico, and Chile. Elsewhere, Mr. Díaz has performed with the Chamber Music Society of Lincoln Center, and the Lydian String Quartet.

Last year, Mr. Díaz was invited to perform the annual William Primrose Memorial Recital in Provo, Utah. In addition, he also performed in recital and as soloist at the 1989 International Viola Congress in California. During December of 1990, Díaz and two colleagues from the National Symphony traveled to Bahrain to perform for U.S. service personnel stationed in the Persian Gulf.

Mr. Díaz began his musical studies at the Chilean Conservatory and continued at the Georgia Academy of Music, where he studied both violin and viola with his father, Manuel Díaz. He later studied with Burton Fine at the New England Conservatory in Boston and Joseph de Pasquale at the Curtis Institute of Music in Philadelphia. Mr. Díaz also holds a degree in industrial design from DeKalb Technical School in Atlanta.

In addition to teaching master classes at many of this country's leading music schools, Mr. Díaz serves on the viola faculty at the Peabody Conservatory in Baltimore and the University of Maryland in College Park.

PEVRE
(Salsa)
Makes 3 cups

Pevre is a Chilean dish most commonly eaten as a side dish with beef or chicken. It also can be eaten as a dip like salsa. Great when mixed in with a bit of avocado. --R.D.

Large (28 oz.) can whole tomatoes, drained
5 to 8 jalapeño peppers, seeds removed
   (seeds can be added later for hotter pevre)
1 large bunch of cilantro
4 or 5 whole scallions

6 cloves of garlic
¼ teaspoon black pepper or to taste
½ teaspoon salt or to taste
2 to 3 tablespoons olive oil
A few sprinkles of chili powder
Avocado (optional)

Mix all the ingredients (except the tomatoes) in a food processor and chop (not too finely or it turns mushy.) For me, the more cilantro the better. It is good to put in not only the leaves but also most of the stems. Add the tomatoes and blend some more. (Again, do not go too long with the food processor or the salsa gets too liquid). Let it set for about 30 minutes.

*WARNING: Handle peppers with great care. The oil from the pepper skin is very hot and can cause great distress if it enters the eye.

Photo: J. HENRY FAIR

TOBY HOFFMAN, VIOLIST

Violist Toby Hoffman enjoys a distinguished international performing career as both soloist and chamber musician. He has appeared with the Buffalo Philharmonic, Prague Chamber Orchestra, National Orchestra of Costa Rica, Florida Orchestra, Flagstaff Festival Orchestra, Savannah Symphony, American Chamber Orchestra, and, in New York, with the New York Youth Symphony at Carnegie Hall as well as the Juilliard Orchestra at Lincoln Center. He performed the world premiere of the "Double Concerto" for Viola, Cello and Orchestra by Joel Hoffman with the Cincinnati Conservatory Orchestra. Mr. Hoffman was also a recitalist on opening day at the recently renovated Weill Recital Hall at Carnegie Hall.

Mr. Hoffman has been a participant in an impressive group of festivals including Ravinia, Saratoga, Marlboro, Aspen, La Jolla, Chamber Music North West, Carmel, Seattle, Vancouver, Sitka Alaska, Newport, Tours France, Gotland Sweden, and Kuhmo Finland. He is a regular participant at the Settimane Musicali Internazionali di Napoli and the Festival di Cremona in Italy, at the invitation of the violin virtuoso Salvatore Accardo. Mr. Hoffman performed with both Maestro Accardo and Maurizio Pollini at the Festival di Napoli at Teatro Alla Scala in Milano and London's Queen Elizabeth Hall. He has been a frequent participant at the Moon Beach Festival in Okinawa as both a teacher and a performer. He also appeared as a guest artist with the Tokyo Chamber Soloists, giving concerts in Tokyo and other cities in Japan. Toby Hoffman is a regular participant at the Stichting Reizend Muziekgezelschap, performing throughout the Netherlands in such cities as Amsterdam, Rotterdam, Den Haag, Utrecht and many others.

Mr. Hoffman appears frequently as a guest artist with the Chamber Music society of Lincoln Center and is a member of Mostly Music in New Jersey with violinist Robert McDuffie and cellist Gary Hoffman. He has also performed with the Theater Chamber Players of Kennedy Center and on the Linton Series in Cincinnati. He has toured several times with Music From Marlboro and performed with the Tokyo String Quartet at Ravinia.

Toby Hoffman is an active recording artist. Recently released as part of an extensive recording project of Mozart, for both video and compact disc with Salvatore Accardo, is the *Sinfonia Concertante* with the Prague Chamber Orchestra, two duos for violin and viola, Divertimento string trio, the six viola quintets, Horn Quintet, Clarinet Quintet, Oboe Quartet and *Eine Kleine Nacht Musik*, all for the Nuova Era Company. Also with Nuova Era, he has recorded the Verdi and Borodin quartets, the Terzetto Bass Quintet and the Piano Quintet by Dvořák, in addition to the Chausson Concerto for the Dynamic Recording Company in Italy. Hoffman has recorded the Joel Hoffman Duo for Viola and Piano for CRI. He has also recorded for the Marlboro Recording Society, Musical Heritage Society, Arabesque and Philips.

Mr. Hoffman comes from a distinguished family of musicians. He studied the violin with his mother, Esther Glazer, until he went to the Juilliard School where he graduated with both bachelor and master degrees in music, studying with Paul Doktor. His various awards and prizes include the Sir John Barbirolli Prize from the Lionel Tertis International Viola Competition in England, prizes from the William Kapell Competition and two consecutive Juilliard Viola Competitions.

Currently, Toby Hoffman is an artist-in-residence at Harvard University.

Mr. Hoffman plays on a 1628 Antonio and Hieronymus Amati viola made in Cremona, Italy, which formerly belonged to Queen Victoria of England.

Page Roberts Hoffman, pianist, is currently pursuing a master of music degree at Juilliard, studying with Peter Serkin. She concertizes throughout the United States as chamber musician and soloist, as well as giving duo concerts with her husband Toby.

Born in Tyler, Texas, Ms. Hoffman made her orchestral debut in 1983, at the age of thirteen, with the Baylor University Orchestra, after winning first prize in their national concerto competition. Since then, she has appeared as soloist with the Rice University Orchestra, the Jupiter Symphony Orchestra, the East Texas Symphony, and the California State University Orchestra in Los Angeles.

CHICKEN PAPRIKASH

Serves 4 to 6

I learned this dish from Toby's mother, Esther Glazer Hoffman, who was a concert violinist, and the teacher of Toby. She now is a painter and resides in New York City. --P.R.H.

1 medium cut-up chicken fryer, minus back (or parts of your choice)	2 tablespoons sweet paprika
1 large Spanish yellow onion, chopped	Salt and pepper to taste
1 tablespoon butter or vegetable oil	1 cup sour cream
	Fresh lemon juice from ½ lemon

Cook the chopped onion in the butter or oil on medium heat until golden, about 15 to 20 minutes. Remove onion, put aside. Place the chicken in the skillet, browning it on both sides. Lower the heat. Return onion to skillet. Cover the chicken and onion with an even distribution of paprika. Add a generous amount of black pepper and a little salt. Cover the skillet and simmer on low heat for about 1 hour. Stir occasionally.

When the chicken is cooked, take out the chicken parts, leaving the juice and onions in the skillet. Over very low heat, stir in the sour cream. Do not let it boil! Depending on how much juice remains from the chicken, the amount of sour cream can vary. The consistency should not be too thick or too thin; it should be gravy-like. Add fresh juice from about half a lemon and return the chicken, covering it with the sauce.

Serve over rice (*I like to use Jasmine or Basmati for their fragrant flavors*).

Photo: ERIK HEINILA

DONALD McINNES, VIOLIST

Professor of viola at the University of Southern California, artist-in-residence at Duquesne University, and guest master teacher at the Yehudi Menuhin School in England and Switzerland, violist Donald McInnes is known in virtually every corner of the music world. He has appeared with such orchestras as the New York Philharmonic, Boston Symphony Orchestra and L'Orchestre Nationale de France, among others, and his career includes associations with many of the world's major artists.

An active recording artist, Mr. McInnes can be heard on Columbia, RCA, Deutsche Grammophon, Angel (EMI) and Laurel labels. 1994 recording activities saw issuance of a CD performed on twelve of the world's greatest violas, and a German Lieder CD album for Delos Records, with Florence Quivar and Armen Guzilimian, which include the Brahms Two Songs for voice,

viola and piano. McInnes also has introduced many new works for viola, including commissions for him by William Schuman, Vincent Persichetti, William Bergsma, Robert Suderburg, and Paul Tufts. In addition, the well-known composer, Thomas Pasatieri, recently finished a new viola sonata for Mr. McInnes. The premier of this work was given by Mr. McInnes last season.

A frequent guest artist and teacher at leading music schools, Mr. McInnes has been associated with the Banff Centre in Canada, the Menuhin Schools in England and Switzerland, the Britten-Pears School for Advanced Musical Studies in England, and, since 1982, has been on the faculty of the Music Academy of the West in Santa Barbara, California, during the summer months. His students can be consistently found in major competitions, teaching positions, and orchestras throughout the world.

ROYALE BLACK AND WHITE CHOCOLATE SOUFFLÉ

Serves 6

This dessert is delicious, festive, and unique. Bon Appétit!! --D.M.

10 soda crackers, finely crumbled

1½ squares of cooking chocolate (dark)

½ cup of sugar, scant measure

1½ cups milk

1 teaspoon vanilla

2 beaten egg yolks

2 egg whites, stiffly beaten

Heavy cream

Cook combined crackers, chocolate, sugar, milk, vanilla and egg yolks in a pan surrounded by boiling water for 10 minutes. Remove from stove. Fold in 2 egg whites, beaten stiff. Turn into 8 x 8-inch baking dish, or similar size, and set in pan of water. (Water should be as high as the baking dish contents or slightly higher).

Bake uncovered in oven for 45 minutes at 350 degrees. Serve at once with heavy cream surrounding each portion of the soufflé.

Photo: Courtesy of Chicago Symphony Orchestra

CHARLES PIKLER, VIOLIST/VIOLINIST

Charles Pikler became a member of the Chicago Symphony Orchestra as a violinist in 1978; however, in 1986 he was named head of the viola section, returning to the instrument he had been playing since his teens.

Born in California, Mr. Pikler studied the piano with his parents before beginning violin lessons at the age of twelve; in Norwich, Connecticut he studied with Ben Ornstein. Later, he entered the University of Connecticut, still studying with Ben Ornstein. He entered the University of Connecticut to pursue a degree in mathematics, but continued his violin studies there under the guidance of Bronislaw Gimpal. Between 1965 and 1971, Mr. Pikler spent his summers at several music festivals, including the Tanglewood Young Artist Program at the Berkshire Music Center, where he studied with Roman Totenberg. He also sharpened his skills in solo appearances with the Hartford Symphony Orchestra, Eastern Connecticut Symphony, and Manchester Civic Orchestra, among others.

Mr. Pikler launched his orchestral career as a violinist in 1971, with the Minnesota Orchestra, later becoming a member of the Cleveland Orchestra (1974-76) and the Rotterdam Philharmonic (1976-78). Although he had viola lessons in his teens, he began to take that instrument more seriously in his early twenties, when he played chamber music with a quartet in Cleveland. He

occasionally was a substitute in the Chicago Symphony viola section and also played viola for six years in the orchestra's ensemble concerts throughout the Chicago area, which he continues to do. Mr. Pikler serves as concertmaster of the Chicago Chamber Orchestra under Dieter Kober, the Sinfonia Orchestra of Chicago under Barry Faldner, the Orchestra of the Apollo Chorus, and the River Cities Philharmonic under Jay Friedman. He has been featured as a viola soloist with the Chicago Symphony Orchestra, as well as a soloist on both violin and viola with other orchestras in the Chicago area.

A chamber music enthusiast, Pikler performs with his own group and with other ensembles, including the Chicago Symphony String Quartet. He has been a guest artist with the Daniel String Quartet in Holland and frequently performs on the WFMT live radio broadcasts. In the summer of 1990, he performed the Viola Concerto by Frank Beezhold, which was written for and dedicated to him, with the Civic Orchestra at Orchestra Hall. He also has recorded the work, in the composer's own arrangement for piano and viola, with pianist Dorothy Shultz. In February 1992, Mr. Pikler toured eastern Europe as concertmaster and soloist with the Chicago Chamber Orchestra, playing his own transcription for viola of Mozart's Concerto in D, K. 218. He has recorded *Don Quixote* with the Chicago Symphony Orchestra under Barenboim for the ERATO label.

RAKOTT KRUMPLI
(Scalloped Potatoes)
Serves 6

The RAKOTT KRUMPLI recipe is from my late grandmother, Irene Landgraf (1890-1975). She was a great Hungarian cook. --C.P.

2½ pounds potatoes (small ones if possible)	1 cup sour cream
6 hard-boiled eggs	Salt and black pepper to taste
¼ pound butter	1 tablespoon paprika

Without peeling, boil potatoes in salted water until tender. Peel potatoes and eggs, let cool. Butter a heatproof glass dish (2-quart). Place in the dish alternate layers of sliced potatoes and sliced eggs until dish is full. Put desired amount of black pepper and melted butter on each layer. Salt to taste. Top layer should be potatoes. Pour remaining melted butter on top. Spread sour cream on top and sprinkle with paprika.

Bake in oven uncovered at 350 degrees for 30 minutes.

Photo: CHRISTIAN STEINER

ELLEN ROSE, VIOLIST

Ellen Rose, a Juilliard School graduate, has served since 1980 as principal violist of the Dallas Symphony, where her orchestral viola solos can be heard on many DSO recordings. She has performed several viola concertos with the DSO and other orchestras and has been a member of the Tesoro Quartet. Besides performing at the Grand Teton Festival with Lionel Party, Ms. Rose has performed as recitalist throughout the U.S., at the Chigiana Institute in Sienna, Italy, the Lincoln Center Library, and the Princeton University Recital Series. In 1991, she and Katherine Collier performed at the Phillips Collection in Washington D.C. She has appeared in chamber music performances with Itzhak Perlman, Pinchas Zukerman, Lynn Harrell and Ralph Kirschbaum.

Ms. Rose is principal violist and faculty member of the Aspen Music Festival, where she collaborates in a special team teaching project with Heidi Castleman and Victoria Chiang. From 1991 to 1992, she was on the viola faculty of the Meadowmount Music School. In 1991, she and Katherine Collier, pianist, recorded a contemporary composition written for her by Margaret Brouwer, which was released on CD by Centaur Records. In January 1995, she and Katherine Collier recorded a collection of Spanish music to be released at a later time. She is viola professor at Southern Methodist University and teaches professional musicians throughout the country. Some master classes include the Cleveland Institute of Music, Oberlin Conservatory, University of Michigan and the Juilliard School.

Ellen Rose has written several transcriptions and arrangements, articles for *A.S.T.A.* and *The Instrumentalist*, and is on the International Advisory Council for the Performing Arts Health Information Services, Inc. Her February 1994 article in *A.S.T.A.* magazine described an educational project of arrangements of orchestral music to aid violists in preparing for orchestral auditions. She was the recipient of Aspen and Tanglewood fellowships and a special Juilliard School Naumberg Award in viola.

ELLEN'S BRATSCHE BARS

Makes 24 bars

WARNING: *Do not add marshmallows to this recipe—I tried it and it doesn't work!* --E.R.

½ cup butter
1½ cups graham cracker crumbs
14 oz. can Eagle brand sweetened
    condensed milk
½ cup chunky peanut butter
1 teaspoon vanilla
1 tablespoon Grand Marnier liqueur

⅓ cup slivered almonds,
    coarsely chopped
⅓ cup pecans, coarsely chopped
⅓ cup walnuts, coarsely chopped
8 oz. of chocolate chips
4 oz. of flaked coconut

Preheat oven to 325 degrees. Melt butter and spread evenly into 9 x 13-inch baking pan. Sprinkle crumbs over butter, smoothing evenly with fingers. Thoroughly mix Eagle brand milk with peanut butter, vanilla and Grand Marnier and spread evenly over crumbs.

Mix all of the nuts together after chopping. Top evenly with chocolate chips, coconut and nuts; press down gently. Bake 25 minutes at 325 to 350 degrees, or until lightly browned.

Cool THOROUGHLY before cutting. Loosely cover any leftovers.

Photo: DOROTHEA VON HAEFTEN

MICHAEL TREE, VIOLIST, GUARNERI STRING QUARTET

Michael Tree was born in Newark, New Jersey, and received his first violin instruction from his father. Later, as a scholarship student at the Curtis Institute of Music in Philadelphia, Mr. Tree studied with Efrem Zimbalist, Lea Luboshutz, and Veda Reynolds. In 1954, the *New York Herald Tribune* wrote, "A 20-year old American violinist, Michael Tree, stepped out upon the Carnegie Hall stage last night and made probably the most brilliant young debut in the recent past...the violinist evidenced not one lapse from the highest possible musical and technical standards." Subsequent to his debut, Mr. Tree has appeared as violin and viola soloist with the Philadelphia, Los Angeles, Baltimore, New Jersey, and other major orchestras. He has also participated in leading festivals, including Marlboro, Casals, Spoleto, and Israel.

As a founding member of the Guarneri String Quartet, Mr. Tree has played in major cities throughout the world. In 1982, Mayor Koch presented the quartet with the New York City Seal of Recognition, an honor awarded for the first time.

One of the most widely recorded musicians in America, Mr. Tree has recorded over 80 chamber music works, including 10 piano quartets and quintets with Artur Rubinstein. Other artists with whom he has recorded include Emanuel Ax, Richard Goode, Jaime Laredo, Yo-Yo Ma, Sharon Robinson, Rudolf Serkin, Isaac Stern, and Pinchas Zukerman. These works appear on the Columbia, Nonesuch, RCA, Sony and Vanguard labels. His television credits include repeated appearances on *The Today Show* and the first telecast of *Chamber Music Live from Lincoln Center*.

Mr. Tree serves on the faculty of the Curtis Institute of Music, Manhattan School of Music, University of Maryland, and Rutgers University.

The members of the Guarneri quartet include (from left to right) Michael Tree, viola, John Dailey, violin, David Soyer, cello and Arnold Steinhardt, violin.

SUNDAY MORNING SPECIAL

The perfect first breakfast after a long tour, even if it's not Sunday. --M.T.

PER PERSON:

½ **cup flour**
2 **eggs, beaten**
½ **cup milk**

1 tablespoon butter
Powdered sugar
Lemon juice

Stir flour and eggs into milk. Melt butter in a skillet or shallow baking dish. Pour milk/flour/egg mixture into the baking dish. Bake in preheated oven at 425 degrees for approximately 20 to 25 minutes. It should rise quite high and be brown on top.

Sprinkle with powdered sugar and lemon juice or add fruits such as berries with maple syrup on it.

Photo: LARRY KENESSKY

KAREN TUTTLE, VIOLIST

Karen Tuttle was born in Lewiston, Idaho. She studied at the Curtis Institute of Music with William Primrose. Ms. Tuttle also studied with Pablo Casals and performed with him in seven Casals Festivals. Ms. Tuttle has participated in six Marlboro Festivals under Rudolf Serkin. She has performed solo repertoire with the Schneider Chamber Orchestra, Scherman "Little Orchestra Society," Saidenberg Chamber Orchestra, and the Philadelphia Little Symphony. In 1959, Ms. Tuttle toured cross-country as viola soloist with the Camera Concerti. Her Carnegie Recital Hall debut was in 1960. She is a member of Schneider, Galamir, and Gotham String Quartets. She has recordings under the Columbia, M.G.M., and Haydn Records labels. Ms. Tuttle has given numerous masters classes in viola and chamber music. She has toured as viola soloist for the Association of American Colleges.

Her faculty appointments include: the Curtis Institute of Music, Peabody Conservatory, Mannes School of Music, Manhattan School of Music, Aspen Music Festival, and the Banff Centre of Performing Arts. She has been on the faculty of the Juilliard School since 1987.

She is a member of Philomusica Chamber Society, New York; and the Theater Chamber Players, Washington, D.C. She is televising all the Haydn string quartets for WNYC.

DATE BONS

Serves 12

The "Date Bons" recipe comes from my grandmother. --K.T.

4 eggs	1 teaspoon baking powder
4 tablespoons boiling water	1 teaspoon vanilla (or to taste)
1 cup sugar	1 cup walnuts, finely chopped
1 cup cake flour	1 heaping cup dates, finely chopped

Blend eggs well but not until foamy. Add boiling water, sugar, flour (little by little), baking powder, vanilla, walnuts and dates.

Place in greased 9 x 9-inch cake pan. Bake at 300 degrees for about 50 minutes or until golden brown. Test with toothpick.

VIOLIN

Photo: © LUCIANO ROMANO

SALVATORE ACCARDO, VIOLINIST/CONDUCTOR

Salvatore Accardo gave his first professional recital in 1954, at the age of 13, with a program that included the Paganini caprices. He was awarded first prize in the Geneva Competition at age 15, and, two years later, became the very first winner of the Paganini Competition. His vast repertoire ranges from pre-Bach to post-Berg and he regularly plays concertos with the world's leading orchestras and conductors.

A renowned recitalist and chamber music player, Accardo formed the Accardo Quartet in 1992, which has made extensive tours and played at the 1995 Salzburg Festival in a concert with Maurizio Pollini.

In recent years, Accardo has also devoted part of his activities to conducting, and he has appeared with a number of important orchestras. At the 1987 Rossini Opera Festival in Pesaro, he made a highly auspicious debut as an opera conductor in a new production of *L'occasione fa il ladro*. In the following years, he conducted this opera and *Così fan Tutte* in Rome and Naples (*Così* also in Monte-Carlo), and in 1992 he returned to Pesaro to conduct the rarely-heard *Messa di Gloria*, in celebration of the 200th anniversary of the birth of Rossini. It was also recorded for a CD release by Ricordi/Fonit Cetra.

From 1993 to 1995, Accardo was music director and principal conductor of the Teatro de San Carlo, Naples, where he conducted Pergolesi's *Il Flaminio* (repeated at the Lille Opera); Rossini's *Mose in Egitto* and *L'occasione fa il ladro*; Haydn's *Il mondo della luna*; the Royal Opera House, Covent Garden production of *Don Giovanni*; and various concerts, including Rossini's *Stabat Mater*. During 1995, he conducted several concerts with the Mitteldeutscher Rundfunk of Leipzig, where he is a regular guest conductor. He conducted the Wiener Symphoniker at the Musikverein, as well as appearing there as a recitalist. Accardo also had concerts with the radio orchestras of Stuttgart and Torino, and tours with the Quartetto Accardo.

In addition to his famous recordings of the complete Paganini concertos and caprices on Deutsche Grammophon, Accardo has an extensive discography, including recently released recordings of a *Homage to Kreisler* recital on Fone, and the Beethoven Violin Concerto and two romances with the La Scala Philharmonic Orchestra, conducted by Carlo Maria Giulini, on Sony Classical.

Salvatore Accardo has always been a strong supporter of young musicians; in 1984 he created a school for string players in Cremona, where he regularly teaches. He was awarded the *Premio Abbiati* by the Italian critics, and Italy's highest honour, the *Cavaliere di Gran Groce*, was bestowed on him by the President of the Italian Republic in 1982.

ITALIAN DINNER FOR 6

PASTA CON ZUCCHINI:
10 to 12 oz. pasta
1 large onion, chopped
20 oz. zucchini, thinly sliced in rounds
4 cloves garlic, chopped

2 tablespoons olive oil
1 cup hot water
Salt and pepper to taste
Parmigiana cheese, grated
Parsley

Chop the onion and slice the zucchini. Chop up the garlic. Place onion and garlic into in a large frying pan with 2 tablespoons of olive oil. Sauté on medium heat for about 10 minutes, raise heat slightly, then add the zucchini and 1 cup of hot water.

Turn down heat to medium and cook zucchini for 20 to 25 minutes, or until tender, stirring occasionally. Meanwhile, boil spaghetti in a pan of water and when ready, place the spaghetti and the mixture on a serving dish with the Parmigiana and parsley.

PARMIGIANA DI MELANZANE:
2 pounds melanzane (baby eggplants)
⅓ to ½ cup olive oil
16 oz. can tomato sauce
3 tablespoons tomato paste

1 teaspoon Italian seasoning
10 oz. mozzarella cheese, thinly sliced
4 oz. Parmigiana cheese, grated
8 oz. mortadella, sliced (Italian salami)
½ cup fresh basilico (basil)

Cut the melanzane into long ⅓-inch thick slices, (about 5 slices per eggplant) and fry in olive oil for about 20 minutes, until soft. Meanwhile, in a medium saucepan, place about ¾ can (12 oz.) of tomato sauce, paste and Italian seasoning, and simmer for 15 minutes.

Layer cooked eggplant in a 2-quart Pyrex dish. On top of this, place the tomato sauce, sliced mozzarella, grated Parmigiana, mortadella (cut into smaller pieces) and basilico. Place in the oven, uncovered, for about one-half hour on medium heat (350 degrees).

SALTIMBOCCA ALLA ROMANA:
1½ pounds veal (shoulder or breast)
Butter and olive oil

½ cup dry white wine
Fresh sage, about 10 leaves
⅓ pound uncooked ham (prosciutto)

Trim extra fat from veal and place veal into a large frying pan. Add a tablespoon each of butter and olive oil, plus ½ cup wine and slowly cook veal, covered, for 1 to 1½ hours, until tender. Remove veal but save pan juices. Break the meat into pieces and place back into pan. Place the sage and slices of ham on top of the veal pieces and add a little extra dry white wine. Heat all ingredients and serve.

MACEDONIA DI FRUTTA:
One of each: banana, peach, apple, orange
3 kiwi
1 cup pineapple chunks

1½ cups strawberries
½ cup mandarin (depending on season)
½ cup pine tree nuts
Juice of 1 lemon

Cut fruit into small pieces, add pine nuts and dress with lemon juice.

Portrait: VICKI THOMPSON (1979)

VICTOR AITAY, VIOLINIST

Victor Aitay joined the Chicago Symphony Orchestra as concertmaster in 1954 at the invitation of Fritz Reiner. Born in Budapest, Hungary, Mr. Aitay studied with Béla Bartók, Ernst von Dohnányi, Zoltan Kodály, and Leo Weiner.

After receiving his diploma from the Franz Liszt Royal Academy, Aitay became concertmaster of the Hungarian Royal Opera and the Philharmonic Orchestras, and he organized the Aitay String Quartet. Shortly after he emigrated to the United States, Mr. Aitay was engaged from 1948 to 1954 as concertmaster of the Metropolitan Opera Company in New York City.

He has performed as a recitalist and as a soloist with the leading orchestras of the United States and Europe. On several occasions he performed at the invitation of the late Pablo Casals at the Casals Festival in Puerto Rico. He has made several appearances as a soloist with the Chicago Symphony, both in Orchestra Hall and on tour, under the direction of Sir Georg Solti.

Mr. Aitay also serves as professor of violin at DePaul University, as music director and conductor of the Lake Forest Symphony, and is the leader of the Chicago Symphony String Quartet. He received the distinguished degree of doctor of fine arts honoris causa from Lake Forest College in 1986. Victor Aitay now holds the title of co-concertmaster emeritus from the Chicago Symphony.

KÖRÖZÖTT
(Hungarian cheese dip)

This dip may be served with toasted rounds, radishes, green peppers, or any other preferred raw vegetables. It makes a delicious stuffing for celery. --V.A.

12 oz. container cream cheese	½ small onion, grated
¼ pound lightly salted butter	½ teaspoon caraway seeds
2 oz. can anchovies, rolled with capers	3 to 4 teaspoons Hungarian paprika
1 teaspoon prepared mustard	

Mix cream cheese with softened butter. Remove anchovies and capers from oil and mash using the back of a fork. Mix all ingredients together, adding enough paprika to achieve a light orange color. Refrigerate.

Photo: CHRISTIAN STEINER

JOSHUA BELL, VIOLINIST

The poetic artistry and musical integrity of Joshua Bell have earned the American-born violinist a position of prominence among the leading musicians of the world. Born in Bloomington, Indiana in 1967, he came to national attention when he won the Seventeen Magazine/General Motors Competition at 14 years of age. His Philadelphia Orchestra debut that same year, followed by his Carnegie Hall debut, an Avery Fisher Career grant, and subsequent exclusive recording contract with London/Decca, created a sensation that rapidly spread throughout the music world. Today, at the age of 30, Joshua Bell has earned a reputation not only as a dynamic performer but as a dedicated and thoughtful musician who has successfully bridged the gap from child prodigy to inspired and mature artist.

Joshua Bell's 1995-96 season began with summer festival engagements in the United States and Europe, including the Hollywood Bowl, Tanglewood, Bath Festival, and London's Hampton Court Festival. Highlights of his North American orchestral engagements for this season included appearances with such orchestras as the Atlanta Symphony, Boston Symphony, Los Angeles Philharmonic, Indianapolis Symphony and the Minnesota and San Francisco Symphony Orchestras. In Europe, he appeared as featured soloist with the Netherlands Radio Orchestra on tour throughout Germany and Austria, in addition to concerts with the Orchestre de la Suisse Romande in Geneva and the Czech Philharmonic in Prague. Recital engagements include concerts at London's Wigmore Hall and major halls of New York, Connecticut, Virginia, Florida, Delaware, Iowa, Singapore and Hong Kong.

Joshua Bell received his first violin at the age of five and became seriously committed to the instrument by the age of twelve. His earliest training began with Mimi Zweig, professor at the Indiana University School of Music, and it was at Indiana University where he met the renowned violinist and pedagogue Josef Gingold, who became his beloved teacher and mentor.

Joshua Bell has performed with many of the world's leading orchestras, including the New York Philharmonic, Chicago Symphony, Cleveland Orchestra, Los Angeles Philharmonic, and major orchestras of Germany, France, Switzerland, England, the Netherlands, Spain, Belgium, Asia and Australia. He has worked with many conductors, including Herbert Blomstedt, Andrew Davis, Christoph von Dohnányi, James Levine, Leonard Slatkin, Juri Temirkanov and David Zinman.

Mr. Bell performs over 100 concerts each season worldwide, including concerto appearances, solo recitals and chamber music. He is interested in exploring the work of living composers and recently performed the world premieres of two pieces written for him: a violin concerto by renowned British composer Nicholas Maw, and *Air* for violin and piano by American composer Aaron Jay Kernis. Joshua Bell is unique among his peers in that he has begun composing his own cadenzas for major violin concertos. His cadenzas for the Brahms, Beethoven and Mozart concertos have received consistent praise from conductors and critics alike. He also enjoys chamber music collaborations and performs with close friends and colleagues, such as Pamela Frank, Steven Isserlis, Olli Mustonen, Jon Kimura Parker and Jean Yves-Thibaudet.

In 1987, Mr. Bell became the first violinist in over a decade to sign an exclusive recording contract with London/Decca records. Since that time, ten recordings have been released, the latest of which features the two Prokofiev Sonatas for violin and piano, with pianist Olli Mustonen. Some of Josh Bell's orchestral recordings include: the two Prokofiev Concertos with the Montreal Symphony and Charles Dutoit; the Tchaikovsky and Wieniawski Concertos with the Cleveland Orchestra and Vladimir Ashkenazy; and the Mendelssohn and Bruch Concertos with the Academy of St. Martin in the Fields and Sir Neville Marriner.

Joshua Bell has been featured on *The Tonight Show* with

Johnny Carson, CBS *Sunday Morning*, CNBC, and a 1993 *Live from the Lincoln Center* broadcast on PBS. He is one of the first classical musicians to be the focus of a music video, which has been broadcast on VH1, Arts & Entertainment and Bravo. He was the subject of a documentary film which was presented on BBC's *Omnibus*, and, most recently, he appeared on A & E's *Biography* of Mozart. Mr. Bell has been featured by *USA Today, New York, Vogue, Mirabella, Interview, Esquire* and *Strings* magazines.

Joshua Bell resides in New York City, and his other interests include basketball, tennis, baseball and golf, as well as chess and computers. He plays on an Antonio Stradivari violin dated 1732, which is known as the "Tom Taylor."

LINGUINI WITH BROCCOLI AND BAY SCALLOPS

Serves 4

This recipe is one of Josh's favorites. However, Josh lets it be known that his truly favorite dish is a gourmet hamburger (rare) with all the toppings. The below tasty recipe comes from a friend of the Bell family, Tako Dwyer, who lives in Springfield, MA. This dish is also quite popular in the kitchen of Josh's mother, Shirley Bell.

1 bunch broccoli (4 to 4½ cups)
¾ pound (12 oz.) linguine (al dente)
Butter
Salt to taste

Pepper to taste
2 teaspoons minced garlic
1 pound bay scallops
⅓ cup Parmesan cheese, grated

Cut broccoli into florets. Slice stem into ¼-inch slices. Blanch for 2 minutes in boiling, salted water, then drain and refresh in cold water.

Cook the pound of linguine until 'al dente' and then drain and toss with butter, salt and pepper to taste. Cover and keep warm.

Heat ¼ cup butter. Add 2 teaspoons of minced garlic. Sauté and then add the broccoli. Heat through. Add pound of bay scallops, ¼ teaspoon pepper and 1 teaspoon salt. Cook about 3 to 4 minutes. Spoon over the pasta and sprinkle with Parmesan.

Photo: LOUIS OUZER

LYNN BLAKESLEE, VIOLINIST

Lynn Blakeslee is professor of violin at the Eastman School of Music. She grew up in Los Angeles where she began studying the violin at the age of four. She studied with Sascha Jacobsen and then with Efrem Zimbalist at the Curtis Institute of Music where she graduated with a bachelor of music degree. A Fulbright grant took her to Vienna, where she received her diploma with high distinction. Her teachers there were Ricardo Odnoposoff and Sandor Vegh. In Europe, Ms. Blakeslee has been concertmaster at Theater an der Wien and was for many years a member of "Die Wiener Solisten." A recipient of the Martha Baird Rockefeller grant, she has given recitals in the major capitals of Europe, recorded for radio and television and for the Lyrinx label, and been soloist with such distinguished orchestras as the Vienna Tonkünstler, Vienna Chamber, Los Angeles Philharmonic, and the Philadelphia Orchestra. Before returning to the United States after 23 years abroad, Lynn Blakeslee served on the faculties of the Mozarteum in Salzburg, the Bruckner Conservatorium in Linz, the Musikschulwerk in Salzburg, and the Casals Festival in Prades, France.

During the summer of 1995, she was on the faculties of the Bowdoin Summer Music Festival in Maine and the Internationale Summer Academie at the Mozarteum in Salzburg .

Ms. Blakeslee maintains a European concert career as first violinist of the Mozarteum String Quintet. In summer of 1996 she returned for the seventh year to her own "Violin Workshop in Auerhof" in Upper Austria.

CHOCOLATE MOUSSE

Serves 6

Serve with whipped cream, cookies, and your imagination. SINFUL! --L.B.

8 oz. bittersweet chocolate
⅓ cup strong black coffee
5 egg yolks, beaten

5 egg whites, beaten
¼ to ⅓ cup rum, brandy or
    other liquor (Grand Marnier)

Melt chocolate with coffee—when melted, add thickly beaten yolks and cool. Add liquor, fold in stiffly beaten egg whites. Put into bowl and chill in refrigerator for at least 5 to 6 hours.

DARK CHOCOLATE BUNDT CAKE
Serves 10 to 12

This cake is courtesy of cellist Alita Rhodes, who is a member of the Santa Barbara Symphony.

1 package devil's food cake mix (*I use the store brand*)
1 small package instant vanilla pudding
½ cup warm water

½ cup oil
1 cup sour cream
1½ cups chocolate chips
4 eggs

Mix all ingredients together except chips. Beat for three or four minutes. Add chips. Bake in greased Bundt pan at 350 degrees for around 50 minutes. Let cool in pan 15 minutes, then remove (usually comes out easily). Enjoy!

Photo: CHRISTIAN STEINER

ANDRÉS CÁRDENES, VIOLINIST

Cuban-born violinist Andrés Cárdenes is a polished performer with ferocious technique and remarkable tonal subtlety who has garnered staggering international acclaim from both critics and audiences. After a recent performance of the Beethoven Violin Concerto with the Pittsburgh Symphony Orchestra (where he holds the position of concertmaster), under the direction of André Previn, Mark Kanny from the *Pittsburgh Post Gazette* wrote: "Cárdenes shone....The slow movement was especially beautiful with the combination of dignity and emotional expression that is one paradoxical element of classical style. Here the character of Cárdenes sonority was at its most affecting."

During the 1994-95 season, in addition to numerous appearances as both soloist and chamber musician, Cárdenes undertook several significant recording projects: the violin concertos of Ricardo Lorenz, Leonardo Balada, and Ramiro Cortes with the Orchestra of St. Luke's; the complete Beethoven sonatas with distinguished pianist David Deveau; and an album of rare short pieces for violin and piano with Chilean pianist Luz Manriquez, entitled *Peaceful Here* and released by Arabesque Recordings.

Since capturing the top American prize in the 1992 Tchaikovsky International Violin Competition in Moscow, Cárdenes has collaborated with such noted conductors as Lorin Maazel, Charles Dutoit, Eduardo Mata, André Previn, David Zinman, Leonard Slatkin, and Sergiu Comissiona, and has appeared with over 70 orchestras worldwide, including those of Pittsburgh, St. Louis, Los Angeles, Houston, Helsinki, Caracas, and Shanghai. A frequent recitalist, Cárdenes has performed in the world's major cultural capitals, including New York, Washington D.C., Paris, London, Mexico City and Moscow.

Cárdenes is currently artist-in-residence at Carnegie Mellon University and a member of the renowned Carnegie Mellon Trio which has performed extensively throughout the United States. Their recording of the Arensky and Tchaikovsky trios drew rave reviews and a Grammy nomination in 1991.

Cárdenes also has been an active teacher for fifteen years, beginning with his appointment to the faculty of Indiana University in 1979. A former student and protégé of the legendary Josef Gingold, he has continued the legacy and discipline of violin playing as professor of music at the Universities of Utah, Michigan, and Carnegie Mellon, and has given numerous master classes at Rice and Columbia Universities, among others. In November 1993, Cárdenes was appointed artistic director of Strings in the Mountains—a festival in Steamboat Springs, Colorado, which brings together some of the finest chamber musicians in the world to play and teach each summer.

A champion of contemporary composers, Cárdenes has premiered and recorded commissioned works ranging from pieces for solo violin to concertos from Ramiro Cortes, Ricardo Lorenz, Edgar Meyer, Fredrick van Rossum, David Canfield, and Mariana Villanueva. His most recent commission is a piano trio by renowned Spanish composer Leonardo Balada, which was premiered by the Carnegie Mellon Trio in September 1994. In December 1994, Cárdenes performed the world premiere of a concerto by Roberto Sierra with the Pittsburgh Symphony, conducted by James de Priest. Arabesque Recordings has recently released his recording of Saint-Saëns's sonatas for violin and piano with pianist Don Stevenson. Cárdenes can also be heard on the Delos, RCA, ProArte, Melodya, Enharmonic, Telarc, and Sony labels.

A Cultural Ambassador for UNICEF from 1980 to 1991, and an indefatigable spokesperson for the arts, Cárdenes has received numerous awards for his community and cultural contributions, most notably from Mayor Tom Bradley of Los Angeles and the Mexican Red Cross.

BLACK BEANS AND RICE
"Moros con Cristianos"
Serves 8

This is my favorite Cuban dish from my mother's culinary repertoire. Be careful with pressure cooker—they are very dangerous if not used properly—explosions can occur! Speaking of explosions, eat this dish with more than one person, as flatulence among the uninitiated can be pretty 'deadly'. --A.C.

1 pound dried black beans
10 cups water (approximately)
⅔ cup olive oil
1 large green bell pepper, sliced
1 large onion, finely chopped
4 garlic cloves, crushed or diced
4 tablespoons vinegar

1 tablespoon margarine
½ teaspoon oregano
1 bay leaf
Dash of cumin
4 teaspoons salt (or to taste)
½ teaspoon pepper
3 cups rice (cook just before serving)

Wash black beans, remove stony residue and other dirt. Put in pressure cooker* with water (water should not be more than 1 inch above bean level). Cook at high pressure for 30 to 45 minutes, allow pressure to go down.

In a large frying pan, sauté green bell pepper, onion and garlic in olive oil for 8 to 10 minutes. As the final step, add ingredients from frying pan along with vinegar, margarine, and spices into pressure cooker. Cook at lower pressure for 40 to 50 minutes, until ingredients are tender.

Cook rice as you would according to package instructions. Serve separately, but combine on plate as desired while eating.

*If a pressure cooker is not available, soak beans overnight in a large bowl, covering beans with 3 inches of water. Discard water, put beans into a 4-quart pot, then cover with 1 inch of water above bean level and bring to a boil. Cook on low heat for 1½ hours, covered. In a large frying pan, sauté green pepper, onion and garlic in olive oil for 8 to 10 minutes. Combine frying pan contents along with vinegar, margarine and spices into pot containing cooked beans. Simmer an additional 30 to 45 minutes, covered, until tender.

NORMAN CAROL, VIOLINIST

Norman Carol is a native of Philadelphia and a graduate of the Curtis Institute of Music, where he studied with Efrem Zimbalist.

Mr. Carol was concertmaster of the Philadelphia Orchestra for 28 years, beginning in 1966. He began his professional career at the age of 17, when he was invited to play with the first violin section of the Boston Symphony Orchestra. He first played with the Philadelphia Orchestra in its inaugural season at the Saratoga Performing Arts Center in 1966.

Mr. Carol has performed with many of the world's finest orchestras, in works such as the Britten, Hindemith, Barber, Conus, Harty, and Nielsen Violin Concertos. He presented the world premiere of the Stanislaw Skrowaczewski Violin Concerto in 1985, which was commissioned for Carol and the Philadelphia Orchestra. He has been on the faculty of the Curtis Institute of Music since 1979. Mr. Carol plays one of the world's finest violins: the ex-Albert Spalding Guarnerius (del Gesu), dating from 1743.

LEMON ORANGE CAKE

My wife's (Elinor) family recipe is from San Francisco....It has become a favorite from coast to coast - north, south, east and west! --N.C.

Lemon cake mix
1 package orange JELL-O
4 eggs, beaten
¾ cup oil
¾ cup water

TOPPING:
Lemon juice to desired
    consistency (about 1 to 2 lemons)
2 cups powdered sugar

Mix all ingredients in bowl, pour into greased pan (9 x 13-inch), bake at 350 degrees for 25 to 30 minutes. While cake is still warm, use a fork or toothpick gently to poke holes all over the top of the cake. Then, with a spoon, drizzle the topping all over the cake and let it run down and over the sides.

A variation of this same recipe can be to use orange cake mix and lemon JELL-O. Substitute fresh orange juice for the lemon juice with the topping; or half lemon juice and half orange juice.

Photo: SPECTRUM STUDIO

COREY CEROVSEK, VIOLINIST

Corey Cerovsek, born to Austrian parents on April 24, 1972, in Vancouver, Canada, now resides in Bloomington, Indiana. The world-renowned violin teacher, Professor Josef Gingold, accepted him as a student in August 1984. At the age of twelve, Corey became the youngest student ever at Indiana University. After only two and a half years of study, during which Corey also completed his Canadian high school diploma through correspondence courses, he graduated with a bachelor of science in music and mathematics, making him the youngest alumnus in the 170-year history of Indiana University. A year later, he received his master of music degree and completed all requirements for a master of mathematics degree. All of his degrees were earned with highest distinction, his having attained a perfect 4.0 GPA. Currently, he stands only a dissertation away from a coveted doctoral degree in music, having already completed all requirements for a doctoral minor in mathematics. He is also the youngest recipient of the School of Music's prestigious Performer's Certificate. For his academic achievements, Corey has four times been awarded Indiana University's Josef Gingold Violin Scholarship, funded by the Dorothy R. Starling Foundation.

Corey has studied piano with Enrica Cavallo-Gulli for the past seven years and made his piano debut in 1988, soloing with the Palo Alto Chamber Orchestra in California and on tour in Australia. Since then, he has also performed concerti on both instruments with great success throughout North America, Europe and the Middle East.

Corey has won countless other prizes and awards in regional, national and international competitions. A four-time winner of the Canadian Music Competitions, he was the only competitor to place first in both violin and piano for two consecutive years. In 1982, he received the highest marks of the entire competition (open to contestants up to age 36 in instruments and voice) and was chosen to play with the London (Ontario) Symphony Orchestra on a nationally-televised gala concert, conducted by Boris Brott. In 1985, he was awarded the Prix d'Honneur of the Prague International Radio Competition. In April 1988, he performed the Bruch G Minor Violin Concerto to great acclaim in a nationally-televised concert with the State Symphony Orchestra of Gottwaldov, Czechoslovakia.

Corey made his orchestral debut in 1981 with the Calgary Philharmonic. He has since appeared with many major orchestras, including the Israel Philharmonic, the Philadelphia, Cincinnati, St. Louis, Baltimore, Toronto, Montreal, and New World Symphony Orchestra. His total appearances include solo performances with over 90 symphony orchestras in North America and Europe, as well as many concerts with various community orchestras.

Corey has been profiled in numerous widely-read publications, including *People,* the *Chicago Tribune,* the *Detroit News,* the *Los Angeles Times, Newsweek, McLeans,* the *Globe and Mail, Saturday Night* magazine, *Reader's Digest, Music* magazine, the *Indiana Alumni* magazine, the *Strad* and *McCalls.* He has appeared twice on *The Tonight Show* with Johnny Carson and Jay Leno, eight times on Robert Schuller's "Hour of Power," on *The David Frost Show* in England, and on the PBS Special *Musical Encounters* (with Professor Gingold). He hosted another segment of this show in December 1993. Corey has been the subject of several mini-documentaries on television in the U.S., Canada, and abroad, including many times on CNN (world-wide and W5 (Canada).

Corey plays a violin made in 1908 by Stefano Scarampella.

CHICKEN AND MUSHROOMS IN BRANDY CREAM
Serves 2 to 3

I've always found this dish to be one of the tastiest in my mother's (Sophia Cerovsek) repertoire. I think that after I turned twenty-one she trusted me not only to cook without destroying the kitchen, but to handle these admittedly rich ingredients responsibly. Since then, I persuaded her to pass on the recipe and I consider it a handy standby—in my opinion, it seems a good deal more sophisticated when served, than it is difficult to make. --C.C.

¼ cup flour
1 teaspoon salt
½ teaspoon pepper
1 whole chicken breast, skinned, boned,
   and cut into bite size pieces
4 tablespoons butter
8 to 10 large mushrooms, trimmed,
   sliced lengthwise through stems*

¼ cup brandy
1 cup heavy cream
2 tablespoons ketchup
2 to 3 dashes Tabasco sauce
1 teaspoon cornstarch dissolved
   in 1 tablespoon water
Salt and pepper to taste
¼ cup minced parsley and
   extra parsley for garnish

Combine flour, salt and pepper. Coat chicken with flour mixture. Rub flour evenly into chicken pieces. Shake off excess.

Heat pan or wok, add 2 tablespoons butter. When sizzling, add chicken pieces and brown lightly on both sides. Remove with slotted spoon. Add remaining butter and mushrooms to pan or wok. Stir-fry over medium heat for about 5 minutes.

Remove mushrooms with slotted spoon. Remove pan from heat. Add brandy, cream, ketchup, Tabasco sauce, and dissolved cornstarch, blend together. Stir over low heat until sauce thickens. Add salt, pepper, chicken and mushrooms. Stir until reheated.

Serve with noodles, rice, or on toast or in patty shells. Sprinkle with parsley.

*Other vegetables like carrots and peas may be added—blanch in boiling water until bright green and slightly soft, but still crunchy.

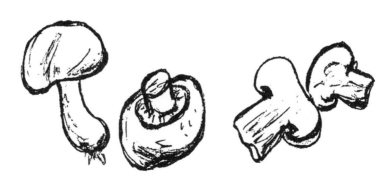

CREAM CHEESE PANCAKES
"Topfen-Palatschinken"
Makes 10, 8-inch pancakes

This recipe was passed along to me by my mother, who tells me she enjoyed it as she grew up in Austria every bit as much as I did back in our home. It's not exactly diet-conscious, but when my friends and I take a break from a few hours of chamber music reading, calories are usually the furthest thing from our minds! If you really are watching the waistline more carefully than this bunch of musicians, feel free to substitute any kind of low-fat cottage or curd cheese for the cream cheese and milk for the heavy cream. We've made the pancakes this way and they're still delicious!

PANCAKES:
2 cups flour
Dash of salt
2 eggs
2½ to 2¾ cups milk (depending on
    the size of the eggs)

FILLING:
½ cup butter
¼ sugar
8 oz. cream cheese
3 eggs (separate yolks from whites)
Lemon rind (1 small lemon)
½ cup raisins
½ cup heavy cream

Work the pancake ingredients into a fine batter and let rest for 30 minutes. Heat a large frying pan or griddle and grease the surface lightly. Pour enough batter into pan to cover surface evenly, brown on both sides, lift out and repeat.

Cream the butter with the sugar, add cream cheese, 2 egg yolks and the lemon rind. Fold in the beaten whites of 3 eggs and the raisins.

Spread filling on pancakes, roll up tightly and place into a buttered ovenproof pan. (The pancakes can be cut to fit the pan). Mix the remaining yolk with cream, pour over pancakes and bake at 350 degrees for about 20 minutes. Sprinkle with sugar and enjoy!

Photo: STEWART POLLENS

STEPHANIE CHASE, VIOLINIST

Described as "one of the violin greats of our era," Stephanie Chase is acclaimed worldwide for performances praised for their technical brilliance, tonal beauty and compelling artistry. With an extensive repertoire that ranges from Vivaldi to Bernstein and features several unusual concerti, Ms. Chase has been presented by numerous orchestras, including those of New York, Chicago, San Francisco, London, Vienna, Mexico City and Israel. Other engagements have taken Ms. Chase to the Far East, including an unprecedented tour of the People's Republic of China as soloist with the Hong Kong Philharmonic.

Ms. Chase began to concertize extensively at the age of nine after winning the Chicago Symphony Orchestra's Youth Competition, appearing on nationwide tours as recitalist and soloist with orchestras. Among her other competition prizes is the Bronze Medal from the 1982 Tchaikovsky International Competition in Moscow, at which the *New York Times* described her as "the most highly praised contestant." In 1987, Ms. Chase was chosen as a recipient of the prestigious Avery Fisher Career Grant.

Born in Illinois to musician parents, Stephanie Chase began her violin studies with her mother at the remarkably early age of two. Subsequent teachers include Sally Thomas of the Juilliard School and the renowned Belgian artist Arthur Grumiaux, who was her mentor during the last ten years of his life. Further studies in chamber music took place at the Marlboro Festival in Vermont, and Ms. Chase continues her interpretative studies with the esteemed American pedagogue William Lincer.

An unusually versatile artist, Ms. Chase is in demand as a period-instrument performer. She made musical history as soloist in a highly acclaimed first recording of Beethoven's masterful Violin Concerto and his romances, performed on Classical-era instruments. This recording, with the Hanover Band under the direction of Roy Goodman, includes original cadenzas composed by Ms. Chase; of it, *BBC Music* magazine states that it is "a perfect premiere...Stephanie Chase has a great sense of style, a matchless technique and flawless intonation..." This performance is available on Cala Records. Ms. Chase is also featured on Classical violin on Granada Television's historical overview, "Man and Music."

Stephanie Chase is a frequent guest of many chamber music festivals worldwide and appears regularly with the Boston Chamber Music Society. She performs on a modernized violin that was made by Petrus Guarnerius of Venice in 1742; her Classical instrument is Tyrolean and dates from the early to middle 18th century.

Ms. Chase makes her home in New York City with her husband Stewart Pollens, who is the associate conservator of musical instruments at the Metropolitan Museum.

LAMB SHANKS CHASE
Serves 4

As soon as there is a hint of coolness in the air, I find myself asking the butcher about the availability of lamb shanks. This homely dish is most appropriate when there is a nip in the air and the cook is not in a rush. It is best served over rice—such as Arborio white, short-grained rice—with a simple mesclun salad afterward. A merlot or even Beaujolais wine will accompany the lamb well.

Although I possess numerous cookbooks—most of them given to me as gifts—I generally cook by instinct, rarely following recipes or measuring ingredients. Cuisines encountered in the course of my concert tours are often an inspiration for my own recipes, although I sometimes cannot wait to return home so the insipid (and badly cooked) meals that generally accompany tour travel can be forgotten by preparing something really tasty (or by going out to one of New York's great ethnic restaurants). --S.C.

1 large, heavy skillet (cast iron is ideal)
1 dutch oven or deep casserole with cover
     (at least 3 to 4 quarts in size)
2 meaty lamb shanks (about 3 pounds)
Salt and ground pepper
Olive oil (optional)
1 leek (white part) washed, coarsely chopped
1 large Vidalia onion (or two medium),
     coarsely chopped (2½ to 3 cups)
5 cloves garlic, chopped

½ medium-sized sweet red bell pepper,
     coarsely chopped
3 plum tomatoes (fresh or canned),
     coarsely chopped (you may
     wish to peel and seed them first)
½ teaspoon each of thyme and rosemary
     (a bit more if fresh)
2 carrots, cut into about ½-inch pieces
⅓ cup balsamic vinegar (or red wine)

Remove any whitish membrane from lamb. Season lamb with salt and pepper. In heavy skillet, add a little vegetable oil and brown lamb shanks on high heat while turning frequently (it is not necessary to flour them first). Once browned, remove and place in casserole dish.

Using the same skillet containing drippings from lamb (add a little olive oil if needed), sauté leek, onion, garlic and red pepper until wilted, then add tomatoes, stirring frequently. Continue until tomatoes lose their firmness, then add thyme, rosemary, and a pinch more of salt.

Preheat oven to 400 degrees. Place carrots around lamb shanks in the casserole. Add vinegar (or wine) to sautéed vegetables, stir and pour mixture over shanks. Cover loosely with lid and place in oven.

Reduce heat to 375 degrees (or slightly less) and cook for at least 1½ hours (lamb will be more tender if it cooks long and slowly), turning shanks over and stirring vegetables every half hour or so. Vegetable mixture will cook down; if lid is on tightly there will be too much liquid. If it seems dry, add either a little water, vinegar or wine.

Remove meat from bones and cut into small pieces. Add to sauce from casserole and serve over rice.

Photo: PAUL HOFFER

VICTOR DANCHENKO, VIOLINIST

The highly esteemed Russian born violinist Victor Danchenko was for many years one of the Soviet Union's premier celebrated soloists. A former pupil of the legendary David Oistrakh, Mr. Danchenko was a Gold Medal winner in the Soviet National Competition and in the World Youth and Student Festival. Then he went on to covet a top prize in the Jacques Thibaud International Competition in Paris, winning the Ysaÿe Gold Medal. Oistrakh personally described Mr. Danchenko as "an excellent violinist who combines superb technical skill with genuine artistry, and a musician with a profound and comprehensive background." More recently, the noted critic Henry Roth described him as "a formidable virtuoso with all admirable musical instincts."

Danchenko's extraordinary artistry leaves no one unmoved. His performances always combine sincere emotion and lyrical mood with technical finesse and virtuoso skill. These special qualities, combined with his usual profound conception of the music and an ability to find the one tone best suited to the style and epoch of whatever he plays, bear witness that here truly is a most sensitive and deep artist always at work to deliver the best and most musically significant performance possible. Therefore, it is understandable that wherever Danchenko has performed, critics have continually lavished upon this exciting virtuoso the most remarkable adjectives to describe his playing. In fact, this has indeed been the case when he has performed throughout the major music capitals of Europe and North America, in such countries as Great Britain, Spain, Italy, and Switzerland.

In addition to his concert activity Mr. Danchenko is also a highly sought-after teacher. He was a member of the violin faculty of the prestigious Cleveland Institute of Music. He is now on the faculties of the Peabody Conservatory of Music and the Curtis Institute of Music.

RUSSIAN PIROGI

Makes 20 biscuits

1 pound ground beef
1 tablespoon olive oil
1 onion, chopped
1 clove garlic, chopped

20 Pillsbury buttermilk biscuits
Salt and pepper
1 egg

Heat 1 tablespoon olive oil. Sauté the onion and garlic for abut 5 minutes and season with salt and pepper. Add ground beef and cook until browned. Put aside. Roll out each biscuit. Place 1 tablespoon ground beef mixture in the center of each biscuit. Moisten the edge with cold water and fold over filling, forming a half moon. Press edges with the tines of a fork to seal.

Put on baking sheet. Mix egg with 1 tablespoon of water and brush top of each biscuit.

Preheat the oven to 375 degrees. Bake for 20 to 30 minutes (a longer time than instructions on biscuit package) until it attains desired crispness. They will have a nice golden top. Eat hot or cold.

VINAIGRETTE

Serves 4

Mr. Danchenko remarked in his recipe that "Vinaigrette" is a very popular and typical Russian vegetable salad. It is also cheap, plain, and delicious.

2 potatoes, not peeled
2 carrots
2 beets
2 kosher pickles, cut into chunks

½ cup sauerkraut
3 tablespoons light olive oil
Salt and pepper

Boil the potatoes, carrots and beets together until tender. Drain and set aside to cool. Peel ingredients and cut into cubes. Mix all the salad ingredients together in a bowl. Add salt, pepper and olive oil and mix. Sprinkle with parsley if you wish.

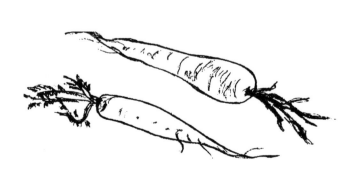

Photo: MAURICE DICTEROW

THE DICTEROWS, VIOLINISTS

Few families can boast the mass of talent that can be seen in the Dicterow family. Violinist Harold and concert pianist Irina are the parents of violinists Glenn and Maurice Dicterow and have had an influence on musical life in America for almost half a century. Harold has been principal second violin of the Los Angeles Philharmonic for over 47 years. His performances with the orchestra many times have taken him all over the world, performing in all the great music centers. His wife, Irina, was born in the Caucases Mountains of southern Russia to an Austrian baroness, studied piano at the Gresina University of Moscow, Canada, and later studied with Josef and Rosina Lhevinne at the Juilliard School. Irina often accompanied her husband and sons in concerts and recitals. Harold and Irina were married in 1944.

One of their talented sons, Maurice, is a family practitioner on staff at one of the community hospitals in the Los Angeles. He plays, in his "spare" time, with the Los Angeles Philharmonic, Glendale Symphony, California Chamber Symphony and in studio recordings.

Few contemporary violinists have been compared favorably with the fabled Isaac Stern, but that is the case with Glenn Dicterow. Dicterow, concertmaster of the New York Philharmonic, received high praise after a solo appearance with the Montreal Symphony Orchestra several years ago. A Canadian critic wrote, "Dicterow is not only a first-class violinist...but (also) a far-reaching soloist. He was able to draw more from the concerto than Stern does in his recording."

Glenn Dicterow made his debut with the Los Angeles Philharmonic at the age of 11 and performed with the New York Philharmonic at age 18. A graduate of the Juilliard School, his mentors included such legendary violinists as Isaac Stern and Jascha Heifetz.

In 1970, Glenn traveled to Moscow, Russia, for the prestigious Tchaikovsky Competition and came away with the Bronze Medal. Not long afterward, Zubin Mehta chose Dicterow as concertmaster of the Los Angeles Philharmonic, at age 27. After being named concertmaster of the Los Angeles Philharmonic, he moved to the same position with the New York Philharmonic four years later. He has held that position for nearly 18 years, performing concurrently as a featured soloist with leading philharmonic orchestras in the United States. Glenn Dicterow also performed for President Ronald Reagan during a state dinner at the White House for the late Indira Gandhi, prime minister of India.

Dicterow currently serves on the faculties of the Juilliard School and the Manhattan School of Music.

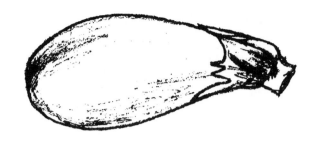

IRINA DICTEROW'S
"POOR MAN'S CAVIAR"

1 medium-sized eggplant
1 large can (28 oz.) of peeled whole tomatoes
1 medium-sized onion, finely chopped
1 clove of garlic, finely chopped

Juice of 1 small lemon or large lime
½ teaspoon each of salt and pepper
Light corn oil, Wesson brand,
    4 tablespoons or more

Bake whole eggplant at 350 degrees on a metal pie plate until inside of eggplant is soft, about 55 to 60 minutes. The eggplant will collapse slightly when soft. Cool eggplant, peel carefully, and cut into small pieces. Put into a bowl. Empty can of tomatoes (drained) into the bowl with the eggplant. Add chopped onion and garlic into bowl. Put lemon or lime juice, about 4 tablespoons, into bowl. Sprinkle salt and pepper into mixture.

Pour light oil, (about 4 tablespoons, or more) into a large frying pan. When oil is hot, carefully add the mixture of eggplant and lower the heat. The mixture needs constant stirring for smooth, creamy consistency. It may be necessary to add more salt, lemon, lime or Wesson oil, if mixture is too dry.

Cooking time is about 50 to 60 minutes or until mixture is perfectly blended and creamy-smooth. Serve on bread. Can be used as dip when cold.

LIME LEMON PIE

1 can Borden's Eagle-brand sweetened,
   condensed milk
Juice of 1 lemon plus enough
   lime juice to total ¾ cup
4 eggs

½ teaspoon cream of tartar
4 tablespoons white granulated sugar
10-inch 'ready made' graham
   cracker crust (comes with pie plate)

Empty the Eagle-brand milk into medium-sized china bowl. Squeeze lime and lemon juice, strain, put into same bowl. Separate eggs, adding yolk of eggs into milk and juice mixture, and put whites of eggs into a <u>smaller china bowl</u>.

Heat oven to 400 degrees and bake crust until it browns. Put pie crust into freezer to cool. Mix milk, juice and eggs to creamy consistency. Whip whites of egg, slowly adding sugar and cream of tartar until mixture is very thick. Pour contents of milk, juice and eggs into cooled pie crust. With a big spoon, spread whipped meringue over the top. Bake pie in 350 degree oven until meringue is slightly brown.

GLENN DICTEROW'S FAVORITE
SCOTCH SHORTBREAD

Makes 1 loaf

1 cup (½ pound) sweet butter
½ cup confectioners sugar

2 cups sifted all-purpose flour

Cream butter well. Beat in sugar gradually and slowly mix in flour. Turn dough onto dry baking sheet. Pat dough into ¾-inch thickness, and into the shape of a circle. Pinch edges of dough all the way around. Make fork marks on top of dough. Chill dough for at least 40 minutes.

Bake dough at 375 degrees for 5 minutes, then reduce heat to 300 degrees and bake for about 45 minutes or longer. Shortbread should be pale gold, not brown. While still warm, cut into wedges.

Photo: TANIA MARA (N.Y.C.)

PAMELA FRANK, VIOLINIST

American violinist Pamela Frank has established an outstanding international reputation across an unusually varied range of performing activity. In addition to her extensive schedule of engagements with prestigious orchestras throughout the world and her recitals on the leading concert stages, she is regularly sought after as a chamber music partner by today's most distinguished soloists and ensembles.

Some highlights of Ms. Frank's 1996-97 season include a tour of Germany with the Academy of St. Martin in the Fields, an American tour with the Baltimore Symphony and a series of family concerts in Japan with Yo-Yo Ma. She makes her first concerto recording for London/Decca, featuring two Mozart violin concertos, with the Tonhalle Orchestra in Zürich, following concert performances there.

Ms. Frank's schedule in 1995-96 included her first tour of Australia, performing with the orchestras of Brisbane, Hobart, Melbourne and Sydney; two tours of Japan for chamber, orchestral and recital engagements; and an American tour with the St. Petersburg Philharmonic Orchestra with conductors Yuri Temirkanov and Mariss Jansons, including a concert at Carnegie Hall. In February of 1996, she appeared on a "Live from Lincoln Center" telecast from Alice Tully Hall, featuring a performance of Schubert's "Trout" Quintet with Emanuel Ax, Rebecca Young, Yo-Yo Ma and Edgar Meyer. The concert coincided with a compact disc release of the "Trout" Quintet by the same artists on Sony Classical.

Ms. Frank's 1994-95 season included her New York Philharmonic debut, performing the Dvořák Violin Concerto with Leonard Slatkin conducting, as well as appearances with the Philadelphia Orchestra, the Orchestre de Paris, the Cleveland Orchestra, the Israel Philharmonic, and the orchestras of Baltimore, Detroit, Milwaukee, Phoenix and Seattle. As recitalist, she performed in London, Paris, Amsterdam, Vienna and New York, where she made her Carnegie Hall recital

debut. She also toured Germany as soloist with the Cincinnati Symphony and returned to Japan for a series of recital and orchestral appearances. At the Berlin Festival, Ms. Frank joined Peter Serkin and Yo-Yo Ma for a trio program and a performance of the Beethoven "Triple Concerto," with Daniel Barenboim leading the Berlin Staatskapelle. Among other chamber music projects, she also joined Mr. Ma for a series of duo recitals and for a tour with Emanuel Ax, Eugenia Zukerman and Paul Meyer in a program of works by Brahms and Schoenberg, including an appearance at Carnegie Hall.

Previous career highlights for Ms. Frank have included festival appearances at Tanglewood, Mostly Mozart, Ravinia, the Hollywood Bowl, Aldeburgh, Colmar, Prague, Grant Park, Riverbend and the Blossom Festival; recital tours with her father, Claude Frank, and with Peter Serkin, both of whom are her frequent collaborators; and concerts with such ensembles as the Vienna Chamber Orchestra under Sandor Vegh, the Boston Symphony Orchestra under Seiji Ozawa, and the Saint Louis Symphony under Leonard Slatkin. Her chamber music engagements have included frequent appearances with the Chamber Music Society of Lincoln Center and with Music from Marlboro on numerous tours. In May 1993, she participated in the Isaac Stern chamber music master classes at Carnegie Hall as part of a group of performer-teachers assisting Mr. Stern.

In the recording studio, Pamela Frank has embarked upon a Beethoven sonata cycle for MusicMasters Classics, with Claude Frank at the piano. The first volume featuring the Sonatas Nos. 1 and 9 ("Kreutzer"), has already been released to exceptional critical acclaim. The three Op. 30 sonatas on this album were just released in the fall of 1996. Ms. Frank has also recorded the Chopin Piano Trio with Emanuel Ax and Yo-Yo Ma for Sony Classical, and is featured on the soundtrack to the film "Immortal Beloved."

Born in New York City, Pamela Frank is the daughter of noted pianists Claude Frank and Lillian Kallir; the three frequently play chamber music both at home and before the public. Ms. Frank began her violin studies at age 5; after 11 years as a pupil of Shirley Givens, she continued her musical education with Szymon Goldberg and Jaime Laredo. In 1985, she formally launched her career with the first of her four appearances with Alexander Schneider and the New York String Orchestra at Carnegie Hall. A recipient of the coveted Avery Fisher Career grant in 1988, she graduated the following year from the Curtis Institute of Music in Philadelphia, where she now resides.

THANKSGIVING STUFFING FROM HELL
Serves *devilish* portions

I always get so carried away cleaning out the cupboards and refrigerator with this "non-recipe" that I often forget the bread cubes themselves! BEWARE!! --P.F.

At least 1 head of garlic, if not 3!!
6 onions, chopped
1 cup carrots, chopped
1 cup celery, chopped
1 bunch scallions, minced
Any spice you can find
'Tons' of currants
'Tons' of yellow raisins

Lots of pecans
Lots of slivered almonds
Lots of chopped walnuts
Pitchers of apple cider
6 eggs
3 more sticks of butter than you think
    necessary
Packages of stuffing: CUBED AND
    GRAIN

Sauté the first 5 items, and add more garlic!

Follow the directions on the back of your basic bags of CUBED AND GRAIN stuffing. Add more water and butter than indicated.

Add all other items, while adding apple cider and raw eggs for moisture.

STUFF your face, and the bird, if you must!

Photo: ROBERT PRESTON

ERICK FRIEDMAN, VIOLINIST

Erick Friedman made his New York debut at the age of fourteen and at seventeen began studying with Jascha Heifetz, with whom he recorded Bach's Concerto for Two Violins. Since then Mr. Friedman has been soloist with many of the world's major orchestras, including the orchestras of Boston, Chicago, London, New York, Philadelphia, Dallas, Berlin, Pittsburgh and Paris. He has appeared with the conductors Steinberg, Sargent, Ozawa, von Karajan, Leinsdorf, Mata and Previn. Friedman has an extensive discography, including many solo and concerto recordings on the RCA label. He is music director and conductor of Garrett Lakes Summer Music Festival in Maryland. As a pedagogue, Mr. Friedman has been associated with the North Carolina School of the Arts and the Manhattan School of Music. In 1983, he was appointed professor and artist-in-residence at Southern Methodist University, a post he held for five years until he joined the Yale School of Music faculty in 1989.

THAI FISH SOUP WITH COCONUT MILK
Serves 6

This dish is prepared for me by my student Ingrid Sweeney. --E.F.

¼ cup dried lemon grass
4 slices dried Laos root
3 cups fish stock or vegetable
  stock or water
2, 14 oz. cans of coconut milk
3 to 6 small red chilies, cut into rounds

3 scallions, minced
2 tablespoons chopped fresh cilantro
¾ pound whitefish fillets, cut into
  bite-size chunks
Juice of 2 limes

Simmer lemon grass and Laos root in 1 cup of stock or water for one-half hour. (Add more liquid to retain the 1 cup). Set aside. Simmer in different medium saucepan remaining stock with coconut milk **uncovered** for 5 minutes. Add chilies, scallions, cilantro and fish to pan; strain lemon grass and Laos mixture, adding liquid to the pan. Simmer all ingredients, except lime, in partially covered pan for 10 to 15 minutes until fish is cooked. Remove from heat.

Stir in lime juice. Taste, then add more lime juice if preferred. Serve hot.

© STEVE SANCHEZ, Bloomington Herald Times

JOSEF GINGOLD, VIOLINIST

Josef Gingold loved to tell the story of how he earned his first fee for playing the violin. Born in Brest, then the Russian Empire, in 1909, his first lessons were at age three from an older brother. A few years later, during World War I, the city was threatened by invading Germans, and the Gingold family were refugees fleeing the war. One night some Russian soldiers entered the refugee barracks that housed the family and many of their neighbors. They asked "Where is the young Josef who plays the violin?"

Everyone froze. Fearing the worst, no one would admit to knowing anyone by that name, but the soldiers laughed and explained that they were having a party and their old 'fiddler' couldn't play at all. They had heard that a young boy named Josef was really good and would he please come and play for them. At that point, a woman began to question the soldier in charge very intensely. Only when she was satisfied with their intention did she allow her little son, whom she shielded behind her, to get his violin and go with the soldiers , but she admonished, "He must be back by midnight!" The soldiers agreed.

The boy played and played and played. The soldiers would call out their favorite tunes, or sing a few bars, and the boy would pick up on it immediately. There was singing and dancing and drinking and merriment, and there was young Josef and his fiddle in the middle of it all. He even found himself helping the old fiddler with some fingering. Finally, not having the constitution of a Tsarist reveler, the boy literally started to fall asleep while he played. The soldier in charge looked at the time; it was 3 a.m. The bleary-eyed troops quickly passed the hat and presented the young fiddler with a hat full of money. Half asleep but not oblivious to the needs of his family and friends, Josef stated emphatically, "we don't need this, we need food!" In a flurry, the soldiers filled a sack with bread and fare from the party. They spirited the young child back to a terror-stricken barracks where Josef's mother was in a frantic state, certain that

she would never see him again. But there he was, fiddle tucked under his arm, with a sack full of food, and money besides. "Such a feast there was in the barracks that night on the delicacies brought by the soldiers," recalled Mr. Gingold many years later. "I knew then, for the first time, that I could make a living playing the violin."

Josef Gingold (1909-1995) was a violinist, teacher, and concertmaster without peer. A student of famed Belgian violinist, Eugène Ysaÿe, Gingold became a member of the NBC Symphony Orchestra under Toscanini, concertmaster of the Detroit symphony, and concertmaster of the Cleveland Orchestra under George Szell. He taught at the Cleveland Music School Settlement, the Meadowmount School (for 30 summers), and was a distinguished professor of music at Indiana University from 1960 until his death. He received many prestigious awards during his lifetime, the latest of which was the American Symphony Orchestra League's Golden Baton Award.

Mr. Gingold pressed several recordings for Columbia and RCA Records. A famous recording of the Kodály Duo for cello and violin was make during his tenure at Indiana University, with his close friend and colleague Janos Starker. His long list of students include many of today's top artists, including such names as Joshua Bell, William Preucil, Jaime Laredo, Philip Setzer, Miriam Fried, Andrés Cárdenes and Corey Cerovsek. He represented the United States as juror in many of the world's major violin competitions, including the Sibelius, Queen Elisabeth, Wieniawski, Paganini, Nielsen, Naumberg, Leventritt and Tchaikovsky competitions. He was founder of the Indianapolis Violin Competition in 1982 and played a major role in shaping the competition for future generations to come.

Mr. Gingold was a remarkable human being, loved by all who knew him. Mr. Gingold truly loved people, and of course, music and the violin.

DAVID'S SCRAMBLED EGGS PRESTO
Serves 4

The author, having grown up in Bloomington, Indiana, had the privilege of a warm and lasting friendship with Mr. Gingold. The author will always remember Mr. Gingold's inspirational and encouraging words, as well as his tremendous warmth and kindness, during his early years of study in Bloomington.

In 1995, the author had a conversation with Mr. Gingold at his home in Bloomington. While talking about Mr. Gingold's days with the Cleveland Orchestra, and at the same time looking at the hand-written egg recipe on paper, Mr. Gingold jokingly remarked in his deep gravelly voice, "David, don't you think the recipe looks too much like a Bruckner Symphony—much, much, much too long!?"

6 **large eggs**
½ **cup cottage cheese (4% fat tastes best)**
2 **tablespoons virgin olive oil**
⅛ **cup chives and/or scallions**
1 **clove garlic, crushed**

⅓ **cup button mushrooms, chopped**
Salt and pepper to taste
Parsley for garnish
Grated Cheddar cheese for topping

Scramble eggs in bowl, mix in cottage cheese. Heat olive oil on medium-high flame, in medium-large frying pan. A Teflon pan is best. (In a Teflon pan oil will not spread out evenly, but collect towards the center—so spread out the oil the best you can). When oil is hot, add chives and/or scallions, garlic and mushrooms.

Sauté several minutes, then add eggs to pan. Cook mixture, while constantly stirring, until eggs are cooked. The consistency may be slightly watery from the cottage cheese.

Garnish with chopped parsley and add a light sprinkling of Cheddar cheese.

Photo: EVA HAITTO

HEIMO HAITTO, VIOLINIST

Heimo Haitto was born in Viipuri, Finland in 1925. At the age of nine, he started to study the violin. Four years later, on February 24, 1939, he made his debut with the Helsinki Philharmonic Orchestra and immediately won the musical attention of Finland. In May of that year, Heimo traveled to London to participate in the international competition of the British Council of Music. Although the youngest competitor, Heimo won the 1939 prize—the biggest musical award in the world.

On his return to Finland, Heimo starred in a Finnish musical film "Pikku Pelimanni" (Little Fiddler), produced by the S. F. Films, which was enthusiastically received. In 1940, he appeared as soloist with the Stockholm Symphony and the Malmo and Oslo Philharmonic Orchestras. His success in these Scandinavian cities was sensational. After bombs destroyed his home in the early days of the Russo-Finnish war, Heimo embarked on a series of benefit concerts for Finnish relief, both in Finland and abroad.

Following that, Heimo came to the United States. He made his American debut with Eugene Ormandy and the Philadelphia Orchestra. Critics liked him and agreed that the predictions of Jean Sibelius, who was following Heimo's career with great interest, had come true.

Capping this came a contract with Paramount Studios, and the motion picture, "There's Magic In Music." Honorably discharged from the United States Army, after two and a half years of service, Heimo began concertizing again when World War II ended. Heimo played under contract with the NBC and Columbia Motion Pictures Studio Orchestra and five years with the Los Angeles Philharmonic, in addition to solo performances with the most important orchestras in the U.S.A., Canada, and Europe.

In 1962, he was concertmaster of the Mexico City Symphony Orchestra, while continuing concert touring to Finland and other European countries.

The next 10 years of Heimo's life were his "wandering years" in the United States, outside of music, as told in the book entitled *Viuluniekka Kulkurina* (Violinist as a Tramp). He returned to music in 1976, resuming a full schedule of teaching, concerts, chamber music, and conducting.

Owing to a serious bone accident and ill health, Heimo Haitto is at present writing his memoirs. The first book appeared in December 1976, the second in 1994, with more to follow.

KARELIAN MEAT STEW
(From Finland)
Serves 6

Heimo today is frugal and simple in his eating habits. We must bear in mind that we (Eva and Heimo) belong to the generation who suffered from scarcity, many times even lack of food during growing-up years because of the poverty of our families.

The Karelian Stew is a popular dish all over this Finland....Heimo wants to pay homage to the province where he was born and educated to be a musician, and then was sadly lost to a big neighbor. Viipuri was the music center of Finland; beautiful, cosmopolitan and charming, where all languages were spoken...it was rightly called "Paris of the North," now all ruined by the Soviets.

This is the original country recipe. These days, less tradition-bound town dwellers prepare variations of the recipe. Those who do not like pork can replace it, for example, with kidney, liver and heart, or merely beef. --Eva H.

1 **pound pork shoulder, all with bones, gristle and connective tissues included**	1 **large onion**
	15 **grains (peppercorns) pepper**
	2 **teaspoons salt**
1 **pound breast of beef (brisket)**	1½ **quarts water**
1 **pound shoulder of mutton**	

Rinse the meats. Cut them into pieces, about the size of eggs. Brown onion with the chunks of pork, beef and mutton, in a dutch oven or an iron skillet that has a lid. Sprinkle pepper and salt over meat, add water to pan, cover, and heat in oven at 300 degrees for 2 hours or longer.

Serve with boiled potatoes and other vegetables, according to preference.

HEIMO'S QUICK-LUNCH OF RAINBOW TROUT

Serves 6

This recipe is Heimo's own creation. In his present state of health, he has to avoid salt. He has always liked to drink milk, but those with lactose intolerance can replace milk with water in the recipe. We have an open-air market around the corner, open from 7 a.m. to 2 p.m. There we can buy fresh vegetables, fruit and eggs direct from the farms, as well as all sorts of fresh fish (lake, sea, also smoked); the variety is great. The rainbow trout are cultivated, as large as small salmon, filleted into halves, the bones removed. There are also huge sea salmon, up to one meter long, a kilo costing more than the "rainbow salmon," as we call it. We prefer the last mentioned—it is delicious!

About 1 pound of fleshy fresh
   rainbow trout, fillet (not salted)
3 large potatoes, peeled (7 cups)
1 medium onion, chopped (2 cups)
½ teaspoon pepper or to taste

1 fish stock cube (Knorr brand)
1 teaspoon dried dill
¼ cup fresh parsley, chopped
Salt to taste
1 quart of milk

Cut the flesh of the trout into pieces the size of sugar cubes. Do the same with the peeled potatoes. Place all the ingredients and spices, except for the fish, into a saucepan large enough to prevent sudden over boiling of the milk.

Put the saucepan on medium flame and watch carefully until the milk boils, stirring delicately. Turn down heat to very low, cover pan with lid, and let ingredients simmer until just tender (about 12 minutes).

Add fish and simmer an additional 8 to 10 minutes. Remove from the burner and let stand for 10 minutes, well-covered with lid.

While the broth is still hot, it is ready to be eaten, complemented perhaps with some rye bread. This recipe is adaptable to personal variations, if salt or stronger spicing is desired.

Photo: BEN SPIEGEL

SIDNEY HARTH, VIOLINIST/CONDUCTOR

One of America's most distinguished artists, Sidney Harth has gained a highly acclaimed international reputation as a violinist, conductor and educator. Mr. Harth's career took off with flying colors when he became the first American to be awarded the Laureate Prize in the Wieniawski Violin Competition in Poland, where he often returned for concert tours. He has served as concertmaster with the New York and Los Angeles Philharmonic orchestras under Zubin Mehta, the Chicago Symphony Orchestra under Fritz Reiner, with the Louisville Orchestra, and has performed concertos and been heard in recitals on five continents.

For several seasons, Harth was music director of the Jerusalem, Israel and Puerto Rico Symphony Orchestras. He also held the post of associate conductor of the Los Angeles Philharmonic and the Louisville Orchestra. Mr. Harth has had many guest conducting and solo engagements throughout the world, including performances in Spain, Israel, Canada, Mexico, Brazil, Great Britain, Russia and Yugoslavia, and with most of the leading orchestras in the United States.

He is a familiar figure at major summer festivals such as Aspen, Banff and Anchorage. He is now conductor of the Northwest Chamber Orchestra in Seattle, Washington.

Born in Cleveland, Sidney Harth began violin studies at the age of four and later attended the Cleveland Institute of Music, studying with Joseph Knitzer. After graduating with the highest honors ever bestowed by the institute, he moved to New York for advanced studies with Michel Piastro and Georges Enesco.

During his academic career, Mr. Harth was the Andrew W. Mellon Professor of Music at Carnegie Mellon University, where he also headed the department of music. For several seasons, he was director of the conducting program at the Mannes College of Music in New York and at the University of Houston. Currently, he is a professor of violin at Yale University and director of orchestral activities at the Hartt College of Music of the University of Hartford in Connecticut.

Sidney Harth records for Vanguard, Louisville Orchestra Series, Musical Heritage and Stradivari records.

PESTO OVER GREEN NOODLES
Serves 4

Pesto can be made with some variations, such as substituting walnuts or pecans for pine nuts. Try adding a little fresh cilantro with the basil leaves. Other hard cheeses such as Parmesan give the pesto an excellent taste.

1 **cup tightly packed, snipped**
    fresh basil
½ **cup snipped parsley**
½ **cup grated Romano cheese**
¼ **cup pine nuts**

1 **clove garlic**
¼ **teaspoon salt**
⅓ **cup olive oil**
Cooked and buttered
    green noodles, hot

Place all ingredients, except oil and noodles, in blender container. Cover container and blend until smooth. Gradually add olive oil, a teaspoon at a time, until mixture is of a soft-butter-consistency. Refrigerate until ready to use. Toss hot buttered noodles and one-half of the pesto together. Serve immediately. Pass around remaining pesto, additional Romano and pine nuts, if desired.

Photo: MARTY UMANS

IDA KAVAFIAN, VIOLINIST, BEAUX ARTS TRIO

The vast range of Ida Kavafian's versatility has gained her a truly unique position in the music world. Internationally acclaimed as one of the few artists to excel on viola as well as violin, Ida Kavafian's musical travels have taken her from solo recitals and orchestral appearances to chamber music, duos with her sister Ani, teaching, and a highly acclaimed career as artistic director.

With a repertoire as diverse as her talents, Ms. Kavafian has electrified recital stages throughout North America, the Far East and Europe. She has appeared as a soloist with leading orchestras both nationally and internationally, including the orchestras of New York, Boston, Pittsburgh, Detroit, Saint Louis, Montreal, Minnesota, Metropolitan (Tokyo), Hong Kong, Buenos Aires and London. Her commitment to contemporary music has led to many world premieres by composers as varied as Toru Takemitsu, who wrote a concerto for her, and jazz great Chick Corea, with whom she has toured and recorded. Her television credits include a solo feature on CBS *Sunday Morning*.

Since her founding membership in the legendary and innovative group TASHI over twenty years ago, Ida Kavafian's chamber music appearances have included many renowned festivals, including Santa Fe, Tanglewood, Ravinia, Mostly Mozart, and Spoleto (Italy and U.S.A.). She has toured and recorded with the Guarneri String Quartet and the Chamber Music Society of Lincoln Center, of which she was an artist member. She continues to perform regularly with her sister Ani Kavafian; together, their television credits include features on CBS *Sunday Morning* and NBC's *Today Show*. Also together, they have recorded Mozart, Moszkowski, and Sarasate for Nonesuch Records.

As a member of the acclaimed Beaux Arts Trio, Ms. Kavafian performs over 100 concerts a year in the major capitals throughout North America and South America, Asia and Europe. Their most recent release on Philips Classics is the Beethoven "Triple" Concerto with the Leipzig Gewandhaus Orchestra under Kurt Masur.

As artistic director, Ms. Kavafian has guided the success of two major festivals: Bravo! Colorado in Vail for seven years, and Music from Angel Fire in New Mexico for ten years. In addition to her own demanding concert schedule, she selects the programming and artists for over forty concerts each summer, including chamber music, jazz, popular, and orchestral.

Born in Istanbul, Turkey, of Armenian descent, Ms. Kavafian's family immigrated to the United States when she was three, settling in Detroit. She began her studies at the age of six with Ara Zerounian, continuing with Mischa Mischakoff, ultimately earning her master of music degree with honors from the Juilliard School, where she was a student of Oscar Shumsky. Ms. Kavafian made her New York debut at the 92nd Street "Y" with pianist Peter Serkin as a winner of the Young Concert Artists International Auditions. She was a recipient of the coveted Avery Fisher Career grant in 1988 and has served on the faculty of Yale University. Her violin is a J. B. Guadagnini, made in Milan in 1751, and her viola was made in 1987 by Peter and Wendela Moes.

Ms. Kavafian resides in Connecticut, where she and her husband, violist Steven Tenenbom, breed, raise, train, and show prize-winning champion Hungarian Vizsla dogs. The name of their kennel is "Opus One Vizslas."

ARMENIAN AROMATIC EGGPLANT
Serves 4 to 5

This is a recipe that I learned, then modified myself, from my mother, who is without a doubt the **World's Greatest Cook!** *Although she never let me help her prepare dinner when I was a child (she always sent me to my room to practice), I stole some peeks while growing up, then tried to duplicate the delicious dishes when I went to live on my own. I would inevitably have to call to consult with her, and we had some of my favorite conversations as a result. --I.K.*

2 medium eggplants, firm, dark and
  not too heavy
2 cloves garlic, finely chopped
Olive oil
2 fresh tomatoes, coarsely chopped

Salt and pepper
1 small (8 oz.) can tomato sauce
2 tablespoons (or to taste) balsamic
  vinegar (wine vinegar is also fine)
1 small (8 oz.) container plain yogurt

Wash, then peel off 3 strips of skin lengthwise down the eggplant, creating a striped effect. Slice eggplants into ½-inch thick pieces (rounds) and salt both sides, placing on paper towels to soak up moisture. Leave for about 45 minutes, turning over a few times, changing paper towels if needed.

While eggplant is 'sweating', sauté garlic in olive oil in medium-sized pan until lightly brown. Add fresh tomato, salt and pepper to taste, and cook over medium-low heat for about 10 minutes. Add tomato sauce, bring to a boil and simmer for another 8 minutes or so. Add vinegar and let simmer for 1 to 2 minutes, just until flavors blend. Let cool.

Preheat broiler. Place eggplant slices in single layer in a large broiling pan or on a cookie sheet and brush both sides with olive oil.

Place under broiler (about 5-6 inches from coil) and cook until evenly light to medium brown. Turn and broil other side. Eggplant should be tender when broiling is completed. *Although eggplant can be fried, I prefer broiling, since it absorbs less oil.* Let cool slightly.

In serving platter, place a single layer of eggplant, spoon yogurt on top almost to cover each individual piece, then add tomato sauce to cover well. Add layers until you have used up the eggplant. The top layer should be the sauce. Serve at room temperature.

One of the advantages of this recipe is that it can be made long ahead of time and kept at room temperature, or even the day before and refrigerated. Be sure to let it set at room temperature for at least an hour before serving. Enjoy!

Photo: BOB ADLER

RAYMOND KOBLER, VIOLINIST

Violinist Raymond Kobler, concertmaster of the San Francisco Symphony since 1980, previously served as associate concertmaster of the Cleveland Orchestra for six years. With that orchestra he appeared as soloist in violin concertos by Glazunov, Mozart, Prokofiev, Sibelius, Tchaikovsky, and Vivaldi. In 1977, he played in the Tippett *Fantasia Concertante on a Theme of Corelli,* under the composer's direction in a special performance before Britain's Prince Charles. Mr. Kobler also served as concertmaster of the Cleveland Orchestra in many recordings under Lorin Maazel and was a soloist at the sixtieth anniversary concert, televised nationally on PBS.

After earning a bachelor of music degree from Indiana University, Mr. Kobler joined the United States Marine White House String Quartet, concurrently earning a master of music degree at Catholic University. Upon leaving the service, he became concertmaster of the National Ballet Orchestra, then joined the National Symphony. Two years later, he was appointed assistant concertmaster of the Baltimore Symphony and appeared there as soloist on many occasions.

Mr. Kobler has been soloist with the San Francisco Symphony many times. The important premieres in which he has been featured include the first United States performances of Sir Michael Tippett's "Triple Concerto" (1981); the North American premiere of the recently discovered Violin Concerto by Janáček (1989);

and the U.S. premiere of the orchestral version of Lutoslawski's *Partita*, with the composer conducting (1991), a work he introduced to San Francisco in its version for violin and piano in 1986. Kobler was soloist in the premieres of chamber works by Elliott Carter and Ellen Taafe Zwilich; gave the first San Francisco Symphony performances of Haydn's Violin Concerto No. 1 (1986); Frank Martin's *Polyptique* (1993); Korngold's Violin Concerto (1994); and in January 1989, he gave the first symphony performances of Bruch's *Scottish Fantasy* since the work was introduced to audiences there in 1919. Other works which Mr. Kobler has performed with the symphony include concertos of Beethoven, Tchaikovsky, Walton, Prokofiev (No. 1), Bartók (No. 2), and Bach (A Minor). He has also been featured in the Bach Concerto for Two Violins (with Yehudi Menuhin), Berg's Chamber Concerto, Bartók's Rhapsody No. 1, and Chausson's *Poeme.*

Raymond Kobler's many other solo appearances include engagements with the Zürich Chamber Orchestra in Switzerland, with which he was featured in Bach's E Major Concerto and in that orchestra's first performance of *The Lark Ascending*, as well as in the European premiere of Glinski's *Rhapsody*.

Mr. Kobler is concertmaster of the Sun Valley (Idaho) Summer Symphony, where he has played and conducted the Beethoven Violin Concerto.

ARROZ CON POLLO
(Chicken and Rice)
Serves 4 to 5

This is one of the many Spanish dishes my mother used to prepare that was always a big hit in our household. My mother, who is Puerto Rican, is a gifted poet (published in two books and four anthologies), and just celebrated her 81st birthday. **Buen Apetito!** *--R.K.*

5 to 6 mixed chicken parts
Salt and pepper
2 tablespoons olive oil
2 cloves garlic, crushed
1 medium-sized green bell pepper, chopped
1 medium-sized onion, chopped
1 teaspoon capers
5 small green olives

2 sprigs fresh tarragon, chopped
2 cups water
2 cups seasoned chicken broth
2 cups white rice (long grain)
Pinch of saffron
Green peas (for garnish)
Red pimento (for garnish)

Skin and wash chicken. Pat dry with paper towel. Season well with salt and pepper. In a large skillet, heat 2 tablespoons of olive oil and cook chicken on medium heat, for 5 to 7 minutes. (Pan should be large enough to hold 4 cups of liquid, 2 cups rice and chicken).

Add to the chicken pieces crushed garlic, green pepper, onion, capers, olives and chopped fresh tarragon. Stir and cook for another 5 minutes.

Add water, chicken broth and rice, plus pinch of saffron. Stir and cover. Turn heat to low and cook for 15 minutes. Stir rice, turning over well and cook another 15 to 18 minutes. Check chicken for doneness. To serve, pour onto a large platter and garnish with cooked green peas and slices of red pimento.

Photo: CHRISTIAN STEINER

ISABELLA LIPPI, VIOLINIST

Violinist Isabella Lippi, whose playing has been described as "...flawlessly shimmering and captivating with warmth and urgent skill" (*Washington Post*, November 1992, Kennedy Center debut), began performing in public at the age of 10 when she toured with the Haag-Leviton Suzuki Performing Group and went on during that year to perform with the Chicago Symphony Orchestra as winner of the Chicago Symphony Youth Concert Auditions. At 17, Ms. Lippi won the first prize in the Illinois Young Performers Competition when she performed as finalist with the Chicago Symphony Orchestra under Maestro Hugh Wolff. After appearing with the Debut Orchestra in Los Angeles performing Tchaikovsky's Violin Concerto, the *Los Angeles Times* critic wrote that she "...exhibited flawless bow control, dazzling listeners with her technical polish and her clean, articulate playing....Her expressive lyricism in the cantabile playing proved captivating."

The 1993-94 season found Isabella Lippi in Spain, where she was the soloist in the Mendelssohn Violin Concerto with the Orquestra Sinfonica de Bilbao and Maestro Theo Alcantara. In the U.S., she performed the Brahms Violin Concerto in New Orleans with the Louisiana Philharmonic and a recital in West Palm Beach, Florida. In January of 1994, Ms. Lippi was featured in a new CD which contains the only solo work for violin and the complete works for violin and piano by Miklos Rosza.

In January 1993, Isabella Lippi made her New York City recital debut at the 92nd Street Y's Tisch Center for the Arts. Other important debuts during the 1992-93 season included recitals at the Kennedy Center for the Performing Arts' Terrace Theater and in the Rising Artists Series as part of the Ravinia Festival. With orchestra, Ms. Lippi has appeared as soloist with the Tulsa Philharmonic, the New World Symphony under Maestro Stanislaw Skrowaczewski, the St. Louis Symphony, the Phoenix Symphony, and the symphonies of New Orleans, San Diego and Waterloo-Cedar Falls,

Iowa. Isabella Lippi appeared in the 1988-89 season with the Moscow Symphony during a Latin American tour in a concert which was broadcast on Mexican National Television; eight concerts throughout Mexico with the Summer Festival Orchestra of the Mexico City Philharmonic; and with the Mexico City Philharmonic, playing concertos by Mozart, Mendelssohn and Sibelius. In addition, she performed as soloist with the Mexico City Philharmonic in a "Tribute to Henryk Szerying," under the director of Enrique Batiz, in a program which was broadcast on Mexican National Television.

In the spring of 1989, Isabella Lippi won the St. Louis Symphony Young Artist Competition, so impressing Maestro Leonard Slatkin that for the first time in the fifty-five year history of the competition the winner, Ms. Lippi, was invited to perform with the symphony in subscription concerts under Maestro Slatkin. The great success of these concerts in May 1989 was reflected in the headline of the *St. Louis Post-Dispatch* which declared "Lippi A Standout, Even Among Virtuosos."

In 1986, Ms. Lippi won the highest honors in the National Foundation for Advancement in the Arts Talent Search and has performed in many cities throughout the United States in events sponsored by that group. She performed at the Kennedy Center in Washington, D.C., after being named a Presidential Scholar in the Arts. She won first place in the 1986 WTTW Young Performers Competition, in a performance with the Chicago Symphony, which was broadcast in the 1988 Young Musician's Foundation National Debut Competition in Los Angeles.

Isabella Lippi was a featured artist on the McGraw-Hill Young Artist series on radio station WQXR in New York, the Mostly Music Series on WNIB in Chicago, KFAC's "Sundays at Seven" in Los Angeles, and in a nationally distributed educational program entitled "Encounters."

Born in Chicago in 1968, Isabella Lippi's teachers have included Robert Lipsett in Los Angeles, Dorothy Delay at the Juilliard School, and Almita and Roland Vamos in Chicago.

RISOTTO WITH VEGETABLES
Serves 4

This recipe was given to me by my Italian aunt who lives in Lucca (a small town outside Florence, Italy). --I.L.

The risotto recipe of Ms. Lippi is quite tasty, but may require some extra 'practice time' to perfect. One must make the rice absorb small doses of broth until the rice swells and becomes firm, yet is tender and creamy.

1 cup Italian Arborio rice	1 medium carrot, cut into small rounds
1 small onion, very finely sliced	4 to 5 cups chicken broth
2 tablespoons extra virgin olive oil	Parmesan cheese
1 medium zucchini, cut into small rounds	Basil or parsley, finely chopped

Over medium heat, brown the very finely sliced onion in oil, adding a few drops of water. Add cut up zucchini and carrots**.** Cook for about 10 minutes.

In the meantime, heat chicken broth in separate pan to near boiling. Add the rice to the vegetables. Gently stir rice several minutes until it begins to brown slightly, then start to add the hot chicken broth, ½ cup at a time. Stir constantly until rice absorbs all the broth. Continue stirring and adding broth ½ cup at a time, or slightly less towards the end, until the rice becomes tender. The whole process should take about 30 to 35 minutes. The texture of the rice should be creamy, but firm. Add salt and pepper to taste.

Immediately before serving, sprinkle on finely chopped fresh basil or parsley. Sprinkle abundantly with Parmesan cheese and serve hot.

For a variation, substitute 2 oz. dried European mushrooms for the vegetables and add ¼ cup dry sherry to the chicken broth.

ALBERT MARKOV, VIOLINIST/COMPOSER

Albert Markov, violinist, composer, teacher and conductor studied at Kharkov and Moscow conservatories under Leschinsky and Yankelevich.

After winning the Gold Medal in the Queen Elizabeth Competition in Brussels, he concertized extensively. Composer Aram Khachaturian wrote in 1966:

"*Albert Markov's activities have had many facets. He is a violinist, teacher and composer. In all spheres of actions he shows a remarkable talent. As a violinist, he is undoubtedly one of our best. As a teacher, he has trained excellent violinists. As a composer, he is remarkable in the originality of his compositions. In summary, Albert Markov is an outstanding musician.*"

After his immigration to the United States in 1975, Albert Markov quite literally burst upon the Western World when he made his sensational debut with the Houston Symphony in May 1976, which prompted the *New York Times* reviewer to write: "The audience roared approval, coming to its feet for three standing ovations, Mr. Markov 'wowed' them with dazzling pyrotechnics."

Following outstanding performances with symphonies and a solo appearance at Carnegie Hall in New York, Markov performed at the Kennedy Center in Washington, D.C., and played to great media acclaim in concert halls in Chicago, Los Angeles, Detroit,

Philadelphia, Houston, Toronto, Montreal and other cities in the U.S., Canada, Mexico and Europe. Leighton Kerner of the *Village Voice*, echoed many other critics when he said, "A fire-eating technician, it was obvious to me that here was a musician of an artistry more powerful than most."

After almost 20 years of absence on the Russian concert stage, Markov returned triumphantly again to Moscow in May, 1994.

His recordings are on Sunrise, Melodia and Musical Heritage labels. His compositions published by Muzica (Russia) and G. Schirmer (U.S.A.) are sonatas for solo and duo violins, three rhapsodies, caprices and others. His recent works are the "Formosa" Suite for Violin and Orchestra, the Violin Concerto (both recorded by Markov with the Russian National Orchestra on the Sunrise label) and the Chamber Symphony.

During the past few years, Markov has been the music director and conductor of the Rondo Chamber Orchestra, regularly appearing both as a soloist and conductor with this orchestra.

Albert Markov is a member of the violin faculty at the Manhattan School of Music. His books *Violin Technique* and *Little Violinist,* published by G. Schirmer, have been a worldwide recognized violin method.

BEET BORSCHT

Serves 6

This delicious borscht recipe comes from master chef Matthew Everson. It has a wonderful flavor; with the combination of white and black pepper giving the borscht a spicy edge to the taste. It may be enjoyed either hot or cold.

5 medium beets, peeled and chopped	2 medium-large onions, quartered
2 medium potatoes, peeled and chopped	and finely sliced

Cover above ingredients with water and bring to a boil, then reduce heat and simmer for 15 minutes.

1 tablespoon vegetable oil	½ teaspoon black pepper
5 cloves of garlic, minced	½ teaspoon white pepper
½ head of green cabbage, shredded	¼ teaspoon ground coriander
½ cup red wine	1 teaspoon salt
2 teaspoons dried mint	Parsley and green onions (for garnish)

Heat a large skillet and sauté for several minutes together the above, then add to the soup. Simmer all for an additional one-half hour and serve with chopped parsley and green onions sprinkled on top.

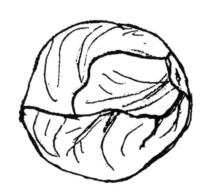

Photo: CHRISTIAN STEINER

ALEXANDER MARKOV, VIOLINIST

Alexander Markov is a distinguished recitalist and orchestral soloist in Europe and North America.

Highlights of recent seasons include performances at the Vienna Musikverein; a tour of the Far East, including performances in Japan, Korea, Hong Kong and Taiwan; concerts in France, Italy, Finland, Portugal and Germany; a United States tour with Sergiu Comissiona and the Jerusalem Symphony Orchestra; his New York debut recital at Carnegie Hall; appearances with Christoph Eschenbach conducting the Mostly Mozart Festival Orchestra at Avery Fisher Hall; two recitals at the 92nd Street Y, the most recent of which was comprised of the complete Paganini Caprices; and concerts with the symphony orchestras of Baltimore, Houston, San Diego, Milwaukee, Edmonton and Seattle.

Mr. Markov's recent recording of the twenty-four Paganini Caprices, Op. 1 (Erato) was released on compact and video disc, (directed by the famed film director, Bruno Monsaingeon). The first video disc to be made of the complete opus, the performance has been televised in France, Germany and Luxembourg, and is scheduled to be televised in England, Switzerland and Italy. Other recordings include the two violin concertos of Paganini and "Encore," a program of short violin pieces.

He was the winner of the Gold Medal in the Paganini Competition, Avery Fisher Concert Grant, Los Angeles National Debut Competition, Waldo Mayo Award and Juilliard Competition.

Born in Moscow in 1963, Alexander Markov began violin studies with his father, concert violinist Albert Markov and immigrated to the U.S. with his parents in 1976.

BAKLAVA
Makes about 30 pieces

This fine recipe comes again from master chef Matthew Everson.

1 pound unsalted butter
1 pound walnuts
1 heaping tablespoon cinnamon
½ teaspoon nutmeg
¾ cup granular sweetener

1 pound phyllo pastry sheets
2 cups light honey
1 cup water
2 teaspoons orange blossom water
Chopped pistachios (for garnish)

Gently melt the butter in a saucepan. Do not boil. In a food processor, coarsely chop the walnuts with the cinnamon, nutmeg and granular sweetener. Brush a 8 x 14 x 2-inch pan with some melted butter, and layer eight phyllo pastry sheets, one at a time, brushing each with butter. Sprinkle a thin layer of the walnut mixture. Continue adding the walnut mixture every three phyllo layers until used up. Make sure there are at least six layers of phyllo on the top of all. Freeze for about one-half hour.

Remove and cut into triangle servings with a sharp knife. On the lower rack, have a tray partially filled with water. In a preheated 325 degrees oven, bake uncovered on the center rack for approximately 2 hours, or until golden brown. Remember to keep water in the lower pan during baking.

In a saucepan, combine and bring to a near boil the honey, water, and orange-blossom water. Simmer very gently for 15 minutes, then let cool. When baklava is baked, remove from the oven and immediately pour the COOL syrup over it.

Garnish with chopped pistachios. Serve at room temperature.

Photo: MATTHEW GILLIS

YURI MAZURKEVICH AND DANA POMERANTS-MAZURKEVICH, VIOLINISTS

Dana Pomerants-Mazurkevich and Yuri Mazurkevich are brilliant representatives of the Soviet violin school, and they both are outstanding pupils of the legendary David Oistrakh, with whom they studied at the Moscow Conservatory for eight years.

Yuri and Dana met and married in Moscow, while studying at the Conservatory. Later, after graduating from Moscow Conservatory, they became faculty members of the Kiev Conservatory and concertized extensively as soloists and as a duo within the U.S.S.R., as well as abroad.

While living in Soviet Union, Dana won prizes in the J. S. Bach International Competition and the George Enesco Contest of violinists, while Yuri received his laureate diplomas in Helsinki, Munich and Montreal.

In 1975, the Mazurkevichs emigrated with their daughter from the Soviet Union to Canada; shortly afterward they joined the faculty of music at the University of Western Ontario. In 1985, Yuri was appointed a professor of violin at Boston University.

Their duo playing, summer teaching and other performing activities include their presence at the Victoria International Festival and Johannesen International School of the Arts in Victoria, Canada.

During their stay in Canada, Yuri and Dana made their highly successful debut as a violin duo in Switzerland, West Germany, Italy, U.S.A., Canada, France, England, Belgium, Australia, Mexico and Hong-Kong.

The Mazurkevich Violin Duo has to its credit many radio and television performances for BBC, CBC, ABC (Australia), Radio France, Radio Moscow, Sender Freies Berlin and many others.

Both artists are recorded on the Melodya, Masters of the Bow and S.N.E. labels.

PLUM CAKE
Makes 16 to 18 servings

Plums are very popular in Russia, therefore plum cake is also a popular dessert. This recipe brings back memories from my childhood days in my native Russia. --D.M.

3 cups sifted flour	½ cup butter
1 cup sugar	½ cup sour cream
3 teaspoons baking powder	4 egg yolks, raw
Rind of 1 lemon (yellow part only)	1¾ to 2 cups plum jam

Combine all dry (first 3) ingredients and rind of lemon together. Cut in butter with pastry blender or knife. Mix sour cream and 4 egg yolks together and add to dry ingredients and working in with a fork. Form into a ball with wax-paper and place in the refrigerator for 1 hour to cool.

Remove dough from refrigerator and divide into halves. Put one part of dough in freezer for an additional 1½ hours. Roll out other part on a floured board to approximately the size of the pan (9 x 14-inch) and put in greased 9 x 14-inch pan, spreading the dough with your fingers to fit the pan. Spread plum jam over dough surface, cover with some wax-paper and return to refrigerator until ready to use. When the other piece of dough is ready, take out of the freezer, remove wax-paper and break up coarsely with a fork and spread over jam. Let pan warm to room temperature before baking.

Preheat oven and bake at 350 degrees for 35 to 45 minutes or until golden in color.

Photo: J. HENRY FAIR

ROBERT McDUFFIE, VIOLINIST

Robert McDuffie is one of America's finest young violinists. Excelling in a career that encompasses concerto appearances, solo recitals and chamber music, Mr. McDuffie is widely known not only for his remarkable interpretation of traditional repertoire but also for his enthusiasm, interest and desire to discover and champion important contemporary works.

Mr. McDuffie performs over 100 concerts worldwide each season. He has appeared as soloist with many of the world's finest symphony orchestras: Chicago Symphony, Philadelphia Orchestra, San Francisco Symphony, Montreal Symphony, Pittsburgh Symphony, St. Louis Symphony, Houston Symphony, Dallas Symphony, Atlanta Symphony, Baltimore Symphony, Cincinnati Symphony, Los Angeles Chamber Orchestra, and the St. Paul Chamber Orchestra, as well as with the Orchestra Teatro La Scala, Santa Cecilia Orchestra, Moscow State Orchestra, Prague Chamber Orchestra, Danish National Radio Symphony Orchestra and the Czech Philharmonic. He has had the privilege of working with such conductors as Christoph Eschenbach, Charles Dutoit, Leonard Slatkin, Herbert Blomstedt, Yoel Levi, Christof Perick, Libor Pesek, Sergiu Comissiona, Vaclav Neumann, Jiri Belohlavek, Hugh Wolff, Jorge Mester, Lawrence Foster and James DePriest. With his devoted colleague Yehudi Menuhin as conductor, Mr. McDuffie has made tours in the United States with the Warsaw Sinfonia and in Europe with the Netherlands Chamber Orchestra.

Mr. McDuffie's 1994-95 concert season began at the Aspen Festival Orchestra in a performance of William Schuman's Concerto for Violin. In July, he played the Bernstein *Serenade* with Hugh Wolff and the Grant Park Festival Orchestra. In August, pianist Misha Dichter, Ralph Kirshbaum, cellist, and Mr. McDuffie created a stir with stellar chamber music collaborations at both the Aspen and Caramoor Music Festivals.

In September, Mr. McDuffie traveled to Rumania for a series of engagements with Sergiu Comissiona and the Bucharest Philharmonic, as well as a recital with pianist Ursula Oppens. In October, he toured South America with Michael Tilson Thomas and the New World Symphony in performances of the Tchaikovsky Violin Concerto, Bernstein Serenade and Barber Violin Concerto. Additional orchestral engagements include the San Francisco Symphony, Atlanta Symphony, debut with the National Symphony Orchestra, St. Paul Chamber Orchestra, Los Angeles Chamber Orchestra, Jacksonville Symphony, Pacific Symphony, Charlotte Symphony and Rhode Island Philharmonic, among others. In March, Mr. McDuffie gave recitals in numerous cities throughout Italy.

Robert McDuffie is well recognized for the enduring appeal he holds for American composers of our time. Composers such as Samuel Barber, Leonard Bernstein, David Diamond, William Schuman and Gian Carlo Menotti sought out McDuffie to perform their music. In 1992, Mr. McDuffie performed the world premiere of Stephen Paulus's Violin Concerto No. 2 at the Aspen Music Festival to honor his former teacher, Dorothy Delay, on the occasion of her 75th birthday. Along with bass-baritone Samuel Ramey and cellist Carter Brey, he recently organized the world premiere performance of Mr. Paulus's *The Long Shadow of Lincoln*, written to honor the 85th birthday of Justice Harry A. Blackmun. Mr. Diamond dedicated his Second Violin Sonata to Robert McDuffie, and in 1991, Mr. McDuffie performed at La Scala in celebration of Menotti's 80th birthday—an engagement specifically requested by the composer.

Mr. McDuffie's debut recording for Angel, the William Schuman Concerto for Violin and Leonard Bernstein's *Serenade*, earned him a 1990 Grammy Award nomination. His first recordings for Telarc will be Viennese works by Kreisler, Lehar and Strauss with Erich Kunzel and the Cincinnati Symphony, and the Cincinnati Pops, followed by the Barber Violin Concerto with the Atlanta Symphony conducted by Yoel Levi.

A native of Georgia, Robert McDuffie has been profiled for NBC's *Today Show*, CBS *Sunday Morning*, PBS's *Charlie Rose Show* and the *Wall Street Journal*. He has performed four private recitals at the request of his close friend Justice Harry A. Blackmun and the United States Supreme Court and in 1992 was recognized as an outstanding Georgian for his contribution to the arts by Georgia's Governor Zell Miller. Mr. McDuffie is a member of the Board of Directors for the Harlem School of the Arts, where he also serves as chairman of the artistic committee. He currently resides in New York City with his wife, Camille Taylor McDuffie, and their children, Eliza and Will.

CHEESE KRISPIES

Makes about 45, 1¼-inch balls

This family favorite recipe was graciously supplied by Camille McDuffie, Robert's wife. It makes for a wonderful appetizer or the perfect afternoon snack.

8 oz. sharp Cracker Barrel
   Cheddar cheese, grated
2 sticks softened butter
2 cups flour

1 teaspoon salt
Dash of Tabasco
¼ teaspoon red pepper
2 cups Rice Krispies

Grate Cheddar cheese in food processor. Work together all ingredients, except for cereal. Add Rice Krispies. Pinch off small balls and press with fork onto non-greased pan. Bake at 300 degrees for at least 30 minutes or until golden brown on tops.

Photo: VIRGINIA SCHMIDT

YEHUDI MENUHIN, VIOLINIST/CONDUCTOR

Yehudi Menuhin was born in New York of Russian Jewish parents and made his violin debut at the age of seven with the San Francisco Symphony in Lalo's *Symphonie Espagnole*, following this a year later with a recital in New York. By the time he was eleven, he had made his historic debuts in Paris and shortly after at Carnegie Hall, at twelve, in Berlin and at thirteen, in London, thus launching himself at an early age on a career that was to take him all over the world for the ensuing decades, playing with all the leading conductors and orchestras. Alongside his renown as a great musician, Lord Menuhin is equally recognized for his committed humanism, exemplified by his interest in and work for the young, for international understanding, and for any of the many other causes he finds close to his synoptic mind and generous spirit.

It was on his first visit to India in 1952, at the invitation of Prime Minister Pandit Nehru with whom he founded a lasting friendship, that he met Ravi Shankar, developing a deep admiration for both him and Indian music. Subsequently they gave many concerts together, from which came their records which sold millions of copies. He donated all the proceeds from the concerts given on his tours of India to charity. In 1960, he was awarded the Nehru Peace Prize for International Understanding. Some thirty years later, in 1992, he was honoured with the title of Ambassador of Goodwill to UNESCO. In 1995, Spain awarded Lord Menuhin the 'Gran Cruz de la Orden del Merito Civil'.

In recognition of the many concerts he gave for the Allied Forces during World War II, flying over from America whenever he could find space in a military plane, Yehudi Menuhin was awarded numerous honours, only a few among which were the Legion d'Honneur and the Croix de Lorraine from France, the Order of Merit from Germany, the Ordre Leopold and the Ordre de la Couronne from Belgium, and from England the Royal

Philharmonic Society's Gold Medal. Queen Elizabeth II bestowed a knighthood on him and gave him the Order of Merit; in 1993, Her Majesty's Government conferred a Life Peerage upon him. He holds honorary doctor of music degrees from 27 universities in different countries, including those of Oxford, Cambridge, St. Andrew's and the Sorbonne as well as being a Freeman of the cities of Edinburgh, Bath, Reims and Warsaw and holding the Gold Medals of the Cities of Paris, New York and Jerusalem. Yehudi Menuhin was also the first Westerner to be made an honorary professor of the Beijing Conservatory in recognition of his concerts in China and of his endeavours in helping many young Chinese violinists to continue their studies in the West.

In 1963, Lord Menuhin achieved one of his greatest ambitions, that of creating a boarding school for young promising musicians. In 1977, he founded the International Music Academy for young graduate string players in Gstaad, Switzerland, the site of his annual Menuhin Music Festival, now in its 38th year, for which he was awarded Swiss citizenship.

Yehudi Menuhin is president and associate conductor of the Royal Philharmonic Orchestra and of the Halle Orchestra, principal guest conductor of the English String Orchestra, principal guest conductor of the Warsaw Sinfonia, and president and principal conductor of the Philharmonia Hungarica.

Yehudi Menuhin made his first record when he was twelve; a year later he began his long association with His Master's Voice/EMI, with which he continued to record. In addition, he has recorded for Deutsche Grammophon (The complete Beethoven sonatas with Wilhelm Kempff) and conducted numerous orchestral works for Philips, Virgin, Nimbus and other labels. A great number of his early recordings were reissued on compact disc on the occasion of his 75th birthday in

1991. Films made in Russia, U.S.A., Canada, France and Hungary, as well as various video recordings, which have already been issued or are scheduled for future release, complete his musical ventures thus far. He has achieved wide success with his autobiography *Unfinished Journey*, *Menuhin Music Guides*, his *The Music of Man*, which accompanies the television series of the same title, and numerous other publications, including two volumes of *Conversations with Menuhin* and *Life-Class, a Collection of Exercises for Mind and Body.*

YEHUDI MENUHIN'S AIGO BOUIDO
(Garlic Soup)
Serves 6 to 8

While enjoying your first bowl of garlic soup, you might never suspect its ingredients. Because the garlic is boiled, its after-effects are at a minimum, and its flavor becomes exquisite, aromatic, and almost undefinable. Along the Mediterranean, "Aigo Bouido" is considered to be very good indeed for the liver, blood circulation, general physical tone, and spiritual health. A head of garlic is not at all too much for 3 pints of soup. For some addicts, it is not even enough. --Y.M.

1 **separated head of garlic or about**	¼ **teaspoon sage**
16 cloves whole, not peeled	¼ **teaspoon thyme**
3 **pints water**	½ **bay leaf**
1 **teaspoon salt or to taste**	4 **parsley sprigs**
Pinch of pepper	3 **tablespoons olive oil**
2 **cloves**	**5-pint saucepan**

Drop the garlic cloves into boiling water and boil 30 seconds. Drain, run cold water over them, then peel. Place the garlic and rest of the ingredients in the saucepan and boil slowly for 30 minutes. Adjust seasoning.

A wire whisk	**2 to 3 tablespoons olive oil**
3 eggs yolks	**A soup tureen**

Beat the egg yolks in the soup tureen for a minute until they are thick and sticky. Drop by drop, beat in the olive oil as would be done in making mayonnaise. Set aside.

Strainer	**4 oz. of grated Swiss or**
Rounds of hard toasted French bread	**Parmesan cheese**

Just before serving, beat a ladleful of hot soup into the egg mixture, drop by drop. Gradually strain in the rest, beating and pressing the juice from the garlic. Serve immediately over bread and cheese. If reheating next day, do not bring to a boil.

Photo: BRIGITTE LACOMBE

MIDORI, VIOLINIST

In 1986, Midori's stunning performance at Tanglewood made front page headlines in the *New York Times*. Mid-performance, two strings broke successively and fourteen-year-old Midori had to switch violins twice in order to continue. As she successfully completed this heroic performance, Leonard Bernstein, the Boston Symphony and the audience gave her a thunderous ovation.

Now, in the second decade of an extraordinary career, Midori has become one of the most celebrated figures in the music world. She is received enthusiastically and with highest praise by the public, critics and colleagues. Midori performs regularly on the great concert stages of Europe, North America, and the Far East. She has recently added an important dimension to her public life through the activities of Midori & Friends, which was established in 1992 to bring the performing arts closer to the lives of children.

Midori was born in Osaka, Japan, in 1971. She made her professional debut at age eleven with Zubin Mehta and the New York Philharmonic. Since then, she has been in consistent and ever-increasing demand worldwide, whether at the White House, Carnegie Hall, the Kennedy Center, the "Tonight Show," "Sesame Street," the Musikverein in Vienna, the Concertgebouw in Amsterdam or the Barbican in London. She has collaborated with such eminent artists as Claudio Abbado, Vladimir Ashkenazy, Daniel Barenboim, Leonard Bernstein, Yo-Yo Ma, Kurt Masur, Zubin Mehta, André Previn, Mstislav Rostropovich, Isaac Stern, and Pinchas Zukerman; and she has performed with such distinguished orchestras as the Berlin Philharmonic, the Boston Symphony, the Chicago Symphony, the Israel Philharmonic, the London Symphony, the Los Angeles Philharmonic, the New York Philharmonic, and the Royal Concertgebouw Orchestra.

Midori has recorded for Phillips and Sony Classical. Her recording of the Paganini Caprices for Solo Violin was nominated for a Grammy Award in 1990. Her most recent release, Encore!, is a collection of miniature pieces for violin and piano. Due for future release is a disc featuring the Sibelius Violin Concerto and Bruch's "Scottish Fantasy."

ALMOND COOKIES

Makes 25 cookies

These cookies come from Midori's collection of baking recipes. She enjoys baking in her spare time and is particularly fond of this recipe.

I love these cookies....I call them "Viennese Waltzes" --M.

1¼ sticks butter (softened)
1 teaspoon vanilla extract
½ teaspoon almond extract
⅓ cup sugar

½ cup fresh almonds, finely ground
1½ cups flour
Powdered sugar

In electric mixing bowl, beat butter, vanilla and almond extracts, and sugar for one minute. Beat in ground almonds and with the mixer at low speed, add in flour and work until completely blended. Take out cookie dough and knead on lightly floured table surface until smooth.

Pinch off small pieces of dough, teaspoon size, and roll between hands until about 3 inches long or slightly less. Put on dry baking sheet, about 1½ inches apart and pinch ends of each roll into crescent 'moon' shape.

Bake for 15 minutes in preheated oven at 350 degrees until lightly browned. Cool when done, move to clean plate and lightly cover with powdered sugar.

450

Portrait: HORACE VERNET, The Library of Congress

NICCOLÒ PAGANINI, VIOLINIST

Born in Italy, Paganini's first musical study was on the mandolin, with his father. Soon, the young Paganini turned to the violin. His last formal study on this instrument was in Parma, with Ghiretti and Alessandro Rolla.

In 1798, when only sixteen years old, Paganini broke with his father and toured on his own. Compulsive gambling became an obsession, causing him to lose his violin to creditors. Fortuitously, a compassionate nobleman presented Paganini with the gift of a Guarnerius instrument. In 1805, he was appointed court solo violinist at Lucca. From 1808-1827, increasingly successful tours were made throughout Italy, culminating with an 1827

triumph in Vienna. At some concerts, this wizard of the violin performed seemingly impossible, sensational pyrotechnical feats, almost circus-like in nature, causing him to be accused of being in league with the devil, in order to attain such fiendishly difficult technical skills. Franz Liszt was so inspired by hearing Paganini that he earnestly sought to develop commensurate technical prowess at the piano.

Increased debauchery in Paganini's personal life, manifest in rampant alcoholism, eventually destroyed his health and he died in Nice in the spring of 1840. His compositions are still standard fare on violinists' concert programs.

The following recipe was discovered in a collection of material purchased for the Library of Congress in the 1940's by Mrs. Gertrude Clarke Whittall as an addition to the Gertrude Clarke Whittall Foundation Collection (a important collection of musical autographs presented to the Library of Congress by Mrs. Whittall). The Paganini collection had originally been assembled by Mrs. Charles Hohn, who, under her maiden name of Maia Bang, enjoyed an enviable reputation as a violin pedagogue. It was Mrs. Hohn's intention to use this material for a biography of Paganini and then find a permanent home for her collection in the Library of Congress. Maia Bang's untimely death in 1940 prevented her from writing the biography, but her other wish was ultimately realized when Mrs. Whittall purchased the collection from the estate of Mr. Charles Hohn, who passed away soon after his wife's death.

I (the author) was very fortunate to have come across this remarkable recipe. During a trip to the Library of Congress in Washington, D.C., I was looking throughout the mammoth library for old recipes and having no luck at all until I happened to ask one of the employees at the desk at the music division how I could possibly find any books that might contain some famous composers recipes. He said he had no idea, but that he did know one of the music library staff had some recipe by Paganini! He then introduced me to Mr. Charles Sens, music specialist at the Library of Congress, who proceeded to give me a copy, in Italian, of a recipe by Paganini for use in my book. Not understanding what was written on the original manuscript, I was quite relieved to find a translation of the ravioli recipe completed by Charles' friend and chamber music partner, Ms. Judy Gardner. Both Charles and Judy are avid cooks as well as accomplished musicians. Many thanks for their generosity.

This recipe has not been altered in any way from the original translation.

PAGANINI'S RAVIOLI

SAUCE:

For a pound and a half of flour, [you will need] 2 pounds of good lean beef to make the sauce. Place some butter in a frying pan and sauté a small amount of minced onion. Add the beef and cook until it begins to brown. In order to thicken the sauce, slowly add a little flour until it browns. Then take some tomato sauce, dilute it with water, and pour into the mixture. Stir well to blend. Finally, add some finely-chopped mushrooms, and that's the sauce.

PASTA:

For the pasta, make a dough without using eggs; adding a little salt to the pasta will improve its consistency. [It is understood that the dough should be made with a pound and a half of flour, based on references to that amount in the directions for the sauce and filling].

FILLING:

For the filling, using the same skillet as before, cook one-half pound lean veal in the sauce. Remove it and chop finely. Take a calf's brain, cook it in water, then remove the skin covering the brain and chop finely. Take some Lugano sausage, remove the skin and chop finely. Take a handful of bovage (known in Nice as "bovaj"), boil it, squeeze until dry, and chop finely.

Take 3 eggs, which are enough for a pound and a half of flour. Beat them well. After mixing all the above mentioned ingredients together with the eggs, add a little Parmesan cheese. And that's the filling.

For a more delicate filling, you can substitute capon for the veal and sweetbreads for the calf's brain. If the filling is too stiff, add some of the sauce. For the ravioli, keep the pasta moist and let it stand, covered, for an hour, so that you'll be able to roll it into thin layers.

Photo: CHRISTIAN STEINER

ITZHAK PERLMAN, VIOLINIST

Itzhak Perlman's uniqueness in the rarefied ranks of superstar musicians stems from something more than his supreme artistic credentials. The combination of talent, charm and humanity in this Israeli-born artist is unrivaled in our time and has come to be recognized by audiences all over the world, who respond not only to his flawless technique but to his communication through the irrepressible joy of making music. President Reagan recognized these qualities when he honored Mr. Perlman with a "Medal of Liberty" in 1986.

Born in Israel in 1945, Mr. Perlman completed his initial training at the Academy of Music in Tel Aviv. He came to New York and soon was propelled into the international arena with an appearance on the Ed Sullivan Show in 1958. Following his studies at the Juilliard School with Ivan Galamian and Dorothy DeLay, Mr. Perlman won the prestigious Leventritt Competition in 1964, which led to a burgeoning worldwide career.

Since then, Itzhak Perlman has appeared with every major orchestra and in recitals and festivals throughout the world. In November of 1987, he joined the Israel Philharmonic for history-making concerts in Warsaw and Budapest, representing the first performances by this orchestra and soloist in Eastern bloc countries. He again made history as he joined the Israel Philharmonic for its first visit to the Soviet Union in April/May 1990 and was cheered by audiences in Moscow and Leningrad who thronged to hear his recital and orchestral performances. In December 1990, Mr. Perlman visited Russia for the second time to participate in a gala performance in Leningrad, celebrating the 150th anniversary of Tchaikovsky's birth.   This concert, which also featured Yo-Yo Ma, Jessye Norman, and Yuri Temirkanov conducting the Leningrad Philharmonic, was televised live in Europe and later broadcast throughout the world; it is now available on home video (RCA/BMG Classics).

Mr. Perlman's recordings on the Angel/EMI, Deutsche

Grammophon, London/Decca, CBS Masterworks/Sony Classical, Erato/Elektra International Classics, and RCA/BMG Classics labels regularly appear on the best-seller charts and have won thirteen Grammy Awards. Among his latest releases is a four-disc 'retrospective' entitled *The Art of Itzhak Perlman* (EMI Classics), which contains a wide variety of the violinist's favorite pieces which he recorded for that label over the last 20 years. Other recent releases feature collaborations with world-class artists such as Daniel Barenboim and the Berlin Philharmonic, performing the Brahms Violin Concerto; Zubin Mehta and the Israel Philharmonic, in a live recording of the Violin Concertos by Castelnuovo-Tedesco and Ben-Haim; and Pinchas Zukerman and Lynn Harrell, in a live recording of Beethoven string trios (all Angel/EMI).

Numerous publications and institutions have paid tribute to Itzhak Perlman for the unique place he occupies in the artistic and humanitarian fabric of our times. *Newsweek* magazine featured him with a cover story in April of 1980; in 1981, *Musical America* pictured him as Musician of the Year on the cover of its *Directory of Music and Musicians*.   Harvard University, Yale University, Brandeis University, Yeshiva University and Hebrew University in Jerusalem are among the institutions which have awarded him honorary degrees.

On television, Mr. Perlman has entertained and enlightened millions of viewers of all ages, on shows as diverse as *The Late Show with David Letterman*, *Sesame Street*, the PBS series *The Frugal Gourmet*, *The Tonight Show*, the *Grammy Awards* telecasts, several *Live From Lincoln Center* broadcasts, and the PBS specials *A Musical Toast* and *Mozart by the Masters*, both of which he hosted. In 1992, the PBS documentary of his historic trip to the Soviet Union with the Israel Philharmonic, entitled *Perlman in Russia* (Angel/EMI video), was honored with an Emmy Award as Best Music Documentary. In July of 1994, Mr. Perlman was seen by millions of viewers when he hosted the U.S. broadcast of the *Three Tenors, Encore*! live from Dodger Stadium in Los Angeles. One of Mr. Perlman's proudest achievements was his collaboration with film score composer John Williams in Steven Spielberg's Academy Award-winning film *Schindler's List* in which he performed the violin solos. His most recent endeavor has been a highly successful recording called *Itzhak Perlman in the Fiddler's House*; a collection of klezmer music featuring Itzhak Perlman with some the world's finest klezmer bands.

His presence on stage, on camera and in personal appearances of all kinds speaks eloquently on behalf of the handicapped and disabled, and his devotion to their cause is an integral part of his life.

Itzhak Perlman lives in New York with his wife Toby and their family.

ITZHAK PERLMAN'S VERY FATTENING CHOPPED CHICKEN LIVERS
Makes about 2½ cups

If you want more tang, add raw chopped onions (that's the way my mother used to make it). Make sure you have plenty of antacids—but it's worth it! --I.P.

1 pound chicken fat
1 pound chicken livers
1 medium onion, finely chopped

3 hard-boiled eggs
Salt and pepper to taste

Render chicken fat. When rendered, add chicken livers, turn off flame, and let livers stew in the hot fat for 6 minutes. Add chopped onion and let it remain until slightly brown and livers are ready. (5 to 6 minutes)

Take out livers—in a very fine colander, let the fat drain—but not too much! Chop together with hard-boiled eggs.

Serve either with matzoh or rye bread.

It is no secret to audiences all over the world that Mr. Perlman is known for his artistry in the kitchen as well as on the concert stage. Several years ago I (the author) was visiting the Interlochen Arts Camp in Interlochen, Michigan. Deciding to grab a bite to eat, I went into a local Italian restaurant called Giovanni's. Upon looking at the menu my eyes caught sight of an unusual type of pizza. Printed at the right and bottom corner of the menu was "The Perlman" Pizza. I spoke to the manager, John Hobbard, about how this name came about. Apparently, Mr. Perlman had come into the restaurant after his performance at the Interlochen Arts Camp. He called over the manager and instructed him exactly how he would like to have a pizza cooked and seasoned. This pizza recipe was so tremendous that Mr. Hobbard decided to include it as a regular item in the menu; naming it after the creator, Mr. Perlman. Unfortunately, this book does not have this recipe, so for you to enjoy this pizza you will have to make a trip up to Interlochen and visit Giovanni's Restaurant!

Photo: © PETER SCHAAF

Photo: SPECTRUM STUDIO

WILLIAM PREUCIL AND GWEN STARKER PREUCIL, VIOLINISTS

During the 1994-95 concert season, William Preucil was selected as the new concertmaster of the Cleveland Orchestra. He was also appointed to the faculty of the Cleveland Institute of Music during the same year.

Mr. Preucil has been first violin of the Cleveland Quartet and professor of music at the Eastman School of Music. The Cleveland Quartet recently ended its association after twenty-six successful concert seasons. Since the formation of the group in 1969, the Cleveland Quartet performed an average of ninety concerts each year in the music capitals of the world. In past seasons, the quartet's concert schedule took them to New York, Washington, Boston, Los Angeles, San Francisco, Toronto, Montreal, London, Paris, Berlin, Frankfurt, Munich, Lisbon, Vienna, Salzburg, Madrid, Helsinki, Seoul, and Tokyo. The quartet has recorded the complete cycle of Beethoven quartets for Telarc Records, and past releases on the Telarc label include compact discs of the music of Mozart, Dvořák, and Schubert.

Prior to joining the Cleveland Quartet, Mr. Preucil served as concertmaster of the Atlanta Symphony Orchestra for seven seasons. During his tenure in Atlanta, Mr. Preucil appeared in over sixty concerto performances with the orchestra; his recording of the Violin Concerto by Stephen Paulus, which was written for and dedicated to him, is available on New World Records. He regularly performs as recitalist and soloist with orchestras around the world, as well as participating in prominent chamber music festivals, such as Seattle, Sitka, Sarasota, Santa Fe and Ernen, Switzerland.

Mr. Preucil began violin studies at the age of five with his mother, Doris Preucil, a leader in the Suzuki movement in the United States. After graduating from the Interlochen Arts Academy, he entered Indiana University to study with Josef Gingold, and was awarded the prestigious Performer's Certificate. He was appointed concertmaster of the Nashville Symphony at the age of twenty-two and also served in that capacity with the Utah Symphony before going to Atlanta in 1982.

Gwen Starker Preucil has been a member of the Nashville and Utah Symphonies and concertmaster of the Atlanta Ballet Orchestra for six years. She received the prestigious Performer's Certificate from Indiana University, where she studied with Josef Gingold and Franco Gulli. In demand as a chamber musician and ensemble player, she appears in many festivals around the world. She also has toured Europe and South America with the Festival Strings Lucerne and has often appeared together with her father, Janos Starker.

PASTA STRADIVARI

Serves 4 to 6

Bill came up with this wonderful recipe entirely on his own and we all adore it. This recipe evolved from years of trying to find the ultimate marinara sauce! We wanted something simple, yet full of flavor and with a nice, thick consistency...and Bill found it! --G.S.P.

Olive oil (to cover bottom of pot)
2 medium-large onions, finely
    chopped (2 cups)
1 large clove of garlic, finely chopped
2, 28 oz. cans of crushed tomatoes
2 to 3 tablespoons basil

2 to 3 tablespoons oregano
3 tablespoons Italian herbs
½ teaspoon pepper
2 bay leaves
3 oz. red wine *(if you happen to be*
    sipping while cooking!)

Thinly cover the bottom of a 5-quart pot with olive oil. Turn heat to medium. When the oil is hot, add the chopped onions and garlic. Take 1½ tablespoons each of the basil, oregano and Italian herbs (reserving the remainder for later) and grind between your palms as you add them to the pot. Cook on medium heat until the mixture begins to brown and flavors mingle. Add the crushed tomatoes and remaining ground spices, pepper, red wine (optional) and bay leaves. Simmer on low heat for 1 hour, uncovered, stirring occasionally.

Serve over cappellini or spaghettini. Recommended wine: Spring Mountain Cabernet Saovignon 1983!

Photo: © GORDON BAER, Cincinnati

PHILLIP RUDER, VIOLINIST

Phillip Ruder, who served as concertmaster of the Cincinnati Symphony Orchestra from 1973 until spring of 1994, assumed a new professional position at the University of Nevada in Reno, in September of 1996. In addition to his teaching and performing responsibilities at the university, Mr. Ruder is currently developing an innovative new program of study to prepare young professionals for a career in the field of orchestral performance.

A native of Chicago, Ruder made his solo debut with the Chicago Symphony at the age of 12, and his New York recital debut in 1963 at the age of 23. As a graduate of the Hartt School of Music, where he studied with Raphael Bronstein, he received both his bachelor and master of music degrees.

Mr. Ruder was the former concertmaster of the Dallas Symphony Orchestra from 1969-1973 and concertmaster of the New Orleans Philharmonic from 1965-1967.

Other prestigious positions include concertmaster of the Grand Teton Music Festival Orchestra (1995), concertmaster at the Aspen Music Festival and the Santa Fe Opera Festival.

His former academic positions have taken Mr. Ruder across the United States. He was a member of the Claremont Quartet, in residence at the North Carolina School for the Arts, in Winston-Salem, with additional performing and teaching residences at the Peabody Institute of Music, the University of Rhode Island and Salem College.

For the past 16 years, Mr. Ruder has been associate music director and resident violinist of the Linton Chamber Music Series in Cincinnati. Mr. Ruder plans to maintain his longtime relationship with the Linton Series by continuing his work as associate artistic director and guest performer.

RUTH RUDER'S APRICOT FLAN PIE

Serves 8 to 9

Ruth developed this recipe for a pie baking contest and won a blue ribbon! --P.R.

3 tablespoons sugar	¾ cup cream
3 oz. blanched almonds	3 eggs
1⅓ cups condensed evaporated milk	3 egg yolks

Caramelize sugar by heating over moderate heat until sugar melts, then pour into bottom of a 9-inch or 10-inch springform pan to cover. Let it cool. Toast almonds until brown, then process with blender or food processor until coarsely but evenly ground. Add condensed milk, cream, eggs and egg yolks. Stir to mix, then blend on high until smooth.

Pour into springform pan with caramelized sugar. Bake in water bath 45 minutes or until set, at 325 degrees. Cool, refrigerate overnight. The next day, invert onto pie crust (see below recipe.) Wipe off any liquid sugar/syrup with a paper towel or clean sponge.

POWDERED SUGAR CRUST

1 stick butter	1 cup flour
½ cup sugar	

Soften butter and mix with flour and sugar. Press into 10-inch (preferably fluted and wide-topped) pie pan. Prick bottom with fork. Bake at 350 degrees for 20 to 25 minutes, or until slightly browned. Remove and cool.

APRICOT GLAZE

28 oz. can apricots (*I use lite syrup but heavy is okay*)	1 teaspoon almond extract
1 to 2 teaspoons cornstarch	Sugar to taste

Reserve all juice from can, decorate top of flan with whole halves of apricot in center and thin slices of apricot around edges, overlapping the slices, like a deck of cards.

Purée remaining apricots, enough to make 1½ cups of glaze in their own juice. Add sugar to taste, cornstarch and almond extract. Heat and stir with a whip until thick and immediately pour over top of apricots and entire pie, sealing to edges of crust. Cool in refrigerator until set.

GOTTFRIED SCHNEIDER, VIOLINIST

Born in Badgastein, Austria, Gottfried Schneider comes from a musical family. His mother was a noted singer and his father conducted the local orchestra. At the age of three he received his first violin lessons. His solo debut with orchestra was given eight years later.

Formal musical education began at the Mozarteum in Salzburg. Subsequent instruction was provided by Otto Buchner (Munich), Max Rostal (Bern), and Ivan Galamian (New York).

Mr. Schneider is a prize winner of such international competitions as the Carl Flesch of London and the Jeunesses Musicales of Belgrade. In addition, he was awarded the Gebruder-Busch Prize and was invited by Rudolph Serkin to his Marlboro Festival in America. Gottfried Schneider, who lives near Munich, plays regularly with such well-known orchestras as the Berliner Philharmoniker, the Bayerische Staatsorchester, the Munchner Philharmoniker and the Wiener Symphoniker.

Numerous radio and television appearances (including a Paganini violin concerto for ZDF), as well as the first recordings of the Dohnányi Violin Concerto and the Domenico Scarlatti violin sonatas, have consolidated his international reputation.

Alongside with his concert performances which lead him all over the world, Gottfried Schneider organizes the "Sylter Sommer" Festival, which he initiated in 1981. He succeeded Sandor Vegh as professor of violin and chamber music at the Düsseldorf Musikhochschule. In 1991, he was appointed professor at the Munich Academy. Gottfried Schneider plays the "Del Comble" Stradivarius of 1728.

CHOCOLATE TREAT

Here is the recipe of a good friend's grandmother. It is easy to make and the result will be amazing. Don't eat too much of it. It would be better to share it with good friends. Serves 8 to 10. --G.S.

8 oz. butter
5 oz. bitter chocolate
6 eggs, separated

8 oz. powdered sugar
6 tablespoons flour

In a pot, melt butter and chocolate. Beat egg yolks and powdered sugar in mixer until foamy. Add the flour and cooled chocolate mixture to the above. Blend the stiffly beaten egg whites gently into the mixture. Put into a 9-inch springform pan. Put into a *cold* oven and turn heat to 360 degrees. Bake for 45 minutes or slightly less. Top and bottom of cake should be dry—inside will be moist.

JAAP SCHRÖDER, VIOLINIST

Dutch violinist Jaap Schröder has pioneered historical performance practice for the violin throughout his long and distinguished career. As chamber musician, soloist and conductor, he has sought out the far reaches of the Baroque and Classical repertoire, as well as attending to the great works of Bach, Haydn and Mozart. Schröder has led many groups, including the Quartetto Esterhazy and Concerto Amsterdam. He also has co-directed the Academy of Ancient Music with Christopher Hogwood in their complete traversal of Mozart symphonies. Mr. Schröder's current performing activities center on two instrument groups: the Smithson Quartet which dedicates itself to works of the Classical period, and the Atlantis Ensemble, which performs 19th century music. Mr. Schröder teaches at the Yale School of Music and at the Luxembourg Conservatory.

SOUPE AUX COURGETTES
(Zucchini Soup)
Serves 6

This recipe is French and comes from my wife, who also is French. --J.S.

2¼ pounds of zucchini (not too big)	3 or 4 wedges of "The Laughing Cow"
¾ quart of water	cheese (a special French processed cheese)
1½ to 2 bouillon cubes	Sour cream
Salt and pepper to taste	Chopped fresh or dried dill

Peel half of the zucchini. For the other half, leave the skin on. Slice all zucchini into about ⅓-inch thick rounds. Put all zucchini in ¾ quart of boiling water. Add bouillon cubes. Salt and pepper to taste. When the zucchini becomes tender, after about 15 minutes, remove from heat. Add cheese and combine well in mixer or blender. Serve very hot, accompanied with 1 tablespoon of sour cream per serving bowl and sprinkled with some dill.

Photo: RAY SANTINI

SERGIU SCHWARTZ, VIOLINIST

Sergiu Schwartz is "the consummate heroic figure possessed of a lion's share of talent, commanding stage presence and abundant technique," wrote the *Los Angeles Times*, and the reviewer of the *Chicago Tribune* noted that "he possesses a sweet tone, an instinctively dramatic way with a phrase and an ability to make every note count," following the artist's performance with the symphony at Chicago's Grant Park Festival. Mr. Schwartz's appearances in the United States, Canada, Europe, and Israel have brought unanimous critical accolades and praise for his beauty of tone, brilliant technique and an artistry of distinctive style and elegance. The *New York Times* reviewed Mr. Schwartz's sold-out New York debut recital at Carnegie's Weill Recital Hall, as winner of the Artists International Competition, as "an impressive, authoritative and surging performance," and wrote following his 1993 recital at the Tisch Center for the Arts of the 92nd Street Y: "What Sergiu Schwartz does with the violin is always accomplished: big, active tone, grand gestures of phrase, color with dark undertones, excellent agility."

This violinist has appeared before the public with orchestras and in recital at major music centers in twenty countries and over forty North American states, including New York's Lincoln Center, 92nd Street Y, Town Hall, Merkin, and Carnegie Recital Halls (where he performed five sold-out New York recitals), Washington's Kennedy Center and the Library of Congress, Royce Hall and Ambassador Auditorium in Los Angeles, as well as in most other major cities in the U.S. and Canada. A frequent guest in London's concert halls, Mr. Schwartz made his London debut at Wigmore Hall in the Outstanding Israeli Artists Series and performed with the London Symphony Orchestra at Barbican Hall. Many of Mr. Schwartz's recitals were broadcast live by classical radio stations in the U.S. and in Europe, including WQXR in New York and the BBC in London, where he performed the S. Coleridge-Taylor Violin Concerto in its BBC world premiere. As recitalist, Sergiu Schwartz appeared in concert series which he shared with distinguished artists, such as José Carreras at Los Angeles' "L'Ermitage," and Itzhak Perlman and Yo-Yo Ma at the 1993 Interlochen Arts Festival. Highlights of his upcoming engagements include appearances with the Slovak Philharmonic during the orchestra's first tour of the United States, the Jerusalem Symphony under Sergiu Comissiona, and a recital in the UCLA concert series at Royce Hall in Los Angeles.

Mr. Schwartz made his recording debut with the London Symphony Orchestra with an "all-Scandinavian" compact disc released by *Vox Unique*, featuring music by Sibelius, Svendsen and Grieg. His most recent disc, comprising the three Spohr Sonatas for violin and harp, was released by EMS Records, Belgium.

Sergiu Schwartz studied violin and chamber music with Ramy Shevelov at the Rubin Academy of Music in Tel Aviv, Israel; he also gained exposure to world-class artists, such as Isaac Stern and Yehudi Menuhin, during master classes at the Jerusalem Music Center. Mr. Schwartz's musical growth was further influenced by Leon Fleisher, Felix Galimir, and Sandor Vegh in chamber music, and by the legendary conductor Sergiu Celibidache. In 1981, Sergiu Schwartz received scholarships from the America-Israel Cultural Foundation and the Juilliard School in New York to study with the distinguished violin teacher Dorothy DeLay. Mr. Schwartz is also the recipient of a National Endowment for the Arts Solo Recitalist fellowship and winner of major prizes in international violin competitions in England, Switzerland, Chile, Israel, and the United States.

In addition to his extensive performing career, Sergiu Schwartz serves on the artist faculty of the Harid Conservatory in Boca Raton, Florida, conducts master classes in the United States and in Europe, and is a regular guest at chamber music festivals in France, Germany, Finland, Switzerland and the United States.

LAMB-STUFFED CABBAGE ROLLS
Makes 24 rolls

*After having **practiced** this recipe, gradually increasing the **tempo** of preparing the ingredients, I can say that my **interpretation** is really true to the original score. I have to give credit to my wife's family (my mother-in-law) in Israel, who inspired this recipe. My wife, Diana, has a professional background in linguistics, travel, and public relations. I might add that she is my toughest critic when I perform.* --S.S.

1 medium cabbage head

FILLING:
1 pound ground lamb
1 cup raw rice
¼ teaspoon cinnamon
¼ teaspoon pepper
¼ teaspoon salt
2 tablespoons lemon juice

1 teaspoon olive oil
2 tablespoons chopped fresh parsley
Water to cover rolls

SAUCE:
28 oz. can no-salt-added whole
    tomatoes or 4 cups peeled and seeded
    fresh tomatoes
4 large garlic cloves, peeled and halved

Wash cabbage and core it deeply enough so that the outer leaves begin to separate from the head.

In a pot large enough to hold the head of the cabbage, bring water to a boil. Dip the head of the cabbage into the boiling water. As the leaves loosen, remove them. Continue removing at least 12 leaves. Scald the leaves in boiling water for 2 minutes. Cool. Cut cooked leaves in half, removing the hard center.

Knead together the lamb, rice, cinnamon, pepper, salt, lemon juice, olive oil and parsley. Place half a cabbage leaf with the cut side toward you. Add 1 or 2 tablespoons of filling on the center of the leaf. Fold the left and right sides of the cabbage over the filling. Roll the leaf away from you, starting with the cut side.

Arrange filled rolls tightly in a non-stick sprayed 9 x 13-inch baking pan. Break the tomatoes into small pieces and pour them with juice over the tops of the rolls. Place the garlic over the tomatoes. Add water to the top of the rolls. Bake uncovered at 350 degrees for 45 minutes.

Photo: CHRISTIAN STEINER

PHILIP SETZER, VIOLINIST, EMERSON STRING QUARTET

Violinist Philip Setzer was born March 12, 1951 in Cleveland, Ohio. He began violin studies at the age of five with his parents, both former members of the Cleveland Orchestra. He later continued his studies with Josef Gingold and Rafael Druian, and with Oscar Shumsky at the Juilliard School. As a founding member of the Emerson String Quartet, one of the premiere chamber ensembles in the world, Setzer performs over 100 concerts each season worldwide. The Emerson Quartet has won two Grammy Awards, including Best Classical Album, and records exclusively for Deutsche Grammophon.

A Bronze Medal recipient, Mr. Setzer was one of only two Americans to place at the 1976 Queen Elisabeth International Competition in Brussels. The other American to receive an award was Eugene Drucker—who alternates with Setzer in the first chair position of the Emerson String Quartet. Mr. Setzer has participated in the Marlboro Music Festival and has appeared as guest soloist with the National Symphony, and on several occasions, with the Cleveland Orchestra. In addition, Setzer has performed with the orchestras of Brussels, Belgium, Anchorage and the New Orchestra of Westchester. In April of 1989, Mr. Setzer premiered Paul Epstein's Matinee Concerto with the Hartt Wind Symphony. The piece, which was dedicated to and written for Mr. Setzer, was performed in Hartford, New York and Boston to favorable critical acclaim. Philip Setzer teaches as visiting professor of violin and chamber music at Hartt Music School at the University of Hartford and resides in New Jersey with his wife Linda and daughter Katia. He plays a violin made by Sanctus Serphin (Venice, 1734).

The members of the famed Emerson Quartet include: (see front cover photo, from left to right)) Eugene Drucker, violin, David Finckel, cello, Lawrence Dutton, viola and Philip Setzer, violin.

EASY GOURMET PASTA

Serves 3 to 4

This is a very tasty recipe which only takes about 20 minutes to prepare. Perfect for the musician on-the-go! The hot pasta cooks the tomatoes and basil slightly, but the effect is one of refreshment, which is why it is better to serve this dish warm instead of hot. --P.S.

½ **pound penne or rigatoni or fusilli**
1 **clove garlic**
2 **tablespoons olive oil**
½ **cup pine nuts**
2 **fresh tomatoes, sliced to bite-size**

¾ **to 1 cup chopped or torn fresh basil leaves (washed carefully)**
Parmesan or Romano cheese (grated)
1 **small package goat cheese (grated)**
Salt and pepper to taste

As you are boiling the water and then cooking the pasta, you can prepare the other ingredients.

Brown the garlic clove (gently) in the olive oil, then remove and discard the garlic and add the pine nuts, again browning gently. Cut up the tomatoes and basil and place them in the bottom of a large bowl.

When pasta is done (do not overcook!), drain and add the still-hot pasta to the bowl. Mix in all the other ingredients, except the grated cheeses, including the oil and pine nuts from the 'browning' pan.

Sprinkle the goat cheese over the mixture and serve warm or at room temperature. Serve with grated Parmesan or Romano cheese on the side. Add more olive oil if it's too dry. Enjoy!!

Photo: KELLY

EUDICE SHAPIRO, VIOLINIST

Eudice Shapiro, who plays the "ex-Wieniawski" Guarnarius violin, has won plaudits as soloist with such famed conductors as Eugene Goossens, Fritz Reiner, William Steinberg, Josef Rosenstock, Igor Stravinsky, Otto Klemperer and Izler Solomon. She has played chamber music concerts with world-famous Artur Schnabel, Bruno Walter, Lili Kraus, Rudolf Firkušný, Jascha Heifetz, Gregor Piatigorsky, Zara Nelsova and Leonard Pennario. Performing recitals throughout Europe, New Zealand, and the Orient, as well as the United States, Eudice Shapiro has received such critical acclaim as "a remarkable American violinist"—"a violinist who surpasses the usual by far"—"one of the finest of violinists."

At the age of twelve, Miss Shapiro was awarded a special scholarship to the Curtis Institute of Music, one of the few students—and the only female student at that time—accepted by violinist Efrem Zimbalist. During her five years at Curtis, she appeared as soloist with the Buffalo and Rochester Orchestras and with the Philadelphia Orchestra at the invitation of Leopold Stokowski.

Following a Town Hall debut, the talented young artist won the National Violin Award of the National Federation of Music Clubs. She enlarged an already active solo career by becoming the first woman concert-mistress-soloist in the Hollywood film and recording industries. She held this position for more than twenty years, and her recorded playing in solo passages has probably been heard by an audience far greater than any other woman violinist in history.

A staunch champion of contemporary music, premier performances of works by Copland, Foss, Kirchner, Milhaud and Stravinsky have been given by Miss Shapiro. Public performances and recordings, with the composers at the piano, have been with Roy Harris, Ingolf Dahl, Leon Kirchner and Peter Mennin. Under the baton of Darius Milhaud, Eudice Shapiro performed his *Concertino de Printemps,* and she was chosen by Igor Stravinsky to play the intricate violin solos in *L'Histoire du Soldat,* with the famed composer as conductor.

Miss Shapiro is professor of violin at the University of Southern California, in Los Angeles. She was the recipient of the Ramo Music Faculty Award, as well as receiving the Outstanding Educators of America Award for recognition of her teaching abilities. She was presented with the Artist Teacher of 1984 Award by the American String Teacher's Association at their National Convention in Chicago.

Some of Miss Shapiro's recordings now on CD include: Hovaness's Tzsaikerk for Solo Violin, Flute, Drums and String Orchestra; Lou Harrison's Concerto for Violin and Percussion Orchestra and Stravinsky's Divertimento and Duo Concertant.

Miss Shapiro has been a chamber music judge in the semi-finals of the Van Cliburn International Competition, and adjudicator for the *Seventeen* magazine and General Motors National Competitions. She is currently the violin artist-teacher at the Manchester Music Festival held each summer in Vermont.

POACHED DISHWASHER SALMON

Honestly, the salmon works, and as to the pie, no one will guess what it is. --E.S.

Wrap fresh, seasoned salmon well in heavy foil and put through full cycle of dishwasher. **DO NOT USE SOAP!**

AVOCADO PIE
Serves 8 to 10

2 nicely-sized avocados
¼ cup lemon juice
14 oz. can of sweet condensed milk

9-inch graham cracker pie crust
Non-dairy whipped topping

Peel avocados and blend with lemon juice and milk until smooth. Put into pie crust and cover with topping. Chill in refrigerator, or freeze.

Photo: DOROTHEA VON HAEFTEN

ARNOLD STEINHARDT, VIOLINIST, GUARNERI STRING QUARTET

Arnold Steinhardt was born in Los Angeles, receiving his early training from Karl Moldrem, Peter Meremblum and Toscha Seidel, and making his solo debut with the Los Angeles Philharmonic Orchestra at age fourteen. He continued his studies with Ivan Galamian at the Curtis Institute of Music and with Joseph Szigeti in Switzerland in 1962 under the sponsorship of George Szell.

Winner of the Philadelphia Youth Competition in 1957, the 1958 Leventritt Award, and Bronze medalist in the Queen Elizabeth International Violin Competition in 1963, Mr. Steinhardt has appeared throughout America and Europe as a recitalist and soloist with orchestras, including the New York Philharmonic and the Cleveland Orchestra.

Mr. Steinhardt is first violinist and a founding member (1964) of the internationally acclaimed Guarneri String Quartet, with which he has made innumerable tours on many continents and recorded dozens of albums for RCA Victor and Philips.

He is professor of violin at the University of Maryland, Rutgers University and the Curtis Institute of Music, where he has directed the Curtis Orchestra in several concerts, including an appearance on French television. Recipient of honorary degrees from the University of South Florida and S.U.N.Y., Binghamton, Arnold Steinhardt has also received an award for distinguished cultural service from the City of New York, presented by Mayor Koch. He is the author of articles which have appeared in the magazines of *Chamber Music America*, *Musical America* and *Keynote*.

Mr. Steinhardt's recordings include Romantic music for violin and piano, which he recorded "direct-to-disk" with pianist Lincoln Mayorga for the audiophile Sheffield label; an album of music for violin and piano by women composers, on Northeastern Records; and a Town Hall label recording of unaccompanied Bach works. In his most recent release on Biddulph CDs, Steinhardt plays violin and viola with pianist brother Victor in works by Robert Fuchs.

The members of the Guarneri String Quartet include Arnold Steinhardt and John Dalley, violins; Michael Tree, viola, and David Soyer, cello. (See page 397 for quartet photo).

ARNIE'S CHILI CON CARNE
Serves 8

3 tablespoons olive oil
3 medium-sized onions, sliced
½ green bell pepper, sliced
1½ pounds lean beef (round steak),
    sliced into 'smallish' cubes
28 oz. can tomatoes, imported Italian plum,
    or equivalent fresh tomatoes, drained
6 oz. can tomato paste
1 to 4 tablespoons chili powder (*I use 4*)

Salt as needed
1 teaspoon cumin (*optional, but for me
    all defining*)
Several drops Tabasco sauce
2 or 3 cloves garlic, thinly sliced
1 bay leaf
Large (40 oz.) can kidney beans
½ cup dry red wine*

In large skillet, heat oil, add sliced onions and bell pepper; cook until onions are tender, but not brown. Sauté beef cubes until cooked and lightly browned. Add all ingredients except kidney beans. Cover and simmer for 45 minutes.

Add beans and cook at least 20 more minutes. *I add ½ cup dry red table wine after drawing off that amount of bean liquid.* Adjust seasoning after beans are added. The total cooking time may be much longer, depending on the desired thickness. Also, the cut of meat will affect time, so check for tenderness of beef while cooking.

Serve with grated 'jack' or Cheddar cheese and sour cream as optional topping.

Photo: DARLENE DELBECQ

HIDETARO SUZUKI AND ZEYDA RUGA SUZUKI, VIOLINIST AND PIANIST

Born in Tokyo, Hidetaro Suzuki made his debut at the age of fourteen and concertized throughout Japan prior to graduating from the Toho School of Music in 1956. He later studied with Efrem Zimbalist at the Curtis Institute of Music in Philadelphia. He has received top prizes in many prestigious international violin competitions, including the Tchaikovsky in Moscow (1962), the Queen Elisabeth in Brussels (Bronze medal in 1963 and Silver medal in 1967), and the Montreal International (Second prize in 1966).

Since his graduation from the Curtis Institute of Music, Mr. Suzuki has been a soloist, conductor, concertmaster, and chamber musician throughout the world, appearing as guest conductor or soloist with the Hong Kong and Japan Philharmonics; Tokyo, NHK, Yomiuri, and Sapporo Symphonies; Toronto, Montreal, and Quebec Symphonies and the CBC Radio Orchestra in Canada; the Concerts Colonne in Paris; L'Orchestre National of French Radio and Television; Belgian National Orchestra; and the Moscow and Minsk Philharmonics.

Mr. Suzuki was appointed concertmaster of the Indianapolis Symphony Orchestra in 1978. Previously, he was concertmaster of the Quebec Symphony Orchestra for fifteen years and professor of violin at the Conservatoire de Musique de la Province de Quebec and at Laval University.

In the chamber music field, Mr. Suzuki founded and performed in the Bay Chamber Concerts in Camden, Maine, from 1961 through 1972, and has been artist-in-residence at the Stratford Festival of Canada, the Marlboro Festival, Chautauqua, Grand Teton, and Blue Hill. He is founder and director of "Suzuki & Friends," now in its fourteenth season, and served as juror for the

Montreal International Violin Competition in 1979, as well as the quadrennial International Violin Competition of Indianapolis in 1982, 1986, 1990, and 1994.

Hidetaro Suzuki is a recipient of the TRACI Award given by the Metropolitan Arts Council for contributions to the "Advancement of Culture in Indianapolis."

Pianist Zeyda Ruga Suzuki's first language is music. At the age of three, she learned how to read music before she learned how to read Spanish in her native Cuba. Since then, her fluency and eloquence in the language of music have transcended cultural and political boundaries. Married to Japanese violinist Hidetaro Suzuki, she and her husband have enjoyed a magnificent global partnership, having toured extensively in the former Soviet Union as well as Canada, France and Japan over the last thirty years.

In North America, Mrs. Suzuki has performed from Maine to Texas, and from Alaska to Florida, in major music centers such as New York City, Chicago, Montreal and Toronto. She has been artist-in-residence at the Stratford, Mont-Orford, Lac St. Jean, Bay Chamber Concerts, Grand Teton, and Steamboat Springs Music Festivals. As a soloist, she has performed with the Havana Symphony, the CMQ Chamber Orchestra of Havana, the Quebec Symphony, the CBC Chamber Orchestra of Quebec, the Tokyo and Sapporo Symphonies, the Hong Kong Philharmonic, the Grand Teton Music Festival Orchestra, the Indianapolis Chamber Orchestra, and the Indianapolis Symphony. As a recording artist, Mrs. Suzuki has recorded several discs for Toshiba-EMI, Select-Canada, and CBC International. Since coming to Indianapolis in 1979, Mrs. Suzuki has been one of the city's most active musicians, presenting the lion's share of the chamber music repertoire for piano in the "Suzuki & Friends" series. Her depth and dedication have captivated the Hoosier audience, inspiring *Arts Indiana* to call her "an Indianapolis treasure," and both the *Indianapolis News* and *Indianapolis Star* to extoll her contributions to the city's musical life.

Zeyda Ruga Suzuki holds diplomas from Havana's Municipal Conservatory and the Curtis Institute of Music in Philadelphia, as well as a doctorate in music from Quebec's Laval University where she served as an assistant professor of chamber music between 1971 and 1979. During 1990-91, she was a visiting professor of piano at Indiana University South Bend, and, in 1992, was a juror for the Fischoff National Chamber Music Competition.

The Suzuki's have raised three children: Kenneth, Nantel, and Elina.

CHAWAN MUSHI
(Japanese Custard)
Serves 10

We love to prepare food together from all parts of the world. These two are our favorite recipes from our native countries: Japan and Cuba. --H.S. & Z.S.

Chicken:
10 raw, finger-tip-sized pieces of chicken breast meat
1 teaspoon shoyu (soy sauce)
1 teaspoon mirin (rice wine)

Mix ingredients and marinate for one-half hour.

Dashi (fish stock):
4½ cups cold water
1½ sheets of Kombu, torn into smaller pieces
1 packet (¾ oz.) Dashi-no-Moto

2 tablespoons mirin (rice wine)
2 teaspoons shoyu (soy sauce)

Using a medium-sized pot, soak Kombu in cold water for 15 to 20 minutes. Add remaining ingredients and bring to a slow boil. Cover pan and gently simmer for 10 minutes. Remove from heat and cool for one-half hour. Remove and discard Kombu.

Custard:
10 custard cups with lids (or use Saran
    wrap to cover)
4½ cups dashi (see above)
2 dried black mushrooms, (soften in
    cold water for about 20 minutes)
Shoyu (soy sauce)

Sugar
5 eggs, beaten
10 small raw shrimp, peeled
Marinated chicken (see above)
Watercress leaves

In a small saucepan, sauté mushrooms in a little butter or margarine with a dash each of soy sauce and sugar; remove and cut into small pieces. Add finely beaten eggs to the fish stock. Mix well. Place equal amounts of shrimp, chicken and mushrooms into each of 10 custard cups. Pour approximately ½ cup fish stock mixture into each cup. Top each cup with one or two watercress leaves.

Place covered custard cups in a wide pot and fill the pot with enough water to bring the water level to about ¾-way up the custard cups contents. Bring water to a boil, partially cover pan with a lid and cook for 10 minutes. Let cool slightly before serving.

FRIJOLES NEGROS CUBANOS
(Cuban Black Beans)
Serves 8

1 pound dried black beans	½ teaspoon pepper
8 cups water	¼ teaspoon dried oregano
½ cup olive oil	1 bay leaf
1 large onion, chopped	2 tablespoons sugar
4 cloves garlic, finely chopped	2 tablespoons vinegar
2 green bell peppers, chopped	2 tablespoons dry wine
4 teaspoons salt	2 tablespoons olive oil

Wash beans and discard any grit or bad beans, put into 4-quart pan with 8 cups of lightly salted water and boil for several minutes. Remove from heat and let stand for 1 hour. After 1 hour, cook beans again in the same water, with pan lid slightly uncovered, until beans are just tender (about 45 minutes).

Heat ½ cup olive oil in frying pan and add onion and garlic, followed by chopped green pepper. Sauté over medium heat for 5 minutes. Add 1 cup of drained beans to pan and mash with other ingredients in pan. (If using a Teflon pan, mash in separate dish so not to mar pan coating). Remove ingredients in frying pan and add to pot of remaining beans, together with salt, pepper, oregano, bay leaf and sugar.

Allow to boil on low heat, with the pan lid ajar, for another hour, then add vinegar and wine. Cook slowly for one additional hour. Add 2 tablespoons of olive oil before serving.

Photo: BRUCE A. FOX, M.S.U. RELATIONS

WALTER VERDEHR AND ELSA LUDEWIG-VERDEHR, VIOLINIST AND CLARINETIST, VERDEHR TRIO

Walter Verdehr was born in Gottschee, Yugoslavia, and received his first violin instruction at the Conservatory of Music in Graz, Austria. As a student at the Juilliard School, he was the first violinist to receive the doctorate there. On a Fulbright scholarship, he studied at the Vienna Academy of Music. Verdehr was a member of the International Congress of Strings faculty for several summers and chairman of the string department at Michigan State University School of Music, where he is a professor of music. He has made numerous appearances as soloist with orchestras in the United States, Czechoslovakia, Austria and Turkey, and has given solo and chamber music recitals in the United States and Europe. The *London Times* called his performance "sweeping and vigorous." The *Vienna Express* stated "he is a perfect violinist with beautiful blossoming tone and noble musicality." He has made solo recordings for Golden Crest records and NETTV.

Elsa Ludewig-Verdehr studied at the Oberlin Conservatory of Music and the Eastman School of Music, which granted her the distinguished Performer's Certificate as well as a doctor of musical arts. She has performed and lectured at numerous international clarinet congresses and for several years participated in the Marlboro Music Festival and touring group. She has appeared frequently in the United States and Canada as recitalist, clinician and soloist with symphony orchestras. With the Richards Wind Quintet, she played in Canada, throughout much of the United States, and at the White House. She was presented the Distinguished Faculty

Award at Michigan State University, where she is professor of music. She has solo recordings on Grenadilla and Mark labels. The *New York Times* called her playing "distinguished and musical." *The Boston Globe* noted her "musical tone and elegant sense of phrasing," while the *Chicago Tribune* wrote of her "virtuosity of a most compelling sort."

An acknowledged leader in the field of new music, the Verdehr Trio has concentrated on defining the personality of the violin-clarinet-piano trio. The members of the Verdehr Trio include Walter Verdehr and Elsa Ludewig-Verdehr, violin and clarinet, and Gary Kirkpatrick, piano. Through its commissioning efforts, over 75 new works written by some of the world's most prominent composers have been added to the chamber music repertoire. To round out its repertoire with Classical and Romantic works, the trio has rediscovered and transcribed many 18th and 19th century pieces for inclusion in its concert programs. The Verdehr Trio has performed throughout the world: in fourteen European countries, the former Soviet Union, the South and Central America, as well as in Asia, Australia, and in more than two-thirds of the United States. Among major concert halls where the trio has appeared are Kennedy Center, Lincoln Center, Vienna's Brahmssaal, Sydney Opera House, London's Wigmore Hall and Purcell Room, IRCAM Centre in Paris, Leningrad's Philharmonic Chamber Hall and the Concertgebouw Chamber Hall in Amsterdam.

SCHÖN ROSMARIN
(Chicken with Garlic and Rosemary)
Serves 5 to 6

Walter and Elsa suggest serving the chicken with cranberry sauce or preserved figs. For wine they recommend a Gewürztraminer from California or Alsace, or a California or Australian Chardanay.

1 medium-sized chicken (3 pound, Amish
   or free range chicken preferred)
Milk (for soaking chicken)
2 or 3 cloves of garlic

1 tablespoon dried rosemary
1 or more tablespoons olive oil
5 to 7 small red potatoes

Let chicken soak in milk for 2 hours (this takes away any fowl taste), then dry off the chicken and place in large baking dish. Slice garlic and distribute several slices in the cavity and over the chicken.

Sprinkle liberally with rosemary and olive oil. Cut potatoes into halves. Preheat oven to 450 degrees and bake chicken for 20 minutes, then add potatoes (cut side down) and continue baking at 350 degrees for an additional 45 to 60 minutes, until chicken is crispy.

Photo: LOUIS OUZER

ZVI ZEITLIN, VIOLINIST

Internationally renowned violinist Zvi Zeitlin has performed with most of the great orchestras of the world under such conductors as Bernstein, Mehta, Kubelik, Dorati, Kord, Levine, Maazel, Mata, Sawallisch, Boulez, Atzmon, Zinman, Gielen, Lochran, Dohnányi and Stravinsky.

In addition to his vast standard repertoire, he has been an outstanding champion of contemporary music by American, European and Israeli composers. Among composers of whose works Zeitlin gave world premieres or first performances in various centers are: Schuller, Druckman, Copland, Foss, Ginastera, Surinach, Ben-Haim, Orgad, Starer, Bloch, Adler, Rochberg, Rorem, Sverre Jordan, William Schuman, Isang Yun, Haubenstock-Ramati, Partos, Schwandtner, Hodkinson, Reynolds, Thea Musgrave, and others.

Born in Russia and raised in Israel, at age eleven he became the youngest scholarship student in the history of the Juilliard School, studying with Sascha Jacobsen, Louis Persinger and Ivan Galamian.

Apart from his solo career, Zeitlin has earned an international reputation as one of the major violin teachers, beginning with a stint on the faculty at the Tanglewood Festival while still a student at Juilliard. Currently he is professor of violin at the Eastman School of Music where he was honored as the first Kilbourn Professor in 1974. As a dedicated chamber music player, he was a founding member of the Eastman Trio, and, for over two decades, has been head of the violin program on the artist faculty of the Music Academy of the West Summer Festival. In earlier years he was a participant for four summers at the Marlboro Music Festival in Vermont and a visiting professor of violin at Indiana University's School of Music.

Zeitlin's recording of the Schoenberg Violin Concerto with the Bavarian State Orchestra under Rafael Kubelik

has recently been reissued by Deutsche Grammophon's 20th Century Classics on CD. He has performed this work with most of the world's foremost orchestras and conductors. The violinist has also recorded all of Stravinsky's violin and piano works for Pantheon Records. Other recordings have been issued by Vox, Turnabout, CRI, and Musical Heritage Society.

Zeitlin has toured Europe frequently, as well as Australia, New Zealand and Hong Kong, to great acclaim. In 1992 he made his fifteenth tour of Central and South America, playing in Mexico, Bolivia and the West Indies. In addition to giving master classes in many of the major universities and music schools of the United States, Zeitlin has taught in the Beijing and Shanghai Conservatories in China; Seoul, Korea; the Jerusalem Music Center in Israel; the Yehudi Menuhin School, the Royal Academy of Music, the Wells Cathedral School and the Guildhall School of Music and Drama in England as well as in Oslo and Trondheim in Norway.

Zeitlin has been a judge in such competitions as Montreal, Indianapolis, John D. Rockefeller and the Concert Artists Guild.

Among the many honors accorded him, the violinist was given the America-Israel Society Award for "his efforts in furthering close cultural ties between the people of the United States and Israel through the medium of music." In April of 1990, he was honored by the Music Fraternity Mu Phi Epsilon as Musician of the Year.

Mr. Zeitlin is the author of numerous articles as well as the editor of a newly unearthed Nardini Concerto for Violin which was published by G. Schirmer. Articles by Mr. Zeitlin on performance practices have appeared in *Strings* magazine in March of 1990, and September of 1995. The second article deals specifically with problems and pitfalls of young performers as they grow from adolescence to adulthood.

CHICKEN CACCIATORE

Serves 5 to 6

When I was on a tour of my native Israel in 1962, after many years in the United States, my wife and I cooked this dish, to the delight of our Israeli relatives, who hitherto had never tasted anything but traditional boiled or roasted chicken. --Z.Z.

1 tablespoon olive oil
3½ pounds chicken cut into serving pieces
2 pounds chopped ripe tomatoes (with juice)
½ cup tomato paste, or more to taste
3 sliced carrots
2 chopped onions, preferably red
3 celery ribs

3 bell peppers: red, green, and orange,
**   if available**
½ pound button mushrooms
4 cloves of garlic, minced
Salt and pepper to taste
½ cup each of fresh basil and oregano
Chicken broth, if needed

Brown chicken in olive oil, then transfer to a large pot. Add tomatoes and tomato paste mixed with 1 cup water and simmer over low heat for about one hour, until chicken is tender. Add vegetables and seasonings. (Add extra broth or water to pot if liquid does not cover ingredients). Simmer for another half hour. Serve with rice.

ARTIST INDEX

FOOD INDEX

ABOUT THE AUTHOR

David Rezits was born in 1957 in Champaign-Urbana, Illinois. Both David's parents are musicians, consequently he began to study piano at age six and cello at age seven. His first cello studies were with his mother, who is a cellist. He spent his formative years in Bloomington, Indiana, later attending Indiana University for his undergraduate music degree. He studied cello with Eva Janzer and Janos Starker during this period. In the year of his graduation he was offered a cello position with the Orquestra Sinfônica Brasileira in Rio de Janeiro, Brazil. David's concerts and travels took him to all parts of Brazil, including two months in the Amazon River region in northern Brazil. He returned to the United States in 1980 to begin working with cellist Bernard Greenhouse at State University of New York at Stony Brook. He also was chosen to be a member of the Stony Brook Graduate String Quartet. David completed his master of music degree at State University of New York in 1982. The following summer, David was on an airplane once again, heading to the Middle East to become principal cellist of the Haifa Symphony in northern Israel. David traveled throughout Israel concertizing during his two seasons with the Haifa Symphony. During the orchestra's 'off season' he made his first trip to Europe and Scandinavia; enjoying the food and culture of this part of the world.

Returning to the United States in 1984, David began a year's apprenticeship in string instrument repair at the Indiana University School of Music. In July of 1985, he was selected to play for one season as associate principal cellist with The Florida Orchestra in Tampa. Upon completion of that contract, he returned again to his hometown of Bloomington.

Due to much pain from long-standing chronic tendinitis in David's left arm, he made the difficult decision to end his cello career and pursue another profession. He resumed studies at Indiana University in January 1987, first concentrating for two years in pre-veterinary medicine, then selecting counseling, in which he received a master of science in education degree three years later.

In 1991, after almost five years away from the cello, and missing his former music life, David decided once again to attempt to play the cello. With tremendous patience he began to restructure his cello technique and "relearn" the instrument. With very encouraging results he slowly began to practice the instrument again and become reinvolved in the music community. He auditioned for the Fort Wayne Philharmonic later that year and was hired as a full-time musician. David also began teaching at colleges in the surrounding areas, including Indiana/Purdue University at Fort Wayne and Huntington College. He currently is instructor of cello at Goshen College, in Goshen, Indiana.

David Rezits has worked with many renowned conductors, including Leonard Bernstein, Seiji Ozawa, Kurt Masur, Gunther Schuller, Maurice Abravanel, Maxim Shostakovich and Robert Shaw. He has been a participant at the Berkshire (Tanglewood), National Music Camp, Music Academy of the West, New College and Grand Teton Music Festivals. In 1993, David performed on his first CD recording entitled *Free Fall*, a collection of compositions by classical guitarist and composer Sulaiman Zai. David spends part of each summer teaching cello in Michigan, at the Blue Lake Fine Arts Camp.

When not writing, cooking, or practicing, David enjoys traveling, hiking, camping, jogging, photography, and reading the veterinary stories of author James Herriot. A strong advocate for the environment, he also participates in concerts as fund-raising events for different environmental groups. He resides in the country on a 200 acre lake and nature preserve in northeastern Indiana.

Photo of David Rezits taken by Spectrum Studio, Kendall Reeves, photographer © 1996 Bloomington, Indiana